This report contains the collective views of an international group of experts and
does not necessarily represent the decisions or the stated policy of the World Health Organization

WHO Technical Report Series

854

PHYSICAL STATUS: THE USE AND INTERPRETATION OF ANTHROPOMETRY

Report of a
WHO Expert Committee

World Health Organization

Geneva 1995

WHO Library Cataloguing in Publication Data

WHO Expert Committee on Physical Status : the Use and Interpretation of Anthropometry
    Physical status : the use and interpretation of anthropometry : report of a WHO expert
    committee.

    (WHO technical report series ; 854)

    1. Anthropometry 2. Health status indicators 3. Nutrition assessment I. Title II. Series

    ISBN 92 4 120854 6   (NLM Classification: GN 54)
    ISSN 0512-3054

The World Health Organization welcomes requests for permission to reproduce or translate its
publications, in part or in full. Applications and enquiries should be addressed to the Office of
Publications, World Health Organization, Geneva, Switzerland, which will be glad to provide
the latest information on any changes made to the text, plans for new editions, and reprints
and translations already available.

Printed in Switzerland
95/10429 – Benteli – 7000

Contents

1. Introduction 1
   References 3

2. Technical framework 4
   2.1 Introduction 4
   2.2 Levels of body composition 4
   2.3 Anthropometric measurements, indices, and indicators 6
       2.3.1 Measurements 6
       2.3.2 Indices 7
       2.3.3 Indicators 8
   2.4 Selection of anthropometric indicators 10
   2.5 Sensitivity and specificity of indicators 12
   2.6 Selection of a best indicator 14
   2.7 Using anthropometry in individuals 16
       2.7.1 Screening with one measurement for targeting an intervention 16
       2.7.2 Assessing response to an intervention 21
   2.8 Using anthropometry in populations 22
       2.8.1 Uses related to decisions 22
       2.8.2 Targeting interventions 24
       2.8.3 Assessing response to an intervention 25
       2.8.4 Ascertaining the determinants and consequences of malnutrition 26
       2.8.5 Nutritional surveillance 26
   2.9 Characteristics of reference data 29
   References 33

3. Pregnant and lactating women 37
   3.1 Introduction 37
       3.1.1 Background 37
       3.1.2 Methodology 38
       3.1.3 Biological significance of anthropometry during pregnancy 40
       3.1.4 Anthropometry as an indicator of nutritional and health status 41
   3.2 Using anthropometry in individuals 47
       3.2.1 Choosing an indicator 47
       3.2.2 Applications of anthropometry for screening pregnant women 56
       3.2.3 Assessing response to an intervention 61
   3.3 Using anthropometry in populations 70
       3.3.1 Targeting interventions 72
       3.3.2 Assessing response to an intervention 79
       3.3.3 Ascertaining the determinants and consequences of malnutrition 80
       3.3.4 Nutritional surveillance 81
   3.4 Population data management and analysis 84
       3.4.1 Sampling considerations 84
       3.4.2 Problem identification 84
       3.4.3 Policy and planning 85
       3.4.4 Programme management and evaluation 86
   3.5 Methods of taking measurements 87
   3.6 Sources and characteristics of reference data 88
       3.6.1 Existing reference data 88
       3.6.2 Criteria for establishing reference data 98
       3.6.3 Recommendations for new reference data 101
   3.7 Relationship between normative reference data and functional outcomes 104

3.8	Populations for which compiled reference data are not pertinent	107
	3.9	The use and interpretation of anthropometry in lactating women	108
		3.9.1 Biological significance of anthropometry during lactation	108
		3.9.2 Selection of individuals	109
		3.9.3 Characteristics for the development of normative reference data	110
		3.9.4 Research needs for lactating women	111
	3.10 Conclusions and recommendations	112
		3.10.1 For practical implementation	112
		3.10.2 For future research and the collection of reference data	114
		3.10.3 For WHO	115
	References	116

4. The newborn infant — 121
   4.1 Introduction — 121
   4.2 Using anthropometry in individual newborn infants — 123
   4.3 Neonatal anthropometric assessment in populations — 128
   4.4 Selection of anthropometric indicators — 129
       4.4.1 Gestational age — 129
       4.4.2 Birth weight — 135
       4.4.3 Birth length — 135
       4.4.4 Birth head circumference — 135
       4.4.5 Proportionality indices — 135
       4.4.6 Other measurements — 135
   4.5 Reference data for size at birth — 136
       4.5.1 Criteria for evaluating existing references — 136
       4.5.2 Size at birth in early gestation — 137
       4.5.3 Size at birth in later gestation — 138
   4.6 Conclusions — 149
   4.7 Recommendations — 153
       4.7.1 General — 153
       4.7.2 For individuals — 153
       4.7.3 For populations — 154
       4.7.4 For WHO — 154
       4.7.5 For Member States — 154
       4.7.6 For future research — 155
   References — 155

5. Infants and children — 161
   5.1 Introduction — 161
       5.1.1 Terminology and clarification of commonly used terms — 162
       5.1.2 Expression and interpretation of anthropometry — 176
       5.1.3 Biological and social significance of anthropometry — 177
       5.1.4 Issues in using anthropometric measurements as indicators of nutritional and health status — 181
       5.1.5 Conditioning the interpretation of anthropometry — 182
   5.2 Using anthropometry in individuals — 183
       5.2.1 Introduction — 183
       5.2.2 Screening children for health and nutritional disorders — 183
   5.3 Using anthropometry in populations — 198
       5.3.1 Introduction — 198
       5.3.2 Targeting interventions — 198
       5.3.3 Assessing response to an intervention — 209
       5.3.4 Ascertaining the determinants of malnutrition — 210
       5.3.5 Ascertaining the consequences of malnutrition — 211
       5.3.6 Nutritional surveillance — 212

5.4 Population data management and analysis   215
   5.4.1 Description of sources of data   215
   5.4.2 Documentation and analysis of coverage rates   215
   5.4.3 Reliability and validity   215
   5.4.4 Data integrity or quality measures   217
   5.4.5 Data compilation and documentation   219
   5.4.6 Data analysis and presentation   219
5.5 Methods of measurement   224
   5.5.1 Height measurements   224
   5.5.2 Weight measurements   224
   5.5.3 Age determination   224
5.6 Sources and characteristics of reference data   224
   5.6.1 Issues related to selection and application of references   224
   5.6.2 Local versus international references   225
   5.6.3 Factors affecting the use and interpretation of growth references   226
   5.6.4 The current international reference (NCHS/WHO reference)   227
   5.6.5 Growth velocity curves   250
5.7 Presentation of anthropometric reference data   251
   5.7.1 For individual-based applications   251
   5.7.2 For population-based applications   252
5.8 Recommendations   253
   5.8.1 Infants   253
   5.8.2 Children   253
References   255

6. Adolescents   263
6.1 Introduction   263
   6.1.1 Background   263
   6.1.2 Biological and social significance of anthropometry   265
   6.1.3 Anthropometry as an indicator of nutritional and health status   270
   6.1.4 Conditioning the interpretation of anthropometry   276
6.2 Using anthropometry in individuals   281
   6.2.1 Introduction   281
   6.2.2 Screening for interventions   281
   6.2.3 Assessing response to an intervention   283
6.3 Using anthropometry in populations   288
   6.3.1 Introduction   288
   6.3.2 Targeting interventions   288
   6.3.3 Assessing response to an intervention   289
   6.3.4 Ascertaining determinants of malnutrition   290
   6.3.5 Ascertaining consequences of malnutrition   291
   6.3.6 Nutritional surveillance   292
6.4 Population data management and analysis   300
   6.4.1 Description of sources of data   300
   6.4.2 Documentation and analysis of coverage rates   301
   6.4.3 Documentation and analysis of reliability   301
   6.4.4 Data compilation and documentation   301
   6.4.5 Data analysis and presentation   302
6.5 Sources and characteristics of reference data   303
6.6 Presentation of findings relative to anthropometric reference data   305
   6.6.1 For individuals   305
   6.6.2 For populations   306
6.7 Recommendations   306
   6.7.1 For Member States   306

	6.7.2 For WHO	306
	6.7.3 For future research and collection of reference data	307
	References	308
7.	Overweight adults	312
	7.1 Introduction	312
	7.1.1 Background	312
	7.1.2 Biological and social significance of overweight	316
	7.1.3 Anthropometry as an indicator of nutritional and health status	327
	7.2 Using anthropometry in individuals	328
	7.2.1 Screening for interventions	329
	7.2.2 Assessing response to an intervention	330
	7.3 Using anthropometry in populations	331
	7.3.1 Targeting interventions	331
	7.3.2 Assessing response to an intervention	331
	7.3.3 Ascertaining determinants of overweight	332
	7.3.4 Ascertaining consequences of overweight	332
	7.3.5 Nutritional surveillance	333
	7.4 Population data management and analysis	334
	7.5 Potential development of reference data	336
	7.6 Recommendations	339
	7.6.1 For practical implementation	339
	7.6.2 For future research	339
	References	340
8.	Thin adults	345
	8.1 Introduction	345
	8.1.1 Background	345
	8.1.2 Terminology	345
	8.2 Biological and social significance of anthropometry	346
	8.2.1 Biological and social determinants of anthropometry	346
	8.2.2 Biological and social consequences of anthropometry	347
	8.3 Anthropometry as an indicator of nutritional and health status	349
	8.3.1 Work capacity	349
	8.3.2 Work productivily	349
	8.3.3 Mortality at low body weight	351
	8.3.4 Morbidity and low body weight	353
	8.4 Interpretation of anthropometry	355
	8.4.1 Considerations of body shape	355
	8.4.2 Low body weight and body composition	356
	8.5 Using anthropometry in individuals	359
	8.6 Using anthropometry in populations	359
	8.6.1 Targeting interventions	359
	8.6.2 Assessing response to an intervention	359
	8.6.3 Ascertaining determinants of malnutrition	360
	8.6.4 Nutritional surveillance	360
	8.6.5 Thinness as a public health problem	361
	8.7 Guidelines for use of anthropometric indicators	362
	8.7.1 Use of BMI with simple cut-off points	362
	8.7.2 Arm and arm muscle circumference	364
	8.7.3 Populations for which the guidelines may not be appropriate	368
	8.8 Recommendations	369
	8.8.1 For practical implementation	369
	8.8.2 For future research	369
	References	370

9. Adults 60 years of age and older 375
  9.1 Introduction 375
    9.1.1 Background 375
    9.1.2 Population variation in anthropometry 378
    9.1.3 Anthropometry as an indicator of nutritional and health status 383
    9.1.4 Interpretation issues in the elderly 389
  9.2 Using anthropometry in individuals 390
    9.2.1 Screening for interventions 390
    9.2.2 Assessing response to an intervention 391
    9.2.3 Assessment of functional ability 392
  9.3 Using anthropometry in populations 393
    9.3.1 Targeting interventions 393
    9.3.2 Assessing response to an intervention 393
    9.3.3 Ascertaining the determinants of thinness and overweight 394
    9.3.4 Ascertaining the consequences of thinness and overweight 394
    9.3.5 Nutritional surveillance 394
  9.4 Methods of taking measurements 395
    9.4.1 Weight 395
    9.4.2 Height 396
    9.4.3 Calf circumference 398
    9.4.4 Subscapular skinfold thickness 398
    9.4.5 Mid-upper arm circumference 398
    9.4.6 Triceps skinfold thickness 399
  9.5 Sources and characteristics of reference data 399
  9.6 Recommendations 405
    9.6.1 For practical implementation 405
    9.6.2 For future research 405
  References 407

10. Overall recommendations 410
  10.1 For Member States 410
  10.2 For WHO 410
  10.3 For research 411

Acknowledgements 412

Annex 1
Glossary of terms and abbreviations 416

Annex 2
Recommended measurement protocols and derivation of indices 424

Annex 3
Recommended reference data 439

WHO Expert Committee on Physical Status:
The Use and Interpretation of Anthropometry

Geneva, 1–8 November 1993

Members

Dr A. Ferro-Luzzi, Unit of Human Nutrition, National Institute of Nutrition, Rome, Italy

Dr C. Garza, Director, Division of Nutritional Sciences, Cornell University, Ithaca, NY, USA

Dr J. Haas, Division of Nutritional Sciences, Cornell University, Ithaca, NY, USA

Dr J.-P. Habicht, Division of Nutritional Sciences, Cornell University, Ithaca, NY, USA (*Chairman*)

Dr J. Himes, Division of Epidemiology, School of Public Health, University of Minnesota, Minneapolis, MN, USA (*Co-Rapporteur*)

Dr A. Pradilla, Department of Epidemiology, University of Valle, Cali, Colombia

Dr L. Raman, National Institute of Nutrition, Indian Council of Medical Research, Hyderabad, India

Dr O. Ransome-Kuti, Former Professor of Paediatrics, University of Lagos, Lagos, Nigeria

Dr J. C. Seidell, Head, Department of Chronic Diseases and Environmental Epidemiology, National Institute of Public Health and Environmental Protection, Bilthoven, Netherlands (*Co-Rapporteur*)

Dr C. Victora, Department of Social Medicine, Faculty of Medicine, Federal University of Pelotas, Pelotas, Brazil (*Co-Rapporteur*)

Dr M. L. Wahlqvist, Monash Medical Centre, Monash University, Melbourne, Australia

Dr R. Yip, Chief, Maternal and Child Nutrition, Centers for Disease Control, Atlanta, GA, USA

Representatives of other organizations

Food and Agriculture Organization of the United Nations (FAO)

Dr R. Weisell, Nutrition Officer, Food Policy and Nutrition Division, Rome, Italy

United Nations Children's Fund (UNICEF)

Dr J. Csete, Nutrition Section, New York, NY, USA

Secretariat

Dr G. A. Clugston, Chief Medical Officer, Nutrition, WHO, Geneva, Switzerland

Dr M. de Onis, Scientist, Nutrition, WHO, Geneva, Switzerland (*Secretary*)

Dr P. Eveleth, Former Deputy Associate Director, National Institute on Aging, National Institutes of Health, Bethesda, MD, USA (*Temporary Adviser*)

Dr M. Kramer, Department of Paediatrics and of Epidemiology and Biostatistics, McGill University, Montreal, Canada (*Temporary Adviser*)

Dr P. Sizonenko, Head, Division of Biology of Growth and Reproduction, Cantonal University Hospital, Geneva, Switzerland (*Temporary Adviser*)

Dr J. Tuomilehto, Department of Epidemiology, National Public Health Institute, Helsinki, Finland (*Temporary Adviser*)

Dr J. Villar, Medical Officer, Special Programme of Research, Development and Research Training in Human Reproduction, WHO, Geneva, Switzerland

Abbreviations

The following abbreviations are used in this report:

AGA	appropriate-for-gestational-age
AMA	arm muscle area
AMC	arm muscle circumference
API	adequate ponderal index
BMI	body mass index
EF	etiological fraction
IUGR	intrauterine growth retardation
LBW	low birth weight
LGA	large-for-gestational-age
LMP	last menstrual period
LPI	low ponderal index
MUAC	mid-upper arm circumference
NCHS	National Center for Health Statistics
NHANES	National Health and Nutrition Examination Survey
OR	odds ratio
PIH	pregnancy-induced hypertension
PPV	positive predictive value
ROC	receiver (or relative) operating characteristics
RR	relative risk
SD	standard deviation
SE	sensitivity
SF	symphysis–fundus (height)
SGA	small-for-gestational-age
SP	specificity
VLBW	very low birth weight

1. Introduction

The WHO Expert Committee on Physical Status: The Use and Interpretation of Anthropometry met in Geneva from 1 to 8 November 1993. Dr F.S. Antezana, Assistant Director-General, opened the meeting on behalf of the Director-General. This meeting was the culmination of a two-year preparatory process, involving more than 100 experts worldwide, which started in 1991 with the establishment of seven subcommittees, and continued with a number of subcommittee meetings, small group workshops, individual and working group contributions, and external reviews. During this process, subcommittees not only reviewed the latest knowledge in their areas, but also, in some cases, moved forward by themselves contributing to the knowledge pool.

The subcommittees received support for their efforts from numerous institutions, organizations, and governments. WHO takes pleasure in drawing attention to these contributions, without which many of the major preparatory activities would have been impossible. All individuals and institutions who contributed to the work are recorded in the Acknowledgements section (page 412).

Each year, 26 million babies are born too small to lead healthy lives, because their mothers were either ill or malnourished. More than 230 million (43%) of all preschool children in the developing world are stunted in their growth because of malnutrition caused by lack of food and by disease. Today, it is expected that this malnutrition will kill about seven million children a year, either directly or by worsening the impact of infectious diseases.

About 15% of non-elderly adults are too thin because of malnutrition and disease, which decrease their productivity and double their rate of premature mortality. At the same time, 150 million adults are overweight, of whom 15 million will die prematurely because of diseases resulting from obesity. In some communities almost all cases of adult diabetes and 40% of cases of coronary heart disease are attributable to body weight in excess of the optimum.

Data such as these on low birth weight, stunting, thinness, and overweight are obtained from measurements of height and weight. Anthropometric measurements assess body size and composition, and reflect inadequate or excess food intake, insufficient exercise, and disease. They demonstrate that deprivation and excess may coexist not only across, but also within, countries and even households, and show too that certain kinds of development and health policy enhance nutrition while others do not. Simple body measurements also permit the selection of individuals, families, and communities for interventions designed to improve not only nutrition but health in general and thus survival.

Anthropometry is the single most universally applicable, inexpensive, and non-invasive method available to assess the size, proportions, and composition of the human body. Moreover, since growth in children and body dimensions at all ages reflect the overall health and welfare of individuals and populations, anthropometry may also be used to predict performance, health, and survival. This report describes appropriate uses and interpretation of anthropometry from infancy to old age. These applications are important for public health and clinical decisions that affect the health and social welfare of individuals and populations.

Over the years, WHO and other specialized agencies of the United Nations system have sought to provide guidance on the appropriate uses of anthropometric indices (1-6). Previously, attention has been focused largely on infants and young children, because of their vulnerability, and on the value of anthropometry in characterizing growth and well-being. Advances during the past decade, however, have demonstrated the relevance of anthropometry throughout life, not only for individual assessments but also for reflecting the health status and social and economic circumstances of population groups. In recognition of these developments, WHO convened an Expert Committee to re-evaluate the value of anthropometric indices and indicators at different ages in assessing health, nutrition, and social well-being. The Expert Committee recognized different needs and applications through the life cycle, and addressed these issues as they relate to pregnant and lactating women, the newborn, infants and children, adolescents, adults, and elderly people (aged 60 years or more).

Paediatricians have long used child growth as an important parameter in evaluating the health and general well-being of children (7). In the nutrition field, low height and/or weight relative to reference data have been used as classic indicators of undernutrition for individuals and groups; similarly, elevated body weight and thickness of subcutaneous fat have become common indicators of overnutrition or obesity.

Recent research has expanded the applications of anthropometry to include predicting who will benefit from interventions, identifying social and economic inequity, and evaluating responses to interventions. Importantly, it has become clear that different uses of anthropometry require different properties of the most appropriate anthropometric indicators, and that appropriate applications and interpretations of anthropometric indicators may be different for individuals and for populations. Further, appropriate indicators for a particular purpose may vary according to the prevalence of a specific problem.

Principles of public health screening (8) and epidemiology are particularly helpful in identifying appropriate anthropometric indicators, and specifying optimum cut-off points for variables (9). Experience with surveillance (2) has contributed to concepts and practices concerning community assessments and "trigger-levels" as a basis for public health decisions.

The Expert Committee was requested to:

- develop recommendations for the appropriate use and interpretation of anthropometry in individuals and populations in various operational settings;

- identify and/or develop reference data for anthropometric indicators when appropriate;
- provide guidelines on how these reference data should be used; and
- identify new or unresolved issues and gaps in knowledge that require further research.

The Expert Committee's report is intended to provide a framework and contexts for present and future uses and interpretation of anthropometry. Technical aspects of this framework are presented in section 2, and specific applications of anthropometry appropriate for a particular physical status or for particular age groups are dealt with in subsequent sections. For some groups, such as adolescents and the elderly, there has been little previous research, and the report provides a basis and impetus for future studies. For other age groups, such as infants and children, the report provides a re-evaluation in the light of current research, and allows for an integrated approach to anthropometry throughout life. It is intended to furnish scientists, clinicians, and public health professionals worldwide with an authoritative review, reference data, and recommendations for the use and interpretation of anthropometry that should be appropriate in many settings.

References

1. Jelliffe DB. *The assessment of the nutritional status of the community.* Geneva, World Health Organization, 1966 (WHO Monograph Series, No. 53).

2. *Methodology of nutritional surveillance. Twenty-seventh Report of a Joint FAO/UNICEF/WHO Expert Committee.* Geneva, World Health Organization, 1976 (WHO Technical Report Series, No. 593).

3. Waterlow JC et al. The presentation and use of height and weight data for comparing nutritional status of groups of children under the age of 10 years. *Bulletin of the World Health Organization*, 1977, **55**:489–498.

4. *Measuring change in nutritional status: guidelines for assessing the nutritional impact of supplementary feeding programmes.* Geneva, World Health Organization, 1983.

5. WHO Working Group. Use and interpretation of anthropometric indicators of nutritional status. *Bulletin of the World Health Organization*, 1986, **64**(6): 929–941.

6. Beaton G et al. *Appropriate uses of anthropometric indices in children: a report based on an ACC/SCN workshop.* New York, United Nations Administrative Committee on Coordination/Subcommittee on Nutrition, 1990 (ACC/SCN State-of-the-Art Series, Nutrition Policy Discussion Paper No. 7).

7. Tanner JM. *History of the study of human growth.* Cambridge, Cambridge University Press, 1981.

8. Wilson JMG, Jungner G. *Principles and practice of screening for disease.* Geneva, World Health Organization, 1968 (Public Health Papers, No. 34).

9. Galen RS, Gambino SR. *Beyond normality: the predictive value and efficiency of medical diagnoses.* New York, Wiley, 1975.

2. Technical framework

2.1 Introduction

Anthropometry has been widely and successfully applied to the assessment of health and nutritional risk, especially in children. Recent publications have refined the interpretation of anthropometric indicators in selected operational settings (*1*), but little guidance has been published concerning other appropriate uses of anthropometry. The implications of specific uses for the choice of indicators and interpretation of findings are not fully understood, even though correct selection of the best anthropometric indicators depends entirely on the purposes for which they are used (*2*).

This section deals with the technical basis underlying the various uses of anthropometric indicators, using principles of applied biostatistics and epidemiology. For the broader audience, these principles are explained without equations; readers interested in a technically more sophisticated treatment are referred to the specialized readings cited.

2.2 Levels of body composition

Full appreciation of the utility of anthropometry requires an understanding of the organizational levels of human body composition. Recently, there have been major advances in conceptual models relating anthropometry to body composition, which provide insight into the physiological mechanisms represented by anthropometry (*3*).

The five organizational levels of body composition and their major compartments are shown in Fig. 1. At the atomic level, the major chemical elements are oxygen, hydrogen, carbon, nitrogen, calcium, and phosphorus. Whole-body measurements of these constituents are usually made with research techniques such as neutron activation analysis, and provide important information. For example, nitrogen balance is an indicator of protein turnover, and total body calcium is an indicator of total bone mineral.

The next level of body composition comprises the major molecular compartments such as water, protein, glycogen, mineral (osseous and non-osseous), and fat (Fig. 2). Water and osseous minerals can be measured directly, but fat, protein, glycogen, and non-osseous minerals must be estimated by indirect techniques. Each of the several methods used to estimate this latter group of constituents relies on assumptions that relate measurable aspects of body composition to the constituent of interest. Anthropometric methods of estimating total body fat and fat-free mass (FFM) are usually developed using one of these indirect techniques.

The cellular level of body composition consists of cells, extracellular fluid (ECF), and extracellular solids (ECS). A widely used model

Figure 1
Five-level model of body composition[a]

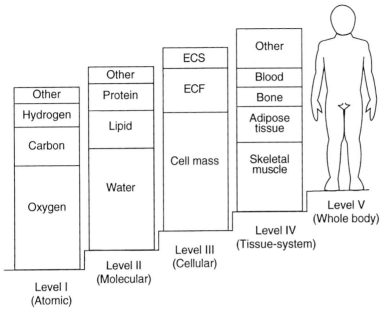

Note: ECS = extracellular solids
ECF = extracellular fluid

[a] Reproduced from reference 3 with the permission of the American Society for Clinical Nutrition.

considers the total cellular mass to be composed of two components – fat (a molecular-level compartment), and the fat-free cell mass referred to as body cell mass (BCM), where most metabolic processes take place. Cells are the body's main functional compartments. Several equations based on anthropometry have been developed to predict body cell mass at the cellular level, although their accuracy is a matter of debate and none is widely used.

The tissue-system level of body composition consists of the major tissues, organs, and systems; thus body weight is equal to adipose tissue + skeletal muscle + bone + blood + residual (visceral organs, etc.). Adipose tissue includes adipocytes, blood vessels, and structural elements, and is the primary site of lipid storage. It is located mainly in the subcutaneous and internal or visceral compartments, with its distribution under hormonal and genetic control.

A steady-state relationship exists between the various body-composition compartments. That is, there are stable quantitative relationships between compartments at the same and different levels of body composition that remain relatively constant over a specified time (usually months or years). This permits information about body composition at various

Figure 2

The major components of body weight [a]

Water, protein, and mineral within the fat-free body mass occur in the average proportions 0.725, 0.195, and 0.08; glycogen is variable at 0.01 to 0.02; 50 to 55% of water is intracellular, with the remainder in the extracellular space.

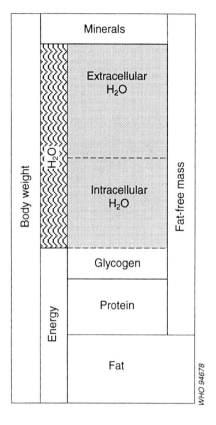

[a] Adapted from reference *3* with the permission of the American Society for Clinical Nutrition.

levels to be derived from anthropometric measurements made at the whole-body level. Both aging and disease affect these quantitative relationships, and anthropometry provides a means of detecting the resultant changes.

2.3 Anthropometric measurements, indices, and indicators

2.3.1 *Measurements*

The basic anthropometry measurements considered here are weight and height, but principles derived from these measures may be applied to other measurements. The methods for collecting recommended data are presented in Annex 2.

2.3.2 *Indices*

Anthropometric indices are combinations of measurements. They are essential for the interpretation of measurements: it is evident that a value for body weight alone has no meaning unless it is related to an individual's age or height (4). Thus, for example, measurements of weight and height may be combined to produce the body mass index (weight/height^2) or a ponderal index (weight/height^3), or weight may be related to height through the use of reference data. In children, the three most commonly used anthropometric indices are weight-for-height, height-for-age, and weight-for-age; other indices are used for different age/physiological groups, such as pregnancy weight gain in pregnant women.

The anthropometric indices can be expressed in terms of Z-scores, percentiles, or percent of median, which can then be used to compare a child or group of children with a reference population. These reporting systems are defined as follows:

- Z-score (or standard deviation score) (5, 6) – the deviation of the value for an individual from the median value of the reference population, divided by the standard deviation for the reference population:

$$\text{Z-score or SD-score} = \frac{(\text{observed value}) - (\text{median reference value})}{\text{standard deviation of reference population}}$$

  A fixed Z-score interval implies a fixed height or weight difference for children of a given age. A major advantage of this system is that, for population-based applications, it allows the mean and standard deviation to be calculated for a group of Z-scores.

- Percentile – the rank position of an individual on a given reference distribution, stated in terms of what percentage of the group the individual equals or exceeds. Thus a child of a given age whose weight falls in the 10th percentile weighs the same or more than 10% of the reference population of children of the same age.

  Percentiles are commonly used in clinical settings because their interpretation is straightforward. However, the same interval of percentile values corresponds to different changes in absolute height or weight, according to which part of the distribution is concerned, and it is therefore inappropriate to calculate summary statistics such as means and standard deviations for percentiles. Moreover, towards the extremes of the reference distribution there is little change in percentile values, when there is in fact substantial change in weight or height status.

- Percent of median – the ratio of a measured value in the individual, for instance weight, to the median value of the reference data for the same age or height, expressed as a percentage.

The main disadvantage of this system is the lack of exact correspondence with a fixed point of the distribution across age or height status. For example, depending on the child's age, 80% of the median weight-for-age might be above or below –2 Z-scores; in terms of health, this would result in different classification of risk. In addition, typical cut-offs for percent of median are different for the different anthropometric indices; to approximate a cut-off of –2 Z-scores, the usual cut-off for low height-for-age is 90%, and for low weight-for-height and low weight-for-age 80%, of the median (7-9).

If the distribution of reference values follows a normal (bell-shaped or Gaussian) distribution, percentiles and Z-scores are related through a mathematical transformation. The commonly used –3, –2, and –1 Z-scores are, respectively the 0.13th, 2.28th, and 15.8th percentiles. Similarly, the 1st, 3rd and 10th percentiles correspond to, respectively, the –2.33, –1.88, and –1.29 Z-scores. It can be seen that the 3rd percentile and the –2 Z-score are very close to each other.

The main characteristics of the three reporting systems are summarized and compared in Table 1. A detailed treatment of their limitations and strengths is to be found elsewhere (9); the brief discussion above is intended to outline the reasons for the Z-score being the preferred system.

The use of indices derived from reference data is appropriate for many purposes, but for other purposes there are better ways of adjusting anthropometric values for age and sex, such as through multivariate analysis (5) or residual analysis (10). However, these methods are in general more suitable for research applications and will not be further discussed here.

It is important to note that all indices derived from age-specific reference data depend for their precision on exact knowledge of age; when this information is not available, use of age-based indices such as height-for-age may result in misclassification (11).

2.3.3 Indicators

The term "indicator" relates to the use or application of indices. The indicator is often constructed from indices; thus, the proportion of children below a certain level of weight-for-age is widely used as an indicator of community status.

The anthropometric indices discussed here all relate to body size and composition. Sometimes this is the only type of relationship that can be inferred; indices should then be referred to as body size or body composition indicators, rather than as nutrition or health indicators. Depending on the circumstances, the same anthropometric index may be influenced equally by nutrition and health, or more by one than by the

Table 1
Comparison of the characteristics of three anthropometric data-reporting systems

Characteristic	Z-score	Percentile	Percent of median
Adherence to reference distribution	Yes	Yes	No
Linear scale permitting summary statistics	Yes	No	Yes
Uniform criteria across indices	Yes	Yes	No
Useful for detecting changes at extremes of the distributions	Yes	No	Yes

other; accordingly it may then be referred to as an indicator of nutrition, or of health, or of both. In some cases, the index may be used as a distal, or indirect, indicator of socioeconomic status or of inequities in socioeconomic status; if the index is genuinely influenced by these factors, even though indirectly through nutrition and health, it may then be referred to as a socioeconomic or equity indicator.

A valid nutritional indicator owes a substantial proportion of its variability to differences in nutrition. For any given indicator, however, this proportion may vary across or within populations. For instance, body mass index (BMI), the ratio of weight to the square of height, is a good indicator of variability in energy reserves in individuals with a sedentary lifestyle, but not in athletes; similarly, low birth weight reflects maternal malnutrition in mothers who are too thin, but not in mothers who are overweight.

It is not uncommon for an indicator to be erroneously interpreted as reflecting nutrition or some other factor, when this is not the case. This may lead to inappropriate targeting of intervention programmes. For example, providing energy supplements to mothers in a particular area on the basis of the prevalence of low birth weight alone will not succeed if smoking is common in the area. For low birth weight to be useful as an indicator of nutritional status within this population, it must be "conditioned" on the nutritional status of the mothers. That is, other factors must be taken into account in assessing the nutritional status of populations from indicators thought to be nutritional. Thus, the prevalence in the population of the nutritional or health factor of concern *conditions* the interpretation of an anthropometric indicator.

Choice and conditioning of indicators should ultimately depend on the decisions that will be made on the basis of the information they yield. Throughout, this report attempts to relate the indicators to the actions that will be taken on behalf of individuals or populations.

2.4 Selection of anthropometric indicators

Anthropometric indicators can be classified according to the objectives of their use, which include the following (the order of listing is dictated by various methodological considerations discussed later):

- *Identification of individuals or populations at risk.* In general, this requires data based on indicators of impaired performance, health, or survival. Depending on the specific objective, the anthropometric indicators must:
    - reflect past or present risk, or
    - predict future risk.

  An indicator may reflect both present and future risk; for instance, an indicator of present malnutrition may also be a predictor of an increased risk of mortality in the future. However, a reflective indicator of past problems may have no value as a predictor of future risk; for example, stunting of growth in early childhood as a result of malnutrition may persist throughout life (*1*), but with age probably becomes less reliably predictive of future risk.

  Indicators of this type might be used in the risk approach to identification of health problems and potential interventions (*12*), although, as discussed below, the risk approach may have little value in predicting the *benefit* to be derived from interventions. An indicator of risk could, however, be appropriately used to assign higher life-insurance rates to obese individuals because of their increased risk of death.

- *Selection of individuals or populations for an intervention.* In this application, indicators must:
    - predict the benefit to be derived from the intervention.

  The distinction between indicators of risk and indicators of benefit is not widely appreciated, yet it is paramount for developing and targeting interventions. Some indicators of present or future risk may also predict benefit, but this is not necessarily the case. Low maternal height, for example, predicts low birth weight, but, in contrast to low maternal weight in the same population, does not predict any benefit of providing an improved diet to pregnant women. By the same token, predictors of benefit may not be good predictors of risk.

  Anthropometry provides important indicators of overall socioeconomic development among the poorest members of a population. Stunting in children and adults reflects socioeconomic conditions that are not conducive to good health and nutrition: thus stunting in young children may be used effectively to target development programmes.

- *Evaluation of the effects of changing nutritional, health, or socioeconomic influences, including interventions.* For this purpose indicators must:
    - reflect response to past and present interventions.

Change of weight-for-height is a good example of an indicator of response in a wasted child being treated for malnutrition. At the population level a decrease in the prevalence of stunting is an indicator that social development is benefiting the poor as well as the comparatively affluent. Similarly, a decrease in the prevalence of low birth weight would indicate success in controlling malaria during pregnancy (*13*).

In describing an indicator of response, the possible lag between the start of an intervention and the time when a response becomes apparent is an important consideration. At the individual level, a wasted infant will respond to improved nutrition first by putting on weight and then by "catching up" in linear growth. At the population level, however, decades may elapse before improvements can be seen in adult height (*14*).

- *Excluding individuals from high-risk treatments, from employment, or from certain benefits.* Decisions regarding an individual's inclusion in, or exclusion from, a high-risk treatment protocol, consideration for employment in a particular setting (e.g. an occupation requiring appreciable physical strength), or admission to certain benefits (e.g. low life-insurance rates) depend on indicators that:

  – predict a lack of risk.

  Anthropometric indicators of lack of risk were once presumed to be the same as those that predict risk, but recent work has revealed that this is not invariably the case (*15*). In the cited studies, indicators of poor growth were less effective in predicting adequate growth than other indicators.

- *Achieving normative standards.* Assessing achievement of normative standards requires indicators that:

  – reflect "normality".

  Some activities appear to have no objectives beyond encouraging individuals to attain some norm. For instance, moderate obesity among the elderly is not associated with poor health or increased risk of mortality, and weight control in this age group is therefore based solely on normative distributions.

- *Research purposes that do not involve decisions affecting nutrition, health, or well-being.* The indicator requirements for these objectives, whether they concern individuals or whole populations, are generally beyond the scope of this report. The need to build appropriate biological, behavioural, and epidemiological models into the analyses often means that some simpler indicators, including some discussed in this report, may be inadequate for research purposes.

There may be differences in the interpretation of anthropometric indicators when applied to individuals or to populations. For example, while a reflective indicator, such as the presence of marasmus, signifies malnutrition in a given child today, a sudden increase of marasmus in a population may be predictive of future famine. The appropriateness of indicators thus depends on the specific objectives of their use, and research is only just beginning to address this specificity and its implications. Little is known, for example, about how the use of different cut-offs for anthropometric indicators fulfils different objectives. Consequently, this report must be largely tentative in its recommendations concerning the coupling of indicators and applications, and should be regarded as a basis for future improvements in research.

2.5 Sensitivity and specificity of indicators

A good indicator is one that best reflects the issue of concern or predicts a particular outcome. Discussion of the methodology for choosing appropriate indicators and cut-offs focuses on risks to health because little work has been done on selection of indicators for other objectives. Risk of mortality is used in the following examples.

Historically, two approaches have been used to identify anthropometric variables that show an association with death. The first uses classical statistical methods that describe relationships between anthropometric indices and death (e.g. ordinary least squares, and logistic regression (5)). The second, discussed below, is based simply on how well the indicator separates those who will die from those who will survive, and is intuitively more obvious to practitioners in public health who are concerned with screening. The two approaches are, however, related (16).

A screening test identifies individuals at risk on the basis of an indicator and a specific cut-off point. Of those who will die, the proportion who are identified as cases by the test is a measure of the *sensitivity* of the screening test. Sensitivity can be improved by changing the cut-off point to identify more people as being at risk. This is illustrated in Fig. 3, which shows the numbers of children at different height-for-age values who died – that is, the sensitivity frequency distribution. As the value of the cut-off point is raised from 65% of median to 100% of median, the sensitivity increases from 0 to 100%, because more children are diagnosed as being at risk. This sensitivity distribution is presented cumulatively in Fig. 4.

Because the sensitivity of a test changes with the cut-off point, sensitivity alone cannot be used in comparing indicators. It is also essential to consider the performance of the screening test in accurately excluding those who will not die. This is the *specificity* of the test; its frequency distribution is also shown in Fig. 3. As the cut-off point is lowered from 105% of median to 67% of median, the proportion of individuals excluded by the test rises, as shown in Fig. 4.

A considerable overlap in anthropometric values between the sensitivity and specificity distributions is apparent in Fig. 3. This is to be expected,

Figure 3
Percentage frequency distribution of height-for-age according to 2-year survival[a]

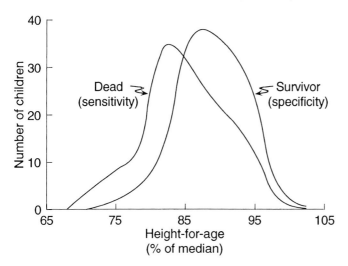

Figure 4
Percentile plot of sensitivity and specificity values for height-for-age as calculated from Fig. 3[a]

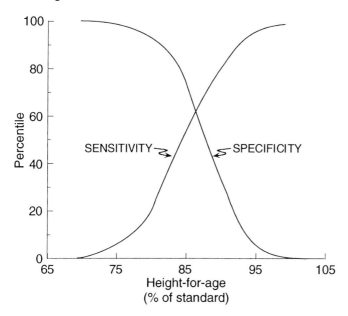

since sensitivity and specificity are inversely related: increasing one (by changing the cut-off point) results in a decrease in the other, as seen in Fig. 4.

Values for sensitivity and specificity are often assumed to be constant for indicators, unaffected by the prevalence or incidence of the condition of interest. Other descriptors of screening tests, however, such as the positive predictive value, are affected by prevalence, which makes them inappropriate for use in comparing indicators across different populations (18).

Specificity and sensitivity will be affected by the underlying biological and behavioural processes that relate the indicator to the outcomes of interest in different settings. For example, in a setting where low birth weight is due mainly to prematurity – which is strongly associated with the early neonatal death rate – its sensitivity as an indicator of mortality will be greater than where it is due mainly to intrauterine growth retardation, which is less strongly associated with the death rate. Thus, for outcomes that may be influenced by several factors, variability in the sensitivity and specificity distributions is to be expected (19). More consistency may be expected of indicators that predict or measure response to an intervention with a well established outcome. For this reason, changes in weight and mid-upper arm circumference are more sensitive than height to short-term seasonal influences (20), but height is generally more responsive than weight to improved food intake in the long term (21).

2.6 Selection of a best indicator

The trade-off between sensitivity and specificity can be represented graphically by plotting probability values for sensitivity against those for specificity at various cut-off points (see Fig. 5) to produce a curve of "receiver (or relative) operating characteristics" (ROC) that permits a comparison of indicators over their whole range. The curves have been linearized by the Z-transformation (5).

For a given specificity, height-for-age has greater sensitivity than weight-for-height (Fig. 5) in identifying those who will die in the subsequent 2 years within the population studied. Accordingly, height-for-age generates fewer errors of classification at every level of sensitivity and specificity than weight-for-height. In this context, therefore, height-for-age is the better indicator. If the curves in the Z-transformed ROC presentation are parallel, one indicator is obviously best over all ranges; if the ROC curves cross, however, one indicator is probably better over one range of values, while the other is better over another range.

Statistical methods for selecting a best indicator have been outlined elsewhere (16). When indicators are to be compared in an effort to select

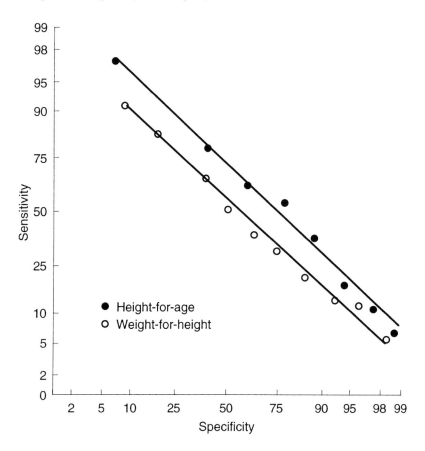

Figure 5

Relationship between sensitivity (%) and specificity (%) for height-for-age and weight-for-height in predicting 2-year survival[a]

the best, results can be misleading if the cut-off point is chosen *before* selection of a particular indicator: there is no *a priori* best cut-off for purposes of comparison.

In the example above, death and survival were the basis for dividing the population into sensitivity and specificity distributions respectively. For identifying the best indicator of response, the population should be divided on the basis of whether or not the treatment was administered (*22*); to predict benefit, and to identify the characteristics associated with best response, the population should be divided into those who respond to the intervention and those who do not.

Using anthropometry in individuals

At the level of the individual, anthropometry is used either to identify a person as being in need of special consideration, or to assess that person's response to some intervention.

2.7.1 *Screening with one measurement for targeting an intervention*

Screening for malnutrition or disease is of value only if effective treatment for the condition is available (*23*). This principle is frequently overlooked in the context of anthropometric screening for malnutrition. Moreover, the anthropometric screen may be the *only* step taken before decisions on intervention are reached, particularly in emergencies. Historically, however, screening has been viewed as simply a *first* step (*23, 24*), i.e. as the first in a sequence of increasingly specific screens leading to effective intervention. It is therefore clear that, the less specific the initial screens are for the intervention envisaged, the more important the subsequent screens become.

An anthropometric screen is based on an indicator for which a suitable cut-off point (or points) is chosen to categorize individuals for different decisions. The crucial questions to be answered by an anthropometric screen are:

- Is the indicator the best one for the decision that must be made? and
- Are the cut-off points the best ones for selecting individuals and ensuring the necessary action?

The first question was addressed in section 2.6; the following section deals with selection of cut-off points.

Selecting the best cut-off point
Universal cut-off points are often recommended but are appropriate only if resources are adequate to handle all individuals selected for intervention and if the intervention causes no adverse side-effects. In such a case, it is unimportant that a high proportion of those who receive the intervention will not benefit from it. The cut-off point should be set at 100% sensitivity, so that all those at risk who *can* benefit from the intervention are treated.

Cut-offs are commonly set on the basis of experience in affluent populations which shows that the proportion of individuals identified by a screen who can benefit is sufficient to warrant further diagnostic steps. These cut-offs are usually described in terms of Z-scores, percentiles, or percent of a normative median because, historically, reference data from healthy populations were used to establish these values. However, these reference data give information only about healthy individuals who cannot benefit from the intervention; they provide no indication of the sensitivity that is relevant for setting the cut-off. Nonetheless, despite the poor theoretical basis for using reference data in this way, these cut-offs have been tested empirically in affluent populations and are now conventional; they should not be abandoned until cut-offs based on sounder principles have been validated.

In certain situations, the specificity distribution of those who cannot benefit from an intervention is important: when the proportion of the population who could benefit is low and the intervention causes adverse side-effects. The introduction of supplementary feeding for a fully breast-fed infant, especially in areas where food contamination and infection are common, probably falls into this category, since the new foods may pose unnecessary health risks to the child (25, 26). It may be that some deficit in nutrition is less harmful than the introduction of potentially contaminated foods, in which case specificity would be more important than sensitivity in setting the cut-off.

Balancing needs and resources in a population
Where resources are insufficient to support intervention for *all* those who might need it, cut-offs should be chosen to maximize the number of at-risk individuals who *can* be treated. Ideally, screening for risk of death should maximize the coverage of those at risk, and at the same time maximize the proportion of those selected who are in fact at risk. The coverage is directly reflected by the sensitivity of the screen. The term "yield" (23) was formerly used for the proportion of those at risk among the total selected, but this has been superseded by "positive predictive value" (24, 27).

Sensitivity and positive predictive value can be readily confused, since the numerator of each ratio (the number of individuals who are at risk and who are identified by the screening test) is the same. This is illustrated in Table 2, where those who are at risk are represented by *B* and *b*, and those not at risk by *N* and *n*. Although the denominators of both proportions include the *B* individuals, they differ in the remaining individuals they include. For sensitivity, a proportion (*b*) of the at-risk individuals are included, who should have been picked up by the screen and were not; they are false-negatives, i.e. individuals falsely diagnosed as not at risk. For the positive predictive value, a proportion (*n*) of the individuals not at risk is included in the denominator; they are false-positives, i.e. individuals falsely diagnosed by the screen as being at risk.

As stated above, the most important principle in screening for an intervention where resources are limited is to select for treatment the greatest number of those who most need it (17). Thus, the screen should identify those in greatest need, and also have the highest positive predictive value. Such a screen will also capture the lowest proportion of individuals who do not need intervention. As presently conceived in anthropometry, the highest positive predictive value is best achieved by moving the cut-off as far as possible from the reference median value. Using risk of malnutrition as an example, the cut-off point for height-for-

Table 2
Sensitivity, specificity, positive and negative predictive values, and prevalence

		Truth		
		Will benefit	Will not benefit	Sum
Diagnosis based on screen	Will benefit	B	n	$B + n$
	Will not benefit	b	N	$b + N$
	Sum	$B + b$	$n + N$	$B + b + n + N$

Sensitivity = $B/(B + b)$ True-positive = B

Specificity = $N/(n + N)$ True-negative = N

Prevalence = $(B + b)/(B + b + n + N)$ False negative = b

Positive predictive value = $B/(B + n)$ False positive = n

Negative predictive value = $N/(b + N)$

age can be set so low that everybody chosen is malnourished. However, there are many others in the population who are malnourished and who would be identified by a higher cut-off. Unfortunately, the higher cut-off also selects individuals who are small but not malnourished, and therefore has a lower positive predictive value. Thus there is usually a trade-off between the positive predictive value and the sensitivity. In many circumstances, when selection for malnutrition is based on low height and weight indices, each increment by which the cut-off is moved towards the reference median delivers the next best positive predictive value compared with the previous cut-off, and also selects those individuals who are the next most malnourished. This is why the cut-off that selects exactly the number of people that can be handled by the intervention selects the most malnourished, with the best positive predictive value, and is therefore the best that can be chosen where resources are limited.

For lack of an appropriate example in anthropometry, a clinical study has been chosen to illustrate this point. The objective was to determine how well early signs and symptoms among young children with diarrhoea predicted the risk of subsequent life-threatening dehydration (28). The sensitivity of each indicator (e.g. vomiting, fever, thirst, six or more stools/day) was plotted against the proportion of all children in the study population who would be selected for close follow-up and intensive intervention. If resources were available for intensive intervention in 25% of the children with diarrhoea, the indicator giving the highest sensitivity for that proportion would be selected. Of course the positive predictive values will change for all of these cut-offs as the prevalence of life-threatening diarrhoea changes, but the order of sensitivity of the indicators will be unchanged.

*Effect of prevalence on positive predictive value and implications for
setting cut-off points*

In contrast to sensitivity and specificity, the positive predictive value
(PPV) always depends on the prevalence of the issue of concern. The
higher the prevalence, the higher the PPV for a given cut-off.

The PPV is determined by the sensitivity and the specificity of the test
and by the prevalence of the condition of interest in the population being
tested. As is evident from Table 2, the more specific a test, the better its
PPV (and thus the greater the confidence that an individual with a
positive test result has the condition of interest). The mathematical
formula relating PPV to sensitivity (SE), specificity (SP) and prevalence
(P) is based on Bayes' theorem of conditional probability (*29*).

$$PPV = \frac{(SE)\,(P)}{(SE)\,(P) + (1-SP)\,(1-P)}$$

This formula shows that a screening test performs well, with moderately
high specificity (90%), if prevalence of the condition in the population
tested is relatively high. At lower prevalences, however, the PPV drops to
nearly zero for the same specificity, and the test is virtually useless for
screening purposes. In summary, the interpretation of a positive test
result varies from setting to setting, according to the estimated prevalence
of the disease or condition of interest.

In a population where malnutrition among children greatly exceeds 50%,
a wasted child is almost certainly malnourished and further diagnostic
screening is superfluous. However, more practical information may be
required before a specific intervention can be implemented. For instance,
if the underlying problem is one of maternal knowledge rather than
the unreliability of the food supply, the nature of the intervention will
differ.

Diagnostic screening for risk and etiological screening thus have
different (though related) objectives, but the primary determinant of
appropriateness in both cases is the positive predictive value.

The basic requirement for using the same percentile or Z-score as the cut-
off point is that it should have the same meaning in different individuals.
This can be true only if the positive predictive value of the test is
constant, which is rare. It must therefore be concluded that universal cut-
off points are less useful than those based on the principle of selecting for
intervention as many people as the available resources can handle. Thus,
where resources are insufficient to treat everybody who is in need, which
is the usual situation among both affluent and poor societies worldwide,
there is no universally ideal cut-off.

Simple, practicable methodologies for choosing cut-offs that take
account of local availability of resources as well as of the number of
people who need the intervention have yet to be developed. Any such

methodology should also provide guidance about additional information that may be needed, the nature of which will vary with prevalence, risk, or benefits sought.

Comparing cut-offs for identifying risk with those for predicting benefit
Little research has examined the relationship between the most efficient cut-offs used to screen for risk and those used to predict benefit, but it seems likely that there are many circumstances in which the two are entirely unrelated. In Fig. 6, for example, neonatal mortality rates at different birth weights among the poor and a more affluent population of the same country are compared. If risk were the only guiding criterion, the most sensible intervention would target infants below, say, 2.5 kg, whether from affluent or poor families. However, assuming that the most efficient intervention would reduce mortality rates among the poor to the levels among the affluent, consideration of potential benefit will direct the intervention to those above this cut-off weight (*30*).

Thus, the choice and use of a cut-off to select individuals for special consideration may differ radically, depending on whether selection is based on prediction of death (risk indicator) or prediction of benefit from improved services (indicator of predicted benefit). This suggests again that the conventional approach of selecting on risk (*12*) and then following up with more specific screens (*23*) may generate conflicting decisions.

Figure 6
Birth-weight-specific mortality of a poor and a more affluent population in the same country

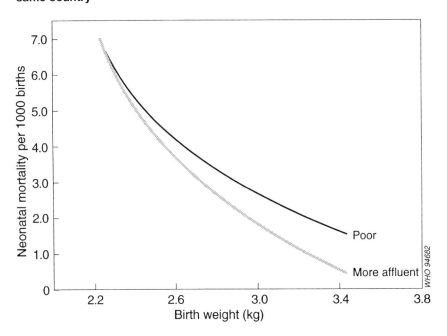

Growth monitoring and screening: changes in size over time
Continuous monitoring is often undertaken for the early detection of health and nutrition problems, particularly during periods when the risk of malnutrition, morbidity, and death is high, as in early childhood or in old age. Measures of satisfactory progress are healthy growth in children and healthy maintenance of body mass in the elderly. In theory, both should be more easily verified by repeated measurements than by comparing attained size with the reference data.

This approach has been widely implemented among children within the larger context of growth monitoring. It is usual practice to ascertain whether the child is growing along a set percentile of reference data. At present, these reference data are cross-sectional, which poses certain problems, particularly in infancy and adolescence (*31*); further research is needed to develop appropriate longitudinal reference data.

Drawing up such data for growth increments is a formidable task, because the distribution of increments around the mean increment of the reference data will depend on the exact intervals between measurements. In practice, few children are measured at set intervals. In the future, it may be possible to compare individual growth data with figures from inexpensive computerized programs based on algorithms derived from reference data.

Even less research has focused on the relationship of growth faltering to responses to interventions than on small attained size, so that few quantitative conclusions can be drawn about the sensitivity distributions and positive predictive values essential for decisions on intervention. The receiver operating characteristics may be much better for incremental than for attained data: increments are a better reflection of present remediable circumstances than is attained size, and may be subject to less genetic variability. All these presumptions, of course, require empirical verification.

In establishing and maintaining a growth monitoring system, a number of other considerations may be just as important as the diagnosis of growth faltering itself. These include increased attention to child health and improvements in access to other services, in social networks, and in the early detection of diseases unrelated to growth.

2.7.2 *Assessing response to an intervention*

In clinical practice change can be assessed from two or more serial measurements in the individual. Public health practice, by contrast, deals with populations and it is thus difficult reliably to assess change over time at the individual level.

Change may also be verified on the basis of a child's achieving some threshold. For instance, a wasted child may be selected to participate in a feeding programme. When the child has regained the level of a given cut-off point – perhaps the same cut-off used in screening for the intervention – he or she can be discharged from the programme. This method, whereby the same screen is used to select for the intervention and to judge satisfactory response, usually shows a high rate of apparent response. However, if individuals are selected for the second measurement on the basis of the first, measuring the same individual twice will often result in spurious improvement. The greater the deviation of the first measurement from the population mean, the more likely it is that the individual will move towards that mean for reasons other than the intervention, including measurement errors and week-to-week variability. Careful account must be taken of this regression towards the mean (*32*). In one study in which they were considered in the context of a feeding programme, these other factors accounted for most of the response, even though prevalence of malnutrition was moderately high (*33*). While this does not detract from the value of the method as a basis for discharging children from a feeding programme, it must be taken into account in judging the effectiveness of the programme.

Anthropometry may also be used for deciding to discontinue an intervention in individuals who fail to respond. In such cases, medical examination may disclose other treatable causes of poor growth.

2.8 Using anthropometry in populations

2.8.1 *Uses related to decisions*

In populations, as in individuals, the major decisions for which anthropometric data are used relate to the types of intervention that are foreseen. Typical applications include decisions on whether or not intervention programmes are needed, to whom they should be delivered, and what their nature will be. These applications are similar to those involved in screening individuals; for populations, however, appropriate decisions are rarely as well established. Programme management, and timely warning and intervention systems to prevent famines and food crises (*34, 35*), for which population approaches have long been used, are probably exceptions to this general rule.

When the implementation of population interventions is planned, it is important to differentiate between relative risk and attributable risk (or, more specifically, the population attributable risk or etiological fraction). The risk of death in a child with a severe anthropometric deficit may be several times greater than that in a child with no deficit, while a child with mild deficits is at an intermediate level of risk. These comparisons refer to relative risks. In a population, however, the number of children with mild deficits will tend to be much greater than that of severely affected children. Thus, although severe deficits are associated with a larger relative risk, the mild deficits may account for the majority of deaths, which is the concept of attributable risk (*24, 36*). At the population level, its implication is that the overall impact of an intervention will be limited if the intervention is delivered only to the most severely affected individuals.

A further important concept in the delivery of population interventions is that displacement of the whole anthropometric curve (Z-score distribution for the anthropometric indicator; see Fig. 7) often occurs in areas where nutritional problems are present. For example, data from many different countries show a very high consistency in the standard deviation of weight-for-height among young children expressed as Z-scores of the international reference. Even under conditions of extreme famine, where the mean Z-score is two or three units below the reference, the value of the standard deviation of Z-scores is very close to unity (*38*). This shows that the entire distribution is shifted, as seen in Fig. 7, so that

Figure 7
Z-score distribution for height-for-age and weight-for-age of Chinese children compared with the NCHS/WHO international reference[a]

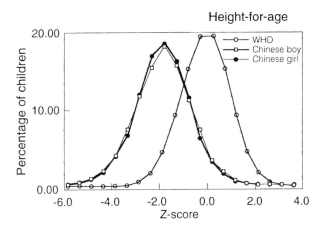

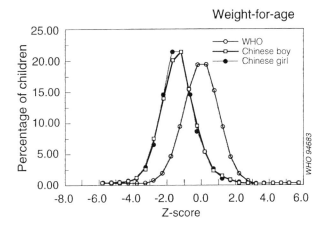

[a] Source: reference *37*.

all individuals, not only those below a given cut-off point, are affected (*39*). Interventions may consequently have to be directed at the whole population, rather than only at those individuals who fall below a given cut-off.

Appropriate use of anthropometry in populations must also take sampling strategies into consideration, including the choice of age ranges, time periods, geographical areas, and socioeconomic groups. Such technical issues as the relationship of sample size to statistical power, specific study designs, and confidence intervals are beyond the scope of this report and are treated elsewhere (*6, 40, 41*). The summary tables of appropriate uses of anthropometry provided in subsequent sections for different age and status groups give initial guidance on some variables to be considered for sampling purposes; however, specific expertise in sampling should be sought before surveys are launched, to ensure that the most important questions can be answered.

Considerations of sample size often result in the need to pool children of different ages, but this procedure is justified only if observed deviations from reference data have the same meaning relative to an intervention at different ages. For example, the cumulative effects of stunting may have ceased by the age of 3 years, so that prevalence values over a wide age range may be difficult to interpret. Assessment of stunting among older children, in whom there is a fixed deficit, will then yield more easily interpretable information regarding the need for long-term intervention. Because the intervention is to be directed towards young children, in whom there is active stunting, rather than towards those who are already stunted, this approach seems paradoxical. Nevertheless, older children provide the sentinel signal for the population to be targeted, even though they will themselves no longer benefit from the intervention. By concentrating monitoring on these "sentinel" children, information can be collected earlier and more cheaply, will be more understandable, and will have greater relevance to decisions regarding actions with longer-term impact.

Sampling considerations must include the appropriate timing of surveys; this is particularly important in such contexts as the alleviation of seasonal food crises. Timing is also a critical aspect of any decision-making process based on anthropometry; the ability to meet deadlines for the collection, compilation, analysis, and presentation of data may be as important as any other consideration. Expertise in designing surveys that are timely is essential if the collected data are to be transformed into information that is relevant and useful for effective public policy and action.

2.8.2 *Targeting interventions*

A screening tool can be used to estimate prevalence by counting the number of individuals in a population who fall below a given cut-off point. Anthropometric indicators can also be used to characterize the status of a population: the mean Z-score, for example, will provide a more accurate estimate of poor anthropometric status than observed prevalence (38), thus reducing the sample size needed for a nutritional survey. In anthropometry, differences in means provide greater statistical power than differences in prevalence in discriminating across target groups (38). Examples of this approach are discussed in more detail in section 5.

Sometimes comparison of the whole population distribution (as shown in Fig. 7) is indicated, rather than just the mean Z-scores or the prevalence below a given cut-off point. In a recent report on a refugee group (42), for example, the death rate among the most severely malnourished was so high that the lower end of the distribution was truncated, leaving the mean hardly affected. A full discussion of appropriate determination of prevalence is included in section 2.8.5.

In principle, targeting of populations, as of individuals, can be based not only on a one-time measurement as discussed above, but also on repeated measurements.

2.8.3 *Assessing response to an intervention*

Assessing the response to interventions requires at least two measurements. If the intervention is likely to affect the anthropometric characteristics of the individual, it is usually more efficient to measure the same individuals twice than different individuals on two occasions, because of the smaller sample size needed to identify a change. In other circumstances, repeated measuring of the same individual makes little sense, especially where prevention of a given condition is the objective of intervention. In such cases, different individuals of the same age are measured to assess reduction in prevalence. It is then essential to take into account any factors that may distort comparability over time, such as selective migration.

The problem of regression to the mean has already been discussed in the context of repeated measurements in the individual. It is less well recognized that the same phenomenon will occur in populations selected for their low initial values, even if the second measurement is not taken in the same individuals as the first.

The same Z-score deviations from the reference data do not necessarily have the same meanings at different ages. It is therefore impossible to interpret change properly unless the effect of age is taken into account.

When the response to specific interventions in a population is monitored, the time delay before the chosen indicator shows evidence of change must be taken into account. For instance, months or years are required to assess the effect on birth weight of improved nutrition during pregnancy, but decades for improvements in birth weight through prevention of childhood malnutrition to become apparent.

2.8.4 *Ascertaining the determinants and consequences of malnutrition*

In general, relating anthropometric indicators of malnutrition to the determinants or consequences of the condition in populations requires careful distinction between non-causal and causal associations. The exception is in targeting, for which causal and non-causal relationships can be equally useful. For example, stunting of an older sibling is a good targeting indicator even though it is not a direct cause of malnutrition in the younger child.

Efforts to infer causality from a single survey must take account of non-causal associations arising from coincident changes across different birth cohorts. For instance, in survey data collected at one specific time, literacy and physical stature in adults may show an inverse relationship with chronological age. The reason for this is that increases in both stature and literacy are the consequences of secular improvements in socioeconomic development that have affected younger adults. This cohort effect, which is a characteristic problem in surveys of older people, is discussed in more detail in section 9. The need for correct modelling of relationships between indicators and determinants and consequences has already been addressed.

2.8.5 *Nutritional surveillance*

Anthropometry provides some of the most important indicators used in nutritional surveillance. The following classification of nutritional surveillance (*34*) is based on the different types of survey mechanisms and other procedures necessary to collect, analyse, and transfer information for use in making decisions that affect nutrition.

Surveillance for problem identification and for policy and programme planning
Prevalence estimates often play a pivotal role in the assignment of government priorities to health problems. True prevalence can be estimated from measured prevalence by taking sensitivity and specificity into account (*43*), and this is often done for specific diseases for which the sensitivity and specificity of a given indicator are precisely calculated through comparison with a clinical or pathological "gold standard". For anthropometric indicators of nutritional status, however, the "gold standard", that is, appropriate nutrition, cannot be measured directly; this presents a difficulty in nutritional surveillance.

The logic of an alternative method of estimating the true prevalence of malnutrition is based on the assumption of a universally applicable specificity distribution. This assumption is closely approximated in young children (*44*), for whom this distribution corresponds to the growth potential of all populations of young children in which there are no stunting or wasting factors, currently represented by the NCHS/WHO reference data.[1] The observed distribution of children in any population is made up of those who have not been stunted or wasted and thus correspond to the NCHS/WHO reference data (specificity distribution), plus stunted and wasted children (sensitivity distribution). The prevalence of stunting and wasting is the ratio of the children in the sensitivity distribution to all children in the population; the sensitivity distribution is obtained by subtracting the specificity population from the total population (45). To the degree that other universally relevant reference data for other healthy conditions (e.g. healthy thinness) can be defined, these reference data can be used as the specificity distribution for counting the unhealthy (e.g. the overweight) in conditions other than childhood malnutrition.

Two new methods have been proposed for estimation of prevalence using the reference data as the specificity distribution (46, 47). The more recent of the two (47) implicitly takes account of the effect of prevalence itself on the results, and is more accurate. This method is also the simpler, does not require a computer, and has good precision when the mean Z-score of the malnourished population is low. In other cases, however, a graphical method (45) using the reference standards as the specificity distribution might have better precision.

Computer methods are available that do not depend on an external standard to define specificity (48). Because they take into account the small genetic differences between populations, they should be intrinsically more precise provided that the sensitivity and specificity distributions are Gaussian.

All the above methods make the assumption that only a proportion of the children are malnourished. Other methods (38), described in section 5, may be used if *all* the children in the population can be assumed to be malnourished.

It is a mistake to compare relatively precise estimates of malnutrition prevalence derived from anthropometry in young children with those of other diseases estimated less precisely or with estimates of malnutrition based on other indicators. Dietary information derived by using cut-offs is particularly misleading in this application (49).

In nutritional surveillance for policy development and programme planning it is crucial to identify those of the most important causal influences that are amenable to interventions. Clear differentiation between analyses designed to *identify* interventions and those designed to *target* interventions is essential.

---

[1] NCHS/WHO growth reference data: reference data for height and weight of US children, originally collected by the National Center for Health Statistics and recommended by WHO for international use (see *Measuring change in nutritional status*, Geneva, World Health Organization, 1983).

Timely warning and intervention systems
Child anthropometry has provided appropriate indicators for targeting food distribution to prevent outright famines. In order to obviate the need for the disruptive social and economic effects of food relief, timely warning and intervention systems should also be capable of averting food crises. Unfortunately, changes in the prevalence of wasting large enough to give reliable warning usually occur too late to permit effective preventive action against food crises (*35*); a longer lead time is essential if the need for emergency food distribution is to be avoided.

The timeliness of information can be improved by preferential sampling of "sentinels", i.e. groups and individuals who signal the advent of food crisis earlier than the rest of the population. However, this early warning may lack specificity, in that it may occur seasonally even when there is no subsequent food crisis in the population. It therefore becomes necessary to follow this first screen with the collection of other more specific information (*34*).

Anthropometric indicators are useful in the late stages of the evolution of food crises (*35*). As famine progresses, however, selective mortality of the most wasted children may make the affected population as a whole appear less severely malnourished than it really is (*42*), and anthropometry must therefore be complemented by mortality information.

Surveillance for programme management
Programme managers require information both for targeting an intervention and for evaluating its success: its efficacy in covering everyone it should, and its efficiency in covering *only* those that it should. These latter two aspects have very different implications for sampling. Efficiency, or yield, can be determined by assessing the positive predictive value on programme participants themselves; assessment of coverage depends on determining sensitivity and thus also requires information on non-participants, which presents a much more difficult task.

Programme managers also need to ensure that the response of participants is as expected. In defining expected responses in situations where participants are screened by anthropometry, it is important to take into account the positive predictive value and regression to the mean.

The impact of the intervention programme on participants is a matter of concern, too, to those who provide the financial resources, who often fail to realize that this cannot be assessed on the basis of data obtained from participants alone. Assessment requires appropriate control groups, and expertise is also needed to model the anthropometric impact properly. Understanding this model is essential both for sampling the individuals for measurement and for analysis of the data.

2.9 Characteristics of reference data

A *reference* is defined as a tool for grouping and analysing data and provides a common basis for comparing populations; no inferences should be made about the meaning of observed differences. A *standard*, on the other hand, embraces the notion of a norm or desirable target, and thus involves a value judgement. Concern has been expressed that, because reference data embody certain characteristics or patterns of normality, they have been widely and inappropriately used to make inferences about the health and/or nutrition of individuals and populations; that is, they have been treated as optimum targets, or standards, and any deviation from these "standards" has been assumed to have a fixed and particular meaning. Much of the justification for this is provided by extensive evidence that, in populations, the effect of ethnic differences on the growth of children is small compared with environmental effects. Thus, for example, there is no reason to believe that the 2–3 cm difference in median height between well nourished 18-year-olds in the Netherlands and France has any health implications, nor that improving the health and nutrition of French youth would be associated with any reduction in the height difference. By contrast, the Expert Committee recommended a body mass index cut-off of ≥30 as a provisional standard of grade 2 overweight (defined in section 7.2.1), applicable to *all* adults, because available data on risks of morbidity and mortality support this. For many other anthropometric characteristics, however, there are insufficient data to permit the specification of standards.

The Expert Committee recognized that release of references by WHO makes it almost impossible to prevent their use as standards for judging the nutritional status of individuals and populations. It is therefore recommended that care should always be taken to choose references that resemble, as far as possible, true standards, so that the same deviation from the reference data has the same biological meaning. For example, because the mean heights of young children from many affluent populations differ little across ethnic groups compared with the socioeconomic variability within a given ethnic group (*44*), it should be possible to construct a standard that represents the growth potential of all children. This may seem surprising in the light of the rather broad distribution of attained heights and weights, generally felt to be of genetic origin, within a well nourished population. However, across most populations there seems to be very little difference in mean growth in height or in its distribution around the mean that is attributable to genetics. A universal standard of height distribution among young children is therefore justified, but it must derive from a population that has fully met its growth potential. For this reason, the most important criterion in choosing the current set of WHO childhood height and weight reference data (*4, 6*) was that it should come from a well nourished population (*50*).

The choice of a sample for developing references or standards thus raises the question of what constitutes a healthy population. At least four definitions exist:

(1) The population lives in a healthy environment. This is the type of population from which the current childhood NCHS/WHO reference data (*4, 6, 7*) have been drawn.

(2) The population lives in a healthy environment and contains no overtly sick or very few clinically sick individuals. This is the type of population from which many national paediatric reference data have been drawn.

(3) The population lives in a healthy environment and contains only individuals whose present good health will be demonstrated by longevity or at least by survival for some years after measurements are taken.

(4) The population lives in a healthy environment and contains only individuals who live healthily according to present prescriptions, for example infants who are breast-fed according to WHO recommendations.

A further definition might cover some combination of the above, such as a population living in a healthy environment, excluding both those who die within some specified time after measurement (see item 3 above) and those who engage in unhealthy practices such as smoking (see item 4).

The first of the above definitions prevailed for children in the past because its advantages, principally total population representation, were felt to outweigh the advantages of the second, especially since the NCHS/WHO reference data were very similar to the best of previous reference data sets based on the second definition. Little work has been done in comparing populations that correspond to the first two definitions with others; section 5 of this report, however, contains a comparison of definitions (1) and (4) in the context of infants who are exclusively breast-fed from birth to 4–6 months of age in accordance with WHO recommendations (*51*).

A related question concerns the extent to which different standards should be used to approximate the ideal, i.e. whether there should be different standards of birth weight according to race, of growth data according to parental size, or of body mass index according to body frame. Possibly, this should depend upon the use to which the standards will be put. For instance, different criteria for assessing mean birth weight according to maternal smoking status might be useful: equal degrees of intrauterine growth retardation have different prognoses for children of smokers and non-smokers. However, in assessing the prevalence of intrauterine growth retardation, controlling for a mother's smoking would be wrong as it would mask an important problem. The theoretical advantage of using different standards for specific purposes may thus be counterbalanced by equally strong theoretical disadvantages. For this reason, when reference data are to be used to make decisions about populations, it is better to use statistical methods to control for differences (such as those associated with different altitudes) within or across populations than to use different standards.

On the level of the individual, different standards have been proposed to take into account intrinsic differences in the expected optimal size associated with, for example, differences in altitude, parental heights, or feeding practices (whether a child is exclusively breast-fed or not). The utility of developing different standards for screening individuals depends essentially on the prevalence of the condition being screened. Unless its variability is low, prevalence has such a large effect on the positive predictive value that errors arising from the lack of separate standards are of little practical significance. In wealthy countries, however, where prevalence is low and therefore shows little variability, the use of separate standards might be justified. In such settings, the positive predictive values of anthropometric screens are so low that further screens generally become necessary. The trade-off between the cost of using multiple standards and the savings made by avoiding further screens remains to be investigated, but computerization of expected optimal growth on the basis of various characteristics of individuals will probably favour the use of individualized standards in wealthy populations. In poorer populations, where the use of different standards does not improve screening and poses considerable managerial problems, single standards should continue to be used.

If reference data are to be used as standards, the criteria for the reference population are of critical importance. The following criteria have been established as desirable, and are briefly reviewed (*50*):

- *"The sample should include at least 200 individuals in each age and sex group"*

  This criterion relates particularly to the precision with which extreme percentiles or Z-scores are calculated. A sample of this size would provide the 5th percentile with a standard deviation of about ± a 1.54 percentile, and is considered acceptable for individual-based applications (such as screening). In population-based applications, the sample size is also sufficiently large to allow differentiation between environmental and genetic effects on growth (*52*).

- *"The sample should be cross-sectional since the comparisons that will be made are of a cross-sectional nature"*

  This is no longer considered essential, since longitudinal data can be presented cross-sectionally with minor adjustments. On the contrary, growth charts derived from cross-sectional data should not be used to monitor longitudinal data (*31*). Where several measurements are made in the same individual, the slope of the line joining successive points on the growth chart is a direct measure of growth velocity. If the slope differs substantially from that of the neighbouring percentile curves, so that the data appear to cross percentiles, this is taken to be an indication of abnormal growth. However, since percentiles are derived from cross-sectional data and are relevant only to single measurements, their application to the interpretation of longitudinal data is inappropriate. This is particularly true during infancy and puberty. Correct interpretation of percentile crossing requires a different set of percentiles, derived from longitudinal data (*31*). Unfortunately, cross-sectional references continue to be widely misused for the interpretation of longitudinal data.

- *"Sampling procedures should be defined and reproducible"*

- *"Measurements should be carefully made and recorded by observers trained in anthropometric techniques, using equipment of well tested design and calibrated at frequent intervals"*

References should also include data on reliability and precision (as is true of the current NCHS/WHO childhood reference) (*53*). Both inter-observer variability and instrument error should be documented, and it is useful, though not essential, to have separate estimates of within- and between-observer components of reliability (*54*).

Where missing data have had to be "imputed" – that is, generated by means of a statistical algorithm based on a number of assumptions – they should be separately identified and the method by which they were derived should be clearly documented. Any "cleaning" procedures used to remove patently spurious data should also be described.

- *"The measurements made on the sample should include all the anthropometric variables that will be used in the evaluation of nutritional status"*

The various measurements taken from a single individual should be compared with reference data derived from a single population. This avoids the inconsistencies that may arise from using several different references for different measurements, such as weight and arm circumference.

- *"The data from which reference graphs and tables are prepared should be available for anyone wishing to use them, and the procedures used for smoothing curves and preparing tables should be adequately described and documented"*

There have been many recent developments in techniques for smoothing curves, which have implications for required sample sizes and accurate representation of the data.

References

1. Beaton G et al. *Appropriate uses of anthropometric indices in children: a report based on an ACC/SCN workshop.* New York, United Nations Administrative Committee on Coordination/Subcommittee on Nutrition, 1990 (ACC/SCN State-of-the-Art Series, Nutrition Policy Discussion Paper No. 7).

2. Habicht J-P, Pelletier DL. The importance of context in choosing nutritional indicators. *Journal of nutrition*, 1990, **120** (Suppl. 11):1519–1524.

3. Wang ZM, Pierson RN Jr, Heymsfield SB. The five-level model: a new approach to organizing body-composition research. *American journal of clinical nutrition*, 1992, **56**:19–28.

4. WHO Working Group. Use and interpretation of anthropometric indicators of nutritional status. *Bulletin of the World Health Organization,* 1986, **64**:929–941.

5. Armitage P, Berry G. *Statistical methods in medical research,* 2nd ed. Oxford, Blackwell, 1987.

6. *Measuring change in nutritional status: guidelines for assessing the nutritional impact of supplementary feeding programmes.* Geneva, World Health Organization, 1983.

7. Dibley MJ et al. Development of normalized curves for the international growth reference: historical and technical considerations. *American journal of clinical nutrition,* 1987, **46**:736–748.

8. Dibley MJ et al. Interpretation of Z-score anthropometric indicators derived from the international growth reference. *American journal of clinical nutrition,* 1987, **46**:749–762.

9. Gorstein J et al. Issues in the assessment of nutritional status using anthropometry. *Bulletin of the World Health Organization*, 1994, **72**:273–284.

10. Esrey SA, Casella G, Habicht J-P. The use of residuals for longitudinal data analysis: the example of child growth. *American journal of epidemiology*, 1990, **131**:365–372.

11. Gorstein J. Assessment of nutritional status: effects of different methods to determine age on the classification of undernutrition. *Bulletin of the World Health Organization,* 1989, **67**:143–150.

12. Backett EM, Davies AM, Petros-Barvazian A. *The risk approach to health care, with special reference to maternal and child health care, including family planning.* Geneva, World Health Organization, 1984 (Public Health Papers, No. 76).

13. Brabin B. An assessment of low birthweight risk in primiparae as an indicator of malaria control in pregnancy. *International journal of epidemiology,* 1991, **20**:276–283.

14. Monteiro CA, Torres AM. Can secular trends in child growth be estimated from a single cross sectional survey? *British medical journal,* 1992, **305**:797–799.

15. Shekar M, Habicht J-P, Latham MC. Is positive deviance in growth the converse of negative deviance? *Food and nutrition bulletin,* 1991, **13**:7–11.

16. Brownie C, Habicht J-P, Cogill B. Comparing indicators of health or nutritional status. *American journal of epidemiology,* 1986, **124**:1031–1044.

17. **Habicht J-P, Meyers DL, Brownie C.** Indicators for identifying and counting the improperly nourished. *American journal of clinical nutrition,* 1982, 35(5 Suppl.):1241–1254.

18. **Galen RS, Gambino SR.** *Beyond normality: the predictive value and efficiency of medical diagnoses.* New York, Wiley, 1975.

19. **Leon ME et al.** Identifying the malnourished within Peru: regional variation in the performance of a nutrition indicator. *International journal of epidemiology,* 1990, 19:214–216.

20. **Briend A et al.** Measuring change in nutritional status: a comparison of different anthropometric indices and the sample sizes required. *European journal of clinical nutrition,* 1989, 43:769–778.

21. **Yarbrough C et al.** Response of indicators of nutritional status to nutritional interventions in populations and individuals. In: Bosch S, Arias J, eds. *Evaluation of child health services: the interface between research and medical practice.* Washington, DC, U.S. Government Printing Office, 1978 (DHEW Publication No. (NIH) 78-1066):195–207.

22. **Stoltzfus RJ et al.** Evaluation of indicators for use in vitamin A intervention trials targeted to women. *International journal of epidemiology,* 1994, 22:1111–1118.

23. *Principles and practice of screening for disease.* Geneva, World Health Organization, 1968 (Public Health Papers, No. 34).

24. **Last JM.** *A dictionary of epidemiology,* 2nd ed. New York, Oxford University Press, 1988.

25. **Victora CG et al.** Evidence for protection by breast-feeding against infant deaths from infectious diseases in Brazil. *Lancet,* 1987, ii:319–322.

26. **Habicht J-P, DaVanzo J, Butz WP.** Mother's milk and sewage: their interactive effects on infant mortality. *Pediatrics,* 1988, 81:456–461.

27. **Vecchio TJ.** Predictive value of a single diagnostic test in unselected populations. *New England journal of medicine,* 1966, 274:1171–1173.

28. **Victora CG et al.** Is it possible to predict which diarrhoea episodes will lead to life-threatening dehydration? *International journal of epidemiology,* 1990, 19:736–742.

29. **Fletcher RH, Fletcher SW, Wagner EH.** *Clinical epidemiology: the essentials.* Baltimore, Williams & Wilkins, 1982:41–58.

30. **Victora CG et al.** Birthweight and infant mortality: a longitudinal study of 5914 Brazilian children. *International journal of epidemiology,* 1987, 16:239–245.

31. **Cole TJ.** Growth charts for both cross-sectional and longitudinal data. *Statistics in medicine,* 1994, 13:2477–2492.

32. **Davis CE.** The effect of regression to the mean in epidemiologic and clinical studies. *American journal of epidemiology,* 1976, 104:493–498.

33. **Rivera JA, Habicht J-P, Robson DS.** Effect of supplementary feeding on recovery from mild to moderate wasting in preschool children. *American journal of clinical nutrition,* 1991, 54:62–68.

34. **Mason JB et al.** *Nutritional surveillance.* Geneva, World Health Organization, 1984.

35. **Brooks RM et al.** A timely warning and intervention system for preventing food crises in Indonesia: applying guidelines for nutrition surveillance. *Food and nutrition,* 1985, **11**:37-43.

36. **Pelletier DL, Frongillo EA Jr, Habicht J-P.** Epidemiologic evidence for a potentiating effect of malnutrition on child mortality. *American journal of public health,* 1993, **83**:1130-1133.

37. **Chang Ying et al.** Nutritional status of preschool children in poor rural areas of China. *Bulletin of the World Health Organization,* 1994, **72**:105-112.

38. **Yip R.** Expanded usage of anthropometry Z-scores for assessing population nutritional status and data quality. In: *Abstracts book no. 1, 15th International Congress of Nutrition (Adelaide).* Adelaide, International Union of Nutritional Sciences, 1993:279.

39. **Rose G.** Sick individuals and sick populations. *International journal of epidemiology,* 1985, **14**:32-38.

40. **Lwanga SK, Lemeshow S.** *Sample size determination in health studies: a practical manual.* Geneva, World Health Organization, 1991.

41. *Conducting small-scale nutrition surveys: a field manual.* Rome, Food and Agriculture Organization of the United Nations, 1990 (Nutrition in Agriculture, No. 5).

42. **Yip R, Sharp TW.** Acute malnutrition and high childhood mortality related to diarrhea. Lessons from the 1991 Kurdish refugee crisis. *Journal of the American Medical Association,* 1993, **270**:587-590.

43. **Rogan WJ, Gladen B.** Estimating prevalence from the results of a screening test. *American journal of epidemiology,* 1978, **107**:71-76.

44. **Habicht J-P et al.** Height and weight standards for preschool children. How relevant are ethnic differences in growth potential? *Lancet,* 1974, i:611-614.

45. **Meyers LD et al.** Prevalences of anemia and iron deficiency anemia in black and white women in the United States estimated by two methods. *American journal of public health,* 1983, **73**:1042-1049.

46. **Mora JO.** A new method for estimating a standardized prevalence of child malnutrition from anthropometric indicators. *Bulletin of the World Health Organization,* 1989, **67**:133-142.

47. **Monteiro CA.** Counting the stunted children in a population: a criticism of old and new approaches and a conciliatory proposal. *Bulletin of the World Health Organization,* 1991, **69**:761-766.

48. **Brownie C, Habicht J-P, Robson DS.** An estimation procedure for the contaminated normal distributions arising in clinical chemistry. *Journal of the American Statistical Association,* 1983, **78**:228-237.

49. *Nutrient adequacy: assessment using food consumption surveys. Report of the Subcommittee on Criteria for Dietary Evaluation of Food Consumption Surveys, Food and Nutrition Board.* Washington, DC, National Academy Press, 1986.

50. **Waterlow JC et al.** The presentation and use of height and weight data for comparing nutritional status of groups of children under the age of 10 years. *Bulletin of the World Health Organization,* 1977, **55**:489-498.

51. The World Health Organization's infant-feeding recommendation. *Weekly epidemiological record,* 1995, **70**:119-120.

52. **Martorell R, Habicht J-P.** Growth in early childhood in developing countries. In: Falkner F, Tanner JM, eds. *Human growth: a comprehensive treatise. Vol. 3: Methodology: ecological, genetic and nutritional effects on growth.* New York, Plenum Press, 1986:241-262.

53. **Marks GC, Habicht J-P, Mueller WH.** Reliability, dependability, and precision of anthropometric measurements. The Second National Health and Nutrition Examination Survey 1979-1980. *American journal of epidemiology,* 1989, **130**:578-587.

54. **Villar J et al.** Perinatal data reliability in a large teaching obstetric unit. *British journal of obstetrics and gynaecology,* 1988, **95**:841-848.

3. Pregnant and lactating women

3.1 Introduction

3.1.1 *Background*

Anthropometric evaluation of nutritional status during the reproductive cycle, particularly during pregnancy, is a widely used, low-technology procedure that may be expected to generate much valuable information, yet it has seldom been rigorously evaluated (*1, 2*). The biological mechanism that underlies the relationship between women's nutritional status and reproductive outcomes is not fully understood except in extreme situations (e.g. famine).

Unlike nutritional evaluation during other periods of life, which is concerned only with the individual(s) in whom measurements are made, measurements made during pregnancy and lactation are expected to reflect both the nutritional status of the woman and, indirectly, growth of the fetus and, later, the quantity and quality of breast milk.

At the clinic level, anthropometric measurements are routinely made on all pregnant women at the time of first contact with the health services and several times thereafter. Information obtained is also routinely incorporated into medical records. The impact of these activities, in terms of benefits for the health of the mother and the fetus or newborn, remains to be demonstrated by randomized controlled trials and has recently been challenged (*2*).

Measurements taken early in pregnancy should be used to evaluate the nutritional status of the woman and to predict how well she can cope with the physiological demands of pregnancy. Unfortunately, this objective is usually neglected, despite clear evidence that, in developing countries, pregnancy and lactation represent a major nutritional drain on the mother (*3*). Among well nourished women, moreover, excessive weight gain during pregnancy, followed by only a brief period of lactation, will be associated with postpartum overweight, increasing the risk of chronic diseases later in life. Measuring a woman's height provides a proxy indicator of childhood growth and skeletal pelvic structure and a good predictor of the risk of cephalopelvic disproportion and obstructed labour, which is a major cause of maternal death in developing countries.

Thus, anthropometric measurements made during the reproductive period should be designed to evaluate women's capacity to deal with the physiological stress of pregnancy, and to identify those women who would benefit most from nutritional interventions.

Perhaps the most widespread use of anthropometric measurements during pregnancy has been in evaluating the risk of fetal growth retardation and selecting women or populations for nutritional interventions aimed at improving fetal growth or prolonging gestation. This application has unfortunately not lived up to expectations (*4, 5*).

Intrauterine growth retardation (IUGR) of nutritional etiology can be a consequence of both low availability of nutrients from a malnourished mother and poor placental transfer of nutrients from a relatively well nourished mother. The latter problem, however, is unlikely to be detected by maternal anthropometry. The association between maternal nutritional status and gestational age at birth is unclear (4). Moreover, the two negative outcomes of principal interest, fetal malnutrition or intrauterine growth retardation and prematurity, are heterogeneous syndromes (6, 7), with maternal nutrition being only one of the causative factors. Improving maternal nutritional status has a significant impact on birth weight only under extreme conditions.

Important methodological issues should be considered when the use of anthropometry during pregnancy is evaluated. There is a strong correlation between preterm delivery and inadequate maternal weight gain, but the fetal contribution to total maternal weight gain cannot be separately determined during pregnancy. Estimation of gestational age, a fundamental issue when considering repeated anthropometric measurements, requires special facilities not usually provided in clinical settings (8), and a high percentage of women are uncertain of the date of their last menstrual period. Failure to give appropriate consideration to issues of this nature has obscured the interpretation of research findings on maternal anthropometry and its clinical application.

In this report, the use and interpretation at the individual and population level of single and serial anthropometric measurements during the reproductive cycle are discussed in the context of both adequate and severely limited health service resources. This approach, combined with a critical evaluation of the literature, is expected to contribute to the most effective, yet practical, use of these important clinical and public health tools.

Implementation of screening programmes and referral systems based on anthropometric measurements during pregnancy may be more feasible than improving the socioeconomic conditions of the population, but should never be considered as a substitute for such improvements.

3.1.2 *Methodology*

Several recent publications have discussed in detail methodological issues related to anthropometry during pregnancy (9, 10). In anthropometric terms, pregnancy is unique in two respects: the period of observation is relatively brief and anthropometric indices change rapidly.

Prepregnancy values of maternal weight, height, or skinfold thickness are only seldom available, although similar values of height will be obtained regardless of when measurements are made. Body weight measured no more than 2 months before conception is an acceptable approximation of prepregnancy weight. If this value is unavailable, a proxy for measured prepregnancy weight may be based on maternal recall or on a measurement made during the first trimester of pregnancy (9). Most epidemiological studies consider that use of recalled prepregnancy weight introduces recall bias, and that use of body weight measured in early pregnancy introduces first trimester weight-gain bias. However, in a study of a group of adolescents in the USA, recalled prepregnancy weight correlated closely with measured weight (11). Moreover, recalled prepregnancy weights obtained by hospital staff and then by research project staff were in close agreement, with an intraclass correlation coefficient of 0.95 (95% confidence interval 0.94–0.96) (1). Prepregnancy weight can be used as an indicator of the need for maternal weight gain and as a predictor of fetal growth, and may contribute to understanding of the biological mechanism of the interaction between nutrition and reproduction.

Total weight gain during pregnancy, perhaps the most commonly used maternal anthropometric indicator, is determined by subtracting prepregnancy weight (or weight in early pregnancy) from the weight in late pregnancy (usually measured just before delivery). Unfortunately, the value of anthropometry in late pregnancy for predicting risk or selecting individuals or populations for interventions is limited; measurements are made after most of the fetal growth has been achieved and interventions to increase birth weight are less effective. It is of greater value for decisions on referral of patients to appropriate facilities for labour, delivery, and neonatal care, and – during lactation – for selecting individuals for interventions.

Additional considerations relevant to components of the weight gain indicator include:

- accuracy of gestational age calculations
- fetal contribution to total weight gain
- the use of postpartum net weight gain vs. late pregnancy weight gain minus fetal weight
- rate of weight gain.

Length of gestation is most commonly estimated from the date of the last normal menstrual period (LMP) as recalled by the woman at the time of her first prenatal visit. The accuracy of this method and its potential for misclassification of growth-retarded and preterm infants have been extensively discussed in the literature (1, 8, 12). However, the effect of errors in recall of LMP or in calculation of gestational age on the rate of weight gain between two prenatal visits appears to be minimal after the first trimester, i.e. from 14 weeks to term (9). In clinical practice in developed countries and in research settings, measurements taken by ultrasound techniques early in pregnancy (16–18 weeks) could improve the accuracy of gestational age estimations. Agreement (to within 2 weeks) between gestational age estimated by early ultrasound measures such as biparietal diameter and femur length or newborn physical evaluation and gestational age estimated by the date of last menstrual period has been used to select the study populations for epidemiological studies of maternal nutrition (8, 13). Where ultrasound is unavailable or women receive no prenatal care until the latter half of pregnancy, symphysis-fundus (SF) height and recalled time of first fetal movements may complement LMP as means of estimating gestational age.

The contribution made by fetus and placenta to total maternal weight gain is almost 40%, and represents approximately 9% of the weight gain before 10 weeks, 23% from 10 to 20 weeks, 41% from 20 to 30 weeks, and 54% from 30 to 40 weeks (14). There is a positive association between total weight gain and fetal growth (or duration of gestation); however, since total weight gain reflects both fetal weight and maternal tissue gain, the weight of the fetus is included in both sides of the prediction equation.

To eliminate the fetal contribution to total weight gain, the use of net weight gain has been suggested, obtained either by subtracting birth weight from total maternal weight gain (9) or by measuring maternal weight immediately after delivery (6, 15). The former method, however, takes no account of other products of conception or of maternal oedema, which together can represent up to 3 kg of the net weight gain (6). The second approach yields a measure of retained maternal weight. These approaches are of greater importance for research on the determinants of pregnancy outcome than for practical applications such as screening for intervention during pregnancy.

The extent of the correlation between total maternal weight gain and low birth weight (LBW) is probably distorted by the inclusion of preterm deliveries in many reports; the lower total weight gain in women who deliver preterm is likely to be a function of the shorter gestation. It has therefore been suggested that use of weight gain per week of gestation or rate of net weight gain during gestation has greater validity (9). Calculations can be made for the total gestational period, or more appropriately, by periods of pregnancy, if available. As is the case for total weight gain, the influence of fetal weight on the rate of weight gain will be less during the first part of pregnancy. Total or net weight gain is divided by the length of gestation and expressed as grams per week of gestation. During the period of linear weight deposition (from about 15 weeks to term) it is more appropriate, if tedious, to perform simple linear regression analysis, using three or more weight values for each woman, and to calculate the rate of weight gain from the linear regression coefficients of weight versus gestational age (6). Although this approach can be used for further statistical calculations in the context of research, it is impractical in clinical settings.

3.1.3 *Biological significance of anthropometry during pregnancy*

Some of the changes that occur during normal human pregnancy can alter the biological meaning of anthropometric measurements. Many of these changes relate to the growth of the fetus and of maternal tissue such as

Figure 8

Pattern and components of maternal weight gain during pregnancy[a]

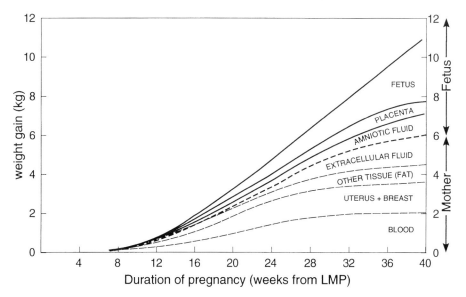

[a] Source: Pitkin RM. Nutritional support in obstetrics and gynecology. *Clinical obstetrics and gynecology*, 1976, **19:**489–513. Reproduced with the permission of the publisher.

the breasts and uterus; others include the increases in body hydration and blood volume that occur quite early in pregnancy. The pattern and components of maternal weight gain during pregnancy are illustrated in Fig. 8.

3.1.4 *Anthropometry as an indicator of nutritional and health status*

Anthropometric indicators may be reflective of past events, predictive of future events, or indicative of current nutritional status. They may also indicate concurrent socioeconomic inequity, risk, or response to an intervention, or predict which individuals will benefit from an intervention. The distinctions between these different types of indicator are fundamental to their usefulness in the context of clinical application, programme implementation and management, and policy and planning.

Indicators of past and present status
Assessment of maternal status during pregnancy is commonly based on height, weight, mid-upper arm circumference, and various measures of skinfold thickness. In addition, maternal weight gain and fundal height may reflect fetal growth status.

Height in adults is a reflection of the interaction of genetic potential for growth and environmental factors that influence realization of that potential. In the more developed countries, genetic potential is the

41

primary determinant of height, since environmental constraints, such as acute and chronic disease, malnutrition, and socioeconomic deprivation, are minimized during the years of linear growth. In less developed countries, by contrast, much of the variation in adult height is the result of environmental influences on linear growth, especially those that affect growth in the first few years of life (16).

Use of maternal height as an indicator of health and nutritional status must therefore take account of the environmental context in which growth occurred. For example, a short woman in a developed country may be at risk of obstetric complications: her relatively small pelvis may be a constraint on vaginal delivery of a normally grown infant. A short woman in a less developed country, on the other hand, may be at high risk of bearing a poorly grown fetus if a poor childhood environment has persisted into her adult years, influencing her current pregnancy. The environmental conditions that lead to poor maternal linear growth may also result in poor growth and suboptimal development of the anatomical and physiological systems that sustain optimal fetal growth or maximize maternal health.

The biological changes that occur during pregnancy may affect the interpretation of maternal height relative to the non-pregnant state. The normal lordosis of pregnancy, for example, has been found to reduce maternal height as pregnancy progresses. This effect is significant enough to conceal increases in maternal height, associated with growth, in teenage mothers (17). In very young adolescents, in whom significant linear growth potential remains, some increase in height may be observed during pregnancy (17), but is likely to be very small (less than 1 cm). Adolescents may be misclassified as being at risk for poor pregnancy outcomes because of short stature relative to adults, when in fact the greater risk derives from other factors associated with adolescent pregnancy.

Body weight measured at various times during pregnancy has been widely used to assess maternal health status. In as much as weight is generally strongly correlated with height, it may serve as a general reflection of the past growth performance of the mother. However, since weight is changeable in adulthood and therefore variable within a given height category, this measure also reflects recent and concurrent health and nutritional status. Because body weight changes rapidly during pregnancy, gestational weight changes are routinely monitored as part of the prenatal care in many settings worldwide (9, 10). Interpretation of these weight changes is constrained by the fact that the various components of body weight may vary differentially depending on health and nutritional status, stage of gestation, and physiological condition, and according to genetic determinants. While total weight may be sensitive to these factors, it lacks specificity as an indicator.

The large variation in weight within a specific height category has given rise to various expressions of weight-for-height, such as the body mass index (BMI). The exact significance of BMI is often difficult to determine. It may be used as an overweight index, on the assumption that excess weight for height reflects excess adiposity; however, while this may be valid for the upper extremes of BMI, it is less reliable for the middle of the population distribution in developed countries. In both developed and less developed countries, a very low BMI is a fairly accurate reflection of severe wasting of both fat and lean tissue (see sections 7 and 8).

Mid-upper arm circumference (MUAC) also reflects past and current status, but is less responsive than weight to short-term changes in health and nutritional conditions. It is relatively stable throughout pregnancy (*10*) and, even when measured relatively late in pregnancy, may be more reflective than weight of prepregnancy conditions. Other measures of limb circumference, such as of the calf (*18*) and thigh (*6*), have been proposed as indicators of status during pregnancy. These sites may involve more dynamic tissue, with changes in circumference reflecting changes in fat, muscle, and/or water specific to pregnancy. Oedema is increasingly common as pregnancy advances. Most pregnant women develop a degree of dependent oedema in the legs, which is considered normal during pregnancy (although pathological oedema can also occur); measurements of the lower body, specifically leg circumferences, may therefore be increased, particularly in late pregnancy.

Measurement of *skinfold thickness* at one or several sites is an increasingly common method of assessing nutritional status, but its use depends on several assumptions. First, skinfolds are assumed to reflect, at least to some degree, the overall distribution of subcutaneous fat. This approaches validity only if skinfold measurements are made at several sites. It is also assumed that the relationship between subcutaneous and total fat is sufficiently constant among populations (or that the factors that influence it are known and controllable) to allow total body fat to be estimated from skinfold measurements. In pregnancy, it is assumed that the relationship between skinfolds and total body fat described for non-pregnant women also applies, since normative data for pregnant women have not been reported. None of these assumptions, however, is likely to be universally valid.

In any individual, the proportion of body fat situated subcutaneously is variable according to certain influences (pregnant/non-pregnant, well/poorly nourished, etc.). In non-pregnant women with unusual fat distributions, skinfold measurements may thus yield very poor indications of total fat. In pregnancy, the situation is complicated by the influence of the various physiological changes on fat distribution and hence on skinfold thickness. Repeated measurements in pregnant women would therefore be unlikely to produce an accurate picture of the changes taking place in total body fat.

Relocation of existing fat stores from central to peripheral sites may occur during pregnancy to facilitate accommodation of the fetus in the abdominal cavity. Thus, increased skinfold thickness on the arms, on the legs, or even on the back may not reflect an increase in the total body fat of a pregnant woman, although these sites are also believed to store the additional fat gained by many women during pregnancy. As pregnancy progresses, the enlarging abdomen makes it increasingly difficult to measure the abdominal skinfold reliably. The skinfold may appear very "thin" where it stretches over the uterine compartment, but since the abdominal skin is having to cover an increasing volume it may actually include an increased amount of subcutaneous fat compared with the prepregnant state.

As mentioned above, oedema may also affect skinfold measurements, particularly those made on the lower extremities in late pregnancy, by changing the composition and compressibility of subcutaneous adipose tissue. In undernourished populations, however, in whom the normal increases in plasma volume may be inhibited by malnutrition, the normal oedema of pregnancy may not be apparent.

Variation in skinfold thickness and circumference of the lower limbs may reflect the hydration status of the mother in middle to late pregnancy. Under the influence of increasing estrogen levels, changes in the water-holding capacity of subcutaneous ground substance allow more water to be held by the skinfold without overt oedema. This may increase the resistance of the skinfold to compression, resulting in an increased skinfold thickness, even when subcutaneous fat has not increased. Decreases in skinfold measurements observable in the first few weeks postpartum may reflect a reversion of the tissues to the non-pregnant hydration level, rather than an acute decline in fat stores.

Symphysis-fundus (SF) height has long been used to gauge the size of the pregnant uterus. Though originally used to assess gestational age (*19*), SF height has been evaluated as an indicator of fetal growth on the premise that the height of the uterus reflects its overall size and that this in turn reflects the size of uterine contents, which are dominated by the fetus by the second half of gestation. SF height has also been used to assess fetal growth deviations at both extremes (small and large for gestational age). In clinical settings its use has relied on single and serial measurements from mid-gestation to term. A recent review of 12 studies (*20*) concluded that SF height was of variable value as a predictor of IUGR. However, large values of SF height in late pregnancy have been used successfully to predict complications of delivery and problems with the newborn (*21*).

Indicators of risk, benefit, and response
In addition to their ability to reflect past and current health and nutritional status, all the measures discussed above have been shown to be related, with differing degrees of association, to various pregnancy outcomes. The ability of measures such as prepregnancy BMI and gestational weight gain to predict risk of LBW and pregnancy complications has led to their widespread acceptance as clinical tools. Later in this section,

results are presented of an extensive analysis of the degree to which some of these measures predict obstetric and neonatal risks. First, however, it is important to discuss the distinction between pregnancy-specific indicators of risk, indicators of benefit, and indicators of response. This requires some consideration of the role of anthropometry in the causal chain that leads from maternal health and nutritional status to pregnancy outcome.

One view of these relationships is presented in Fig. 9, taken from a recent report by the Institute of Medicine (9). This figure was developed to focus attention on the causes and consequences of variation in gestational weight gain. However, it also demonstrates the role played by other anthropometric factors in relation to pregnancy outcomes and as potential confounders or modifiers of the effects of weight gain on these outcomes.

The use of terms such as "determinant" and "consequence" implies causality, and all the relationships shown in Fig. 9 between maternal weight gain and its determinants or consequences are in some way assumed to be causal. This is important because any clinical or public health intervention designed to affect a particular anthropometric indicator will be ineffective in improving outcome for the mother or fetus/child if the associations between that indicator and the outcome(s) are not causal. Notwithstanding, the anthropometric indicator may still be valuable if it helps to identify women who might benefit from the intervention. Short maternal height in a chronically undernourished population, for example, may help to identify those at risk of LBW although it will not be influenced by an intervention that improves dietary energy intake during pregnancy. An indicator such as low weight gain during pregnancy, on the other hand, may identify women whose fetuses would benefit from a dietary intervention, and the intervention in turn may also improve the mothers' weight gain.

Another view of the distinctions between the concepts of risk, benefit, and response at the population level is illustrated in Fig. 10. As shown, maternal anthropometric deficits and physiological changes are among the several consequences of maternal malnutrition.

The more direct, or proximal, nutrition-related causes of these are past and current dietary intake, morbidity, physical activity, and the reproductive experience, which affect the state of maternal nutritional depletion or repletion. Non-nutritional causes include smoking and pregnancy-induced hypertension (PIH), which affect maternal physiology and neonatal development. More distal causes relate to maternal knowledge and behaviour, household resources, and environmental conditions. Although causal frameworks like this are commonplace, their more subtle implications for choosing and interpreting indicators are often overlooked.

Malnutrition as such is not shown in Fig. 10 because it is not directly measurable. Anthropometric deficits are often used as indicators of malnutrition, but for heuristic purposes it is best to consider these as consequences of poor diet and health status, along much the same lines as

Figure 9

Schematic summary of potential determinants, consequences, and effect modifiers for maternal weight gain[a]

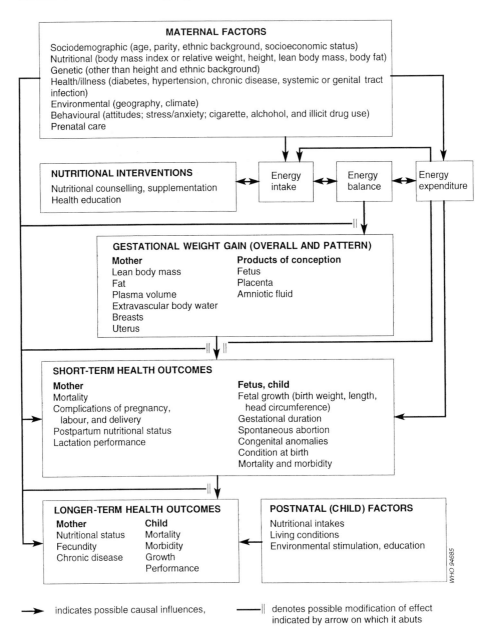

[a] Reproduced from reference 9 with permission from *Nutrition during pregnancy*. Copyright 1990 by the National Academy of Sciences. Courtesy of the National Academy Press, Washington, DC.

Figure 10
Selected causes and consequences of maternal malnutrition

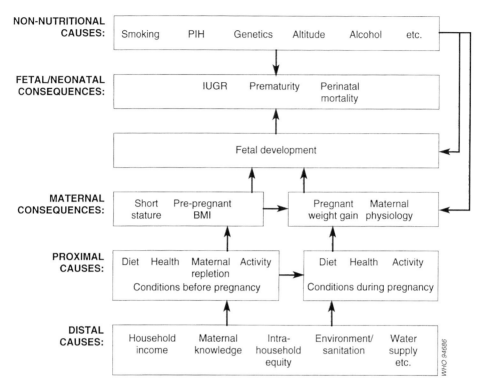

other consequences. The common practice of placing malnutrition in the centre of such a diagram can be misleading when, as is often the case, malnutrition is assumed to be fully or largely captured in anthropometric characteristics. Conversely, the figure explicitly shows "maternal physiology" and "fetal development" as outcomes of nutritional and non-nutritional influences, even though they are not directly observable; they are important factors which may mediate, modify, or confound the relationships between causal indicators and indicators of consequences.

3.2 Using anthropometry in individuals

In choosing an indicator of maternal status during pregnancy from a number of candidate indicators, the crucial question is, "For what purpose will the indicator be used?"

3.2.1 *Choosing an indicator*

Anthropometric indicators have two primary uses – the targeting of interventions and the assessment of response to interventions. Matching indicators to application thus involves recognizing that a particular disease is relevant, determining whether there is a treatment and how to identify (screen) women for the treatment, and evaluating the effectiveness of the treatment. The process of identifying the screening and response indicators necessarily involves assessing the degree to which a screening indicator identifies a subgroup that is more responsive to the treatment or, in epidemiological terms, the degree of effect modification achieved by the screening indicator. This can be done by several methods, but must recognize the prevalence of the poor outcome that is to be affected and the percentage of the population that is identified as at risk by the indicator. Finally, the selection of indicators will depend on practical and logistic considerations that include the availability of human and material resources, the timing and frequency of prenatal visits, and the acceptability of the measuring procedure to the women concerned.

This approach has been extensively developed for screening preschool-age children for malnutrition (22) and to a lesser degree for screening individual pregnant women (10). In a WHO collaborative study, this rationale also served as the basis for the analytical design applied to the evaluation of maternal anthropometry and pregnancy outcomes (23). This multicentre study supplements the findings in recent reviews on maternal anthropometry (9, 10) and on determinants of LBW (24), and serves as an excellent source of information to assist in the selection of appropriate maternal anthropometric indicators for screening.

None of the current literature has addressed the selection process as thoroughly and systematically as described above. Most of the previous emphasis has been on screening individuals at risk of poor pregnancy outcomes; the following discussion of indicators for screening individual women relies heavily on the published results of the WHO Collaborative Study with occasional reference to other supporting work.

The WHO Collaborative Study

The WHO Collaborative Study on Maternal Anthropometry and Pregnancy Outcomes (23) examined the relationships between maternal anthropometry and various pregnancy outcomes in separate studies of 25 population groups located throughout the world. Data were collected by local investigators from 1959 to 1989. They represent approximately 111 000 women for whom anthropometric data were collected repeatedly from early pregnancy to term. Among the various outcomes included in the data set, the most commonly reported are birth weight, gestational age, and pregnancy complications. The relative risks (or odds ratios where appropriate) of various deleterious outcomes based on maternal anthropometry were computed for each study. The results across studies were then combined into a meta-analysis.

The following outcomes were examined: LBW (<2500 g), preterm delivery (gestation <37 weeks), small for gestational age (SGA) or IUGR (birth weight <10th percentile for gestational age), assisted (nonspontaneous) delivery, pre-eclampsia (diastolic pressure >90 mmHg[1] with proteinuria and/or oedema), and postpartum haemorrhage (during first 24 hours). Fetal outcomes were fairly easily defined, but maternal complications were more difficult; in many studies there were no records of complications or the criteria (e.g. pre-eclampsia) were poorly specified. For these analyses, only the studies that yielded reliable data were included.

The maternal anthropometric indicators used were: height, weight, and BMI before pregnancy or during the first trimester, and at the 20th, 28th, and 36th weeks; weight gain between these various time points; and mid-upper arm circumference (MUAC) in early pregnancy.

Sample size for the 25 studies varied from 286 to 16 481, with a mean of about 4200; all but four studies had over 1000 subjects. Sample mean birth weights ranged from 2633 to 3355 g. The prevalence of LBW ranged from 4.2 to 28.2%, of SGA from 5.8 to 54.2%, and of preterm delivery from 4.6 to 56%. In the 14 studies that reported it, assisted delivery ranged from 2.2 to 27.6%; pre-eclampsia ranged from <1 to 15.4% in 11 studies, and postpartum haemorrhage from 0.5 to 4.4% in six studies. The individual studies produced similarly variable mean values for anthropometry. Mean maternal height ranged from 148 to 163 cm in 24 studies and mean prepregnancy weight from 42.1 to 65.6 kg in 23 studies. In 17 studies, mean weight at 20 weeks ranged from 44.0 to 64.6 kg, at 28 weeks from 45.5 to 65.3 kg, and at 36 weeks from 47.5 to 67.3 kg. Mean MUAC ranged from 21.9 to 25.4 cm in the 13 studies that reported it.

Odds ratios (ORs) were computed for each outcome by each indicator for each study that yielded relevant data. Since the values for each indicator varied greatly, the various studies were organized into between three and five groups, or clusters, identified according to similar statistical distributions of the indicator within the cluster. The distribution of the indicator was described for each cluster and the lowest 25% identified as the "at risk" portion of the sample.

Logistic regression was used to compute ORs for each study sample based on the risk of an outcome in the lowest quartile relative to the risk of the outcome in the highest three quartiles. The individual study ORs were then combined and an overall OR was computed for each of five pregnancy outcomes by each indicator.

The results of this analysis are summarized in Table 3. The first six indicators listed represent basic anthropometry in different stages of pregnancy. These are followed by a second set of derived indicators, such as BMI and weight gain, computed from the basic anthropometric data. The third set represents the results of an analysis of all the indicators in

---

[1] 90 mmHg = 12.0 kPa.

the first two sets, but only for those subjects in each study whose heights were below the population median height. This simulates a two-stage screening process, and is an indirect test of how the indicators would perform in the most stunted members of a population. Finally, the fourth set of results also simulates the two-stage screening, but uses prepregnancy weight below the population median weight as the first level of screening. The numbers enclosed in boxes represent combined ORs that are relatively high and for which the 95% confidence interval does not include 1.0, i.e. an indication of a significantly greater risk than expected by chance. Numbers that are underlined indicate a significant "protective effect" of the lower values of an indicator.

For almost all indicators, ORs are significantly greater than 1.0 for SGA and, therefore, for LBW. As pregnancy progresses towards term, ORs increase for measures of attained weight and weight gains from the prepregnancy period. The measures of weight gain appear to be more strongly related to risk of LBW and SGA if they include the initial weight measured at 20 weeks. Generally, the ORs increase substantially from the single-level screening to the two-level screening in which either short stature or low prepregnancy weight is considered as the first screening indicator. For predicting preterm delivery, measurements taken before pregnancy or in the first trimester have significant ORs in the range 1.20–1.49. Indicators related to weight gain vary widely, with some indicators (weight gain from 20 to 28 weeks) showing ORs between 1.43 and 1.86 and others (weight gain from prepregnancy to 20 or 28 weeks) showing ORs below 1.0, suggesting a protective effect of low cumulative weight gain.

Anthropometric indicators are less strongly related to complications of pregnancy and labour than to fetal growth. In general, ORs are less than 1.0; significant ORs suggest a reduced risk of complications in subjects with indicators in the lower quartile compared with the upper three quartiles of anthropometry. An important exception is the increased risk of assisted delivery in short women (OR = 1.61).

Interpretation of these results should take account of certain limitations to the analysis. Meta-analysis has been applied only recently in epidemiology, and there is still considerable debate about its validity and utility. In addition, potential bias in the combined ORs may be introduced by the method used to establish the cut-off points for each of the indicators examined in this study.

While ORs provide valuable quantitative estimates of the relationship between several anthropometric indicators and important outcomes of pregnancy, they represent only the first step in testing the utility of the indicator. The next step is to determine the optimum cut-off point for discriminating between women destined to have adverse outcomes and those destined to have favourable outcomes. This requires an analysis of the sensitivity, specificity, and positive predictive values (PPV) for those indicators with the best ORs (25, 26).

Table 3
Summary of estimated combined odds ratios (ORs) from the WHO Collaborative Study[a]

Note: Indicators with relatively high ORs for elevated risk are outlined; indicators predictive of low relative risk are underlined.

Predictors	IUGR or SGA	LBW	Preterm	Assisted delivery	Pre-eclampsia	Postpartum haemorrhage
Basic anthropometry						
Maternal height	1.91	1.72	1.20	1.61	0.88	0.72
Mid-upper arm circumference	1.63	1.93	1.22	0.88	0.69	0.65
Prepregnancy weight	2.55	2.38	1.42	1.00	0.71	0.71
Attained weight by week 20	2.77	2.43	0.99	1.04	—	0.96
Attained weight by week 28	3.03	2.41	0.89	0.91	0.87	0.97
Attained weight by week 36	3.09	2.59	—	0.87	0.71	0.68
Derived indicators						
Prepregnancy BMI	1.87	1.87	1.33	0.76	0.75	0.87
BMI by week 20	2.11	1.66	0.75	0.73	1.30	1.40
BMI by week 28	2.31	1.90	0.91	0.67	0.91	1.22
BMI by week 36	2.26	1.88	—	0.68	0.69	1.08
Weight gain: pp[b] to week 20	1.87	1.53	0.47	1.00	1.13	0.63
Weight gain: pp to week 28	1.85	1.53	0.78	0.75	0.82	0.81
Weight gain: pp to week 36	2.06	1.68	—	0.73	0.60	0.63
Weight gain: weeks 20 to 28	1.71	1.64	1.43	0.73	0.79	1.04
Weight gain: weeks 20 to 36	1.75	1.72	—	0.81	0.29	1.15
Weight gain: weeks 28 to 36	1.47	1.24	—	0.89	0.66	0.72

Table 3 (continued)

Predictors	IUGR or SGA	LBW	Preterm	Assisted delivery	Pre-eclampsia	Postpartum haemorrhage
Mothers of small stature						
Prepregnancy weight	2.99	2.63	1.49			
Attained weight by week 20	3.24	2.59	1.09			
Attained weight by week 28	3.56	2.65	0.95			
Attained weight by week 36	3.46	2.97	—			
Weight gain: pp[b] to week 20	2.79	1.96	—			
Weight gain: pp to week 28	2.85	2.09	—			
Weight gain: pp to week 36	3.20	2.30	—			
Weight gain: weeks 20 to 28	2.64	2.68	1.86			
Weight gain: weeks 20 to 36	2.67	2.82	—			
Weight gain: weeks 28 to 36	2.24	1.82	—			

Sensitivity, specificity, and PPV all depend on the relationship between a risk factor and a given outcome. However, the risk factor may be a statistical "marker" of the outcome without necessarily being the cause of it. To the extent that the success of an intervention depends on the causal link between the risk factor and the outcome, the etiological fraction (EF; also called the population attributable risk) will also be important. The EF is the proportion by which the incidence rate of the adverse outcome in a given population would be reduced if exposure to the risk factor were eliminated. It depends on both the relative risk (or OR) associated with exposure and the prevalence of exposure in the population. The EF is particularly important for those anthropometric indicators that will be targets for intervention, such as weight and BMI. For example, the EF associated with low gestational weight gain will indicate the maximum impact in reducing the incidence of a given outcome achievable by an intervention capable of ensuring adequate weight gain for all pregnant women in the population. EFs are therefore useful in defining the

Table 3 (continued)

Predictors	IUGR or SGA	LBW	Preterm	Assisted delivery	Pre-eclampsia	Postpartum haemorrhage
Mothers of low prepregnancy weight						
Attained weight by week 20	3.87	2.50	0.97			
Attained weight by week 28	4.02	2.75	1.07			
Attained weight by week 36	3.79	2.83	—			
Weight gain: pp[b] to week 20	5.58	2.71	—			
Weight gain: pp to week 28	5.36	3.49	—			
Weight gain: pp to week 36	5.63	3.36	—			
Weight gain: weeks 20 to 28	2.81	2.15	1.71			
Weight gain: weeks 20 to 36	2.49	1.68	—			
Weight gain: weeks 28 to 36	2.68	1.77	—			

[a] Reference 23.
[b] pp = prepregnancy.

magnitude of expected effect of public health action designed to reduce adverse outcomes in a given community.

Finally, the feasibility of any risk assessment/management programme depends on the proportion of women who will be identified as at risk; adequate facilities, economic resources, and numbers of personnel must be available to deal with their subsequent referral and treatment. The anthropometric measurements chosen for risk assessment, as well as the cut-off points used to define risk, must take account of these practical aspects to avoid overburdening the health care system and to promote the efficient use of limited resources.

Relatively few studies have considered any of these factors, and none has considered all of them, in making recommendations for the use of maternal anthropometry. An analysis of misclassification was undertaken in the WHO Collaborative Study. While the analysis is rather restrictive and suffers from some of the same limitations as the estimates of ORs, the results are informative. With cut-off values fixed at the 25th percentile of the cluster in which it was placed, each individual study was examined for sensitivity (SE) and specificity (SP) for each indicator relative to each outcome. If more than 40% of the studies met the criteria of SP>.7 and SE>.35 for a given indicator versus LBW and SGA (SE>.30 for preterm), the indicator was tagged as potentially useful for screening. The analysis is summarized in Table 4.

For predicting LBW, maternal prepregnancy weight and achieved weights at 20, 28, and 36 weeks performed equally well; about 50% of the studies met the criteria and had similar ORs in the range 2.4-2.6. When LBW is broken down into its components of SGA and preterm delivery, the results are generally as expected. The indicators that perform well in predicting LBW also perform well in predicting SGA, with similar sensitivity and slightly higher ORs. For predicting risk of preterm delivery, only prepregnancy weight and prepregnancy BMI met

Table 4

Summary of preliminary sensitivity (SE) and specificity (SP) analysis of various anthropometric indicators in pregnancy in 21 studies in the WHO Collaborative Study[a]

Anthropometric indicator	No. of studies[b]	% of studies meeting criteria[c]	Min. SE[d] (%)	Max. SE[e] (%)	OR (95% CI)[f]
Outcome = low birth weight					
Prepregnancy weight	21	62	35	47	2.38 (2.1-2.5)
Attained weight at 20 weeks	15	53	36	56	2.43 (2.0-2.8)
Attained weight at 28 weeks	14	50	38	52	2.41 (2.1-2.7)
Attained weight at 36 weeks	17	47	38	47	2.59 (2.2-2.9)
Outcome = small for gestational age					
Prepregnancy weight	20	50	36	52	2.55 (2.3-2.7)
Attained weight at 20 weeks	15	40	38	49	2.77 (2.3-3.2)
Attained weight at 36 weeks	17	53	36	50	3.09 (2.7-3.4)
Outcome = preterm delivery					
Prepregnancy weight	20	45	31	54	1.42 (1.3-1.5)
Prepregnancy BMI	20	40	31	39	1.33 (1.1-1.4)

[a] Reference *23*.
[b] Number of studies for which data exist for both outcome and indicator.
[c] Percentage of eligible studies with SP>.7 at cut-off of 25th percentile.
[d] Lowest sensitivity observed in studies with SP>.7.
[e] Highest sensitivity observed in studies with SP>.7.
[f] Combined odds ratio of all studies with 95% confidence interval (CI).

the criteria in over 40% of the studies. These same indicators had moderate combined ORs (1.33 and 1.42).

The major limitation of this analysis is that it does not allow for different cut-off values of the indicators across individual studies. The fact that the specificity criteria were met in 40% of the studies provides strong support for the general applicability of these predictors across many populations. However, the data should be re-examined using a series of common cut-off values, and the results compared across studies at the same cut-off values. This would help in determining the type of reference that should be developed: a reference with a common absolute cut-off, several references with a common relative cut-off value, or several (perhaps regional) references with different relative and absolute cut-off values.

Other evidence
The results of the analysis by the WHO Collaborative Study (*23*) generally confirm the findings of another meta-analysis in which the determinants of LBW were examined (*24*) (summarized in Table 5). This analysis relies on a thorough review of 895 studies published between 1970 and 1984. Strict criteria were applied to select studies with appropriate study design including variables that allow inference of potential causal determinants of LBW. However, relatively few studies provided the information needed to estimate relative risk (RR). Determined on the basis of low prepregnancy weight, the RR of preterm delivery was 1.25 compared with the OR of 1.42 in the WHO Collaborative Study. Kalkwarf (*27*) reports significant ORs of 1.42 (95% confidence interval = 1.25–1.60) and 1.37 (CI = 1.27–1.49) for prepregnancy BMI below 18.5 for 7312 white and 6730 black births, respectively, in the US National Collaborative Perinatal Project (NCPP). Kramer found no studies published before 1984 that showed a convincing relationship between the risk of preterm delivery and either maternal height or weight gain. However, in the NCPP Kalkwarf (*27*) has shown ORs of 1.65 (CI = 1.42–1.92) and 1.62 (CI = 1.46–1.79) for white and black women, respectively, for risk of preterm delivery when gestational weight gain was 100 g/week (the population 10th percentile) between 20 weeks and delivery. This compares with an OR of 1.43 (CI = 1.1–1.7) for weight gain between the 20th and 28th weeks in the WHO Collaborative Study.

In examining the risk of SGA from low anthropometric values, Kramer (*24*) reported RRs of 1.27 for maternal height, 1.84 for prepregnancy weight, and 1.98 for total gestational weight gain, compared with ORs from the WHO Collaborative Study of 1.91, 2.55, and 2.06, respectively. Kalkwarf (*27*) reported ORs of 1.83 and 1.44 for SGA in white and black women, respectively, from maternal prepregnancy BMI below 18.5, which are similar to the OR of 1.87 reported for the WHO Collaborative Study. Current evidence suggests the existence of biologically important correlations between many anthropometric indicators and fetal outcomes of pregnancy.

Table 5
Summary of anthropometric "determinants" of preterm delivery and intrauterine growth retardation[a]

Anthropometric indicator	Preterm delivery		IUGR[b]	
	RR[c] (no. of studies)	EF @ prevalence[d]	RR[c] (no. of studies)	EF @ prevalence[d]
Maternal height < 158 cm	1.0 (4)	–	1.27 (2)	6.3% @ .25 14.5% @ .63 18.5% @ .85
Prepregnancy weight < 54 kg	1.25 (3)	6.3% @ .27 10.3% @ .46 14.0% @ .65	1.85 (1)	11.9% @ .15 19.6% @ .29 28.7% @ .48
Total gestational weight gain < 7 kg	1.0 (1)	–	1.98 (2)	13.6% @ .16 36.6% @ .59

[a] Source: reference 24.
[b] As inferred from SGA.
[c] Relative risk; number of studies meeting criteria for inclusion in meta-analysis is given in parentheses.
[d] Etiological fraction (%) at various prevalence rates; not computed if RR = 1.0, i.e. EF = 0.

In addition, Kramer (24) computed the EF for the three anthropometric indicators used in Table 5, reporting results only for those relationships found to be significant. Since EF varies as a function of prevalence of the risk factor in the population, results are reported for several prevalence rates. As an example of the interpretation of Table 5, intervention in a population where the prevalence of low body weight was 27%, resulting in the elimination of prepregnant weights below 54 kg, would reduce the incidence of preterm deliveries by 6.3%. Elimination of low prepregnant weight in a population of similar prevalence (.29) would result in a 19.6% reduction in the incidence of SGA.

3.2.2 *Applications of anthropometry for screening pregnant women*

On the basis of information provided by the WHO Collaborative Study (23), the detailed literature reviews of the Institute of Medicine report (9), and the Pan American Health Organization publication on maternal anthropometry (10), criteria were identified for the selection of nutritional indicators to be applied to individuals. These are listed in Table 6.

For anthropometric measurements made only once during pregnancy, generally at the time of a woman's first contact with the health care system, mid-upper arm circumference, height, weight (prepregnancy or early pregnancy, and attained weight at any stage during pregnancy), weight-for-height, and calf circumference were identified as of possible value in predicting maternal and fetal outcomes.

Table 6
Considerations in the selection of a nutritional indicator during pregnancy and lactation

1. Why is an indicator needed?
    - Screening for a nutritional intervention for the mother during pregnancy or lactation
      - to improve her nutritional state if she is underweight
      - to minimize complications during pregnancy (e.g. toxaemia, prolonged labour, need for assisted delivery)
      - to minimize maternal mortality.
    - Screening for a nutritional indicator to improve fetal health by:
      - reducing growth retardation
      - reducing preterm delivery
      - reducing morbidity/mortality.

2. Which instruments (scales, measuring tapes, etc.) are available?

3. What constraints are there on the availability of personnel and/or services?

4. Which nutritional indicators are available?

5. Is there any evidence of an association between these indicators and the outcomes of interest?

6. What are the biological bases for these associations? For what are these indicators proxy measures?

7. What is the minimum number of measurements required?

8. Are there reference data:
    - normative?
    - predictive of risk?

9. How are these references expressed? What data must be collected?

10. Is there any evidence that when applied to individuals or at clinic level the primary outcome is improved (randomized clinical trials)?

Mid-upper arm circumference is largely independent of gestational age and regarded as a proxy indicator of maternal prepregnancy weight or early pregnancy weight; it changes very little during pregnancy (*10*). Although the correlation between prepregnancy weight and MUAC is statistically significant, in most of the studies reported by WHO (*23*) this association is too weak to permit MUAC to substitute for prepregnancy BMI in individuals.

Table 7 lists sensitivity and specificity for several proposed MUAC cut-off points for the identification of pregnant women at risk of LBW, SGA, and neonatal morbidity. In Brazil, with an LBW rate of 23%, Lechtig (*28*) used a cut-off point of <23.5 cm and calculated a positive predictive value of 45% (*n* = 445, sensitivity 77%, specificity 71%). Thus, even where incidence of LBW is high, using this indicator to target interventions (to increase either birth weight or referrals for delivery at

Table 7
The use of maternal arm circumference for the prediction of neonatal outcomes[a]

Country	MUAC (cm)	RR	Sensitivity (%)	Specificity (%)	Outcome
Bangladesh	< 22.5	–	73	41	Neonatal morbidity
Brazil	< 23.5	–	77	71	Low birth weight
Chile	24	2.6	–	–	IUGR[b]
Guatemala	< 22.5 (14 days postpartum)	1.5	24	84	Low birth weight

[a] Adapted from reference *10* with permission. Copyright Pan American Health Organization, Washington, DC.
[b] As suggested by SGA.

tertiary centres) yields a high percentage of false-positive cases, i.e. women who are unlikely to benefit from the interventions.

Short maternal height has been associated with an increased risk of IUGR in several populations, and cut-off points between 140 cm and 150 cm have been proposed for screening. The WHO Collaborative Study (*23*) reports individual ORs and confidence intervals for the prediction of LBW from a cluster-specific definition of short maternal stature in each of 24 studies. Results are illustrated in Fig. 11. In most studies ORs are above 1.5 and the lower limits of the confidence interval are consistently above 1.0; exceptions are Guatemala, Lesotho, Malawi, and Viet Nam. The OR for all studies combined is 1.7 with a 95% confidence interval of 1.6–1.8 (see Table 3). Unfortunately, although specificity exceeded 70% in only four of the studies, sensitivity was very low (36–41%) for the detection of SGA at a height cut-off equal to the 25th percentile of a cluster-specific distribution.

Short maternal height has also been shown to be associated with an increased risk of surgical delivery and intrapartum caesarean section among primigravidae (*29*). It could be of practical use for referring women for hospital delivery in areas where there are many home deliveries.

Results from the WHO Collaborative Study show that there is a strong correlation between a single measure of maternal weight late in pregnancy and SGA and LBW. While weight alone has a higher OR than BMI, it is a particularly good indicator when applied only to short women or those with low prepregnancy weights (Table 3). Rosso (*30*) also reports a strong relationship between weight-for-height at term and birth weight (Table 8). This indicator, even measured late in pregnancy, could be used for referral of women for delivery at facilities offering special care for the newborn.

Figure 11

Estimated odds ratios and 95% confidence intervals for low birth weight by maternal height[a]

Note: The ORs are for maternal height below the lowest quartile cut-off point vs. height above the highest quartile cut-off point.

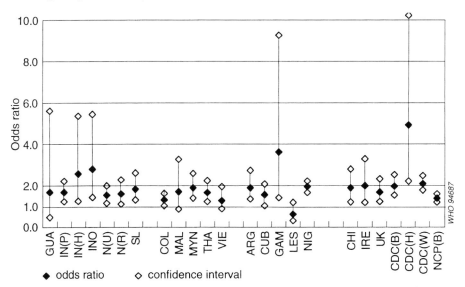

◆ odds ratio   ◇ confidence interval

[a] Source: reference *23*.

Key:

GUA	= Guatemala	ARG	= Argentina
IN(P)	= India (Poona)	CUB	= Cuba
IN(H)	= India (Hyderabad)	GAM	= Gambia
INO	= Indonesia	LES	= Lesotho
N(U)	= Nepal (urban)	NIG	= Nigeria
N(R)	= Nepal (rural)	CHI	= China
SL	= Sri Lanka	IRE	= Ireland
COL	= Colombia	UK	= United Kingdom
MAL	= Malawi	CDC(B)	= USA (blacks) (Centers for Disease Control)
MYN	= Myanmar	CDC(H)	= USA (Hispanics)
THA	= Thailand	CDC(W)	= USA (whites)
VIE	= Viet Nam	NCP(B)	= USA (blacks) (National Collaborative Perinatal Project)

Much of the foregoing discussion of these studies is summarized in Table 9, which provides a structure for evaluating various anthropometric indicators for screening pregnant women. The table is divided into four parts, of which two (A and B) pertain to single examinations in settings with either low or adequate resources, the third (C) to multiple examinations where resources are adequate, and the fourth (D) to assessment of responses to interventions. Columns 1 and 2 deal with the purposes of screening or of evaluating an intervention and with what will actually be done for the individual woman as a result. The target populations and the type of anthropometric measurements are covered in columns 3 and 4, anthropometric indices and units of measurement in

Table 8
Influence on birth weight of weight-for-height of healthy, low-income Chilean women at term[a]

Weight-for-height (% of standard)	No. of subjects	Mean birth weight[b] (SD) (g)	Mean birth weight adjusted for height (g)
< 105	360	3224 (402)	3328
105–109	290	3219 (387)	3323
110–114	220	3264 (347)	3368
115–119	260	3327 (370)	3431
120–124	273	3419 (361)	3523
125–129	212	3501 (402)	3605
130–134	178	3486 (375)	3590
135–139	140	3555 (389)	3659
> 139	235	3642 (403)	3746

[a] Reproduced, with permission, from reference 10 (p. 179). Copyright Pan American Health Organization, Washington, DC.
[b] Liveborn, full-term infants; both sexes combined.

column 5, and the stage of pregnancy at which measurements should be made in column 6. Only the indices known to be related to the specific outcomes of interest are reported; in many cases, further evaluation of sensitivity, specificity, positive predictive value, and etiological fraction in specific applications and for particular situations would be necessary before final recommendations could be made. However, where current knowledge has identified a best index for a particular purpose, this is identified in the table.

Column 7 deals with reference data and criteria for judgement, i.e. the cut-offs applied to the various indices; these are not necessarily the references and cut-offs recommended by the Expert Committee, but those used by specific authors to generate the results summarized in column 8. Further information that may be relevant to the interpretation of anthropometric measurements is presented in column 9.

Where screening has involved multiple examinations of pregnant women (parts C and D of Table 9), the most common anthropometric measurement has been weight change. Depending on the purpose of screening, weight change may be determined over a short (several weeks) or long (the whole of gestation) period. Short-term weight change is generally determined early enough in pregnancy to allow for intervention to improve fetal growth; in the longer term, weight change may be used to identify women who should be referred to appropriate facilities for labour and delivery or for neonatal care.

In general, correlation between pregnancy outcome and weight change is weaker than that between outcome and a single determination of weight at any stage during pregnancy. This may be partly explained by greater error of measurement in determining weight change than in determining a single weight, and by the fact that a single weight determination also includes variation due to height. The WHO Collaborative Study (*23*) reported very high ORs (5.4–5.6) for the risk of SGA determined on the basis of weight gain from a low prepregnant value to 20, 28, or 36 weeks. Although many weight-gain charts have been used in prenatal care (*9, 31*), no single chart has proved to be useful over the whole range of applications covered by Table 9.

3.2.3 *Assessing response to an intervention*

Evaluation of the response of an individual woman to a nutritional or health intervention during pregnancy requires at least two anthropometric measurements – before and after the intervention. The indicator selected for the evaluation must be one that exhibits sufficient variation during pregnancy to be sensitive to intervention. Changes in values may be expressed as net difference between the two measurements, as percentage change from the baseline value, or as rate of change. Suitable indicators for the purpose are weight gain during pregnancy, changes in thigh and subscapular skinfolds, and changes in symphysis–fundus height, all of which are roughly linear after the first trimester of pregnancy (*6, 9, 32*). Normative data are available for these indicators, and the reports cited here present rates of change, with standard deviations, by week of gestation.

For clinical applications, it has been recommended that a sequential plot be made of maternal weight or weight increase for comparison with rate of weight gain of reference populations (*9*). Rate of weight gain can be calculated from the individual plots and compared with rates reported for normal healthy women who give birth to infants of normal birth weight (*6*).

Data on the effects of dietary changes on weight gain during pregnancy in six studies of maternal supplementation have recently been reviewed (*33*). It appears that unequivocal changes in maternal weight gain are seen only among women near starvation and, to a lesser degree, those who are clinically undernourished. For other women, even those at socioeconomic risk, the effects of these supplements on weight gain have been very modest and related to diet in early pregnancy, type of supplement, and prepregnancy weight (*33*). The use of these indicators for evaluating the impact of interventions aimed at improving maternal weight at the individual level require further evaluation, and it is not yet clear at this point whether the practice of weighing pregnant women at every prenatal visit should continue, particularly among healthy, well nourished women (*2*).

Table 9
Summary of recommendations for screening individual pregnant women for interventions

1	2	3	4	5
Uses: what will be done for the individual?	For what purpose?	Target group	What to measure	Indices and units

A. Low resource settings (no scales available), one examination to screen for poor pregnancy outcomes

1	2	3	4	5
Refer for further evaluation if available; advise on or supplement diet	Prevent IUGR or treat newborn to prevent morbidity/death	Population at risk of IUGR	Mid-upper arm circumference	Absolute; cm (independent of gestational age)
			Calf circumference	Absolute; cm (independent of gestational age)
			Height[a]	Absolute; cm (independent of gestational age)
Refer for delivery at facility with neonatal care	Prevent neonatal morbidity/ death due to prematurity	Population at risk of preterm delivery	Height[a]	Absolute; cm (independent of gestational age)
Refer for delivery	Prevent labour/delivery complications	Primiparas and history of dystocia	Height[a]	Absolute; cm (independent of gestational age)
Advise on or supplement mother's diet	Prevent depletion of maternal stores for lactation	Population with chronic undernutrition	Calf circumference	Absolute; cm (independent of gestional age)

6	7	8	9
Stage of pregnancy	Criteria for judgement (cut-offs)	Rationale for anthropometry	Other factors for interpretation
Any time during pregnancy	< 20.7 cm or < 23 cm; limited criteria for judgement (*23, 10*)	For IUGR: RR=2.6 (*10*), RR=1.6 (*23*). Assesses body composition; proxy for prepregnancy weight	Limited value; modest sensitivity and specificity
Late in pregnancy	Not reported (*18*)	Best SE at 0.5 SP for IUGR (*18*); may reflect fat and lean tissue, also oedema (may be harmful or beneficial)	Promising, but not common measurement
Any time during pregnancy	Population-specific reference; likely cut-offs 147–153 cm (*23*)	RR=1.91 (*23*) RR=1.27(*24*) Proxy for past nutrition/ health status and SES	Limited use alone; poor sensitivity and specificity
Any time during pregnancy	Population-specific cut-offs,140– 150 cm (*23*)	RR=1.00 for preterm (*24*) RR=1.20 (*23*)	Limited use; poor sensitivity and specificity
Any time during pregnancy	Population-specific cut-offs, 140– 150 cm (*23*)	RR=1.62 for assisted delivery (*23*) Proxy for small pelvis	
Any time during pregnancy	None cited (*18*)	Identifies women who respond to postpartum supplement to improve lactation (*18*)	Mid-upper arm circumference may also be used but was not tested

Table 9 *(continued)*

1	2	3	4	5
Uses: what will be done for the individual?	For what purpose?	Target group	What to measure	Indices and units

B. Adequate resources (scales available), one examination (by early in second trimester) to screen for poor pregnancy outcomes

Refer for further evaluation; advise on diet; dietary or medical intervention	Prevent IUGR or treat new-born to prevent morbidity/death[b]	Population at risk of IUGR	Weight (measured or recalled) and height	BMI
			Weight	Absolute; kg
			Weight	Weight for gestational age[a]; % of reference; kg
			Weight and height	BMI
Prevent preterm delivery or refer for neonatal care	Prevent new-born morbidity/ death due to prematurity[b]	Population at risk of preterm delivery	Weight and height	BMI[a]
			Weight	Absolute; kg

6	7	8	9
Stage of pregnancy	Criteria for judgement (cut-offs)	Rationale for anthropometry	Other factors for interpretation
Measured during first trimester (or recalled early enough to intervene)	Population-specific 25th percentile (17–21 pre-pregnancy) (23)	RR=1.87 for BMI (23)	Recalled weights may not be reliable
	Population-specific 25th percentile (40–53 kg) (23)	For absolute weight: RR=2.55, high sensitivity and specificity (23); RR=1.84 (24). Indicates general body composition and health status	Absolute weight better than BMI; first screen for short stature improves RR for weight to 2.9 (23)
Measured during second trimester	Below % reference cut-offs (9), below population-specific 25th percentile (40–53 kg @ 20 weeks 43–57 kg @ 28 weeks) (23)	RR=2.77 @ 20 weeks, RR=3.03 @ 28 weeks, good sensitivity and specificity	First-stage screen for short stature improves RR for weight to 3.2–3.5 (23)
	Population-specific 25th percentile (19–22 @ 28 weeks)	RR=2.11–2.31 for BMI, good sensitivity and specificity (23)	Absolute weight better than BMI
Measured during first trimester (or recalled weight)	Population-specific 25th percentile (17–21 prepregnancy) (23)	RR=1.33, moderate sensitivity and specificity for prepregnant BMI	Best prediction in populations with lowest mean BMI
	Population-specific 25th percentile (40–53 prepregnancy) (23)	RR=1.42, moderate sensitivity and specificity for prepregnant weight (23); RR=1.25 (24)	Prediction not improved by first screen for short stature

Table 9 *(continued)*

1	2	3	4	5
Uses: what will be done for the individual?	For what purpose?	Target group	What to measure	Indices and units
Refer for delivery at facility with neonatal care	Prevent labour/delivery complications[b]	Population at risk of complications and of limited access to assisted delivery	Weight and height	BMI
Advise on or supplement diet	Prevent depletion of maternal stores for lactation[b]	Population with chronic undernutrition	Weight and height	BMI

C. Adequate resources (scales available), multiple examinations (by mid-pregnancy and at least twice before delivery) to screen for poor pregnancy outcomes

1	2	3	4	5
Refer for further evaluation; advise on diet; dietary or medical intervention	Prevent IUGR[c]	Population at risk of IUGR	Weight	Absolute rate of weight gain; kg/week
				Absolute gain from prepregnancy weight; kg
			Weight and height	Absolute rate of weight gain; kg/week
	Prevent IUGR or refer for newborn care to prevent morbidity/death[c]	Population at risk of IUGR	Uterine (symphysis–fundus) height[d]	SF height relative to gestational age; cm

6	7	8	9
Stage of pregnancy	Criteria for judgement (cut-offs)	Rationale for anthropometry	Other factors for interpretation
Measured during first trimester (or recalled weight)	Population-specific 25th percentile (17–21 prepregnancy) (23)	RR=0.76 for BMI v. assisted delivery (23)	Height performs better than BMI. Note low BMI reported as "protective"
Any time during pregnancy	Below % reference population	Low body mass before or during pregnancy may persist after delivery	No observation found in literature
Up to 30 weeks' gestation	Population-specific 25th percentile (0.05–0.30 kg/ week between 20 and 28 weeks) (23)	RR=1.7 for weight change between 20 and 28 weeks	Not tested at other cut-off values
	Population-specific 25th percentile from weight gain chart (1 kg at 20 weeks, 3 kg at 28 weeks) (23)	RR=1.8 for total weight gain up to 20 or 28 weeks (23). Measures maternal and fetal tissue gain	
Up to 30 weeks' gestation	As above for weight gain between 20 and 28 weeks, and total weight gain to 20 or 28 weeks, but only in women of height or pre-pregnant weight below population mean	For short women: RR=2.64 for weight change from 20 to 28 weeks; RR=2.8 for total weight gain to 20 or 28 weeks (23). RR=5.6 for women with lowest prepregnant weight (23)	Not tested at other cut-off values
20–40 weeks' gestation	Below 10th percentile for gestational age (various reference data used) (20)	Proxy for fetal size. SE=0.5–0.7, SP=0.8–0.9 from 12 studies (20)	Useful in low resource area with multiple visits

Table 9 (continued)

1	2	3	4	5
Uses: what will be done for the individual?	For what purpose?	Target group	What to measure	Indices and units
Refer for further evaluation; advise on diet; dietary or medical intervention	Prevent preterm delivery[c]	Population at risk of preterm delivery	Weight[a]	Absolute rate of weight gain; kg/week
				Absolute total weight gain; kg
			Weight and height[a]	Absolute total weight gain; kg
Refer for delivery at facility with neonatal care	Prevent newborn morbidity/ death due to IUGR[e]	Population at risk of IUGR and with access to neonatal care	Weight[a]	Absolute total weight gain; kg
				Absolute rate of weight gain: kg/week

6	7	8	9
Stage of pregnancy	Criteria for judgement (cut-offs)	Rationale for anthropometry	Other factors for interpretation
20–40 weeks' gestation	Population-specific 25th percentile (0.05–0.3 kg/ week) (23)	RR=1.43 for weight change from 20 to 28 weeks, RR=0.47 for total weight gain to 20 weeks, poor sensitivity and specificity (23).	
	Population-specific 25th percentile (0–1 kg by 20 weeks) using provisional weight gain charts (23)	RR=1.6 for weight gain after 20 weeks (27).	Low total weight gain reported as "protective"
	As above, but in women below population mean height	RR=1.86 for weight change 20 to 28 weeks in shortest women (23)	
20–40 weeks' gestation	Population-specific 25th percentile (3.0–7.6 kg) for total weight gain to 36 weeks from provisional charts (23)	RR=2.06 for total pregnancy weight gain, RR=1.71 for weight change from 20 to 36 weeks	Allows use of measurements late in pregnancy, assuming there is a facility available for neonatal care
	Population-specific 25th percentile (0.05–0.32 kg/ week) for weight gain 20–36 weeks (23)	RR=3.20 for total pregnancy weight gain, RR=2.67 for rate of gain from 20 to 36 weeks in shortest women	
	First screen on height or prepregnant weight below population mean	RR=5.63 for total pregnancy weight gain, RR=2.49 for rate of gain from 20 to 36 weeks in women with lowest prepregnant weight (23)	

Table 9 *(continued)*

1	2	3	4	5
Uses: what will be done for the individual?	For what purpose?	Target group	What to measure	Indices and units

D. Assessing response to an intervention during pregnancy: adequate resources (scales available), mothers seen periodically from early pregnancy (examined at least twice before delivery)

Refer for further evaluation; advise on diet; dietary or medical intervention	Prevent adverse effects on fetus (IUGR, preterm delivery)	Population at risk of adverse pregnancy outcomes	Weight, gestational age	Rate of weight gain[a]; kg/week
	Prevent maternal complications (e.g. toxaemia)	Population at risk of complications	Weight, gestational age	Rate of weight gain; kg/week
	Prevent depletion of maternal tissue for postpartum adaptations	Population at risk of under-nutrition or with low initial weight for gestational age	Weight, gestational age	Rate of weight gain; kg/week
			Thigh skinfold, gestational age (25–35 weeks)	Rate of fat gain; mm/week

[a] Indices/measurements recommended by the Expert Committee.
[b] Indicators listed in Part A may also be used.
[c] Indicators listed in Part B may also be used.
[d] Multiple measurements over time improve reliability.
[e] Indicators listed for preventing IUGR (column 2) may also be used.

Unfortunately, there are no published data documenting the rate of change in thigh and subscapular skinfolds or symphysis–fundus height after a nutritional or health intervention during pregnancy that would support its use for monitoring individuals.

3.3 Using anthropometry in populations

For many years anthropometric indicators have been used for assessing the nutritional status of populations in the context of surveys at national or community level, as a component of surveillance or monitoring

6	7	8	9
Stage of pregnancy	Criteria for judgement (cut-offs)	Rationale for anthropometry	Other factors for interpretation
20-35 weeks' gestation	Rate of weight gain greater than average (to allow for compensation)	Expected accumulation of maternal/fetal tissue due to intervention	Amount of weight gained will depend on the intervention and its effects on specific components (fat, muscle, water, fetus)
Mid-pregnancy to term	Rate of weight gain within normal range	Expected changes in hydration following treatment	
Throughout pregnancy (especially last trimester)	Sufficient excess weight gain to compensate for deficiency	Correction of inadequate balance of dietary intake, energy expenditure, and fetal demands, which leads to imbalance/depletion of fat and muscle	
	Positive gain		Subscapular skinfold may also be useful

systems, and for evaluating supplementary feeding programmes (*34*) or more general health/nutrition programmes (*35*). They are justifiably considered to be valid and practical indicators of the overall socioeconomic and environmental conditions of populations, especially young children, and have become increasingly accepted as such by international organizations and national governments (*22*).

While the widespread use of anthropometric indicators as tools in planning and policy-making is a positive trend in general, their value in programmes designed to improve the nutritional status of a population is potentially far greater than is currently realized. Two major factors constrain achievement of this potential. First, there is a need for much greater perceptual clarity concerning the interpretation and use of anthropometric indicators for different purposes. Second, much of the research on anthropometric indicators fails to address the most urgent gaps in knowledge concerning their use in the context of policy and planning.

The conceptual issues discussed in this section relate primarily to maternal and fetal health, and research needs are highlighted as appropriate.

Figure 10 illustrates the relationship between nutritional and non-nutritional causes and consequences of maternal malnutrition and the way in which maternal anthropometric indicators may be used as measures of both outcomes and risk factors at the population level. Using a format identical to that of Table 9, Table 10 summarizes recommendations for the use of maternal anthropometry in populations. Much of the "evidence" that supports these uses is indirect and therefore extrapolated to the population level.

3.3.1 *Targeting interventions*

Targeting interventions to particular geographical areas or socioeconomic groups is the most common and best known application for anthropometric indicators, notably child indicators which are especially well suited to the purpose. Broad-based development programmes, for example, may well be targeted according to the prevalence of stunting among children, which closely reflects local socioeconomic conditions. In such cases, short stature is used as an indicator of socioeconomic inequity, and may often be combined with other considerations, such as literacy levels and housing quality (*36*). In economically disadvantaged populations, short stature in adults could also be used as an indicator of socioeconomic inequity.

As they relate to maternal anthropometry, socioeconomic indicators would include BMI among women (non-pregnant and non-lactating, or standardized for stage of pregnancy and lactation) as an overall indicator of the factors that affect women's energy balance (diet, workload, morbidity, reproductive demands). The importance of nutritional status as a factor in reproductive outcomes as well as maternal mortality makes a strong argument for the validity and usefulness of maternal BMI as an indicator of socioeconomic inequity. The same indicators may be used at the individual level to rank women according to degree of deprivation and to target resources to the most deprived, again using the underlying concept of socioeconomic inequity. However, in populations not characterized by energy deficiency (e.g. in developed countries), the significance of anthropometric indicators may be quite different; indeed, the correlation between BMI and socioeconomic status of adult women in developed countries is likely to be the opposite of that in developing areas.

Indicators of socioeconomic inequity are the simplest to develop because they are required only to rank individual women or population groups from lowest to highest with respect to the measurement. The measurement may be chosen to reflect past inequities (height), recent inequities (weight-for-height in undernourished populations), or current inequities (dietary intake). The underlying assumption is that the measurement reflects some or all of the proximal or distal causes of maternal malnutrition (see Fig. 10), but no assumptions are made about the functional consequences of low indicator values or likely responses to the interventions proposed. For screening purposes, choice of cut-off points for inequity indicators may be governed strictly by the availability of resources for intervention.

By contrast, use of indicators of risk demands greater knowledge of the functional consequences of low indicator values. For instance, short maternal stature, low prepregnant BMI, and poor weight gain are all indicators of risk for IUGR, as are non-anthropometric factors like cigarette smoking and high altitude. Indicators of risk are often used when the principal concern is to prevent a particular adverse outcome (e.g. IUGR), or to ameliorate or prevent its consequences (e.g. neonatal morbidity or mortality related to IUGR). Risk indicators are preferred for the second of these purposes, unless the underlying reasons for the risk are well understood or can be ascertained, and are amenable to solution with the interventions available. They are often used for both purposes on the sometimes questionable assumption that causes are well known, can be ascertained, and are amenable to the available interventions.

Indicators of risk identify women who are more likely than average to have a specified outcome (e.g. IUGR); however, it does not necessarily follow that these women will benefit from the available interventions. For instance, short women are at risk for IUGR, but the degree to which they will benefit from supplementary feeding may actually depend less on height than on BMI. Risk indicators can be developed from observational studies, whereas predictors of benefit must be developed on the basis of intervention design and may vary according to the nature of the intervention.

These distinctions between indicators of inequity, risk, and benefit have important implications for how the indicators are used and interpreted. As mentioned above, inequity indicators can be used to target broad-based interventions designed to improve socioeconomic conditions. However, use of maternal height (as an indicator of risk for IUGR) to target more narrowly-based interventions (e.g. supplementary feeding programmes to prevent IUGR) may represent a misuse of the indicator:

Table 10
Summary of recommendations for screening populations of pregnant women for interventions and monitoring response[a]

1	2	3	4	5
Uses: what will be done for the individual?	For what purpose?	Target group	What to measure	Indices and parameters

A. Targeting of interventions: one examination

1	2	3	4	5
Targeting for equity those deprived of access to social/ health/nutrition services	Ensure equit-able access to services and reduce causes of maternal malnutrition	Population with socio-economic inequities and poor energy intake	Height	Absolute; means of functional groups[b]
			Weight, height, gestational age	Absolute weight or BMI; Z-score, % of gestation-specific mean[b]
Targeting interventions (supplementary feeding, vouchers, newborn care facilities, etc.) to those at risk of poor pregnancy outcomes	Prevent IUGR or provide access to neonatal care of IUGR infants; reduce presumed causes of maternal malnutrition and ameliorate poor outcomes for newborn or mother		MUAC	Absolute; prevalence below cut-off value (no correction for gestational age)
			Calf circumference	
			Height	
			Weight, height	Absolute weight or BMI
			Weight, height, gestational age	Absolute weight or BMI for gestational age[b]

6	7	8	9
Stage of pregnancy	Criteria for judgement (cut-offs)	Rationale for anthropometry	Other factors for interpretation
Any time during pregnancy	Rank by mean values for functional group/region; choice of intervention group depends on resources available	Measure of past inequity; socio-economic status related to anthro-pometry (10)	Cut-off to be age-adjusted for young teenagers
		Measure of current inequities (9, 10)	BMI preferred if recent inequities are to be considered
Any time during pregnancy	Cut-off may be population-specific, ranking by prevalence; choice of intervention groups depends on resources available	RR=2.6 for IUGR (10); assess body composition	Only as good as causal inference
		High sensitivity for IUGR (18); assess body composition	
		RR=1.9 (23); assess past nutrition/health and socioeconomic status	Cut-off to be age-adjusted for teenage mothers
First trimester measure or pre-pregnant recall		RR=1.84 for BMI RR=2.55 for weight (23)	Recalls unreliable; ab-solute weight includes effects of short stature
During second half of pregnancy		RR=2.77 @ 20 weeks, 3.03 @ 28 weeks for weight; RR=2.11 @ 20 weeks, 2.31 @ 28 weeks for BMI (23)	

Table 10 *(continued)*

1	2	3	4	5
Uses: what will be done for the individual?	For what purpose?	Target group	What to measure	Indices and parameters
Targeting interventions (supplementary feeding, vouchers, newborn care facilities, etc.) to maximize benefit by reducing poor pregnancy outcomes	Prevent IUGR or provide access to neonatal care of IUGR infants; reduce presumed causes of maternal malnutrition and ameliorate poor outcomes for newborn or mother	Population with socioeconomic inequities and poor energy intake	Weight, height, gestational age	Absolute weight or BMI for gestational age[b]

B. Assessing response to intervention: at least two examinations

Evaluating long-term response to nutrition interventions, to allow subsequent modification	To ensure adequate nutrients are available to the fetus[c]; to add to mother's reserves for lactation	Women with nutritional deficits	Weight, gestational age	Weight gain, kg/week, over at least a 4-week period[b]; prevalence below cut-off; mean rate can also be used
			Thigh skinfold	Fat gain, mm/week, over at least a 4-week period[b]; prevalence below cut-off; mean rate can also be used

[a] The only uses listed in this table are for targeting interventions and assessing responses to interventions. Ascertaining determinants and consequences of malnutrition with the population as a unit of analysis has not been undertaken to any great extent. This type of ecological analysis is usually a first step to guide further studies at the individual level, which provide more definitive indication of the cause–effect relationship. Uses of nutritional surveillance are described in the text and are based on the same rationale as that presented in this table.

[b] Indices/measurements recommended by the Expert Committee.

[c] This assumes that, in the evaluation of most interventions, the response will be observed in the mother. The response is most likely to be reflected in the outcome of pregnancy; maternal anthropometric changes reflect intermediate or mediating mechanisms.

6	7	8	9
Stage of pregnancy	Criteria for judgement (cut-offs)	Rationale for anthropometry	Other factors for interpretation
	Cut-off may be population-specific, ranking by pre-valence; choice of intervention groups depends on resources available	No data: possibly the same indicators as listed above for targeting risk	First stage screen for height improves RR for weight to 3.3–3.5 (23)
20–32 weeks' gestation or 2nd and 3rd trimesters	Change in means or prevalence of low values of weight gain	Significant maternal weight gain following supple-mentation in selected popu-lations (33)	Total weight gain up to any date in late pregnancy is also useful if prepregnant weight is available
25–35 weeks' gestation	Change in means or prevalence of low values of weight gain	Rapid change in selected skinfolds during late preg-nancy (6)	Subscapular skinfold may also be useful

maternal stunting reflects conditions that prevailed during the women's early childhood and may have little relevance to their current nutritional status. Thus, since maternal height is not necessarily predictive of benefit, supplementary feeding may not be an appropriate intervention. These theoretical considerations obviously need to be tested in appropriate research involving both maternal and neonatal outcomes (mortality and morbidity).

Targeting supplementary feeding programmes on the basis of maternal BMI involves three implicit assumptions:

- low maternal BMI is caused by chronically low energy intake by mothers in this population (rather than by morbidity-related factors shown in Fig. 10);

- low intake is caused by inadequate access to food at the household level (rather than by inequitable distribution of food within the household); and

- the food provided by the programme will be preferentially available to women (pregnant, lactating, or non-pregnant non-lactating) and will not substitute for the home diet.

An additional assumption is that supplementary feeding is preferred as an intervention to other measures that might be designed to reduce workload (e.g. labour-saving technology or changes in organization of labour in households and communities) or reproductive burden (child-spacing). Thus, the targeting of a particular intervention on the basis of anthropometric indicators presupposes that deficits in weight or height have specific, well understood causes that will be successfully dealt with by the intervention. In other words, assumptions are made about both causality and the efficacy of the chosen intervention.

Another aspect of the distinction between indicators of risk and benefit relates to the fact that two individuals (or populations) may attain the same value for a given measurement in different ways, which has strong implications for the types of intervention that would be most effective. For example, there is a well known relationship between birth weight and risk of mortality. Given that maternal diet and weight gain during pregnancy are determinants of birth weight, it might be expected that improved diet and weight gain would increase birth weight and decrease infant mortality correspondingly. However, it is also well known that the risk of neonatal mortality at a given birth weight is higher for preterm infants than for those who are SGA (37, 38). It is therefore unlikely that mortality in these two groups would be reduced to the same extent by a given intervention such as dietary supplementation. At a population level, it follows that the expected impact of improved maternal nutritional status on infant mortality will vary according to the pre-existing distribution of LBW across the SGA and preterm categories. This would explain, for instance, why dietary intervention during pregnancy would have little or no impact on infant mortality in the USA (where most LBW is due to prematurity) but might have an important impact in populations with widespread and severe energy deficiency (where most LBW is a result of IUGR and a relatively large proportion of infant deaths can be attributed to SGA).

The above examples illustrate the general point that a given anthropometric indicator may be a valid indicator of inequity or risk, but will not necessarily predict benefit. Despite their profound implications, the distinctions between the different types are not generally appreciated by users of anthropometric indicators. As noted, development of indicators of benefit requires the use of intervention designs in which the differential impact of a given intervention can be examined across subgroups of women defined according to anthropometric indicators or other easily measured characteristics. Relatively little research has been done in this area, and apparently none that relates to maternal mortality as an outcome.

3.3.2 *Assessing response to an intervention*

Whereas predictors of benefit are useful for planning purposes in identifying the individuals or population groups who should receive a specific intervention, indicators of response are more valuable for assessing the effects of an intervention. An indicator useful for the one purpose may not necessarily be useful for the other. For instance, supplementary feeding for women of short stature (an indicator of risk for IUGR) will not increase their height but may well improve their weight gain; thus weight gain is the better indicator of response. A less obvious example is supplementary feeding of pregnant women with moderately low BMI (an indicator of risk); depending upon the degree of undernutrition in the population, the intervention may have more significant impact on birth weights than on any index of maternal anthropometry.

The concept of responsiveness of indicators is important because it suggests alternative ways of evaluating the impact of interventions on individuals and populations; it is also another factor to consider in interpreting the results of evaluation. For example, Beaton & Ghassemi (34) suggested that the failure of most studies to find any anthropometric impact of child feeding programmes might be explained by the extra energy provided by the dietary supplement being used for greater physical activity rather than for growth: though conjectural, this serves to underline the point that indicators used to screen individuals or target populations may not be those in which an impact is expressed.

Thus, anthropometric indicators need not lie on the causal pathway linking two events. They may simply be convenient markers of causal processes, which explains why they may indicate risk but may not be predictive of benefit or responsive to intervention. Low birth weight is a good indicator of infant mortality risk, and in some populations a proportion of LBW is a result of maternal undernutrition; in certain settings, however, improvement of maternal nutritional status may have no significant impact on infant mortality (*39*). Similarly, weight gain may be poor among pregnant women in a population with a high incidence of morbidity during pregnancy, and the latter may have important effects on fetal development; in such a case, dietary intervention may well improve weight gain yet fail to improve the outcome of pregnancy.

3.3.3 *Ascertaining the determinants and consequences of malnutrition*

Anthropometric indicators are often used as outcome variables for analysing the determinants of malnutrition in research and planning settings. They are also used to ascertain the consequences of malnutrition; in many cases they are well suited to this purpose but, as in previous examples, problems may arise if anthropometry is equated too closely and uncritically with nutritional status itself.

Small-for-gestational-age, for example, has several non-nutritional causes (smoking, altitude, pre-eclampsia) and is also susceptible to various nutritional influences that operate at different stages in the mother's life. In any given country it may be relevant to health policy to determine the contribution made by maternal malnutrition to SGA. Short maternal stature, low prepregnant BMI, and poor weight gain during pregnancy all reflect maternal malnutrition, and the contribution of all three variables to the risk of SGA could be estimated by means of an observational study (implying the use of risk indicators). However, a study of the effects on fetal growth of dietary supplementation during pregnancy may seriously underestimate the contribution of maternal malnutrition to SGA, depending upon the relative influence of nutritional and non-nutritional factors in the local population and upon the effects on SGA of short stature and prepregnant BMI. It is also essential to consider the distribution of nutritional status in the population; dietary supplementation in a reasonably well nourished population would not be expected to have an effect on birth weight. Theoretically, therefore, a study of the contribution made by maternal malnutrition to SGA would require the normalization of nutritional status at all stages of the mother's development, from infancy (and probably *in utero*) through adulthood and pregnancy. This hypothetical study would inevitably yield different results from the observational study described above. The anthropometric indicators used in the latter case reflect a variety of non-nutritional socioeconomic and health problems with independent effects on SGA, and thus result in overestimation of the importance of nutrition. Risk indicators, on the other hand, do not necessarily reflect the direct effects that dietary intervention may have on fetal development, with no corresponding response in maternal anthropometry, and the importance of nutrition is therefore underestimated.

3.3.4 *Nutritional surveillance*

Most experience in the use of anthropometry for nutritional surveillance is based on children rather than on women in the reproductive years or on newborn infants. The one notable and important exception is low birth weight, which has been advocated as an important surveillance and general health indicator. This section relates the principles of inequity, risk, benefit, and response to the interpretation and use of LBW in surveillance systems, and to the potential uses of maternal anthropometry in different types of surveillance system.

It should be stressed that "surveillance" is used here primarily in the context of assisting decisions that affect populations rather than individuals; the use of anthropometry for patient screening and monitoring is covered in section 3.2.2. The focus is on three types of surveillance: for problem identification, for policy-making and planning, and for programme management and evaluation (*40*).

Birth weight
Because it can be interpreted as an indicator of inequity, risk, benefit, and response, low birth weight has numerous possible uses in surveillance. It reflects inequities in the conditions affecting women (throughout life, not only in pregnancy); it can predict (or be used as a proxy for) the risk of neonatal and infant mortality; it can predict which population groups may benefit from improved antenatal care of women and neonatal care of infants; and, assuming that interventions are well chosen and properly implemented, it can be a very responsive indicator for evaluation purposes. However, the potential also exists for misusing the indicator. This potential relates to the examples given earlier:

- LBW alone does not indicate the relative contribution made by prematurity and SGA;
- prematurity and SGA have different causes and will respond differently (or not at all) to various interventions; and
- prematurity and SGA have different consequences for the newborn and require different forms of neonatal and infant intervention.

So long as these distinctions are recognized, and the relative contributions of prematurity, SGA, and other, antecedent, causes are known, the indicator is valuable for targeting and evaluating interventions designed to prevent either LBW itself or its consequences (e.g. mortality). The value of LBW as an indicator can be further increased by careful selection of cut-off points and by means such as restricting its interpretation to term infants only.

Maternal anthropometry
Although maternal anthropometry has not been used for population surveillance to date, there are sound justifications for this application. There is growing recognition of the significance of maternal nutritional

status not only for successful reproduction but also for the health and social status of women in general. Acceptance of maternal anthropometric indicators as indicators also of socioeconomic inequity can strengthen the advocacy needed to translate this recognition into policy; implementation of policy, in turn, will be supported by the use of the indicators for targeting and evaluation of interventions. The primary application of maternal anthropometry is concerned mostly with conditions of undernutrition rather than overnutrition, although this depends on the context.

If interventions are to be targeted on the basis of a general concern about socioeconomic inequity, the mean of labile maternal measurements or prevalence of low values would appear useful. This assumes that maternal stature reflects past conditions too distant in time to relate reliably to current conditions. However, if interventions are to be targeted on the basis of risk of adverse outcomes, the choice of indicators, parameters (means vs. prevalence), and cut-off points becomes critical. In this case, low (or very low) maternal stature may well be a strong predictor of the risk of IUGR (or of delivery complications or maternal mortality) and may be preferred to more labile indicators. Maternal stature may also be a valuable indicator if the actions it is to guide relate to improving obstetric and neonatal care facilities to prevent or ameliorate the consequences of LBW (resulting from IUGR or preterm delivery). Stature may be less useful than maternal BMI or gestational weight gain if the actions relate to prevention of IUGR itself. For evaluating the impact of interventions, the best indicator is the one that is most responsive to the particular intervention; this would not be maternal stature (except perhaps in relation to early adolescent pregnancy), but could be one of several others, such as BMI at various stages in the reproductive cycle, gestational weight gain, or postpartum weight loss.

The principal distinction between the optimal maternal indicators of risk, benefit, or response may be determined more by the choice of cut-off point than by the choice of indicator *per se*. Depending on the situation, the cut-off point that is optimal for predicting risk (providing maximum sensitivity and specificity) may be higher or lower than that required to predict benefit. Although there has been insufficient research on this issue, the following considerations are obviously pivotal:

- the nature of the outcome (e.g. prematurity, IUGR, LBW, neonatal mortality, delivery complications, maternal mortality, postnatal maternal depletion);
- the nature of the intervention (e.g. energy supplementation, iron/folate supplementation, reduced workload, child-spacing, malaria prophylaxis);
- the distribution of the anthropometric measurement in the population (i.e. percentage of the population below various cut-off points);
- the prevalence of the outcome; and

- the importance in the population of the cause targeted by the intervention relative to other causes (i.e. the population attributable risk).

A single anthropometric indicator (e.g. weight at 20 weeks' gestation) may be used to predict who is at particular risk of a given adverse outcome (e.g. IUGR), predict who will benefit from a given intervention (e.g. energy supplementation), and identify those who have responded to the intervention (e.g. prolonged child-spacing since the previous birth), but the most efficient cut-off point for each will be different and will vary according to various combinations of outcomes and interventions. Unfortunately, in the absence of empirical evidence on this point, it is usually assumed that the same cut-off point is relevant for all purposes. For example, the cut-off point for LBW is generally set at 2500 g to predict infant mortality, but the same cut-off is often used uncritically to evaluate the impact of maternal dietary supplementation.

These considerations suggest that the impact of surveillance would be enhanced by greater knowledge of the efficiency of various indicators and cut-off points for predicting risk, benefit, and response. For example, a great deal of policy-making and planning is (or should be) prompted initially by concern about a particular pregnancy outcome (e.g. IUGR). To describe the distribution of risk for IUGR (or its correlate, SGA) in a population, a reasonable anthropometric indicator would be a maternal characteristic (and cut-off point) that most efficiently predicts the risk of IUGR (assuming that data on birth weight and/or gestational age themselves are not available). This information would be useful in allocating resources to programmes that ameliorate either the consequences of IUGR or the particular causes of IUGR in the population concerned. It would also be useful for allocating "block" resources to decentralized levels, leaving the decision concerning the most appropriate interventions to planners at those levels. In other circumstances, however, it may be desirable to allocate resources for a specific intervention (e.g. supplementary feeding). In this case the most appropriate indicator, rather than one of risk, would be a maternal characteristic (and cut-off point) that most efficiently predicts the populations most likely to benefit from supplementary feeding. Use of a combination of indicators, such as maternal height and weight in pregnancy, maternal prepregnancy BMI and weight gain, or maternal BMI and season (e.g. pre/post-harvest), may provide the best prediction in some situations. In evaluating the effects of specific programmes (e.g. dietary supplementation) over time, the characteristic (and cut-off point) should be one known to be responsive to the particular intervention.

Given that the maternal characteristics and cut-off points are reasonably similar for each of the applications discussed above, the "best" choice for surveillance purposes would be a single indicator, which would simplify the process. However, if there are large differences between the "most efficient" characteristics and cut-off points for different purposes, the cost and complications of using several indicators may be fully justified by the improvements in targeting resources for maximum impact, although there has been insufficient research on this topic to guide a rational choice of indicators.

3.4 Population data management and analysis

3.4.1 *Sampling considerations*

At the population level the principal uses of anthropometry in the area of public health and social development are:

- to determine the nature and extent of nutrition-related problems;
- to target resources to population groups, on the basis of equity considerations according to the risk of abnormality, or according to the probability that the population would benefit from the available interventions; and
- to evaluate the response of the population to the chosen intervention(s).

It is important to distinguish these three applications of anthropometry from research on the development and testing of anthropometric indicators. Research applications may require samples that are representative of a known population group and longitudinal measurements on the same individuals over time. These requirements may or may not be relevant to public health applications involving anthropometric indicators.

3.4.2 *Problem identification*

Maternal anthropometric indicators are nonspecific and simply reflect, among other conditions, the nutritional status of women in the population. They do not, of themselves, indicate the causes of any imbalances, but may be used in conjunction with other information to confirm the existence of public health problems. Problems may include inadequate dietary intake of energy, protein, or other nutrients, and the excessive physical demands of morbidity, heavy workload, or high reproductive burdens. In formulating actions to improve maternal anthropometry it is important to understand the relative importance of these problems in the population. First, however, the emphasis should be on documenting the extent of each problem in order to promote awareness among policy-makers and stimulate interest in identifying the causes of and solutions to the problem.

For promoting awareness, samples can be cross-sectional and need not always be representative; longitudinal samples are necessary only if gestational weight gain is the indicator to be used, or if it is impossible for women to recall important events needed for data standardization. In documenting nutritional status during pregnancy, for example, it would be important to know the gestational stage of each woman in the sample in order to compare the measurements with reference values for the same stage. If the conception date (or LMP) cannot be recalled with accuracy, it may be necessary to obtain longitudinal data, note the date of delivery, and use this as a reference point for assigning anthropometric measurements made earlier to the appropriate stages of pregnancy. Similar considerations apply to the postpartum and inter-partum periods (although to a lesser extent by 6–12 months postpartum).

The representativeness of samples may be an important issue in some settings where a high degree of bias is suspected in "convenience" samples (e.g. clinic populations), although this is not necessarily true when data are collected simply for the purpose of identifying problems.

In countries with high attendance at antenatal clinics, the absolute number of women with low anthropometric values may be sufficiently high to indicate the existence of a serious problem, even if there is sampling bias. Where clinic attendance is very low, it may be possible to determine the direction of bias among clinic attenders; for instance, comparison of maternal education levels may suggest that clinic attenders are generally among the more educated, and this will indicate the potential direction of bias in the prevalence of maternal malnutrition derived from clinic data. Data from referral hospitals may have extreme levels of bias (because patients are those who are very sick or at high risk) and might best be analysed separately from non-referral clinics.

3.4.3 *Policy and planning*

The principal decisions involved in policy-making and planning concern the targeting of resources towards population groups defined according to various criteria: physiological (pregnant, lactating, or neither), demographic (maternal age, parity, reproductive history), socioeconomic (occupation, ethnic group, income, social class), or geographical (region, district, etc.). Physiological and geographical criteria are the most commonly used. Each of these groups can be ranked according to the prevalence of maternal anthropometric deficits to determine which should receive priority "attention". Attention may take the form of specific interventions (e.g. supplementary feeding) if the causes of the deficits are well known, of a "package" of basic maternal interventions, or of more detailed investigation of the causes of deficits to facilitate selection and design of the most appropriate interventions.

Longitudinal samples are unnecessary for these purposes unless there is reason to suspect serious recall errors. Even where recall errors exist, the ranking of the various population groups may not be affected unless the degree of error varies across these groups. When the decisions to be made are based on prevalence trends over time, rather than on cross-sectional prevalence, time-series data will be necessary but need not rely on serial measurements in the same individuals.

The primary criterion for judging the importance of representativeness of samples is the degree to which it may affect decisions that are based on the ranking of population groups. If non-representative samples show the same direction and extent of bias in all geographical regions, targeting decisions will not be adversely affected. Similarly, if the direction and extent of bias do not change over time, targeting decisions based on time trends will not be adversely affected. Seasonal trends, however, represent a special case of lability over time: the composition of clinic samples may well vary according to seasonal incidence of morbidity and to constraints of travel time or accessibility that affect attendance at clinics. In practice, the direction and extent of bias, and its lability over time, are seldom known, and representative samples are consequently preferable.

In many practical settings it may actually be preferable to use clinic samples, despite the existence and variability of bias. This is because many of the resources to be targeted are intended to be delivered at the static health facilities rather than to the general population. In this case the relevant statistics concern the number of needy women who attend the clinics in each area and the types of service that they require. The number of needy women in the catchment area as a whole is largely irrelevant unless there are mobile clinics or other ways of reaching the non-attenders. A strong case can be made for using the available resources to reach the remote and underserved communities, but in reality few countries have the infrastructure necessary to support such an approach.

3.4.4 *Programme management and evaluation*

Anthropometric data have several potential uses in programme management and evaluation:

- monitoring the degree of coverage (percentage of needy being covered) and yield (percentage of those covered who are needy) achieved by the programme;
- monitoring the degree to which prevalence is changing and moving in the expected direction; and
- evaluating the net impact of the programme (i.e. changes in anthropometric indicators that are attributable to the programme).

The three applications have different sampling requirements and involve different design considerations.

Coverage and yield

Coverage and yield are common process indicators (*40*). Yield can be estimated from samples from the programme itself, whether or not these are representative. Coverage, by contrast, requires population-based (i.e. representative) samples from the catchment areas. By their nature, programme management decisions based on these statistics require certain longitudinal data, even if only in the form of a baseline assessment and periodic reassessments. Yield can be easily assessed on a regular basis, since it requires information only on programme participants; coverage is probably assessed less frequently because of the need for community-based samples to achieve representativeness.

Adequacy evaluation

Adequacy evaluation can include process indicators like coverage and yield; it can also involve evaluation of "gross impact" – the overall change in outcome indicators of maternal anthropometry. Discussion here focuses on the latter aspect. Programme managers and administrators need to know whether the general trend in outcome indicators is in the expected direction; even if such a trend cannot be wholly attributed to the effects of the programme, it provides some indication of whether the programme is having the intended impact. The samples for analysis are drawn from among programme participants and are thus not necessarily representative of the population as a whole. Certain longitudinal data are essential. These may be obtained from several measurements of the same women at different stages in the programme cycle (on entry and at various points after entry), with the "delta value" (i.e. change in anthropometry) aggregated for all women of similar characteristics. They may also take the form of a single measurement on each woman at a particular point of interest in the programme cycle (e.g. on entry or at last visit). The specific requirements will vary according to the nature of the programme and the degree to which the design of the information system makes allowance for various sources of bias and confounding.

Impact evaluation

Impact evaluation differs from adequacy evaluation principally in attempting to determine the degree of change in outcome indicators that is directly attributable to the programme. It therefore involves more extensive sampling as well as a variety of other design and analytical considerations, although requirements will vary according to the desired level of plausibility in the results. Clearly, the cost of impact evaluation is closely related to the required level of plausibility.

Within this framework, the essential requirement of all impact evaluations is that they estimate the change in outcome indicators among programme participants compared with the levels of change among non-participants. Thus, non-participants must also be sampled, and measurements at two separate times are required in both groups to provide longitudinal data. In general, these samples should be chosen to be representative of a larger population of interest, although circumstances frequently do not allow this.

3.5 Methods of taking measurements

Measurements recommended for use during pregnancy and lactation are weight, height, mid-upper arm and calf circumferences, thigh skinfold thickness, and symphysis–fundus height. Techniques for taking these measurements are described in Annex 2. For some of these measurements, pregnancy imposes certain constraints. Specific problems related to the reliability of skinfold thickness, for example, which is affected by problems related to compressibility, have already been discussed (see section 3.1.4). The measurement of SF height is unique to pregnancy and has been described by Belizán et al. (*32*), while measurement errors for weight, height, arm and calf circumference, and skinfold in non-pregnant women have been described elsewhere and generally apply to measurements made during pregnancy. Estimates of measurement error for most of the maternal anthropometric indicators have been reported by Villar et al. (*1*), with interclass correlations for height, weight, SF height, and gestational age in over 200 replicate measures of 0.82, 0.99, 0.92, and 0.98, respectively.

3.6 Sources and characteristics of reference data

The reference data needed to evaluate maternal anthropometric indicators are generally variable in quality; in some cases, there are no reference data. For certain indicators (height, attained weight, mid-upper arm and calf circumference) the interpretation is cross-sectional, while for others (weight gain, skinfold change) it is longitudinal through different stages of pregnancy. Nearly all reference data are normative, in that they are based either on data from the general population or, in the case of attained weight and weight gain, on data from women selected on the basis of favourable pregnancy outcomes. Only prepregnancy weight-for-height reference data have been established in populations with a proven health risk, and then only on the basis of long-term mortality (see sections 7 and 8). Few of the reference data have been based on pregnancy or postpartum outcomes, including maternal mortality, and none has analysed the differences in the distribution of indicators between mothers with favourable outcomes and those with unfavourable outcomes. Such an analysis is essential for the selection not only of appropriate normative data but also of the best cut-off values for each indicator relative to specific outcomes.

Existing reference data and proposals for the development of more useful references where necessary are discussed in the following section.

3.6.1 *Existing reference data*

Reference data for the assessment of anthropometry in pregnant women derive from several different sources, but there has been no attempt to standardize them.

Height
Height has generally been evaluated relative to local reference standards. In well nourished populations, most adults achieve their maximum linear growth potential by the age of about 18 years, and reference standards have been established from surveys of representative populations of

healthy, non-institutionalized individuals. In the USA, for example, the age- and sex-stratified reference data from the National Health and Nutrition Examination Surveys (NHANES) have been used (*41*). Since mean final achieved height varies across developed countries (*42*), locally derived reference data are probably necessary for some population groups. However, there has been no test of differences in the predictive value of specific height cut-off values for unfavourable pregnancy outcomes such as SGA, preterm delivery, or the need for assisted delivery across populations with similar or different mean heights.

Assessment of height in undernourished populations, of whom a large proportion fail to achieve maximum growth potential, poses different problems. Short stature in these settings is more likely to reflect past deficits, the causes of which still persist. Because variations in height between well nourished and undernourished populations have different causes, very different intervention strategies may be required to deal with unfavourable outcomes (SGA, preterm delivery) that are apparently similar yet perhaps of very different etiology. Moreover, the much higher prevalence of the risk factor (i.e. short height) in undernourished populations has implications for allocation of scarce resources in settings where many women are identified as at-risk. The best cut-off points may therefore differ according to outcome and underlying causes, as well as with the availability of interventions that focus on maternal height. This last factor is particularly important for population level assessments; the best cut-off for height will be the value that selects only the number of women for whom resources are sufficient to implement intervention. Of course, this assumes that height is in fact the best indicator of risk for the outcome of interest. In fact, for all the fetal outcomes examined by the WHO Collaborative Study (*23*), weight was generally a better indicator of risk than height. Only assisted delivery was predicted better by height than by weight. However, the WHO analysis suggests that initial screening on the basis of height can improve the predictive power of other anthropometric indicators. This two-stage screening requires further testing, first for misclassification (especially false-positives whose taller stature would exclude otherwise high-risk women from further consideration), and then for optimal cut-off values for height that ensure the least misclassification and the best correlation of the second-stage indicator with the outcome.

Prepregnancy or early pregnancy weight and weight-for-height
Reference data for prepregnancy or early pregnancy weight are generally derived from the same types of survey as height references. It should be recognized that weight used alone may also represent variation in height; as a result its predictive power will be somewhat stronger than that of weight adjusted for height. From the literature it is clear that larger mothers have larger babies; what is less clear are the independent effects of weight and height, and how they work together, perhaps with height

modifying the effect of weight on various outcomes. The results of the WHO Collaborative Study (23) suggest that both low prepregnancy or early pregnancy BMI and short stature are significant independent risk factors for LBW, SGA, and preterm delivery; the ORs for both indicators are similar in magnitude but not as high as those for weight alone (Table 3). For clinical and public health applications the use of weight alone may be sufficient, but for research into the biological relationships, the independent, combined, and interactive effects of weight and height require clarification.

The Institute of Medicine (9) recommends the use of BMI for assessment of prepregnant nutritional status in well nourished populations. The reference standards proposed are based on the Metropolitan Life Insurance Company tables of desirable body weight-for-height (43). The percentage of desirable weight-for-height is converted to BMI and the cut-off values that distinguish underweight and overweight from normal weight correspond to approximately 90% and 120% of the Metropolitan Life reference. These desirable weights-for-height are based on a functional relationship between weight and life expectancy, but there is no indication that they also correspond to levels of obstetric risk for the mother or fetus, or of postpartum maternal health or lactation performance.

Attained weight during pregnancy

Attained weight measured at any time during pregnancy has generally been compared with reference weight gain charts. These charts have a long history, which has been described by Haas (31) and the Institute of Medicine (9). The first chart to be widely used was derived from data on 60 women from Philadelphia who were measured throughout pregnancy, gained an average of 10.9 kg by term, and had healthy pregnancy outcomes (44). A subsequent chart was based on 2868 healthy, primiparous British women with good pregnancy outcomes, who gained an average of 12.5 kg (45). These two became the basis for most weight gain charts that are used in the USA today.

The Institute of Medicine (9) has proposed a series of provisional charts (see Fig. 12) based on a nationally representative sample of US women who delivered full term (39–41 weeks), normally grown (3000–4000 g) infants without complications. The references were developed to reflect different weight gains associated with three categories of prepregnancy BMI. Ranges of accumulated weight gain are given only at term, since no data existed at the time on variation in achieved weights at various stages of pregnancy for an appropriate reference population. More recently, longitudinal data have been tabulated on 1185 women from San Francisco who had favourable pregnancy outcomes (Abrams, unpublished data reported in 31). None of these normative reference charts has been tested for the overlap of distributions in women with favourable and unfavourable outcomes: the large variation in total weight

Figure 12

Provisional weight gain charts according to prepregnancy body mass index (BMI)[a]

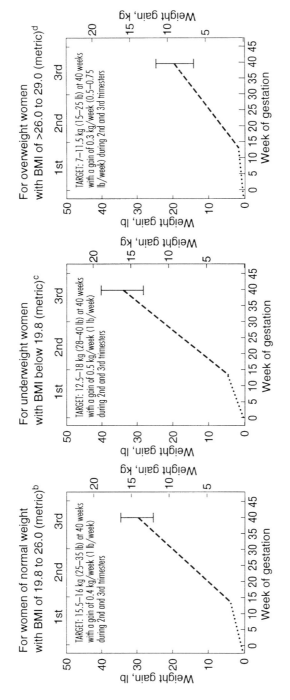

For women of normal weight with BMI of 19.8 to 26.0 (metric)[b]

TARGET: 15.5–16 kg (25–35 lb) at 40 weeks with a gain of 0.4 kg/week (1 lb/week) during 2nd and 3rd trimesters

For underweight women with BMI below 19.8 (metric)[c]

TARGET: 12.5–18 kg (28–40 lb) at 40 weeks with a gain of 0.5 kg/week (1 lb/week) during 2nd and 3rd trimesters

For overweight women with BMI of >26.0 to 29.0 (metric)[d]

TARGET: 7–11.5 kg (15–25 lb) at 40 weeks with a gain of 0.3 kg/week (0.5–0.75 lb/week) during 2nd and 3rd trimesters

[a] Reproduced from reference 9 with permission from *Nutrition during pregnancy*. Copyright 1990 by the National Academy of Sciences. Courtesy of the National Academy Press, Washington, DC.

[b] Assumes a gain of 1.6 kg (3.5 lb) in the first trimester and the remaining gain at a rate of 0.44 kg/week (0.97 lb/week).

[c] Assumes a gain of 2.3 kg (5 lb) in the first trimester and the remaining gain at a rate of 0.49 kg/week (1.07 lb/week).

[d] Assumes a gain of 0.9 kg (2 lb) in the first trimester and the remaining gain at a rate of 0.3 kg/week (0.67 lb/week).

Figure 13

Chart designed for use in monitoring weight gain during pregnancy, considering prepregnancy weight-for-height as a percentage of a standard[a]

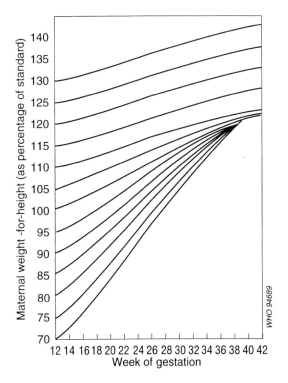

gain from Institute of Medicine charts (*9*) suggests that it may not be possible to detect clearly different distributions in populations of this type. The 15th and 85th percentiles of total weight gain in the normative data used to produce the Institute of Medicine recommendations are 7.3 and 18.2 kg, respectively. In the San Francisco normative data the coefficient of variation in weight at various stages of pregnancy ranges from 90% at 13–14 weeks to 30% in the third trimester (Abrams, unpublished data reported in *31*).

A reference chart based on theoretical calculations of proportional weight gain has been proposed by Rosso (*30*) as an alternative to those based on normative data. This chart (see Fig. 13) is based on the assumption that total weight gain in most women should equal 20% of the ideal prepregnant weight-for-height. Use of the chart requires a knowledge of weight, height, and gestational age at any stage of pregnancy. Given height, ideal body weight can be estimated from a nomogram based on Metropolitan Life Insurance charts (*43*). Current body weight is then presented as a percentage of the ideal weight and plotted on the curve (see Fig. 13). The application of these curves to undernourished populations, where prepregnancy BMI for a large proportion of women is below 18.5, is of questionable validity. For many of these women expectations of weight gain during pregnancy in order to compensate for prepregnancy deficits may be unrealistic. The curves are now being used to target women in Chile for a national food supplementation programme; evaluation results were not available at the time of preparation of this report.

The WHO Collaborative Study (23) provides insight into an approach for creating reference curves of attained weight. Though provisional, the curves produced show important features that are likely to be retained in the final version.

As described in section 3.2.1, the studies were first assigned to groups by cluster analysis according to the final weight achieved during pregnancy. Four clusters or country groups were identified, ranked from the lowest to the highest mean attained weight at 36 weeks of pregnancy. Each was then divided into three subgroups on the basis of birth weight (<2500 g, 2500–3000 g, and >3000 g). The weight gain curves for each country group according to birth weight are shown in Fig. 14. In all four, the curves for birth weights over 3000 g are clearly distinct from those for the two lighter birth-weight subgroups. Final attained maternal weights for the heaviest birth-weight subgroups are 55, 61, 65, and 73 kg for groups G1 to G4, respectively. It appears that women who deliver infants weighing over 3000 g have very different weights throughout pregnancy from mothers who deliver smaller infants, which suggests that this subgroup may be a suitable basis for constructing a normative reference.

As a next step, assuming that the definition of the normative population for these indicators is satisfactory, more generic curves are prepared, to reflect accumulated weight gain from the beginning of pregnancy. The curves developed for each group are shown in Fig. 15; all four represent the weight gain pattern of women who delivered infants weighing over 3000 g. Of these, the three curves from groups of less developed countries (G1, G2, G3) are very similar, with a total weight gain of about 10.5 kg. In contrast, women from Ireland and the UK (G4) gain about 3 kg more, and their weight gain pattern is almost identical to that proposed as a reference by the Institute of Medicine (9). The similarity of the curves for groups G1, G2, and G3 might suggest that a single reference could be appropriate for these undernourished populations. However, it is important that this observation be validated with other outcomes (such as obstetric complications and lactation performance) before a definitive reference is recommended. Also, basing a reference on "positive deviants" (i.e. those who do well despite an environment where nutrition is not optimal, as in the countries of groups G1 to G3) is unwarranted (see section 2.9). It is also important to recognize any additional benefits of the extra 3 kg gained by the women in G4 (such as extra fat to

Figure 14

Pregnancy weight gain curves, by country group, for mothers with infants in different birth-weight (BW) categories[a]

Notes
1. The initial weight is based on the average prepregnant weight for that group
2. Group 1 = India (Poona), Nepal (rural), Nepal (urban), Sri Lanka
   Group 2 = Indonesia, Myanmar, Thailand, Viet Nam
   Group 3 = China, Colombia, Malawi
   Group 4 = Ireland, United Kingdom

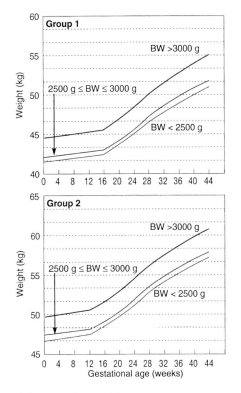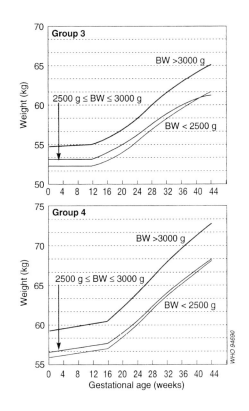

[a] Source: reference *23*.

support lactation). Even though the pregnancy outcome is comparable across groups, G4 represents populations living in a "healthier" environment, which might lend support to this group serving as a normative reference. The final reference curve should present the median weight for gestational age of the normative population, along with lines representing -2, -1, +1, and +2 SD units.

It would then be desirable to test different cut-off values of maternal weight for their ability to identify women with poor pregnancy outcomes; sensitivity, specificity, and PPV would be examined at various cut-off values, at various gestational ages, relative to the risk of delivering an infant weighing less than 3000 g. Depending on the reasons for using maternal weight as the indicator (for screening for risk, response, or

Figure 15

Cumulative pregnancy weight gain by week of gestation for women delivering infants of birth weight >3000 g, by country group[a]

Note: G1, G2, G3, G4 refer to the country groups shown in Fig. 14.

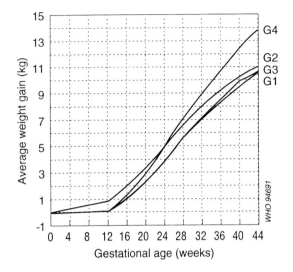

[a] Source: reference *23*.

benefit, or for estimating population characteristics), different cut-off points might be identified (see section 2) and could be added to the curves presented in Fig. 15.

In the meantime, a practical approach to using the results currently available is proposed, but should be fully field-tested and evaluated before being widely used.

Screening for risk of SGA to identify individuals for supplementary feeding can take advantage of the strong correlation shown in the WHO Collaborative Study between attained weight measured after mid-pregnancy and risk of SGA. As can be seen in Fig. 15, in countries with significant rates of undernutrition in women (i.e. groups G1, G2, and G3), the median weight gain was similar for all mothers whose infants' birth weights were above 3000 g: approximately 2.5, 6, and 8.5 kg from the time of conception to 20, 28, and 36 weeks, respectively. The 25th percentile was approximately 4 kg below the median in each group. For countries with no major undernutrition during pregnancy (group G4), median weight gain by mothers whose infants' birth weights were above 3000 g was 3, 7, and 10.5 kg, respectively, at 20, 28, and 36 weeks of gestation. The 25th percentile was about 6 kg below the median. Using these data to select the 25th percentile of attained weight at various stages of pregnancy, attained weight can be estimated from the following algorithm:

Estimation of 25th percentile attained weight at different stages of pregnancy derived from median weight of non-pregnant women (W$_{np}$)

Level of undernutrition in pregnant women	Weight (kg) below which increased risk of SGA is expected		
	20 weeks	28 weeks	36 weeks
High	$W_{np} - 1.5$	$W_{np} + 2$	$W_{np} + 4.5$
Low	$W_{np} - 3$	$W_{np} + 1$	$W_{np} + 4.5$

This calculation requires the median weight, W_{np}, of non-pregnant women aged 20-29 years. This figure should be available (or readily measurable) for each ethnic group in each country. Use of the 25th percentile as a cut-off point is based on its association with an increased risk of SGA and its selection of a feasible proportion of women for treatment; in situations where more or fewer resources are available, the cut-off can be adjusted accordingly. Over time, a progressively smaller proportion of women should fall below this cut-off; initially it should be around 25%.

This approach to screening takes no account of other maternal characteristics, such as height, that may affect its efficiency. Results from the WHO Collaborative Study suggest that it should be possible to improve screening efficiency by first choosing women who fall below the population median height and then weighing them during pregnancy. These cut-off values should be subjected to an analysis of misclassification to test their efficiency in identifying women who would benefit from supplementation, and to see to what extent a two-stage selection procedure (height then weight) improves screening efficiency.

Weight gained during pregnancy
Although the charts described above are often referred to as "weight gain" charts they are actually "weight accumulated" charts in that they reflect what have been called "distance curves" (*46*). Actual weight gains should be expressed per unit time and plotted as velocity curves; only one true velocity curve has been published (*47*), and that relates to pregnant adolescents. A more common and practical expression of weight gain is the amount of weight gained between consecutive prenatal examinations and expressed as weight gain per week or per month. The Institute of Medicine (*9*) recommends a weekly gain of 0.4 kg during the second and third trimesters for women of normal prepregnant BMI, 0.5 kg for those who are underweight, and 0.3 kg for overweight women. Gains at the upper end of the range (3 kg/month) are suggested as reason for further evaluation of the mother; at the lower end of the range, gains of less than 0.5 kg/month by overweight women and less than 1 kg/month by women of normal weight should be cause for concern.

In the WHO Collaborative Study (*23*), preliminary analysis of monthly weight gain patterns in women delivering babies weighing more than

Figure 16

Mean monthly pregnancy weight gain and cumulative weight gain of mothers with infants of birth weight > 3000 g[a]

Note: Groups 1, 2, 3, 4 are the country groups shown in Fig. 14.

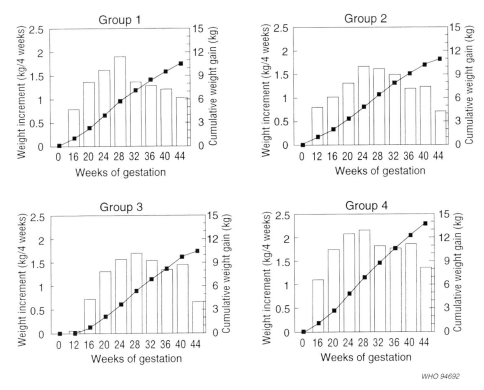

WHO 94692

[a] Source: reference *23*.

3000 g suggests consistency with the recommendations of the Institute of Medicine (Fig. 16). In developing countries gains of 1.5 kg/month during the last two trimesters are consistent with good pregnancy outcomes, while in developed countries gains of about 2.0 kg/month produce the same outcomes relative to adequate birth weight. Monthly weight gain seems to diminish somewhat in both populations from the second to the third trimester of pregnancy. No information on the distribution (standard deviation, percentiles) was reported for women with the more favourable outcomes, but means and standard deviations for all women, irrespective of pregnancy outcome, indicate considerable variation within clusters of populations (coefficient of variation 50 to 79% during mid-pregnancy). Villar et al. (*6*) report average gains of 375.1 g/week after 16 weeks of pregnancy for 105 healthy Guatemalan women who delivered infants with a mean birth weight of 3211 g (LBW = 4.8%), which is the same as that reported by the WHO Collaborative Study (*23*).

Mid-upper arm and calf circumference
Reference data for mid-upper arm circumference have been discussed at length by Krasovec & Anderson (*10*). Local reference data were generally used and based on cut-off values that range from 21 to 23 cm to identify women likely to have LBW infants. While MUAC seems to increase somewhat during pregnancy, the mean increases reported by Krasovec & Anderson are very small (generally less than 0.5 cm). These authors also suggest that MUAC measured at any time during pregnancy be used in place of maternal prepregnancy weight when scales are not available. This approach, however, should be validated before reference data are developed for application during pregnancy, since it implies that MUAC, like prepregnant BMI, may be used as both a screening indicator and a conditional factor for interpreting gestational weight gain. Recently, maternal calf circumference has been suggested as an effective screening indicator for risk of LBW and poor lactation performance (*18*), but no reference data specific to pregnancy are available and there is some question as to whether reference data for non-pregnant women are applicable. The lack of normative data from populations in developing countries where the measure may be most useful, and the fact that oedema is likely to affect the measure (improving its correlation with outcomes), suggests that more research is needed to evaluate the potential usefulness of this indicator. If possible, such research should include maternal mortality and morbidity outcomes in countries with poor health resources.

Skinfold thickness
Reference data on skinfold thickness specific to pregnancy have not been developed. In the relatively few studies that have used skinfolds throughout pregnancy (*3, 6, 9*), large changes in skinfold thickness at the medial anterior thigh site have been noted. Changes in skinfold thickness at many sites may be unrelated to body fat, especially during late pregnancy, and reference data based on non-pregnant relationships between skinfolds and total body fat are therefore not necessarily valid for extrapolation to body fat during pregnancy. By extension, the correlation between pregnancy outcomes and skinfold thickness (or its change during pregnancy) may not be simply a reflection of the mobilization of body fat stores to support fetal growth but may also involve other factors, such as changing hydration levels.

3.6.2 Criteria for establishing reference data

Criteria for describing normative reference data apply also to the establishment of functional cut-off points depending on local needs, resources, and applications.

Distance and velocity curves
Velocity is the rate of change of an anthropometric measurement and, by analogy, distance is the current value of that measurement (*46*). Although they are strongly correlated, the two should be considered separately.

Distance measurements are height, prepregnant weight, weight at any stage of pregnancy, MUAC, and skinfold thickness. Most weight gain charts are actually distance curves, indicating attained weight at a given point in pregnancy. However, if weight at conception is shown as zero, these curves can be considered as measuring velocity from time zero (usually date of LMP) to the point of measurement, provided that gain is divided by the elapsed time.

The most widely used velocity measurement is velocity of weight gain. For research applications, it is important to distinguish between gross gain and gain net of infant and products of conception; for simple prediction of risk, especially risk of LBW, IUGR, or macrosomia (rather than maternal nutritional status *per se*), the distinction is probably less relevant. Velocity of weight gain should also be adjusted for gestational age, since it is not linear throughout pregnancy. There is a wide choice of time intervals over which velocity can be measured, e.g. first, second, or third trimester, weekly, monthly, etc., which should be compared when charts are prepared. It is also important to consider measurement errors and timing of normal antenatal checks.

Velocity can be adjusted for, or considered independently of, distance; the two approaches may yield different results, so both should be investigated.

Conditional standard
An alternative to distance or velocity is a conditional or regression-based standard (*48*), which takes into account the possibility that optimal velocity is linearly related to distance, as proposed by Rosso (*30*). The conditional standard answers the question: What weight (or weight gain) is to be expected at the end of pregnancy, given the prepregnant weight?

Choice of reference data
Population. The ideal reference population is one in which the incidence of poor pregnancy outcomes is low. Assuming that obesity contributes to adverse pregnancy outcomes, this is unlikely to be a European or North American population, where overweight is a major problem. An African, Asian, or Central or South American population would be suitable, possibly one composed of relatively privileged people living in a healthy environment. Although the reference may be defined for a selected healthy population, it is essential that information is also collected on the population that is excluded by reason of poor pregnancy outcomes; this will permit the analysis necessary to establish functional cut-off points.

An alternative approach, and one that is easier to handle statistically, is to use two contrasting populations, one to define the lower limits of normal and the other the upper limits. The aim would be to identify ranges of anthropometric values within which birth outcome is generally good.

A further option would be a very large study, such as that of Naeye (*49*) with a sample size of 45 000, which used perinatal mortality rate as the outcome measure. The large sample size ensures that the extremes of maternal height, weight-for-height, and weight gain are adequately represented. This is important if valid predictions are to be made for small and/or thin women. The data used were collected between 1959 and 1966 by the Collaborative Perinatal Project, and strongly influenced the 1970 recommendations of the US National Academy of Sciences on pregnancy weight gain. Although the data are now fairly old, they have the advantage of being unaffected by the recent trend to increasing obesity.

A further advantage is the use of perinatal mortality, rather than birth weight, as the outcome measure; since this is raised at both extremes of maternal anthropometry, the optimal central region can be identified unambiguously by fitting quadratic (U-shaped) regression curves relating mortality to anthropometry. The WHO Collaborative Study on maternal anthropometry (23) could also provide data to set these criteria, since it had both a large sample size (111 000) and a large number (25) of different populations from many different countries.

Study design. Ideally, reference data should be based on longitudinal studies, with anthropometric measurements made before and throughout pregnancy, and for 6-12 months postpartum. Measurements should be related to birth outcome, postnatal infant development, and maternal postpartum nutritional status. A cross-sectional study relating prepregnancy anthropometry to birth outcome would clarify the importance of achieved anthropometric values, particularly height, weight, and upper arm circumference.

Study size. For fully longitudinal studies with more common outcomes (SGA, preterm birth, etc.), a sample of about 1000 women may be adequate. A larger sample, of perhaps 2000, may be required for cross-sectional studies of similar outcomes. Perinatal and infant mortality studies require a very large sample, in excess of 10000. All of these sample sizes are dependent on the prevalence of the outcome in the population being studied.

Data. Desired measurements include height at the start of pregnancy (and at the end for adolescent populations), weight throughout, and arm and calf circumference, if possible. It is important to standardize measurement techniques, with periodic inter- and intra-observer comparisons. Data should also be collected on maternal race, parity, age, general health, and pregnancy complications, and on birth weight, gestational age, and sex of infants. Data of high quality are essential; this is especially true of gestational age, since any indicator that changes during pregnancy carries the potential for misclassification (8).

Analysis. Each available outcome measure should be used in turn for each of the analyses. Birth weight and gestational age should also be analysed as binary outcomes (LBW and preterm, respectively), and birth weight should be related to gestational age (small (SGA), appropriate (AGA), or large (LGA) for gestational age).

Cross-sectional regression analysis should be used to relate height and prepregnant weight to outcome. Distinctions should be made between weight alone, height alone, weight and height together, and weight corrected for height (i.e. weight-for-height). For the last of these, it is also possible to regress log weight on log height to determine whether BMI is the best weight-for-height index, or whether another power of height, e.g. (height)^3, is better.

The results of this analysis can be used to identify ranges of weight and/or height associated with an acceptable outcome. It is important to look for non-linear relationships between anthropometry and outcome, particularly U-shaped curves related to mortality, to simplify the search for suitable cut-offs. For example, the probability of SGA or macrosomia as it relates to maternal weight and height can be modelled to identify the central region where the risks of both are low. Other maternal outcomes can be similarly combined to generate an optimal anthropometric profile.

The analyses should be extended to include velocity, particularly of weight gain during different periods of pregnancy. Velocity of gain in arm circumference, however, is unlikely to be informative.

Gross weight gain during pregnancy includes the weight of the fetus and products of conception. A more realistic impression of the correlation between weight gain and birth weight is obtained by using net rather than gross weight gain. However, this has little value in clinical or public health applications where prediction of adverse pregnancy outcomes is desired, since net gain cannot be calculated until *after* delivery.

The results of all analyses should be tested for their predictive power at the individual level by calculating sensitivity, specificity, and positive and negative predictive values. If these are not satisfactory there is little justification for putting forward anthropometric recommendations, unless it is made clear that they are for groups of women, not individuals.

3.6.3 *Recommendations for new reference data*

The recommendations in this section for reference data applied to specific indicators are based on the general principles discussed in the previous section.

Height
The reference for height of pregnant women should be cross-sectional and, in order to test for secular trends, especially in undernourished populations, and to examine when linear growth stops during adolescence, should sample across the reproductive age span of 15 to 50 years. The sample for the reference should represent healthy women who are likely to have reached their genetic growth potential, and who have had a favourable pregnancy outcome (gestational age between 37 and 42 weeks, birth weight between 3000 and 4000 g, no complications of pregnancy, labour, or delivery). It should be drawn from the general

population to which the reference is to be applied, so that height distribution can be compared for sub-populations with favourable outcomes (the specificity distribution) and sub-populations with specific unfavourable outcomes (the sensitivity distribution). This will allow the relationship between height and outcomes to be tested and the utility of height as an indicator of risk to be determined.

If height meets the criterion of significant correlation with outcome, the sensitivity, specificity and positive predictive value can be estimated from these data in order to compare height with other candidate indicators and to determine the best cut-off point for any particular proposed use (25, 50). This analysis should also take account of potential modification of the height/outcome relationship by maternal age, parity, and perhaps other known factors such as socioeconomic status or race that may serve as useful first-level screening criteria. For example, it may be necessary to use different cut-off values for adolescent and adult mothers in screening for risk of cephalopelvic disproportion or SGA, or height may prove to be a useful measure only for women of a specific population subgroup. The size of the sample drawn from the reference population must be large enough to allow the third or fifth percentiles to be established with confidence. Selection of the total sample size to test for cut-off points must take into consideration the number of cases of unfavourable outcome needed to produce clinically and statistically significant measures of association. Data that meet many of these requirements are available from the WHO Collaborative Study (23).

Height should be measured according to standard procedures (see Annex 2). Careful note should be made of major deviations in technique, such as whether the subject wore shoes, whether height was actually measured or simply recalled, and the certainty of age.

It would be useful to compare the results of this analysis with those from the general population of women of reproductive age in whom other short-term and long-term health risks are predicted from height.

Prepregnant weight or body mass index
Determination of appropriate reference standards for prepregnant BMI or weight should follow guidelines similar to those described for height. Since BMI reflects different etiologies and thus different associations for the same pregnancy outcomes, consideration should be given to the need for population-specific references. For example, in populations with marginal protein–energy nutritional status, variations in BMI reflect variations in lean body mass and all of its correlates (iron status, energy and protein reserves, physical activity, etc.). In contrast, BMI variation in populations with adequate protein and energy intakes generally reflects degrees of adiposity and obesity at one end of the distribution, and levels of lean body mass that are often related to greater physical fitness (less fatness) at the lower end of the distribution. The pregnancy-related consequences of variation in BMI may therefore differ widely between

populations. The contribution made by inter-population variation in body proportions (leg-to-trunk length ratio) to BMI variation, and the functional significance of this during pregnancy, is unresolved. Other issues that may have to be separately resolved for each population include the choice between weight and BMI as an appropriate indicator, which will also depend on the human resources needed to take and interpret the measurements.

Reference data for MUAC should follow similar guidelines.

Achieved weight and weight gain
Since serial measures are required for reference data on both achieved weight and weight gain during pregnancy, a longitudinal study is required that links achieved weight and/or weight increments with outcomes. Gestational age should be measured as accurately as possible: for application of the references, interpretation of achieved weight requires good estimates of gestational age. Interpretation of short-term weight gain does not require the same accuracy in gestational age, provided that increments are measured over short time periods (4-6 weeks). It is important to recognize that the relationship of weight or weight gain to outcomes may differ depending on specific characteristics of the mother, such as prepregnancy BMI, height, parity, age, and race. This should be formally tested to determine whether certain subgroups require separate references. Weight charts used to screen women at the first prenatal visit should be constructed with a series of mean and median weights at various weeks of gestation for a population with favourable pregnancy outcomes. To determine optimal cut-off values at each stage of pregnancy and for various outcomes, the trend line that is obtained by following these points should be bounded on both sides by lines of risk determined by the results of misclassification analysis. If optimal cut-off values have not been determined, -2, -1, +1, and +2 standard deviations (SD) should be plotted at each gestational age where a mean (or median) is known, and lines drawn to connect similar SDs across gestational age. These lines should be smoothed in ways similar to those described later for child growth curves (see section 5). This approach has been described by the Institute of Medicine (9).

Short-term weight gain may be expressed in two ways. A velocity curve can be used, similar to those used to assess child growth. The difficulty with this approach is that measures of variation or cut-off points of risk will vary with the length of the measurement interval; calculations then become necessary for every patient in whom measurements are taken over a different time frame from that used in the reference. Generally, where health care personnel have only minimal education and training, velocity curves are not well accepted. A more acceptable approach is to prepare a table of "optimal" weight gain that uses short (daily or weekly) intervals from which the health worker can easily calculate optimal gain over the time interval he or she is using. Alternatively, the table may be designed with recommendations expressed as various options depending on the elapsed time between measurements; for example, there may be separate columns for observations made every 1, 2, 3, or 4 weeks. Regardless of how the recommendations are presented, however, it is essential that they include upper and lower limits of risk or SDs based on analysis similar to that described above for other indicators.

Skinfold thickness
Reference data for skinfold thickness can be constructed following similar guidelines to those described for achieved weight, and perhaps for weight gain, if a case can be made for a good association between skinfold change and specific outcomes. A major limitation of this approach is that it could result in a large number of reference curves or tables, each one specific to a certain sub-population and to certain outcomes. It would be valuable, but possibly difficult, to develop criteria that allow multipurpose reference data to be used with maximal efficiency.

3.7 Relationship between normative reference data and functional outcomes

The distinctions between indicators of socioeconomic inequity, risk, benefit, and response – discussed earlier – have profound implications for the construction of reference data for anthropometry at all stages in the life cycle, but little systematic attention has been given to these by the international bodies responsible for constructing reference data and advising on their appropriate uses. This section clarifies the issue and suggests the type of research required for further development.

The concept that underlies the construction and interpretation of current reference data is based on the specificity distribution for anthropometric characteristics. In other words, current reference data describe the distribution of anthropometric traits in an ostensibly healthy, well nourished population with favourable pregnancy outcomes. This concept has the greatest validity in the case of height of preschool children because it is possible to identify populations (e.g. the USA) in which the observed distribution and its moments can be assumed to reflect the variation in genetic potential within a population reasonably free of disease and environmental deprivation. In the past, this approach has also been used more uncritically for weight and weight-for-height of preschool children, although the existence of obesity among US infants and children is now recognized and invalidates the assumption that the population is "healthy and well nourished" in this respect. The definition of the specificity distribution for weight, weight-for-height, and related characteristics, in contrast to that for height, will require more knowledge about the long-term consequences of deviations in these characteristics at early ages. The situation is similar for anthropometry during pregnancy where short-term (pregnancy outcomes, maternal morbidity and mortality) and long-term (maternal depletion, obesity later in life) consequences need to be examined.

It should be emphasized that the specificity distribution indicates only the extent to which a particular woman deviates from the median of a healthy population; it does not indicate the probability of suffering an adverse outcome at some time in the future. The latter requires empirical evidence on the sensitivity distribution, i.e. the probability of suffering a given adverse outcome, which is in turn dependent on the prevalence of the outcome. As shown in Fig. 17, this distribution may deviate from the specificity distribution by a large or small amount, reflecting the steepness of the rise in risk as deviation from the median increases. The quantitative relationship between the two distributions (i.e. the distance between them) can only be determined empirically.

The importance of this lies in the fact that the "conventional" cut-off points based on the specificity distribution (e.g. 3rd percentile) have no intrinsic value for predicting the risk of adverse outcomes such as SGA, preterm delivery, obstetric complications, neonatal or maternal mortality. In general, it is safe to assume that the risk of a given adverse outcome increases at some point as deviation from the median of the specificity distribution increases, but the location of that point and the steepness of the increase in risk beyond that point cannot be predicted without empirical support. It follows that the most efficient screening cut-off point for predicting an outcome cannot be identified by using only the specificity distribution; knowledge of the sensitivity distribution and the prevalence of the outcome is also necessary.

As shown in Fig. 17, similar concepts apply to the development of indicators of benefit. In this case it would be desirable to compare the distributions of those who benefit from a given intervention and those who derive little or no benefit with respect to a measurement taken before intervention. For example, the mid-pregnancy weight of women who benefited from supplementation could be compared with the weight of those who did not. ("Benefit" might be defined as a higher birth weight or postpartum maternal BMI than was predicted on the basis of other characteristics, e.g. height, MUAC, previous LBW, poor socioeconomic status.) With this information it would be possible to identify the most efficient cut-off point for identifying women likely to benefit from supplementation. Note that the definition of "benefit" can be based on the same measurements as those used to predict who will benefit or on different measurements; in this example, benefit might be defined relative to SGA, or to maternal weight at some point after the intervention.

Finally, indicators of response refer to characteristics that are capable of changing in response to a given intervention. In the above example, indicators of response may be fetal growth, maternal anthropometry during or after intervention, or, less obviously, such characteristics as

Figure 17

Characteristics of an indicator that predicts benefit from an intervention[a]

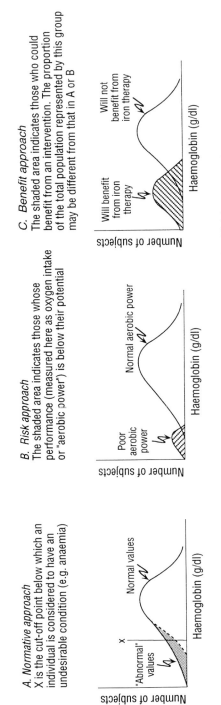

A. Normative approach
X is the cut-off point below which an individual is considered to have an undesirable condition (e.g. anaemia)

B. Risk approach
The shaded area indicates those whose performance (measured here as oxygen intake or "aerobic power") is below their potential

C. Benefit approach
The shaded area indicates those who could benefit from an intervention. The proportion of the total population represented by this group may be different from that in A or B

maternal physical activity. It is important to note that indicators of response need not be the same as indicators of risk or predictors of benefit; indeed, some indicators are intrinsically more responsive to interventions in ways that do not necessarily conform to *a priori* expectations. Beaton & Ghassemi (*34*) suggested that physical activity might be a more appropriate indicator of response to supplementary feeding in children than anthropometric indicators, even though the latter may be useful in predicting who will benefit and are also good indicators of risk of adverse outcomes such as mortality. Similarly, Wolgemuth et al. (*52*) noted that dietary supplementation of road workers in Kenya did not result in greater work productivity, but anecdotal evidence suggested that workers were more active in the domestic sphere. It has also been noted that height of infants or young children is more responsive to supplementary feeding than is arm circumference or skinfold thickness (*53*). As illustrated by these examples, the responsiveness of indicators is a particularly important attribute for evaluation of programme impact.

In contrast to indicators of risk and benefit, there is no particular need for reference data for indicators of response. Instead, it has been suggested that responsiveness should be viewed as a continuous variable, such that different indicators may be characterized as being more or less responsive than others (*53*). The proposed formula for responsiveness is $0.5 \, (\text{response/SD})^2$, where response is the difference between the mean value of the indicator in treated and control groups and SD is the pooled standard deviation of the two groups before treatment. As more is learned about the responsiveness of various indicators to different interventions, it will be possible to select more carefully those that are appropriate in a given situation.

It should be stressed that empirical evidence is not currently sufficient for constructing reference data based on risk or benefit, nor is it adequate for guiding the selection of the most efficient indicators of response. These are priority areas for future research, especially as regards the development of predictors of benefit. This can be addressed through careful design of evaluation components in small- or large-scale intervention programmes and appropriate analysis of data. In time, such research would improve the targeting, screening, and evaluation of those same programmes and would assist in similar activities in programmes implemented elsewhere. Thus, it is suggested that these gaps in knowledge be addressed in the context of action programmes rather than separate research projects. Although this will require some increased investment in evaluation and analysis, the cost-effectiveness of such an approach is likely to be far greater than that of separate research.

3.8 Populations for which compiled reference data are not pertinent

Since the only compiled reference data currently in use are from developed countries, there is some question of their usefulness in less developed areas. Total gestational weight gains are generally 4–5 kg greater in advantaged than in disadvantaged or undernourished populations. Moreover, when the two types of population are compared on the basis of similar birth weights and gestational ages, women from developed countries apparently gain about 3–4 kg more than those in less developed areas who produce infants of the same size (Fig. 14), suggesting that reference data for weight gain (either total or incremental) derived from developed countries may be excessive. This requires further investigation in relation to other pregnancy outcomes, including maternal body stores necessary to support lactation and prevent postpartum nutritional depletion and its sequelae.

The WHO Collaborative Study (23) provided reasonable evidence to suggest that, for pregnancy risk, there are different absolute cut-off values of maternal height for different populations. This should be investigated more thoroughly, using the WHO collaborative data with different cut-off values for each population represented in the data set.

For other measures, such as arm and calf circumference, there is insufficient evidence in the literature to allow different reference data to be recommended for different populations. Only after better information is available on the relationship of these indicators to specific outcomes can the question of reference data be considered.

Current reference data do not take into consideration potential modifying factors that may influence the interpretation of risk in relation to cut-offs. These factors include extremes in maternal age and parity, and pre-existing or current diseases such as diabetes, malaria, and anaemia.

3.9 The use and interpretation of anthropometry in lactating women

3.9.1 Biological significance of anthropometry during lactation

Changes in weight and body composition that occur during lactation underlie the biological basis for anthropometric assessment of lactating women, and the same rationale that governs the use of anthropometric measurements as indicators of nutritional risk or predictors of benefit from intervention applies to lactating women. A lack of reference data, however, limits the application of anthropometry to lactating women.

Lactation is the most energetically demanding phase of the human reproductive cycle. The total energy cost of producing milk is estimated to be 2930 kJ/day during the first 6 months of lactation and 2090 kJ/day during the next 18 months (54). Normally, fat deposited during pregnancy (about 4 kg, but this is highly variable) is mobilized postpartum to meet the energy costs of lactation (55).

Fat seems to be deposited preferentially in pregnancy, notably in the back and upper thighs, but not over the arms. This same pattern has been observed in different populations (6, 56). However, the increase of skinfold thicknesses cannot be attributed solely to deposition of fat, since, in most body sites, it is followed by a decrease at the time of parturition (6). During lactation lipolysis is higher in the femoral than in the abdominal region.

Thereafter, weight loss is slow and stabilizes at about 4-6 months. This is variable, however, and depends on socioeconomic status, weight gained during pregnancy, energy intake, and pattern of breast-feeding. It is useful to summarize the weight changes that occur at two levels of nutritional status. In well nourished lactating women, changes are generally minor and gradual. Weight losses are highest in the first 3 months of lactation (57-61) and are generally reported to be greater in women who breast-feed exclusively (58-60, 62). Skinfold thickness also tends to reflect weight changes, with most measurement sites showing decreased thickness as lactation progresses (56-59, 63, 64). An exception is the apparent gain in triceps skinfold thickness reported by several authors (56, 58, 59, 63-65). Among undernourished women, gestational weight gain and postpartum weight loss are lower than in well nourished women (6, 66-75). Although published values for milk composition of women from developing countries differ substantially, lower nutrient levels have usually been found in undernourished women (57, 62, 68, 76).

3.9.2 *Selection of individuals*

At present, anthropometric measurements cannot be used effectively to assess the nutritional status of individual lactating women. Moreover, no anthropometric indicators of risk for undesirable outcomes or of benefit from medical or nutritional interventions have been developed specifically for lactating women (77).

Nutritional status of the mother during lactation depends on many factors such as past nutritional status, weight gain in pregnancy, immediate postpartum weight loss, duration and intensity of lactation, dietary intake, and physical activity. Studies conducted worldwide have consistently noted that weight loss during lactation is much greater in the first month because of the shedding of extra water, tissue, and, to some extent, fat accrued during pregnancy.

While the limited literature reviewed here on changes in maternal weight is useful for establishing a basis for anthropometric assessment of nutritional status during lactation, it is only a first step towards developing anthropometric indicators. The purpose for which these indicators will be used must be considered. If it is for screening women at risk of poor postpartum outcomes, more extensive information on the nature of these outcomes and how they are affected by maternal nutrition will be required. Knowledge in this area is very limited at present and the research conducted thus far has not reported results in a manner that is easily interpreted for evaluation of indicators of risk. Even the definition of desirable outcomes presents problems. Lactation performance is certainly one area for investigation; however, the difficulties associated with evaluating the quantity and quality of breast milk as well as the definition of optimal growth in breast-fed infants (see section 5) suggest that more research is needed before progress can be made with identification and validation of indicators of risk for lactating women. Analysis of outcomes should also consider mothers' health and well-being during and after lactation. These considerations include resumption of menstruation, depletion and repletion of nutritional stores, and development of a risk profile for various chronic diseases.

3.9.3 *Characteristics for the development of normative reference data*

Normative reference data are not available to identify nutritionally "at risk" groups of lactating women (76). In populations in which anthropometric indices reflect food availability, nutritional vulnerability should be indicated by body weight, skinfold thicknesses, and arm and calf circumferences. Poor gestational weight gain may predict poor lactation performance, because fat stores may be inadequate to subsidize the energy costs of lactation. Although extensive data are available on the milk production of women of varying nutritional status, they have not been used to develop indicators of lactation performance.

Since no reference data exist for assessing nutritional status during lactation and very little research has been conducted in this area, only provisional criteria can be recommended for lactating women. There is evidence that poor maternal postpartum status, reflected in low BMI, is associated with poor lactation performance and poor infant growth, which suggests that BMI may be a useful indicator of postpartum nutritional status. However, the level of BMI below which there is a risk of poor lactation or infant growth has not been reported. It is possible to estimate a level based on the lower limit of BMI (<18.5) suggested for thin adults in section 8, adjusted for the average weight (4 kg) retained by mothers following an acceptable pregnancy weight gain (10.5–12.0 kg) and enough time for postpartum hydration to have equilibrated (2–4 weeks). This results in an estimated cut-off for BMI of 20.3 at 1 month postpartum for women 150 cm tall. BMI may be expected to decline steadily throughout the first 6 months of lactation, at which point the non-pregnant non-lactating value of 18.5 can be used as a cut-off for identifying women at risk.

Only a limited number of studies have attempted to assess upper levels of BMI during lactation. However, in the light of the recommendations for modest gestational weight gain by overweight and obese women (9), it is likely that the upper limits of BMI recommended for non-pregnant, non-lactating women (see section 7) would apply to lactating women as well.

To develop normative reference data for individuals, anthropometric measurements would have to be recorded longitudinally in a population of well nourished, healthy, lactating women and related to their lactation performance. Anthropometric changes in lactating women have been documented in a number of studies, but few of these have assessed lactation performance. Acceptable limits of postpartum weight and body compositional changes would be defined on the basis of lactation performance. In prolonged lactation, success would be at the expense of maternal stores. Development of anthropometric reference data for lactating women would require ancillary data on age, parity, prepregnant weight, gestational weight gain, and the intensity (exclusive or partial) and duration of breast-feeding. An evaluation of lactation performance would require data on milk volume, milk composition, and growth in infant weight and length.

Evidence to date does not suggest an association between maternal anthropometric indices and early lactation performance in well nourished populations. In prolonged lactation, maternal adipose stores may limit lactation performance if dietary intake is restricted.

Normative reference data based on anthropometric changes in well nourished populations are unlikely to be applicable to lactating women in undernourished populations because of significant differences in height, weight, and gestational weight gain between the populations. Moreover, sensitive indicators may be population-specific; for example, the triceps skinfold thickness is indicative of milk fat concentration in Bangladeshi and Gambian women, but not in American women (*67, 68*).

Evidence of an association between poor nutritional status and compromised lactation performance supports the development of anthropometric indicators within populations of nutritionally vulnerable lactating women. In undernourished populations, anthropometry will reflect both past and present food availability. Critical anthropometric thresholds should be definable, below which restricted maternal diet and limited tissue reserves are inadequate to meet the energy demands of lactation.

3.9.4 *Research needs for lactating women*

Reference data are needed for estimation of the prevalence of under-nutrition among lactating women in the population, and can be developed on the basis of available data from well nourished women. This should take account of different patterns of weight gain during pregnancy and different breast-feeding patterns. The same reference data would be used to screen individual lactating women for interventions.

To predict risk of maternal malnutrition or of individual women producing insufficient milk to maintain normal infant growth, there is a need for risk indicators. No indicators of risk of adverse maternal or infant outcomes are available at present, and research on their development is essential. Candidate indicators include maternal body weight or its change over a short period of time, maternal calf circumference, change in maternal skinfold thickness over a short period of time, and poor infant growth during exclusive breast-feeding.

Indicators are also needed that will predict benefits to the individual lactating woman or her breast-feeding infant of an appropriate intervention. Candidate indicators include maternal body weight or change in weight over a short period, maternal skinfold thicknesses or change in thicknesses over a short period of time, infant milk intake, and the ability to maintain exclusive breast-feeding of infants up to 6 months of age.

Candidate indicators for evaluating the response of individual lactating women to an appropriate intervention include changes in maternal body weight and skinfold thicknesses, change in infant milk intake, and the proportion of women who are able to breast-feed exclusively. Most of these indicators have been used in a recent randomized study of nutritional intervention in Guatemala (78).

3.10 Conclusions and recommendations

3.10.1 For practical implementation

Conclusions

Anthropometry in some form will continue to be a routine part of prenatal examinations throughout the world. This report has identified several applications of anthropometry that are useful in specific circumstances, depending on the availability of resources and the potential for intervention to achieve favourable pregnancy outcomes. The criterion of utility for most anthropometry examined in the report is a degree of association between the anthropometric indicator and the risk of a specific undesirable outcome such as SGA, preterm delivery, delivery complications, and, to a lesser degree, postpartum maternal depletion. In very few instances have the sensitivity, specificity, and positive predictive value of these relationships been examined to test for misclassification of individuals for risk of poor outcome or response to interventions. Any recommendations for the use of specific anthropometry summarized in Tables 9 and 10 are therefore provisional. The analysis of misclassification undertaken by WHO (23) is, conceptually, an appropriate next step in the evaluation of indicators that show significant association with pregnancy outcomes. However, there is a need for further analysis of sensitivity, specificity, and positive predictive value at different cut-offs for the various indicators. Within these limitations, it is possible to rank the various indicators, as applied to individuals in clinical settings, according to their ORs (Table 3), sensitivities, and specificities (Table 4) for different outcomes and with different levels of logistic support.

When resources are limited (i.e. no scales are available), short height may be useful as a screening instrument owing to modest ORs (1.2 to 1.9) for several outcomes. However, it is likely that the use of height will result in considerable misclassification. The appropriate height cut-off for screening will depend on local conditions, such as resources for intervention. Calf circumference is a more promising indicator but must be investigated in several different settings. Thus far, only maternal height seems to be a reliable predictor of the need for assisted delivery; research on its relationship to maternal mortality is needed, especially among disadvantaged populations.

When scales are available and properly used, attained body weight at any time during pregnancy appears to be the most useful screening indicator for SGA. However, further testing of the potential for misclassification is needed and, if the results are sufficiently promising, proper reference data must be developed. Weight measurements should be taken early enough in pregnancy to allow appropriate intervention. Attained weight at 20 weeks of gestation is useful for screening for dietary supplementation, although earlier assessment is preferred. Later assessment can be useful for referring mothers for delivery to a health facility where SGA and preterm infants can receive special care. The utility of weight measured during pregnancy is improved if short height is used as a first level of screening; body mass index alone is less useful than this two-stage screening approach, and further analysis of misclassification in two-stage screening is needed. Calf circumference may also prove more useful than some of the more "sophisticated" indicators. Weight gained between two examinations is less useful than a single measurement of weight as a predictor of poor pregnancy outcome. Change in thigh skinfold thickness appears to have greater potential as a specific indicator of maternal body composition change, and is related to fetal growth and postpartum maternal body stores.

Recommendations to countries
1. To screen women for risk of delivering SGA babies when scales are unavailable, height should be measured at any stage of pregnancy and deviations from local norms should be interpreted with regard to resources available for supporting interventions.

2. When scales are available, women should be weighed as early in pregnancy as possible to screen for risk of SGA babies. Maternal weight for gestational age should be compared with a reference similar to that shown in Fig. 15 for advantaged populations. Until more appropriate references are available, the same reference may be used for less well nourished populations, but cut-off levels for screening individuals should be set lower and should take account of local resource availability.

3. For monitoring the response of individuals in all populations to interventions during pregnancy, weight changes between successive examination should be determined during the final two trimesters and compared with existing cut-off guidelines set by the Institute of Medicine (9).

4. Since the application and interpretation of anthropometry during pregnancy are likely to differ from country to country, each country should develop its own cut-off values for each relevant indicator, using methodologies described in this report.

5. Countries should develop nutritional surveillance systems that cover the collection and analysis of data on national problems of pregnancy and lactation, and appropriate action.

3.10.2 *For future research and the collection of reference data*

1. Many of the practical recommendations in this report are based on the composite analysis of 25 studies reported by the WHO Collaborative Study (*23*). Further analysis of these data is required to establish the precise ORs for different anthropometry versus different pregnancy outcomes. Research of this type should also be undertaken using other data sets not included in the WHO study in order to broaden knowledge in this area; this should include analysis of sensitivity, specificity, and positive predictive value of various indicators and cut-off points for different pregnancy outcomes in relation to specific purposes and the resources available in different settings.

2. Most of the pregnancy outcomes used for the evaluation of maternal anthropometry in this report are commonly reported in the research literature, but other important outcomes in the areas of fetal, neonatal, and maternal morbidity and mortality, as well as fertility, should also be tested. More research is urgently needed on maternal postpartum consequences of anthropometric variation during pregnancy, especially in relation to lactation performance, resumption of ovarian function, and repletion (or further depletion) of maternal nutrient stores. Some of the common outcome measures should be refined. Classifications such as SGA, preterm and assisted delivery, and maternal morbidity are themselves subject to further subclassification, and the resulting subgroups are likely to be more homogeneous with regard to both causes and consequences; maternal anthropometry may be more effective as an indicator of risk for some of the more specific outcomes and unrelated to risk of others.

3. Studies of anthropometric risk factors for poor pregnancy outcomes will also benefit by expansion of the analysis to include both long-term outcomes (infant death, poor postnatal cognitive development) and important intermediate measures (SGA, risk of preterm delivery, breast milk quantity and quality). This would allow more precise causal pathways to be identified and the validity of using commonly measured intermediate variables as outcomes to be established. In general, research is needed to establish the biological bases of the anthropometric correlates of specific pregnancy outcomes. For example: What is short maternal stature actually measuring as it relates to increased risk of SGA? What proportion of maternal weight

gain is represented by maternal tissues that will support the pregnancy or later lactation?

4. Many of the newer applications of anthropometry have been validated in only a few isolated situations. Validation of calf circumference and thigh skinfold measurements should be extended to different populations and settings. The recommended weight gain chart of Rosso (*30*) should be tested for screening efficiency in populations where maternal malnutrition is prevalent, and the algorithm proposed by WHO to screen women for supplementation by using a single weight measurement from the second half of pregnancy should be evaluated. Systematic evaluation of multi-stage screening approaches that employ a cascade, or sequence, of measurements is also needed.

5. The comprehensive treatment of maternal anthropometry of under-nourished population groups should be extended to populations where excess energy balance is more common. It is also important to consider the effects of maternal obesity and high weight gain on such pregnancy outcomes as SGA, macrosomia, preterm delivery, complications of labour and delivery, postpartum maternal weight retention, and infant and maternal morbidity. Some research recommendations in this area were made by the Institute of Medicine report (*9*), which focused primarily on gestational weight gain of women from more developed countries, and more results are starting to appear in the literature (*79*). An extensive list of research recommendations for women from less developed countries has already been compiled by Krasovec & Anderson (*10*).

Completion of even part of this research agenda will help to establish criteria for reference data for assessing the nutritional status of women during pregnancy. Continued analysis of data sets from the WHO Collaborative Study (*23*) for misclassification relative to various pregnancy outcomes is particularly important. Choice of indicators and cut-off values requires an analysis of indicators relative to commonly defined outcomes across a variety of clinical and public health settings in several different population groups that reflect geographical, demographic, ethnic, and socioeconomic variation.

3.10.3 *For WHO*

1. WHO should facilitate research on anthropometry of women during the reproductive years, based especially on the data from the WHO Collaborative Study (*23*). Analysis of these data should be extended to include different population groups and various maternal and infant postpartum outcomes.

2. WHO should assist in the development of methods that will allow countries to establish locally relevant cut-off values for the anthropometric indicators recommended in this report. Data from the WHO Collaborative Study could serve as a useful resource in this effort.

4. WHO should facilitate the development of simple algorithms for the application and interpretation of anthropometry during pregnancy and lactation, and for integrating anthropometry into health care strategies.

5. WHO should assist countries in establishing surveillance systems to identify solutions to health and nutrition problems in women of reproductive age.

References

1. Villar J et al. Perinatal data reliability in a large teaching obstetric unit. *British journal of obstetrics and gynaecology*, 1988, **95**:841–848.

2. Dawes MG, Green J, Ashurst H. Routine weighing in pregnancy. *British medical journal*, 1992, **304**:487–489.

3. Merchant K, Martorell R. Frequent reproductive cycling: does it lead to nutritional depletion of mothers? *Progress in food and nutrition science*, 1988, **12**:339–369.

4. Kramer MS et al. Maternal nutrition and spontaneous preterm birth. *American journal of epidemiology*, 1992, **136**:574–583.

5. Villar J, Belizan JM. The evaluation of the methods used in the diagnosis of intrauterine growth retardation. *Obstetrical and gynecological surveys*, 1986, **41**:187–199.

6. Villar J et al. Effect of fat and fat-free mass deposition during pregnancy on birth weight. *American journal of obstetrics and gynecology*, 1992, **167**:1344–1352.

7. Savitz DA, Blackmore CA, Thorp JM. Epidemiologic characteristics of preterm delivery: etiologic heterogeneity. *American journal of obstetrics and gynecology*, 1991, **164**:467–471.

8. Kramer MS et al. The validity of gestational age estimation by menstrual dating in term, preterm, and postterm gestations. *Journal of the American Medical Association*, 1988, **260**:3306–3308.

9. Institute of Medicine. *Nutrition during pregnancy. Part 1: Weight gain*. Washington, DC, National Academy Press, 1980.

10. Krasovec K, Anderson MA, eds. *Maternal nutrition and pregnancy outcomes: anthropometric assessment*. Washington, DC, Pan American Health Organization, 1991 (Scientific Publication, No. 529).

11. Stevens-Simon C, McAnarney ER, Coulter MP. How accurately do adolescents estimate their weight prior to pregnancy? *Journal of adolescent health care*, 1986, **7**:250–254.

12. Wilcox AJ, Horney LE. Accuracy of spontaneous abortion recall. *American journal of epidemiology*, 1984, **120**:727–733.

13. Launer L, Villar J, Kestler E. Epidemiological differences among birthweight and gestational age subgroups of newborns. *American journal of human biology*, 1991, **3**:425–433.

14. Hytten FE. Weight gain in pregnancy. In: Hytten FE, Chamberlain G, eds. *Clinical physiology in obstetrics*. Oxford, Blackwell, 1980:193–233.

15. **Lawrence M, McKillop FM, Durnin JVG.** Women who gain more fat during pregnancy may not have bigger babies: implications for recommended weight gain during pregnancy. *British journal of obstetrics and gynaecology*, 1991, **98**:254–259.

16. **Martorell R, Habicht J-P.** Growth in early childhood in developing countries. In: Falkner F, Tanner JM, eds. *Human growth: a comprehensive treatise*, 2nd ed., Vol. 3. New York, Plenum Press, 1986:241–262.

17. **Scholl TO, Hediger ML, Ances IG.** Maternal growth during pregnancy and decreased infant birth weight. *American journal of clinical nutrition*, 1990, **51**:790–793.

18. **González-Cossío T, Flores F, ARCIU Group.** Validity of maternal calf circumference to identify risk of intrauterine growth retardation (IUGR). *The FASEB journal*, 1992, **6**(5):A1683.

19. **McDonald E.** Mensuration of the child in the uterus with new methods. *Journal of the American Medical Association*, 1906, **47**:1979–1983.

20. **Jacobsen G.** Prediction of fetal growth deviations by use of symphysis–fundus height measurements. *International journal of technology assessment in health care*, 1992, **8**(Suppl. 1):152–159.

21. **Hughes AB et al.** Symphysis–fundus height, maternal height, labor pattern, and mode of delivery. *American journal of obstetrics and gynecology,* 1987, **156**: 644–648.

22. **Beaton GH et al.** *Appropriate uses of anthropometric indices in children : a report based on an ACC/SCN workshop.* New York, United Nations Administrative Committee on Coordination/Subcommittee on Nutrition, 1990 (ACC/SCN State-of-the-Art Series, Nutrition Policy Discussion Paper No. 7).

23. Maternal anthropometry and pregnancy outcomes: a WHO collaborative project. *Bulletin of the World Health Organization*, 1995, **73** (Suppl.).

24. **Kramer MS.** Determinants of low birth weight: methodological assessment and meta-analysis. *Bulletin of the World Health Organization*, 1987, **65**:663–737.

25. **Habicht J-P.** Some characteristics of indicators of nutritional status for use in screening and surveillance. *American journal of clinical nutrition*, 1980, **33**: 531–535.

26. **Galen RS, Gambino SR.** *Beyond normality: the predictive value and efficacy of medical diagnoses.* New York, Wiley, 1975.

27. **Kalkwarf HJ.** *Maternal weight gain during pregnancy and risk of preterm delivery: effects on neonatal mortality and public health impact* (Dissertation). Ithaca, NY, Cornell University, 1991.

28. **Lechtig A.** Predicting risk of delivering low birth weight babies: which indicator is better? *Journal of tropical pediatrics*, 1988, **34**:34–41.

29. **Merchant KM, Villar J.** Effect of maternal supplementation on risk of perinatal distress and intrapartum cesarean delivery. *The FASEB journal*, 1993, **7**:A282.

30. **Rosso P.** A new chart to monitor weight during pregnancy. *American journal of clinical nutrition*, 1985, **41**:644–652.

31. **Haas JD.** Weight gain in pregnancy. In: Krasovec K, Anderson MA, eds. *Maternal nutrition and pregnancy outcomes: anthropometric assessment.* Washington, DC, Pan American Health Organization, 1991 (Scientific Publication, No. 529): 29-51.

32. **Belizan JM et al.** Diagnosis of intrauterine growth retardation by a simple clinical method: measurement of uterine height. *American journal of obstetrics and gynecology*, 1978, **131**:643-646.

33. **Susser M.** Maternal weight gain, infant birth weight, and diet: causal sequences. *American journal of clinical nutrition*, 1991, **53**:1384-1396.

34. **Beaton GH, Ghassemi H.** Supplementary feeding programs for young children in developing countries. *American journal of clinical nutrition*, 1982, **35**(4, suppl.): 863-916.

35. **Habicht J-P, Butz WP.** Measurements of health and nutrition effects of large-scale nutrition intervention projects. In: Klein RE et al., eds. *Evaluating the impact of nutrition and health programs*. New York, Plenum Press, 1979:133-182.

36. **Valverde V et al.** Uses and constraints of school children's height data for planning purposes: national experiences in Central America. *Food and nutrition bulletin*, 1986, **8**(3):42-48.

37. **Lubchenco LO, Searls DT, Brazie JV.** Neonatal mortality rate: relationship to birth weight and gestational age. *Journal of pediatrics*, 1972, **81**:814-822.

38. **Haas JD, Balcazar H, Caulfield I.** Variation in early neonatal mortality for different types of fetal growth retardation. *American journal of physical anthropology*, 1987, **73**:467-473.

39. **Garner P, Kramer MS, Chalmers I.** Might efforts to increase birthweight in undernourished women do more harm than good? *Lancet*, 1992, **340**:1021-1023.

40. **Mason JP et al.** *Nutritional surveillance*. Geneva, World Health Organization, 1984.

41. **Abraham S, Johnson CL, Najjar MF.** *Weight by height and age for adults 18-74 years*. Hyattsville, MD, US Department of Health, Education, and Welfare, 1979 (Vital and Health Statistics: Data from the National Health Survey, Series 11, No. 208).

42. **Eveleth PB, Tanner JM.** *Worldwide variation in human growth*. Cambridge, Cambridge University Press, 1990.

43. **Metropolitan Life Insurance Company.** New weight standards for men and women. *Statistics bulletin*, 1959, **40**:1-4.

44. **Tompkins WT, Wiehl DG.** Nutritional deficiencies as a causal factor in toxemia and premature labor. *American journal of obstetrics and gynecology*, 1951, **62**:898-919.

45. **Thomson AM, Billewicz WZ.** Clinical significance of weight trends during pregnancy. *British medical journal*, 1957, **1**:243-247.

46. **Tanner JM.** *Growth at adolescence; with a general consideration of the effects of hereditary and environmental factors upon growth and maturation from birth to maturity*, 2nd ed. Oxford, Blackwell, 1962.

47. **Hediger ML et al.** Patterns of weight gain in adolescent pregnancy: effects on birth weight and preterm delivery. *Obstetrics and gynecology*, 1989, **74**:6-12.

48. Cameron N. Conditional standards for growth in height of British children from 5.0 to 15.99 years of age. *Annals of human biology*, 1980, **7**:331-337.

49. Naeye RL. Weight gain and the outcome of pregnancy. *American journal of obstetrics and gynecology*, 1979, **135**:3-9.

50. Habicht J-P, Meyers LD, Brownie C. Indicators for identifying and counting the improperly nourished. *American journal of clinical nutrition*, 1982, **35**(5, suppl.): 1241-1254.

51. Rasmussen K, Habicht J-P. Malnutrition among women: indicators to estimate prevalence. *Food and nutrition bulletin*, 1989, **11**:29-37.

52. Wolgemuth JC et al. Worker productivity and the nutritional status of Kenyan road construction laborers. *American journal of clinical nutrition*, 1982, **36**:68-78.

53. Habicht J-P, Mason J, Tabatabi H. Basic concepts for the design of evaluation during programme implementation. In: Sahn DE, Lockwood R, Scrimshaw NS, eds. *Methods for the evaluation of the impact of food and nutrition programs*. Tokyo, United Nations University, 1984 (UNU Food and Nutrition Bulletin, Supplement No. 8).

54. *Energy and protein requirements. Report of a Joint FAO/WHO/UNU Expert Consultation*. Geneva, World Health Organization, 1985 (WHO Technical Report Series, No. 724).

55. Hytten FE. Nutrition. In: Hytten FE, Chamberlain G, eds. *Clinical physiology in obstetrics*. Oxford, Blackwell, 1980.

56. Taggart NR et al. Changes in skinfolds during pregnancy. *British journal of nutrition*, 1967, **21**:439-451.

57. Butte NF et al. Effect of maternal diet and body composition on lactational performance. *American journal of clinical nutrition*, 1984, **39**:296-306.

58. Manning-Dalton C, Allen LH. The effects of lactation on energy and protein consumption, postpartum weight change and body composition of well-nourished North American women. *Nutrition research*, 1983, **3**:293-308.

59. Brewer MM, Bates MR, Vannoy LP. Postpartum changes in maternal weight and body fat deposits in lactating vs nonlactating women. *American journal of clinical nutrition*, 1989, **49**:259-265.

60. Ohlin A, Rossner S. Maternal body weight development after pregnancy. *International journal of obesity*, 1990, **14**:159-173.

61. Morse EH et al. Comparison of the nutritional status of pregnant adolescents with adult pregnant women. II. Anthropometric and dietary findings. *American journal of clinical nutrition*, 1975, **28**:1422-1428.

62. Paul AA, Müller EM, Whitehead RG. Seasonal variations in energy intake, body-weight and skinfold thickness in pregnant and lactating women in rural Gambia. *Proceedings of the Nutrition Society*, 1979, **38**:28A.

63. Forsum E, Sadurskis A, Wager J. Estimation of body fat in healthy Swedish women during pregnancy and lactation. *American journal of clinical nutrition*, 1989, **50**:465-473.

64. Forsum E, Sadurskis A, Wager J. Resting metabolic rate and body composition of healthy Swedish women during pregnancy. *American journal of clinical nutrition*, 1988, **47**:942-947.

65. **Dugdale AE, Eaton-Evans J.** The effect of lactation and other factors on post-partum changes in body-weight and triceps skinfold thickness. *British journal of nutrition*, 1989, **61**:149–153.

66. **Kramer FM et al.** Breastfeeding reduces maternal lower body fat. *Journal of the American Dietetic Association*, 1993, **93**:429–443.

67. **Prentice A, Prentice AM, Whitehead RG.** Breast-milk fat concentrations of rural African women. 2. Long-term variations within a community. *British journal of nutrition*, 1981, **45**:495–503.

68. **Brown KH et al.** Lactational capacity of marginally nourished mothers: relationships between maternal nutritional status and quantity and proximate composition of milk. *Pediatrics*, 1986, **78**:909–919.

69. **Schutz Y, Lechtig A, Bradfield RB.** Energy expenditures and food intakes of lactating women in Guatemala. *American journal of clinical nutrition*, 1980, **33**:892–902.

70. **Ebrahim GJ.** *Cross-cultural aspects of breast-feeding. Breast-feeding and the mother*. Amsterdam, Elsevier, 1976 (Ciba Foundation Symposium, No. 45): 195–204.

71. **Adair LS, Pollitt E.** Seasonal variation in pre- and postpartum maternal body measurements and infant birth weights. *American journal of physical anthropology*, 1983, **62**:325–331.

72. **Adair LS, Pollitt E.** Outcome of maternal nutritional supplementation: a comprehensive review of the Bacon Chow study. *American journal of clinical nutrition*, 1985, **41**:948–978.

73. **Adair LS, Pollitt E, Mueller WH.** Maternal anthropometric changes during pregnancy and lactation in a rural Taiwanese population. *Human biology*, 1983, **55**:771–787.

74. **Adair LS, Pollitt E, Mueller WH,** The Bacon Chow study: effect of nutritional supplementation on maternal weight and skinfold thickness during pregnancy and lactation. *British journal of nutrition*, 1984, **51**:357–369.

75. **Calloway DH, Murphy SP, Beaton GH.** *Food intake and human function: a cross-project perspective*. Berkeley, CA, University of California, 1988.

76. **Rasmussen KM.** Maternal nutritional status and lactational performance. *Clinical nutrition*, 1988, **7**:147–155.

77. **Institute of Medicine (U.S.) Subcommittee on Nutrition during Lactation.** *Nutrition during lactation*. Washington, DC, National Academy Press, 1991.

78. **González-Cossío T et al.** Food supplementation during lactation increases infant milk intake and proportion of exclusive breastfeeding. *The FASEB journal*, 1991, **5**:A917.

79. **Johnson JWC, Longmate JA, Frentzen B.** Excessive maternal weight and pregnancy outcome. *American journal of obstetrics and gynecology*, 1992, **167**:353–372.

4. The newborn infant

4.1 Introduction

It is universally acknowledged that size at birth is an important indicator of fetal and neonatal health in the context of both individuals and populations. Birth weight in particular is strongly associated with fetal, neonatal, and postneonatal mortality, and with infant and child morbidity (*1, 2*).

Size at birth reflects two factors: duration of gestation and rate of fetal growth. It must therefore be considered with respect to gestational age, otherwise the increase in size that occurs with age will lead to severe confounding of growth and maturity. In general, bigger babies are more mature babies and – since it is well known that immature infants (particularly extremely preterm infants, i.e. those born at < 32 weeks) are at much higher risk for mortality, morbidity, and impaired development – failure to consider gestational age leads to major problems in interpretation that can hinder decision-making at both clinical and public health levels (*3*).

Growth is defined as an increase in size over time, and documentation of increasing size thus requires two or more serial measurements. During fetal life, however, serial measurements are feasible only with ultrasound and have not proved to be sufficiently valid or precise (ultrasound estimation of fetal weight has a high coefficient of variation) to serve as a standard for assessing fetal growth (*4*). Moreover, ultrasound measurements are not truly anthropometric and are thus beyond the scope of this report.

Body size is obviously proportional to age, not only in the fetus but throughout childhood until the time of skeletal fusion. Thus an infant's size at birth reflects the *average* growth rate for that infant from conception to birth, although not necessarily a steady rate, since there may have been periods of rapid and slow growth. Problems will arise, however, if the distribution of size at birth of different infants born at different gestational ages is used to make inferences about "normal" fetal growth. It is important to stress the limitations of a cross-sectional approach based on different infants, and to question how well any chart derived in this way reflects the longitudinal growth of fetuses of the same gestational age (*5*). There is some evidence that preterm infants are somewhat smaller than fetuses of the same gestational age who remain *in utero* (*6-8*). This may partly reflect the fact that some of the determinants of fetal growth and length of gestation overlap: pre-eclampsia, for example, and other hypertensive disorders that impair fetal growth also increase the risk of preterm delivery (*9, 10*). Although this overlap may reflect shared underlying biological mechanisms, it is common practice in modern obstetrics for labour to be induced in mothers in whom poor fetal growth has been diagnosed. Thus if infants whose delivery is induced because of retarded growth are not excluded from the data, their smaller size for gestational age will reduce the average size of all infants born at that age (*11*).

At the other end of the gestational age spectrum, there is also some (albeit more indirect) evidence that fetuses who remain unborn post-term may not have grown at the same rate as those born earlier. Fetal size is considered to be one of the determinants of the onset of labour, and the flattening (or even negative slope) of some fetal growth curves after 40 or 41 weeks of gestation may reflect both the slowing of growth due to placental insufficiency (as demonstrated by the presence of oligo-hydramnios, placental grade III, meconial amniotic fluid, or abnormal Doppler indices), and the earlier birth of faster-growing fetuses.

This inherent problem of deriving fetal growth standards from anthropometric measurements of newborn infants may have less relevance to the first 20-24 weeks of gestation, when elective, induced abortions are performed for indications unrelated to fetal growth (i.e. for reasons other than chromosomal or other genetic abnormalities of the fetus). This should not affect measurements of fetal weight or other body dimensions provided that abortion is induced by means of prostaglandin or hysterotomy rather than saline (which dehydrates the fetus). The situation changes, however, when *all* fetuses are included, since a large number of births during weeks 20 to 24 are spontaneous and probably related to factors that *do* affect fetal growth. From week 24 onwards, however, it should be kept in mind that fetal growth curves based on anthropometric measurements of different infants born at different gestational ages may not be valid, particularly pre- and post-term.

The determinants of fetal growth have been the subject of considerable research (*2, 9, 12-17*), and it is now clear that, despite some of the areas of overlap alluded to above, these differ considerably from the etiological determinants of gestational duration (*10, 12, 15-19*). In particular, maternal stature, prepregnancy weight, and energy intake during gestation all have important influences on the rate of fetal growth (*9, 12-17*), but much less, if any, effect on the duration of gestation (*10, 12, 15-19*). Genetic (including racial) and inter-generational effects also bear primarily on fetal growth (*12, 20-24*); cigarette smoking affects both fetal growth and gestational duration, but the effect is considerably greater on the former (*9, 10, 12, 19*). Only a few other determinants, such as infections (*25, 26*), maternal cocaine use (*27, 28*), and prepregnancy and gestational hypertension (particularly severe pre-eclampsia) (*9, 10*) also affect both outcomes.

Impairments in fetal growth can have adverse consequences in infancy and childhood in terms of mortality, morbidity, growth, and performance (*1, 2, 29*). It has even been suggested that restriction of fetal growth may increase the risk of ischaemic heart disease, hypertension, obstructive lung disease, and diabetes in adulthood (*30, 31*). This is an important area for future follow-up studies of growth-retarded infants or, where reasonable perinatal information is available, for retrospective cohort studies.

Using anthropometry in individual newborn infants

Weight-for-gestational-age at birth is often used to categorize an individual infant as having experienced normal, subnormal (small-for-gestational age or intrauterine growth retardation), or supranormal growth *in utero*. The classification most frequently used is: small-for-gestational-age (SGA or IUGR), appropriate-for-gestational-age (AGA), and large-for-gestational-age (LGA), although, strictly speaking, SGA and IUGR are not synonymous (*33*). Some SGA infants (e.g. those born to short mothers) may merely represent the lower tail of the "normal" fetal growth distribution, while other infants who have been exposed to one or more growth-inhibiting factors may actually meet the criteria for AGA (e.g. those born to tall, well nourished cigarette-smokers). In individual cases, however, it is usually very difficult to determine whether or not the observed birth weight is the result of true *in utero* growth restriction, and classification of an infant as IUGR is therefore based on the established cut-off for SGA. In fact, the higher the SGA rate, the greater the likelihood that SGA is a result of IUGR.

Various criteria (i.e. cut-off points) have been used as the dividing lines between these three categories. Those most commonly used are based on percentiles of a distribution of birth-weight-for-gestational-age derived from an accepted reference population; the 10th percentile is used most frequently as the cut-off between SGA and AGA, and the 90th percentile between AGA and LGA. Other definitions, such as < -2 or $> +2$ standard deviations (Z-scores) from the reference mean, have also been applied. One recent approach has based the classification on relative weight (the so-called fetal growth ratio or, more correctly, "relative birth weight ratio"), in which the birth weight of an infant is expressed as a fraction or percentage of the mean birth weight (again derived from some reference population) for that infant's gestational age (*32*). Thus, infants who weigh $< 85\%$ of the mean can be classified as SGA, and those weighing $>115\%$ of the mean as LGA. These latter definitions are analogous to those used to classify under- and overnourished populations of older children and adults. However, although 85% of the mean birth weight at term is very similar to the 10th percentile, for preterm infants this cut-off could represent a much higher percentile. If this principle is applied across a range of gestational ages, the prevalence of SGA and LGA will vary with maturity. The use of 85% of the mean as a cut-off point therefore cannot be recommended for use without evidence that the coefficient of variation for birth weight remains fairly constant at different gestational ages.

Regardless of which definition is used, the classification of a newborn as either SGA or LGA has implications for diagnosis, prognosis, surveillance, and treatment. SGA infants are more likely to have congenital anomalies (*34*), and the observation that an infant is growth-retarded often prompts a more careful physical examination or even laboratory tests such as karyotype determination to ascertain whether such an anomaly is present. Laboratory cultures of biological samples and serological tests of the mother and infant may occasionally reveal a previously unsuspected intrauterine infection. The diagnosis of SGA may also prompt closer examination of the placenta and reveal evidence of infarction, single umbilical artery, velamentous insertion of the cord, or previously unsuspected disease in the mother.

Regardless of the cause of the growth retardation, a severely growth-retarded fetus or infant is at markedly increased risk of death, hypogly-caemia, hypocalcaemia, polycythaemia, and neurocognitive complications of pre- and intrapartum hypoxia (i.e. *in utero* malnutrition is associated with *in utero* deprivation of oxygen) (*2, 35*). Close monitoring of blood glucose, calcium, haematocrit (erythrocyte volume fraction), and circulatory adequacy in the neonatal period will allow timely intervention and should reduce the risk of adverse secondary sequelae. Diagnosis of SGA should also prompt actions to support breast-feeding and – in affluent populations where weaning foods are hygienically safe – may indicate the need for instituting a high-energy diet to maximize the potential for catch-up growth in the first few postnatal months. Over the long term, growth-retarded infants may exhibit permanent mild deficits in growth and neurocognitive development (*2, 29*).

The diagnosis of LGA can also be important for the individual infant. Large infants are at increased risk of birth trauma (including clavicular fracture and brachial plexus injury), and of asphyxia secondary to obstructed labour. The most common concern is maternal diabetes, which may or may not have been diagnosed before or during pregnancy; here, too, monitoring (particularly for the development of hypoglycaemia) may be important to permit prompt institution of glucose therapy and thus prevent adverse sequelae.

Various proportionality indices have been used to relate different dimensions of fetal growth, particularly among growth-retarded infants. The most commonly used of these is Rohrer's ponderal index, which is defined as 100 times the birth weight (in grams) divided by the cube of birth length (cm^3). Infants with high ponderal indices are relatively heavy for length (or, equivalently, relatively short for weight); those with low ponderal indices are thin, with low weight-for-length. Although the ponderal index at birth is usually evaluated with reference to the gestational age of the SGA infant, it may be preferable to refer it to birth weight (*32*). Since body proportions change during the course of gestation, proportionality for size may provide a better index than proportionality for age for assessing how growth following the onset of some growth-inhibiting influence is distributed among different body compartments, compared with its distribution in infants who continue to grow normally.

Several publications have developed the concepts of proportionate (also called Type 1, symmetric, or "stunted") and disproportionate (Type 2, asymmetric, or "wasted") growth retardation (*36–38*), although the importance of the distinction is still under discussion. Body proportionality at birth may capture information about the timing of growth retardation as well as the nutritional status of the newborn. Much of the discussion about the effect of timing of onset of IUGR on body proportionality has been based on early data from Streeter (*39*) and more recent data from Gruenwald's report on body weight, length, and placental and organ weight (*40*), both of which are in agreement with the diagrammatic velocity curves published by Tanner (*41*). Recent evidence indicates that proportionality among IUGR infants is strongly confounded by the severity of the growth retardation or deficit in nutritional status (*32*) and that, given reliable estimates of gestational age, disproportionate IUGR infants tend to be more severely growth-retarded than their proportionate counterparts. Analysis of data thus requires that the severity of IUGR be controlled. For example, data from Canada demonstrate that, once severity has been accounted for, proportionality appears to be of little if any etiological (*9*) or prognostic (*35*) importance; in the latter study, however, an independent increased risk of stillbirth was associated with a high length-for-weight ratio (OR 1.24, 95% CI 1.03–1.48).

A recent small study that used three ultrasound measurements to monitor the fetal growth pattern of 71 SGA infants (most of them with adequate ponderal index), concluded that, given the birth weight and gestational age of the newborn, body proportionality (e.g. ponderal index) does not contribute further to the judgement of fetal growth rate (*42*). On the other hand, several large studies from different populations support the independent association between indicators of body proportionality at birth and a number of important neonatal or infant health outcomes. In the USA, Conlisk (*43*) studied the risk of neonatal mortality for proportionate and disproportionate infants using stratified analysis by 400-g groups and logistic regression analysis to control for birth weight. The results showed that both black and white disproportionate infants are at higher risk of mortality at lower birth weights than proportionate infants, but at lower risk at birth weights above 2400 g (black) and 2800 g (white). Interaction of birth weight and proportionate groups was significant for both blacks ($P=0.05$) and whites ($P=0.04$). The effect of birth weight on mortality was significantly greater for disproportionate than for proportionate infants at birth weights < 2200 g (black) and < 2600 g (white); risk was lower at higher birth weights.

In a cohort of 5539 term newborns studied in Argentina (*44*), an increased risk of postnatal morbidity was demonstrated in infants who were SGA and of low ponderal index (LPI) compared with the groups of normal birth weight and of SGA/adequate ponderal index (API), adjusted for sex, birth weight, gestational age, and hospital of birth. A study of 3450 term SGA infants in Guatemala (*45*) again demonstrated that, after adjusting by birth weight, the risk of neonatal morbidity was higher in the SGA/LPI than in the SGA/API group. In both developing and developed countries, SGA newborns estimated to have experienced slow head growth before the 26th week of gestation (as documented by serial ultrasound measurements) and those with API at birth (indicating proportionate retardation of growth in weight and length) have consistently demonstrated the lowest developmental performance during childhood (46-49).

Finally, Williams et al. (50) classified IUGR infants by their ponderal index at birth and followed them up at 7 and 18 years of age to study their blood pressure patterns. At age 7 years, sex- and weight-adjusted systolic and diastolic blood pressure were significantly higher in those who were classified IUGR/API. By age 18, the mean adjusted systolic blood pressure was 121.8 mmHg (16.2 kPa) in the IUGR/API group compared with 118.8 mmHg (15.8 kPa) in the IUGR/LPI group (P=0.13; n=29). No differences were observed in diastolic blood pressure.

Proportionality indices may well prove to be useful for predicting outcome in SGA babies, particularly where there is no reliable information on gestational age, but further research is clearly needed on this subject.

Where valid assessment of gestational age is unavailable (as in many settings in developing countries), size at birth, and particularly birth weight, can be used as the basis for decisions regarding surveillance and referral of small infants. Birth weight below 2500 g (LBW) is a reasonable cut-off for instituting surveillance and/or referral for the detection and treatment of early complications of preterm birth or IUGR. However, it should be noted that, because of "rounding", the prevalence of LBW will be underestimated. In settings with a very high prevalence of fetal growth retardation, a locally determined lower cut-off (e.g. <2250 g or <2000 g) may be preferable to avoid overwhelming the health care system with mildly growth-retarded infants who are at lower risk for serious adverse sequelae. Local cut-offs and the methodology for their selection have already been discussed in section 2.

Surveillance of LBW, preterm infants for complications should include monitoring of oxygenation and respiratory status (including the signs and symptoms of respiratory distress syndrome and neonatal apnoea), indications of neonatal sepsis (e.g. apnoea, poor feeding, vomiting, jaundice), and neurological complications possibly caused by intra-ventricular haemorrhage (coma, seizures, apnoea, or focal neurological deficit). Where adequate surveillance and treatment are not possible locally, or the response to treatment is unsatisfactory, infants should be referred to an appropriate health care establishment. Surveillance and referral are even more important for very-low-birth-weight (VLBW) infants, i.e. those with birth weights below 1500 g, who are usually extremely preterm.

Table 11 summarizes the recommendations for the use of anthropometric measures in individual newborn infants.

Table 11

Summary of recommendations for screening individual newborn infants for interventions

1	2	3	4	5	6	7	8
Uses: what will be done for the individual?	For what purpose?	Target group and setting	What to measure and how often	Indices	Criteria for judgement (cut-offs)	Rationale for anthropometry	Other factors for interpretation
Determine how well the infant grew *in utero* and whether it is at risk for complications of IUGR or preterm birth. Monitor blood glucose, Ca, Hb; refer if necessary; prescribe high-energy diet; follow growth; or monitor oxygenation, respiratory status, and signs of sepsis; refer if necessary	Reduce morbidity/ mortality, optimize long-term growth and performance	All newborn infants Hospital, home, or other birth setting, as soon as possible after birth	Gestational age, sex, birth weight, length Single measurement	1. Birth weight and ponderal index for gestational age and sex 2. Birth weight	1. <10th, >90th percentile; Z-score <-2, >+2 2. <2500 g, <1500 g	Size for gestational age	Validity of gestational age; race; reliability of length measurements

4.3 Neonatal anthropometric assessment in populations

The prevalence of SGA (based on a common reference population) can be used to select populations that should be targeted for interventions. Fetal growth is clearly influenced by maternal size, health, and nutrition; data consistently show larger fetuses (particularly at term) in developed countries than in developing countries (9). When SGA rates are unavailable, the prevalence of LBW can be used as a proxy. Preterm birth rates also appear to be higher in developing countries (51, 52) and among poor populations in developed countries (2), although most of the difference in the incidence of LBW between developed and developing countries is due to a disproportionately high incidence of LBW/SGA (52). However, SGA prevalence is preferable both for targeting and for assessing response, because few interventions have been found to prevent preterm birth.

Recommended cut-off levels for triggering public health action have not been established, but it seems reasonable to target those populations with double the prevalence (i.e. >20% for SGA and >15% for LBW) found in developed countries. Population-wide interventions might include nutritional supplementation, antismoking campaigns, and malaria prophylaxis. Within a given population, response to intervention can be assessed by monitoring SGA rates (or VLBW and LBW if gestational age is not available) over time.

Targeting of interventions and assessing response can also be based on LBW and VLBW rates used not as proxies for SGA but as indicators of the need for health care facilities to treat the complications of SGA or preterm birth. LBW and VLBW rates in excess of 15% and 2%, respectively, suggest a population at high risk for fetal and infant mortality and morbidity, and for long-term adverse effects on childhood growth and performance. Trends in developed countries over the past 20 years show that, with no reduction in the prevalence of LBW and VLBW, fetal and infant mortality can be dramatically reduced by optimal care of such infants. Monitoring overall and birth-weight-specific fetal and infant mortality is therefore essential in assessing the response to interventions.

Anthropometric assessment of newborn infant populations is an important research tool for studying the determinants and consequences of impaired (or excessive) fetal growth. Although many of the determinants (maternal height, prepregnancy weight, gestational weight gain, smoking, etc.) and early consequences (stillbirth, birth asphyxia, neonatal hypoglycaemia and hypocalcaemia, etc.) probably retain their importance across different populations, their prevalence varies considerably and so, therefore, does their public health importance as reflected by the etiological fraction (population attributable risk). Moreover, specific local factors may play an important etiological role that would justify new epidemiological studies in settings where novel risk factors are suspected, such as maternal tobacco-chewing, exposure to indoor smoke, malaria or other tropical diseases, and HIV infection.

Similarly, although the immediate, life-threatening sequelae of severe IUGR are probably similar in all populations, the longer-term consequences for child growth, development, and performance may differ across populations because of interaction with adverse postnatal influences in disadvantaged populations, including socioeconomic and nutritional factors as well as the level of medical care available. Investigation of such environmental factors and of interventions that reduce adverse health sequelae should receive high priority in developing countries where the prevalence of SGA is high.

Anthropometric assessment of newborn infants can also be important in the context of nutritional surveillance. Periodic assessment of a population over time may reveal changes in the prevalence of SGA (or LBW as a proxy) that could signal the effects of famine, epidemic infectious disease, or other adverse environmental circumstances.

Table 12 summarizes the uses of anthropometric measurements for assessment in populations.

4.4 Selection of anthropometric indicators

4.4.1 *Gestational age*

Although the assessment of gestational age does not come under the heading of anthropometry, it is mentioned first because any size-for-age measurement requires a reasonably valid and precise measure of age. In most cases, particularly in developing countries, gestational age is assessed by calculating the number of completed weeks since the beginning of the last menstrual period (LMP). Because of potential difficulties with maternal recall and biological problems such as delayed ovulation, early non-menstrual bleeding wrongly interpreted as a period, and undetected miscarriages (i.e. without bleeding), gestational age calculated on this basis is often erroneous, particularly at the extremes of the gestational age distribution (i.e. preterm and post-term) (53).

Early (< 20 weeks) ultrasonic measurement of the biparietal diameter (and/or femoral length, crown–rump length, or abdominal circumference) could be considered the "gold standard" for assessment of gestational age (53-56). Unfortunately, rigorous evaluation of this "better" assessment in randomized controlled trials has failed to reveal any benefit to maternal and perinatal health (57-60), and it cannot be recommended for routine use in all pregnant women. Other methods, such as assessment of fundal height or quickening, are often used in clinical practice to confirm (or discredit) LMP-derived gestational age. Physical or neurological examination of the newborn infant has also been commonly employed in hospitals in both developed and developing countries, although this has been found to produce significant overestimates of gestational age for

Table 12
Summary of recommendations for uses of anthropometry in populations of newborn infants

1	2	3	4	5	6	7	8
Uses: what will be done for the population?	For what purpose?	Target group and setting	What to measure and how often	Indices	Criteria for judgement (cut-offs)	Rationale for anthropometry	Other factors for interpretation
Targeting of interventions							
Improve maternal nutrition, reduce maternal smoking, provide malaria prophylaxis: to improve fetal growth	Reduce morbidity/mortality, and optimize long-term growth and performance	Newborn infants in populations with high prevalence of SGA (or LBW)	Gestational age, sex, birth weight, chest circumference	1. Birth weight for gestational age and sex	1. >20% below 10th percentile; >5% with Z-score <−2	Size for gestational age or size only	Validity of gestational age assessment; racial distribution
Develop facilities (including transport and other infrastructure) for care of IUGR and preterm infants		Hospital, home, or other birth setting, as soon as possible after birth	Single measurement	2. Birth weight	2. >15% below 2500 g; >2% below 1500 g		
				3. Chest circumference	3. >15% below 29 cm		

Table 12 (continued)

1	2	3	4	5	6	7	8
Uses: what will be done for the population?	For what purpose?	Target group and setting	What to measure and how often	Indices	Criteria for judgement (cut-offs)	Rationale for anthropometry	Other factors for interpretation
Assessing response to an intervention							
Determine whether size at birth (fetal growth) has improved and whether fetal or infant mortality has declined	Reduce morbidity/mortality, and optimize long-term growth and performance	Newborn infants in populations with high prevalence of SGA (or LBW) Hospital, home, or other birth setting, as soon as possible after birth	Gestational age, sex, birth weight Measured every 1–2 years	1. Birth weight for gestational age and sex 2. Birth weight	1. >20% below 10th percentile; > 5% with Z-score <−2 2. >15% below 2500 g; >2% below 1500 g	Size for gestational age or size only	Changes in methods of gestational age assessment or in racial distribution
Discontinue, modify, or continue intervention							

Table 12 (*continued*)

1	2	3	4	5	6	7	8
Uses: what will be done for the population?	For what purpose?	Target group and setting	What to measure and how often	Indices	Criteria for judgement (cut-offs)	Rationale for anthropometry	Other factors for interpretation
Ascertaining determinants of malnutrition							
Identify the determinants of IUGR Improve maternal nutrition, reduce maternal smoking, provide malaria prophylaxis, modify other determinants	Reduce morbidity/mortality, and optimize long-term growth and performance	Newborn infants in populations with high prevalence of SGA (or LBW) Hospital, home, or other birth setting, as soon as possible after birth	Gestational age, sex, birth weight Single measurement	Birth weight for gestational age and sex	>20% below 10th percentile; > 5% with Z-score <−2	Potential maternal or environmental determinants of IUGR	Validity of gestational age assessment; racial distribution

Table 12 (continued)

1	2	3	4	5	6	7	8
Uses: what will be done for the population?	For what purpose?	Target group and setting	What to measure and how often	Indices	Criteria for judgement (cut-offs)	Rationale for anthropometry	Other factors for interpretation
Ascertaining consequences of malnutrition							
Determine whether IUGR impairs child health, growth, and performance Improve infant nutrition and stimulation	Reduce morbidity/mortality, and optimize long-term growth and performance	Newborn infants in populations with high prevalence of SGA (or LBW) Hospital, home, or other birth setting, as soon as possible after birth	Gestational age, sex, birth weight Single measurement	Birth weight for gestational age and sex	>20% below 10th percentile; > 5% with Z-score <-2	Fetal, infant, and child mortality, morbidity, growth, and development	Validity of gestational age assessment; racial distribution

Table 12 (continued)

1	2	3	4	5	6	7	8
Uses: what will be done for the population?	For what purpose?	Target group and setting	What to measure and how often	Indices	Criteria for judgement (cut-offs)	Rationale for anthro-pometry	Other factors for inter-pretation
Nutritional surveillance							
Determine whether there is evidence of recent problems impairing fetal growth

Detect new adverse influences (e.g. famine, increased maternal smoking, malaria epidemic) | Reduce morbidity/mortality, and optimize long-term growth and performance | Newborn infants in populations at risk for increased prevalence of SGA | Gestational age, sex, birth weight

Measured every 1–2 years | Birth weight for gestational age and sex | >20% below 10th percentile; > 5% with Z-score <−2 | Size for gestational age | Validity of gestational age assessment; racial distribution |

134

very preterm infants (*61-63*). Nevertheless, these methods, particularly in some of their simplified versions (*64, 65*), could be most useful for assessing gestational age of infants weighing ≥1500 g at birth in large field evaluations where other methods are not available (*45*).

4.4.2 *Birth weight*

The most widely used anthropometric indicator of size is birth weight, for which mechanical and electronic scales provide reasonably valid and precise readings. As discussed above, most diagnostic classifications of fetal growth for both individuals and populations are based on birth-weight-for-gestational-age.

4.4.3 *Birth length*

Birth length is another indicator of neonatal size, which can be used when birth weight is not available and which frequently provides useful additional information, since some infants with low weight-for-age may be of relatively normal length at birth. Several authors have argued that a discrepancy between weight and length deficits may be of etiological and prognostic importance. However, birth length is measured far less precisely than birth weight (*32*), owing to variations in posture and muscle tone among newborn infants, and considerable training is required to obtain reasonably reproducible measurements.

4.4.4 *Birth head circumference*

Birth head circumference-for-age can be measured more reproducibly than birth length (*32, 66*), although the presence of head moulding (particularly after a difficult or forceps-assisted delivery) may affect the measurement. As with birth length, head circumference (as an indicator of brain volume) may provide important diagnostic and prognostic information beyond that provided by birth weight alone.

4.4.5 *Proportionality indices*

The most commonly used index of neonatal body proportionality relates birth weight to birth length: Rohrer's ponderal index = 100 times the birth weight (in grams) divided by the cube of birth length (cm^3). Other proportionality indices that relate head circumference to length, for example, or chest circumference to length have been studied occasionally, but further research would be needed to show that they offer any advantage over the indicators already mentioned.

4.4.6 *Other measurements*

Skinfold thickness has been used to assess newborn adiposity, but the determinants and consequences of variation in this measurement have not been shown to differ from those of the anthropometric indices discussed in the foregoing paragraphs. Since measurement of skinfold thickness is relatively imprecise, it is not currently recommended for purposes of routine assessment.

In developing countries, where scales may be unavailable for measuring birth weight, other anthropometric measurements – including chest, arm, thigh, and calf circumferences – have been used as proxy measures of newborn size (67-70).

Arm and chest circumferences were considered as surrogates for birth weight in a recent multicentre WHO study of 400 births (67). Both indicators demonstrated high correlation coefficients with birth weight and high positive predictive values for LBW. The use of chest circumference alone is recommended, however, because it is simpler to measure and because little additional information is provided by the arm measurement. Cut-offs of 29 and 30 cm are suggested, with < 29 cm for the identification of "highly at risk" and ≥29 but <30 cm for "at risk" newborns. Studies in India (69, 70) have evaluated the usefulness of calf circumference of the newborn as a proxy indicator for birth weight; results showed a strong correlation between the two. The sensitivity of calf circumference for identification of LBW infants is as high as 95%, compared with 80-85% for other measurements, while specificity is similar to that of other measurements, i.e. 80%. Using a cut-off of 10 cm, it was possible to identify 98% of infants with birth weights below 2.5 kg Thus, calf circumference can be also used as a simple screening tool for LBW.

A recently published report established interesting data on abdominal circumference at birth; small circumference was associated with raised serum concentrations of low-density lipoprotein cholesterol in adult life (71).

4.5 Reference data for size at birth

4.5.1 Criteria for evaluating existing references

Over the past 40 years, many investigators have proposed reference data as standards for assessment of fetal growth by clinicians, public health practitioners, and researchers. Most data have come from North America or western Europe, but have varied considerably in terms of sample size, representativeness (some being hospital- or clinic-based and others population-based), racial and socioeconomic characteristics of the population studied, sex stratification (unisex or sex-specific references), inclusion or exclusion of multiple births and of infants with major congenital anomalies or intrauterine infections known to reduce fetal growth, and methods for assessing gestational age. Unfortunately, few investigators have attempted to relate these reference data (or deviations therefrom) to subsequent infant and child mortality, morbidity, and performance.

Clear trade-offs in sample size, representativeness, and validity of gestational age estimates are involved in choosing between hospital- and population-based sources of reference data. For example, data derived from a single hospital centre are likely to be based on relatively small sample sizes that may or may not be representative of the larger population of infants to whom the references are to be applied. Differences between one hospital (or even one delivery room) and another in calibration of balances, terminal digit preference, and rounding practice may lead to small differences in birth weight distributions. On the other hand, data quality control for gestational age measurement is often better than for population-based measurements. In most older references, gestational age was based on maternal recall of LMP, whereas many recent references have modified the LMP estimates by prenatal clinical assessment, exclusion of infants with improbable birth weights for their gestational age, or, more recently, early (before 20 weeks) ultrasound measurement of the fetal biparietal diameter and/or other body dimensions.

References derived from geographically-based populations usually rely on information provided by birth certificates; these have the advantages of large sample populations and improved representativeness. The large numbers are essential for reasonably precise estimation of birth weight (and other anthropometric measurements) at very early gestational ages, particularly in the tails of the distribution (e.g. SGA and LGA). Unfortunately, quality control of assessment of gestational age is often much poorer than in studies based on a single hospital. Misleading interpretations are likely unless it is recognized that data for pre- and post-term births are less likely than data for term infants to provide valid indications of average growth *in utero*.

These trade-offs in sample size, representativeness, and validity of gestational age estimation are highlighted in discussion of specific reference data in section 4.5.3. The references discussed do not comprise a complete list, but represent a selection of those most frequently used or mentioned by clinicians and researchers, or those with one or more noteworthy characteristics.

4.5.2 *Size at birth in early gestation*

The most frequently cited early fetal growth reference is that for length (and length velocity) suggested by Tanner (*41*) in his textbook on human growth. Despite Tanner's statement that "between 18 and 28 weeks, there are almost no useful data", several earlier and more recent studies based on prostaglandin and hysterotomy abortions appear to provide pertinent and valid information (*72-74*). Tanner's curves, which he describes as "diagrammatic, based on several sources of data", include detailed information from Gruenwald (*40*) and suggest a slowing of length growth velocity by 20 weeks; other published studies, however, are extremely consistent in showing no fall-off in velocity of linear growth (length, biparietal diameter) and continued exponential growth in weight from 6 or 8 weeks until well into the third trimester. Nevertheless, it is clear from ultrasound measurements of biparietal diameter and crown–heel length, as well as from anthropometric data on preterm newborns, that length reaches 70% of its mean value at term by 26–28 weeks, while only 32% of the term weight is achieved by this time. Although the evidence is fairly meagre, no large sex- or race-specific anthropometric differences are apparent in the first two trimesters.

4.5.3 Size at birth in later gestation

Tables 13 and 14 summarize the relevant characteristics of selected fetal growth references published in the literature. One of the earliest references for later gestation is based on all births that occurred during 1947 in Birmingham, England, for which sex, birth weight, and gestational age of the babies were known ($n = 16\,749$) (75). Because it is population-based, the original reference sample (*all* Birmingham births for 1947) is probably representative, at least of urban England at the time. Unfortunately, however, the fact that gestational age was unknown for nearly 25% of that original sample may have biased the curves upwards if those infants were undergrown relative to those included in the reference, whose gestational age was known. Moreover, gestational age was apparently based on maternal recollection of LMP. The sample size is reasonable, but the small number of births at low gestational age leads to considerable instability of the curves at those gestations. Although the curves are sex-specific, they are not restricted to singletons, and infants with congenital malformations are not excluded.

A second reference that is still in common use, particularly in the United Kingdom, is based on the weight of 46 703 singleton births in Aberdeen, Scotland, from 1948 to 1964 (76). Its advantages over the earlier reference (75) include a larger sample size, restriction to singleton births, fewer infants of unknown gestational age, and correction of uncertain gestational ages (in completed weeks) on the basis of available obstetric information. It also provides separate references according to parity. (As discussed below, it is clear that average birth weights are lower in first than in subsequent births, but less clear whether birth-weight-specific mortality, morbidity, and other health outcomes differ according to parity and therefore whether parity-specific references should be used.)

Perhaps the most widely used reference is that of Lubchenco et al. (77, 78), which is derived from a single hospital and constructed from weights, lengths, and head circumferences of 5635 liveborn Caucasian infants of white and Hispanic mothers of predominantly low socio-economic status living at moderately high altitude near Denver, Colorado, USA. Multiple births were included, but infants with incompatible birth weight/gestational age combinations were excluded. Gestational ages are based on LMP and reported to the nearest week. The appeal of this reference is twofold: the published graphs are easy for

Table 13

A comparison of selected fetal growth reference data characteristics

Reference	Location	Source	Characteristics	Exclusions	Measurements	Stratification	Gestational age	No. of subjects, n
Gibson & McKeown (75)	Birmingham, England	All births 1947	Urban, white	None	Birth weight	Sex	Completed weeks (LMP)	16 749
Thomson et al. (76)	Aberdeen, Scotland	90% of births 1948–1964	Urban, white	Illegitimate and multiple births, macerated stillbirths, fetal malformations	Birth weight	Sex, parity	Completed weeks (confirmed LMP)	46 703
Lubchenco et al. (77, 78)	Denver, CO, USA	1 hospital 1958–1961	High altitude, low socioeconomic status, white and Hispanic	Stillbirths, malformations affecting BW, maternal diabetes, "incompatible" BW/GA	Birth weight, length, and head circumference	None	Nearest week (LMP)	5 635
Gruenwald (81)	Baltimore, MD, USA	1 hospital late 1950s to early 1960s	[not specified]	Multiple births, malformations affecting BW	Birth weight	None	Nearest week (corrected LMP)	13 732
Usher & McLean (82)	Montreal, Canada	1 hospital 1959–1963	Urban, white	Stillbirths, multiple births, major congenital anomalies, maternal diabetes, severe IUGR	Birth weight, length, head circumference, and others	None	Nearest week (LMP)	300

Table 13 (continued)

Reference	Location	Source	Characteristics	Exclusions	Measurements	Stratification	Gestational age	No. of subjects, n
Babson et al. (83)	Portland, OR, USA	2 hospitals 1959–1966	Urban, white, high socioeconomic status	Stillbirths, multiple births	Birth weight	Sex	Nearest week (confirmed LMP)	39 895
Brenner et al. (73)	Cleveland, OH, USA	1 hospital 1962–1969	Urban, white (high socioeconomic status) and black (low socioeconomic status)	Antepartum stillbirths, multiple and breech births, congenital anomalies, pre-eclampsia	Birth weight	Corrections for sex, race, and parity	Nearest week (LMP)	30 722
Williams et al. (84)	California, USA	All births 1970–1976	Mixed races and socioeconomic status	None	Birth weight	Sex, non-Hispanic white, singleton vs. multiple birth	Completed weeks (corrected LMP)	2 288 806
David (85)	North Carolina, USA	All births 1975–1977	Mixed races and socioeconomic status	Stillbirths	Birth weight	None	Completed weeks (corrected LMP)	195 867
Lawrence et al. (86); Niklasson et al. (87)	Sweden	Healthy 79% of all births 1977–1981	Predominantly white	Stillbirths, multiple births, pregnancy complications affecting BW, major malformations	Birth weight, length, and head circumference	Sex	Completed weeks (confirmed LMP)	362 280

Table 13 (continued)

Reference	Location	Source	Characteristics	Exclusions	Measurements	Stratification	Gestational age	No. of subjects, n
Arbuckle et al. (88)	Canada	All births 1986–1988	Mixed races and socioeconomic status	Stillbirths	Birth weight	Sex, singleton vs. twin	Completed weeks (corrected maternal or physician reports)	1 110 093

Table 14

Selected fetal growth reference data: comparison of birth weight (in grams) for gestational age (GA)

Reference	Stratum[a]	GA = 28 weeks			GA = 32 weeks			GA = 36 weeks			GA = 40 weeks			GA = 42 weeks		
		10%ile	50%ile	90%ile	10%ile	50%ile	90%ile	10%ile	50%ile	90%ile	10%ile	50%ile	90%ile	10%ile	50%ile	90%ile
Gibson & McKeown (75)	B		1262[b]			1966[b]	2610		3087[b]	3580		3559[b]	4110		3623[b]	4220
	G		1230[b]			1857[b]	2660		2996[b]	3480		3428[b]	3930		3487[b]	4020
Thomson et al. (76)	B				1360	1930		2380	2950		2920	3490		3010	3590	
	G				1270	1900		2270	2850		2780	3340		2850	3410	
Lubchenco et al. (77, 78)	B	915	1205	1570	1320	1760	2280	2105	2745	3385	2700	3290	3880	2730	3310	3995
	G	870	1140	1530	1250	1675	2330	1960	2630	3335	2630	3160	3720	2630	3210	3840
Gruenwald (81)	Overall		1075[b]			1770[b]			2876[b]			3270[b]			3411[b]	
Usher & McLean (82)	Overall		1113[b]			1727[b]			2589[b]			3480[b]			3513[b]	
Babson et al. (83)	Overall	695	1118	1691	1351	1861	2453	2173	2697	3414	2880	3448	4045	3039	3618	4288
Brenner et al. (73)	Overall	770	1150	1660	1310	1810	2500	2190	2650	3290	2750	3280	3870	2830	3410	4060
Williams et al. (84)	W, non-Hispanic B	762	1184	1661	1348	1979	2727	2278	2910	3591	2944	3534	4154	3086	3665	4276
	W, non-Hispanic G	678	1102	1645	1219	1861	2619	2169	2788	3450	2817	3389	4005	2936	3513	4094

Table 14 (*continued*)

Reference	Stratum[a]	GA = 28 weeks			GA = 32 weeks			GA = 36 weeks			GA = 40 weeks			GA = 42 weeks		
		10%ile	50%ile	90%ile	10%ile	50%ile	90%ile	10%ile	50%ile	90%ile	10%ile	50%ile	90%ile	10%ile	50%ile	90%ile
David[c] (85)	Overall	840	1107	1360	1320	1789	2240	2200	2812	3420	2830	3380	3930	2960	3551	4170
Lawrence et al. (86);	B		1152[b]			1941[b]			2875[b]			3646[b]			3810[b]	
Niklasson et al. (87)	G		1070[b]			1833[b]			2769[b]			3506[b]			3642[b]	
Arbuckle et al. (88)	B	880	1190	1480	1460	1910	2360	2300	2830	3450	3030	3580	4170	3200	3790	4420
	G	800	1100	1420	1350	1790	2320	2210	2750	3360	2910	3430	4000	3070	3620	4200

[a] B = boys, G = girls, W = white
[b] Mean value.
[c] Cited publication gives no tables for 10th and 90th percentiles; for these percentiles, birth weights were estimated from graphs.

clinicians to use, and birth weight/gestational age categories are related to neonatal mortality (79) and long-term morbidity (80). Despite recognition that the curves are considerably lower than the other references under discussion, because of the low socioeconomic status of the reference sample and the fetal growth-restricting effect of high altitude, they continue to be used by many clinicians and researchers.

Gruenwald (81) developed a birth weight reference from singleton births in the late 1950s and early 1960s, based on a combination of data on 1232 surviving infants obtained in an earlier study and on 12 500 consecutive births at a single hospital in Baltimore, Maryland, USA. Estimation of gestational age (to the nearest week) was based on corrected LMP; the modest sample size results in few births at early gestational ages. Gruenwald was one of the first investigators to note the apparent bimodality of the birth weight distribution in preterm infants and to attribute this to errors in gestational age assessment based on LMP. He was able to smooth the reference curves for early gestational ages by basing them on the predominant distribution at each gestational age, which suggested that the higher, second mode was the result of underestimation of true gestational age in a significant proportion of the births alleged (on the basis of LMP) to be preterm.

Usher & McLean (82) based their reference curves on liveborn, singleton, white infants at a single hospital in Montreal. Gestational age to the nearest week was estimated on the basis of LMP. The sample size was only 300, and there was no separation of the sexes. Although consecutive births were used for higher gestational ages during a single year (1959), recruitment of subjects continued for four additional years to increase the numbers of infants born at low gestational age. Despite its very small sample size, this study has the advantages of including birth length, head and chest circumference, and a variety of proportionality indices, and of relying on a single trained observer using standardized measurement techniques.

One popular American birth weight reference is based on nearly 40 000 singleton, liveborn, Caucasian infants of middle-class mothers delivering in two maternity hospitals in Portland, Oregon, USA, in 1959-1966 (83). Gestational age was calculated to the nearest week from maternal recall of LMP. Birth weight distributions at early gestational ages did not exhibit true bimodality, but were positively skewed.

A study of 30 722 singleton, liveborn infants without malformations at a single hospital in Cleveland, Ohio, USA, from 1962 to 1969 (73) provides another popular American birth weight reference. Breech deliveries and infants of mothers with pre-eclampsia were excluded. All gestational ages were based on LMP and reported to the nearest week. The sample was about half white and half black; most white, but few black, mothers were private patients. Sex- and race-specific references are not provided, but "correction factors" are given to adjust the single curve for these variables.

A more recent multiracial birth weight reference has the dual advantages of being population-based and of using an extremely large sample (more than two million births in California over the study period 1970-1976 (*84*)). Gestational ages are reported in completed weeks; a computer algorithm was used to adjust any that seemed suspicious (those associated with high birth weights belonging to a second mode, as previously reported (*81*)). Curves are presented separately for singleton boys and girls (Figs. 18 and 19) and for multiple births (Fig. 20). Race-specific curves are not presented, but data are provided for non-Hispanic whites. A distinctive feature is the availability of neonatal mortality at various gestational ages and birth weights.

In a population-based reference of all live births 1975-1977 in North Carolina, USA, a computer algorithm was again used to correct underestimated LMP-based gestational ages (in completed weeks) of preterm infants (*85*). However, this approach resulted in the exclusion of, rather than adjustment for, infants whose birth weights appeared to correspond to a second (higher) mode. The resulting curves are unisex and not race-specific.

A recently published Swedish reference (*86, 87*) is based on birth weight, length, and head circumference measurements in 362 280 "healthy" Swedish infants born 1977-1981. Stillbirths and multiple births were excluded, as were infants with congenital malformations and those whose mothers had growth-inhibiting complications of pregnancy. One major advantage of this reference is that gestational age (in completed weeks) was based on LMP only when the LMP estimate was in agreement (±2 weeks) with the results of ultrasound or other clinical assessment. Statistical techniques were used to transform the skewed distributions of birth weight into normal distributions and to derive objectively smoothed curves. However, the exclusion of infants whose mothers experienced pregnancy complications appears to have resulted in reference curves that are somewhat higher at term than the others under discussion. Moreover, there is no information on perinatal viability in the various birth-weight-for-gestational-age categories.

Over one million births in Canada from 1986 to 1988 have provided another recent reference (*88*). Gestational ages in completed weeks were reported by mothers or, in Quebec, by the attending physicians, and thus reflect ultrasound and other obstetric estimates as well as LMP. Exclusion from the analysis of infants with birth weights more than two interquartile ranges above the 75th percentile or below the 25th percentile reduced the otherwise falsely elevated 90th percentile curves for preterm infants. No statistical or other smoothing procedures were used.

Two additional references are currently under development. In Montreal, Usher and colleagues are deriving a new reference based on more recent births at the same hospital as their earlier reference (*82*), but using a much larger sample size and sex stratification. Most importantly, data are being restricted to infants whose gestational age, estimated by LMP, has

Figure 18
Birth weight percentiles and perinatal mortality rates (per 1000) for single female births[a]

Note: The mean birth weight–gestational age combination is marked with a black dot. Down the right-hand side are the birth-weight-specific rates for all gestational ages, and across the top are the gestational-age-specific rates for all birth weights. The birth-weight/gestational-age-specific mortality rates, computed on the basis of 2-week gestation and 250-g weight intervals, are plotted within the square corresponding to the appropriate intersection of the birth-weight/gestational-age grid. For example, the perinatal mortality rate for infants weighing between 3251 and 3500 g and of 40 and 41 completed weeks of gestation is 3.1. The perinatal mortality rate for the birth-weight group 3251–3500 g for all gestational ages is 4.0 per 1000, and the perinatal mortality rate for the 40- to 41-week gestational age group for all birth weights is 5.0.

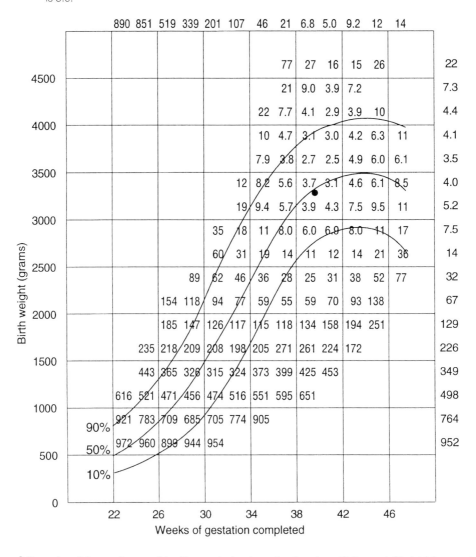

Figure 19
Birth weight percentiles and perinatal mortality rates (per 1000) for single male births[a]

Note: For explanation, see Fig. 18.

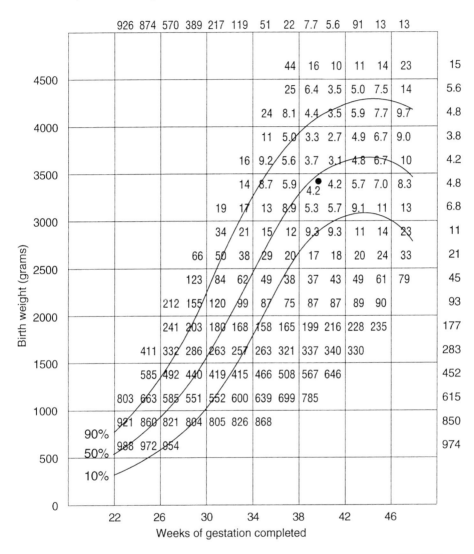

WHO 94695

[a] Reproduced from reference *84* with permission from the American College of Obstetricians and Gynecologists.

Figure 20

Birth weight percentiles and perinatal mortality rates (per 1000) for multiple births[a]

Note: For explanation, see Fig. 18.

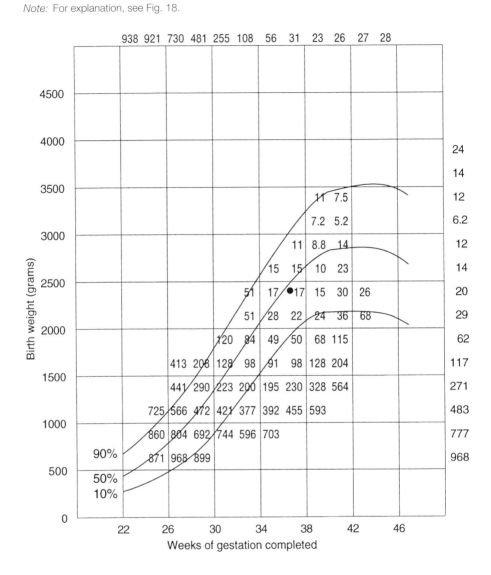

[a] Reproduced from reference *84* with permission from the American College of Obstetricians and Gynecologists.

been confirmed (±7 days) by ultrasound, early in the second trimester. This reference would be most applicable to infants whose mothers are confident of their menstrual dates and those whose gestational age has been determined by early ultrasound. However, the routine use of ultrasound is rare in developing countries and may decrease in developed countries in the light of recent published clinical trials that have shown it to produce no improvement in perinatal outcomes (57-60).

A very different, but equally valuable, approach is being taken by Yip and colleagues (unpublished data) at the Centers for Disease Control in the USA. Sex-, race- and altitude-specific references are based on vital records of singleton, socially advantaged infants for the whole USA over the period 1980-1987; this is highly advantageous in terms of both sample size and representativeness. Problems with determining gestational age are dealt with by a regression approach that allows extrapolation of growth curves from newborns of higher gestational ages to those (such as preterm deliveries) whose gestational ages have been overestimated.

Despite the many differences in calendar time, population characteristics, exclusions, and methods of estimating gestational age, the similarities among the various references are more striking than their differences (Tables 13 and 14). Several distinct patterns emerge. Girls weigh less than boys, even at 28 weeks of gestation, and the difference increases with advancing gestational age. The references of Lubchenco et al. (77, 78) and Brenner et al. (73) begin to lag behind the others by 32 weeks. In the former, the lag is probably caused by the growth-restricting effect of moderately high altitude, although low socioeconomic status may also play a role (probably mediated, at least in part, by maternal cigarette smoking). (The high 10th percentile values at 28 weeks suggest a systematic overestimate of gestational age.) In the latter case, the lag is probably due to the large proportion of black infants born to mothers of low socioeconomic status. The low 10th percentile values at 28 and 32 weeks in the reference from North Carolina (85) probably reflect the algorithm-induced exclusion of higher-weight infants at those gestational ages. Birth weights in the recent Swedish (86, 87) and Canadian (88) references do not exceed those of the other tabulated references until term; higher post-term birth weights may reflect the increasing availability of obstetrically confirmed gestational ages in those countries.

4.6 Conclusions

Because the effects on fetal growth of differing sex, race, and exposure to growth-promoting and growth-inhibiting environmental influences do not appear to diverge until the late second or early third trimesters, any of the recently published early-gestation reference curves (or a meta-analysis based on several of them) could be used for developing a single fetal growth standard up to at least 24-26 weeks (72-74). In later gestation, however, the existing curves differ to some degree. The fact that growth varies according to fetal sex and race, and maternal height, weight, parity, gestational nutrition, cigarette smoking, and numerous environmental influences does not necessarily mean that separate curves are required for each specific combination of these determinants. Indeed, the recent suggestion that fetal growth curves should be "customized" according to maternal determinants (89) simply begs the question as to whether an infant who is small for age because the mother is short is "equivalent" to an infant who is small because the mother is from India, was thin before pregnancy, or smoked cigarettes during pregnancy.

Until more is known about determinant-specific fetal and child health outcomes, the use of determinant-specific growth curves may result in "controlling" out the adverse effects of growth-inhibiting influences during gestation, and lead to the under-identification of individual infants and populations in need of intervention. Such specific curves are therefore not recommended. Moreover, regional and international comparisons are facilitated by the use of a single reference (or, at most, a small number of references) for fetal growth.

The case for sex-specific curves, however, appears unassailable. Starting at about the third trimester, female fetuses are, on average, smaller than male fetuses. All else being equal, however, the prognosis for mortality and morbidity of girls is better than that of boys born at the same weight-for-gestational-age.

Many investigators have also argued for race-specific curves. Several within-country studies have shown that, before 34–36 weeks' gestation, black infants are larger than white infants; thereafter the pattern reverses (2, 90-92). A similar pattern was recently reported among Hawaiian, Filipino, and Japanese infants (93). However, most of these studies have relied on gestational age estimated from LMP, and it is therefore possible that some gestational ages before 36 weeks may have been underestimated in black infants, although a very recent study of native and immigrant Chinese infants with gestational age confirmed by early ultrasound shows a similar trend (Wen SW, Kramer MS, unpublished data).

Although it has not been possible to distinguish nature from nurture in explaining the differences in mean birth-weight-for-gestational-age between different racial groups, it is difficult to imagine any environmental influence that would lead to faster growth early in the third trimester and slower growth later on. Unless evidence is produced to the contrary, differences in the rate of growth at different periods of gestation seem likely to be genetically determined. Such differences appear to support the case for race-specific curves, although a multiplicity of standards would hinder comparison at the international level. As Goldenberg et al. have shown (94), differences in method of assessing gestational age, socioeconomic status, and altitude, use of singleton versus multiple births, and inclusion versus exclusion of stillbirths or infants with congenital anomalies are probably far more responsible than race for the differences between the existing reference curves.

In summary, race-specific references should not be used where race is associated with other risk factors, such as poor nutrition or low socioeconomic status. Current knowledge does not confirm large genetic differences in birth weight among various populations and therefore does not support the use of separate, race-specific reference curves.

Further research is needed to identify those determinants of fetal growth that influence mortality, morbidity, and performance *independently* of their effects on growth. Although it is quite clear that the use of sex-specific reference curves is justifiable, additional research is needed using large populations and ultrasound confirmation of gestational age to assess whether infants of different races born at a particular weight-for-gestational-age are at substantially different risks for important health outcomes. Similar research is needed for infants born to mothers of different parity and stature, to determine whether infants who are born small because their mothers are primiparous or of short stature are at the same risk for adverse sequelae as those of equivalent size who are small because their mothers have pre-eclampsia or smoke cigarettes. Until the answers to those questions are available, the use of a single, sex-specific international reference has much to recommend it.

Although none of the reference curves published or under development meets all desirable criteria (Table 13), several appear to come close. The best are probably those from California (*84*), Sweden (*86, 87*), and Canada (*88*) (see Table 15). The Canadian reference is the most recent, but there are irregularities in extreme percentiles at low gestational ages because no smoothing technique was used. The Swedish reference is slightly dated, but the statistically smoothed curves and presentation of means plus and minus multiples of the standard deviations make it quite useful for the diagnosis of SGA and LGA. As this is based on a selected "healthy" population (of mothers and newborns) it could be of value when a growth chart from a population that has achieved a high level of its growth potential is needed for purposes of international comparison.

The Committee considered that the multiracial reference of Williams et al. (*84*) represents the best option presently available. Of the total births, 9.9% were blacks, 25.8% whites with Spanish surnames, 59.2% non-Spanish whites, and 5.1% other non-white minorities. The reference is well known, it is based on a large sample size at the lower end of the gestational age distribution, and it is comparable to many other candidate curves. More importantly, perhaps, it provides data on the relationship between birth-weight-for-gestational-age and neonatal mortality (unfortunately, not presented by sex). Thus, the criteria for diagnosis of SGA and LGA can be based on perinatal risk rather than arbitrary statistical cut-offs, as well as on considerations of cost that will ultimately determine the proportion of newborns for whom interventions can be made available (see section 2).

Table 15
Comparison of three selected reference data sets for newborn infants

Criteria	Williams et al. (84)	Lawrence et al. (86) Niklasson et al. (87)	Arbuckle et al. (88)
Years of data collection	1970–1976	1977–1981	1986–1988
Sample size	2 288 806	362 280	1 110 093
Representativeness	Population-based	Population-based, of "healthy" newborns	Population-based
Validity of gestational age	LMP and clinical estimation	LMP in agreement with ultrasound and clinical estimation	LMP, ultrasound, and clinical estimation
Smoothed for suspicious GAs	Yes	Yes	No
Race	Multiracial (9.9% black, 25.8% Hispanic whites, 59.2% non-Hispanic whites, 5.1% other)	Single-race (Swedish)	Multiracial (9% "visible minorities")
Socioeconomic status	All births	High	All births
Stratification by sex	Yes	Yes	Yes
Multiple births	Stratified	Excluded	Stratified
Congenital malformations	Included	Excluded	Included
Maternal pathologies and intrauterine infections	Included	Excluded	Included
Quality of data source	Birth registration certificate	Birth registration certificate	Birth registration certificate
Relates reference data to outcome	Yes	No	No
From a population where neonatal care and outcomes are "reasonably good"	Yes	Yes	Yes
Level of current use	Wide	Very limited	Very limited

Reference curves for singleton boys and girls, as well as multiple births, are provided in Figs 18–20.

The way in which a reference is interpreted and the clinical and public health decisions that will be based upon it are probably more important than the choice of reference. Criteria for diagnosis of SGA or LGA should be based on evidence of increased risk for mortality, morbidity, or impaired performance. Future research should therefore attempt to identify a range of fetal growth associated with optimal long-term health outcomes, as well as ranges associated with specific adverse outcomes. These results may lead to the use of cut-offs other than the traditional 10th and 90th percentiles, these new cut-off points may vary with gestational age. New references should provide the 3rd, 5th, 10th, 15th and 25th percentiles so that health planners and practitioners can identify the portion of the population they need to work with, and should also present the information according to Z-scores (e.g. -3, -2, -1, 0 (mean), +1, +2, and +3) since the Z-score system will probably be more widely used in the future. Where management decisions for individual infants are based on their size for age, available options for intervention should be rigorously tested and shown to do more good than harm. Similarly, public health policy-makers should ensure that interventions designed to "improve" an abnormal fetal growth distribution are truly beneficial to mothers and their infants.

Based on all the above considerations, recommendations for specific activities and future research are made in section 4.7.

4.7 Recommendations

4.7.1 *General*

1. Any of the recently published data on early gestation can be used up to 26 weeks.

2. No "customized" curves or curves specific to particular determinants of birth weight should be used.

3. The birth-weight-for-gestational-age, sex-specific, single/twins curve developed by Williams et al. (*84*) is recommended. The 10th percentile of the curve should be used for the classification of SGA.

4. Race-specific curves are not currently recommended for most situations. However, the appropriateness of using race-specific reference data for some populations with low infant mortality should be evaluated.

4.7.2 *For individuals*

1. Percentiles of a distribution of birth-weight-for-gestational-age are recommended as the ideal indicator, with cut-offs at the 10th (SGA) and 90th (LGA) percentiles.

2. Where gestational age is unavailable, birth weight < 2500 g is recommended as the LBW cut-off. However, in settings with a very high prevalence of SGA, a cut-off of < 2250 g or even < 2000 g can be applied to avoid overwhelming the health services. A cut-off of < 1500 g is recommended as the VLBW cut-off for identifying newborn infants who should be given highest priority for referral to higher levels of care.

3. If scales are unavailable and birth weight cannot be determined, chest circumference should be measured; newborns with chest circumference < 29 cm should be designated as "highly at risk" and those with circumference ≥ 29 cm but < 30 cm as "at risk". It should be noted, however, that this measure has been validated only in terms of its relationship to birth weight and not to perinatal outcomes.

4.7.3 *For populations*

1. Prevalence of SGA in excess of 20% is recommended as the cut-off for triggering public health action. In the absence of information on gestational age, prevalence > 15% of either LBW or chest circumference < 29 cm may be used as a proxy cut-off.

2. As indicators of the need for health facilities (rather than as a proxy for SGA), LBW prevalence exceeding 15% and VLBW prevalence exceeding 2% are recommended.

3. Birth-weight-specific fetal and infant mortality should be monitored for evaluating response to interventions.

4.7.4 *For WHO*

The Expert Committee recommends that WHO should promote the research needed in the following areas:

1. Assessment and development of fetal growth reference data suitable for international applications.

2. Birth weight coefficients of variation by gestational age.

3. Further development of the LBW/SGA databank at present organized by WHO.

4. Assistance to Member States in improving their reporting systems for data on birth-weight-for-gestational-age.

5. Producing the means and SDs (Z-scores) from the reference of Williams et al. (*84*).

4.7.5 *For Member States*

The Expert Committee recommends that Member States should:

1. Encourage the systematic collection of population-based data on birth-weight-for-gestational-age (or its proxy indicators).

2. Implement simplified data collection systems for all deliveries.

3. Encourage the collation of birth weight records and infant death certificates to relate birth-weight-for-gestational-age data to population-based outcomes.

4.7.6 *For future research*

The Expert Committee recommends research to:

1. Explore how risk factors that affect fetal growth influence newborn mortality, morbidity, and performance, independently of fetal growth effects.

2. Explore further the relationship between maternal morbidity and newborn anthropometric measurements.

3. Explore the association between size and proportionality at birth and long-term physical and developmental outcomes, including health conditions into adulthood.

4. Explore the association between birth-weight-for-gestational-age and newborn outcomes in developing countries.

References

1. McCormick MC. The contribution of low birth weight to infant mortality and childhood morbidity. *New England journal of medicine,* 1985, **312**:82-90.

2. Institute of Medicine/National Academy of Sciences. *Nutrition during pregnancy.* Washington, DC, National Academy Press, 1990.

3. Kramer MS. Birth weight and infant mortality: perceptions and pitfalls. *Paediatric and perinatal epidemiology,* 1990, 4:381-390.

4. Little GA. Fetal growth and development. In: Eden RH, Boehm FH, eds. *Assessment and care of the fetus: physiological, clinical, and medico-legal principles.* Norwalk, CT, Appleton & Lange, 1990:1-5.

5. Wilcox AJ. Birth weight, gestation, and the fetal growth curve. *American journal of obstetrics and gynecology,* 1981, **139**(8):863-867.

6. Ott WJ, Doyle S. Normal ultrasonic fetal weight curve. *Obstetrics and gynecology,* 1982, **59**(5):603-606.

7. Weiner CP et al. A hypothetical model suggesting suboptimal intrauterine growth in infants delivered preterm. *Obstetrics and gynecology,* 1985, **65**(3):323-326.

8. Secher NJ et al. Growth retardation in preterm infants. *British journal of obstetrics and gynaecology,* 1987, **94**:115-120.

9. Kramer MS et al. Determinants of fetal growth and body proportionality. *Pediatrics,* 199, **86**:18-26.

10. Kramer MS et al. Maternal nutrition and spontaneous preterm birth. *American journal of epidemiology,* 1992, **136**:574-583.

11. Yudkin PL et al. Influence of elective preterm delivery on birthweight and head circumference standards. *Archives of disease in childhood,* 1987, **62**:24-29.

12. Kramer MS. Determinants of low birth weight: methodological assessment and meta-analysis. *Bulletin of the World Health Organization,* 1987, **65**:663-737.

13. Stein ZA, Susser M. Intrauterine growth retardation: epidemiological issues and public health significance. *Seminars in perinatology,* 1984, **8**:5-14.

14. Keirse MJ. Epidemiology and aetiology of the growth retarded baby. *Clinical obstetrics and gynaecology*, 1984, **11**:415-436.

15. Wen SW et al. Intrauterine growth retardation and preterm delivery: prenatal risk factors in an indigent population. *American journal of obstetrics and gynecology*, 1990, **162**:213-218.

16. Abrams B, Newman V. Small-for-gestational-age birth: maternal predictors and comparison with risk factors of spontaneous preterm delivery in the same cohort. *American journal of obstetrics and gynecology*, 1991, **164**:785-790.

17. Barros FC et al. Comparison of the causes and consequences of prematurity and intrauterine growth retardation: a longitudinal study in southern Brazil. *Pediatrics*, 1992, **90**(2 Pt 1):238-244.

18. Kalkwarf HJ. *Maternal weight gain during pregnancy and risk of preterm delivery: effects on neonatal mortality and public health impact* [Dissertation]. Ithaca, NY, Cornell University, 1991.

19. Kramer MS. Effects of energy and protein intake on pregnancy outcome: an overview of the research evidence from controlled clinical trials. *American journal of clinical nutrition*, 1993, **58**:627-635.

20. Johnstone F, Inglis L. Familial trends in low birth weight. *British medical journal*, 1974, **3**:659-661.

21. Klebanoff MA et al. Low birth weight across generations. *Journal of the American Medical Association*, 1984, **252**:2423-2427.

22. Goldenberg RL et al. Black-white differences in newborn anthropometric measurements. *Obstetrics and gynecology*, 1991, **78**(5 Pt 1):782-788.

23. Leff M et al. The association of maternal low birthweight and infant low birthweight in a racially mixed population. *Paediatric and perinatal epidemiology*, 1992, **6**:51-61.

24. Alberman E et al. The contrasting effects of parental birthweight and gestational age on the birthweight of offspring. *Paediatric and perinatal epidemiology*, 1992, **6**:134-144.

25. Taha T-el-T, Gray RH, Mohamedani A. Malaria and low birth weight in Central Sudan. *American journal of epidemiology*, 1993, **138**:318-325.

26. Villar J, Klebanoff M, Kestler E. The effect on fetal growth of protozoan and helminthic infection during pregnancy. *Obstetrics and gynecology*, 1989, **74**:915-920.

27. Zuckerman B et al. Effects of maternal marijuana and cocaine use on fetal growth. *New England journal of medicine*, 1989, **320**:762-768.

28. Petitti DB, Coleman C. Cocaine and the risk of low birth weight. *American journal of public health*, 1990, **80**:25-28.

29. Teberg AJ, Walther FJ, Pena IC. Mortality, morbidity, and outcome of the small-for-gestational-age infant. *Seminars in perinatology*, 1988, **12**:84-94.

30. Barker DJP. The intrauterine origins of cardiovascular and obstructive lung disease in adult life. The Mark Daniels Lecture 1990. *Journal of the Royal College of Physicians of London*, 1991, **25**:129-133.

31. Barker DJP. The fetal origins of diseases of old age. *European journal of clinical nutrition*, 1992, **46**(Suppl. 3):S3-S9.

32. **Kramer MS et al.** Body proportionality and head and length "sparing" in growth-retarded neonates: a critical reappraisal. *Pediatrics*, 1989, **84**:717–723.

33. **Altman DG, Hytten FE.** Intrauterine growth retardation: let's be clear about it. *British journal of obstetrics and gynaecology*, 1989, **96**:1127–1132.

34. **Khoury MJ et al.** Congenital malformations and intrauterine growth retardation: a population study. *Pediatrics*, 1988, **82**:83–90.

35. **Kramer MS et al.** Impact of intrauterine growth retardation and body proportionality on fetal and neonatal outcome. *Pediatrics*, 1990, **86**:707–713.

36. **Rosso P, Winick M.** Intrauterine growth retardation. A new systematic approach based on the clinical and biochemical characteristics of this condition. *Journal of perinatal medicine*, 1974, **2**:147–160.

37. **Miller HC, Merritt TA.** *Fetal growth in humans*. Chicago, Year Book Medical, 1979.

38. **Villar J, Belizan JM.** The timing factor in the pathophysiology of the intrauterine growth retardation syndrome. *Obstetrical and gynecological survey*, 1982, **37**:499–506.

39. **Streeter GL.** Weight, sitting height, head size, foot length and menstrual age of the human embryo. *Contributions to embryology*, 1920, **11**:134–170.

40. **Gruenwald P.** Intrauterine growth. In: Stave U, ed. *Perinatal physiology*. New York, Plenum Publishing Corporation, 1978:1–18.

41. **Tanner JM.** *Foetus into man: physical growth from conception to maturity*. Cambridge, MA, Harvard University Press, 1979:37–51.

42. **Petersen S, Larsen T, Greisen G.** Judging fetal growth from body proportions at birth. *Early human development*, 1992, **30**:139–146.

43. **Conlisk E.** *The heterogeneity of low birth weight as it relates to the black–white gap in birthweight specific neonatal mortality* [Dissertation]. Ithaca, NY, Cornell University, 1993:64–73.

44. **Caulfield LE et al.** Differences in early postnatal morbidity risk by pattern of fetal growth in Argentina. *Paediatric and perinatal epidemiology*, 1991, **5**:263–275.

45. **Villar J et al.** The differential neonatal morbidity of the intrauterine growth retardation syndrome. *American journal of obstetrics and gynecology*, 1990, **163**(1 Pt 1):151–157.

46. **Villar J et al.** Heterogeneous growth and mental development of intrauterine growth-retarded infants during the first 3 years of life. *Pediatrics*, 1984, **74**:783–791.

47. **Fancourt R et al.** Follow-up study of small-for-dates babies. *British medical journal*, 1976, **1**:1435–1437.

48. **Parkinson CE, Wallis S, Harvey DR.** School achievement and behaviour of children who are small-for-dates at birth. *Developmental medicine and child neurology*, 1981, **23**:41–50.

49. **Harvey DR et al.** Abilities of children who were small-for-gestational-age babies. *Pediatrics*, 1982, **69**:296–300.

50. **Williams S, St George IM, Silva PA.** Intrauterine growth retardation and blood pressure at age seven and eighteen. *Journal of clinical epidemiology*, 1992, **45**:1257–1263.

51. Puffer RR, Serrano CV. *Patterns of birthweights*. Washington, DC, Pan American Health Organization, 1987 (Scientific Publication No. 504).

52. Villar J, Belizan JM. The relative contribution of prematurity and fetal growth retardation to low birth weight in developing and developed societies. *American journal of obstetrics and gynecology*, 1982, **143**:793-798.

53. Kramer MS et al. The validity of gestational age estimation by menstrual dating in term, preterm, and postterm gestations. *Journal of the American Medical Association*, 1988, **260**:3306-3308.

54. Okonofua FE, Atoyebi FA. Accuracy of prediction of gestational age by ultrasound measurement of biparietal diameter in Nigerian women. *International journal of gynaecology and obstetrics*, 1989, **28**:217-219.

55. Reece EA et al. Dating through pregnancy: a measure of growing up. *Obstetrical and gynecological survey*, 1989, **44**:544-555.

56. Todros T et al. The length of pregnancy: an echographic reappraisal. *Journal of clinical ultrasound*, 1991, **19**:11-14.

57. Ewigman G et al. Effect of prenatal ultrasound screening on perinatal outcome. RADIUS Study Group. *New England journal of medicine*, 1993, **329**:821-827.

58. Newnham JP et al. Effects of frequent ultrasound during pregnancy: a randomised controlled trial. *Lancet*, 1993, **342**:887-891.

59. Bucher HC, Schmidt JG. Does routine ultrasound scanning improve outcome in pregnancy? Meta-analysis of various outcome measures. *British medical journal*, 1993, **307**:13-17.

60. LeFevre ML et al. A randomized trial of prenatal ultrasonographic screening: impact on maternal management and outcome. RADIUS Study Group. *American journal of obstetrics and gynecology*, 1993, **169**:483-489.

61. Mitchell D. Accuracy of pre- and postnatal assessment of gestational age. *Archives of disease in childhood*, 1979, **54**:896-897.

62. Shukla H et al. Postnatal overestimation of gestational age in preterm infants. *American journal of diseases of children*, 1987, **141**:1106-1107.

63. Alexander GR et al. Validity of postnatal assessment of gestational age: a comparison of the method of Ballard et al. and early ultrasonography. *American journal of obstetrics and gynecology*, 1992, **166**:891-895.

64. Capurro H et al. A simplified method for diagnosis of gestational age in the newborn infant. *Journal of pediatrics*, 1978, **93**:120-122.

65. Ballard JI, Novak KK, Driver M. A simplified score for assessment of fetal maturation of newly born infants. *Journal of pediatrics*, 1979, **95**(5 Pt 1):769-774.

66. Bhushan V, Paneth N. The reliability of head circumference measurement. *Journal of clinical epidemiology*, 1991, **44**:1027-1035.

67. Use of a simple anthropometric measurement to predict birth weight. WHO Collaborative Study of Birth Weight Surrogates. *Bulletin of the World Health Organization*, 1993, **71**:157-163.

68. Dusitsin N et al. Development and validation of a simple device to estimate birthweight and screen for low birthweight in developing countries. *American journal of public health*, 1991, **81**:1201-1205.

69. Raman L, Neela J, Balakrishna N. Comparative evaluation of calf, thigh and arm circumference in detecting low birth weight infants – Part II. *Indian pediatrics*, 1992, **29**:481-484.

70. Neela J et al. Usefulness of calf circumference as a measure for screening low birth weight infants. *Indian pediatrics*, 1991, **28**:881-884.

71. Barker DJP et al. Growth in utero and serum cholesterol concentrations in adult life. *British medical journal*, 1993, **307**:1524-1527.

72. Birkbeck JA, Billewicz WZ, Thomson AM. Foetal growth from 50 to 150 days of gestation. *Annals of human biology*, 1975, **2**:319-326.

73. Brenner WE, Edelman DA, Hendricks CH. A standard of fetal growth for the United States of America. *American journal of obstetrics and gynecology*, 1976, **126**:555-564.

74. Kaul SS, Babu A, Chopra SRK. Fetal growth from 12 to 26 weeks of gestation. *Annals of human biology*, 1986, **13**:563-570.

75. Gibson JR, McKeown T. Observations on all births (23,970) in Birmingham, 1947: VI. Birth weight, duration of gestation, and survival related to sex. *British journal of social medicine*, 1952, **6**:152-158.

76. Thomson AM, Billewicz WZ, Hytten FE. The assessment of fetal growth. *Journal of obstetrics and gynaecology of the British Commonwealth*, 1968, **75**:903-916.

77. Lubchenco LO et al. Intrauterine growth as estimated from liveborn birth-weight data at 24 to 42 weeks of gestation. *Pediatrics*, 1963, **32**:793-800.

78. Lubchenco LO, Hansman C, Boyd E. Intrauterine growth in length and head circumference as estimated from live births at gestational ages from 26 to 42 weeks. *Pediatrics,* 1966, **37**:403-408.

79. Lubchenco LO, Searls DT, Brazie JV. Neonatal mortality rate: relationship to birth weight and gestational age. *Journal of pediatrics*, 1972, **81**:814-822.

80. Lubchenco LO, Delivoria-Papadopoulos M, Searls D. Long-term follow-up studies of prematurely born infants. II. Influence of birth weight and gestational age on sequelae. *Journal of pediatrics*, 1972, **80**:509-512.

81. Gruenwald P. Growth of the human fetus. I. Normal growth and its variation. *American journal of obstetrics and gynecology*, 1966, **94**:1112-1119.

82. Usher R, McLean F. Intrauterine growth of live-born Caucasian infants at sea level: standards obtained from measurements in 7 dimensions of infants born between 25 and 44 weeks of gestation. *Journal of pediatrics*, 1969, **74**:901-910.

83. Babson SG, Behrman RE, Lessel R. Fetal growth. Liveborn birth weights for gestational age of white middle class infants. *Pediatrics*, 1970, **45**:937-943.

84. Williams RL et al. Fetal growth and perinatal viability in California. *Obstetrics and gynecology*, 1982, **59**:624-632.

85. David RJ. Population-based intrauterine growth curves from computerized birth certificates. *Southern medical journal*, 1983, **76**:1401-1406.

86. Lawrence C et al. Modelling of reference values for size at birth. *Acta paediatrica Scandinavica, Suppl.*, 1989, **350**:55-69.

87. Niklasson A et al. An update of the Swedish reference standards for weight, length and head circumference at birth for given gestational age (1977-1981). *Acta paediatrica Scandinavica*, 1991, **80**(8-9):756-762.

88. Arbuckle TE, Wilkins R, Sherman GJ. Birth weight percentiles by gestational age in Canada. *Obstetrics and gynecology*, 1993, **81**:39-48.

89. Gardosi J et al. Customised antenatal growth charts. *Lancet*, 1992, **339**: 283-287.

90. Hoffman HJ et al. Analysis of birth weight, gestational age, and fetal viability, U.S. births, 1968. *Obstetrical and gynecological survey*, 1974, **29**:651-681.

91. de Araujo AM, Salzano FM. Parental characteristics and birthweight in a Brazilian population. *Human biology*, 1975, **47**:37-43.

92. Taffel S. *Factors associated with low birthweight, United States 1976*. Washington, DC, US Government Printing Office, 1980 (DHEW Publication, No. (PHS) 80-1915; Vital Statistics Series 21, No. 37).

93. Crowell DH et al. Race, ethnicity and birth-weight: Hawaii 1983 to 1986. *Hawaii medical journal*, 1992, **51**:242-255.

94. Goldenberg RL et al. Intrauterine growth retardation: standards for diagnosis. *American journal of obstetrics and gynecology*, 1989, **161**:271-277.

5. Infants and children

5.1 Introduction

A number of reports have addressed the appropriate use and interpretation of anthropometry in infancy and childhood (*1-4*). This section is intended to update these reports and to discuss topics that they did not cover fully.

The use and interpretation of growth measurements may differ significantly according to whether they concern the individual (for clinical purposes) or an entire population (for public health purposes). The structure of this section reflects this important difference. Emphasis is placed on the assessment of physical status by measurement of height, weight, and mid-upper arm circumference. Other anthropometric measurements may be of relevance in specific clinical and research settings, particularly in developed areas, but these are not covered in detail. Greater emphasis is also given to problems of less developed areas, to children under 5 years old, to problems of undernutrition (rather than overnutrition), and to public health considerations rather than clinical applications, all of which are relevant to most of the world's children, particularly those at greatest health and nutritional risks.

The proper assessment and interpretation of physical status are of little value without appropriate action to improve the health and nutritional status of the individual child or of the population of interest. This section of the report therefore focuses on the applications and interpretation of anthropometry, although its scope does not include the detailed prescription or subsequent evaluation of intervention activities. It also addresses the growth patterns of infants fed according to current WHO recommendations and the relevance of such patterns for the development of growth curves. Increased recognition of the immediate benefits of breast-feeding for health, nutrition, and child-spacing has led to widespread efforts to promote exclusive breast-feeding from birth to 4-6 months of age; thereafter, children should continue to be breast-fed, while receiving appropriate and adequate complementary foods, up to 2 years of age or beyond (*5*).

Anthropometric indices are used as the main criteria for assessing the adequacy of diet and growth in infancy. Application of these criteria, however, has become difficult as the scientific and clinical communities have realized that growth patterns observed over the past 30-50 years, among presumably normal infants, vary according to diet (*6*). This is especially problematic when failure to understand these variations may lead to inappropriate decisions on supplementary feeding of fully breast-fed infants – a dangerous change where the new foods may be contaminated or of poor nutritional quality. The outcomes of premature weaning are an increased risk of infectious illness, the replacement of human milk by foods of inferior nutritional value, and reduced contraceptive protection for the mother. On the other hand, too long a delay in introducing complementary foods may result in wasting and stunting.

In the light of the importance of these issues, the growth of breast-fed infants living under favourable environmental conditions has been examined to determine whether it differs substantially from accepted international references for weight-for-age, height-for-age, and weight-for-height, and whether any differences are of practical significance to clinical practice and public health policy. The relative merits of references based upon current practices compared with those derived from populations following current health-related recommendations were of particular importance to these considerations.

5.1.1 *Terminology and clarification of commonly used terms*

Three commonly used anthropometric indices are derived by comparing height and weight measurements with reference curves: height-for-age, weight-for-age, and weight-for-height. Although these indices are related, each has a specific meaning in terms of the process or outcome of growth impairment. Moreover, the ranges of the deficit of physical status based on each index vary significantly across populations. In non-emergency situations, prevalence levels of low height-for-age tend to be substantially greater than those of weight-for-height, even in the Indian subcontinent where low weight-for-height is particularly prevalent (7).

Deficits in one or more of the anthropometric indices are often regarded as evidence of "malnutrition". However, it should not be assumed that such deficits are solely the result of nutrient or energy deficit (often, in turn, equated with a lack of food intake). A significant deficit in a physical measurement, indicating past or current malnutrition at the cellular level, could be due to a primary lack of food, to an increased rate of nutrient utilization (as in many infectious diseases), and/or to impaired absorption or assimilation of nutrients. The combination and interaction of these processes contribute to much of the deficit in growth or physical status observed in less developed areas. Thus, anthropometric findings alone do not define the specific processes that are leading to malnutrition: interpretation of a growth deficit depends on the indices used, on the causes of the deficit, and on the socioeconomic status of the population under study.

To some, "malnutrition" implies the severe form of wasting characterized by the clinical conditions of marasmus and kwashiorkor. However, the term also encompasses milder forms of undernutrition, characterized by a significant deficit in one or more of the anthropometric indices. The terms "malnutrition", "undernutrition", and "protein–energy malnutrition" have all been widely used to describe abnormal anthropometric findings and have an important role in advocacy, but their use should be properly qualified whenever possible. In particular, they should not be equated exclusively with hunger or inadequate dietary intake. Furthermore, abnormal anthropometric findings related to excess intake, with resulting overweight or obesity, also indicate a form of malnutrition. It would be helpful to qualify the term "malnutrition" with specific anthropometric parameters, for example by describing results as "malnutrition based on low weight-for-height".

Whenever the term "malnutrition" is used without qualification in this section, it refers to the syndrome that results from the interaction between poor diet and disease and leads to most of the anthropometric deficits observed among children in the world's less developed areas.

Table 16 summarizes the most useful terms for describing anthropometric abnormalities.

Table 16
Common terms for height- and weight-based anthropometric indicators

Anthropometric indicator	Terms describing outcomes	Terms describing process	Explanation
Low height-for-age	Shortness	–	Descriptive
	Stunted	Stunting (gaining insufficient height relative to age)	Implies long-term malnutrition and poor health
Low weight-for-height	Thinness	–	Descriptive
	Wasted	Wasting (gaining insufficient weight relative to height, or losing weight)	Implies recent or continuing current severe weight loss
High weight-for-height or high body mass index	Heaviness	–	Descriptive
	Overweight	Gaining excess weight relative to height, or gaining insufficient height relative to weight	Implies obesity
Low weight-for-age	Lightness	–	Descriptive
	Underweight	Gaining insufficient weight relative to age, or losing weight	Implies stunting and/or wasting
High weight-for-age	Heaviness	–	Descriptive
	Overweight	Gaining excess weight relative to age	Implies overweight as a result of obesity

Height-for-age

Height-for-age reflects achieved linear growth and its deficits indicate long-term, cumulative inadequacies of health or nutrition. Two related terms – length and stature – are also used. Length refers to the measurement in a recumbent position, and is often used for children under 2–3 years of age who cannot stand well. Standing height measurement is often referred to as stature. For simplification, the term height is used here to cover both measurements.

Low height-for-age: shortness and stunting. "Shortness" is the descriptive definition of low height-for-age. It implies nothing about the reason for an individual's being short, and can reflect either normal variation or a pathological process. "Stunting" is another commonly used term but one that implies that shortness is pathological; it reflects a process of failure to reach linear growth potential as a result of suboptimal health and/or nutritional conditions.

In less developed areas, where the prevalence of low height-for-age is substantial, it may be safely assumed that most short children are stunted; it is therefore appropriate to use the term stunting to represent low height-for-age. However, where the prevalence of low height-for-age is low (that is, near the expected level), most children with low height-for-age are genetically short, and it is then inappropriate to assume that short children are stunted.

The worldwide variation of prevalence of low height-for-age (below –2 SD of the NCHS/WHO reference) is considerable, ranging from 5 to 65% among the less developed countries (7). In many such settings, prevalence starts to rise at the age of about 3 months; the process of stunting slows down at around 3 years of age, after which mean heights run parallel to the reference.

In areas of high prevalence, therefore, the age of the child modifies the interpretation of height-for-age. For younger children (under 2–3 years), low height-for-age probably reflects a continuing process of "failing to grow" or "stunting"; for older children, it reflects a state of "having failed to grow" or "being stunted" (4).

Because height deficits result from a long-term process, the term "chronic malnutrition" is often used to describe low height-for-age and seems to imply that poor nutrition or inadequate food consumption is the cause of the observed deficit. It fails to differentiate between a deficit associated with a past event and one associated with a long-term, continuing process, yet this differentiation has major implications for intervention. For these reasons, general use of "chronic malnutrition" as a synonym for low height-for-age should be discouraged.

High height-for-age: tallness. High height-for-age, or tallness, is an indicator with little public health significance and is not discussed in this report. It may, however, be of clinical concern, especially in developed areas, since rare endocrine disorders such as growth-hormone-producing tumours may be manifest as excessive linear growth.

Weight-for-height

Weight-for-height reflects body weight relative to height. Its use carries the advantage of requiring no knowledge of age (which may be difficult to assess in less developed areas). However, it is important to note that weight-for-height does not serve as a substitute for height-for-age or weight-for-age, since each index reflects a different combination of biological processes: although they may share common determinants, they cannot be used interchangeably.

Low weight-for-height: thinness and wasting. The proper description of low weight-for-height is "thinness", a term that does not necessary imply a pathological process. The term "wasting", on the other hand, is widely used to describe a recent and severe process that has led to significant weight loss, usually as a consequence of acute starvation and/or severe disease. Children may also be thin as a result of a chronic dietary deficit or disease; for those in whom thinness is known to be due to one of these pathological processes, use of the term wasting is appropriate. The term can also be applied to populations in which the prevalence of thinness substantially exceeds the 2–3% expected on the basis of normal distribution; in such populations, it is probable that most thin children will be wasted.

In contrast to low height-for-age, low weight-for-height in non-disaster areas is of relatively constant prevalence, usually less than 5% (7) (see Table 17). The Indian subcontinent, where higher prevalences are found, is an important exception. Typically, the prevalence of low weight-for-height shows a peak in the second year of life.

The terms "acute malnutrition", "current malnutrition", and "severe malnutrition" – like chronic malnutrition – are often wrongly used as synonyms for wasting or low weight-for-height. Lack of evidence of wasting in a population does not imply the absence of current nutritional problems: stunting and other deficits may be present (8). On the other hand, low weight-for-height may not always be of recent onset; it may be the result of a chronic condition in some communities.

High weight-for-height: overweight and obesity. "Overweight" is the preferred term for describing high weight-for-height. Even though there is a strong correlation between high weight-for-height and obesity as measured by adiposity, greater lean body mass can also contribute to high weight-for-height. On an individual basis, therefore, "fatness" or "obesity" should not be used to describe high weight-for-height. However, on a population-wide basis, high weight-for-height can be considered as an adequate indicator of obesity, because the majority of individuals with high weight-for-height are obese. Strictly speaking, the term obesity should be used only in the context of adiposity measurements, for example skinfold thickness.

Table 17
Height-for-age, weight-for-height, and weight-for-age Z-scores

Country	Year	Age (years)	% below -2 Z-scores	Mean Z-score	SD
Height-for-age Z-scores					
Armenia	1993	0.5-5	6.2	-0.41	1.17
Bolivia	1982	0.5-5	40.5	-1.66	1.31
	1989	0.5-3	29.1	-1.43	1.36
Brazil	1986	0.5-3	24.7	-1.32	1.32
Burundi	1987	0.5-3	40.9	-1.75	1.34
Colombia	1986	0.5-3	21.0	-1.19	1.19
Dominican Republic	1986	0.5-3	16.5	-1.02	1.31
Egypt	1980	0.5-5	36.2	-1.62	1.14
	1988	0.5-3	24.1	-1.20	1.34
El Salvador	1988	0.5-5	32.9	-1.51	1.15
	1993	0.5-5	24.3	-1.24	1.17
Ghana	1988	0.5-3	24.8	-1.31	1.28
Guatemala	1987	0.5-3	56.7	-2.15	1.31
Iraq	1992	0.5-5	24.6	-1.23	1.22
Jordan	1974	0.5-3	25.6	-1.23	1.21
	1978	0.5-3	23.3	-1.23	1.16
	1984	0.5-3	16.7	-0.91	1.20
	1990	0.5-3	7.2	-0.61	1.05
Lebanon	1978	0.5-3	21.1	-0.88	1.39
	1990	0.5-3	6.9	-0.48	1.15
Morocco	1987	0.5-3	21.5	-1.24	1.36
Nepal	1975	0.5-5	69.0	-2.60	1.26
Nigeria (Ondo)	1987	0.5-3	30.9	-1.46	1.28
Occupied Palestinian Territories (Gaza)	1974	0.5-3	19.3	-1.10	1.13
	1978	0.5-3	21.1	-1.13	1.21
	1984	0.5-3	20.4	-0.99	1.28
	1990	0.5-3	7.6	-0.49	1.11
Occupied Palestinian Territories (West Bank)	1978	0.5-3	25.0	-1.23	1.23
	1984	0.5-3	15.5	-0.94	1.11
	1990	0.5-3	6.3	-0.42	1.15
Romania	1991	0-2	7.3	-0.29	1.16
	1991	2-5	8.5	-0.44	1.23
Senegal	1986	0.5-3	22.5	-1.20	1.18
Sri Lanka	1978	0.5-5	57.4	-2.26	1.18
	1987	0.5-3	26.3	-1.38	1.15

Table 17 (*continued*)

Country	Year	Age (years)	% below -2 Z-scores	Mean Z-score	SD
Height-for-age Z-scores (*continued*)					
Syria	1978	0.5–3	20.3	-1.12	1.13
	1990	0.5–3	15.7	-0.97	1.14
Thailand	1987	0.5–3	18.0	-1.07	1.08
Togo	1977	0.5–5	33.5	-1.53	1.22
	1988	0.5–3	24.3	-1.31	1.29
Trinidad and Tobago	1987	0.5–3	4.6	-0.28	1.09
Uganda	1989	0.5–3	38.4	-1.73	1.37
USA (American Indian)	1989	2–5	4.8	-0.13	1.11
USA (Asian refugee)	1980	2–5	18.4	-0.94	1.18
	1984	2–5	12.2	-0.72	1.14
	1989	2–5	7.7	-0.32	1.18
USA (black)	1989	2–5	3.3	-0.10	1.12
USA (Hispanic)	1989	2–5	3.3	-0.14	1.17
USA (white)	1989	2–5	5.1	-0.23	1.09
Yemen	1979	0.5–5	57.6	-2.21	1.24
Zimbabwe	1989	0.5–3	27.2	-1.39	1.18
Weight-for-height Z-scores					
Armenia	1993	0.5–5	1.0	0.20	0.91
Bolivia	1982	0.5–5	0.8	0.36	0.88
	1989	0.5–3	1.4	0.21	1.04
Brazil	1986	0.5–3	1.5	0.17	0.94
Burundi	1987	0.5–3	6.5	-0.49	1.02
Colombia	1986	0.5–3	1.6	0.17	1.03
Dominican Republic	1986	0.5–3	2.5	-0.04	0.97
Egypt	1980	0.5–5	4.1	-0.32	0.97
	1988	0.5–3	1.5	0.17	0.98
El Salvador	1988	0.5–5	2.2	-0.13	1.01
	1993	0.5–5	1.3	-0.09	0.91
Ghana	1988	0.5–3	10.2	-0.72	0.95
Guatemala	1987	0.5–3	2.4	-0.01	0.93
Haiti	1978	0.5–5	9.1	-0.74	0.98

Table 17 (*continued*)

Country	Year	Age (years)	% below -2 Z-scores	Mean Z-score	SD
Weight-for-height Z-scores (*continued*)					
Iraq	1992	0.5-5	2.8	-0.32	0.97
Iraq (Kurds)[a]	1991	0-2	8.9	-0.80	0.96
		2-6	1.5	-0.11	0.89
Jordan	1974	0.5-3	6.3	-0.47	1.04
	1984	0.5-3	1.7	0.09	1.09
Lebanon	1978	0.5-3	4.7	-0.27	1.07
	1990	0.5-3	4.2	-0.32	0.97
Morocco	1987	0.5-3	2.6	-0.02	1.02
Nepal	1975	0.5-5	13.2	-1.09	0.84
Nigeria (Ondo)	1987	0.5-3	7.2	-0.55	0.94
Occupied Palestinian Territories (Gaza)	1974	0.5-3	5.0	-0.44	0.97
	1978	0.5-3	2.4	-0.03	0.99
	1984	0.5-3	2.0	0.20	1.09
	1990	0.5-3	1.8	-0.01	0.94
Occupied Palestinian Territories (West Bank)	1978	0.5-3	3.9	-0.12	1.08
	1984	0.5-3	1.6	-0.02	0.92
Romania	1991	0-2	2.8	-0.13	1.01
	1991	2-5	2.3	-0.17	0.93
Senegal	1986	0.5-3	6.2	-0.47	1.07
Somalia[a]	1993	0.5-6	37.1	-1.74	1.17
Sri Lanka	1978	0.5-5	21.5	-1.38	0.80
	1987	0.5-3	15.5	-0.98	0.89
Sudan (southern)[a]	1993	0.5-6	71.9	-2.58	1.11
Syria	1978	0.5-3	1.9	-0.33	0.85
	1990	0.5-3	4.4	-0.39	0.97
Thailand	1987	0.5-3	6.4	-0.56	0.98
Togo	1977	0.5-5	4.5	-0.52	0.90
	1988	0.5-3	3.9	-0.27	1.11
Trinidad and Tobago	1987	0.5-3	4.0	-0.25	1.13
Uganda	1989	0.5-3	2.0	0.06	0.96
USA (American Indian)	1989	2-5	0.8	0.47	1.00
USA (Asian refugee)	1980	2-5	3.6	-0.17	1.00
	1984	2-5	3.1	-0.15	1.04
	1989	2-5	2.7	-0.04	1.01

[a] Survey conducted during emergency or under disaster conditions.

Table 17 (*continued*)

Country	Year	Age (years)	% below −2 Z-scores	Mean Z-score	SD
Weight-for-height Z-scores (*continued*)					
USA (black)	1989	2–5	2.1	0.07	1.03
USA (Hispanic)	1989	2–5	1.2	0.29	1.07
USA (white)	1989	2–5	1.8	0.11	0.96
Yemen	1979	0.5–5	11.3	−0.95	0.88
Zimbabwe	1989	0.5–3	1.4	0.19	1.03
Weight-for-age Z-scores					
Armenia	1993	0.5–5	4.7	−0.34	1.04
Bolivia	1982	0.5–5	12.4	−0.84	1.07
	1989	0.5–3	11.4	−0.73	1.20
Brazil	1986	0.5–3	10.2	−0.71	1.17
Burundi	1987	0.5–3	32.5	−1.53	1.21
Colombia	1986	0.5–3	8.7	−0.62	1.15
Dominican Republic	1986	0.5–3	9.5	−0.66	1.15
Egypt	1980	0.5–5	23.6	−1.27	1.15
	1988	0.5–3	11.6	−0.72	1.18
El Salvador	1988	0.5–5	16.8	−1.04	1.01
	1993	0.5–5	11.5	−0.86	1.01
Ghana	1988	0.5–3	25.2	−1.36	1.17
Guatemala	1987	0.5–3	30.4	−1.44	1.17
Haiti	1978	0.5–5	37.5	−1.60	1.19
Iraq	1992	0.5–5	13.3	−0.82	1.16
Jordan	1974	0.5–3	20.3	−1.17	1.08
	1978	0.5–3	17.2	−1.03	1.00
	1984	0.5–3	6.5	−0.54	1.02
	1990	0.5–3	5.2	−0.55	0.97
Lebanon	1978	0.5–3	15.7	−0.78	1.19
	1990	0.5–3	7.9	−0.61	1.04
Morocco	1987	0.5–3	12.3	−0.79	1.23
Nepal	1975	0.5–5	69.4	−2.39	0.93
Nigeria (Ondo)	1987	0.5–3	26.9	−1.34	1.10
Occupied Palestinian Territories (Gaza)	1974	0.5–3	18.2	−1.06	1.07
	1978	0.5–3	1.1	−0.75	1.08
	1984	0.5–3	6.0	−0.49	0.99

Table 17 (*continued*)

Country	Year	Age (years)	% below −2 Z-scores	Mean Z-score	SD
Weight-for-age Z-scores (*continued*)					
Occupied Palestinian	1978	0.5–3	14.9	−0.93	1.08
Territories (West Bank)	1984	0.5–3	7.5	−0.63	0.98
Romania	1991	0–2	4.9	−0.25	1.08
	1991	2–5	6.2	−0.49	1.04
Senegal	1986	0.5–3	18.1	−1.10	1.10
Sri Lanka	1978	0.5–5	78.3	−2.38	0.91
	1987	0.5–3	38.3	−1.65	1.03
Syria	1978	0.5–3	12.8	−0.97	0.95
Thailand	1987	0.5–3	19.0	−1.13	1.11
Togo	1977	0.5–5	26.2	−1.36	1.04
	1988	0.5–3	16.2	−1.01	1.37
Trinidad and Tobago	1987	0.5–3	6.6	−0.43	1.22
Uganda	1989	0.5–3	17.7	−1.06	1.21
USA (American Indian)	1989	2–5	1.5	0.20	1.18
USA (Asian refugee)	1980	2–5	12.3	−0.77	1.20
	1984	2–5	8.4	−0.61	1.24
	1989	2–5	4.7	−0.31	1.21
USA (black)	1989	2–5	3.3	0.10	1.12
USA (Hispanic)	1989	2–5	1.8	0.09	1.26
USA (white)	1989	2–5	5.1	−0.23	1.09
Yemen	1979	0.5–5	56.1	−2.09	0.96
Zimbabwe	1989	0.5–3	10.4	−0.72	1.12

Weight-for-age

Weight-for-age reflects body mass relative to chronological age. It is influenced by both the height of the child (height-for-age) and his or her weight (weight-for-height), and its composite nature makes interpretation complex. However, in the absence of significant wasting in a community, similar information is provided by weight-for-age and height-for-age, in that both reflect the long-term health and nutritional experience of the individual or population. Short-term change, especially reduction in weight-for-age, reveals change in weight-for-height.

Low weight-for-age. "Lightness" has been proposed as a descriptive term for low weight-for-age, while "underweight" has been used to refer to the underlying pathological process. Although there is some inconsistency with the use of overweight (which refers to excessive weight-for-height), the term underweight has been widely used to describe the condition in high-prevalence areas, just as stunting and wasting are employed in the context of low height-for-age and low weight-for-height.

Because low weight-for-age reflects low height-for-age, low weight-for-height, or both, the term "global malnutrition" has been used to describe this indicator, which may encompass "chronic malnutrition" and/or "acute malnutrition". For the reasons discussed above, this term should be avoided.

The worldwide variation of low weight-for-age and its age distribution are similar to those of low height-for-age (7).

High weight-for-age. High weight-for-age is seldom used for public health purposes because other indicators, such as high weight-for-height, are more useful in the evaluation of overweight as a proxy for obesity. The proper descriptive term for high weight-for-age would be "heaviness" (for consistency with lightness for low weight-for-age). Because few children have high weight-for-age as a result of tallness, for practical purposes high weight-for-age reflects high weight-for-height or overweight.

Other anthropometric indices

Some of the large number of available anthropometric indices are described below, although few have achieved such widespread use as the height- and weight-based measurements already discussed.

Mid-upper arm circumference. Mid-upper arm circumference (MUAC) has been proposed as an alternative index of nutritional status for use where the collection of height and weight measurements is difficult, including emergency situations such as famines or refugee crises. In these situations, low MUAC, based on a fixed cut-off point such as 12.5 cm, has been used as a proxy for low weight-for-height or wasting. Comparisons of the two indicators, however, show that they are poorly correlated (9, 10). In community-based studies, on the other hand, MUAC appears to be a superior predictor of childhood mortality compared with height- and weight-based anthropometric indicators (11-14). This has led to the proposal of MUAC as an additional screening tool in non-emergency situations.

The key operational advantages of MUAC include the portability of measuring tapes and the fact that a single cut-off value (12.5 or 13.0 cm) can be used for children under 5 years of age. The use of a fixed cut-off value was based on the observation in normal, well fed Polish children that MUAC increased by only about 1 cm between the ages of 1 and 4 years (15, 16). However, this assumption of age independence may not reflect the true pattern of mid-upper arm growth, and the use of a fixed cut-off may result in wasting being overdiagnosed among younger children and underdiagnosed among older ones (17).

Mean MUAC values across ages for the NCHS sample of children in the USA and for a cohort of Malawian children are shown in Fig. 21. Both populations show a definite age-dependent increase of approximately 2 cm in MUAC between the ages of 6 and 59 months. When a unisex MUAC-for-age reference was constructed from the NCHS data (see Annex 3) and applied to the Malawian children, important differences were observed between the age-specific prevalences of low MUAC-for-age Z-scores and of low MUAC based on a cut-off of 13.0 cm (Fig. 22). A fixed MUAC cut-off therefore resulted in a large proportion of young children being identified as positive cases, which explains the apparently poor correlation of low MUAC with low weight-for-height. Since mortality among infants and younger children, regardless of their anthropometric status, is higher that than among older children, low MUAC based on a fixed cut-off seems to have been an excellent predictor of childhood mortality in many studies (*11-14*).

A one-year follow-up of the Malawian children provided an opportunity to examine the predictive value of MUAC for mortality, with and without taking age into account. Table 18 compares the sensitivity, specificity, and positive predictive value of eight indicators divided into two groups: those using absolute cut-offs (MUAC, weight, height, and age) and those that are age-adjusted (MUAC-for-age, height-for-age, weight-for-height, and weight-for-age). To ensure comparability, the cut-offs were chosen to correspond to the 20th percentile for the distribution of each index, so that 20% of the children would be screen positives. It is evident that the

Figure 21
Mean mid-upper arm circumference for children in the USA (NCHS) and in Malawi, aged 6–59 months

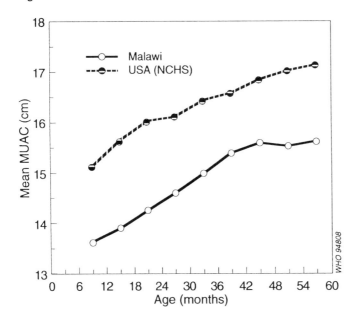

Figure 22

Age-specific prevalences of low MUAC in Malawian children aged 6–59 months, according to two different cut-offs

Prevalence of absolute MUAC below 13.0 cm

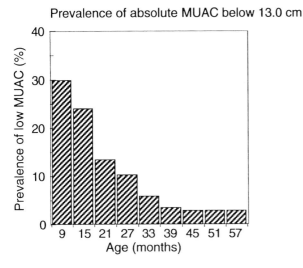

Prevalence of MUAC-for-age below −2 Z-scores of the NCHS/WHO reference

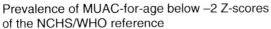
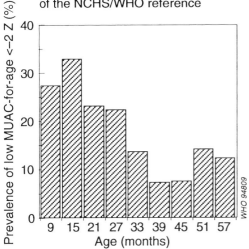

WHO 94809

superior performance of MUAC declined significantly after adjustment for age (low MUAC-for-age). In fact, the MUAC performance in predicting mortality is comparable to that of age, height, or weight based on fixed cut-offs (Table 18). The recommended reference data (see Annex 3) include the MUAC-for-age reference based on children in the USA aged 6 to 60 months from the samples collected for the first and second National Health and Nutrition Examination Surveys (NHANES I and II).

Table 18

Comparison of the performance of age and of various anthropometric indicators in predicting one-year mortality among a cohort of Malawian children aged 6–59 months

	Sensitivity (%)	Specificity[a] (%)	Positive predictive value (%)
Fixed cut-offs			
Age <14.2 months	41.5	81.1	6.0
MUAC <13.5 cm	37.0	80.1	5.1
Height <72.6 cm	45.7	80.8	5.9
Weight <8.3 kg	43.9	81.3	6.4
Age-adjusted cut-offs (Z-scores)			
MUAC-for-age <-1.97	30.9	80.6	4.4
Height-for-age <-3.28	28.4	80.2	3.5
Weight-for-age <-2.49	27.2	80.5	3.9
Weight-for-height <-1.19	27.1	80.6	3.6

[a] All cut-off points were chosen to select approximately 20% of the children as screen positives.

Although MUAC is confounded by age when a fixed cut-off is used, it is still of value for certain applications. For example, it seems to perform nearly as well as height-, weight-, and age-based measurements and may be easier to determine in many situations. In many settings, too, it is desirable to give priority to younger children who are more vulnerable to morbidity and mortality. However, for proper interpretation of MUAC with regard to nutritional status or to its etiological relationship to functional outcomes, the application of an MUAC-for-age reference is indicated, because of the significant increase of MUAC up to the age of 5 years.

Current evidence from Bangladesh (Bloom M, personal communication) suggests that MUAC-for-age provides comparable information to weight-for-height in the context of nutritional surveillance of populations. The usefulness of MUAC-for-age underlines the need to evaluate properly the less commonly used index of MUAC-for-height, including the use of the QUAC stick (*18*), which is a simple means of adjusting MUAC cut-offs according to height; MUAC-for-height might prove to be an adequate proxy for MUAC-for-age.

Using MUAC-for-age reference data in the field is no more complicated than using a weight-for-height reference, which is commonly done during rapid nutrition surveys. Moreover, the equipment required to measure MUAC is much simpler than that for measuring weight and height. One disadvantage of using MUAC-for-age in the field, however, is the need to determine age, which is often difficult. Another limitation worth noting is the relatively large variability in MUAC measurements, especially when they are made by inexperienced field workers; an error of 0.5 cm is small in terms of height measurements but has much greater significance for MUAC. For this reason, more time and effort are needed for proper staff training and standardization of MUAC. The height-based QUAC stick, however, is much easier to use than an anthropometer because it does not require reading of a measurement.

Body mass index. Body mass index (BMI) is calculated by dividing weight in kilograms by the square of height in metres. In adults it is used with age-independent cut-offs to define overweight or thinness (see sections 7 and 8). It has also been used for older children and adolescents, but not widely used for young children because of its variation with age. Thus, in addition to the calculation or use of a table or nomogram required to obtain the BMI value, it is also necessary to refer to a BMI-for-age curve to interpret the calculated value. Furthermore, there is no widely-used paediatric BMI reference, nor does the development of one seem useful at this stage.

Skinfolds. Skinfold measurements assess the thickness of subcutaneous tissue and are widely used for assessing obesity among adults. Used alone, however, they are of limited value for assessing the degree of wasting because they fail to take into account changes in muscle mass. In addition, high intra- and inter-individual variation, the cost of equipment, and the lack of widely acceptable reference data preclude their application for children for the diagnosis of either over- or under-nutrition, unless highly skilled individuals are available to perform the measurements.

Head circumference. Head circumference (occipital–frontal circum-ference) is often used in clinical settings as part of health screening for potential developmental or neurological disabilities in children. Both small and large circumferences are indicative of health or developmental risk. The measurement is of less value for assessing nutritional status or for monitoring the response to nutritional interventions, except in infants (*19*).

Proxies for length. There are methodological and practical limitations to obtaining accurate measurements of infant length, particularly in environments where equipment and personnel are inadequate for undertaking measurements as currently standardized. Potential proxies include leg (or fibular) and arm (or ulnar) length, as well as head circumference. If these proxies are valid indicators of length throughout infancy and can be shown to be easier to measure accurately, they would permit indirect assessments of stunting without cumbersome measurements of total length. This issue merits further research.

5.1.2 *Expression and interpretation of anthropometry*

Evaluation of the anthropometric status of an individual or of a population requires the use of growth standards or references. As mentioned above, WHO has recommended the use of height and weight reference data for populations studied by the US National Center for Health Statistics – the NCHS/WHO reference (2). For the reporting of height-for-age, weight-for-height, weight-for-age, and MUAC-for-age relative to the reference, three different systems are commonly used: Z-scores (standard deviation scores), percentiles, and percent of median values. These are discussed in section 2 and summarized below.

The Z-score or standard deviation value system
The Z-score system expresses the anthropometric value as a number of standard deviations or Z-scores below or above the reference mean or median value. A fixed Z-score interval implies a fixed height or weight difference for children of a given age. For population-based uses, a major advantage is that a group of Z-scores can be subjected to summary statistics such as the mean and standard deviation.

The percentile system
The percentile refers to the position of an individual on a given reference distribution. Percentiles are commonly used in clinical settings because their interpretation is straightforward. However, the same interval of percentile values corresponds to different changes in absolute height or weight, according to which part of the distribution is concerned. Statistical calculations, such as the mean and standard deviations, are thus inappropriate for percentile values. Moreover, the lack of change in percentile values near the extremes of the reference distribution, when in reality there is a substantial change in weight or height status, represents a further disadvantage of this system.

The percent of median system
Anthropometric measurements can also be expressed as a percentage of the median value of the expected reference. The principal disadvantage of this system is a lack of exact correspondence with a fixed point of the distribution across age or height status. For example, depending on the child's age, 80% of the median weight-for-age might be above or below –2 Z-scores, and could therefore be taken to indicate different risks in terms of health. Also, the proposed cut-offs for percent of median are different for each of the three common indices. For example, to approximate a cut-off of –2 Z-scores, the commonly used cut-off for low height-for-age is 90% of the median, while for low weight-for-height it is 80%.

The key features of the three reporting systems for height-, weight-, and MUAC-based indices (20) have already been summarized in Table 1. Of the three systems commonly used for expressing anthropometry, the Z-score system is to be preferred. This is consistent with an earlier recommendation of a WHO working group (3).

5.1.3 *Biological and social significance of anthropometry*

Malnutrition is often portrayed as part of a vicious cycle that also includes poverty and disease, the three components being interrelated and each contributing to the occurrence and persistence of the others. Anthropometric deficits may therefore act through the other two components of the cycle and lead to further malnutrition. Socioeconomic and political changes that improve health and nutrition conditions can break the cycle, as can specific interventions in the areas of nutrition, health, and related sectors. A detailed review is beyond the scope of this report, but the proper interpretation of anthropometry requires a general understanding of these issues.

Biological and social determinants of anthropometry

In environments where there are no adverse influences on growth, small differences in the growth patterns of children of different ethnic groups result in a worldwide height variability of about 1 cm in 5-year-old children (*21*). By far the greatest part of worldwide variation can be attributed to differences in socioeconomic status: a review of data on preschool children from several countries revealed differences of up to 12% in height and 30% in weight according to socioeconomic class (*22*).

Of the major determinants of, or events leading to, malnutrition, some are more distant (or distal) and some are more immediate (or proximal) to the outcome. The proximal factors are inadequate dietary intake and disease. The distal factors are socioeconomic in nature and do not influence anthropometric status directly, but do so through intermediate and proximal determinants via a number of causal pathways. For example, poverty can lead to low levels of parental education, poor water supply and sanitation, scarce resources for buying food, poor food availability, and inadequate health care, all of which contribute to a greater risk for disease and poor energy and nutrient intake. Cultural factors, influenced by social and economic background, also play an important role in the etiology of poor growth. Examples include the duration of breast-feeding, hygiene practices that lead to food contamination, and child-care practices, including food taboos. These intermediate-level determinants will lead to the most important proximal determinants of poor growth, namely inadequate dietary intake and infectious diseases.

In general, the causes of a high prevalence of wasting, including acute food shortage, increased rates of diarrhoea, or economic crises, are obvious. The causes of elevated prevalences of stunting, other than the general socioeconomic status of the population, are less easily identified.

Energy and nutrient intake. It is widely accepted that much of the global childhood stunting and wasting is the result of deficiencies in energy and protein intake, hence the term "protein–energy malnutrition", commonly used to describe growth deficits. Dietary intake includes the consumption of energy, macronutrients, and micronutrients, and its impact on linear growth, ponderal growth, and attained height and weight of children has been demonstrated in supplementation trials (*23*). Because the food provided in these trials contained energy, macronutrients, and micronutrients, it is not possible to separate the effects of energy on anthropometry from those of specific nutrients. The major role of inadequate energy intake in the anthropometric deficits observed in less developed areas is well known, but there is increasing evidence that deficiencies of micronutrients such as vitamin A, iron, and zinc may also play a significant role (*24-26*).

Infectious disease. The role of infectious diseases in determining growth has been studied extensively in recent years. Infections may adversely affect growth by reducing appetite and thus food intake, decreasing nutrient absorption, increasing metabolic requirements, or causing direct nutrient loss (*23*). Of all infectious diseases, diarrhoea has the most marked effect on anthropometric status, and several longitudinal studies in different parts of the world have reported its negative impact on child growth (*27*). Food supplementation may offset the negative impact of diarrhoea on attained height (*28*). At the population level, the relative effects of diarrhoea on anthropometric status are greater at higher baseline prevalences (*23*). Although upper respiratory infections do not seem to affect growth, pneumonia and other lower respiratory tract infections have a deleterious effect (*29*). Measles and malaria have been associated with poor growth in the Gambia (*30*), and anthelminthic treatment of intestinal parasites has been shown to improve child growth.

Biological and social consequences of abnormal anthropometry

Abnormal anthropometry, including deficits in weight and height gain as well as excess weight gain, has significant short- and long-term health consequences. The framework for examining the consequences of abnormal anthropometry is outlined in the following paragraphs.

Short- and long-term consequences. To a large extent, the time-span studied depends on the indicator being considered. For acute anthropometric deficits such as wasting due to diarrhoea, the very short-term consequences, including mortality, may occur within days. Using childhood obesity as an example, the most immediate prediction is that of risk of obesity during adolescence and, later, in adulthood. The next level of prediction is the risk of hypertension, diabetes, and hypercholesterolaemia. The third level is the risk of developing ischaemic heart disease, and the final level the risk of mortality. This chain of events must be taken into account when studying the predictive value of abnormal anthropometry.

Age. The prevalence of anthropometric deficits changes with age. Low weight-for-height, for example, peaks in the second year of life, while low height-for-age may start very early, at around 3 months of age, with prevalence decreasing at around 3 years. The same anthropometric indicator, therefore, has different meanings or different predictive values at different ages. A high prevalence of low height-for-age among 1-year-olds indicates current health and nutrition problems in the population (stunting). Among 5-year-olds, it reflects a past problem in the children already affected (stunted), but may also indicate that there is active, concurrent stunting among younger children in the population.

Low weight-for-age among young children is more likely to reflect the prevalence of low weight-for-height, but at later ages it is more closely associated with the prevalence of low height-for-age.

Nature of the outcome. The major outcomes of malnutrition may be classified in terms of morbidity (incidence and severity), mortality, psychological and intellectual development, and consequences in adult life (adult size, work and reproductive performances, and risk of chronic diseases).

- *Childhood morbidity.* Several authors have examined the association between anthropometry and morbidity. While there is some debate about whether malnutrition leads to a higher incidence of diarrhoea, there is little doubt that malnourished children tend to have more severe diarrhoeal episodes in terms of duration, risk of dehydration or hospital admission, and associated growth faltering (27-29, 31). The risk of pneumonia is also increased in these children (32).

- *Childhood mortality.* A number of studies carried out during both emergency and non-emergency situations have demonstrated the link between increased mortality and increasing severity of anthropometric deficits (33, 34). Data from six longitudinal studies on the correlation between anthropometric status and mortality of children aged 6–59 months have been recently subjected to a meta-analysis (35), which revealed a strong log-linear or exponential association between the severity of weight-for-age deficits and mortality rates in all studies with adequate sample size and appreciable baseline mortality. The excellent fit of the log-linear model suggests that there is no clear threshold on the weight-for-age scale for increased mortality (see Fig. 23).

Since mild to moderate deficits are by far the most common, the actual proportion of deaths (population attributable risk) due to such deficits is greater than that due to severe deficits (35), even though the relative risk is greater in individuals with severe deficits.

At the conventional cut-off level, weight-for-age had the highest predictive ability, followed by height-for-age; weight-for-height was the weakest predictor of long-term mortality. It should be noted, however, that the predictive capacities for death were low for all anthropometric indicators (34).

This analysis also revealed a synergism, with the effect of malnutrition being greatest in populations with high morbidity and mortality, and vice versa. The correlation between anthropometry and

Figure 23

Log of mortality per 1000 children per year, by weight-for-age status, based on six different studies[a]

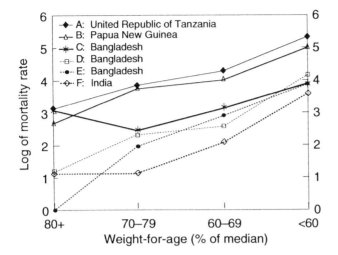

[a] Reproduced from reference *35* with the permission of the publisher. Copyright American Public Health Association.

mortality is therefore expected to vary according to the death rate among well nourished individuals in each population, since malnutrition does not increase the incidence of disease as much as it increases the case-fatality rate.

- *Child development and school performance.* There is good evidence that poor growth or smaller size is associated with impaired development (*36*), and a number of studies have also demonstrated a relationship between growth status and either school performance or intelligence (*37*). This cannot be regarded as a simple causal relationship, however, because of the complex environmental or socio-economic factors that affect both growth and development. An intervention study in Jamaica indicated that the developmental status of underweight children can be partly improved by food supplementation, but that greater improvements are achieved through intellectual stimulation (*38*).

- *Adult-life consequences.* Childhood stunting leads to a significant reduction in adult size, as clearly shown by a follow-up of Guatemalan infants who, two decades earlier, had been enrolled in a supplementation programme (*39*). One of the main consequences of small adult size resulting from childhood stunting is reduced work capacity (*40*), which in turn has an impact on economic productivity at the national level.

Maternal size is associated with specific reproductive outcomes. Short women, for example, are at greater risk for obstetric complications because of smaller pelvic size. There is also a strong association between maternal height and birth weight which is independent of maternal body mass (*41*). There is thus an inter-generation effect (*42*), since low-birth-weight babies are likely to have anthropometric deficits at later ages (*43*).

Limited evidence has also been produced to link overweight in childhood to adult morbidity and mortality (*44-46*).

5.1.4 *Issues in using anthropometric measurements as indicators of nutritional and health status*

Anthropometric measurements have been used widely as indicators or proxies for various conditions related to health and nutrition. On an individual basis, abnormal anthropometry itself does not generally provide specific etiological information. For example, a child may be "abnormally" short as a result of infection, inadequate food intake, or psychosocial deprivation, or because of endocrine, metabolic, or other diseases. In areas with a high prevalence of low height-for-age, however, it is reasonable to classify most short children as stunted or malnourished. In such settings, reduction in stature is probably a generalized phenomenon, not restricted to children who fall below the cut-off for low height-for-age (*47*). In other words, the height distribution of the entire population is shifted downward. Strictly speaking, therefore, a diagnosis of growth failure should not be restricted to children below the cut-off but should be applied to almost all children. Evidence for population-based changes of anthropometric status is provided in sections 5.4.5 and 5.4.6.

The need for index-specific interpretation

On a population basis, both the prevalence of abnormal anthropometry and the mean Z-score serve as useful indicators of the health and nutrition problems of the community. A high prevalence of low height-for-age indicates poor nutrition, high morbidity from infectious disease, or – most often – both. A high prevalence of low weight-for-height is indicative of severe recent or current events, for example starvation or outbreaks of infectious diseases such as diarrhoea or measles. Such "diagnostic" information provides the basis for assessing the nature and severity of the problem, which can be helpful for planning appropriate action. Each anthropometric indicator thus has a different meaning, and indicators should not be used interchangeably.

Defining abnormal anthropometry

In general, abnormal anthropometry is statistically defined as an anthropometric value below –2 standard deviations (SD) or Z-scores (< 2.3rd percentile), or above +2 SD or Z-scores (>97.7th percentile) relative to the reference mean or median. These cut-offs define the central 95% of the reference distribution as the "normality" range. In some cases, the 5th and 95th percentiles are used, with the central 90% as the normality range. It should be noted that the convention of using the central 90% or 95% of a given distribution to define cut-offs or reference ranges does not truly define the "normal" range from the point of view of health or nutrition; rather, it is used as a guide to facilitate clinical screening or population-based surveillance. Obviously, a child who was originally at +2 Z-scores and falls to, say, –1.5 Z-scores because of malnutrition will show wasting despite remaining above the –2 cut-off (*48*). The presence of oedema in kwashiorkor will also affect a child's body weight (*49*).

Anthropometric measurements as process and outcome indicators
In the selection and application of anthropometric indices, it is useful to distinguish between their multiple roles as indicators of health and nutrition problems. Anthropometry may be related to past exposures (reflective), to present processes (concurrent), or to future events (predictive); anthropometric indicators may also predict risk, benefit, or response. Moreover, anthropometric outcome indicators may be close to (proximal or direct) or distant from (distal or indirect) the events of interest.

The sensitivity, specificity, and predictive value of an indicator also depend on its nature, the cut-off used, the specific risk under consideration, the age of the child, and the prevalence of the condition in the population. The functional classification of anthropometric measurements as indicators of health or nutritional events is discussed in detail in section 2.

5.1.5 *Conditioning the interpretation of anthropometry*

The interpretation of abnormal anthropometry will vary according to a number of circumstances. The most important factor is the *prevalence* of the condition of interest within a given population, since the positive predictive value of the indicator is related to prevalence. This is particularly relevant because health and nutrition problems differ markedly in their prevalence in developed and less developed areas.

Age is a clear effect-modifier in the interpretation of anthropometry. For example, the predictive value for mortality of a given anthropometric indicator tends to decrease with age. Since age is a strong predictor of mortality, independent of anthropometric status, it may also confound this relationship.

In some parts of the world, *sex* is an important factor in the evaluation of anthropometric status, because boys and girls may be treated differently in matters that affect their health and nutrition. Further, as discussed in section 5.1, *feeding mode* in infancy also conditions the interpretation of anthropometry.

5.2 Using anthropometry in individuals

5.2.1 *Introduction*

The interpretation of abnormal anthropometry in an individual child varies according to the prevalence of malnutrition in the community, while the appropriate follow-up action depends on the availability of resources. Thus, although there are common principles that guide the use of anthropometry in individuals, a clear distinction should be made between developed and less developed settings.

The main applications of anthropometry to individuals are listed in Table 19. For practical purposes, most of these applications are concerned with the nutritional care of infants and screening for high-risk children, including growth monitoring, selection of children for supplementary and therapeutic feeding, and diagnosis of failure to thrive and of overweight. Children who are selected for intervention may require further evaluation to determine the causes of poor growth and to provide treatment when applicable. Once intervention measures have been initiated, anthropometry may also be used to assess response.

5.2.2 *Screening children for health and nutritional disorders*

Applications in less developed areas

Growth monitoring. Valuable anthropometric information can be obtained from repeated measurements of each child or from growth monitoring (row A in Table 19). Although growth charts are based on cross-sectional data, they are also useful for following the growth pattern of individuals, particularly during childhood. During infancy and adolescence, however, percentile crossing is common and does not necessarily indicate abnormal growth (*50*). Incremental growth references or growth velocity curves can also be applied when there is a need to monitor children who have already been found to have significant deficits in growth status or growth patterns that cause concern.

All the major conditions that give rise to most growth deficits in developed areas (see below) also occur in less developed areas. However, their relative contribution to the overall high prevalence of stunting or wasting is small; instead, recurrent common childhood diseases, especially diarrhoea, as well as poor intake of energy, proteins, and micronutrients, are the main contributing factors. For this reason, the overall approach to screening, follow-up, and intervention in less developed areas for children with abnormal growth patterns is very different from that applied in developed settings, even though anthropometry is still used to screen for those children at greater risk of concurrent health and nutritional disorders. Because malnutrition is common, the positive predictive value of anthropometric deficits is high. It is then reasonable to embark on specific interventions without further evaluation for other possible organic disorders or normal variability.

Table 19
Summary of recommendations for use of anthropometry in individual infants and children

1	2	3	4	5
Uses: what will be done for the individual?	For what purpose?	Target group and setting	What to measure, what information to collect, and how often	Indices

Screening for interventions

1	2	3	4	5
A Identification of infants/children with poor health and nutrition for interventions specifically tailored to causes of poor growth: • breast-feeding support • nutrition education • supplementation of infant/child and mother • prevention and treatment of diarrhoea	To prevent malnutrition. To sustain or improve: • health • growth • psychomotor development • well-being • future productivity and reproductivity	Attenders at growth-monitoring centres, including: • community weighing posts • maternal and child health clinics • primary health care clinics Communities in less developed areas	Weight Length or height (if possible) Age Sex (if sex-specific growth curves are used) At least two measurements as part of growth-monitoring and promotion programme: every 1–3 months depending on age and need	Deviations from curves of: • weight v. age Attained status in • weight-for-age • weight-for-height • height-for-age
B Identification of infants/children who need supplementary food and treatment for disease (particularly diarrhoea)	To prevent malnutrition. To improve: • survival • health • development • well-being	Attenders at: • growth-monitoring centres • maternal and child health clinics • primary health care clinics • food distribution centres • feeding centres	Weight Length or height MUAC Age One or multiple measurements	Weight-for-height MUAC-for-age (for children 1–5 years of age)

184

6	7	8	9
Demographic characteristics	Criteria for judgement (cut-offs)	Rationale for anthropometry	Other factors for interpretation
Infants and children: • commonly under 5 years of age • priority under 3 years of age	Depends on resources. Common conventions: • direction of curve (flat; downwards) • no growth ≥ twice • <-2 Z-scores of curve • <2.3rd percentile of curve	Adequacy of weight gain; additional information often required to assess causes	Socioeconomic status Feeding practices Birth weight Sanitary practices Health care practices (e.g. immunizations) Current health status Other nutritional disorders
Infants and children: • commonly under 5 years of age • priority under 3 years of age	Depends on resources. Common for moderate prevalence situation: • <-2 Z-scores of weight-for-height or MUAC-for-age • locally set	Adequacy of food intake relative to needs	Feeding practices Immunization status Morbidity Other nutritional disorders

Table 19 (continued)

1	2	3	4	5
Uses: what will be done for the individual?	For what purpose?	Target group and setting	What to measure, what information to collect, and how often	Indices

Screening for interventions (continued)

1	2	3	4	5
B Identification of infants/children who need supplementary food and treatment for disease (particularly diarrhoea)	To prevent malnutrition. To improve: • survival • health • development • well-being	Communities in developing areas with poor avail-ability or distribution of food (including disaster and refugee camps)	Weight Length or height MUAC Age One or multiple measurements	Weight-for-height MUAC-for-age (for children 1–5 years of age)
C Identification of infants/children who need thera-peutic feeding and treatment for disease (particu-larly diarrhoea) in emergency situations	To treat severe malnutrition and related conditions. To improve: • survival • health • development • well-being	Attenders at: • nutrition rehabilitation centres • hospitals Rapid surveys of disaster and refugee camps	Clinical signs of marasmus and kwashiorkor Weight Length or height MUAC Age	Weight-for height MUAC MUAC-for-age Clinical signs (oedema, etc.)
		Disaster and refugee situations in developing areas	One measure-ment	
D Identification of infants/children with organic diseases or "failure to thrive" who need treat-ment for under-lying diseases	To improve growth To treat under-lying diseases	Attenders at: • paediatric clinics • hospitals Developed areas with adequate food availability	Weight Length or height Age Sex One or multiple measurements	Deviation from curves of: • weight v. age • height v. age Absolute or relative change in: • weight-for-age • height-for-age • low weight-for-height

6	7	8	9
Demographic characteristics	Criteria for judgement (cut-offs)	Rationale for anthropometry	Other factors for interpretation
Infants and children: • commonly under 5 years of age • priority under 3 years of age	Depends on resources. Common for moderate prevalence situation: • <-2 Z-scores of weight-for-height or MUAC-for-age • locally set	Adequacy of food intake relative to needs	Feeding practices Immunization status Morbidity Other nutrition disorders
Infants and children: • under 5 years of age	Depends on resources. Common for severe prevalence situation: • clinical signs • <-3 Z-scores of weight-for-height or MUAC-for-age	Risk of death in the short term	Clinical diseases Other nutritional disorders
	• <11.5 cm MUAC • locally set		
Infants and children: • birth to 10 years	Depends on resources. Common conventions: • direction of curve (flat; downwards) • no growth in ≥ 2 periods • <-2 Z-scores	Need for intervention against cause of growth failure	Feeding practices Current health status Other nutritional disorders Family interactions

Table 19 (continued)

1	2	3	4	5
Uses: what will be done for the individual?	For what purpose?	Target group and setting	What to measure, what information to collect, and how often	Indices

Screening for interventions (continued)

1	2	3	4	5

E Identification of infants/children who are over-weight for inter-ventions to promote modifi-cations in diet and increased physical exercise	To prevent future morbidity, such as heart disease or diabetes. To improve: ● health ● well-being ● long-term-
	  survival
		Attenders at: ● paediatric
		  clinics ● school
		  health pro-
		  grammes
			Weight Length or height Skinfold thicknesses Age Sex
			
			One measurement
				Weight-for-height

Assessing response to an intervention

1	2	3	4	5

F Monitoring the growth of infants/ children diagnosed with malnutrition or growth faltering for continuation, modification, or discontinuation of growth promotion interventions	To improve nutrition and health until adequate growth status is achieved	Attenders at: ● growth-
		  monitoring
		  and
		  promotion
		  centres
		
		Communities in developing areas with growth-monitoring and promotion programmes
			Weight Length or height Age Sex
			
			Monthly measurements
				Following curves of: ● weight-for-age Attained status in: ● weight-for-age ● weight-for-
				  height ● height-for-age

G Monitoring response of severely malnour-ished infants/ children to thera-peutic feeding for continuation, modification, or discontinuation of feeding and disease treatment (mainly diarrhoea)	To improve nutritional status until risk of death is minimized and supplementary food no longer needed	Attenders at supplementary: ● feeding
		  centres ● food dis-
		  tribution
		  centres ● nutrition
		  rehabilitation
		  centres ● other thera-
		  peutic feeding
		  centres, includ-
		  ing hospitals
			Weight Length or height Clinical signs Age Sex
			
			Weekly to monthly measurements
				Following curves of: ● weight-for-age Achieved status in: ● weight-for-
				  height ● weight-for-age ● clinical signs
				  (oedema, etc.)

6	7	8	9
Demographic characteristics	Criteria for judgement (cut-offs)	Rationale for anthropometry	Other factors for interpretation
Infants and children: • all ages	Weight-for-height >+2 Z-scores	Need for intervention based on extent of obesity	Skinfold measures Dietary intake and feeding patterns Exercise patterns Current health status Other nutritional disorders Family interactions
Infants and children: • commonly under 5 years of age • priority under 3 years of age	Depends on resources. Common conventions for discontinuing: • direction of curve (upwards) • positive Z-score trend	Effectiveness of growth-monitoring programme in achieving weight gain and catch-up growth	Changes in practices identified as leading to growth failure Current health status Other nutritional disorders
Infants and children: • commonly under 5 years of age • priority under 3 years of age	Depends on resources. Common conventions for discharge: • Z-score above –2 SD • locally set	Adequacy of supplementary food to meet nutritional needs and improve anthropometric status	Supplementary intake Home dietary intake (substitution) Immunization status Current health status Other nutritional disorders

Table 19 (continued)

1	2	3	4	5
Uses: what will be done for the individual?	For what purpose?	Target group and setting	What to measure, what information to collect, and how often	Indices

Assessing response to an intervention (continued)

1	2	3	4	5
G Monitoring response of severely malnourished infants/children to therapeutic feeding for continuation, modification, or discontinuation of feeding and disease treatment (mainly diarrhoea)	To improve nutritional status until risk of death is minimized and supplementary food no longer needed	Communities in developing areas or disaster and refugee camps	Weight Length or height Clinical signs Age Sex Weekly to monthly measurements	Following curves of: • weight-for-age Achieved status in: • weight-for height • weight-for-age • clinical signs (oedema, etc.)
H Monitoring response to therapy of infants/children treated for organic disorders or "failure-to-thrive", for continuation, modification, or discontinuation of treatment for underlying disease and/or family/social interactions	To improve nutritional, psychological, and health status until risk of "failure-to-thrive" is minimized	Attenders at: • paediatric clinics • hospitals Developed areas	Weight Length or height Age Sex Weekly until discharge (but daily for hospitalized infants)	Following curves of: • weight-for-age • height-for-age Absolute or relative change in: • weight-for-age • weight-for-height • height-for-age
I Monitoring response of overweight infants/children to exercise and modifications in diet, for continuation, modification, or discontinuation of efforts to promote these	To reduce health risks associated with overweight	Attenders at: • paediatric clinics • school health programmes Developed[1] and developing[2] areas	Weight Length or height Skinfold thicknesses Age Sex Monthly until discharge	Weight-for-height

[1] Generally lower socioeconomic status.
[2] Generally higher socioeconomic status.

6	7	8	9
Demographic characteristics	Criteria for judgement (cut-offs)	Rationale for anthropometry	Other factors for interpretation
Infants and children: ● commonly under 5 years of age ● priority under 3 years of age	Depends on resources. Common conventions for discharge: ● Z-score above –2 SD ● locally set	Adequacy of supplementary food to meet nutritional needs and improve anthropometric status	Supplementary intake Home dietary intake (substitution) Immunization status Current health status Other nutritional disorders
Infants and children: ● birth to 10 years	Discontinuation based on establishment of satisfactory growth pattern	Adequacy of therapy for improving anthropometric status	Changes in practices that led to growth failure Current health status Other nutritional disorders
Infants and children: ● all ages	Reduction of weight-for-height Z-score	Adequacy of efforts to promote dietary changes and exercise to reduce body fat	Changes in skinfold thicknesses Changes in food intake and eating pattern Exercise patterns Current health status Other nutritional disorders Family interactions

Growth monitoring as part of primary health care represents the major individual-based screening effort in less developed areas.

A growth-monitoring programme can be described as periodic assessment of child growth and, when indicated, the institution of appropriate action to maintain or improve growth and health. The principal measurement is usually weight, and plotting the values on a growth curve constitutes the main screening activity in the primary health care setting. The position of a single measurement on the weight chart is of less importance than the pattern of growth over time. Growth faltering, or a significant deviation from the expected weight gain, is a matter for concern and warrants evaluation, treatment, or both, even though the measurement may still be above the established cut-off. A general rule of thumb for clinical purposes is crossing more than one of the percentile lines (of the NCHS/WHO growth chart). Failure to gain weight between two successive measurements is another indicator of possible health problems. Such empirical recommendations are likely to be subject to variation in different age ranges and according to the frequency of the measurements. There has been no comprehensive evaluation of this type of screening practice.

Growth monitoring should be regarded as part of overall intervention or promotion activities in the areas of health and nutrition (51). Educational activities include breast-feeding support, and timing and selection of complementary food and appropriate weaning foods. Likely reasons for individual growth faltering must be determined by the health worker, who can also provide immunizations and treatment for infections. Ideally, growth monitoring should not be a stand-alone activity, but part of a broader community-based programme to improve primary health care, education, and sanitation. It remains to be shown that growth monitoring by itself is effective without other, concurrent efforts to improve health and nutrition, or that growth monitoring is essential when other programmes are fully functional (52). There are, however, a few well documented cases of a reduction in malnutrition in areas where growth monitoring is part of an integrated project for health and nutrition improvement; the Tamil Nadu Integrated Nutrition Programme in India and the Iringa Project in the United Republic of Tanzania are two examples (53, 54).

Interventions should be initiated for children attending growth-monitoring programmes who are diagnosed with growth faltering or malnutrition, and response must be assessed (row F in Table 19). Weight gain is the primary response indicator, while achieved weight-for-age, height-for-age, and weight-for-height may also contribute to decisions on whether to continue, discontinue, or modify the intervention.

Screening for supplementary or therapeutic feeding. In many situations in less developed areas, particularly during emergencies, longitudinal assessment of growth may not be possible, and a single measurement should then be used to determine the need for intervention.

A child's anthropometric status relative to the reference, whether expressed as a Z-score or as a percentile, represents a probability statement of that child being part of the healthy distribution (specificity). It is not a statement about the probability that the child is unhealthy (positive predictive value). However, the further away a measurement is from the central part of the distribution, the greater the likelihood of health and nutritional disorders, although this depends on the prevalence of the disorders in the population (55). The cut-off points commonly used, based on the central 95% of the distribution (–2 to +2 Z-scores), were selected for screening purposes and to facilitate population-based monitoring. For individual-based applications, the cut-offs can be adapted according to the local prevalence of malnutrition and the availability of resources for intervention. The major exception to this is a situation in which the risk of morbidity and mortality below a particular cut-off value is markedly increased: the identification of very wasted children (e.g. weight-for-height below –3 Z-scores) for therapeutic feeding is an example.

In areas with a high prevalence of malnutrition, it is common practice to select children with low weight-for-height (or sometime low weight-for-age) for preferential enrolment in feeding programmes. The underlying assumption is that these anthropometric indicators are capable of predicting benefit from the intervention. On the other hand, selecting children for a feeding programme on the basis of height-for-age or weight-for-age in the absence of wasting is difficult to justify because it is not clear that these children will benefit.

During emergency or refugee situations, high rates of severe malnutrition justify a programme in which very malnourished children are kept at the feeding centre for intensive feeding. Such an approach, commonly referred to as a therapeutic feeding programme (row C in Table 19), may be life-saving for severely wasted children (weight-for-height below –3 Z-scores). For less severely affected children, the provision of extra food to individuals or families (beyond the normal family ration) is often called a supplementary feeding programme (row B in Table 19). The choice of a cut-off for accepting children in the programme will be affected by the availability of resources for supplementation, but whenever possible all children under 3 years of age should be supplemented. The effectiveness of such programmes as part of emergency relief efforts has not been fully evaluated. Age is an important factor for predicting the benefits of supplementation: younger children are likely to show improvement in growth, older children less likely. This has been shown in supplementation studies in Guatemala (56).

In most feeding programmes, weekly weight gain is the main parameter used to indicate response (row G in Table 19). Other indicators, such as achieved weight-for-age or weight-for-height and the presence of oedema or other clinical signs may also be useful.

Applications to developed areas

Malnutrition is rare in developed areas, and the positive predictive value of anthropometric screening for the condition is therefore very low. More complex screens are necessary to differentiate between malnutrition and other causes of small size in affluent populations.

Diagnosis of failure-to-thrive. In developed countries, the main purpose of routine growth measurements in clinical settings is to screen children for medical conditions that would improve with medical therapy or intervention (row D in Table 19). Upon further evaluation, some of the abnormal anthropometry will be attributable to concurrent problems that can be dealt with by a specific intervention; some indicators, however, may be reflective of past problems, and some could represent normal variations or false-positives in the screening procedure.

The major medical conditions for which anthropometry can be used as a reflective indicator include the following:

- *Organic disorders.* These encompass both congenital and acquired disorders or abnormal function of the endocrine system or the metabolism (including enzymatic defects), and gastrointestinal dysfunction, especially malabsorption. A pattern of poor weight gain or low height-for-age diagnosed during early childhood is often the first sign of these disorders. In essence, a significant deviation from the normal growth pattern in infancy or early childhood in a developed area has a high predictive value for organic disorders. During treatment of these conditions, anthropometry may be used to monitor response.

- *Chronic disease.* Any significant systemic disorder of long duration can result in poor growth as a consequence of poor food intake and metabolic disturbance. Severe chronic disease is the most common cause of wasting in children in developed areas; examples include severe forms of anaemia, tuberculosis, and human immunodeficiency virus (HIV) infection. In such cases, the degree of growth retardation can serve both as an indicator of the severity of the primary disease and as an indicator of response to therapy.

- *Non-organic failure to thrive.* One major cause of extremely poor growth, especially during infancy, is severe psychosocial disturbance in the family, resulting in so-called non-organic failure to thrive. The spectrum of underlying problems includes inappropriate feeding practices, failure to recognize poor growth and development, poor maternal–infant bonding, child neglect, and inadequate parenting. The condition may present as poor weight gain, low weight-for-height, or both.

- *Constitutional shortness.* A diagnosis of constitutional shortness applies to children who are short without any pathological reasons. Often these children show delays in bone age and late puberty; the result is a longer growth period but a final adult height in the normal range. Therapy with genetically engineered human growth hormone is now available and has been used in older children who are short even though they have no definite growth hormone deficiency. The effectiveness and health implications, however, are unclear, so that this report makes no recommendation for selecting and monitoring these children.

The success of any intervention in children diagnosed with failure to thrive should be monitored (row H in Table 19). Both weight and height gain are used as indicators of response, with growth followed at regular, usually weekly, intervals.

Diagnosis of overweight. In many developed countries, overweight among children is becoming a matter of increasing concern; the same is true for the more affluent in less developed countries. Anthropometry can be used to screen overweight children (row E in Table 19), who will then be subject to weight control interventions including increased exercise and modifications in diet. Screening activities are usually carried out in paediatric clinics or in schools, using the conventional indicator of weight-for-height, with a cut-off of +2 Z-scores.

For the clinical monitoring of progress of children diagnosed as overweight, indicators of response include reductions in weight-for-height or weight-for-age, as well as absolute weight loss over a specified period of time (row I in Table 19).

Special applications relevant to infancy

The selection of indices for anthropometric assessment during infancy depends on the age of the infant, as do the purposes of measuring growth status and the types of intervention that are appropriate during the first year of life. In addition to conventional uses, individual anthropometric assessments during infancy may be carried out for the following purposes:

- assessment of the adequacy of intake of breast milk or breast-milk substitutes;
- assessment of the appropriate age for introduction of complementary foods;
- evaluation of the adequacy of the weaning diet; and
- assessment of response to counselling on improved feeding practices.

Based on current recommendations for exclusive breast-feeding of infants from birth to 4-6 months and for breast-feeding plus appropriate and adequate complementary foods up to or beyond 2 years of age, and on the fact that growth slows considerably in all infants after the first 6 months, the applications of anthropometry in infants should consider the age intervals 0-4, 4-6, and 6-12 months.

Birth to four months. Exclusive and frequent breast-feeding should be actively supported in developing countries, where several studies have shown that exclusive breast-feeding is associated with lower infant mortality and morbidity, better growth during the first 4 months, and prolonged postpartum amenorrhoea (*5, 57-64*). Partial breast-feeding is less protective (*57-59*). When contraceptive use is low, a longer period of lactational amenorrhoea is likely to lead to a greater interval between successive births, which may also benefit the health of the mother and her infants.

Nutritional supplementation (with energy, protein, and/or micronutrients) of malnourished lactating women is used to ensure adequate quantity and quality of breast milk and prevent maternal depletion. Although the evidence regarding the impact of pre- or postnatal energy supplementation on lactation performance is inconclusive, undernourished women may well benefit from such interventions (*65, 66*). The correlation between the fat content of human milk, which is the major source of energy for the infant, and maternal body composition is well documented (*67, 68*). In some populations, maternal supplementation with certain micronutrients (particularly vitamins such as vitamin A, B_6, B_{12}, and riboflavin) may be warranted to ensure adequate concentrations in breast milk (*65*).

Four to six months. The support of exclusive and frequent breast-feeding remains a high priority for infants aged 4-6 months because it offers both nutritional advantages and protection against infection. The nutritional supplementation of malnourished lactating women may be even more important during this period, when the likelihood of maternal depletion is greater. If these two interventions are not adequate, it may be necessary to provide nutrient-dense complementary foods or micronutrient supplementation.

The period from 4 to 6 months after birth is considered a time of transition, when some breast-fed infants require foods in addition to breast milk to provide certain key nutrients such as iron and zinc which are known to be essential for adequate growth (*25, 26, 69-71*). However, because complementary foods tend to reduce breast-milk intake (*72, 73*), their introduction should be delayed as long as possible to maximize the nutritional and immunological protection provided by breast-feeding.

Educational programmes to foster hygienic preparation and storage of weaning foods are likely to result in improved infant growth in disadvantaged populations; this transition period is the key time to target such programmes.

Six to twelve months. The second 6 months of life are associated with marked growth faltering in many disadvantaged populations (*74*). Interventions appropriate for this period include those listed for infants aged 4-6 months, except that complementary foods should be given several times each day while breast-feeding is continued. Educational programmes to encourage frequent feeding (including breast-feeding) are also appropriate.

In less developed countries, growth faltering may be the result of termination of breast-feeding or of the inadequate quantity or poor nutritional and hygienic quality of complementary foods (62). The optimal nutritional composition of weaning foods for children in such environments is still under active investigation, but it is clear that nutrient density – particularly of micronutrients – is of critical importance. This may also be a concern among affluent populations and might explain the lower growth rate of infants who are only partially breast-fed.

In affluent populations, too, concerns regarding the development of obesity may become an issue in late infancy. In most cases, obese infants do not remain obese later in life (75-77), and there is no evidence that restricting intake during the first 12 months is effective in reducing the later risk of obesity. However, parents may be counselled to modify inappropriate infant feeding practices or choice of foods.

Interventions for the prevention and appropriate management of infections are also applicable at each of the age intervals discussed. The synergistic relationship between nutritional status and infection is particularly apparent during infancy (74).

Frequency of measurements in infancy. The frequency of measurements is of particular relevance during infancy, and depends on the average growth rate (which declines with age), the measurement error for each index, and the purpose of the anthropometric assessment. In cases where failure to thrive is suspected or a child's response to treatment is being monitored, frequent measurements are clearly essential, although gains or losses over short intervals must be interpreted with caution. For routine monitoring, a suggested guideline for weight increments is that "no interval be so short that the difference between the 5th and 50th percentiles (in grams per interval) would be less than 180 gm – about the size of a single feeding", and for length increments that "no interval be so short that the difference (in centimetres per interval) between the 5th and 50th percentiles would be less than 0.4 cm – about the size of the measurement error" (78). The magnitude of measurement error depends on the apparatus used and the training of the anthropometrists.

Using these guidelines, Guo et al. (79) recommended that 1 month intervals are appropriate during the first 6 months of life, but that longer intervals (e.g. 2 months) may be more appropriate thereafter. However, growth-monitoring programmes often continue with monthly measurements throughout infancy, since these are useful for the early detection of growth faltering and the promotion of improved nutrient quality and safety of complementary and weaning foods. This is particularly critical during the second 6 months of life, the period of greatest faltering in growth. None the less, in assessing the adequacy of growth rate it is important to guard against over-interpretation of data from frequent measurements, since infants may exhibit marked growth spurts or decelerations during the first year of life (*80*). For example, an infant measured just before a growth spurt may be falsely diagnosed as faltering.

5.3 Using anthropometry in populations

5.3.1 *Introduction*

Collection of anthropometric data at the population level can help in the definition of health and nutritional status for purposes of programme planning, implementation, and evaluation. Assessment may take the form of a once-only cross-sectional endeavour or a continuing, longitudinal activity. In either case, the objective is the same – identification of concurrent or past health or socioeconomic problems, and prediction of future risk and potential response to intervention programmes.

Commonly, nutritional surveillance is defined as the continuous monitoring of the physical status of a population, based on repeated surveys or on data from child health or growth-monitoring programmes. However, with its emphasis on the nature of measurement activities, this is a rather narrow definition. A broader concept would emphasize the use of nutritional information to promote, manage, and evaluate programmes aimed at improving health and nutritional status. This broader view includes programmes and interventions as essential components of nutritional surveillance, with the data collection and monitoring system being only one part of the overall surveillance activities.

In this section, nutritional surveillance is treated as a major operational approach for population-based applications of anthropometry, including targeting interventions and assessing their effectiveness, as well as research on the determinants and consequences of malnutrition. All of these specific activities are essential for the planning, implementation, and management of nutrition programmes. Specific issues and functions related to nutritional surveillance, such as information collecting systems and warning systems for famine, are discussed, and Table 20 provides detailed information on the application of anthropometry at the population level.

5.3.2 *Targeting interventions*

Anthropometry can be used to verify the existence of a nutritional problem in a population and to assess its magnitude. Such information is essential for directing programme resources to populations or communities with the greatest health and/or nutritional needs. In this context, anthropometric assessment provides an indication of risk as well as of socioeconomic development, but is used primarily as an indicator of benefit for selecting those communities likely to gain most from a proposed intervention. An analogy may be drawn with observations of individual children, among whom the most malnourished tend to derive the greatest benefit from therapy, the assumption being that the worst-off communities will respond best to appropriate interventions. This is supported by the fact that the growth status of children improves as the socioeconomic conditions of their community improve, the effect being most marked when the baseline level is lowest.

The choice of operational anthropometric indicators for programme targeting depends on the nature of the intervention being considered (see rows A–D in Table 20) as well as on the prevalence of anthropometric deficits. For example, height-for-age is suitable for targeting a wide range of interventions because it both reflects the cumulative effects of socioeconomic, health, and nutrition problems (Table 20, rows A and B) and varies widely from place to place. Stunting is a predictor of risk and, because it is strongly correlated with socioeconomic status, reflects the overall level of development. It may also be an appropriate indicator of benefit at the community level. If wasting is uncommon, weight-for-age may be as useful as height-for-age for ranking communities.

Although the height-for-age of older children is reflective of past nutritional and environmental conditions and is not particularly amenable to interventions, it may indicate conditions currently being experienced by younger children in that community. School height censuses, such as those conducted in several countries of Central and South America, may therefore be useful for targeting purposes (Table 20, row B).

The prevalence ranges shown in Table 21 have been used by WHO to classify levels of stunting and underweight for global monitoring purposes (7). Such classification is valuable for summarizing prevalence data from diverse sources and can be used for targeting purposes. It should be borne in mind, however, that this classification was not based on correlations with functional outcomes and simply reflects a convenient statistical grouping of prevalence levels from different countries. Moreover, the designations of prevalence as "low" and "medium" should be interpreted cautiously and not be taken as grounds for complacency. Since only 2.3% of the children in a well-nourished population would be expected to fall below the cut-off, the "low" weight-for-age group includes communities with up to four times that expected prevalence, and the "medium" group communities with up to an eight-fold excess.

For targeting food supplementation in areas where wasting is common, weight-for-height is the ideal indicator of benefit (Table 20, row C), although its usefulness is limited by the fact that prevalence of wasting is

Table 20

Summary of recommendations for uses of anthropometry in populations of infants and children

1	2	3	4	5
Uses: what will be done for the population?	For what purpose?	Target group and setting	What to measure, what information to collect, and how often	Indices

Targeting interventions

1	2	3	4	5
A Identify areas of greatest need to target appropriate nutrition interventions (breast-feeding support, supplementation of mothers, weaning education, etc.). Determine priorities for allocation of resources	To improve the equity of: • survival • health • development • well-being • future productivity and reproductivity	Representative surveys, preferably by age range. Communities (or geographical or political units) in less developed areas	Weight Length or height Age Sex (if sex-specific references are used) One measurement	Weight-for-age Weight-for-height Height-for-age
B Identify areas of greatest need to target health and economic interventions to vulnerable areas/ population groups. Determine priorities for allocation of resources	To improve the equity of: • health care • economic development	Data collected in political or geographical areas of decision-making for resource allocation: • surveys • school height censuses Communities (or geographical or political units) in less developed areas	Height Age Sex One measurement	Height-for-age

6	7	8	9
Demographic characteristics	Criteria for judgement (cut-offs)	Rationale for anthropometry	Other factors for interpretation
Children: • under 5 years of age	Depends on resources Based on prevalence above "expected" values of 2.3% (<–2 Z-scores) Based on difference from the "expected" • mean Z-score of 0 • SD of Z-score of 1	Extent and magnitude of malnutrition: • number of areas needing intervention • population groups needing intervention • types and combinations of interventions	Socioeconomic status Food availability and cost Infant/young child feeding practices Sanitary resources and practices Health care coverage Morbidity prevalence Prevalence of other nutritional disorders
Children: • under 5 years of age • school age (6–10 years)	Depends on resources Based on prevalence above "expected" values of 2.3% (<–2 Z-scores) Based on difference from the "expected" • mean Z-score of 0 • SD of Z-score of 1	Low socioeconomic status	Major occupations and sources of income Transportation infrastructure Food availability and cost Sanitary resources Health care resources

Table 20 *(continued)*

1	2	3	4	5
Uses: what will be done for the population?	For what purpose?	Target group and setting	What to measure, what information to collect, and how often	Indices

Targeting interventions *(continued)*

C Determine the severity of the disaster/emergency and the need for and quantity and content of relief food rations. Determine priorities for allocation of resources	To reduce rates of: <ul><li>mortality</li><li>morbidity</li><li>malnutrition</li></ul> Disaster and emergency situations in less developed areas	Rapid assessment surveys	Weight Height MUAC Clinical signs of marasmus and kwashiorkor Age One measurement	Weight-for-height MUAC-for-age (for children aged 1–5 years only)
D Identify areas of greatest need to target interventions to reduce food and fat consumption and/or to increase physical exercise	To reduce rates of obesity. To improve the equity of: <ul><li>survival</li><li>health</li><li>well-being</li></ul>	Representative surveys Communities (or geographical or political units) in developed (though often poor) areas	Weight Height Age Sex One measurement	Weight-for-height

6	7	8	9
Demographic character-istics	Criteria for judgement (cut-offs)	Rationale for anthropometry	Other factors for inter-pretation
Children: • under 5 years of age • under 100 cm in height if age is unavailable	Depends on resources Based on preva-lence above "expected" values of 2.3% (<-2 Z-scores) Based on difference from the "expected" • mean Z-score of 0 • SD of Z-score of 1 MUAC-for-age <-2 Z-scores	Extent and magnitude of malnutrition: • severity and type • number of people affected	Frequency of diarrhoea Mortality Food supply Baseline status before emergency
Children: • all ages	Prevalence above +2 Z-scores of weight-for-height	Extent and magnitude of overnutrition: • number of areas needing intervention • population groups needing intervention • types and combinations of interventions	Dietary background Secular trends in overweight

Table 20 *(continued)*

1	2	3	4	5
Uses: what will be done for the population?	For what purpose?	Target group and setting	What to measure, what information to collect, and how often	Indices

Assessing response to an intervention

E Assessing response to a non-specific intervention (e.g. agriculture, socioeconomic development) for decision on its improvement or discontinuation	Make more efficient use of resources	Representative sample of areas receiving the intervention, and possibly of control areas without the intervention Communities (or geographical or political units) in less developed areas	Weight Length or height Age Sex Measured once if intervention/ control design is used, at least twice if before/ after design is used	Weight-for-age Height-for-age Weight-for-height
F Assessing response to specific interventions (e.g. supplementation, growth-monitoring, disease control) to establish their efficacy	Disseminate intervention to other population groups	Well defined intervention and control groups, randomly allocated if possible Communities in less developed areas	Weight Length or height Age Sex Data on risk factors Measured at least twice in each group (intervention or control)	Weight velocity Height velocity Weight-for-height Weight-for-age Height-for-age

6	7	8	9
Demographic character- istics	Criteria for judgement (cut-offs)	Rationale for anthropometry	Other factors for inter- pretation
Children: ● under 5 years of age	Changes in mean Z-score Changes in prevalence of deficits	Improvements in nutritional status over time that may be attributed to the intervention	Nature of the intervention and biological plausibility Concomitant changes in confounding factors
Children: ● under 5 years of age	Significant difference in growth velocity between intervention and control groups	Improvements in nutritional status over time that may be attributed to the intervention	Biological plausibility Changes in process indicators Confounding factors

Table 20 (continued)

1	2	3	4	5
Uses: what will be done for the population?	For what purpose?	Target group and setting	What to measure, what information to collect, and how often	Indices

Identifying determinants of malnutrition

1	2	3	4	5
G Identifying modifiable risk factors for anthropometric deficits, as well as high-risk subgroups	Reduce the prevalence of malnutrition through preventive strategies and special care for high-risk groups	Population-based sample of children Communities in less developed areas	Weight Length or height Age Sex Data on risk factors Measured once in cross-sectional studies, at least twice in longitudinal studies	In cross-sectional studies: • weight-for-age • height-for-age • weight-for-height In longitudinal studies, also: • weight velocity • height velocity
H Identifying modifiable risk factors for overweight, as well as high-risk subgroups	Reduce the prevalence of overweight through preventive strategies and special care for high-risk groups	Population-based sample of children Communities in less developed areas	Weight Length or height Age Sex Data on risk factors Measured once in cross-sectional studies, at least twice in longitudinal studies	In cross-sectional studies: • weight-for-height In longitudinal studies, also: • weight velocity

Predicting consequences of malnutrition

1	2	3	4	5
I Predicting the health consequences of anthropometric deficits to promote the survival of children at nutritional risk through appropriate interventions	Increase survival and equity	Community-based sample Communities in less developed areas	Weight Length or height Age Sex MUAC Morbidity and survival rate Measured at least once for anthropometric baseline data	Weight-for-age Height-for-age Weight-for-height MUAC-for-age

6	7	8	9
Demographic character-istics	Criteria for judgement (cut-offs)	Rationale for anthropometry	Other factors for inter-pretation
Children: • under 5 years of age	Prevalence below –2 Z-scores	Magnitude and significance of association be-tween proposed risk factors and anthropometric deficits	Confounding factors Possible biases
Children: • all ages	Prevalence above +2 Z-scores	Magnitude and significance of association be-tween proposed risk factors and overweight	Confounding factors Possible biases
Children: • under 5 years of age • special attention for children under 3 years of age	Prevalence groups: • <–2 Z-scores • <–3 Z-scores	Magnitude and significance of association be-tween malnutrition and subsequent morbidity, mortality, and development	Confounding factors Possible biases Losses to follow-up

Table 21

Proposed classification of worldwide prevalence ranges of low height-for-age and low weight-for-age among children under 5 years of age

Prevalence group	Prevalence ranges (% of children below −2 Z-scores)	
	Low height-for-age (stunting)	Low weight-for-age (wasting)
Low	< 20	<10
Medium	20–29	10–19
High	30–39	20–29
Very high	≥ 40	≥ 30

Figure 24

Major generalized downward shift of entire weight-for-height distribution during severe famine in southern Sudan, March, 1993

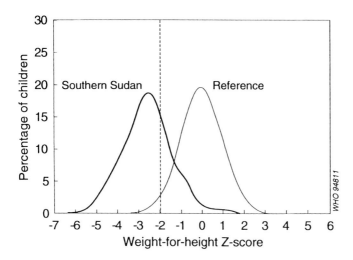

often low and may vary little between communities. In such circumstances, MUAC-for-age may be a more appropriate indicator. Weight-for-height is the anthropometric indicator of choice for targeting interventions against obesity (Table 20, row D) since it reflects concurrent conditions leading to overnutrition.

In the population approach to targeting, all children from a high-prevalence group receive the intervention, whether or not individual anthropometric values are below the cut-off; in the individual screening approach, intervention is limited to children below the cut-off. It may be argued that the population approach is more likely to promote equity and development since, within a high-prevalence group, there is a tendency for all children to fail to achieve their genetic potential for growth (*47*). Improved conditions shift the whole distribution positively, rather than affecting only those children below the cut-off. A good example is the marked improvement in the anthropometric status of Asian refugee children whose families became immigrants of the USA (*81*).

During acute deterioration of nutritional status as a result of starvation or infectious diseases, the increased prevalence of low weight-for-height or wasting is also associated with an overall downward shift of the weight-for-height distribution in the affected population (*82*). For example, Fig. 24 shows the dramatic downward shift of the weight-for-height distribution, relative to the reference, that occurred during the 1993 famine in southern Sudan; the prevalence of wasting reached the unprecedented level of 65% (*83*). Recent re-analysis of several worldwide surveys revealed a consistent pattern of variance of all three height- and weight-based anthropometric indices, independent of the level of malnutrition (*84*) (see also Table 17). This provides further support for the idea that factors that cause changes in nutritional status tend to affect all children in the population, not just those near the lower end of the distribution. For this reason, population-based interventions to improve health or nutrition must target not the "worst-off" children within each community but *all* children among the "worst-off" communities.

5.3.3 *Assessing response to an intervention*

Anthropometry at the population level also finds major application in indicating response to specific or nonspecific interventions. The latter include changes in economic or agricultural conditions, which contribute to improved growth via better health care, sanitation, or food supply. In general, these interventions are evaluated by observational means such as comparing child growth before and after the intervention period (Table 20, row E); an example is the marked secular change in growth among Palestinians detected through repeated surveys (*47*). In this type of evaluation, the outcome measures are differences in population means or in the proportion of the population below a given cut-off. Growth velocity data from individuals are not generally used because the long-term nature of the intervention results in different children being examined during each round of the evaluation: those examined in the first survey will have grown out of childhood when the later measurements are made.

Specific interventions include programmes for disease control, growth monitoring, and nutritional supplementation. Their proper evaluation often requires controlled trials (row F in Table 20). Useful examples are provided by trials conducted in rural Guatemala from 1969 to 1977, which demonstrated a long-term effect of nutritional supplementation on intellectual performance, body size, and work capacity (*39*), and the 1973–1980 trial in Colombia, which showed a protective effect of supplementation against the stunting effect of diarrhoea (*28*). In trials of this nature, sequential measurements are usually taken to allow comparison of mean growth velocities in the intervention and control groups.

Apart from the purely observational assessment of nonspecific interventions and the experimental approach of trials, several quasi-experimental designs may be used for evaluating response. In an evaluation of a Catholic Church child survival programme in Brazil, for example, 60 communities within the programme were compared with 60 matched control communities. Anthropometric measurements were made of 15 children from each community, but no differences were found between the two sets of communities (85). Since measurements were taken on a single occasion, the comparison had to be based on achieved size, including height-for-age, weight-for-height, and weight-for-age.

Stunting and wasting often fail to show strong correlation either on an individual or on a population basis (8, 20), and the selection of appropriate anthropometric indicators for evaluating the response to an intervention is therefore critical and dictated by the study design, the type of intervention, and baseline levels. Since almost all less developed areas have substantial levels of stunting and low weight-for-age, changes in the prevalence of these deficits or in mean Z-scores are useful for assessing long-term, nonspecific community interventions. Low weight-for-height is of limited value in many areas because its baseline prevalence is often low; it can, however, be a useful indicator of responses (86).

When the same children are to be measured more than once to evaluate response to specific interventions, several alternatives exist in the choice of indicator. For example, mean changes in height-for-age or weight-for-age Z-scores would be suitable for evaluating response to a dietary intervention, as would height or weight velocities if the intervention and control groups were matched or adjusted for age. For assessing short-term response, such as in a diarrhoea control trial, changes in weight-for-height or in absolute weight would be more useful indicators. Regardless of the indicator or combination of indicators selected, the use of mean values (Z-scores or growth velocities), together with the proportion of children below a given cut-off, will give greater precision than the latter alone, particularly when sample size is relatively small (84).

5.3.4 *Ascertaining the determinants of malnutrition*

Anthropometry may be used at the population level for identifying the determinants of malnutrition in a particular setting (row G, Table 20). As discussed above, the main determinants of anthropometric status are dietary intake and infection, both of which are themselves affected by more distal determinants. Epidemiological studies are useful for identifying these distal risk factors at the population level and in deciding on appropriate interventions.

In extreme and acute situations, the determinants of low weight-for-height are relatively easy to define since they are currently active. For example, severe energy deficits are the main cause of the extremely high levels of wasting seen recurrently in Ethiopia, Somalia, and Sudan (33); this is confirmed by the rapid response to re-feeding interventions. Another extreme example is provided by the 1991 Kurdish refugee crisis, during which the elevated prevalence of wasting among young children was the result of widespread and prolonged diarrhoea within a 1-month period of inadequate food supply (82).

In non-disaster situations, the determinants of low weight-for-height may be identified by comparing wasted and non-wasted children, using a cross-sectional or case-control study design. An alternative is to use the Z-scores of weight-for-height as a continuous outcome variable, which usually results in increased statistical power compared with the use of a cut-off, particularly where wasting is rare.

A similar approach may be used for studying the determinants of stunting. Unlike wasting, however, stunting is reflective of long-term and cumulative influences, and its determinants are therefore more difficult to identify; this is particularly true of dietary intake and morbidity patterns. Investigation of the determinants of overweight in a population is affected by similar difficulties, because of the long-term influence and indirect nature of possible risk factors (row H, Table 20).

Observational studies of the determinants of anthropometric deficits and imbalances have therefore to overcome a number of methodological problems. Confounding is particularly important; any variable associated with socioeconomic status will tend also to be associated with anthropometric deficits or imbalances. Definitive answers can be provided only by intervention studies, but ethical and pragmatic considerations often preclude such an approach. Carefully designed observational studies, meticulously analysed and interpreted in the light of biological plausibility, will therefore continue to be the major source of information on determinants of anthropometric status.

5.3.5 *Ascertaining the consequences of malnutrition*

In the public health context, levels and types of anthropometric deficits or imbalances may indicate the risk of morbidity and mortality (Table 20, row I). Predictive capacity depends on the indicator chosen, on the specific risk under consideration, on the age of the children, and on the baseline levels of anthropometric deficit, morbidity, and mortality. Findings from one particular setting may therefore not be applicable elsewhere. Much research in this area has focused on defining the indicator that has the greatest positive predictive value for adverse outcomes such as mortality. There is continuing debate, for example, on whether MUAC is superior to weight-for-height for predicting short-term mortality in emergency situations. For non-emergency situations, it has been found (*34, 35*) that weight-for-age has the highest predictive value followed by height-for-age; weight-for-height is the poorest predictor of mortality within the following year.

5.3.6 *Nutritional surveillance*

Nutritional surveillance systems require the timely collection of appropriate information for programme operation. Indicators of benefit and response, rather than of risk alone, are preferable for surveillance purposes since they allow the targeting and evaluation of interventions. Data from surveillance systems are useful for all the applications listed in Table 20, and the major data-collecting systems and some specific applications are reviewed in the paragraphs that follow. The handling and reporting of anthropometric data are detailed in section 5.4.

Figure 25
Association between crude mortality rates and the prevalence of low weight-for-height of children under 5 years of age (<80% median weight-for-height NCHS/WHO reference population) in 41 refugee camps[a]

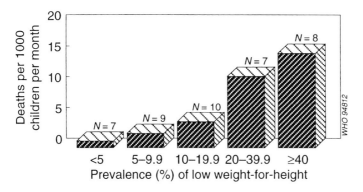

[a] Source: reference *33*.

Table 22
Severity index for malnutrition in emergency situations based on prevalence of wasting and mean weight-for-height Z-score for children under 5 years[a]

Classification of severity	Prevalence of wasting (% of children <-2 Z-scores)	Mean weight-for-height Z-score
Acceptable	< 5	>-0.40
Poor	5-9	-0.40 to -0.69
Serious	10-14	-0.70 to -0.99
Critical	≥ 15	≤-1.00

[a] Modified from reference *87*.

Assessment during emergency situations
In situations such as famines or refugee crises, rapid anthropometric surveys are useful for determining the need for and type of relief rations and for establishing priorities for the allocation of resources (Table 20, row C) (*33*). These surveys rely on weight-for-height or MUAC for assessing the extent of the disaster. The prevalence of low weight-for-height (below -2 Z-scores) among children under 5 years of age can be used to characterize the severity of the situation (*87*) as it is strongly predictive of concurrent crude mortality of the population. This relationship between crude mortality and low (<80% of median) weight-for-height is illustrated in Fig. 25 for 41 refugee settings; increased mortality is apparent when prevalence of malnutrition exceeds 5% (*33*).

Table 22 shows a proposed classification of the severity of malnutrition according to the prevalence of wasting and the mean weight-for-height Z-score for children under 5 years of age. Designation of a prevalence of wasting in excess of 5% as elevated is based on the observation that this level is seldom reached except when there is acute stress as a result of severe food shortage or disease outbreaks (*7*) (see also Table 17). The major exceptions are the countries of southern Asia, where prevalence is often 10% and above in normal circumstances – apparently a chronic condition related to poor health and nutrition.

Proper usage of MUAC as an indicator requires the application of an MUAC-for-age reference, and the performance of low MUAC-for-age compared with that of low weight-for-height during emergency situations should be further evaluated.

Information collection and management systems
There are two principal approaches to the collection of nutritional surveillance information: special surveys (single or repeated), and continuous monitoring systems based on anthropometric data from existing programmes.

Nutrition surveys. The major uses of nutrition surveys are:

- *To characterize nutritional status*: to measure the overall prevalence of anthropometric deficits as well as variations with age, sex, socio-economic status, geographical area, etc.
- *Targeting*: to identify populations and sub-populations with increased nutritional needs.
- *Evaluation of interventions*: to collect baseline data before and at the end of programmes aimed at improving nutrition.
- *Monitoring*: to monitor secular trends in nutritional status.
- *Advocacy*: to raise awareness of nutritional problems, define policy, and promote programmes.
- *Training and education*: to motivate and train local teams to undertake nutritional assessment.

Commonly used approaches include community-based surveys of under-5-year-olds, school height censuses, and rapid nutrition surveys during disaster.

The first of these usually involves the collection of data on height-for-age, weight-for-age, and weight-for-height, and is the method most often used to obtain national or regional data on nutritional status. School height censuses are often conducted to assess long-term trends; height-for-age is used as a reflective or concurrent indicator of socioeconomic status and equity. Rapid nutrition surveys are discussed on page 213.

If they are to be useful, surveys must follow standardized procedures and be based on a representative sample of sufficient size. For repeat surveys, these requirements, particularly as regards sampling, are especially important. During emergency situations, however, representativeness may not be feasible because of limited time and lack of a population sampling frame.

Continuous monitoring systems. Continuous collection of anthropometric and health data from clinics and programmes is often described as "nutritional surveillance", but this is a rather narrow definition of the activity. In contrast to surveys, continuous monitoring systems offer the advantages of using actual programme data for feedback to the health workers and providing more timely programme evaluation.

Initial development is often difficult, but if a data collection system is properly designed and sustainable, it can provide useful information on time trends. The system need not cover all clinics or health units in a country or area: a selected subset can serve as sentinel sites for surveillance purposes. Though desirable, it is not essential that these sites cover a representative sample of the population, but it is important that their catchment population should remain unchanged. For example, if a public clinic is privatized, the prevalence of stunting may fall in the surveillance data even though there are no actual changes in the underlying population.

Application of nutritional surveillance in special conditions: timely warning
Monitoring of nutritional status is part of the overall warning system for severe food shortages and famine. Other early warning indicators include weather or rainfall patterns, crop failures, food production and distribution figures, unemployment rates, and market food prices. Anthropometric indicators, even concurrent changes in weight-for-height, are relatively late elements in the overall warning system: by the time changes are detected, significant morbidity and mortality have already occurred. Anthropometry is thus a useful ancillary tool for following the later stages of evolution of food crises, but reliance on anthropometry alone for timely warning is unwarranted. Data on such matters as weather or food production should be the basis for planning and action (88).

Nevertheless, anthropometric data may provide timely warning of the need for intervention in other health sectors. For example, a seasonal pattern of wasting in a given community may provide the impetus for specific interventions such as food supplementation or training in diarrhoea case-management. Similarly, high rates of wasting in a crowded refugee camp may imply an urgent need for measles immunization and vitamin A distribution, as well as food supplementation.

5.4 Population data management and analysis

Greater uniformity in the handling and analysis of population-based anthropometric data is essential to facilitate the comparison of growth status information across populations and over time. Much of what has been recommended elsewhere (*1-3*) for the use and presentation of population-based anthropometric data has been incorporated in the discussion that follows.

5.4.1 *Description of sources of data*

Proper description of a survey or surveillance system requires at least the following information:

- characteristics of the population
- month, year, and season (winter/spring/summer/autumn; or dry/wet) during which data were collected
- sources of the data within the population: household, clinic, or school
- methods and procedures for data collection
- purpose of data collection
- individual and agency responsible for collection of data
- training and standardization procedures for the measurements
- type of sampling (if applicable)
- type of weighing and measuring equipment; recumbent or standing height.

5.4.2 *Documentation and analysis of coverage rates*

For survey coverage to be properly defined and for determining the representativeness of the sample, information on the sampling strategy and likely biases, such as losses and refusals, is essential. Assessment of coverage and representativeness requires a comparison of the socio-demographic profile of the sub-population monitored with that of the general population. When data are obtained from a health or nutrition programme, it is often difficult to define the characteristics of non-participants in the programme without a special coverage survey.

5.4.3 *Reliability and validity*

Precision of the estimate
For population-based data or findings, the precision of the estimate of prevalence or mean Z-score can be assessed from the confidence interval,

which depends on the sample size and the complexity of the survey design. Required precision also depends on how the information will be used. In general, if the prevalence of a condition is high, lower levels of precision can be tolerated. For example, a 95% confidence interval of ±5% (absolute precision) would seem reasonable for an estimated prevalence of stunting near 50% (a relative precision of $^5/_{50}$ or 10%), but the same absolute precision would be unacceptable for a prevalence level of 10% (a relative precision of $^5/_{10}$ or 50%).

Accuracy of the estimate

Accuracy, that is the extent to which a sample-based estimate for a given population truly reflects the actual physical status of the population, is a function of the adequacy of the sampling procedure and of the quality of measurement methods. If the sample size is adequate and representative of the population, the findings are likely to be accurate.

Verification of accuracy is best done by remeasurement of a sub-sample of the original sample by individuals who are fully qualified in anthropometric procedures. Regular calibration of measuring equipment is also essential. The types of survey result that may indicate inaccuracy of the overall anthropometric estimate include:

- a resulting mean Z-score that is significantly higher than the expected zero value for reference;
- a variance or standard deviation greater than expected; and
- inconsistencies between the estimates based on height-for-age and those based on weight-for-age.

Poor estimates of age are also a frequent cause of inaccurate overall estimates.

Validity of the population-based finding

Anthropometric indicators, including low weight-for-height, low height-for-age, and low MUAC, cannot be interpreted without considering their ecological context. For example, a high prevalence of wasting without evidence of increased mortality must bring into question the validity of the findings. Thus, valid conclusions about the nutritional status of a population require supporting information beyond anthropometric findings. Cross-validation or internal validity between different indicators is one approach: for example, high rates of low height-for-age in the absence of high rates of low weight-for-age would be a matter for concern. External validity checks require additional information such as socioeconomic, morbidity, and mortality data.

It is frequently necessary to validate the functional meaning of an anthropometric finding for specific populations or settings. For example, high weight-for-height, a proxy for obesity, may be less reflective of adiposity among Hispanic populations than among other ethnic groups because of differences in lean body mass (*89*).

5.4.4 *Data integrity or quality measures*

Several steps are involved in assessing the quality of anthropometric data. Both the internal and external validity checks discussed above are appropriate means of assessment.

Quality of age estimates

The quality of age data may be directly assessed by means of a frequency distribution or histogram of age in months. Signs of low accuracy include strong digit preference or "heaping" at multiples of 6 or 12 months. In samples of children under 5 years of age, roughly the same proportion (about 20%) would be expected in each 1-year age grouping. In general, if age is not based on actual date of birth, the quality of the data is inadequate for assessment of height-for-age and weight-for-age. For infants and young children, the effect of expressing age in completed months as opposed to rounded months can result in a substantial difference in the interpretation of height-for-age and weight-for-age (*90*). Age should therefore be computed to the nearest one-tenth of a month and should be based on date of birth.

Quality of anthropometric measurements

Height and weight distributions may also be affected by heaping. Excesses of recorded height or weight values ending with ".5" or ".0" are strong evidence of inadequate measurement techniques; height and weight measurements should be recorded to the nearest 0.1 cm and 0.1 kg, respectively. The best evidence for the quality of measurements is provided by records of blinded repeat measurements over short intervals to estimate measuring precision (*2*) or over longer intervals to estimate reliability (*91*).

Missing and improbable values

The proportion of measurements that are missing or biologically implausible can be a helpful index for data quality assessment. For example, if the proportion of Z-scores below -6 or above +6 exceeds 1%, the quality of the data is doubtful. It is important to document the frequency of such implausible measures before excluding them from the analysis. Such extreme values may be caused by errors in the anthropometric measurement itself or in the reported age. Common mistakes include the recording of weight as height or vice versa, and recording the wrong birth year so that the age of the child is incorrect.

For the purpose of analysis, values more than 4 Z-score units from the observed mean Z-score are likely to be errors and may be treated as missing values. The exclusion criteria can be even more restrictive for some indicators; for example, beyond the age of 1 year it is very rare for a child to have a height-for-age Z-score greater than +3.0. In populations not under significant nutritional stress, a weight-for-height Z-score below

-3.0 is rare. The recommended exclusion criteria for anthropometric values that are most likely to represent errors can be summarized as:

- *Flexible exclusion range*: 4 Z-score units from the observed mean Z-score, with a maximum height-for-age Z-score of +3.0. For example, if the mean height-for-age Z-score of the study population is -2.0, values less than -6.0 and greater than +3.0 would be excluded in the analysis.

- *Fixed exclusion range* (suitable when the observed mean Z-score is above -1.5):

height-for-age Z-score	< -5.0 and > +3.0
weight-for-height Z-score	< -4.0 and > +5.0
weight-for-age Z-score	< -5.0 and > +5.0

Distribution or standard deviation of Z-scores

The observed standard deviation (SD) value of the Z-score distribution is also useful for assessing data quality. With accurate age estimates and anthropometric measurements, the SD of the observed height-for-age, weight-for-age, and weight-for-height Z-score distribution should be relatively constant and close to the expected value of 1.0 for the reference distribution.

A recent analysis of multiple large-scale nutrition surveys was based on data available to the USA's Centers for Disease Control, including several rapid nutrition surveys undertaken during emergency situations. After applying the exclusion criteria described above, the standard deviations of the height-for-age, weight-for-age, and weight-for-height Z-score distributions from the majority of survey populations ranged within approximately 0.2 units of the expected value (*84*), as follows:

height-for-age Z-score:	1.10 to 1.30
weight-for-age Z-score:	1.00 to 1.20
weight-for-height Z-score:	0.85 to 1.10

The observed means and standard deviations of the anthropometric Z-score distribution for each survey are listed in Table 17. In several surveys where age was not based on date of birth, the standard deviation of the Z-score distribution ranged from 1.4 to 1.8, even after the exclusion of values regarded as likely errors (*84*).

This consistent finding of a nearly constant variance, or SD, in height- and weight-based Z-score distributions provides an opportunity to assess data quality. Studies with an SD outside the above ranges require closer examination for possible problems related to age assessment and anthropometric measurements. For example, if the SD value of the height-for-age Z-score distribution decreases with increasing age, poor technique for length measurement might be suspected, which may be the result of the greater difficulty in measuring infants properly. Inaccurate age assessment of older children may result in an SD value of the height-for-age distribution that increases with age.

It is less common to encounter a Z-score distribution with an SD value that is lower than expected. In the case of the weight-for-height Z-score distribution, a small SD may suggest increased mortality among children with the lowest weight-for-height, resulting in a more homogeneous sample (82).

5.4.5 *Data compilation and documentation*

For population-based data management, proper documentation of data processing, exclusion criteria, and treatment of missing values is essential. The proportion of cases or measurements excluded because of suspected errors should also be reported to provide a measure of data quality.

5.4.6 *Data analysis and presentation*

Anthropometric data for populations should always be presented according to sex and age groups (2, 3). The following age stratification is recommended:

minimum: 0-23, 24+ months (if age unavailable, < 85 cm or ≥ 85 cm)

acceptable: 0-11, 12-23, 24-59, 60+ months

best: 0-5, 6-11, 12-17, 18-23, 24-35, 36-47, 48-59, 60-71 months, etc.

Of the three reporting systems used to express anthropometric data in relation to a reference – percentiles, percent of median, and Z-scores – only Z-scores are recommended for analysis and presentation because of the various advantages cited in section 5.1.2 (20). For population-based assessment, including surveys and nutritional surveillance, there are two ways of expressing anthropometry-based results using Z-scores. One is the commonly used cut-off-based prevalence and confidence interval for the indicators; the other includes the summary statistics of the Z-scores – mean, median, SD, standard error, and frequency distribution.

Prevalence-based reporting
For consistency with clinical screening, prevalence-based data are commonly reported using a cut-off value, often -2 and +2 Z-scores (see section 5.2.2). The rationale for this is the statistical definition of the central 95% of a distribution as the "normal" range, which is not necessarily based on the optimal point for predicting functional outcomes. This definition has been called the "classic prevalence" (see Fig. 26).

The use of -2 Z-scores as a cut-off ensures that 2.3% of the reference population will be classified as malnourished even if they are truly "healthy" individuals with no growth impairment. Hence, 2.3% can be

Figure 26

Approaches for estimating "true" prevalence of malnutrition (shaded area) in a population

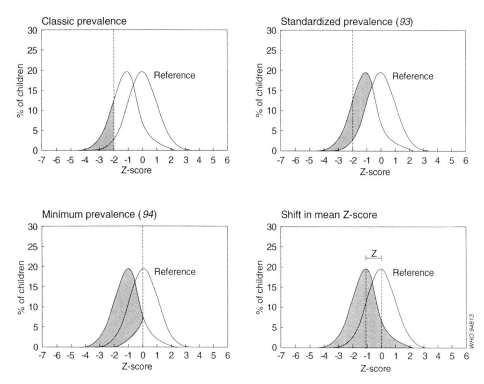

regarded as the baseline or expected prevalence. For this reason, proper assessment of the prevalence of a condition requires the subtraction of the baseline prevalence from the observed prevalence. In the case of low height-for-age, worldwide prevalences are often many times greater than the expected level of 2.3% (7), and failure to subtract the baseline level is unlikely to affect the interpretation of findings. In some countries, however, a cut-off of <-1 Z-score has been proposed, which has an expected prevalence of 16% in the reference population. Failure to subtract this value will obviously create the impression of a substantial level of nutritional problems. Since routine subtraction of the expected prevalence of 16% is unlikely, the use of the -1 Z-score cut-off is not recommended. For the same reasons, defining children with Z-scores between -1 and -2 as "mildly" malnourished is not recommended.

One reason for selecting a higher cut-off value to define malnutrition is to improve the precision of the prevalence estimate or increase the power of a given survey without expanding the sample size. An alternative is to define the prevalence as the proportion below the median (or 0 Z-score) after subtracting the expected prevalence of 50%. This method of estimating prevalence has been called the "median shift" (92).

Two further alternatives to the "classic prevalence" have been proposed: the "standardized prevalence" (93) and the "minimum prevalence" (94). Both methods attempt to improve on the shortcomings of the fixed cut-off prevalence, which often gives the impression – incorrect in most of the less developed areas – that all individuals above the cut-off level are "normal" or "well nourished". These proposed alternative methods both use theoretical considerations to define the prevalence of malnutrition and overcome the weaknesses of a fixed cut-off.

Mora (93) proposes a "standardized prevalence estimate", which is based on the proportion of individuals of the observed distribution who fall outside the reference distribution (Fig. 26). The method proposed by Monteiro (94), the "minimum prevalence", is based on the assumption that, in a population with a high prevalence of malnutrition, there are two sub-populations: one "malnourished" with a distribution shifted downward from the reference and the other "non-malnourished" with a distribution overlapping the reference. The non-malnourished proportion is calculated by doubling the percentage of children who are above the reference mean or median; the remaining proportion is the minimum prevalence estimate (Fig. 26). Both modified approaches have a fixed relationship with the cut-off-based prevalence, but the minimum prevalence gives a higher estimate than the standardized prevalence.

A major advantage of these alternative approaches is that, when the observed distribution is the same as the reference distribution, as is often the case for weight-for-height, the prevalence would be zero, rather than at an artificial baseline level of 2.3% based on the -2 Z-score cut-off.

Both proposed methods are used strictly to estimate the severity of the deficit in a population; unlike "classic prevalence", they do not identify which individuals are affected. In fact, both represent a significant improvement in defining the level of malnutrition in a population by not focusing only on severely affected children at the low end of the distribution. This is especially important in the light of recent evidence that the less severe forms of malnutrition create a greater burden on mortality (35).

Mean Z-score-based reporting
An alternative to the prevalence-based approach for expressing severity of anthropometric deficits or malnutrition is the calculation of summary statistics of the Z-scores, including mean and standard deviation. The mean Z-score, though less commonly used, has the advantage of describing the nutritional status of the entire population directly, without resorting to a subset of individuals below a set cut-off (Fig. 26). As an index of severity for malnutrition, it also addresses the conceptual shortcomings that "standardized prevalence" and "minimum prevalence" are intended to overcome by not assuming that only those individuals below the cut-off are affected.

The calculation of mean Z-score is straightforward in a computer-based operation, and mean Z-score value corresponds to the graphical presentation of the Z-score distribution.

A mean Z-score significantly lower than zero – the expected value for the reference distribution – usually means that the entire distribution has shifted downward, suggesting that most, if not all, individuals have been affected. This is confirmed by the examination of data from multiple population-based surveys. Both secular trends in height-for-age or weight-for-age and deterioration of weight-for-height during emergency situations are accompanied by a generalized shift of the entire distribution, not just a change in its shape or skewness (47, 81, 82, 95). Figure 24 provides an example of high rates of wasting being a result of a generalized downward shift of the entire weight-for-height distribution (83). Another example of a downward shift of the entire height- and weight-for-age distributions may be seen in Fig. 7.

Using the mean Z-score as an index of severity for health and nutrition problems results in increased awareness that, if a condition is severe, an intervention is required for the entire community, not just those who are classified as "malnourished" by the cut-off criteria (96). Plotting the entire distribution of the Z-scores against the reference distribution is helpful in representing the nutritional status of the population (Figs 7, 24, 26).

Because the standard deviation of the Z-score distribution for height- and weight-based indices is usually within 0.2 SD units of the expected value of 1.0, and since this value can be computed directly, the mean and SD of the Z-score distribution can be used to estimate the fixed-cut-off prevalence (84). Table 17 confirms the constancy of the standard deviations of Z-score distributions in numerous countries and for widely varying nutritional status. The main advantage of such an indirect estimate is that the required sample size is smaller than that needed to observe the actual prevalence at a fixed cut-off. This is analogous to the fact that, for a given sample size, the precision is greater for determining the median than it is for estimating the 3rd percentile.

The conversion of mean Z-score to a prevalence based on < -2 Z-scores is as follows:

Option 1:   probit [(-2 - observed mean Z-score)/SD]

Option 2:   assuming SD is 1.0:

                  probit (-2 - observed mean Z-score)

The probit function is a complex equation, not given here, that converts Z-score values to cumulative percentiles. For example, for a survey with a mean weight-for-height Z-score of -0.9 and an SD of 1.0, the probit function of [-2 - (-0.9)] or -1.1 is 0.14, meaning that 14% of the children would fall below the -2 SD cut-off. Table 23 allows mean Z-scores to be converted to estimated prevalences below -2 SD.

Table 23
Estimated prevalence below –2 SD after conversion from a given mean Z-score

Mean Z-score	Prevalence (%)	Mean Z-score	Prevalence (%)
–3.0	84	–1.0	16
–2.5	69	–0.9	14
–2.4	66	–0.8	12
–2.3	62	–0.7	10
–2.2	58	–0.6	8
–2.1	54	–0.5	6.7
–2.0	50	–0.4	6.0
–1.9	46	–0.3	4.5
–1.8	42	–0.2	3.6
–1.7	38	–0.1	2.8
–1.6	34	0	2.3
–1.5	31	+0.1	1.8
–1.4	27	+0.2	1.4
–1.3	24	+0.3	1.1
–1.2	21	+0.4	0.8
–1.1	18	+0.5	0.6

In summary, the following information should be included when population-based anthropometric data are reported:

- general characteristics of the population and circumstances (e.g. local or displaced; emergency or non-emergency; increased mortality, etc.)
- sample size
- design of the survey or surveillance system
- measurement methods
- method of determining age
- proportion of data missing or excluded because of likely error, and the exclusion criteria
- prevalence based on a fixed cut-off, e.g. < -2 Z-scores
- confidence interval of the prevalence estimate
- mean Z-scores, with 95% confidence interval or standard error of the mean
- standard deviation of Z-scores
- frequency distribution plot of the Z-scores against the reference distribution.

A complete report for a population sample should include sex and age group stratifications as well as stratification by other characteristics of special interest such as feeding mode for infants.

5.5 Methods of measurement

The basic measurement methods for height and weight are covered in detail elsewhere (97) and described in Annex 2.

5.5.1 *Height measurements*

Height measurements can be based on recumbent length or standing height. In general, length measurements are recommended for children under 2 years of age, and height measurements for others; this is partly because these were the procedures used in the current NCHS/WHO international reference (2). However, it is difficult to obtain accurate height measurements for 2–3-year-old children – especially when they are uncooperative – and many surveys now measure the length of children of up to 5 years of age.

In general, length or height is measured and reported to the nearest 0.1 cm, even though this is less than the measurement error of nearly 0.5 cm. For any child, the length measurement is approximately 0.5–1.5 cm greater than the height measurement. It is therefore recommended that, when a length measurement is applied to a height-based reference for children over 24 months of age (or over 85 cm if age is not known), 1.0 cm be subtracted before the length measurement is compared with the reference.

5.5.2 *Weight measurements*

Weight measurements are reported to the nearest 0.1 kg. Ideally, weight should be determined with the child wearing no clothing. However, for cultural and social reasons, the common practice is for the child to wear one layer of undergarments.

5.5.3 *Age determination*

Whenever possible, information on age should be obtained from a written birth record or similar document, with verbal information on date of birth from the mother or primary care-giver as the second choice. Only as a last resort should information be based on reported age. For computer-based anthropometric applications, age should be calculated in months to at least one decimal place.

5.6 Sources and characteristics of reference data

5.6.1 *Issues related to selection and application of references*

Most references are composite growth curves based on a mixture of infants and children with varied health and nutritional status and medical histories. Such curves are intended to serve as a reference point for screening and monitoring, not as an absolute criterion for defining "malnutrition" or pathology (3). In practice, however, current growth curves are used as a standard and specific decisions are made on the basis of cut-off points. Issues related to the selection and application of references are discussed in detail in section 2.9.

The traditional, normative approach to building a reference includes choosing, for example, a representative sample of young children from a developed country. An alternative approach is to justify a reference on the basis of recommended rather than existing practices. In infancy, this might define the reference population as well nourished and healthy children whose feeding mode and health care during the first year follow established recommendations for breast-feeding and immunization, and might include consideration of prenatal health practices and birth weight. These issues are further discussed below in the context of development of infant growth curves.

5.6.2 *Local versus international references*

An international reference is clearly needed to allow comparison of the nutritional status of populations in different parts of the world. There is evidence that the growth in height and weight of well fed, healthy children, or children who experience unconstrained growth, from different ethnic backgrounds and different continents is reasonably similar, at least up to 5 years of age (21, 98). While it is accepted that there are some variations in the growth patterns of children from different racial or ethnic groups in developed countries, these are relatively minor compared with the large worldwide variation that relates to health, nutrition, and socioeconomic status (22). For this reason, a common reference has the advantage of uniform application, allowing international comparisons without loss of its usefulness for local application (99); this outweighs the disadvantage of the common reference taking no account of minor racial and ethnic variations.

Beyond the inherent lack of value for international comparisons, there are several reasons for not developing a local reference or standard (100):

- many populations in less developed areas experience growth deficits as a result of poor health and nutrition, and any reference developed from such populations therefore has less screening value for the detection of health and nutritional disorders;
- significant secular changes in growth status within a relatively short period of time may render a local reference less useful for clinical screening;
- proper reference development is not a task that can be undertaken easily or frequently; and
- development of local references is very costly.

5.6.3 *Factors affecting the use and interpretation of growth references*

A number of non-pathological factors may influence the growth status of infants and children; some have the potential to alter the interpretation of growth status at both the individual and the population level.

- *Feeding practice.* Breast-fed infants living under favourable conditions in various geographical areas have been reported to follow negative trends relative to the NCHS/WHO weight-for-age, and possibly length-for-age, percentiles during the latter half of the recommended period of exclusive breast-feeding, i.e. after the third month, and to sustain those negative trends during the ensuing period of *ad libitum* mixed feeding of breast milk and solid foods. The magnitude of negative deviations often appears to be sufficient for health workers to make possibly faulty decisions regarding the adequacy of growth in infants following current WHO feeding recommendations. This possibility is of special concern in developing countries where breast-feeding is the key to survival or, at the very least, to the avoidance of severe infectious morbidity.

- *Racial and ethnic variation.* Evidence exists for the following racial and ethnic variations, although these are relatively minor compared with variations that relate to socioeconomic status:

  - weight-for-height status is lower for children of the Indian sub-continent (*8*)

  - Hispanic children in Central and South America appear to have higher weight-for-height status (*8, 89*)

  - black children are of lower birth weight and smaller size during infancy, but exceed the size of white children after 2–3 years of age (*101*).

- *Sex.* In the age range of concern (birth to 10 years) the average weights and heights of boys are consistently greater than those of girls. Sex-specific references are therefore recommended, except possibly in disaster situations where simplification of procedures may require the use of combined-sex references.

- *Size at birth.* Birth size and intrauterine growth status appear to be strong determinants of growth status later in childhood even in the birth-weight range commonly accepted as normal (2.5–4.0 kg). Intrauterine growth-retarded infants grow more slowly than preterm infants of the same birth weight (*43*).

- *Parental stature.* Parental size, especially height, is a determinant of both birth weight and later childhood growth.

- *Altitude.* The environmental factor that has most effect on growth but is not associated with socioeconomic status is altitude (or oxygen partial pressure); high altitude leads to reduced birth weight and lesser subsequent growth (*102*).

With the exception of sex and possibly of infant feeding mode, few of the factors discussed here seem to warrant a separate reference to accommodate the observed variations. However, awareness of these factors can be valuable in adjusting for possible variations when comparisons are made across groups.

Regardless of the approach taken, the definition of the reference population must include consideration of variability. A reference with an inappropriately small variability will result in more children classified as being of clinical concern than a reference with more variability. Since references are intended for international use, they should reflect the variability observed cross-nationally (and, to an extent, that due to genetic differences) in well nourished, healthy populations.

5.6.4 *The current international reference (NCHS/WHO reference)*

Background and history

The original National Center for Health Statistics/Centers for Disease Control (NCHS/CDC) growth curves were formulated in 1975 by combining growth data from four sources to serve as a reference for the USA (*103*). The reference for ages 0-23 months is based upon a group of children in the Fels Research Institute Longitudinal Study from 1929 to 1975. It reflects growth of children who were fed primarily with infant formula and who were of restricted genetic, geographical, and socio-economic background, which does not provide strong justification for its use as a reference. The height curve for this part of the reference was based on recumbent length or supine measurement (the Fels curves). The reference from 2-18 years was based on data from three representative surveys conducted in the USA from 1960 to 1975; the height curves for this age range were based on standing height measurement (the NCHS curves). It was intended that length measurements be interpreted with the Fels curves, and height measurements with the NCHS curves. The fact that this reference was made up from two unrelated samples or sets of curves is its major limitation; ideally, a reference should be based on a single set of curves or on a single survey sample.

In 1978, the NCHS/CDC reference was adopted by WHO as the international reference. In 1980, a software version of the reference for mainframe computers was developed by CDC to facilitate the interpretation of growth data from surveys or clinical studies. In order to formulate the software-based reference, the original height or weight distributions were slightly modified by a normalization procedure (*104*). This normalized reference can provide percentiles and Z-scores of weight-for-age, height-for-age, and weight-for-height.

Throughout the 1980s, several microcomputer-based software versions of the NCHS/WHO reference were developed and supported by CDC and WHO (*105*). These have contributed significantly to the wide acceptance of the concept of the international reference by simplifying the handling of anthropometric data from surveys, surveillance, and clinical studies.

Comparison of current NCHS/WHO reference data with the growth of breast-fed infants

There are many reports in the literature regarding negative deviations from the NCHS/WHO reference in the growth of breast-fed infants (*106*). These prompted an examination of the growth of infants fed according to WHO feeding recommendations, which include breast-feeding exclusively for the first 4-6 months and breast-feeding plus complementary foods until at least 12 months of age, and comparison with the reference data. Further comparisons were made between the growth of other groups of infants and both the reference data and the data for breast-fed infants.

Building of the "breast-fed set" curves. A survey of investigators with data on growth of breast-fed infants was undertaken. The criteria for inclusion of data in the initial review were:

- data available on growth during the first 12 months of life for a sample of at least 20 infants who were fully breast-fed for at least 4 months;
- measurement intervals no greater than 2 months during the first 6 months of life and no greater than 3 months during the second 6 months;
- information available on duration of breast-feeding, use of supplementary milks, formulas, and solid foods, and timing of their introduction; and
- documentation of socioeconomic conditions consistent with the achievement of growth potential.

Seven sets of data fulfilled these criteria and were examined in detail: two from the USA and one each from Canada, Denmark, Finland, Sweden, and the United Kingdom (*106, 107*). Standard anthropometric procedures were used in all the studies to measure infant weight and length.

The countries, number of subjects, and recruitment criteria for each of these seven studies are shown in Table 24. The "number eligible" refers to the number of infants who met the criteria for inclusion in the pooled analysis, which were that they had been breast-fed for at least 4 months, been given no solid foods before 4 months, and received no formula or other milks before 4 months. These criteria correspond to the category of "predominantly breast-fed" as defined by WHO (*108*), but it should be noted that some infants may have received other milks or formulas on an occasional basis (not daily) – the investigators generally did not exclude or fully document such cases.

Preterm or low-birth-weight infants were excluded from five of the seven studies, and three studies also excluded large-for-gestational-age infants.

Of the 453 infants followed in the seven studies, 226 were breast-fed for at least 12 months. These infants are referred to subsequently as the "breast-fed set". Of these 226, 141 were not regularly given formula or other milks in the first year of life; more than half the infants were

Table 24
Characteristics of the studies providing data for the growth curves of breast-fed infants (the "breast-fed set")[a]

Country of study	Dates of study	No. of subjects	No. eligible "A"[b]	No. eligible "B"[c]	Recruitment criteria	Reference
Canada	1977–1980	398	63	23	Term, healthy	109
Denmark	1987–1989	91	32	14	Singleton, term, healthy; birth weight between 10th and 90th percentiles	110
Finland	1981–1982	202	144	68	Singleton, term, healthy, AGA; mother healthy, non-smoker	111
Sweden	1979–1980	314	61	9	Healthy	112
United Kingdom	1984–1989	279	44	27	Singleton, healthy, > 35 weeks' gestation	113
USA	1986–1991	119	50	47	Singleton, term, birth weight > 2500 g; planned to be breast-fed to 12+ months; mother healthy	114
USA	1987–1991	71	59	38	Term, healthy, AGA	115

[a] Source: reference 106.
[b] Criteria for inclusion: breast-fed for at least 4 months *and* no solid foods before 4 months *and* no formula or other milks before 4 months.
[c] Criterion for inclusion: breast-feeding continued to at least 12 months.

not given solid foods until 6 months or later. Eligibility by duration of breast-feeding and age at introduction of formula or other milk is shown in Table 25.

Levels of maternal education were high in the three studies that reported on this, with an overall mean of 15.4 years of education. Mean birth weights in the seven studies ranged from 3414 to 3605 g.

The Z-score patterns of infants in the "breast-fed set" relative to the NCHS/WHO reference are shown in Fig. 27. Mean weight-for-age declined continuously from 2 to 12 months to a low of almost -0.6 SD at

Table 25
Number of eligible subjects by breast-feeding duration and age at introduction of milk or formula[a]

Breast-feeding duration	No. of infants given milk or formula			
	at 4–5 months	>6 months but before termination of breast-feeding	6 months and after termination of breast-feeding	Total
4-5 months	10	0	0	10
6-8 months	45	21	12	78
9-11 months	26	65	48	139
12+ months	20	65	141	226
Total	101	151	201	453

[a] Source: reference *106*.

Figure 27
Mean Z-scores of infants in the "breast-fed set", relative to the NCHS/WHO reference

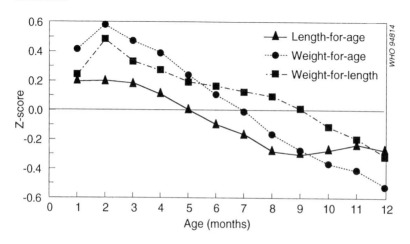

12 months. Length-for-age declined less, with the mean Z-score tending to stabilize or increase after 8 months; the mean value at 12 months was approximately -0.3 SD. Mean weight-for-length at 12 months was also below the NCHS/WHO reference median (approximately -0.3 SD). The declining Z-scores observed during the period of complementary feeding are difficult to interpret, but it is possible that these are artifacts resulting from technical problems in the construction of the NCHS/WHO reference as discussed in section 5.6.4. The declines may also be a consequence of specific weaning practices within the population studied, of other physiological effects attributable to continued breast-feeding, or of unidentified characteristics in the populations used to construct the NCHS/WHO reference and the "breast-fed set".

There was a return towards the current reference medians for weight-for-age, length-for-age, and weight-for-length between 12 and 24 months in most of the studies that provided data on this age range. While data at 24 months are insufficient for determining whether the median value for breast-fed infants would coincide with the NCHS/WHO median, they do suggest that this may be the case.

Variance of the "breast-fed set" data. One of the objectives of analysing the growth of infants fed according to WHO recommendations was to examine the variance of the anthropometric indices. This is critical for the creation of reference data because the Z-score or percentile lines, as well as the statistically defined cut-off values, depend on the "spread" of values in the original data set. If a reference population is "too" homogeneous, the distribution of values will be unacceptably narrow, resulting in cut-off values closer to the median than would be the case for a more heterogeneous reference population.

Standard deviations in weight and length for the "breast-fed set", compared with the SDs from the current NCHS/WHO reference data, are shown in Figs 28 and 29. For both boys and girls, SDs from the "breast-fed set" are smaller than those from the NCHS/WHO reference. However, the impact on cut-off values (e.g. ±2 SD) depends not only on the SD, but also on the placement of the median value. Because of this, the difference in cut-off values between the "breast-fed set" and the current reference depends on infant age, as shown in Figs 30-33. In the first 6-8 months, when the median for the "breast-fed set" is higher than the NCHS/WHO median, the -2 SD values for the former are higher than those based on the latter. After approximately 8 months, when the median for the "breast-fed set" is lower than the current reference median, the -2 SD values for the former are lower than (for weight) or similar to (for length) those based on the latter. For the same reasons, the +2 SD values for the "breast-fed set" are similar to those of the NCHS/WHO reference during early infancy, but later are considerably lower.

The distribution of birth weights is one major factor that may account for the lower variance of the "breast-fed set" compared with the current reference. Most of the studies of breast-fed infants excluded preterm or

Figure 28
Standard deviation of weight (kg) in the "breast-fed set" compared with the NCHS/WHO reference

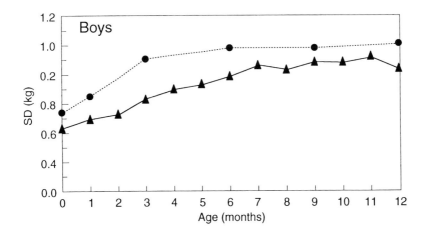

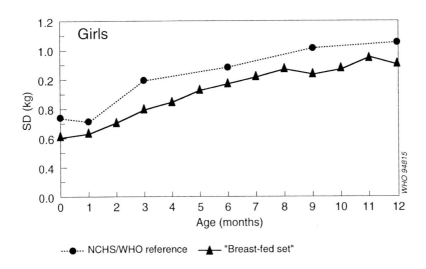

···●··· NCHS/WHO reference   ▲ "Breast-fed set"

Figure 29
**Standard deviation of length (cm) of infants in the "breast-fed set" compared with
the NCHS/WHO reference**

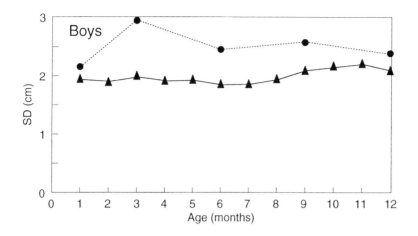

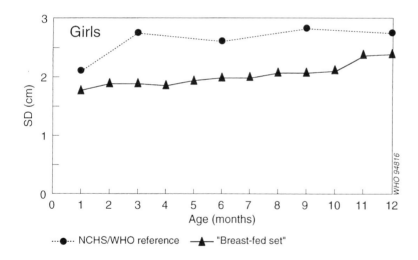

····●··· NCHS/WHO reference   ▲ "Breast-fed set"

Cut-off values of 2 Z-scores below the median weight, according to the "breast-fed set" and to the current NCHS/WHO reference

Cut-off values of 2 Z-scores below the median length, according to the "breast-fed set" and to the current NCHS/WHO reference

Figure 32
Cut-off values of 2 Z-scores above the median weight, according to the "breast-fed set" and to the current NCHS/WHO reference

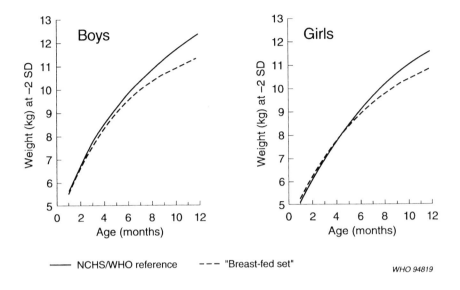

Figure 33
Cut-off values of 2 Z-scores above the median length, according to the "breast-fed set" and to the current NCHS/WHO reference

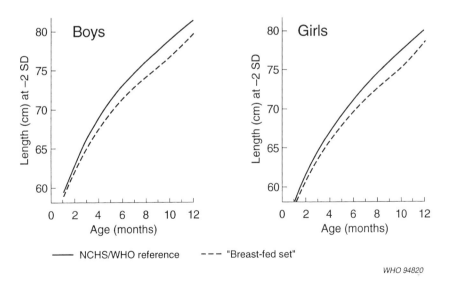

low-birth-weight infants, and several also excluded large-for-gestational-age infants. In addition, the samples included families of a generally high educational level, living under favourable environmental conditions. Mean birth weight in the "breast-fed set" was similar to that of a representative sample of white infants in the USA who met certain criteria indicative of low risk (gestational age ≥ 37 weeks; mother married and at least 20 years of age; at least one parent completed high school) (*116*) (Figs 34 and 35), but the SD was about 70 g lower ($P < 0.05$; Table 26). Considering only the three studies in the "breast-fed set", which did not use any exclusion criteria (*109, 112, 113*), the birth weight SDs were generally quite similar to that of the "low risk" USA population. However, the birth weight SD of the "breast-fed set" was about 120 g lower than that of the Fels data set (*117*) from which the NCHS/WHO reference was derived ($P < 0.005$; see Table 25). It is likely that there were more low-birth-weight infants in the Fels study than in the "breast-fed set". This may be due, at least in part, to "healthier" practices during pregnancy among mothers who choose to breast-feed for the first 12 months; alternatively, mothers of low-birth-weight infants may have more difficulty breast-feeding to 12 months (*118*).

Comparison of the growth of infants from different populations with the "breast-fed set" curves. To determine the potential impact of using a new growth chart based on breast-fed infants, data from several "test" populations were evaluated against both the "breast-fed set" and the NCHS/WHO reference (*106, 107*). The test populations were: breast-fed infants from poor populations in developing countries (India, Peru), breast-fed infants from a range of socioeconomic backgrounds (from five countries included in a study organized by the UNDP/UNFPA/WHO/ World Bank Special Programme of Research, Development and Research Training in Human Reproduction (HRP)), and formula-fed infants from affluent populations.

The data from India come from a cross-sectional study conducted by Anderson (*119*) of predominantly breast-fed infants under 6 months of

Table 26
Means and standard deviations of birth weights from various data sets[a]

Data set	Birth weight ± SD (grams)	
	Boys	Girls
Breast-fed infants	3509 ± 419	3450 ± 405
White USA infants from low-risk population (*116*)	3565 ± 492	3423 ± 470
Fels Research Institute (*117*)	3400 ± 561	3250 ± 530
Formula-fed counterparts	3485 ± 530	3400 ± 458

[a] Source: reference *106*.

Figure 34
Birth weights of the "breast-fed set" infants compared with low-risk infants (boys) in the USA

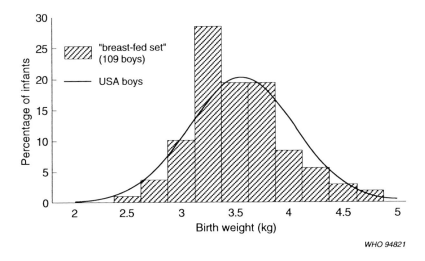

Figure 35
Birth weights of the "breast-fed set" infants compared with low-risk infants (girls) in the USA

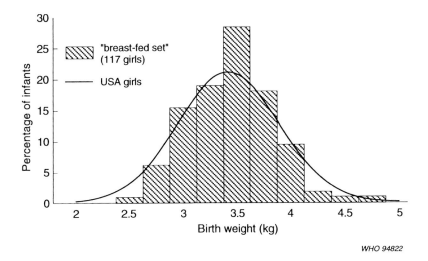

age. The Z-scores for these infants, calculated using either the current NCHS/WHO reference or the "breast-fed set", are shown in Fig. 36. Regardless of the basis for comparison used, the weights and lengths of Indian infants at birth are very low. The Z-scores are more negative relative to the "breast-fed set"; this would be expected, since medians for the "breast-fed set" during the first 6 months are higher than for the current reference. The shape of the Z-score pattern is also quite different, resulting in different interpretations of the timing of growth faltering. When compared with the current reference, the mean weight-for-age Z-score of the Indian infants increased between birth and 3 months, but then declined between 3 and 6 months. In contrast, when compared with the "breast-fed set", the Indian infants show a slight decline in weight-for-age from birth to 1 month, but an increase in mean Z-scores occurred thereafter and was sustained until 5 months. Declining status in weight-for-age would therefore be identified at 3 months using the NCHS/WHO reference but not until 5 months using the "breast-fed set". If these differences persist after the envisaged corrections to the NCHS/WHO reference data versus a breast-fed data-set reference, this has potentially

Figure 36

Weight-for-age, length-for-age, and weight-for-length mean Z-scores of rural Indian infants, compared with the current NCHS/WHO reference and with the "breast-fed set"

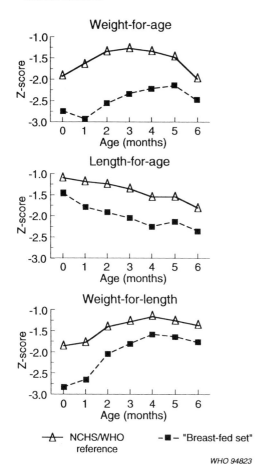

important implications for the optimal timing of complementary feeding of breast-fed infants.

The mean length-for-age Z-scores of the Indian infants were also lower when the "breast-fed set" was used rather than the current NCHS/WHO reference. In contrast to the pattern of weight-for-age, which increased in the early months, the mean length-for-age Z-scores of the Indian infants declined from birth, regardless of the basis for comparison used.

The mean weight-for-length Z-scores of the Indian infants were low at birth, particularly with respect to the "breast-fed set", but increased thereafter to approximately -0.5 using the current reference and -1.0 using the "breast-fed set".

The same data are shown in Fig. 37, expressed in terms of the percentage of infants below -2 Z-scores of the current NCHS/WHO reference or of the "breast-fed set". Using the current reference, 20-55% of infants would be classified as underweight (i.e. below -2 SD) during the first 6 months, compared with 50-75% using the "breast-fed set". The percentage classified as stunted would be 25-40% using the current reference and 40-60% using the "breast-fed set". Low weight-for-length was common at birth (45-80%), but much less so at 2-6 months (10% or less using the current reference and 20-30% using the "breast-fed set").

Similar analyses were carried out for infants from a squatter community on the outskirts of Lima, Peru. The analyses were restricted to 52 infants who were predominantly breast-fed and were measured every month during the first year of life (*120*). The Z-score values are shown in Fig. 38. Mean weight-for-age Z-scores of the Peruvian infants increased

Figure 37
Percentages of rural Indian infants with weight-for-age, length-for-age, or weight-for-length below the –2 Z-score cut-off value, according to the current NCHS/WHO reference and to the "breast-fed set"

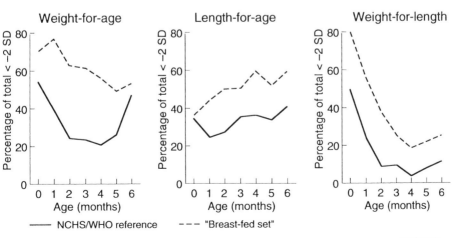

WHO 94824

in early infancy using either basis for comparison; as with the Indian infants, however, a decline began at 3 months using the current reference but not until 4–5 months using the "breast-fed set". On the other hand, the mean length-for-age Z-score declined by 3 months regardless of which basis was used for comparison. The mean weight-for-length Z-scores using the "breast-fed set" were somewhat lower from 1 to 4 months than those derived using the current reference, but from 5 to 12 months the results were very similar with either data set.

Figure 38

Weight-for-age, length-for-age, and weight-for-length mean Z-scores of peri-urban Peruvian infants compared with the current NCHS/WHO reference and with the "breast-fed set"

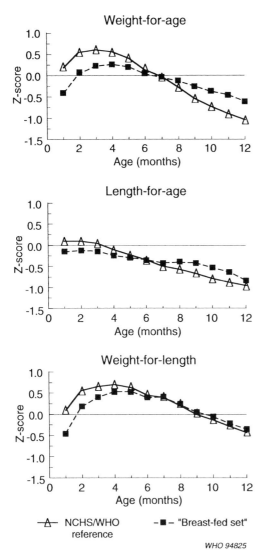

Figure 39

Percentages of peri-urban Peruvian infants with weight-for-age, length-for-age, or weight-for-length below the –2 Z-score cut-off value, according to the current NCHS/WHO reference and to the "breast-fed set"

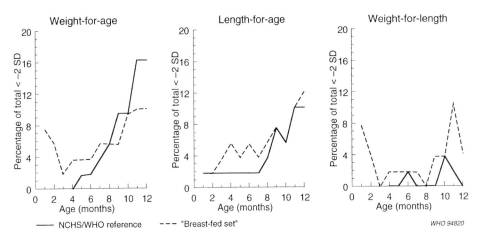

The proportions of Peruvian infants below the -2 Z-scores cut-off are shown in Fig. 39. The percentage classified as underweight during the first 6 months was somewhat higher using the "breast-fed set" (4-8%) than using the current NCHS/WHO reference (0-2%), but after 8 months the situation was reversed: by 12 months the percentage underweight was about 10% using the "breast-fed set" compared with 16% using the current reference. The percentage classified as stunted was relatively low (2-6%) during the first 6 months using either basis for comparison; after 6 months the prevalence of stunting increased, but results were similar using either basis for comparison. Relatively few infants were classified as low in weight-for-length: 0-8% using the "breast-fed set" and 0-4% using the current reference.

Data for a formula-fed test population are illustrated in Figs 40 and 41. These data came from the DARLING (*114*; *n*=45) and the EURONUT studies (Haschke et al., unpublished data; *n*=148); all infants included were breast-fed for 3 months or less. Using the current NCHS/WHO reference, the mean weights-for-age of the formula-fed cohort were higher than the median for the first 8 months but relatively close to the median at 9-12 months. In contrast, the mean weight-for-age Z-scores generated using the "breast-fed set" began close to the median but increased thereafter to an average of about +0.6 at 12 months. Mean length-for-age and weight-for-length Z-scores after 6 months were also higher using the "breast-fed set". The percentage of formula-fed infants classified as above +2 Z-scores is shown in Fig. 41. About 7% of formula-fed infants would be classified as high in weight-for-length at 10-12 months using the "breast-fed set", compared with 3% or less using the current reference.

Data from the HRP Study conducted in eight centres in Chile, Egypt, Hungary, Kenya, and Thailand were also used as a test population (*121*). The weights of 2478 infants were measured. Of these, 1273 infants were measured at each of the planned times: 1.5 months and at months 2 to 12. Nearly all infants (98%) were breast-fed (two or more feedings per day) to at least 12 months. About one-third of the infants (30%) were fully breast-fed to at least 4 months, then partially to at least 12 months; the remaining two-thirds (68%) were fully breast-fed for less than

Figure 40

Weight-for-age, length-for-age, and weight-for-length mean Z-scores of USA and European formula-fed infants compared with the current NCHS/WHO reference and with the "breast-fed set"

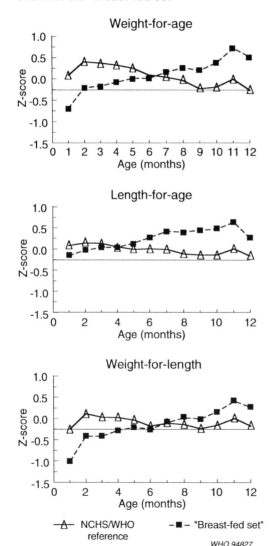

Figure 41
Percentages of USA and European formula-fed infants with weight-for-age, length-for-age, or weight-for-length above the +2 Z-score cut-off value, according to the current NCHS/WHO reference and to the "breast-fed set"

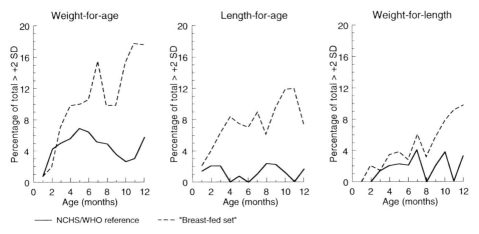

WHO 94828

4 months, but partial breast-feeding continued for at least 12 months. Figure 42 shows that, using the current NCHS/WHO reference, the mean weight-for-age Z-scores began somewhat higher than the median, fell below the median at 5 months, and averaged approximately -0.6 by 12 months. In comparison with the "breast-fed set", the mean Z-scores were very stable from 2 to 12 months, at about -0.3. The percentage of infants below -2 Z-scores at each month is shown in Fig. 43. In the first 6 months, the percentage classified as underweight was relatively low: 3-6% using the "breast-fed set" and less than 2% using the current reference. In the second 6 months, the percentage classified as underweight increased to about 11% at 12 months using the current reference but to only 6% using the "breast-fed set".

These findings suggest that the interpretation of the growth of infants can vary substantially according to whether the current reference or the "breast-fed set" data are used.

Revision of the reference in view of problems with the current NCHS/WHO reference

Height-for-age disjunction. Using the software-based reference for interpreting growth data from large surveys or studies, the mean Z-score of height-for-age and the prevalence of low height-for-age consistently showed an abrupt change at 2 years of age (*122*). In fact, there is a significant disjunction in the height curve between the length-based Fels curves for children under 2 years of age and the height-based NCHS curves for older children. A recent study examined the nature and magnitude of the possible disturbance of the current NCHS/WHO

Figure 42
Mean weight-for-age Z-scores of infants enrolled in the HRP Study compared with the current NCHS/WHO reference and with the "breast-fed set"

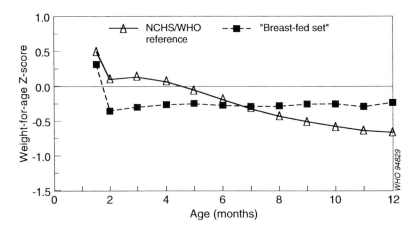

Figure 43
Percentages of infants enrolled in the HRP Study with weight-for-age below the –2 Z-score cut-off value, according to the current NCHS/WHO reference and to the "breast-fed set"

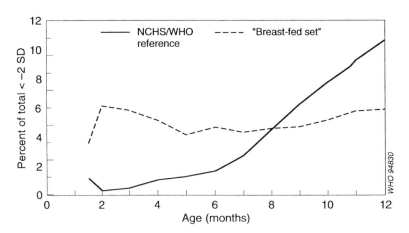

reference by using growth data from more recent representative surveys in the USA (*104*). The original procedures for constructing the current curves were also assessed to determine the possible reasons for the irregularities observed. The areas of "disturbance" can be summarized as follows:

- *The infancy deviation.* The height-for-age curve is lower than the length status of the Fels sample from 1 to 6 months of age, which resulted in an overestimation of observed length values at this age. This deviation is related to a lack of measurement points between 3 and 6 months in the original Fels data.

- *The early deviation.* From 12 to 24 months of age, the height-for-age curves are higher and the weight-for-height curves lower than the actual growth status of the USA reference sample. This deviation is the result of Fels children being taller than those in the USA representative samples, and is a problem if the reference is assumed to reflect the growth pattern of children in the USA.

- *The late deviations.* From 24 to 36 months of age, the height-for-age curve is lower than the height status of the USA reference sample; the weight-for-height curve is higher. However, from 36 to 72 months of age, the height-for-age curve is slightly higher than the actual height status. These deviations are the result of small sample sizes and inadequate statistical assumptions, as well as of the procedures used for construction of curves.

- *The 24-month disjunction.* There is a marked discrepancy in estimated height status immediately before and after 24 months of age. This represents the combined effect of an underestimation of height status with interpretation of the Fels sample length-based curves and an overestimation of height status with the height-based curves from the USA sample at 24 months of age. In essence, this is the net result of the early and late deviations. The magnitude of this disjunction is approximately half a standard deviation or 1.8 cm.

Figure 44 uses the mean height-for-age Z-score across age for four racial groups of low-income children in the USA, monitored by CDC to illustrate the significant changes described above (*101*). The impact of the 24-month disjunction on the prevalence of low height-for-age for these children is illustrated in Fig. 45. The magnitude of these inconsistencies or deviations warrants caution when the current reference is used to interpret the growth status of children covering a wide age range, as in surveys or in the context of growth monitoring.

Issues related to upward skewness of reference population. The height distributions of children of a given age are normally (symmetrically) distributed. By contrast, the distributions of weight-for-age and weight-for-height, though normal in some developed countries, are skewed towards the higher end in others. In fact, the current NCHS/WHO reference based on children in the USA is markedly skewed, reflecting a substantial level of childhood obesity. Using such a reference as a "standard" for optimal growth or health is unwarranted since the upward skewness may reflect an "unhealthy" characteristic of the sample. In addition, given the secular trends of increased overweight in both children and adults observed in the USA and in some other populations, it is of concern that, unless this issue is dealt with, future references will tend to be further and further to the right, thereby resulting in the misclassification of overweight children as "normal".

One potential solution is to use the standard deviation of the lower half of the distribution to model the upper half. The main justification for this is

Figure 44

Mean height-for-age Z-scores across age for four ethnic groups of low-income USA children monitored by the CDC Pediatric Nutrition Surveillance System, illustrating the marked shift in mean Z-scores across the 24-month disjunction[a]

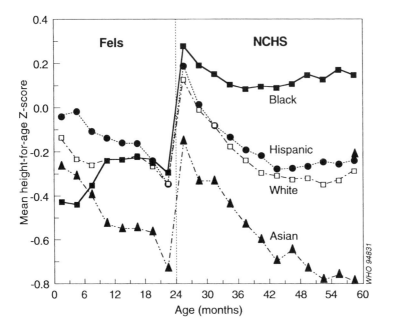

[a] Reproduced with permission from reference *101*. Copyright CRC Press, Boca Raton, Florida

Figure 45

Change in prevalence of low height-for-age of low-income USA children monitored by the CDC Pediatric Nutrition Surveillance System, illustrating the impact of the 24-month disjunction

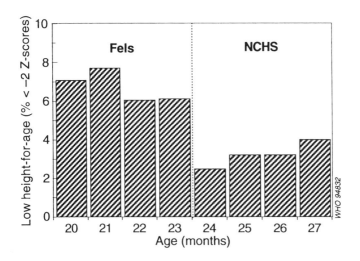

that variations in the lower half of the weight distributions among developed countries (populations with unconstrained growth) are relatively small. However, since there is insufficient knowledge of the normality of weight distribution in children of different ages, the issue of skewness should be the subject of further research.

Efforts to revise the current NCHS/WHO reference. Because of the potential for misinterpretation of anthropometric data resulting from the problems with the current reference discussed above, a revision was carried out by CDC in 1990 to correct some of the irregularities. The revision added further data from the original USA national survey to expand the sample size and provide more reliable curves, as well as to reduce the use of the Fels sample for 12 to 24 months. In addition, different statistical procedures were developed to ensure greater accuracy of the formulated curve. Figure 46 shows that the gap in height values between the Fels curves and the NCHS curves was reduced from the original 2.5 cm to 0.5 cm after the revision. However, this reflects only the difference between recumbent length and standing height, which was small in this case since the children were properly stretched for the length measurement (see section 5.5.1). Figure 47 shows the extent of the late deviation of the NCHS curve after 24 months.

Since a national representative sample of USA children under 12 months of age was not available, the Fels sample was retained for this age group. However, a new procedure, based on modelling the individual growth pattern, was used to overcome the inadequate measurement points for the sample. Unlike the original reference, where the Fels and the NCHS curves were kept as separate sets, the revised reference merged them at 12 months of age to create a single set, since an adequate fit was observed at this age.

Figure 46

Height-for-age disjunction at 24 months of the current NCHS/WHO reference and of the revised NCHS reference

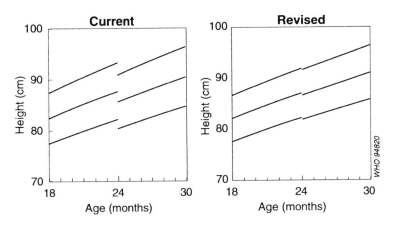

Figure 47

Comparison of the current NCHS/WHO reference and the revised NCHS reference in height-for-age after 24 months

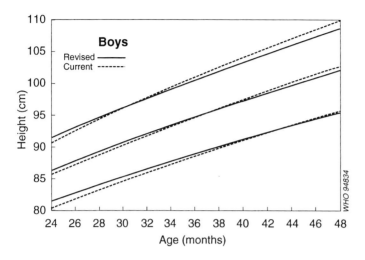

Adoption of the revised curves as the updated international reference for general use is not recommended, but the revised reference should be made available to researchers when it is necessary to compare height- and weight-based measures across age (see Figs 44 and 45) or to assess changes over time for a cohort of children. There are several reasons for not recommending their adoption for general use. One is that the most recent USA national nutrition survey (NHANES III), which has an expanded sample size for younger children, will offer a more definitive update of the reference curves for the USA by the late 1990s, and two changes in a decade would be too disruptive. A second reason is that the formulation of a truly international reference based on carefully conducted surveys covering broad populations from several countries might be more acceptable than data from a single country. The following characteristics are desirable if data sets are to be included in the reference:

- several countries should be included, among them less developed ones;
- they should be based on healthy populations with unconstrained growth (not necessarily representative); the definition of healthy populations is important in deciding whether or not the choice should take infant feeding modes into account (see section 5.6.4, page 227, and section 2.9);
- sample sizes and procedures should be adequate;
- the raw data should be available.

The following characteristics are also desirable, although not essential:

- the age range from birth to adolescence should be covered by most data sources;

- quality control and measurements should be standardized and standardization procedures should be documented;
- for adolescents, measures of sexual maturity should be available;
- secular trends in growth should be small or absent.

Conclusions and comments

The Expert Committee concluded that the current NCHS/WHO reference is inadequate and therefore recommends the development of a new weight and length reference for use in all infants. Infants fed according to WHO recommendations and living under conditions that favour the achievement of genetic growth potential grew less rapidly than, and deviated significantly from, the reference. Differences in growth patterns were most notable after 4–6 months. While it is probable that differences in growth patterns in the first 4–6 months were due mostly to technical inadequacies of the current reference, the same is unlikely to be true of growth differences in later periods. The lesser gains in length after 4–6 months in breast-fed infants supplemented *ad libitum* are sufficiently marked to concern both those who use the NCHS/WHO reference as a standard to assess the adequacy of feeding practices and those who regard maximum length as a reflection of optimum health.

It may be concluded that the present WHO feeding recommendations, as practised in affluent populations, did not result in maximum growth during the first year; the growth of these infants was not assessed at later ages. The assumption of an equivalence of maximum with optimal growth provides the rationale for the development of cut-offs based on the NCHS/WHO reference, although it has never been reviewed explicitly by an expert group. Current WHO feeding recommendations, on the other hand, are based on an expert review (5). The Expert Committee recognized that future scientific advances and worldwide improvements in sanitation may make it necessary to modify recommendations, but considered that current recommendations are based on the best wisdom available.

At present, therefore, it would be reasonable to select a population of infants fed according to the WHO recommendations as a basis for comparing growth patterns. Additionally, the reference sample should be chosen from a population of infants who live in "healthy" environments that do not limit growth, and who are representative of characteristics which influence the normal variance in growth, e.g. birth weight and parental height. The sample should also be sufficiently large to allow reasonable precision in estimates of the more extreme percentiles of weight and length distributions. The results of the pooled analyses (*106*) reveal a relatively low variability in growth which is of concern. Further investigation regarding the observed variance is recommended. The final specification of a reference population, however, requires further consideration and research of the issues discussed.

The possible role of complementary foods in determining growth patterns is of special concern. It is therefore recommended that the effects of the quality of complementary foods on growth and other health outcomes from 4 months onwards be examined in advantaged populations. Such information is essential to develop cut-off values for specific populations. The Expert Committee was concerned that the lack of this information makes it difficult both to evaluate growth in the latter half of infancy and to identify the etiology and measure the rates of stunting and/or wasting within and between populations.

In summary, it is a matter of urgency to clarify the reasons for, and consequences of, the difference in growth between partially breast-fed and non-breast-fed infants older than 4–6 months; it may be, for instance, that complementary foods currently given to breast-feeding infants in affluent populations contain insufficient micronutrients for optimal growth.

If it were found that the different growth patterns resulting from divergent feeding practices are, in fact, compatible with short- and long-term health, there would be strong practical reasons for maintaining a single anthropometric reference for infants. Consideration should be given to the development of cut-offs from a single reference which facilitate the most effective nutritional management of infants, particularly of those who are exclusively breast-fed.

Further evaluation of the feasibility of using reference data based on infants breast-fed for at least 12 months is also recommended. Growth curves based on the pooled analyses (*106*) should be used in research settings to assess the growth of exclusively and partially breast-fed infants and of infants fed formula from birth. The proposed studies should include cohorts from both advantaged and disadvantaged populations. The objectives of the proposed research are the identification of problems encountered (e.g. by health care providers) in the interpretation of such curves, and of the benefits or adverse consequences that may result from changes (relative to the current NCHS/WHO reference) in the proportions of infants classified as faltering, stunted, wasted, or obese or overweight, regardless of feeding mode.

5.6.5 *Growth velocity curves*

Growth velocity curves will detect growth faltering earlier than attained growth charts, but are more difficult to interpret and require repeated measurements at regular intervals. Moreover, growth over short periods of time shows high variability; together with the low precision of some measurements, this will limit the ability to detect growth changes. Sound decision-making requires the use of time intervals during which the expected growth is greater than the combined errors of two repeated measurements.

An important area for research is comparison of the sensitivity and specificity of the simplified procedures for assessing incremental growth (e.g. weight gain versus no change in weight versus weight loss in a specified number of months, or failure to gain a specified amount of weight in a given period) with a procedure based on incremental growth charts. Another relevant issue is the effect of the wide variability in normal growth rates on the use and interpretation of growth velocity reference data.

5.7 Presentation of anthropometric reference data

5.7.1 *For individual-based applications*

Growth curves
The most common format for the current NCHS/WHO chart consists of curves for the 5th, 10th, 25th, 50th, 75th, 90th, and 95th percentiles. This has the disadvantage of unequal intervals from one percentile curve to another which means, in the visual monitoring of growth faltering, that crossing percentile lines gives rise to different interpretations in different areas of the chart. The difficulty in plotting additional curves below the third percentile is a further disadvantage of the percentile-based chart.

To adhere to the current recommendations for expressing height- and weight-based anthropometric data, future growth curves should use Z-score values instead of the current percentiles. A proposed new format would consist of a family of curves using a fixed Z-score interval, starting at –4 Z-scores as the lowest curve and with +3 Z-scores as the highest; the curves would be made up of full Z-score intervals (–4, –3, –2, –1, 0, +1, +2, +3).

Operational research is required on the best design of charts incorporating Z-score lines for field use, including the number and location of lines, colour schemes, and other characteristics that may facilitate their use and interpretation. This system would have the advantages of providing a uniform interpretation of crossing lines in different areas of the chart, as well as being suitable for following the growth patterns of children located significantly below –2 Z-scores.

Criteria for one-time assessment
As a screening tool for current potential health or nutritional disorders, the one-time measurement is of limited value in the case of height-for-age and weight-for-age unless the value is clearly distant from the distribution for the population to which the child belongs. A value judgement for screening will therefore depend on local circumstances and resources. If the current international growth curves were used in an area where the mean height-for-age Z-score is near –1.0, a child with a Z-score below –3.0 would be regarded as an outlier if the –2 Z-score cut-off is used for screening. Thus, a Z-score-based growth curve would be easier for local adaptation – as discussed in section 2 – than

the current format of percentile curves ranging from the 5th to the 95th percentile.

As regards weight-for-height, the greater global uniformity of the baseline level of wasting other than at the time of a disaster (less than 5% of children below –2 Z-scores) suggests that this cut-off would be adequate for most areas. A possible exception is the case of children in and near the Indian subcontinent, where prevalences of wasting are consistently around or above the 10% level, and a slightly lower cut-off could therefore be adopted.

Criteria for repeated measures

For growth monitoring or detection of growth faltering between infancy and adolescence, the Z-score-based growth curves also represent a more functional tool. As mentioned elsewhere in this section and in 5.1.2, an absolute change in Z-score units for a specified time period is more useful than a given change in percentile values, as the latter would give rise to different interpretations according to where in the distribution the initial value was located. For example, a reduction of 10 percentile points means very little actual weight change near the central part of the distribution, but a much larger change in the outer tails.

No uniform criteria for defining growth faltering are currently available, although practical definitions such as "no growth in two consecutive periods" have been suggested. Further research is needed to assess the predictive value of different operational recommendations. Nevertheless, the adoption of Z-score-based monitoring charts would be a major step towards establishing more objective criteria for defining growth faltering.

5.7.2 *For population-based applications*

Issues relevant to population-based applications have been discussed in section 5.4. As for Z-score-based approaches, beyond the adoption of the <-2 cut-off for low height-for-age, weight-for-age, and weight-for-height, a reference mean Z-score of 0 and a standard deviation of 1 are important benchmarks for interpreting observed population-based data.

One recurrent proposition is the use of functional outcomes to define the cut-off point for anthropometric indices as an alternative to using a cut-off based on statistical distribution or on criteria such as –2 Z-scores. In principle, an outcome-based criterion would be the most desirable approach for the application of any anthropometric or other index. However, two limitations prevent this being a practical proposition. One is the fact that it is difficult to acquire longitudinal follow-up data with sufficient sample size, range of age, and co-variates to construct reference criteria based on functional outcomes. The second is that, even if such data can be acquired, the relationship between anthropometric indices and outcomes is unlikely to be fixed from area to area; multiple studies would therefore be necessary to define the best cut-off for each local setting.

5.8 Recommendations

5.8.1 *Infants*

It was concluded that international references based on data from infants who live in environments that favour achievement of the genetic potential for growth and whose nurture follows WHO health recommendations, particularly those that relate to feeding, merit closer evaluation. Available data were insufficient to allow the development of a new reference; however, existing data indicated a need for a new reference to be constructed on the basis of the approach used by WHO in selecting infants for pooled analyses (*106*). Among the chief concerns of the Expert Committee in developing this view was the limited value of the current NCHS/WHO reference in assisting health workers and other providers of child care with the optimal nutritional management of infants.

The following specific recommendations are not listed in priority order, but reflect needs and gaps in knowledge identified by the Committee's deliberations:

1. A new reference is needed, which will improve the nutritional management of infants.

2. The reference population should reflect current health recommendations, particularly in view of the frequent use of references as standards.

3. The practical value of using reference data based on infants whose care follows WHO feeding recommendations should be evaluated in a broad range of settings.

4. The effects of different complementary foods on the growth of such infants merits close investigation.

5. Research is needed to identify proxies for length.

6. Criteria should be developed for the evaluation of abnormal growth.

7. Reference data based on other anthropometric measurements (e.g. skinfold thickness, arm and head circumferences) should be evaluated.

5.8.2 *Children*

Application of anthropometry

1. All applications should provide a proper description of the indicator, cut-off level, and reference used.

2. Different anthropometric indicators reflect different processes and outcomes, and they should not be used interchangeably.

3. A given anthropometric indicator has a different predictive value for risk and outcome in different settings, depending on the prevalence of health and nutritional disorders associated with that indicator. The indicator should therefore not be interpreted in a generalized fashion.

4. Because anthropometric findings are nonspecific indicators of multiple past and current processes, and because the make-up of the processes and their interaction vary, proper interpretation requires that other factors, such as socioeconomic status, disease prevalence, and dietary content, be taken into consideration.

5. In clinical applications, anthropometry is a screening tool for detecting children at greater risk of health or nutritional disorders; it should not be viewed as a diagnostic label for "malnutrition".

6. In population-based applications, a high prevalence of anthropometric deficit is indicative of significant health and nutritional problems in a given population or community. However, since the entire population is at risk, and not just those children below the cut-off, the cut-off point should be used only to facilitate the application of the indicator.

7. In the case of low weight-for-height or wasting, a common international baseline of < 5% can be recommended for management decisions during an emergency because this is the level frequently observed at other times.

8. In general, mid-upper arm circumference is not recommended as a substitute for weight- and height-based indices. Its proper application requires the use of age-specific reference data to permit interpretation of findings as MUAC-for-age.

9. For population-based applications, the mean Z-score of the anthropometric indices can be an adequate index of severity and may be used in place of the prevalence-based index.

10. For population-based applications, an international reference can be used adequately for cross-comparison and monitoring purposes; for individual-based applications, the screening cut-off can be adapted to local conditions.

11. The Z-score system is to be preferred for the reporting and use of anthropometric indices, because of its advantages in the context of activities based on single and multiple measurements. Clinical application requires the use of Z-score-based growth curves.

12. Since age is a major modifier for interpreting growth status, proper age grouping should be used in the analysis and interpretation of data.

13. From the point of view of intervention, it is important to differentiate between "failing to grow" and "failed to grow".

14. Indicators of response should be chosen for the purpose of monitoring changes.

Revision and development of an international reference
1. The current NCHS/WHO reference has significant technical drawbacks, especially for population-based applications; it should be updated or replaced in the near future.

2. The revised CDC reference, which corrects the major technical defects of the NCHS/WHO reference, can be used for special purposes for proper comparison of data across age, or for research purposes, but it is not recommended for general application as a substitute for the current NCHS/WHO reference.

3. Updating an existing reference or adopting a new reference is a major global undertaking and should be done as infrequently as possible. For this reason, the next reference needs to be a well developed one.

4. Apart from a major revision to replace the current reference for the USA, a new reference based on data from many countries can be developed within a common framework; in the long term, this would avoid the use of a single country's growth status as a worldwide "standard".

5. As well as the development of a more acceptable international reference, efforts should also focus on appropriate use of the reference. The reference should be used as a general guide for screening and monitoring, not as a fixed standard to be rigidly applied to children from different ethnic and socioeconomic backgrounds and of different health and nutritional status.

6. The development of multiple growth curves to serve as a standard for children from different backgrounds is an achievable concept as a computer-based operation. For general application, however, it would be operationally difficult because of the hundreds of charts that would be needed; the development of a true paediatric growth standard is therefore not recommended.

7. The previous WHO policy of using a single international reference is reaffirmed.

References

1. Waterlow JC et al. The presentation and use of height and weight data for comparing the nutritional status of groups of children under the age of 10 years. *Bulletin of the World Health Organization*, 1977, 55:489–498.

2. *Measuring change in nutritional status: guidelines for assessing the nutritional impact of supplementary feeding programmes.* Geneva, World Health Organization, 1983.

3. Use and interpretation of anthropometric indicators of nutritional status. WHO Working Group. *Bulletin of the World Health Organization*, 1986, 64:929–941.

4. Beaton GH et al. *Appropriate uses of anthropometric indices in children: a report based on an ACC/SCN workshop.* New York, United Nations Administrative Committee on Coordination/Subcommittee on Nutrition, 1990 (ACC/SCN State-of-the-Art Series, Nutrition Policy Discussion Paper No. 7).

5. The World Health Organization's infant-feeding recommendation. *Weekly epidemiological record,* 1995, 70:119-120.

6. Whitehead RG, Paul AA. Growth charts and the assessment of infant feeding practices in the western world and in developing countries. *Early human development*, 1984, **9**:187–207.

7. de Onis M et al. The worldwide magnitude of protein–energy malnutrition: an overview from the WHO Global Database on Child Growth. *Bulletin of the World Health Organization*, 1993, **71**:703–712.

8. Victora CG. The association between wasting and stunting: an international perspective. *Journal of nutrition*. 1992, **122**:1105–1110.

9. Gayle HD et al. Arm circumference v. weight-for-height in nutritional assessment: are the findings comparable? *Journal of tropical pediatrics*, 1988, **34**:213–217.

10. Trowbridge FL, Staehling N. Sensitivity and specificity of arm circumference indicators in identifying malnourished children. *American journal of clinical nutrition*, 1980, **33**:687–696.

11. Bairagi R. On validity of some anthropometric indicators as predictors of mortality. *American journal of clinical nutrition*, 1981, **34**:2592–2594.

12. Briend A, Zimicki S. Validation of arm circumference as an indicator of risk of death in one to four year old children. *Nutrition research*, 1986, **6**:249–261.

13. Chen LC, Chowdhury A, Huffman SL. Anthropometric assessment of energy-protein malnutrition and subsequent risk of mortality among preschool aged children. *American journal of clinical nutrition*, 1980, **33**:1836–1845.

14. Trowbridge FL, Sommer A. Nutritional anthropometry and mortality risk. *American journal of clinical nutrition*, 1981, **34**:2591–2592.

15. Jelliffe DB. *The assessment of the nutritional status of the community*. Geneva, World Health Organization, 1966 (WHO Monograph Series, No. 53).

16. Shakir A, Morley D. Measuring malnutrition. *Lancet*, 1974, **i**:758–759.

17. Hall G, Chowdhury S, Bloem M. Use of mid-upper-arm circumference Z-scores in nutritional assessment. *Lancet*, 1993, **341**:1481.

18. Sommer A, Loewenstein MS. Nutritional status and mortality: a prospective validation of the QUAC stick. *American journal of clinical nutrition*, 1975, **28**: 287–292.

19. Malina RM et al. Head and chest circumferences in rural Guatemalan Ladino children, birth to seven years of age. *American journal of clinical nutrition*, 1975, **28**:1061–1070.

20. Gorstein J et al. Issues in the assessment of nutritional status using anthropometry. *Bulletin of the World Health Organization*, 1994, **72**:273–284.

21. Martorell R. Child growth retardation: a discussion of its causes and of its relationship to health. In: Blaxter KL, Waterlow JC, eds. *Nutritional adaptation in man*. London, John Libbey, 1985:13–30.

22. Habicht J-P et al. Height and weight standards for preschool children. How relevant are ethnic differences in growth potential? *Lancet*, 1974, **i**:611–614.

23. Pinstrup-Andersen P et al. *World Bank Health Priorities Review: protein energy malnutrition*. Washington, DC, The World Bank, 1992.

24. West KP Jr et al. Vitamin A supplementation and growth: a randomized community trial. *American journal of clinical nutrition*, 1988, **48**:1257–1264.

25. Chwang LC, Soemantri AG, Pollitt E. Iron supplementation and physical growth of rural Indonesian children. *American journal of clinical nutrition*, 1988, **47**: 496-501.

26. Golden MHN, Golden BE. Effect of zinc supplementation on the dietary intake, rate of weight gain and energy cost of tissue depletion in children recovering from severe malnutrition. *American journal of clinical nutrition*, 1981, **34**:900-908.

27. Tompkins A, Watson F. *Malnutrition and infection: a review*. London, Clinical Nutrition Unit, Centre for Human Nutrition, London School of Hygiene and Tropical Medicine (ACC/SCN State-of-the-Art Series, Nutrition Policy Discussion Paper No. 5).

28. Lutter CK et al. Nutrition supplementation: effects on child stunting because of diarrhea. *American journal of clinical nutrition*, 1989, **50**:1-8.

29. Victora CG et al. Pneumonia, diarrhea and growth in the first four years of life. A longitudinal study of 5914 Brazilian infants. *American journal of clinical nutrition*, 1990, **52**:391-396.

30. Rowland MGM, Cole TJ, Whitehead RG. A quantitative study into the role of infection in determining nutritional status in Gambian village children. *British journal of nutrition*, 1977, **37**:441-450.

31. Briend A. Is diarrhoea a major cause of malnutrition among the under-fives in developing countries? A review of available evidence. *European journal of clinical nutrition*, 1990, **44**:611-628.

32. Victora CG et al. Risk factors for pneumonia in a Brazilian metropolitan area. *Pediatrics*, 1994, **93**(6 Pt 1):977-985.

33. Toole MJ, Malkki RM. Famine-affected, refugee, and displaced populations: recommendations for public health issues. *Morbidity and mortality weekly report*, 1992, **41**:1-25.

34. Pelletier D. *Relationships between child anthropometry and mortality in developing countries*. Ithaca, NY, Cornell University, 1991 (Cornell Food and Nutrition Policy Program, Monograph 12).

35. Pelletier D, Frongillo EA Jr, Habicht J-P. Epidemiologic evidence for a potentiating effect of malnutrition on child mortality. *American journal of public health*, 1993, **83**:1130-1133.

36. Pollitt E et al. Early supplementary feeding and cognition. *Monographs of the Society for Research in Child Development*, 1993, **58**:1-116.

37. McGuire JS, Austin JE. Beyond survival: children's growth for national development. *Assignment children*, 1987, **2**:3-52.

38. Grantham-McGregor SM et al. Nutritional supplementation, psychosocial stimulation and mental development of stunted children: the Jamaican study. *Lancet,* 1991, **338**:1-5.

39. Martorell R et al. Long-term consequences of growth retardation during early childhood. In: Hernández M, Argente J, eds. *Human growth: basic and clinical aspects*. Amsterdam, Elsevier, 1992:143-149.

40. Spurr GB, Barac-Nieto M, Maksud MG. Productivity and maximal oxygen consumption in sugar cane cutters. *American journal of clinical nutrition*, 1977, **30**:316-321.

41. **Kramer MS.** Determinants of low birth weight: methodological assessment and meta-analysis. *Bulletin of the World Health Organization*, 1987, **65**:663-737.

42. **Klebanoff MA, Yip R.** Influence of maternal birth weight on rate of fetal growth and duration of gestation. *Journal of pediatrics*, 1987, **111**:287-292.

43. **Binkin NJ et al.** Birth weight and childhood growth. *Pediatrics*, 1988, **82**: 828-834.

44. **Javier-Nieto F, Szklo M, Comstock GW.** Childhood weight and growth rate as predictors of adult mortality. *American journal of epidemiology*, 1992, **136**: 201-213.

45. **Mossberg HO.** 40-year follow-up of overweight children. *Lancet*, 1988, ii: 491-493.

46. **Abraham S, Collins G, Nordsieck M.** Relationship of childhood weight status to morbidity in adults. *HSHMA health reports*, 1971, **86**:273-284.

47. **Keller W.** The epidemiology of stunting. In: Waterlow JC, ed. *Linear growth retardation in less developed countries*. New York, Raven Press, 1988 (Nestlé Nutrition Workshop Series, Vol. 14).

48. **Van den Broeck J, Meulemans W, Eeckels R.** Nutrition assessment: the problem of clinical-anthropometrical mismatch. *European journal of clinical nutrition*, 1994, **48**:60-65.

49. **Gómez F et al.** Mortality in second and third degree malnutrition. *Journal of tropical pediatrics*, 1956, **2**:77-83.

50. **Cole TJ.** Growth charts for both cross-sectional and longitudinal data. *Statistics in medicine*, 1994, **13**:2477-2492.

51. **Griffiths M.** *Growth monitoring*. Washington, DC, World Federation of Public Health Associations, 1985.

52. **George SM et al.** Evaluation of effectiveness of good growth monitoring in south Indian villages. *Lancet*, 1993, **342**:348-352.

53. *India – Tamil Nadu Integrated Nutrition Project. Completion report*. Washington, DC, The World Bank, 1990.

54. **WHO/UNICEF.** *The Joint WHO/UNICEF Nutrition Support Programme in Iringa, Tanzania: 1983-1988 evaluation report*. New York, Defense for Children International – USA, 1989.

55. **Galen RS, Gambino SR.** *Beyond normality: the predictive value and efficiency of medical diagnosis*. New York, Wiley, 1975.

56. **Martorell R.** Body size, adaptation and function. *Human organization*, 1989, **48**:15-20.

57. **Victora CG et al.** Evidence for protection by breast-feeding against infant deaths from infectious diseases in Brazil. *Lancet*, 1987, ii:319-322.

58. **Brown KH et al.** Infant-feeding practices and their relationship with diarrheal and other diseases in Huascar (Lima), Peru. *Pediatrics*, 1989, **83**:31-40.

59. **Popkin BM et al.** Breast-feeding and diarrheal morbidity. *Pediatrics*, 1990, **86**: 874-882.

60. **de Zoysa I, Rea M, Martines J.** Why promote breast-feeding in diarrhoeal disease control programmes? *Health policy and planning*, 1991, **6**:371-379.

61. Feachem RG, Koblinsky MA. Interventions for the control of diarrhoeal diseases among young children: promotion of breast-feeding. *Bulletin of the World Health Organization*, 1984, **62**:271–291.

62. Seward JF, Serdula MK. Infant feeding and infant growth. *Pediatrics*, 1984, **74**(4 Pt 2):728–762.

63. Perez A. The effect of breastfeeding promotion on the infertile postpartum period. *International journal of gynaecology and obstetrics*, 1990, **31**(Suppl. 1):57–59.

64. *Breast-feeding and child spacing: what health workers need to know*. Geneva, World Health Organization, 1989 (unpublished document WHO/MCH/FP/88.1, available on request from Maternal and Child Health and Family Planning, World Health Organization, 1211 Geneva 27, Switzerland).

65. Institute of Medicine. *Nutrition during lactation*. Washington, DC, National Academy Press, 1991.

66. Brown KH, Dewey KG. Relationships between maternal nutritional status and milk energy output of women in developing countries. In: Picciano MF, Lonnerdal B, eds. *Mechanisms regulating lactation and infant nutrient utilization*. New York, Wiley-Liss, 1992:77–95.

67. Brown KH et al. Lactational capacity of marginally nourished mothers: relationships between maternal nutritional status and quantity and proximate composition of milk. *Pediatrics*, 1986, **78**:909–919.

68. Prentice A, Prentice AM, Whitehead RG. Breast-milk concentrations of rural African women. 2. Long-term variations within a community. *British journal of nutrition*, 1981, **45**:495–503.

69. Aukett MA et al. Treatment with iron increases weight gain and psychomotor development. *Archives of disease in childhood*, 1986, **61**:849–857.

70. Walravens PA, Hambridge KM, Koepfer DM. Zinc supplementation in infants with a nutritional pattern of failure to thrive: a double-blind, controlled study. *Pediatrics*, 1989, **83**:532–538.

71. Dirren H et al. Zinc supplementation and infant growth in Ecuador. In: Allen LH, King JC, Lonnerdal B, eds. *Nutrient regulation during pregnancy, lactation and infant growth*. New York, Advances in Experimental Medicine and Biology, 1994.

72. Stuff JE, Nichols BL. Nutrient intake and growth performance of older infants fed human milk. *Journal of pediatrics*, 1989, **115**:959–968.

73. Heinig MJ et al. Intake and growth of breast-fed and formula-fed infants in relation to the timing of introduction of complementary foods: the DARLING Study. *Acta paediatrica*, 1993, **82**:999–1006.

74. Martorell R, Habicht J-P. Growth in early childhood in developing countries. In: Falkner F, Tanner JM, eds. *Human growth: a comprehensive treatise*. New York, Plenum Press, 1986:241–262.

75. Dietz WH. Childhood obesity: susceptibility, cause, and management. *Journal of pediatrics*, 1983, **103**:676–686.

76. Rolland-Cachera MF et al. Influence of body fat distribution during childhood on body fat distribution in adulthood: a two-decade follow-up study. *International journal of obesity*, 1990, **14**:473–481.

77. Shapiro LR et al. Obesity prognosis: a longitudinal study of children from the age of 6 months to 9 years. *American journal of public health*, 1984, **74**:968–972.

78. Fomon SJ. Reference data for assessing growth of infants. *Journal of pediatrics*, 1991, **119**:415–416.

79. Guo SM et al. Reference data on gains in weight and length during the first two years of life. *Journal of pediatrics*, 1991, **119**:355–362.

80. Lampl M, Veldhuis JD, Johnson ML. Saltation and stasis: a model of human growth. *Science*, 1992, **258**:801–803.

81. Yip R, Scanlon K, Trowbridge F. Improving growth status of Asian refugee children in the United States. *Journal of the American Medical Association*, 1992, **267**:937–940.

82. Yip R, Sharp TW. Acute malnutrition and high mortality related to diarrhea. Lessons from the 1991 Kurdish refugee crisis. *Journal of the American Medical Association*, 1993, **270**:587–590.

83. Herwaldt BL et al. Crisis in southern Sudan: where is the world? *Lancet*, 1993, **342**:119–120.

84. Yip R. Expanded usage of anthropometry Z-scores for assessing population nutritional status and data quality [Abstract]. In: *Proceedings of the 15th International Congress of Nutrition, Adelaide, 1993.* Adelaide, Smith-Gordon, 1993:279.

85. Victora CG et al. *Avaliação da Pastoral da Criança em dois Municipios do Maranháo* [Evaluation of the Children's Pastorate in two municipalities of Maranháo State]. Brasilia, United Nations Children's Fund, 1990.

86. Brown KH, Black RE, Becker S. Seasonal changes in nutritional status and the prevalence of malnutrition in a longitudinal study of young children in rural Bangladesh. *American journal of clinical nutrition*, 1982, **36**:303–313.

87. *Report of the Consultation on Rapid Nutrition Assessment in Emergencies.* Alexandria, World Health Organization Eastern Mediterranean Regional Office, 1992 (unpublished document WHO-EM/NUT/114-E/L, available on request from Nutrition, World Health Organization, 1211 Geneva 27, Switzerland).

88. Brooks RM et al. A timely warning and intervention system for preventing food crises in Indonesia: applying guidelines for nutrition surveillance. *Food and nutrition*, 1985, **11**:37–43.

89. Martorell R et al. Short and plump physique of Mexican-American children. *American journal of physical anthropology*, 1987, **73**:475–487.

90. Gorstein J. Assessment of nutritional status: effects of different methods to determine age on the classification of undernutrition. *Bulletin of the World Health Organization*, 1989, **67**:1443–1450.

91. Marks GC, Habicht J-P, Mueller WH. Reliability, dependability, and precision of anthropometric measurements. The Second National Health and Nutrition Survey 1976–1980. *American journal of epidemiology*, 1989, **130**:578–587.

92. Dallman PR, Yip R, Johnson C. Prevalence and causes of anemia in the United States, 1976 to 1980. *American journal of clinical nutrition*, 1984, **39**:437–445.

93. Mora JO. A new method of estimating a standardized prevalence of child malnutrition from anthropometric indicators. *Bulletin of the World Health Organization*, 1989, **67**:133–142.

94. Monteiro CA. Counting the stunted children in a population: a criticism of old and new approaches and a conciliatory proposal. *Bulletin of the World Health Organization*, 1991, **69**:761–766.

95. Chang Ying et al. Nutritional status of preschool children in poor rural areas of China. *Bulletin of the World Health Organization*, 1994, **72**:105-112.

96. Rose G. Sick individuals and sick populations. *International journal of epidemiology*, 1985, **14**:32-38.

97. *How to weigh and measure children: assessing the nutritional status of young children in household surveys.* New York, United Nations Department of Technical Cooperation for Development and Statistical Office, 1986.

98. Graitcher PL, Gentry EM. Measuring children: one reference for all. *Lancet*, 1981, ii:297-299.

99. Agarwal KN et al. *Growth performance of affluent Indian children (under-fives). Growth standard for Indian children.* New Delhi, Nutrition Foundation of India, 1991 (Scientific Report No. 11).

100. Sullivan K et al. Growth references. *Lancet*, 1991, **337**:1420-1421.

101. Yip R, Scanlon K, Trowbridge FL. Trends and patterns in height and weight status of low-income US children. *Critical reviews in food science and nutrition*, 1993, **33**:409-421.

102. Yip R, Binkin NJ, Trowbridge FL. Altitude and child growth. *Journal of pediatrics*, 1988, **113**:486-489.

103. Hamill PVV et al. Physical growth: National Center for Health Statistics percentiles. *American journal of clinical nutrition*, 1979, **32**:607-629.

104. Dibley MJ et al. Development of normalized curves for the international growth reference: historical and technical considerations. *American journal of clinical nutrition*, 1987, **46**:736-748.

105. Fichtner RR et al. Report of the Technical Meeting on Software for Nutrition Surveillance. *Food and nutrition bulletin*, 1989, **11**:57-61.

106. *An evaluation of infant growth – a summary of analyses performed in preparation for the WHO Expert Committee on Physical Status: the use and interpretation of anthropometry.* Geneva, World Health Organization, 1994 (unpublished document WHO/NUT/94.8).

107. An evaluation of infant growth: the use and interpretation of anthropometry in infants. *Bulletin of the World Health Organization*, 1995, **73**:165-174.

108. *Indicators for assessing breast-feeding practices: report of an informal meeting, 11-12 June 1991, Geneva, Switzerland.* Geneva, World Health Organization, 1991 (unpublished document WHO/CDD/SER/91.4, available on request from Diarrhoeal Disease Control, World Health Organization, 1211 Geneva 27, Switzerland).

109. Yeung DL. *Infant nutrition*. Toronto, Canadian Public Health Association, 1983.

110. Michaelsen KF et al. Weight, length, head circumference and growth velocity in a longitudinal study of Danish infants. *Danish medical bulletin*, 1994, 4:577-585.

111. Salmenpera L, Perheentupa J, Simes MA. Exclusively breast-fed healthy infants grow slower than reference infants. *Paediatric research*, 1985, **19**:307-312.

112. Persson LA. Infant feeding and growth – a longitudinal study in three Swedish communities. *Annals of human biology*, 1985, **12**:41-52.

113. Whitehead RG, Paul AA, Cole TJ. Diet and the growth of healthy infants. *Journal of human nutrition and dietetics*, 1989, 2:73–84.

114. Dewey KG et al. Growth of breast-fed and formula-fed infants from 0 to 18 months: the DARLING study. *Pediatrics*, 1992, 89(6 Pt 1):1035–1041.

115. Krebs NF et al. Growth and intakes of energy and zinc in infants fed human milk. *Journal of pediatrics*, 1994, 124:32–39.

116. Yip R, Li Z, Chong WH. Race and birth weight: the Chinese example. *Pediatrics* 1991, 87:688–693.

117. *NCHS growth curves for children, birth–18 years.* Washington, DC, U.S. National Center for Health Statistics, 1977 (Department of Health, Education and Welfare Publication No. (PHS) 78-1650).

118. Barros FC et al. Birth weight and duration of breast-feeding: are the beneficial effects of breast-feeding being overestimated? *Pediatrics*, 1986,78:656–661.

119. Anderson MA. *The relationship between maternal nutrition and child growth in rural India* [Dissertation]. Boston, MA, Tufts University, 1989.

120. Dewey KG et al. Growth patterns of breast-fed infants in affluent (United States) and poor (Peru) communities: implications for timing of complementary feeding. *American journal of clinical nutrition*, 1992, 56:1012–1018.

121. World Health Organization Task Force for Epidemiological Research on Reproductive Health. Progestogen-only contraceptives during lactation: I. Infant growth. *Contraception*, 1994, 50:35–53.

122. Dibley MJ et al. Interpretation of Z-score anthropometric indicators derived from the international growth reference. *American journal of clinical nutrition*, 1987, 46:749–762.

6. Adolescents

6.1 Introduction

6.1.1 *Background*

Adolescence is a significant period of human growth and maturation; unique changes occur during this period and many adult patterns are established. The proximity of adolescence to biological maturity and adulthood may provide final opportunities to implement certain activities designed to prevent adult health problems.

Adolescence begins with pubescence, the earliest signs of development of secondary sexual characteristics, and continues until morphological and physiological changes approximate adult status, usually near the end of the second decade of life. This section considers individuals of about 10-24 years of age, which includes both those considered by WHO as "adolescents" (10-19 years) (1) and those defined as "youth" (15-24 years) by the United Nations. Human growth and maturation are continuous processes, and transitions from childhood and into adulthood are not abrupt; the period of adolescence encompasses rapid changes in physical growth and maturation, and in psychosocial development. It is characterized by low prevalences of most infectious and chronic diseases, but high health risks associated with substance abuse, sexually transmitted diseases, pregnancy, and accidental and intentional injuries (2).

Anthropometry is especially important during adolescence because it allows the monitoring and evaluation of the hormone-mediated changes in growth and maturation during this period. Moreover, because growth may be sensitive to nutritional deficit and surfeit, adolescent anthropometry provides indicators of nutritional status and health risk, and may be diagnostic of obesity. The study and understanding of this period of rapid changes are, at once, important and difficult.

The rapid changes during adolescence include increases in body dimensions, i.e. growth, and progressive attainment of adult status, i.e. maturation. While growth and maturation progress in concert within individuals, they may exhibit appreciable independence when viewed across or among individuals. For example, at menarche – which presages adult reproductive function – girls are taller than premenarcheal peers at the same chronological ages; nevertheless, there is considerable variation in actual stature (and chronological age) at menarche.

The timing of maturational events varies within healthy children primarily because of genetic factors (3). Adolescence is characterized by the onset of major maturational events, principally the spurt in somatic growth and the accompanying appearance of secondary sexual characteristics, menarche, and spermarche. Accordingly, even among healthy youth, there is marked variation in the timing of these maturational changes, so that growth evaluation based exclusively on chronological age may be inaccurate or misleading, especially when applied to individuals. Bone age, or skeletal maturation, can be used as a measure of maturation, but this requires special equipment and expertise. To complicate the picture further, both growth and maturational timing may be affected by environmental and health factors, so that it is difficult to separate the normal variability due to genetics and hormonal changes during adolescence from changes that are environmentally induced.

Adolescence is also a period of increased nutritional requirements. Rapid accretion of new tissue and other widespread developmental changes are accompanied by increased nutritional requirements relative to the childhood years. For example, more than 20% of total growth in stature and up to 50% of adult bone mass are achieved during adolescence (4), resulting in a 50% increase in the calcium requirement. In addition to the increased iron needs of the expanding red cell mass and myoglobin in newly gained muscle tissue, adolescent girls have a further iron requirement – up to 15% – to compensate for menstrual blood losses (5).

Many important changes in psychological and social development take place during adolescence – a period that signals the entrance of individuals into the world of adults. Potential for pregnancy and parenthood, educational choices, occupational commitment, interpersonal relationships, and citizenship are only a few of the new concerns and responsibilities that challenge adolescents and that may be confusing. Many of the responses to the transition to adulthood may include behaviours that have direct implications for health, e.g. dieting, smoking, alcohol consumption, sexual activity, substance abuse, violence. Sometimes, the lack of opportunities associated with poverty or the choices concerning education and occupation may have indirect long-term effects on health.

While adolescence is clearly an important period in human development, it has often failed to receive the attention given to earlier periods in childhood with regard to health-related uses and interpretations of anthropometry. The prevalence of undernutrition in adolescence is considerably lower than that in early childhood, and the need for anthropometry has seemed less pressing. Historically, the rapid changes in somatic growth in adolescence, the problems of dealing with variation in maturation, and the difficulties involved in separating normal variations from those associated with health risks have all discouraged workers from developing a body of knowledge about adolescent anthropometry that would link it directly with health determinants and outcomes (6). As a result, clinicians and public health workers have been left with relatively few tools for meeting the need to evaluate adolescents.

The emergence of obesity and its sequelae as public health problems, particularly in developed countries, has renewed interest in the adolescent anthropometric antecedents of adult obesity and associated risk factors. However, relatively little detailed methodological work has been carried out concerning specific cut-offs, predictive values, and attributable risks. The Expert Committee's intention was to bring together available information on a wide range of uses and applications of adolescent anthropometry to form a basis for future work and discussion.

6.1.2 *Biological and social significance of anthropometry*

Available information linking adolescent anthropometry to biological and social factors is primarily descriptive and relational; for example adolescents from an affluent society are taller than less affluent adolescents of the same age, and body mass index (BMI) in adolescents is positively correlated with diastolic blood pressure. Such findings are critical to the understanding of anthropometric variability, patterns of development, and important correlates of anthropometric dimensions. Published studies have identified important determinants and consequences of anthropometric variation, and generated or confirmed important etiological hypotheses regarding adolescent body dimensions. Much less work has been done to extract from these data the specific information required for using adolescent anthropometric dimensions as indicators of health and nutritional status (7).

Biological and social determinants of anthropometry
The greatest source of variation in anthropometric dimensions is that associated with the adolescent growth spurt, which is experienced by almost all children although it may differ in timing, intensity, and duration. Even within individual children there are small but systematic differences in the timing of the adolescent spurts for different dimensions; the age of peak adolescent velocity for the length of the tibia, for example, precedes the peaks for the ulna and for total stature (8).

Because adolescent changes follow rather systematic sequences, some maturational events can be used as indicators of the timing of the adolescent spurt across different situations or groups of children. For example, the time of menarche is easily established by questionnaire, and its timing usually follows that of peak height velocity by 14–18 months; variation in age at menarche is therefore frequently used to indicate variation in the overall timing of adolescence within and among populations (see Table 27).

The variations in mean age at menarche are the result of genetic and environmental differences. Differences between rural and urban groups or between poor and better-off girls within given areas should be due primarily to differences in health-related concomitants of socioeconomic status: nutrition, hygiene, health care, etc. Of course, social or economic distinctions may include ethnic or genetic differences in some situations. A lowering of mean age at menarche may be seen in some populations (9), and such secular change signals improvement in health-related

Table 27
Age at menarche in selected populations[a]

Country and area/population		Year	Mean age (years)	SE
Brazil, São Paulo state	well-off	1978	12.2	0.03
	poor	1978	12.8	0.03
Cuba	Havana	1973	12.8	0.01
	rural areas	1973	13.3	0.01
India	Madras, well-off	1975	12.9	0.10
	Warangel, poor	1975	14.1	0.10
	Hyderabad, rural areas	1977	14.6	0.08
Iraq, Baghdad	well-off	1969	13.6	0.06
	poor	1969	14.0	0.05
Netherlands	all	1980	13.3	0.04
Papua New Guinea	Bundi, highlands	1967	18.0	0.19
	Kaipit, lowlands	1967	15.6	0.25
Poland	Warsaw	1976	12.7	0.03
	rural areas	1976	13.4	0.02
Sudan, Khartoum	better-off	1980	13.4	0.14
	poor	1980	14.1	0.18
USA	European origin, all	1968	12.8	0.04
	African origin, all	1968	12.5	0.11
Zaire	better-off, urban areas	1979	13.2	0.67
	poor	1979	14.7	0.04

[a] Reproduced from reference *9* with the permission of the publisher.

factors sufficient to allow more rapid maturation at the time of adolescence. In Norway, for example, the mean age of menarche decreased from 15.6 years for women born in 1860 to 13.3 years for women born after 1940 (*10*).

Because of the dramatic growth changes during the adolescent spurt, it is important to identify the measures of maturation that are most appropriate for use with anthropometric indicators of health and nutritional status in individuals and populations. Many measures of somatic maturation have been proposed, and the principal measures used during adolescence, their applicability, and limitations on their use are presented in Table 28. Ideal maturational indicators would be appropriate for both individuals and populations, highly valid, and measurable with high reliability; there should be many sources of reference data, few limitations on the use of the indicators, and few special requirements (for extensive training or expensive equipment). Age at menarche probably comes closest to satisfying all the criteria, but may be a culturally

Table 28
Principal measures of maturation during adolescence

Measure	Appropriate for individuals	Appropriate for populations	Practical measurement reliability[a]	Validity[b]	Reference data[c]	Special requirements limitations[d]
Males and females						
• Peak height velocity age	X		H	H	VF	B, D, I, J
• Pubic hair stage	X	X	M	M	M	D, F
• Axillary hair stage	X	X	M	M	F	D, F
• Number of permanent teeth		X	H	L	VF	D
• Skeletal age	X	X	H	H	F	A, C, E, G
Males only						
• Genitalia development	X	X	M	M	M	D, F
• Testicular volume (calipers)	X	X	H	H	VF	B, D, F
• Testicular volumes (models)	X	X	H	H	F	B, D, F
• Spermarche		X	L	H	VF	A, C, E, F, I
• Adult voice	X	X	M	M	VF	D, H
Females only						
• Menarche	X	X	H	H	VM	F
• Breast development	X	X	M	H	M	D, F

---

[a] Reliability: L = low (intraclass reliability coefficient $R \leq 0.65$); M = medium ($0.65 < R \leq 0.85$); H = high ($R > 0.85$).

[b] Validity (criterion) relative to general somatic maturation indicators during pubescence. L, M, and H as for reliability.

[c] Reference data: VF = very few; F = few; M = many; VM = very many.

[d] A = expensive procedures; B = some equipment required (beyond printed instructions and pictures); C = highly specialized equipment and facilities needed; D = more than usual training required; E = very specialized training and skilled personnel required; F = procedure may be culturally or personally objectionable; G = ionizing radiation required; H = methods not standardized; I = multiple observations or long-term longitudinal data required; J = only useful retrospectively

sensitive topic for enquiry in some situations; moreover, menarche usually occurs late in the adolescent spurt, i.e. later than desirable as a signal of concurrent or imminent spurt-related growth changes.

To a significant extent, the variation in adolescent body size and the timing of maturational events is determined by normal genetic inheritance (*11*) in populations whose environment allows expression of the genotype. Where health-related factors limit full genetic expression, observed growth and maturation (the phenotype) will reflect the environment more than the inherited potential. Variation in adolescent growth may also reflect environmental influences that were active earlier in life. Consequently, it is difficult in any particular situation to determine the degree to which the observed levels of adolescent growth result from purely environmental effects and the timing of these effects. Obviously, a wide range of abnormal clinical syndromes with specific genetic etiologies may also affect adolescent growth, but of such a small proportion of all children that they are not considered here.

Adolescent anthropometry varies significantly worldwide (*9*). Many of the differences observed according to chronological age categories are attributable to variation in maturational timing, and diminish when the timing of the adolescent spurt is considered. It is clear, however, that growth differences among groups are related to nutritional status, socioeconomic levels, degree of industrialization/urbanization, and altitude of residence. For individual adolescents, growth may be limited by such factors as prolonged undernutrition, infection, and chronic disease. There is considerable evidence that significant compensatory or catch-up growth is possible when the growth-limiting condition is remedied (*12*); for instance, children who have spent their childhood in poverty and are then adopted into more affluent families may show catch-up growth and early pubertal development, reaching a final height in the normal range (*13*).

For populations, some cross-sectional studies have shown that groups living in adverse circumstances may experience some catch-up during adolescence without specific intervention (*14*). Nevertheless, detailed studies in Guatemalan adolescents indicate that those who were stunted in early childhood continue to be stunted to the same degree throughout adolescence if they remain in the same environment (*15*). There have been no studies to determine whether groups of growth-retarded children respond to nutritional and health interventions with compensatory growth during the adolescent years. Clearly, if this were possible, it would have important public health implications in view of the adverse consequences of stunting in adulthood.

Careful measurement of the growth of long bones reveals that significant linear growth may continue in adolescent girls who become pregnant (*16*). The added weight of pregnancy, however, may cause sufficient compression of intervertebral discs and postural distortion to reduce total stature and give the impression of a pregnancy-related cessation of statural growth. Little information is available regarding the impact of lactation on the growth of adolescent girls.

Certain aspects of adolescent behaviour may have implications for growth and health. The extremes of nutritional intake in excessive dieting and eating disorders, including anorexia nervosa and obesity, may be reflected in somatic growth, body composition, and menstrual function. Intensive physical training has been shown to alter the hypothalamic-pituitary axis in adolescent girls, with associated alteration in menstrual function and bone density (17). In an extreme case, world-class girl gymnasts who trained 22 hours/week and exercised strict weight control showed significantly reduced growth potential and rates of growth in height (18).

Biological and social consequences of anthropometry

The precise mechanisms that link adolescent anthropometry with concurrent or subsequent health and social outcomes are uncertain, and impacts on health may differ according to the timing of the adverse influences associated with growth deficiencies. Nevertheless, consistent associations and patterns are apparent, and anthropometric variation has sufficient biological coherence as a morphological manifestation of growth and body composition to allow some useful inferences. Because there is little frank disease during adolescence, it is particularly important to consider the degree to which adolescent anthropometry may predict risk factors or disease in adulthood.

Adolescent anthropometry may have social as well as biological implications. Body dimensions and some secondary sexual characteristics are evident to others, and may have culturally defined, psychosocial connotations, many of which relate to "coming of age" or attaining social maturity and independence.

Concurrent consequences. Short stature and low body mass during adolescence may be determinants of concurrent functional impairment. Short stature in adolescents resulting from prior chronic undernutrition is associated with reduced lean body mass and deficiencies in muscular strength and working capacity (19). Acute weight loss in adolescent girls, such as occurs in famine situations and anorexia nervosa, is associated with secondary amenorrhoea and other menstrual dysfunction (20, 21).

Although there is little frank disease in adolescence of the types associated with obesity in adults, overweight and obesity during this period are associated with risk factors for obesity-related diseases. Variations in body mass, subcutaneous fatness, and total body fat in adolescents are significantly associated with variations in blood pressure and blood levels of lipoproteins, glucose, and insulin in many populations of developed countries (22, 23). There are few data concerning concurrent associations between the pattern of fat distribution in adolescents and risk factors for later chronic diseases, but some findings suggest that the importance of trunk or abdominal fat is established in the adolescent years (*23, 24*).

Future consequences. In adolescent girls, short stature that persists into adulthood is associated with increased risks of adverse reproductive outcomes. Risks for low birth weight, cephalopelvic disproportion, dystocia, and caesarean section are increased in the shortest mothers (*25, 26*). Low body mass in adolescent girls has been shown to be associated with reduced bone mass in early adulthood (*27*), and may result in a greater risk of postmenopausal osteoporosis and its sequelae. It is not known whether the chronic undernutrition and low body mass observed during adolescence in large populations of many developing countries are specific risk factors for later osteoporosis.

Recent data from the USA on overweight during adolescence indicate that young people with the highest relative weight or BMI are at increased risks for some adult chronic diseases and for all-cause mortality (*28, 29*). Shorter-term longitudinal studies indicate that elevated body weight and BMI in adolescents are predictive of risk factors for chronic disease in early adulthood (*30, 31*).

Ecological analyses across populations indicate that mean size at adolescence is related to the incidence of some cancers (*32*). For example, mean stature at 14 years of age was correlated ($r^2 = 0.62$) with age-adjusted breast cancer mortality rates in 28 populations (*33*). These findings have been interpreted in the light of the environmental determinants of adolescent size across populations: the most rapid rates of growth and maturation during adolescence may confer additional risk for development of cancer, and it may be that this risk is associated with an affluent lifestyle.

6.1.3 *Anthropometry as an indicator of nutritional and health status*

It is clear from the foregoing discussions that anthropometry has been used during adolescence in many contexts related to nutritional and health status. However, there are no well defined criteria or cut-off values that relate to specific risks or aspects of health in the individual. In many cases, little information is available regarding any associations with past, concurrent, or future health risks. Most available data have considered anthropometric dimensions as continuously distributed variables, so that associations with health can be documented, but have seldom been analysed to provide the optimum cut-offs necessary for development of anthropometric indicators. For example, in industrialized countries, BMI during adolescence is significantly and positively correlated with concurrent diastolic blood pressure; that is, there is a recognized association between BMI and blood pressure. However, no study has yet established the exact BMI cut-off values (or BMI percentiles for age) that are most appropriate for identifying those adolescents at highest risk of current or later hypertension. In the absence of specific health-related cut-offs, it has become conventional to adopt the less desirable option of using statistically determined cut-offs. Continuing the example above, the ≥85th percentile BMI-for-age, relative to appropriate reference data, might be designated as "at risk" of elevated diastolic blood pressure. Because of the positive correlation of BMI with blood pressure, individuals in this upper portion of the BMI distribution will, on average, have the highest diastolic pressure; unfortunately, both the validity characteristics (sensitivity, specificity, predictive values) of such default cut-offs and the actual associated risks of hypertension remain unknown.

Because of the lack of work in this area, available data are insufficient to allow different cut-offs to be specified for different uses of the same indicators. It is quite likely that the best cut-off for one purpose is far from ideal for another, but better definitions must await the results of further research.

The anthropometric indicators recommended for adolescents are presented in Table 29. The indicators use as reference data those collected by the National Center for Health Statistics (NCHS) in the USA. In some cases, local reference data may be required or other local factors must be considered; these are discussed in the context of specific uses.

Until now, WHO has made no specific recommendations for adolescent anthropometry, but advocated the NCHS reference data for younger children (39), which include standard deviations (SD) and percentiles of height and weight through the adolescent years. The Expert Committee therefore considered whether the current NCHS/WHO reference data

Table 29
Recommended cut-off values and original sources of reference data[a] for adolescents

Indicator	Anthropometric variable[b]	Cut-off values	Original references
Stunting or low height-for-age	Height-for-age	< 3rd percentile or < -2 Z-scores	*34*
Thinness or low BMI-for-age	BMI-for-age	< 5th percentile	*35, 36*
At risk of overweight	BMI-for-age	≥ 85th percentile	*35, 36*
Obese	BMI-for-age TRSKF-for-age SSKF-for-age	≥ 85th percentile BMI *and* ≥ 90th percentile TRSKF *and* ≥ 90th percentile SSKF	*35, 36* *37, 38*

[a] For reference data see Annex 3.
[b] TRSKF = triceps skinfold thickness
   SSKF = subscapular skinfold thickness

were the most appropriate for adolescents, or whether other reference data should be recommended. While other reliable reference data for anthropometry are available, the Committee deemed it essential that all variables included in the reference data were measured on the same population. It was also considered desirable that there be continuity in reference levels from age to age.

The cut-off value for stunting during adolescence (< 3rd percentile, or <-2 Z-scores) is the same as that traditionally used during early childhood. Although the expected prevalence of stunting during adolescence is much lower, the recommended cut-off provides both a standardized definition and continuity with the younger ages.

Body mass index was recommended as the basis for anthropometric indicators of thinness and overweight during adolescence (40). Weight-for-age was considered uninformative or even misleading in the absence of corresponding information on height-for-age; conventional approaches to the combined use of height-for-age and weight-for-age to assess body mass are awkward and have yielded biased results (41).

Weight-for-height reference data have the advantage of requiring no knowledge of chronological age. However, the weight/height relationship changes dramatically with age (and probably with maturational status) during adolescence; consequently, at a given height, the weight corresponding to a particular percentile is not the same for all ages, so that the meaning of a given weight-for-height percentile differs with age. For the same reasons, relative weights calculated within categories of height during adolescence are appropriate only when used within narrow age categories (41). Available distributions of weight within categories of height have not been smoothed properly, and the wide range of heights and ages required makes presentation of reference data complex.

Because of these various limitations, BMI-for-age was recommended as the best indicator for use in adolescence: it incorporates the required information on age, it has been validated as an indicator of total body fat at the upper percentiles (42), and it provides continuity with recommended adult indicators. Moreover, reference data of high quality are available. Although BMI has not been fully validated as an indicator of thinness or undernutrition in adolescents, it provides a single index of body mass, applicable at both extremes.

Considerable discussion focused on the appropriateness for international comparison of BMI data from adolescents in the USA. The very high upper percentile levels at any given age, and the marked skewing of the age-specific distributions toward higher values when compared with many other well nourished populations were of particular concern. At the levels of median BMI-for-age and lower percentiles, there is much less variation among well nourished populations (40).

As an example, selected age-specific BMI percentiles for US children (35, 36) are compared with those for French children (43) in Fig. 48. The

Figure 48
Selected percentiles of BMI-for-age for US and French boys[a]

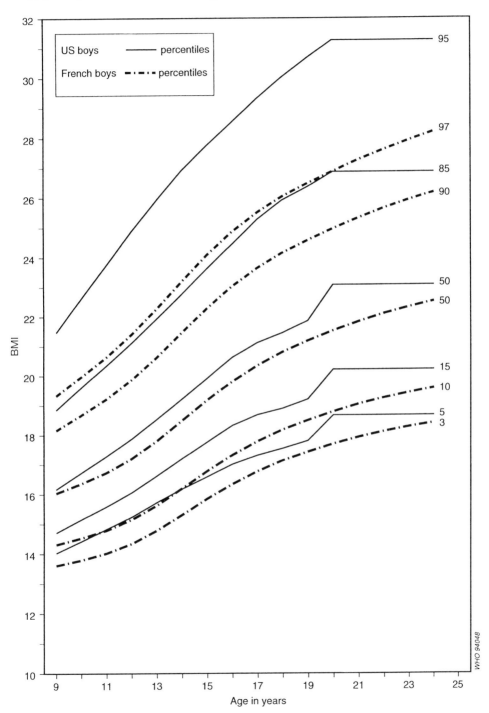

[a] Adapted from references *36* and *43*.

median curve for BMI in US boys is above that for the French boys, especially at the older ages, and the 5th percentile is between the French 3rd and 10th percentiles across the ages presented. Major differences are evident, however, in the skew of the upper percentiles for US boys and in their absolute levels. The 85th percentiles of BMI for US boys exceed the 90th percentiles for the French boys, and approximate the 97th percentiles. These differences mean that between two and five times more US boys than French have a BMI greater than the USA 85th percentile. Comparisons of BMI distributions for US and French girls during adolescence have yielded similar results, although the age patterns of population differences change somewhat.

Little is known regarding specific levels of BMI in adolescence and the relationships with concurrent or future risk or response to interventions. Nevertheless, the Expert Committee concluded that the elevated and skewed levels of the upper percentiles of the BMI distributions for US children, and for children with similar patterns in other developed countries (44) do *not* provide a desirable pattern that should be used as a healthy goal for adolescents internationally. For uniform reporting purposes, however, and in the absence of other data specifying optimum cut-off values for BMI in adolescence, it was recommended that the BMI-for-age data for US children be used on a provisional basis until better reference data for adolescent growth are available. This meets the requirement for reference data for height-for-age and BMI-for-age to be derived from the same reference population. Future research should focus specifically on determining cut-off points for indicators, including BMI, based on functional outcomes.

NCHS did not produce smoothed percentile curves of BMI specifically intended for use as reference data, although summations of the raw data are available in technical reports. The NCHS data are in the public domain and several investigators have therefore published percentiles of BMI-for-age, including the adolescent years. The final recommendation was that BMI data for the whole USA population compiled and published by Must et al. (35, 36) should be used: the sampling weights were used correctly in calculating the national estimates, percentiles recommended for cut-offs are presented, and percentiles were smoothed mathematically across ages in an acceptable manner. These tables are presented in Annex 3.

The Expert Committee recommended BMI-for-age cut-off values for adolescents to be considered at risk of overweight (Table 29). Because BMI is an inexact measure of total body fat, use of the term "obesity" was limited to those who are at risk of overweight *and* have high levels of subcutaneous fat. Designating individuals as at risk for overweight favours efforts to prevent obesity and provide guidance on weight control. Adolescents who are at risk of overweight may show other risk factors for future obesity-related disease, e.g. high blood pressure, elevated serum lipoproteins, and elevated insulin and glucose levels. In the absence of these risk factors, adolescents at risk of overweight should not require additional therapy or advice.

Despite the pressing need for a definition of obesity, there are insufficient data to allow firm standards to be specified with confidence. The combination of elevated BMI (≥85th percentile) and high subcutaneous fat (≥90th percentile for both subscapular and triceps skinfolds) is intended to maximize specificity in identifying those adolescents who are overweight and over-fat (*42*); none the less, recommendations for adolescent obesity must be considered as provisional because of inadequate evidence of the universal applicability of these particular cut-offs. For example, little is known about obesity in populations where BMI distributions during adolescence are known to be substantially lower than the NCHS/WHO reference data, e.g. India. Are those Indian adolescents at the upper extremes of BMI and subcutaneous fatness at the same risks for subsequent obesity-related disease as the most overweight US youth? Some data suggest they may be (*45*). Full answers to these and other questions are required before the recommendations for standards of adolescent obesity can be considered more than provisional.

For populations, the Expert Committee recommended the reporting of frequencies of BMI by age groups according to the recommended BMI reference data, and of adolescents with BMI ≥30 by age. In the later years of adolescence, patterns of BMI-related diseases and mortality risks are similar to those in young adults (*30, 46*). In many countries, there will be few adolescents with BMI ≥30. The reporting cut-off of ≥30 thus provides continuity with the definition of overweight for adults.

Reference data for annual height or weight increments have been generated for some populations in developed countries (e.g. Belgium, England, Ireland, Spain, USA). Some of these reference data include the extremes to be expected in children who mature early or late. These "longitudinal" reference data may be useful for following individual patients over several years, but have not been widely used in public health settings because of difficulty in application. The meaning of a single increment considered relative to chronological age is difficult to interpret unless the phase of the growth spurt is known for the individual adolescent. Assessment of sexual maturation or of some other aspect of maturation is essential for the interpretation of incremental growth status in adolescence.

Accurate assessment of adolescent growth increments relative to the timing of peak height velocity is only possible retrospectively, some time after the peak has passed, and this has little value for timely intervention in adolescents at risk. In research settings and in certain clinical situations, however, long-term data on patterns of incremental growth are important for describing and analysing the characteristics of the adolescent growth spurt. Aligning the pattern of height velocity or weight velocity according to peak height velocity of appropriate reference data allows evaluation of the patterns, rates, and timing of adolescent growth of individuals (*3*). This information is important for monitoring growth in certain diseases and genetic syndromes, and may be useful in evaluating the effects of surgical treatment of growth-related tumours and some hormonal therapies.

No incremental or longitudinal reference data were recommended for widespread use.

6.1.4 *Conditioning the interpretation of anthropometry*

Sex

Because of the considerable differences in size and in the timing of the adolescent spurt (and associated growth changes) between the sexes, anthropometric data must be presented separately for each sex during adolescence.

Age

The most intense phase of the adolescent growth spurt lasts for 2–3 years. Because of the transient nature of adolescent growth patterns, the age intervals for collecting and presenting anthropometric data should be shorter than those used during middle childhood; 6-month intervals are recommended because of the variation among individuals (and between sexes) in the timing of the adolescent spurt. Rate of growth in adolescence is relatively rapid and 6-month increments are sufficiently large to be detectable and meaningful relative to expected measurement errors (*47*). About 2 years after the peak height velocity, growth velocity slows, and measurement intervals should then be increased to 1 year until statural growth ceases.

Physiological events

Maturation. The timing of the adolescent spurt and the associated changes in anthropometric dimensions are maturational phenomena. However, there are few anthropometric reference data that truly incorporate maturational status into the evaluation scheme, such as weight-for-age references appropriate only for postmenarcheal girls, or standardized correction factors for stages of sexual maturity. Maturational status must therefore be used to interpret the meaning of anthropometric indicators of nutritional and health status based on chronological age.

Suitable information on maturation should be collected whenever possible. The use of two maturational events for each sex is recommended to help interpret anthropometric reference data during adolescence, ideally one marker signalling the beginning of the adolescent spurt in each sex, and one indicating that peak velocity for height and associated changes has passed (see Fig. 49):

Figure 49

Approximate timing of recommended maturational events relative to peak height velocity (PHV) in boys and girls

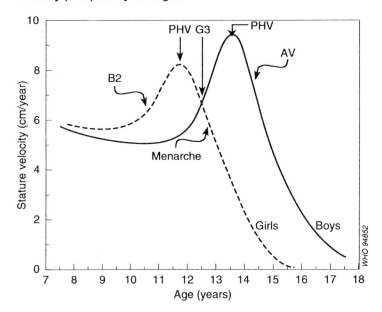

B2 = breast stage 2
G3 = genitalia stage 3
AV = adult voice

- At least breast stage 2 (B2): yes/no
  The start of breast development precedes peak velocity of height by about 1 year. It is identified by examination and can be used as an indicator that the adolescent spurt has begun.
- Menarche attained: yes/no
  Menstruation usually begins a little more than 1 year after peak velocity in height. Menarche is determined by questioning and indicates that most of the adolescent growth spurt has been completed.
- At least genitalia stage 3 (G3): yes/no
  Adolescent changes in the penis, characterizing G3, precede peak velocity in height by about 1 year. This stage is identified by examination and can be used as an indicator that the adolescent spurt has begun.
- Attainment of adult voice (AV): yes/no
  In boys, adult voice is attained about 1 year after the peak velocity in height. It is determined by questioning and indicates that most of the adolescent growth spurt has been completed.

By combining information on these maturational events, which indicate the approximate beginning and ending of the most intense part of the growth spurt, adolescents can be grouped into general categories related

Table 30
General interpretations of recommended maturational events for use with reference data

Boys

Adult voice	At least genitalia stage 3	
	Yes	No
Yes	*Post-pubescent:* boy has probably passed peak velocity for stature and completed most of adolescent growth	This combination of events should not occur in normal children
No	*Pubescent:* boy has begun, but probably not completed, the adolescent spurt	*Prepubescent:* boy has not yet entered the adolescent spurt

Girls

Menarche	At least breast stage 2	
	Yes	No
Yes	*Post-pubescent:* girl has probably passed peak velocity for stature and completed most of adolescent growth	This combination of events should not occur in normal children
No	*Pubescent:* girl has begun, but probably not completed, the adolescent spurt	*Prepubescent:* girl has not yet entered the adolescent spurt

Table 31
Estimated median ages for maturational events for NCHS/WHO reference population

Maturational stage	Median age (years)
Boys	
Genitalia stage 3	12.4
Peak height velocity	13.5
Adult voice	14.5
Girls	
Breast stage 2	10.6
Peak height velocity	11.7
Menarche	12.8

to their maturational status (Table 30). Such maturational groupings may be too crude for some specialized or research purposes, but should be sufficient for routine interpretation of anthropometric reference data.

Based on the estimated median ages of attainment of these maturational markers in the NCHS/WHO reference population in the USA (Table 31), more specific guidance can be given on the use of maturational indicators in conjunction with the recommended anthropometric reference data, particularly in the case of low height-for-age.

When the NCHS/WHO reference data were smoothed, the ages at peak velocity for median stature were inadvertently advanced by about 6 months in girls and 8 months in boys compared with the raw data and are therefore slightly different from those given in Table 31. However, because the recommended use of maturational status relies on markers of the beginning and ending of the adolescent spurt, this shift in peak velocity should not affect the usefulness of the recommended indicators. It is important to note that the timing of maturational events is given here only for use with the NCHS/WHO reference data, and may not have health or other clinical implications; other sources should be consulted for designations of maturational precocity or delay that may have clinical significance (*48*).

The recommended maturational markers were selected for several reasons. It was considered important to focus on adolescent changes associated primarily with the gonadal hormones, i.e. the estrogens and testosterone. By determining only that development of breasts or penis (genitalia) has begun, more difficult distinctions between successive stages of development are avoided. Genitalia stage 3 (G3) was selected primarily because its timing relative to peak height velocity in boys is similar to the relative timing of breast stage 2 (B2) in girls; moreover, it is characterized by marked penis development which can be readily observed and reliably rated (*49*).

Attainment of adult voice (AV) is not commonly used as an indicator of maturation in boys but it was recommended to provide an indicator of the passing of peak velocity. It is important to specify that this indicator is not the so-called "breaking" of the adolescent boy's voice, but the subsequent stage of attainment of the adult voice. Adult voice is easier to distinguish than adult stages of genitalia (G5) and pubic hair (PH5), which would provide similar maturational information. The timing of AV in boys relative to peak velocity is similar to the relative timing of menarche in girls; it has been assessed as a reliable and valid indicator of peak velocity (*50, 51*).

Some investigators have made use of developmental stages of secondary sexual characteristics based on self-reports from adolescents, aided by written descriptions or line drawings (*52*). Some success has been achieved, but reports are available only for white adolescents in the USA. Self-reports have been found to be insufficiently precise to be used for

Table 32
Mean or median age of attainment of recommended indicators of maturation[a]

Country	Mean/median age of attainment of maturational indicator (years)		
	G3	**Boys**	AV
Brazil	12.4		14.6
Cuba	13.6		—
England	12.9		—
Sweden	13.1		15.0
Switzerland	12.9		—
	B2	**Girls**	Menarche
Cuba	10.8		13.1
England	11.2		13.5
Hong Kong	10.7		13.4
South Africa (Bantu)	11.3		14.2
Switzerland	10.9		13.4

[a] Reproduced from reference 9 with the permission of the publisher.

individuals and, possibly, to vary according to ethnic origin. Self-reports of B2 and G3 are not recommended for widespread use.

The Expert Committee recommended that testicular volume should be measured by palpation and compared with models, in situations where these procedures are acceptable (53). A testicular volume of 4 ml signals the beginning of pubescent changes and precedes G3 by about 1 year; a volume of 12 ml indicates that peak velocity has passed (54).

Selected median ages of attainment for the recommended indicators of maturation are given in Table 32, which provides examples of the variation in timing and intervals that may be expected. These indicators have been fully considered in the context of general growth and maturation (55).

Pregnancy. Pregnancy in adolescent girls is clearly associated with many changes in body dimensions and composition that may be reflected in anthropometry. Some information on expected anthropometric changes is available (16), but there are no widely applicable reference data suitable for evaluating the anthropometric status of pregnant adolescents. If pregnant or lactating girls are included in an evaluation of adolescents, they should be identified as such so that possible effects on measurements of weight, circumferences, or fatness may be considered.

Unfortunately, understanding of how and to what extent such measures are affected is poor, and much more research is needed on the effects of pregnancy and lactation on adolescent maternal growth.

6.2 Using anthropometry in individuals

6.2.1 *Introduction*

Specific recommended uses of anthropometric indicators for individual adolescents are outlined in Table 33. For the most part, the recommended cut-off values for indicators are those given in Table 29; when other factors are needed, or desirable, for interpretation of the anthropometric indicators, this is indicated in Table 33.

6.2.2 *Screening for interventions*

Stunting

In the absence of other more appropriate local criteria, stunting in adolescents should be defined using <-2 SD (Z-scores) or <3rd percentile relative to the NCHS/WHO reference data for height-for-age (*39*). Thinness should be evaluated by BMI and the general maturational category determined; the cause of stunting should be sought as a basis for deciding on appropriate interventions.

In primary health care or field settings, the principal aim should be to identify stunted adolescents who may benefit from improved nutrition or treatment of other underlying problems, so that they may be evaluated further. However, interventions will provide benefit only when sufficient time remains before maturation for response to occur, and should therefore focus on premenarcheal girls and prepubertal or early pubertal boys in whom the adolescent growth spurt is unlikely to have been completed. Attainment of breast stage 2 and genitalia stage 3 confirms that pubescence has begun and may be used to interpret the reference data. In girls, menarche indicates that peak stature velocity has passed and the likelihood of response to intervention is low; the same is true of attainment of adult voice in boys. In this setting, observation of parental heights as unusually short for the population may suggest inherited short stature; physical examination may identify obvious pathology as an underlying cause of stunting.

Adolescents referred to secondary or tertiary medical settings on the basis of possible stunting are evaluated to determine the underlying causes and the appropriate treatment (particularly of underweight individuals). Clinical examinations and hormonal or other biochemical studies are required, and complete sexual maturity ratings, including testicular volume for boys, allow better assessment of maturational progress. In some countries such as the former Czechoslovakia (*56*) and the USA (*57*), where parents and children are thought to have approached their genetic growth potential, evaluation of adolescent stature may take into account average parental stature and the contribution of normal inheritance.

Thinness

In emergency situations, immediate action is required to identify those at greatest risk of death from starvation. Approximate age, visual assessment of extreme emaciation, and wasting of muscle and subcutaneous tissues are sufficient to identify those who require immediate feeding. Pregnant or lactating adolescents should also be identified because of their additional nutritional needs. At times, the inability to walk or work may be important in identifying the individuals who are most in need.

Thin or undernourished adolescents identified in primary health care or public health settings may be given nutritional guidance or referred for further evaluation. In general, BMI-for-age <5th percentile is recommended as a provisional cut-off for identifying those in need of intervention, but local cut-offs may also be chosen that take account of the availability of resources to manage the patient load. (Section 2 provides a full discussion of local cut-offs.) Medical histories and physical examinations are important for determining underlying pathology. Referral of thin or undernourished adolescents to secondary or tertiary medical settings will allow more comprehensive maturational assessments and physical examination.

At risk of overweight

Adolescents whose BMI is ≥85th percentile are considered to be at risk of overweight. (The term "obese" is reserved for individuals who are at risk of overweight *and* have excess subcutaneous fat.)

In areas where adolescent obesity is prevalent, those who are at risk of overweight may be identified in primary health care or public health settings and possibly evaluated further. In the USA, where large numbers are at risk of overweight, an additional second-level serial screen has been suggested to identify overweight adolescents with obesity-related risk factors, e.g. high blood pressure, hypercholesterolaemia, family history of cardiovascular disease or diabetes mellitus (58).

Adolescent obesity is usually identified in secondary or tertiary medical settings, where advice and treatment may be provided. Adolescents with BMI ≥85th percentile *and* triceps skinfold and subscapular skinfold thicknesses both ≥90th percentile are considered obese. (The additional requirements of extreme skinfold thicknesses exclude athletes and others who may be overweight because of high muscularity.) Skinfold thicknesses at both limb (triceps) and trunk (subscapular) sites were included to accommodate different distributions of subcutaneous fat. Complete sexual maturity rating (SMR) and other maturity indicators facilitate interpretation of the anthropometric reference data. Assessment of menstrual function is required because of the frequent associations of abnormalities with polycystic ovary disease; assessment of family medical history, and risk factors for cardiovascular disease and diabetes mellitus are important for considering specific pathologies and treatments.

6.2.3 *Assessing response to an intervention*

Stunting

When stunted adolescents are referred to secondary or tertiary medical settings, the intention is to improve growth in height. Some hormonal treatments may require 3-monthly visits and other less intense therapies 6-monthly visits. The expected measurement errors for adolescent height, the expected rates of normal adolescent growth, and the variations in adolescent growth make it unlikely that significant growth of an individual will be detected over 3-month periods except during the most rapid phases of the adolescent spurt and if rapid catch-up were to occur. Intervals of 6 months, however, are sufficiently long to allow significant height increments to be detected throughout most of adolescence. Three-monthly visits may be required for monitoring the side-effects of treatments and to enhance compliance with treatment regimens, rather than for the evaluation of growth *per se*.

Treatments for stunting can be appropriately evaluated on the basis of Z-scores of height-for-age and increases in Z-scores. Patterns of change and timing of height responses relative to treatments may be as important as absolute change in height. Complete SMR and other maturational measures, including skeletal age, allow evaluation of the differential progress in growth and maturation in response to treatments. Biochemical studies may be required to monitor some treatments.

Obesity

Obese adolescents may be treated in secondary or tertiary medical settings to reduce excess body fat and prevent obesity-related sequelae. Three-monthly measurements are required to monitor changes in percentiles of BMI-for-age and thicknesses of triceps and subscapular skinfolds, and to maintain compliance with treatment regimens. Generally speaking, emphasis should be placed on slowing the rate of BMI gain, rather than on lowering BMI. Changes in skinfold thicknesses require special monitoring relative to maturational patterns during adolescence, because the patterns differ from the more familiar shapes of reference data for height or BMI. SMR, including assessment of menarcheal status and testicular volume, allows closer monitoring of maturation, and histories of diet and physical activity are important for evaluating treatment-related behaviour and compliance with treatment. Absolute changes in weight will probably be monitored by the adolescents themselves, but weight changes should be explained to them in the context of expected normal growth and relationship to height.

Table 33
Summary of recommendations for use of anthropometry in individual adolescents

Uses: what will be done for the individual?	For what purpose?	Setting for measurement activities	Demographic characteristics	Indices and frequency of measurement	Criteria for judgement (e.g. cut-offs)[a]	What is being assessed?	Other factors for interpretation[b]
Screening for interventions							
Assessment of stunting in order to: • refer • evaluate further • provide information and advice	To diagnose the problem underlying short stature	Primary health care, public health, or field setting	Premenarcheal girls; boys before AV	Height-for-age; determined once	< 3rd percentile or <-2 Z-scores or locally defined cut-offs	Stunting induced by environmental or genetic factors or metabolic pathology	**Menarcheal status, AV** *B2, G3, weight, parental height, physical examination*
Assessment of stunting in order to: • improve nutrition • treat underlying causes	To reduce growth deficits	Secondary or tertiary medical setting	Premenarcheal girls, and boys before AV, referred for shortness	Height-for-age; determined once	< 3rd percentile or <-2 Z-scores or locally defined cut-offs	Stunting induced by environmental or genetic factors or metabolic pathology	**Menarcheal status, SMR, AV, history, physical examination** *Testicular size, height velocity, parental height, weight, clinical and biochemical studies as indicated*

Table 33 (continued)

Uses: what will be done for the individual?	For what purpose?	Setting for measurement activities	Demographic characteristics	Indices and frequency of measurement	Criteria for judgement (e.g. cut-offs)[a]	What is being assessed?	Other factors for interpretation[b]
Screening for interventions (continued)							
Assessment of thinness in order to: • provide food	To prevent death from starvation	Emergency field situation	All adolescents where there is high prevalence of starvation	Single visual assessment	Emaciation; vitality	Muscle and tissue wasting	**Ability to walk and work, pregnancy, lactation**
Assessment of thinness in order to: • refer • evaluate further • provide information and advice	To identify cases of poor nutrition and metabolic pathology	Primary health care, public health, or field setting	All adolescents	BMI-for-age; determined once	< 5th percentile or locally defined cut-offs	Body mass	**Physical examination, medical history, ability to work, menarcheal status, AV** *B2, G3*
Assessment of thinness in order to: • improve nutrition	To provide further evaluation or treatment	Secondary or tertiary medical setting	All adolescents referred for treatment of undernutrition	BMI-for-age; determined once	< 5th percentile or locally defined cut-offs	Body mass	**Menarcheal status, AV, physical examination, SMR** *Testicular size*

Table 33 *(continued)*

Screening for interventions *(continued)*

Uses: what will be done for the individual?	For what purpose?	Setting for measurement activities	Demographic characteristics	Indices and frequency of measurement	Criteria for judgement (e.g. cut-offs)[a]	What is being assessed?	Other factors for interpretation[b]
Assessment of risk of overweight in order to: ● refer ● evaluate further ● provide information and advice	To identify those at risk of obesity and prevent obesity-related sequelae	Primary health care, public health, or field setting	All adolescents where there is high prevalence of overweight or obesity	BMI-for-age; determined once	≥85th percentile or locally defined cut-offs	Excess body mass, body fat	**Menarcheal status, AV** *B2, G3, physical examination*
Assessment of obesity in order to: ● provide advice or treatment	To diagnose, prevent, or treat obesity	Secondary or tertiary medical setting where there is high prevalence of overweight or obesity	Adolescents referred for overweight or obesity	BMI-for-age; skinfold thickness-for-age; determined once	≥85th percentile BMI, ≥90th percentile triceps skinfold, and ≥90th percentile subscapular skinfold	Excess body mass, body fat, metabolic risk factors	**Menarcheal status, AV, SMR, physical examination, menstrual function, family history** *Testicular size, blood pressure, lipoprotein fractions, blood glucose and insulin*

286

Table 33 (continued)

Uses: what will be done for the individual?	For what purpose?	Setting for measurement activities	Demographic characteristics	Indices and frequency of measurement	Criteria for judgement (e.g. cut-offs)[a]	What is being assessed?	Other factors for interpretation[b]
Assessing response to interventions							
Assessment of stunting in order to: • continue or modify treatment	To improve growth	Secondary or tertiary medical setting	Premenarcheal girls, and boys before AV, under care for growth deficits	Height-for-age; determined 3- or 6-monthly according to therapy	Increase in Z-scores	Growth response to therapy	**Menarcheal status, AV, SMR** *Height velocity, weight, skeletal age, testicular size, appropriate bio-chemical studies, compliance*
Assessment of obesity in order to: • continue or modify treatment	To prevent obesity-related sequelae	Secondary or tertiary medical setting	Adolescents under care for obesity	BMI-for-age or skinfold thickness-for-age; determined 3-monthly	Decrease in age-specific percentiles	Loss of excess body mass and body fat	**Menarcheal status, menstrual function, AV, SMR** *Testicular size, weight, diet history, activity history, compliance*
Assessment of thinness in order to: • continue or modify treatment	To improve weight gain, prevent under-nutrition	Primary, secondary or tertiary medical setting	Adolescents under care for undernutrition	BMI-for-age; determined 3-monthly	Increase in age-specific percentiles	Gain in body mass	**Menarcheal status, menstrual function, AV, SMR** *Testicular size*

[a] For reference data see Annex 3.
[b] AV = adult voice; SMR = sexual maturity rating.
Factors in **bold type** are necessary for interpretation of indicators; factors in *italics* may be required in certain circumstances.

Thinness
Thin adolescents may be treated in primary, secondary, or tertiary medical settings. Three-monthly assessments maintain compliance with treatment and allow monitoring of short-term gains in BMI-for-age. In some areas where adolescents treated for undernutrition have BMI levels well below the 5th percentile for age of the recommended reference data (see Annex 3), it may be necessary to develop local cut-offs or reference data in order to monitor response to treatment for thinness. Maturational indicators improve interpretation of the BMI reference data, and assessment of normal menstrual function or secondary amenorrhoea may aid evaluation of the severity of the undernutrition and response to treatment.

6.3 Using anthropometry in populations

6.3.1 *Introduction*

Recommended uses of anthropometric indicators during adolescence for groups or populations are outlined in Table 34. Generally, the recommended criteria for judgement closely parallel those for individuals and, for the same indicator, are uniform across various purposes.

For many population uses, it is recommended that median ages for maturational indicators (menarche, B2, G3, adult voice) be obtained by probit or similar analyses as explained in section 6.4.4. The population values for maturation facilitate interpretation of the group anthropometric data, adjusted for maturation differences, and provide group estimates of developmental outcomes that are sensitive to many health-related changes. (See maturation adjustment procedures for populations in section 6.4.5.) It is also desirable to present the maturational data for populations as cumulative distributions of attainment across age. This procedure and its interpretation are also outlined in section 6.4.5.

6.3.2 *Targeting interventions*

Thinness
Identification of populations with an excess proportion of thin adolescents in regions where prevalence of undernutrition or protein-energy malnutrition is high is important for designing, initiating, or modifying intervention programmes, and for allocation of resources. While prevalence of thinness is important for all adolescents, it is of special concern in premenarcheal girls and in boys before attainment of adult voice because of increased nutritional needs to support growth and development during the adolescent spurt. Summary statistics (mean, SD) for BMI within age and sex groups, and the frequency below the 5th percentile of BMI-for-age should be reported. In regions where local distributions of BMI are substantially below those of the recommended

reference data (Annex 3), it may be necessary to develop local cut-offs. Median ages of maturational markers facilitate comparisons with other populations.

At risk of overweight
In areas where prevalence of adolescent overweight is thought to be high, actual prevalence can be estimated by an anthropometric survey. Such a survey is also required for the design or modification of intervention programmes, which may include additional risk screening, health education, community activities, or media campaigns. Based on the BMI reference data (Annex 3), frequencies should be reported for adolescents ≥85th percentile, who should be considered as being at risk of overweight. In addition, mean, median, and SD of BMI and frequency of BMI ≥30 should be reported by age and sex groups. Because the distribution of BMI within adolescent age groups may be skewed towards higher values, the median provides a better estimate of central tendency than does the mean. Skewness is especially prominent in groups with high prevalence of overweight relative to the reference data.

Population distributions of several obesity-related outcomes may be useful. Triceps and subscapular skinfold thicknesses allow evaluation of measures of subcutaneous fatness *per se*, and are more specific for obesity and excess body fat than BMI alone. Abdominal and hip circumferences and their ratio can be highly indicative of many obesity-related risks, diseases, and mortality in adulthood, although their significance in adolescence is not well understood. Measurement of blood pressure is a non-invasive procedure and will provide an assessment of population patterns of a major obesity-related risk factor for subsequent cardiovascular disease.

6.3.3 *Assessing response to an intervention*

Thinness
In community or population programmes designed to reduce the prevalence of thinness or protein–energy malnutrition, responses of adolescents may be evaluated using frequencies of BMI relative to either the recommended reference data or more appropriate local reference data. In some situations of prevalent undernutrition or protein–energy malnutrition, secular change in the prevalence of thinness may be an important indicator of overall social or economic improvement. Surveys should be undertaken at least every 5 years during periods of socioeconomic change or while programmes are in progress, otherwise every 10 years. In the event of war, natural disaster, or marked, unexpected economic success or failure, more frequent surveys may be required to monitor rapid changes. The timing of other surveys may be linked to needs of specific programmes and may be more frequent than 5-yearly.

Mean and SD of BMI should be reported, and frequencies of BMI-for-age <5th percentile, (or below locally defined cut-offs). Median ages of maturation indicators facilitate interpretation of mean BMI, cumulative distributions of maturation indicators provide full information on patterns of sexual maturity, and the frequency of abnormal menstrual function provides a measure of secondary amenorrhoea and severity of thinness.

At risk of overweight
Response to population interventions in adolescents at risk of overweight may be evaluated by prevalence of BMI categories for at risk of overweight (≥85th percentile) and obesity within age and sex groups. Intervention programmes will be conducted in areas where prevalence of adolescent overweight and obesity is known to be high. All adolescents should be surveyed, and mean, median, and SD of BMI should be reported by age and sex groups. The appropriate frequency of such surveys depends upon the needs of specific interventions.

To evaluate secular changes in the prevalences and summary statistics for BMI (mean, median, SD) by age and sex, 5- or 10-yearly surveys of adolescents should be conducted in areas with a high prevalence of risk of overweight or obesity. The results of these evaluations are important for understanding the impact of specific programmes, and as controls or background comparisons for accurate assessment of the effects of programmes targeted to particular segments of the population.

Median ages of attainment of maturation indicators facilitate evaluation of the mean BMI, and distributions of more specific obesity-related risk factors (elevated skinfold thickness, abdomen:hip ratio, blood pressure) are helpful for determining the responses to interventions.

6.3.4 *Ascertaining determinants of malnutrition*

Stunting
The prevalence of adolescent stunting may be used as an indicator of prior health or nutritional deficits in a population where the prevalence of stunting is thought to be high. Insufficient studies have been published to allow specification of the exact ages at which adolescent stunting may have occurred. Retrospective interpretation where prevalence of adolescent stunting is high makes it possible to say only that active stunting occurred at some time in the past, perhaps very early in life. Variation in prevalence of stunting across ethnic, social, or geographical areas may be interpreted as an indicator of a history of inequity sufficient to be manifested in growth patterns. Identification of specific determinants associated with adolescent stunting may be important for the design of interventions to modify these determinants and for the formulation of policy.

Mean and SD for height and height Z-scores within age and sex groups, and frequencies of <−2 SD or <3rd percentile of the NCHS/WHO reference data (39) should be reported. In areas where distributions of adolescent height are considerably below those of the NCHS/WHO reference data, locally defined cut-offs should be used and reported accordingly. Median ages of attainment of maturational indicators are useful for interpreting the population means for height, and potential prior environmental determinants of stunting should be evaluated in the context of local conditions.

Thinness

In areas where adolescent undernutrition or chronic protein–energy malnutrition is prevalent, frequency of low BMI-for-age (<5th percentile) may be used within age and sex groups. The determinants of adolescent thinness may include factors of much shorter duration and closer proximity in time than the determinants of adolescent stunting. Survey results may be useful for identifying specific determinants, and for designing policies for the prevention or remedy of thinness, or for the promotion of equity among regions or population subgroups. Mean and SD of BMI and frequencies of <5th percentile of the BMI-for-age reference (Annex 3) should be reported for age and sex groups. In areas where distributions of BMI indicate that the <5th percentile cut-off is unsatisfactory, locally defined cut-offs should be used (see section 2). Median ages for attainment of maturation indicators may facilitate interpretation of the mean BMI, and assessment of menstrual function allows further evaluation of the severity of thinness and related secondary amenorrhoea. Potential concurrent environmental determinants of low BMI should be considered.

At risk of overweight

Determinants of adolescent overweight may be identified in a survey of all adolescents in areas where prevalence of the risk of overweight or obesity is high. Survey results are important for the design of interventions and formulation of policies to reduce risks of obesity-related sequelae. Mean, median, and SD of BMI, and frequencies of adolescents considered at risk of overweight (≥85th percentile and BMI ≥30) should be reported within age and sex groups. Median ages for maturational markers are needed for interpretation of data on mean or median BMI. Potential prior and concurrent determinants of adolescent overweight or obesity should be evaluated, and more specific measures of subcutaneous fatness and fat distribution will allow attention to be focused on excess fat *per se*, rather than on the risk of overweight.

6.3.5 *Ascertaining consequences of malnutrition*

Stunting

In areas where adolescent stunting is prevalent, it is important to determine the risks of related adverse consequences. All adolescents should be studied, but girls are of special concern because of the potential impacts of stunting on reproductive function. Stunting should be reported as frequencies < -2 SD or $<$3rd percentile relative to the NCHS/WHO reference data for height-for-age (39). In areas where adolescent height distributions are substantially below those of the recommended reference, locally defined cut-offs may need to be developed. Mean and SD for height and height Z-scores should be reported for sex and age groups, and median ages of attainment of maturational indicators are required for interpretation of the mean height data. Functional indicators of strength, physical performance, and reproductive outcomes should also be evaluated.

At risk of overweight
Concurrent and future consequences of adolescent overweight may be determined by survey in areas where prevalences of overweight and obesity are high. Surveys may be conducted for research purposes only or may focus specifically on the development of population interventions or formulation of public health policy. The ultimate goal of such surveys is to reduce obesity-related sequelae. Concurrent consequences can be evaluated with a single survey, but determination of future consequences requires repeated surveys, perhaps several years apart. Because frank obesity-related disease is rare during adolescence, most concurrent consequences will be risk factors for adult diseases, e.g. high blood pressure, hypercholesterolaemia, hyperinsulinaemia. Repeated surveys may allow assessment of adult risk factors or disease as consequences of adolescent overweight. Frequencies of adolescents with BMI $\geq$30 and those considered at risk for overweight ($\geq$85th percentile) relative to the reference data should be reported. In addition, means, medians, and SD for BMI should be reported for age and sex groups. Median ages of attainment of maturational indicators facilitate proper interpretation of the BMI data, and more specific measures of subcutaneous fatness and fat distribution provide a more accurate focus on excess fatness. Probable risk factors related to cardiovascular disease and carbohydrate metabolism should be among the possible consequences evaluated.

6.3.6 *Nutritional surveillance*

Stunting
Surveillance can yield information on adolescent stunting that is important to programmes and policies focusing on long-term change of social and economic conditions. Such surveillance should be conducted every 3 years or with a frequency appropriate to local needs, programmes, and resources. Means and SD for height and height Z-scores relative to the reference data should be reported. Frequencies of adolescents < -2 SD or $<$3rd percentile relative to the NCHS/WHO reference data (39) should be reported for age and sex groups, and median ages at attainment of sexual maturity indicators are necessary for interpretation of the mean height data. Probable risk factors for stunting and other variables of relevance to existing programmes and policies should be evaluated.

Table 34
Summary of recommendations for uses of anthropometry in adolescent populations

Uses: what will be done for the population?	For what purpose?	Setting for measurement activities	Demographic characteristics	Indices and frequency of measurement	Criteria for judgement (e.g. cut-offs)[a]	What is being assessed?	Other factors for interpretation[b]
Targeting of interventions							
Assessment of thinness in order to: • design, initiate, or modify programmes • reallocate resources	To identify areas at risk and describe the population	Survey in areas of high prevalence of thinness or protein–energy malnutrition	All adolescents; priority for premenarcheal girls, and boys before AV	BMI-for-age; determined once	< 5th percentile or locally defined cut-offs	Prevalence of low body mass	**Menarche, B2, G3, AV (median ages)** *Cumulative distributions by age, menstrual function*
Assessment of risk of overweight in order to: • design, initiate, or modify programmes • reallocate resources	To identify populations at risk of obesity-related sequelae	Survey in areas of high prevalence of overweight or obesity	All adolescents	BMI-for-age; determined once	≥ 85th percentile or BMI ≥ 30	Prevalence of excess body mass	**Menarche, B2, G3, AV (median ages)** *Cumulative distributions by age, distributions of triceps and subscapular skinfolds; abdomen and hip circumference, AHR, blood pressure*

Table 34 (*continued*)

Assessing response to interventions

Uses: what will be done for the population?	For what purpose?	Setting for measurement activities	Demographic characteristics	Indices and frequency of measurement	Criteria for judgement (e.g. cut-offs)[a]	What is being assessed?	Other factors for interpretation[b]
Assessment of thinness in order to: • allocate resources • continue or modify programmes	To improve nutrition and health, evaluate secular change	Survey in areas of high prevalence of thinness or protein–energy malnutrition	All adolescents	BMI-for-age; determined 5- or 10-yearly or according to needs and programmes	< 5th percentile or locally defined cut-offs	Environmentally induced low body mass	**Menarche, B2, G3, AV (median ages)** *Cumulative distributions by age, menstrual function*
Assessment of risk of overweight in order to: • allocate resources • continue or modify programmes	To improve nutrition and health, evaluate secular change	Survey in areas of high prevalence of overweight or obesity	All adolescents	BMI-for-age; determined 5- or 10-yearly or according to needs and programmes	≥ 85th percentile or BMI ≥ 30	Excess body mass	**Menarche, B2, G3, AV (median ages)** *Cumulative distributions by age, distributions of triceps and subscapular skinfolds; abdomen and hip circumference, AHR, blood pressure*

Table 34 (continued)

Ascertaining determinants of malnutrition

Uses: what will be done for the population?	For what purpose?	Setting for measurement activities	Demographic characteristics	Indices and frequency of measurement	Criteria for judgement (e.g. cut-offs)[a]	What is being assessed?	Other factors for interpretation[b]
Assessment of stunting in order to: • evaluate determinants • design interventions • formulate policy	To prevent stunting, promote equity	Survey in areas of high prevalence of shortness	All adolescents	Height-for-age; determined once	< 3rd percentile or < –2 Z-scores or locally defined cut-offs	Prevalence of stunting	**Menarche, B2, G3, AV (median ages)** *Potential prior environmental determinants, cumulative distributions by age, weight*
Assessment of thinness in order to: • evaluate determinants • design interventions • formulate policy	To prevent thinness, promote equity	Survey in areas of high prevalence of thinness or protein–energy malnutrition	All adolescents	BMI-for-age; determined once	< 5th percentile or locally defined cut-offs	Prevalence of thinness	**Menarche, B2, G3, AV (median ages) potential concurrent environmental determinants** *Cumulative distributions by age, menstrual function*

Table 34 (continued)

Ascertaining determinants of malnutrition (continued)

Uses: what will be done for the population?	For what purpose?	Setting for measurement activities	Demographic characteristics	Indices and frequency of measurement	Criteria for judgement (e.g. cut-offs)[a]	What is being assessed?	Other factors for interpretation[b]
Assessment of risk of overweight in order to: • evaluate determinants • design interventions • formulate policy	To prevent risks of obesity-related sequelae	Survey in areas of high prevalence of overweight or obesity	All adolescents	BMI-for-age; determined once	≥ 85th percentile or BMI ≥ 30	Prevalence of overweight	**Menarche, B2, G3, AV (median ages) potential prior and concurrent environmental determinants** *Cumulative distributions by age, menstrual function, distributions of triceps and subscapular skinfolds, abdomen and hip circumferences, AHR, blood pressure*

Table 34 *(continued)*

Uses: what will be done for the population?	For what purpose?	Setting for measurement activities	Demographic characteristics	Indices and frequency of measurement	Criteria for judgement (e.g. cut-offs)[a]	What is being assessed?	Other factors for interpretation[b]
Ascertaining consequences of malnutrition							
Assessment of stunting in order to: • evaluate stunting-related sequelae • design interventions • formulate policy	To reduce health risks	Survey in areas of high prevalence of shortness	All adolescents, but especially girls	Height-for-age; determined once	< 3rd percentile or < –2 Z-scores or locally defined cut-offs	Stunting and risk of related adverse consequences	**Menarche, B2, G3, AV (median ages)** *Cumulative distributions by age, reproductive outcomes, weight, strength and functional indicators*
Assessment of risk of overweight in order to: • evaluate obesity-related sequelae • design interventions • formulate policy	To reduce health risks	Survey in areas of high prevalence of overweight and obesity	All adolescents	BMI-for-age; determined once for concurrent consequences, several times for future consequences	≥ 85th percentile or BMI ≥ 30	Excess body mass and risk of related adverse consequences	**Menarche, B2, G3, AV (median ages), probable risk factors (e.g. blood pressure, blood lipid, glucose and insulin levels)** *Cumulative distributions by age, distributions of triceps and subscapular skinfolds, abdomen and hip circumferences, AHR*

Table 34 (*continued*)

Uses: what will be done for the population?	For what purpose?	Setting for measurement activities	Demographic characteristics	Indices and frequency of measurement	Criteria for judgement (e.g. cut-offs)[a]	What is being assessed?	Other factors for interpretation[b]
Nutritional surveillance							
Assessment of stunting in order to: • modify programmes • allocate resources	To maintain or improve nutrition and health, promote equity	Surveillance in community or in areas of high prevalence of shortness	All adolescents	Height-for-age; determined 3-yearly or according to needs, programmes, or resources	< 3rd percentile or < –2 Z-scores or locally defined cut-offs	Environmentally induced linear growth deficits	**Menarche, B2, G3, AV (median ages) probable risk factors** *Cumulative distributions by age*
Assessment of thinness in order to: • modify programmes • allocate resources	To maintain or improve nutrition and health, promote equity	Surveillance in community or in areas of high prevalence of thinness	All adolescents	BMI-for-age; determined annually or according to needs, programmes, or resources	< 5th percentile or locally defined cut-offs	Low body mass	**Menarche, B2, G3, AV (median ages), probable risk factors** *Cumulative distributions by age*

Table 34 (continued)

Nutritional surveillance (continued)

Uses: what will be done for the population?	For what purpose?	Setting for measurement activities	Demographic characteristics	Indices and frequency of measurement	Criteria for judgement (e.g. cut-offs)[a]	What is being assessed?	Other factors for interpretation[b]
Assessment of risk of overweight in order to: • modify programmes • allocate resources	To maintain or improve nutrition and health, promote equity	Surveillance in community or in areas of high prevalence of overweight	All adolescents	BMI-for-age; determined annually or according to needs, programmes, or resources	≥ 85th percentile or BMI ≥ 30	Excess body mass	**Menarche, B2, G3, AV (median ages)** *Cumulative distributions by age*

[a] For reference data see Annex 3.

[b] AV = adult voice; AHR = abdomen:hip circumference ratio.

Factors in **bold type** are necessary for interpretation of indicators; factors in *italics* may be required in certain circumstances.

Thinness

Adolescent thinness is more sensitive to short-term changes in the environment than is adolescent stunting and should therefore be included in annual surveillance protocols in areas where the condition is prevalent or where timely warning systems relate to undernutrition. Frequent surveillance of undernutrition will be most effective where there are programmes and policies in place that allow rapid initiation of interventions for thinness. Means and SD for BMI, and frequencies of <5th percentile of the BMI-for-age reference (Annex 3) should be reported; locally defined cut-offs, used in areas of very high prevalence, should also be reported. Probable risk factors for thinness and related variables should be included in the surveillance, and median ages at attainment of maturation stages are useful for interpretation of mean BMI data.

At risk of overweight

In some areas where there is concern about adolescent overweight, surveillance may include adolescent anthropometry. Mean, median, and SD of BMI for age and sex groups should be reported, as should frequencies of adolescents with BMI ≥30 and of those considered at risk of overweight (≥85th percentile) relative to the reference data for BMI-for-age (Annex 3). Median ages of attainment of maturity indicators are necessary to interpret the mean BMI data. Probable risk factors related to adolescent overweight should be included in the surveillance, so that interventions can be initiated within existing programmes, if necessary.

6.4 Population data management and analysis

6.4.1 *Description of sources of data*

In some situations and for some purposes, anthropometric data for adolescents may be obtained from sources other than formal public health surveys. Schools and communities in many areas routinely measure the height and weight of adolescents. When such data are considered, every effort should be made to document the actual population included, the measurement protocols used, and any factors that might bias findings (such as height measured with shoes on). If acceptable protocols and equipment have been used and obvious sources of bias can be accommodated, such "ready-made" data may provide useful concurrent or even historical assessments of growth status. Any generalization of these data to populations other than those from whom data were recorded should be cautious, because the clinic or school sample may be a select group within the total population. It is unlikely that indicators of maturation will have been collected routinely in other than clinical settings.

Little is known regarding the reliability and validity of adolescent self-reports of height and weight, although a few studies in the USA suggest that self-reports are probably biased toward lighter weights than those actually measured (59); self-perception is undoubtedly influenced by cultural and other values. Self-reports of adolescent height and weight are therefore not recommended for routine assessments of individuals or groups.

6.4.2 *Documentation and analysis of coverage rates*

For some studies, data on menarcheal age have been collected retrospectively by the recall method. Properly applied, this approach can provide unbiased estimates of the mean age at menarche for groups, although random error is increased relative to data collected prospectively (60). A common error in recall studies is to use adolescents to provide the most up-to-date data possible, which almost always results in the mean age of menarche being underestimated. In a population of adolescent girls, some will not yet have begun to menstruate and therefore cannot be used in calculating the mean age of menarche. Any survey that uses recalled ages of menarche should involve only women of an age when all will have begun to menstruate; in practical terms, the minimum age for inclusion in such recall surveys should be at least 4 years (≈ 4 SD) above the anticipated mean age at menarche for the population concerned. Hediger & Stine (61) have provided statistical methods for calculating unbiased estimates of age at menarche when only some of the girls have begun to menstruate.

6.4.3 *Documentation and analysis of reliability*

Sexual maturity ratings are based on categorical judgements of qualitative criteria. Consequently, documentation and analysis of reliability differ from those for conventional anthropometric dimensions, for which statistical models of reliability are based on continuously distributed variables. Initial training in maturity rating should include familiarization with written and pictorial criteria, and, in the case of adult voice, with recorded examples. Repeated blind assessments of examples of known maturity status can provide estimates of reliability. Evaluation of reliability and validity of these categorical assessments should include analysis using the kappa coefficient or a similar statistical method to correct for inter-observer agreements (62).

6.4.4 *Data compilation and documentation*

The Expert Committee recommended that median ages of attainment of indicators of maturation such as B2, G3, menarche, and adult voice be collected for populations to facilitate the interpretation of adolescent anthropometry. Such population estimates are best determined by the status quo method (9): in a survey, maturational status is determined for each individual. The frequencies of status within age groups are analysed using probit, logistic, or similar models to yield the median age of occurrence, i.e. that age at which 50% of the population has attained the maturational status (*63, 64*). Approximations of median ages of maturational events in populations can be determined graphically, based on the same survey data. An example of this approach is provided in section 6.4.5.

6.4.5 *Data analysis and presentation*

The Expert Committee suggested that cumulative distributions of maturation indicators be presented by age when possible; Fig. 50 provides the appropriate example of cumulative distribution by age of menarche in girls from the Netherlands (*65*). Estimates of the median age at menarche, or other percentiles, can be obtained from the curve.

Frequencies of maturational status should be reported in tabular form, preferably for age groups covering no more than 6 months. For graphical presentation, a mathematical (logistic) curve should ideally be fitted to the observed frequencies, but smooth curves fitted by eye can also provide approximate estimates of selected percentiles. One of the advantages of using the entire cumulative distribution is that it allows for evaluation of the extremes of the distribution as well as of the central tendency. In many populations, the adolescents who are most delayed maturationally are those at greatest risk of poor health and

Figure 50
Cumulative distribution of menarche in Dutch girls[a]

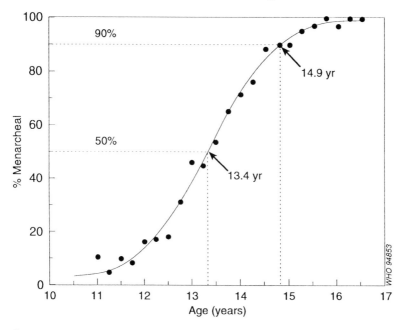

[a] Reproduced from reference *65* with the permission of the publisher.
  Median age at menarche is determined at the age when 50% of girls have attained menarche; 90th percentile for age at menarche is the age at which 90% of girls have attained menarche.

undernutrition, and may thus be the most likely to respond to interventions.

When population estimates of maturational status are available, age-specific means or medians for anthropometry may be adjusted for rates of maturation that differ from the reference data (Table 31). When mean or median values of anthropometric variables are calculated for an adolescent population, mean chronological age for that sample should also be calculated; population median ages of maturation can then be compared with those in Table 31. The population estimates of median maturational age are subtracted from the corresponding NCHS estimates, and, on the basis of that difference, the years or fractions of a year are added to (or subtracted from) the mean chronological age of the population sample. Age-specific data for the sample can then be compared with reference data for that age. The resultant comparisons correct for differences in maturation rate. If different maturity indicators give slightly variant differences in maturation rates, the differences should be averaged and the average used as the adjustment for maturation.

The following is an example of maturity adjustment for interpretation of an age-specific population mean. A mean height of 151 cm for a population of girls aged exactly 14.0 years approximates the 10th percentile, or –1.4 Z-scores, relative to the NCHS/WHO reference data (*39*). From a survey of this same population it is determined that the median age for breast stage 2 is 12.2 years and median age of menarche is 14.2 years. Calculating the differences in maturational timing from Table 31 yields –1.6 years for breast stage 2 (10.6–12.2) and –1.4 years for age at menarche (12.8–14.2), with an average of –1.5 years for the two indicators. Subtracting 1.5 years from 14.0 years (the chronological age associated with the mean height) gives 12.5 years. When the mean of 151 cm is compared with the NCHS/WHO reference data at 12.5 years, it now slightly exceeds the 25th percentile, and is at –0.5 Z-score, which represents the height status of these girls relative to the reference data at a similar level of maturity. In other words, this type of maturity adjustment for populations allows comparisons to exclude average effects that accompany differences in maturational rate.

6.5 Sources and characteristics of reference data

The source population for the recommended reference data for adolescents consists of non-institutionalized adolescents living in the USA. This recommendation is consistent with previous recommendations of WHO for younger children (*6, 66*) and with the recommendations of the Expert Committee concerning infants and children (see section 5). Details of the demographic characteristics of the samples and of measurement and analysis procedures are to be found in the original references cited in Table 29 and in earlier WHO publications (*6, 39, 66*).

The coordination and consistency of the recommendations for adolescent reference data and cut-offs with those of childhood and adulthood should be noted. The same source population and reference data are recommended during adolescence as in childhood, so that there is complete continuity. Because no reference data, only cut-offs, are recommended for adults, there is no incompatibility of reference data *per se*.

Stunting is defined identically in childhood and during adolescence as <-2 Z-scores relative to the NCHS/WHO reference data, although there are differences between some of the other anthropometric indicators and cut-offs recommended for childhood and adolescence. The preferred indicator for thinness and overweight in childhood is weight-for-height, while BMI-for-age is recommended in adolescence. Weight-for-height reference data should not be used for any children who show indications that pubescence has begun, irrespective of their height-for-age: BMI-for-age should be used to evaluate overweight and thinness in pubescent children and individuals from 10 to 24 years of age. Recommended indicators for overweight and thinness are Z-scores in childhood and percentiles in adolescence: no satisfactory Z-scores have been developed for BMI during adolescence. Because the source population is the same during both age periods, medians of weight, height, and weight-for-height at the end of childhood correspond to medians of BMI-for-age at the beginning of adolescence. Recommended cut-off values of weight-for-height and BMI-for-age should be used during the transition from childhood to adolescence, remembering that -2 Z-scores in weight-for-height will be lower than the 5th percentile for BMI-for-age and that +2 Z-scores of weight-for-height will be substantially greater than the 85th percentile recommended to designate risk of overweight in adolescents.

The NCHS/WHO reference data for height are available only until 18 years of age in each sex (*39*). The Expert Committee did not recommend any general reference data for height in adulthood because of the wide international variation, the lack of understanding of genetic and environmental determinants, and the inability to intervene. If reference data for height are required for ages 18 to 24 years, the values at 18 years provided in the NCHS/WHO reference may be used if there are no more appropriate local reference data available.

At the end of adolescence, the recommended cut-offs for BMI-for-age for thinness (5th percentile, 20–24 years) are 18.66 for males and 17.38 for females. Corresponding cut-offs of BMI-for-age designating risk of overweight (85th percentile, 20–24 years) are 26.87 and 26.14 for males and females, respectively. While there is general correspondence of the late adolescent values with adult BMI designations of grade 1 thinness (<18.5), and grade 1 overweight (≥25.0), it is recommended that, for individuals between 18 and 24 years, any guidance given should take appropriate account of the transition to adult definitions. For populations aged 18-24 years, prevalences should be reported using both the adolescent and adult cut-offs, to facilitate understanding of the development of BMI during this transitional period and to minimize confusion arising from the use of different cut-off values.

The recommended reference data are pertinent to the evaluation of growth of all adolescents. Deviations from the reference data, however, may be interpreted differently, according to the individuals or groups concerned and the purposes of the anthropometric evaluation. Reference data should not be interpreted as growth optima; rather, they describe the growth of a single, well nourished population (the USA) and should be used as benchmarks to facilitate common definitions and communication.

For some purposes, reference data based on local populations may be required. In some populations, for example, the distribution of BMI in late adolescence may be so much lower than the reference data that use of the 5th percentile has little value for identifying risk. In other cases, the setting of local cut-offs may reflect available resources as well as the portion of the population likely to be in need of intervention. (Further aspects of local cut-offs are addressed in section 2.)

6.6 Presentation of findings relative to anthropometric reference data

6.6.1 *For individuals*

One-time assessment
Results for individual adolescents should include:

- sex, age, date of examination
- anthropometric dimensions in measured units
- percentiles or Z-scores relative to reference data and chronological age (from graphs or tables)
- maturation status
- any conditions that may affect anthropometry, e.g. pregnancy, pathology
- interpretation of anthropometric status.

Repeated measurements
While the Expert Committee made no recommendations for longitudinal reference data, multiple measurements were recommended for assessing responses to interventions (Table 33). No specific quantitative criteria were recommended for evaluating anthropometric responses; successful responses may differ under varying conditions. A graphical record of repeated visits allows serial plotting of an adolescent's progress relative to the reference percentiles; the pattern, as well as the absolute magnitude, of response may be evaluated, or used as a tool for educating and advising the adolescent.

6.6.2 *For populations*

Measures of central tendency

Means or medians of adolescent anthropometric variables should ideally be reported for 6-month age groups within each sex. When larger age groups are used, patterns of anthropometry and interpretation relative to the reference data are more difficult. When means or medians are compared with the reference data, they should be compared at the mean or median age of the sample, and adjusted for maturity status of the population as described in section 6.4.5.

Presentation of distribution information

Reporting of means of anthropometric variables should include the sample size and the standard deviations or standard error of the mean. Some measure of dispersion should also be included when medians for groups are presented; the 25th and 75th percentiles are often chosen for this purpose.

The anthropometric cut-off values presented in Table 29 provide convenient and meaningful definitions for reporting prevalences in adolescent populations. If local cut-offs that differ from those in Table 29 are used, prevalences should be reported on the basis of both recommended and local cut-offs.

6.7 Recommendations

6.7.1 *For Member States*

It is recommended that Member States:

1. Incorporate anthropometric surveys for adolescents into existing health monitoring or health information systems.

2. Determine whether local cut-off points are required for adolescent anthropometry and if so, develop cut-offs on the basis of local uses, patterns, resources, needs, and experience.

3. Strengthen training of health and education workers in the methods, applications, and significance of adolescent growth and development, and the use of anthropometric indicators.

4. Include adolescent growth and development in health education curricula.

6.7.2 *For WHO*

It is recommended that WHO:

1. Facilitate development of widely applicable protocols for regular countrywide anthropometric surveys, including surveys of adolescents.

2. Develop simple, practicable methods for choosing local cut-offs that take account of local circumstances, and provide technical assistance to Member countries for developing locally defined anthropometric cut-offs.

3. Facilitate in-country training, education, and support for health and education workers in the area of adolescent growth and development.

4. Facilitate the development of a comprehensive research agenda to address the areas in which the Expert Committee has concluded that further knowledge is essential.

5. Facilitate development of information and materials relating to maturation assessment and use of maturational indicators that are applicable across ethnic and racial groups and in many settings.

6. Foster the inclusion of adolescent growth and health in national and international discussions and agendas on child health and nutrition.

7. Promote the development and establishment of international reference growth data based on data from countries.

6.7.3 *For future research and collection of reference data*

It is recommended that future research and collection of reference data should focus on:

1. Determining the most appropriate cut-off values (in terms of their specificity, sensitivity, and positive predictive values) for anthropometric indicators in adolescents, based on functional and health-related outcomes.

2. Determining whether identification of adolescents at risk and of responses to interventions can be improved by incorporation of maturational status into anthropometric reference data or use of reference data conditional upon maturational status.

3. Determining whether compensatory, or catch-up, growth occurs in response to public health interventions in adolescents.

4. Determining the effects of adolescent pregnancy and lactation on maternal growth, and developing anthropometric reference data for the evaluation of pregnant or lactating adolescents.

5. Determining the degree to which the large disparities in late adolescent stature observed across populations are the result of genetic rather than environmental influences.

6. Determining the validity of BMI for identifying adolescents at greatest risk of undernutrition and related functional impairment.

7. Determining whether patterns of fat distribution of adolescents are predictive of later obesity-related risks of disease.

8. Determining the adult consequences of adolescent thinness and stunting.

9. Developing a core of knowledge, plus materials and effective approaches, as a basis for the incorporation of adolescent growth and development into health education curricula.

10. Establishing goals and protocols for an international data set for growth reference data.

References

1. *Young people's health – a challenge for society. Report of a WHO Study Group on Young People and "Health for All by the Year 2000".* Geneva, World Health Organization, 1986 (WHO Technical Report Series, No. 731).

2. *Health needs of adolescents. Report of a WHO Expert Committee.* Geneva, World Health Organization, 1977 (WHO Technical Report Series, No. 609).

3. Tanner JM. *Growth at adolescence; with a general consideration of the effects of hereditary and environmental factors upon growth and maturation from birth to maturity*, 2nd ed. Oxford, Blackwell, 1962.

4. Garn SM, Wagner B. The adolescent growth of the skeletal mass and its implications to mineral requirements. In: Heald FP, ed. *Adolescent nutrition and growth*. New York, Meredith, 1969:139-162.

5. National Research Council. *Recommended dietary allowances*, 10th ed. Washington, DC, National Academy Press, 1989.

6. Use and interpretation of anthropometric indicators of nutritional status. WHO Working Group. *Bulletin of the World Health Organization*, 1986, **64**:929-941.

7. *Methodology of nutritional surveillance. Report of a Joint FAO/UNICEF/WHO Expert Committee.* Geneva, World Health Organization, 1976 (WHO Technical Report Series, No. 593).

8. Roche AF, Davila GH. Differences between recumbent length and stature within individuals. *Growth*, 1974, **38**:313-320.

9. Eveleth PB, Tanner JM. *Worldwide variation in human growth*, 2nd ed. Cambridge, Cambridge University Press, 1990.

10. Brudevoll JE, Liestol K, Walloe L. Menarcheal age in Oslo during the last 140 years. *Annals of human biology*, 1979, **6**:407-416.

11. Malina RM, Bouchard C. *Growth, maturation, and physical activity.* Champaign, IL, Human Kinetics Books, 1991.

12. Largo RH. Catch-up growth during adolescence. *Hormone research*, 1993, **39**(Suppl. 3):41-48.

13. Proos LA. Anthropometry in adolescence – secular trends, adoption, ethnic and environmental differences. *Hormone research*, 1993, **39**(Suppl. 3):18-24.

14. Kulin HE et al. The effect of chronic childhood malnutrition on pubertal growth and development. *American journal of clinical nutrition*, 1982, **36**:527-536.

15. Martorell R et al. Long-term consequences of growth retardation during early childhood. In: Hernández M, Argente J, eds. *Human growth: basic and clinical aspects. Proceedings of the Sixth International Congress of Auxology, Madrid, Spain, 15-19 September 1991.* Amsterdam, Elsevier, 1992:143-149.

16. Scholl TO et al. Maternal growth during pregnancy and lactation. *Hormone research*, 1993, **39**(Suppl. 3):59-67.

17. Dhuper S et al. Effects of hormonal status on bone density in adolescent girls. *Journal of clinical endocrinology and metabolism*, 1990, **71**:1083-1088.

18. Theintz GE et al. Evidence for a reduction of growth potential in adolescent female gymnasts. *Journal of pediatrics*, 1993, **122**:306-313.

19. Spurr GB. Effects of chronic energy deficiency on stature, work capacity and productivity. In: Schürch B, Scrimshaw NS, eds. *Chronic energy deficiency: consequences and related issues*. Lausanne, International Dietary Energy Consultancy Group, 1988.

20. Keys A et al. *The biology of human starvation*. Minneapolis, University of Minnesota Press, 1950.

21. Scott EC, Johnston FE. Critical fat, menarche, and the maintenance of menstrual cycles: a critical review. *Journal of adolescent health care*, 1982, 2:249-260.

22. Smoak CG et al. Relation of obesity to clustering of cardiovascular disease risk factors in children and young adults. The Bogalusa Heart Study. *American journal of epidemiology*, 1987, **125**:346-372.

23. Baumgartner RN et al. Associations between plasma lipoprotein cholesterols, adiposity and adipose tissue distribution during adolescence. *International journal of obesity*, 1989, **13**:31-41.

24. Gillum RF. The association of the ratio of waist to hip girth with blood pressure, serum cholesterol and serum uric acid in children and youths aged 6-17 years. *Journal of chronic diseases*, 1987, **40**:413-420.

25. Camilleri AP. The obstetric significance of short stature. *European journal of obstetrics, gynaecology, and reproductive biology*, 1981, **12**:347-356.

26. Harrison KA. Predicting trends in operative delivery for cephalopelvic disproportion in Africa. *Lancet*, 1990, **335**:861-862.

27. Smith EL. Bone concerns. In: Shangold MM, Mirkin G, eds. *Women and exercise: physiology and sports medicine*. Philadelphia, Davis, 1988:79-87.

28. Must A et al. Long-term morbidity and mortality of overweight adolescents. A follow-up of the Harvard Growth Study of 1922 to 1935. *New England journal of medicine*, 1992, **327**:1350-1355.

29. Javier-Nieto F, Szklo M, Comstock GW. Childhood weight and growth rate as predictors of adult mortality. *American journal of epidemiology*, 1992, **136**: 201-213.

30. Johnson AL et al. Influence of race, sex and weight on blood pressure behavior in young adults. *American journal of cardiology*, 1975, **35**:523-530.

31. Lauer RM, Lee J, Clarke WR. Factors affecting the relationship between childhood and adult cholesterol needs. The Muscatine Study. *Pediatrics*, 1988, 82:309-318.

32. Micozzi MS. Functional consequences from varying patterns of growth and maturation during adolescence. *Hormone research*, 1993, **39**(Suppl. 3):49-58.

33. Micozzi MS. Cross-cultural correlations of childhood growth and adult breast cancer. *American journal of physical anthropology*, 1987, **73**:525-537.

34. Hamill PVV et al. Physical growth: National Center for Health Statistics percentiles. *American journal of clinical nutrition*, 1979, **32**:607-629.

35. Must A, Dallal GE, Dietz WH. Reference data for obesity: 85th and 95th percentiles of body mass index (wt/ht^2) and triceps skinfold thickness. *American journal of clinical nutrition*, 1991, **53**:839-846.

36. Must A, Dallal GE, Dietz WH. Reference data for obesity: 85th and 95th percentiles of body mass index (wt/ht^2) – a correction. *American journal of clinical nutrition,* 1991, **54**:773.

37. Owen GM. Measurement, recording, and assessment of skinfold thickness in childhood and adolescence: report of a small meeting. *American journal of clinical nutrition*, 1982, **35**:629-638.

38. Johnson CL et al. *Basic data on anthropometric measurements and angular measurements of the hip and knee joints for selected age groups 1-74 years of age*. Washington, DC, National Center for Health Statistics, 1981 (Vital and Health Statistics, Series 11, No. 219; Department of Health and Human Services Publication, No. (PHS) 81-1669).

39. *Measuring change in nutritional status: guidelines for assessing the nutritional impact of supplementary feeding programmes*. Geneva, World Health Organization, 1983.

40. Rolland-Cachera MF. Body composition during adolescence: methods, limitations and determinants. *Hormone research*, 1993, **39**(Suppl. 3):25-40.

41. Cole TJ. Weight-stature indices to measure underweight, overweight, and obesity. In: Himes JH, ed. *Anthropometric assessment of nutritional status*. New York, Wiley, 1991:83-112.

42. Himes JH, Bouchard C. Validity of anthropometry in classifying youths as obese. *International journal of obesity*, 1989, **13**:183-193.

43. Rolland-Chachera MF et al. Body mass index variations: centiles from birth to 87 years. *European journal of clinical nutrition*, 1991, **45**:13-21.

44. Hernández M et al. *Curvas y tablas de crecimiento* [Growth curves and tables]. Madrid, Fundación F. Orbegozo, 1988.

45. Gupta AK, Ahmad AJ. Childhood obesity and hypertension. *Indian pediatrics*, 1990, **27**:333-337.

46. Hoffmans MDAF, Kromhout D, de Lezenne Coulander C. The impact of body mass index of 78,612 18-year-old Dutch men on 32-year mortality from all causes. *Journal of clinical epidemiology*, 1988, **41**:749-756.

47. Himes JH. Minimum time intervals for measurements of growth in recumbent length or stature of individual children. In: Hernández M, Argente J, eds. *Human growth: basic and clinical aspects. Proceedings of the Sixth International Congress of Auxology, Madrid, Spain, 15-19 September 1991*. Amsterdam, Elsevier, 1992:106.

48. Hung W, August GP, Glasgow AM. *Pediatric endocrinology*. New York, Medical Examination Publishing Company, 1978.

49. Nicholson AB, Hanley C. Indices of physiological maturity: derivation and interrelationships. *Child development*, 1953, **24**:3-38.

50. Young HB et al. Evaluation of physical maturity at adolescence. *Developmental medicine and child neurology*, 1968, **10**:338-348.

51. **Hagg U, Taranger J.** Menarche and voice change as indicators of the pubertal growth spurt. *Acta odontologica Scandinavica*, 1980, **38**:179-186.

52. **Morris NM, Udry JR.** Validation of a self-administered instrument to assess stage of adolescent development. *Journal of youth and adolescence,* 1980, **9**: 271-280.

53. **Zachmann M et al.** Testicular volume during adolescence. Cross-sectional and longitudinal studies. *Helvetica paediatrica acta*, 1974, **29**:61-72.

54. **Hagg U, Karlberg J, Taranger J.** The timing of secondary sex characteristics and their relationship to the pubertal maximum of growth in boys. In: Carlson DS, ed. *Orthodontics in an aging society*. Ann Arbor, MI, Center for Human Growth and Development, 1989:167-179.

55. **Cameron N.** Assessment of growth and maturation during adolescence. *Hormone research*, 1993, **39**(Suppl. 3):9-17.

56. **Prokopec M.** Nomogram k stanovení strední vysky rodicu akorekce vysky deti podle vysek rodicu [Nomogram for the determination of average height of parents and of the correction for the height of children in relation to the height of their parents]. *Ceskoslovenska paediatrica*, 1973, **28**:557-558.

57. **Himes JH, Roche AF, Thissen D.** Parent-specific adjustments for evaluation of recumbent length and stature of children. *Pediatrics*, 1985, **75**:304-313.

58. **Himes JH, Dietz WH.** Guidelines for overweight in adolescent preventive services: recommendations from an Expert Committee. *American journal of clinical nutrition*, 1994, **59**:307-316.

59. **Himes JH, Story M.** Validity of self-reported weight and stature of American Indian youth. *Journal of adolescent health*, 1992, **13**:118-120.

60. **Damon A et al.** Age at menarche of mothers and daughters with a note on accuracy of recall. *Human biology*, 1969, **41**:160-175.

61. **Hediger ML, Stine RA.** Age at menarche based on recall information. *Annals of human biology*, 1987, **14**:133-142.

62. **Fleiss JL.** *Statistical methods for rates and proportions*, 2nd ed. New York, Wiley, 1981.

63. **Finney DJ.** *Probit analysis*, 3rd ed. Cambridge, Cambridge University Press, 1972.

64. **Freeman DH.** *Applied categorical data analysis.* New York, Dekker, 1987.

65. **Van Wieringen JC et al.** *Growth diagrams 1965 Netherlands: Second National Survey on 0-24-year-olds.* Groningen, Wolters-Noordhoff, 1971.

66. **Waterlow JC et al.** The presentation and use of height and weight data for comparing the nutritional status of groups of children under the age of 10 years. *Bulletin of the World Health Organization*, 1977, **55**:489-498.

7. Overweight adults

7.1 Introduction

7.1.1 *Background*

When intake of energy exceeds energy expenditure, the excess is stored, in the form of triglycerides, in adipose tissue. Although energy storage is fundamental in allowing survival when food is scarce, excessive body fat, or obesity, is associated with increased mortality and morbidity. Obesity may be defined as the degree of fat storage associated with clearly elevated health risks. However, fat mass in the human body is difficult to measure under field conditions, and the practical definition of obesity is therefore based on the body mass index (BMI), also known as Quetelet's Index, which relates height to weight (weight (kg)/height^2 (m^2)). Because BMI does not measure fat mass or fat percentage and because there are no clearly established cut-off points for fat mass or fat percentage that can be translated into cut-offs for BMI, the Expert Committee decided to express different levels of high BMI in terms of degrees of overweight rather than degrees of obesity (which would imply knowledge of body composition).

For adults, the Expert Committee proposed classification of BMI with the cut-off points 25, 30, and 40 for the three degrees of overweight described in section 7.2.1. This classification is based principally on the association between BMI and mortality. These cut-off points of the body mass index can be translated into height and weight tables (see Annexes 2 and 3). The following points are important in interpreting the cut-offs:

- The recommended cut-offs are appropriate for identifying the extent of overweight in individuals and populations, but do not imply targets for intervention.
- The broad ranges of BMI do not imply that the individual can fluctuate within this range without consequence; for example, for an individual of height 1.75 m, the BMI range of 18.5–25 covers a weight range of 20 kg (see Annex 3, Table A 3.10). Weight gain in adult life may be associated with increased morbidity and mortality independently of the original degree of overweight.
- The cut-off points for degrees of overweight should not be interpreted in isolation but always in combination with other determinants of morbidity and mortality (disease, smoking, blood pressure, serum lipids, glucose intolerance, type of fat distribution, etc.).

Many recommendations on overweight use similar cut-off points (*1*) and most focus on weight-loss therapy in individuals who have reached at least grade 2 overweight (BMI 30.00–39.99). However, long-term, sustained weight loss appears to be difficult to achieve; most overweight individuals who lose an appreciable amount of body weight later regain it. Repeated treatment of overweight may thus lead to "weight cycling", which may itself be associated with adverse health consequences. Although most intervention studies have demonstrated a reduction in cardiovascular risk with weight loss, there are some reports of increased mortality from all causes, as well as from coronary heart disease, in people who have lost weight. These studies are observational and do not discriminate between voluntary weight loss (by dieting) and involuntary loss (as a result of illness), but the fact remains that there are no long-term intervention studies that show a clear-cut decrease in morbidity and mortality as a consequence of sustained weight loss. The present state of knowledge may therefore be summarized as follows:

- Weight gain is associated with increased morbidity and mortality.
- Overweight is associated with increased morbidity and mortality.
- Weight cycling may be associated with increased morbidity and mortality.
- Weight loss in overweight is difficult to sustain, is still of uncertain benefit to health in the long term, and may lead to weight cycling.

In view of these findings, the primary prevention of overweight should be the main concern. Unfortunately, little is known about how excessive weight gain with age can be prevented in modern societies. In individuals who are already overweight, weight control should be undertaken with the aim of normalizing the disorders and metabolic risk factors associated with excess weight rather than of weight loss as a target *per se*.

Overweight is a major public health issue. Grade 2 overweight (see section 7.2.1) is relatively common in most industrialized societies and also in many less modernized cultures: data compiled recently show that the prevalence among 20- to 60-year-olds is about 10–20% among whites in the USA and most countries of Europe (*2*). Prevalence is high (20–40%) among women in eastern European and Mediterranean countries and black women in the USA. Even higher prevalences are observed among American Indians and Hispanic Americans, and on the Pacific islands (*3*), with probably the highest rates in the world among Melanesians, Micronesians, and Polynesians (Table 35). In some African and Asian countries prevalence is much lower but in countries of South America and the Caribbean the prevalence of grade 2 overweight may be close to that in many European countries (Table 36).

In addition to the large differences between countries, prevalence of overweight within countries can vary substantially. This can largely be linked to variations in socioeconomic status and/or degree of urbanization; for instance, the prevalence of overweight has been found to be relatively high in certain professional groups in Bombay, India (*8*).

The method used to establish BMI cut-off points has been largely arbitrary. In essence, it has been based upon visual inspection of the relationship between BMI and mortality: the cut-off of 30 is based on the point of flexion of the curve. Studies in this area have usually suffered from certain methodological drawbacks (*9*); moreover, most have been

Table 35
Age-standardized prevalence of body mass index ≥ 30 in adults aged 25–69 years in various island populations of the Pacific and Indian Oceans[a]

Population		Year	Age-standardized prevalence[b] (%)	
			Men	Women
Caucasian				
Australia	Urban	1989	11.1	12.7
Chinese				
Mauritius		1987	6.2	4.9
		1992	2.1	6.0
Creole				
Mauritius		1987	3.8	13.3
		1992	8.0	20.7
	Rodrigues	1992	9.8	31.1
Indian				
Fiji	Urban	1980	4.3	20.0
	Rural	1980	2.8	9.5
Mauritius		1987	3.3	11.3
		1992	5.1	16.2
Melanesian				
Fiji	Urban	1980	17.8	40.8
	Rural	1980	9.4	24.2
Loyalty Islands		1979	10.5	25.0
Papua New Guinea				
Coast	Urban	1991	36.3	64.3
	Rural	1991	23.9	18.6
Highlands		1991	4.7	5.3
Micronesian				
Kiribati	Urban	1981	29.8	34.5
	Rural	1981	11.8	13.1
Nauru		1975/76	61.7	69.4
		1982	67.5	76.4
		1987	64.8	70.3
Polynesian				
Loyalty Islands		1979	5.0	31.3
Niue		1980	21.0	36.0
Rarotonga		1980	39.0	49.6
Tuvalu		1977	24.0	47.5

Table 35 (*continued*)

Population		Year	Age-standardized prevalence[b] (%)	
			Men	Women
Polynesian (continued)				
Wallis Islands	Urban	1980	35.9	65.4
	Rural	1980	24.1	48.1
Western Samoa	Urban	1978	38.8	59.1
		1991	58.4	76.8
	Rural	1978	17.7	37.0
		1991	41.5	59.2

[a] Adapted from references *4, 5,* and *6.*
[b] Standardized to Segi's world population. (See: Segi M. *Cancer mortality for selected sites in 24 countries (1950-57).* Sendai, Tohuku University School of Medicine, 1960.)

Table 36
Proportion of overweight adults in countries of Africa, South America/Caribbean, and Asia[a]

Country	Year	Proportion (%) of population of BMI:	
		25.00–29.99	≥ 30
Africa			
Congo (women)	1986/87	11.8	3.4
Ghana	1987/88	17.1	0.9
Mali	1991	6.4	0.8
Morocco	1984/85	18.7	5.2
Tunisia	1990	28.6	8.6
South America/Caribbean			
Brazil	1989	25.1	8.6
Cuba	1982	26.9	9.5
Peru	1975/76	24.8	9.0
Asia			
China	1982	7.2	1.0
India	1988/90	3.0	0.5

[a] Adapted from reference *7.*

conducted among people living in western Europe or the USA. It may therefore be necessary to revise the classification of overweight in terms of BMI based on health risk.

7.1.2 *Biological and social significance of overweight*

Biological and social determinants of overweight

Interaction of genetic and environmental factors. Overweight is always the product of a positive energy balance resulting from relatively low energy expenditure and/or relatively high energy intake. Social, cultural, and behavioural factors are important determinants of both components, but it is also clear that excess weight gain in affluent circumstances may result from a genetic predisposition. What remains unclear is the mechanism through which genetic factors exert their influence; it is probable that many genes are involved, affecting both energy expenditure and energy intake (*10*).

Figure 51
Schematic representation of the transition of a society from poverty to affluence and its relevance to changes in anthropometry

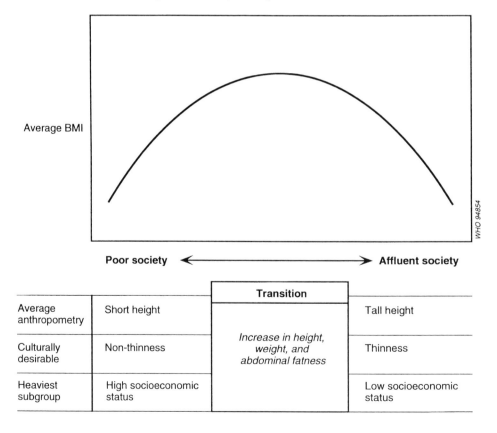

	Poor society	Transition	Affluent society
Average anthropometry	Short height		Tall height
Culturally desirable	Non-thinness	*Increase in height, weight, and abdominal fatness*	Thinness
Heaviest subgroup	High socioeconomic status		Low socioeconomic status

The expression of overweight requires a certain level of food availability above which the relative contributions of genetics and environment probably vary within and across populations. High-fat diets combined with low levels of physical activity play an important role in the increase of overweight that accompanies the transition from poverty to affluence (Fig. 51). In an affluent population of individuals with similar socio-economic values and resources, genetic factors become relatively more important in determining which individuals will become obese.

The "thrifty genotype" hypothesis (11) postulates that populations exposed to inadequate or fluctuating food supplies are genetically selected for a high level of efficiency in caloric utilization or fat storage. When more food becomes available, this efficiency may lead to an increase in the prevalence of overweight and non-insulin-dependent diabetes mellitus.

Secular trends in the prevalence of overweight. According to the NHANES study in the USA, the prevalence of overweight seems to have been stable in the white population during the period 1960-1980 but to have increased among non-whites, particularly black males (12). In the 1980s the prevalence of overweight remained stable or increased in Australia, Finland, the Netherlands, Sweden, and the UK (13-15). Since then, there seems to be no indication of a decrease in the prevalence of overweight in these affluent countries despite increased commercial and other interests in promoting leanness; on the contrary, the prevalence of overweight may be increasing further.

Trend analyses of populations among whom overweight is now common (e.g. Pima Indians in the USA, and Fijians, Maltese, Melanesians, Nauruans, and Samoans) are fragmentary (Table 35), but it is clear that the condition was uncommon before the adoption of sedentary lifestyles and high-fat diets. Data from Mauritius, for example, show that the prevalence of combined grade 2 and 3 overweight has increased by approximately 50%. Studies of Aborigines in Australia have shown that a return to their original lifestyle reduces the prevalence of overweight and other cardiovascular risk factors (16).

Biological determinants

- *Age and sex.* In many affluent countries the prevalence of grades 1 and 2 overweight in men increases with age up to about 55 years, then levels off before finally decreasing somewhat in old age. In women, prevalence continues to rise until old age and then levels off. These observations generally come from cross-sectional studies and the age, period, and cohort effects have not usually been separated. In postmenopausal women, and to a lesser degree in men, BMI increases with age even when body weight remains stable, because of the age-associated decline in stature. Although age-specific mean BMI is usually lower in premenopausal women than in men, the overall prevalence of overweight is generally higher in women. Some studies report that obese adults gain most of their excess weight in early adult life (*17*); the incidence of substantial weight gain may be highest among those who are already overweight in early adulthood (*18*).

- *Pregnancy and lactation.* In cross-sectional studies from affluent countries, body mass index usually increases with the number of pregnancies. There are only a few longitudinal studies that include prepregnant weight as well as appropriate controls. A 1987 literature review revealed that mean body weight at different times after delivery was 0.5–2.4 kg higher than prepregnant weight. Among some 6000 Finnish women who were followed for 5 years, the mean (adjusted) weight gain for women with one child was 0.2 kg and for those with two or more children 0.6 kg (*20*). The relative risk of gaining 5 kg or more in these women depended on their level of education. Thus, the relative risk (compared with those of a high educational level and with no children) was 0.6 for women of high educational level and with two or more children, but 2.8 and 3.3 for similar mothers of intermediate and low educational level respectively. In a large prospective study of 2295 Swedish women, mean weight gain following one pregnancy was 1.5 kg (*21*); about 14% of the women gained more than 5 kg. Factors associated with a weight gain of more than 5 kg were higher prepregnancy BMI, greater weight gain during pregnancy, limited breast-feeding, and cessation of smoking during pregnancy. (The effects of lactation on weight are discussed in section 3.) It may therefore be that the influence of pregnancy in the development of overweight is preventable by educating women on optimal weight gain.

Sociocultural determinants

- *Socioeconomic status/educational level.* In most affluent societies, there is an inverse relationship between educational level and prevalence of overweight. Sobal & Stunkard (*22*) reviewed the relationship between socioeconomic status (usually measured as educational level and/or profession) and prevalence of overweight. Of 20 studies from Europe covering the period 1949–1988 and providing data on women, 16 showed an inverse association between socio-economic status and overweight, and only four showed no association. Of the 33 studies in men, 21 showed an inverse association between socioeconomic status and overweight prevalence, five showed no association, and seven a positive association. Most of the studies that showed a positive association in men were performed in the 1950s, 1960s, and early 1970s. For example, 19 studies were carried out in men in the UK up to 1988; the average year of publication of the four studies that showed a positive association between prevalence of overweight and socioeconomic status was 1961, but for the 11 that showed an inverse association it was 1975.

Figure 52
Household diet and adiposity in Brazil, according to dietary staples[a]

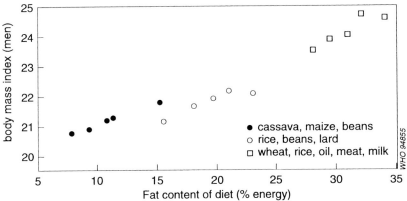

[a] Source: reference 23.

As mentioned earlier, overweight may be seen as a visible indicator of wealth and status in societies where food is scarce. Brazil is an example of a country in which there is a clear positive association between socioeconomic status (measured as income rather than educational level) and average BMI (23). It has been suggested that this association is mediated by the fat content of the diet: see Fig. 52.

- *Marital status.* Longitudinal data from the USA showed that women who got married were more likely to gain weight subsequently, even after adjustment for their educational level and family income. Generally speaking, however, those who divorced lost some weight (24). Similarly, data from a 5-year study in Finland showed that men and women who got married during that period were at twice the risk of gaining 5 kg or more compared with men and women who were already married and stayed married during the period of study (17). These findings suggest that major changes in lifestyle connected with marriage may promote weight gain in affluent societies.

In some traditional societies, there are pressures on women both to gain weight and to remain overweight during reproductive life. An example of this is the custom of "fattening huts" for elite pubescent girls in certain communities in West Africa (25). Such practices reflect cultural perceptions and values related to overweight.

Behavioural determinants

- *Smoking habits.* Reports that the use of tobacco lowers body weight began to appear more than 100 years ago, but detailed studies have been reported only during the past 10 years or so (26). In most populations, smokers weigh somewhat less than ex-smokers;

individuals who have never smoked fall somewhere between the two. The physiological mechanisms involved include alterations in energy intake and expenditure, induced by changes in insulin homeostasis, lipoprotein lipase activity, the activity of the sympathetic nervous system, physical activity, and preferences in food consumption (26). The most important effects of smoking, however, seem to be those on basal metabolic rate and the thermic effect of food (27). In Finland, the inverse relation between smoking and body weight became considerably weaker among women and disappeared among men over the period 1982–1987 (28). A cluster of habits unfavourable to health, such as high intake of alcohol and saturated fat, was apparent among young Finnish smokers. Heavy smoking was also associated with increased BMI among young men in the Netherlands (29), and similar associations have been observed in the USA (30). These observations may suggest that, in populations in which there is growing health awareness and an increasing proportion of people who stop smoking, the remaining smokers are those whose lifestyles carry significant health risks.

Cessation of smoking is associated with weight gain. It has been reported that, after adjustment for age, average weight gain in men who stop smoking is about 3 kg and in women 4 kg (31). The same study reported risk of substantial weight gain (i.e. 10 kg or more) as much higher in people who stop smoking than in non-smokers.

Many recent studies have shown that smoking is also associated with an increased abdominal fatness at each BMI level (32). This relationship may be mediated by changes in the levels of sex hormones and glucocorticosteroids as a result of smoking; it may also be partly explained by a clustering of physical inactivity, smoking, and alcohol consumption.

- *Physical activity.* Individuals who are relatively inactive are more likely to gain weight than those who frequently engage in physical activity. The relative risk of gaining 5 kg or more during a 5-year follow-up study among inactive Finns was 1.6 in women and 1.9 in men (20). A prospective study of adults in the USA showed that remaining physically active is associated with the prevention of age-related weight gain (33). Moreover, there is now substantial evidence linking increased physical activity to a more favourable fat distribution (a lower proportion of visceral fat at a given BMI) (32).

- *Alcohol consumption.* A recent review of 31 studies (16 in the USA) concluded that the relationship between alcohol consumption and adiposity was generally positive for men and negative for women (34). Only three of these studies were prospective, but the two that examined changes in alcohol intake found that, as intake increased over a period of either 4 or 18 years, weight increased significantly.

This finding contrasts with the results of cross-sectional studies, which generally showed a negative association between overweight and alcohol intake, especially for women. The results were inconsistent both within and between the sexes, and the criteria usually employed to establish causality were not met. The data were not consistent across diverse populations in direction, strength, or gradation of association, which suggests diverse patterns of intake. On the one hand, some experimental studies suggested that metabolism of alcohol may not lead to formation of ATP (and therefore may have zero caloric value in the body); on the other hand it was shown that alcohol may reduce fat oxidation and thus contribute to excess fat storage in the body (*35*). It has also been suggested that there is a relationship between alcohol intake and abdominal fatness, although the evidence is inconclusive (*32*).

Biological and social consequences of overweight

Overweight and mortality. It has been widely concluded that the relationship between BMI and mortality is U-shaped or J-shaped. Some studies, however, usually small and of short duration, report no association between BMI and mortality (*36*). The minimum follow-up period necessary seems to be about 5 years and the sample size at least 7000 individuals for there to be sufficient power to detect the positive association between BMI and mortality (*36*). The causes of death at different ends of the U- or J-shaped curve are strikingly different: the high mortality at low BMI is dominated by digestive and pulmonary disease, but at high BMI it is related predominantly to cardiovascular disease, diabetes mellitus, and gallbladder disease. It is sometimes argued that the high mortality at low BMI is due to the confounding presence of smoking and disease and that the relationship between BMI and mortality may in fact be linear. A study of 8828 Seventh-Day Adventist men, among whom such confounding effects are minimal, demonstrated such a linear association, with the lowest mortality among the leanest men (BMI < 20) (*37*).

It has been pointed out (*9*) that most studies published up to 1987 suffered from methodological drawbacks. These drawbacks include:

- Failure to control for cigarette smoking. Since smoking is a strong risk factor for mortality and is also more common among those with a low BMI, failure to control for smoking will lead to an overestimation of the importance of thinness to mortality. Stratification is recommended in analyses for smoking behaviour.
- Failure to eliminate early mortality from the analysis of prospective data may confound the weight/mortality association. Clinical or subclinical illness present before inclusion of an individual in a study could be the reason for, rather than a consequence of, reduced body weight. Failure to adjust for early mortality will thus result in underestimation of overweight-related mortality.

- Inappropriate adjustment for intermediate risk factors such as hypertension, hyperlipidaemia, and diabetes. Control for these intermediate risk factors is likely to lead to an underestimation of the risks associated with overweight.
- Most studies were carried out in predominantly white populations in Europe and the USA.

Troiano and colleagues (*38*) performed a meta-analysis on the relationship between BMI and mortality in adult Caucasian men and women (with elderly cohorts excluded). The Caucasian male sample was based on 17 studies with 37 sub-studies (17 of which were from the USA) representing more than 350 000 men and over 38 000 deaths. The female sample was based on six studies with 12 sub-studies representing about 250 000 women and 13 700 deaths. The authors concluded that the relationship between BMI and mortality is U-shaped and that mortality was increased at a high BMI (>29-30). Minimum mortality for white men who were 50 years of age at entry and were followed for 30 years was at BMI between 24 and 25 (Fig. 53). Although the meta-analysis did not stratify according to age, it can be assumed that the curvature may be even more pronounced at lower ages and minimum mortality shifted somewhat to the left in the acceptable BMI range of 18.5-25. The curves that included smokers and did not exclude individuals on the grounds of disease showed higher levels of mortality but no distinct minimum. The curvature was also much less pronounced for analyses with shorter follow-up (10 years).

For women, no studies have been reported that have both included long follow-ups and separated the effects of smoking. For combined smoking and non-smoking women other than in the USA, with 10 years of follow-up, the curvature was less pronounced and minimum mortality was at a

Figure 53

Predicted relationship between BMI and all-cause mortality for white men 50 years old at entry, with 30-year follow-up[a]

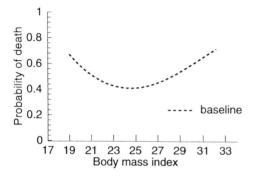

[a] Source: reference *38*.
Baseline = non-smoking US cohorts with exclusions for disease at entry.

BMI of approximately 25. Adjusting for the effect of smoking increased the nadir, which suggests that minimum mortality among non-smoking women would be at BMI less than 25.

A recent Japanese study showed a J-shaped relationship between BMI and mortality, remarkably similar to those in Europe and the USA, with minimum mortality at a BMI of around 22 (*39*).

Overweight and morbidity

- *Overweight and coronary heart disease.* Overweight is associated with an increased prevalence of cardiovascular risk factors such as hypertension, unfavourable blood lipid concentrations, and diabetes mellitus. Although there is a lack of controlled data on decreasing mortality after weight reduction, it is well known that overweight-related risk factors are improved by weight reduction. On the basis of changes in risk factors induced by spontaneous weight reductions in the Framingham study (*40*), it was estimated that a 10% reduction in body weight would correspond to a 20% reduction in the risk of developing coronary heart disease (CHD). Observational studies of weight loss and subsequent mortality, however, have been unable to confirm a reduction in the risk of CHD following weight loss (*41*). Weight cycling has been found to be associated with increased risk of CHD, and this may be particularly harmful in non-obese individuals (*42*).

  The relationship between BMI and CHD has usually been found to be linear, but the level of risk is modified by ethnicity, age, sex, and smoking habits. Elsewhere, it has been calculated that about 40% of the incidence of CHD was attributable to a BMI above 21 and was therefore potentially preventable (*43*).

  In prospective studies in which fat distribution was assessed by skinfolds or circumferences, abdominal fatness was a significant risk factor for CHD independently of BMI (*44*). Abdominal fatness is associated with increased levels of insulin and triglycerides and decreased levels of HDL-cholesterol (*45*). In addition, abdominal fatness may be associated with haemostatic and fibrinolytic factors, which also contribute to an increased risk of myocardial infarction.

- *Overweight and stroke.* Despite the clear relationship between overweight and hypertension (see below), it has been concluded that overweight is not among the major risk factors for stroke (*46*), although three prospective studies (two in women, one in men) have shown that abdominal fatness may be associated with increased risks for stroke independently of BMI. Barrett-Connor suggested that smoking habits and alcohol intake may be among the variables that partly explain the association between fat distribution and stroke (*47*).

- *Overweight and hypertension.* Increased body weight is associated with elevated blood pressure, and weight loss in hypertensive individuals is generally accompanied by a reduction in blood pressure. According to the results of a meta-analysis, a weight loss of 1 kg is associated with a decrease of 1.2–1.6 mmHg in systolic and 1.0–1.3 mmHg in diastolic blood pressure (*48*).[1] In individuals who regain weight after weight loss, it has been observed that blood pressures remain below baseline levels (*49*). The relationships between overweight and hypertension may sometimes be biased by artificially high readings of blood pressure resulting from increased arm circumference in overweight (*50*).

  A number of studies have suggested that lean hypertensive individuals may be at greater risk of CHD than obese hypertensives (*51*), which may partly reflect the different etiologies of hypertension in lean and obese people. Hazardous lifestyles, particularly involving smoking and high alcohol intake, which contribute to both leanness and risk of death, cannot be ruled out as causative factors in the excessive mortality among lean hypertensives.

  Weight loss is recommended for all obese hypertensive individuals. The beneficial effects of weight loss on both blood pressure and the need for antihypertensive medication are mediated through related changes such as reduced cardiac output and blood volume (*51*). Body fat distribution seems to predict hypertension independently of BMI. Increased insulin concentrations have been suggested as playing a role in both the association between BMI and abdomen:hip circumference ratio and blood pressure (*52*).

- *Overweight and non-insulin-dependent diabetes mellitus.* Overweight is a well-established risk factor for non-insulin-dependent diabetes mellitus (NIDDM). The duration of overweight seems to be important, and involuntary weight loss often precedes diagnosis of the condition. Although overweight is associated with poor glucose tolerance and hyperinsulinaemia (insulin resistance), which can be reversed in the short term with weight loss, the long-term benefits of weight loss for the risk of both NIDDM and complications have not been properly studied. During an 8-year follow-up of 113 861 women in the USA, aged 30–55 years, the risk of developing NIDDM increased with increasing BMI (*53*). Compared with women with a BMI below 22, risk was increased 20-fold for women with a BMI between 29 and 31, and more than 60-fold for those with a BMI above 35. Within the total cohort, 90% of diagnoses of NIDDM were attributable to a BMI greater than 22. Adult weight gain of more than 5 kg in 8 years was associated with a significantly increased risk of

---

[1] 1 mmHg = 0.133 kPa.

NIDDM, and weight gain after the age of 18 was also associated with an increased risk. However, risks were no different in women with and without a family history of diabetes mellitus.

The causal role of overweight in the development of NIDDM is supported by evidence that weight loss in NIDDM improves glucose tolerance and reduces the need for hypoglycaemic drugs. Moreover, experimental overweight in normal young men reduces insulin sensitivity, and the effect is reversible with weight loss (54).

In addition to many cross-sectional studies, an increasing number of prospective studies show that abdominal fatness is associated with an increased incidence of NIDDM (52). The most up-to-date hypothesis for a mechanism is increased accumulation of visceral fat leading to increased levels of free fatty acid in the portal vein which, in turn, diminish hepatic insulin clearance. Altered muscle morphology in abdominal fatness and relatively high concentrations of androgens in women with high abdomen:hip circumference ratios may also be involved, but the causal role of these factors remains unclear (52).

- *Overweight and gallbladder disease.* The risk of gallbladder disease is more pronounced in women than men. Overweight is a major risk factor for the development of gallstones, particularly those made of cholesterol rather than the pigmented stones containing bilirubin. The relationship between BMI and the risk of gallstones appears to be approximately linear. Supersaturation of the bile with cholesterol, which results from the relative hypersecretion of biliary cholesterol, is a necessary condition for the formation of gallstones, and this is more frequent in obese patients; it may also result as a short-term response to dieting (55). In the Nurses' Health Study (56), the relative risk of gallstone formation in women with a BMI above 32, compared with those with a BMI below 20, was 6. Independently of the degree of overweight, weight gain was associated with an increased risk. Long-term weight loss did not protect against the incidence of gallstones.

A high abdomen:hip circumference ratio has been found to be related to cholecystectomy independently of BMI in American and Dutch women (57, 58). The relationship between abdominal fatness and gallbladder disease may be a result of the increase in the hypersecretion of biliary cholesterol that is associated with increased serum lipid levels, or an effect of hyperinsulinaemia associated with abdominal overweight, which stimulates hepatic cholesterol synthesis.

- *Overweight and osteoarthritis.* The pathogenesis of osteoarthritis and the risk factors for the condition are not well understood, but there is increasing evidence that overweight is associated with osteoarthritis in several joints (59). Specifically, an association has been found between overweight and osteoarthritis of the knee but not of the hips; the evidence is inconsistent for osteoarthritis of the feet. Overweight has also been shown to be associated with osteoarthritis of the non-weight-bearing joints, such as those in the hands, which may be a reflection of the metabolic consequences of overweight. Overweight-related conditions such as diabetes mellitus, hyperuricaemia, or hypercholesterolaemia, which may influence cartilage degradation, may act together with excessive mechanical stress on the joints in producing osteoarthritis (59). The results of cross-sectional studies should be interpreted with caution, because the limitations imposed by osteoarthritis on physical activity may, in turn, contribute to the development of overweight. Prospective studies have not substantiated this concern, however. The important health implications of the association between overweight and osteoarthritis were illustrated by the finding of a significantly increased risk of disability among obese Finnish men and women because of arthroses of the knee and hip (60).

- *Overweight and cancer.* A review of prospective and retrospective studies of the association between overweight and cancer of the colon, rectum, prostate, breast, ovaries, and endometrium (61) reached the following conclusions:

  - Overweight and the risk of endometrial cancer increase in direct proportion.
  - Overweight probably increases the risk of postmenopausal breast cancer; the case-control studies have yielded more consistent results than prospective studies. Weight gain after menopause may be a risk factor independent of the degree of overweight and further aggravate the problem.
  - The relationships between overweight and cancer of the colon, rectum, ovaries, and prostate are uncertain; reported associations are inconsistent between and within sexes and across populations.

  Fat distribution may be related to some types of cancer independently of overweight (62). Links between abdominal fatness and endometrial and breast cancer reported by some investigators have not been confirmed by others.

- *Overweight and other disorders.* Overweight is positively, and abdominal fatness negatively, associated with the presence of varicose veins (58). Abdominal fatness and overweight have been associated with some endocrine disorders and infertility (63). Overweight may also lead to important social and economic disadvantages (64) as well as psychosocial problems; however, the existence of a causal association and the direction of causality (i.e. the particular role played in the association by stigmatization of overweight and dieting) remain unclear, especially as regards the relationship between overweight and psychosocial problems. At least one epidemiological study suggested that overweight, particularly abdominal fatness in women, is associated with accident proneness and use of drugs for psychological problems (65).

Overweight has been found to increase the risk of reflux oesophagitis and hiatus hernia (66), although severe oesophagitis causes dysphagia and leads to weight loss. Sleep apnoea is common in overweight people and has been found to be an independent risk factor for CVD; it also causes daytime sleepiness, which increases the risk of traffic accidents (67).

7.1.3 *Anthropometry as an indicator of nutritional and health status*

Body mass index as a measure of body fatness
Body mass index appears to be a good indicator of the deposition of excess energy as fat in adult white men and women living in Europe and North America. It is probably less appropriate in other populations who differ in body build and body proportions. Using BMI to classify individuals according to fatness may result in misclassification because of the varying contributions of bone mass, muscle mass, and fluid to body weight. The percentage of body fat increases with aging and is higher in women than in men, but these differences may not be revealed by BMI. For instance, a BMI of 30 in Dutch men implies a body fat content of about 30% at age 20 years and about 40% at age 60; in women aged 20 and 60, these figures are 40% and 50%, respectively (68). Equations that included BMI, sex, and age for these same adults were shown to predict body fat percentage relatively accurately (r^2 about 0.8, SEE about 4%) (68); this prediction error is similar to values obtained with other more elaborate methods such as measurement of skinfold thickness or bioelectrical impedance.

Similar problems may occur in the classification of body fat distribution by abdomen:hip circumference ratio. Different contributions of muscle mass and bone structure as well as stature and abdominal muscle tone may lead to different associations between abdomen:hip ratio and visceral fat accumulation. Abdominal fatness may imply different health risks for different racial groups (69) and at different ages (70). These issues complicate the future development of universal cut-off points for abdomen:hip circumference ratio.

Modifiers of the relationship between overweight and health risks
Within populations, a BMI in excess of 30 is associated with elevated blood pressure and increased risk of coronary heart disease and non-insulin-dependent diabetes mellitus, as previously discussed. It seems, however, that some populations are more vulnerable to the effects of high BMI than others. This may be partly explained by differences in body composition, body build, and fat distribution, but also by the underlying cause of overweight and the genetic predisposition to the development of certain diseases associated with overweight. For instance, overweight resulting from the combination of inactivity with a diet high in saturated fat and low in antioxidants may have different consequences with respect to development of hyperlipidaemia and coronary heart disease from

overweight that results from excess weight gain by individuals with relatively low metabolic rates but adequate physical activity and dietary habits. In addition, the combination of high BMI with one or more different risk factors (e.g. smoking, hypertension, hyperlipidaemia, diabetes mellitus) may lead to different risks of developing disease.

History of overweight may contribute to variations in health risks associated with overweight. Three issues should be considered: age of onset, duration, and weight fluctuation patterns. Overweight *per se* has no immediate effect on the occurrence of chronic disease despite short-term changes in metabolic profiles and mechanical consequences; with increasing duration of overweight, however, the impacts become greater. Early onset usually implies long duration of overweight: weight gain leading to overweight in adult life has been shown to be associated with increased risk of several chronic diseases. There are, however, a number of unresolved issues in this regard, particularly the modifying effects of abdominal fatness and of smoking cessation.

As mentioned earlier, data on the health effects of weight cycling are inconclusive but it may be that its adverse effects are more pronounced in people who are not overweight (*42*).

It has also been suggested that overweight may be less hazardous to health in certain populations, for instance black women (*3*). This is in accordance with the findings that abdominal fatness may be less strongly associated with risk factors for cardiovascular disease and diabetes in black women than in white (*69*). In other comparisons, for instance, between southern Asians and whites living in London and between Mexican-Americans and Anglo-Americans living in Texas, it was concluded that Asians and Mexican-Americans have higher risks of developing non-insulin-dependent diabetes mellitus than Caucasians of similar BMI (*71, 72*). This could be largely explained by differences in fat distribution (abdomen:hip circumference ratios are relatively high in Asians and Mexican-Americans). It has been further speculated that previous long-term malnutrition predisposes to increased abdominal fatness.

7.2 Using anthropometry in individuals

Body mass index and abdomen:hip circumference ratio are used to classify individuals in terms of overweight and abdominal fatness, respectively. Misclassification may occur but should be limited since anthropometric variables have to be interpreted in combination with other risk factors. For longitudinal assessment, variation in body weight or single (abdomen or hip) circumferences will be sufficient because – in contrast to children, adolescents, and the elderly – long-term weight change in adults will predominantly reflect change in fat mass. Furthermore, simple measurements may be the most informative for assessing the outcome of interventions in individuals.

7.2.1 *Screening for interventions*

When individuals have been classified according to BMI, their risk profile should be ascertained in terms of risk factors (abdomen:hip circumference ratio, smoking and dietary habits, physical activity, blood pressure, serum lipids, glucose) as well as of family history of certain disorders (premature coronary heart disease, non-insulin-dependent diabetes, hypertension). Because a large proportion of the adult population in industrialized societies will be overweight or obese, and because weight-loss therapy is ineffective unless closely supervised and followed up, not all overweight or obese individuals will qualify for intervention. Priorities should be given to those at highest risk, with the primary focus on reducing the risk profile rather than on weight loss *per se*. The following scheme may be adopted:

1. Measure height and weight and calculate body mass index.

2. Classify according to BMI:

   normal range: BMI 18.50–24.99

   grade 1 overweight: BMI 25.00–29.99

   grade 2 overweight: BMI 30.00–39.99

   grade 3 overweight: BMI $\geq$ 40.00

Annexes 2 and 3 of this report provide complete and more simplified versions, respectively, of BMI tables that will facilitate the use of BMI in the field; a nomogram is also provided in Fig. A2.1 (Annex 2).

3. For individuals with BMI 18.50–24.99: avoid becoming overweight. There are no recommendations for weight loss.

   For individuals with BMI 25.00–29.99: avoid weight gain. Before recommending any type of intervention, assess other risk factors. If there are additional risk factors (high abdomen:hip ratio, hypertension, hyperlipidaemia, glucose intolerance or NIDDM, strong family history of diabetes mellitus or premature coronary heart disease), recommend a healthy lifestyle that will contribute to improvement of the risk profile: cessation of smoking, increased physical activity, reduced intake of (saturated) fat. Moderate weight loss is recommended but weight loss *per se* should not be the primary target of intervention. A large proportion of the adult population will usually fall into this category, and most will receive advice on healthy nutrition and physical activity appropriate for the general population. Regular (yearly) weight measurement will be helpful in monitoring weight development, and weight histories should be noted. Individuals who have continued to gain weight (e.g. > 5 kg during the previous 2 years) should be identified for weight maintenance programmes designed to halt the weight gain.

For individuals with BMI 30.00–39.99: the same recommendations as for grade 1 overweight, although the prevalence of risk factors and of overweight-associated disorders that require medical attention is usually markedly higher and moderate weight loss is therefore more urgently recommended. In many populations, the proportion of adults falling into this category is still considerable, and treatment priorities will have to be set on the basis of, among other things, the prevalence of health problems in the community concerned. The higher the prevalence of chronic diseases such as diabetes and CVD, the greater is the need for individuals with BMI 30.00–39.99 to lose weight. In other words, the potential impact of weight modification in preventing these problems is likely to be influenced by the disease rates in the population. The risks related to grade 2 overweight in adults depend on other, coexisting, risk factors for chronic noncommunicable diseases. Obese individuals with no additional risk factors or conditions that require medical supervision may be referred to self-help organizations. Such organizations are effective if their leaders have sufficient training in the principles of healthy weight loss (a maximum of about 0.5 kg/week) and of balanced nutrition. For individuals with conditions that do require medical supervision, the focus should be on normalizing the risk factors or alleviating health problems (e.g. improving respiratory function or arthritis in weight-bearing joints) rather than on achieving weight loss *per se*.

For individuals with BMI ≥ 40: intensive action to reduce weight. The proportion of adults with grade 3 overweight is small; for these individuals, weight loss *per se* may be the primary target and options such as surgical treatment for obesity should be considered (*73*).

7.2.2 *Assessing response to an intervention*

Until recently, the response to intervention was usually assessed in terms of attaining "ideal body weight" or reducing weight to below a certain BMI cut-off or "percentage over ideal body weight". It is no longer clear that such goals are optimal. For some people they are unrealistic: in most obese individuals they imply large sustained weight losses, which few are able to achieve unless they are enrolled in long-term pro-grammes with extensive follow-up (e.g. >5 years). Moreover, substantial improvements in risk-factor profiles have been documented in obese individuals who lost only moderate amounts of weight and would still be classified as overweight or obese (*74*). Finally, there is no evidence that large weight losses either have beneficial effects or reduce mortality, and the more extreme diets needed to produce large weight losses may increase the likelihood of relapse (*75*). More realistic responses would therefore be:

- The normalization of risk factors or health conditions that is associated with any amount of weight loss in overweight individuals.

- Prevention of (further) weight gain in obese and non-obese subjects. Weight should be assessed at regular intervals (e.g. once a year), perhaps at routine check-ups.

7.3 Using anthropometry in populations

Overweight is an excellent indicator of energy imbalance caused by a combination of excessive energy intake and insufficient energy expenditure. Even small daily deviations from ideal energy balance can lead to substantial increases in body weight over time; for example, a consistent average daily excess energy intake of 168 kJ (39 kcal$_{th}$) (equivalent to 1 dl of carbonated soft drink) will theoretically lead to a weight gain of 15.6 kg over 10 years. Overweight is thus a sensitive indicator of a chronic energy imbalance that would probably not be detected by cross-sectional surveys of energy intake and energy expenditure in individuals. Moreover, it is a widespread condition in many industrialized societies and notoriously difficult to treat; interventions should therefore aim largely towards its prevention. In the community setting, treatment of all obese adults by physicians is neither rational nor feasible. To establish the need for, and priorities of, preventive interventions, the magnitude of the problem in a particular population must be defined with data derived from representative population surveys; the prevalence of BMI $\geq$ 30 can be used as the principal indicator.

7.3.1 *Targeting interventions*

Anthropometric data can be used to estimate the population-specific risks for various noncommunicable diseases. However, the genetic differences between different populations give rise to two major concerns in the use of anthropometric variables. First, they influence the degree of risk associated with excess body weight, and second, they are also important in determining the kinds of disease that may occur as a result of overweight. For instance, hypertension and hyperlipidaemia are common in obese Caucasian populations, but less common in American Indians and peoples of the Pacific islands, among whom diabetes is more frequent.

7.3.2 *Assessing response to an intervention*

Anthropometry is also used in populations to evaluate programmes of health promotion and disease prevention, in which the prevention and control of overweight may play an important role. While simple indicators may be useful for targeting communities, more detailed information is usually desirable for evaluation of prevention programmes. Since overweight in adult populations is a result of dietary habits and other aspects of lifestyle, and is associated with other metabolic abnormalities, it is important that due attention is given to these associated factors in the evaluation of prevention programmes. Age-specific and age-standardized proportions of the population above a certain BMI cut-off can be used for evaluation, as can trends in the median or other percentiles of BMI. (BMI is usually not normally distributed; distribution is skewed to the right, so means may not be useful for evaluation without logarithmic transformation.)

To evaluate interventions designed to prevent the development of overweight in populations who are not yet obese, it is essential to assess longitudinal weight development. The efficacy of a specific prevention programme can be judged by comparison of populations who have received the intervention with similar populations who have not. Evaluation of treatment interventions (designed to treat obesity or overweight associated with risk factors or medical conditions that improve with weight loss), weight development of treated and untreated individuals should be followed on a population basis. For both types of intervention, the follow-up period should be at least 5 years.

7.3.3 *Ascertaining determinants of overweight*

If secular trends in overweight are to be understood, information about possible determinants is desirable. The prevalence of overweight is affected by the overall stage of socioeconomic development of a given population. There is a link between low socioeconomic status and overweight in societies that have an abundance of food and in which other basic needs are fulfilled, and between high socioeconomic status and overweight in societies in which food is scarce (see Fig. 51).

The most obvious determinants of overweight are physical inactivity and high energy intake (generally in high-fat diets). Other factors known to be associated with, or to modify the effect of, significant weight gain are ethnicity/race, family history of overweight and its consequences, socioeconomic factors such as educational level (a low level is associated with higher risk for weight gain with aging), smoking (cessation may be associated with major weight gain), and parity (high parity may be associated with major weight gain).

7.3.4 *Ascertaining consequences of overweight*

The consequences of overweight are partly determined by the patterns of disease in the population. Among populations in which overweight is associated with relative affluence, mortality is dominated by infectious disease, and life-expectancy is low (as in most societies in Europe at the turn of the 19th century and in many developing countries at present), overweight may be relatively advantageous and associated with comparatively low mortality. Conversely, in societies in which affluence predisposes to high rates of diabetes mellitus and coronary heart disease, overweight will be associated with increased mortality risks.

Overweight is also associated with an increased incidence of coronary heart disease, diabetes mellitus, gallbladder disease, and musculoskeletal disorders. More immediate consequences are the increased levels of risk factors for these noncommunicable diseases, for instance dyslipidaemia, glucose intolerance, hypertension, and hyperuricaemia.

Sample size and follow-up time should be adequate for the purposes of the study. Study of the relationship between BMI and mortality, for example, may require a sample of at least 7000 individuals followed for at least 5 years.

7.3.5 *Nutritional surveillance*

Problem identification

The magnitude of the problem of overweight in populations and its geographical, sex, racial, ethnic, and socioeconomic distribution can be identified by the stratification of sufficiently large random population samples according to sex, age, and race. Details of urbanization, ethnicity, and socioeconomic status should also be recorded, and it is important to document other risk factors such as hypercholesterolaemia, hypertension, and smoking habits in the sample population. In women, menopause influences weight and the pattern of fat distribution as well as their health consequences, and this too should be documented.

Anthropometry can be used for surveillance of risk factors for chronic diseases in populations. This requires repeated measurements in random population samples at regular intervals. Besides height and body weight, abdominal and hip circumferences should also be measured. In many populations, lifestyle and nutrition have undergone radical changes over a relatively short period of time; different birth cohorts may therefore have developed differently in terms of anthropometric indicators, which may complicate interpretation. Increases in abdominal fatness in populations undergoing such changes may provide sensitive indication of an emerging public health problem of overweight and its consequences. Cross-sectional data on height and body weight are available for most adult populations, but data for other indicators are limited.

Monitoring of overweight on a population basis should be performed using independent cross-sectional surveys, either continuously or at regular intervals. Detecting a reliable trend in risk factors requires analysis at many points in time. Five-yearly surveys may be used to detect a trend; continuous monitoring can be even more sensitive in revealing responses to interventions.

Long-term planning

The prevention and treatment of overweight calls for long-term follow-up of weight maintenance. Long-term planning should involve preventive strategies that focus on educating people in the principles of adequate nutrition and physical activity and their role in weight control, and about socioeconomic aspects of overweight and weight gain.

National policies for the treatment and prevention of overweight should be developed and complemented by plans for implementing weight control as an integral activity in the control of hypertension, dyslipidaemia, and diabetes. To be effective, prevention of overweight in the community requires a multisectoral approach rather than purely medically oriented programmes. This may include, for example, the development of economic incentives or disincentives for the purchase of certain foods, determining the availability of particular foods, controlling the layout of supermarkets and the content of advertising in the media, and ensuring that town planners make provision for facilities for safe and regular physical activity.

Timely warning

Surveillance of body weight and BMI in the population is essential to provide information that can be used for timely warning. "Timely" in this context is a long-term concept and not concerned with acute problems. The interpretation of the rate and magnitude of change in anthropometric indices of overweight depends on the prevalence of overweight and its consequences in the population in question. A steep increase in the prevalence of overweight and a steep slope of weight gain by age or time in the population as a whole is a general warning that overweight is becoming a public health problem. An increase in abdominal fatness can provide further evidence of unfavourable developments in the population that would justify an intensification of preventive measures.

For programme management

Effective programme management calls for population-specific data on the prevalence of overweight, the relationship between age and BMI, trends in mean BMI and the prevalence of overweight, and the association of overweight with other risk factors among programme participants. These data should be complemented with risk estimates for major diseases associated with overweight in the target population.

7.4 Population data management and analysis

Participation rates in population surveys vary markedly; usually they are about 90% at best and may often be as low as 50–60%. There is recognized bias resulting from lesser participation among lower socioeconomic groups, smokers, and heavy alcohol drinkers; in addition, people with chronic diseases are often less interested in taking part in population risk factor surveys. This will have an effect on the distribution of anthropometric parameters and on prevalence estimates of overweight, because these parameters correlate with the factors that govern participation. Survey participation bias must therefore be estimated as accurately as possible.

Variability between and within observers should be assessed by the repetition of measurements on the same subjects by the same and different observers under standardized conditions and at short time intervals. Outliers at the lower and upper ends of the distribution of the measured parameters must be confirmed; the criteria should be defined in advance and the validity of unusual values should be confirmed at the survey site. Last digit preference and preference/avoidance of certain values should be analysed for the whole sample and for each observer. Time trends in overall and observer-specific values should be documented, particularly if the survey period is long. Original raw data should remain available for analysis.

Mean values of anthropometric parameters, plus 95% confidence intervals and standard deviations, medians, percentiles, and proportion of subjects with BMI in the ranges 25.00–29.99, 30.00–39.99, and ≥ 40.00 should be reported by sex, age, and race. Age grouping will depend on the sampling frame and sample selection: for instance, if the sample is stratified by age at 5- or 10-year age intervals, data should be documented using the same age intervals.

Ideally, population data on anthropometric parameters in adults should be presented by sex and 5-year age groups (assuming that the sample selection allows for such grouping). Any other stratification used in the sample selection (geographical, ethnic, socioeconomic, etc.) should also be taken into account in the presentation of data. Summary statistics will require proper adjustment for age and other variables used in sample selection (effect modifiers and confounding factors).

The use of indices (BMI and abdomen:hip circumference ratio) may not be entirely appropriate for assessing the functional outcomes of overweight unless an analysis of primary data (weight, height, circumferences) is also provided.

It is important to analyse the association of anthropometric parameters and/or indicators of overweight with various outcome parameters such as morbidity variables (prevalence of diabetes, hypertension, coronary heart disease, etc.), disability (osteoarthritis, activities of daily living, occupational limitations), and levels of physiological risk factors (blood pressure, blood levels of glucose, insulin, lipids). It should be kept in mind, however, that selective mortality associated with either overweight or underweight can influence these relationships, particularly the age-relation of anthropometric parameters and outcome measures in cross-sectional assessments. It is therefore important to supplement cross-sectional data with longitudinal data on the health effects of overweight in different populations.

In analysing data, it is also important to pay attention to such major determinants of body weight as diet, physical activity, smoking, and alcohol consumption.

Secular changes in overweight are of interest for:

- anticipating and preventing increases in the level of overweight in a population;
- revealing a decline in the level of overweight in a population;
- evaluating the contribution of community-based educational or intervention programmes to any decline in overweight;
- assessing the extent to which trends in determinants of overweight are affecting average body mass index or the prevalence of overweight in the population;
- predicting trends in overweight-related morbidity and mortality (e.g. in conjunction with trends in other risk factors for cardiovascular disease);
- linking levels of overweight with changes in population composition (e.g. because of migration).

7.5 Potential development of reference data

Because the prevalence of overweight varies widely from country to country, and because there are no indications that different populations with the same distributions of BMI have similar relative and attributable risks of morbidity and mortality associated with different degrees of overweight, there is currently no obvious need for reference data for BMI in adults. If sufficient data are collected in the future, however, reference data or even standards could be developed.

In order to understand the distribution of BMI values in a healthy population, it is important that data are derived from populations with no problems of nutrition (underfeeding and overfeeding), and that individuals in the population do not smoke and do not suffer from any chronic or acute disease.

Figures 54–57 give examples of the presentation of such data derived from the WHO MONICA Project (76). The frequency and cumulative distribution of BMI values for non-smoking subjects aged 25–34 years in the eight populations with the lowest coronary heart disease mortality were plotted. The curves produced can be regarded as typical for a healthy, non-smoking young adult population with relatively long life-expectancy.

The recommended cut-off points of BMI refer to cross-sectional data only. It has been proposed in this section that weight fluctuations, weight gain, and weight loss are in themselves indicators of risk; it is not currently possible to recommend uniform cut-offs for such weight changes which would allow the identification of high-risk groups. Further research is needed in this area.

Anthropometric data for the potential development of reference data or standards should cover at least weight and height, plus age, sex, race, socioeconomic status, presence of disease, and smoking habits. If

Figure 54
Proportional frequency of body mass index values in eight MONICA populations: men aged 25–34 years[a]

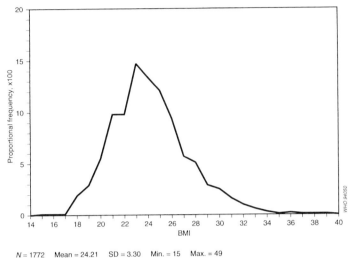

N = 1772   Mean = 24.21   SD = 3.30   Min. = 15   Max. = 49

[a] The WHO MONICA Project has provided these unpublished data from the database described in reference *76*. BMI data for the eight Caucasian populations with the lowest mortality from coronary heart disease were pooled.

Figure 55
Proportional frequency of body mass index values in eight MONICA populations: women aged 25–34 years[a]

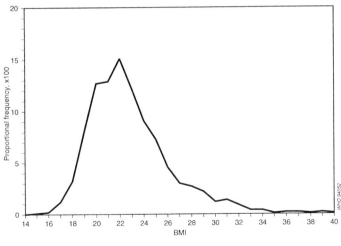

N = 1847   Mean = 22.90   SD = 3.57   Min. = 14   Max. = 44

[a] The WHO MONICA Project has provided these unpublished data from the database described in reference *76*. BMI data for the eight Caucasian populations with the lowest mortality from coronary heart disease were pooled.

Figure 56

Inverse cumulative distribution of body mass index values in eight MONICA populations: men aged 25–34 years[a]

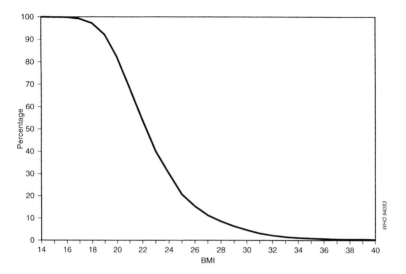

[a] The WHO MONICA Project has provided these unpublished data from the database described in reference 76. BMI data for the eight Caucasian populations with the lowest mortality from coronary heart disease were pooled.

Figure 57

Inverse cumulative distribution of body mass index values in eight MONICA populations: women aged 25–34 years[a]

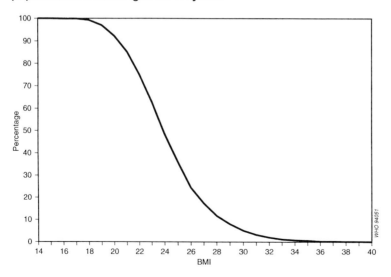

[a] The WHO MONICA Project has provided these unpublished data from the database described in reference 76. BMI data for the eight Caucasian populations with the lowest mortality from coronary heart disease were pooled.

subjects measured are pregnant or receiving any kind of treatment that might influence weight (including dieting on their own initiative), this should be noted. Information on other (cardiovascular) risk factors should also be documented, as should weight history.

In the future, it may be possible to develop better anthropometric indicators of fatness and distribution in adults; indicators that would monitor change in visceral fat distribution would be particularly important.

7.6 Recommendations

7.6.1 *For practical implementation*

Recommendations to Member States
It is recommended that Member States employ anthropometric techniques to:

1. Assess and monitor levels and trends of adult overweight, BMI, and abdominal fatness and their association with health outcomes.

2. Establish national policies and guidelines for the prevention and control of overweight in adults and evaluate their implementation and outcome.

3. Develop and evaluate programmes for the primary prevention of overweight and abdominal fatness in adults, particularly as part of measures for the prevention of noncommunicable diseases.

4. Facilitate the research necessary to implement clinical and public health action; this should include comparative studies of health consequences of overweight in adults.

Recommendations to WHO
WHO should foster the collection and analysis of existing data (and, where necessary, of new data) on height, weight, and abdomen and hip circumferences to establish the prevalence and trends in overweight and abdominal fatness and their associations with health outcomes.

7.6.2 *For future research*

The following areas were considered to be of particular importance for future research.

1. Development of anthropometric indicators and cut-off points for total body fatness and visceral fat in relation to health outcomes, appropriate for certain subgroups of age, sex, and race.

2. Comparison and surveillance (monitoring) of standardized anthropometric parameters and their distribution among different populations.

3. Identification of the genetic and environmental determinants, and their interactions, of overweight and fat distribution in different populations.

4. Validation of new and existing techniques recommended for use in researching overweight, fatness, and abdominal fatness.

5. Cohort studies of anthropometric indicators and their subsequent risk for noncommunicable diseases and premature mortality, to be carried out in representative samples of populations in different ethnic groups.

6. Development of methods for the assessment of the health implications of various indicators of overweight, fatness, and abdominal fatness.

7. Research on the health effects of voluntary and involuntary weight changes and weight fluctuation.

8. Intervention studies to prevent and control overweight, and evaluation of their feasibility, effects, and impact.

References

1. Garrow JS. *Treat obesity seriously – a clinical manual.* London, Churchill Livingstone, 1981.

2. Seidell JC, Deerenberg I. Obesity in Europe – prevalence and consequences for use of medical care. *Pharmacoeconomics*, 1994, **5**(Suppl. I):38-44.

3. Kumanyika SK. Special issues regarding obesity in minority populations. *Annals of internal medicine*, 1993, **119**:650-654.

4. Hodge AM et al. Prevalence and secular trends in obesity in Pacific and Indian Ocean island populations. *Obesity research,* 1995, **3**(Suppl. 2):77-87.

5. Hodge AM et al. Dramatic increase in the prevalence of obesity in Western Samoa over the 13-year period 1978-1991. *International journal of obesity and related metabolic disorders*, 1994, **18**:419-428.

6. *Mauritius Non-Communicable Disease Intervention Program: report on 1992 disease and risk factor prevalence and incidence study.* Melbourne, International Diabetes Institute, 1993.

7. Shetty PS, James WPT. *Body mass index: a measure of chronic energy deficiency in adults.* Rome, Food and Agriculture Organization of the United Nations, 1994 (Food and Nutrition Paper No. 56).

8. Dhurandhar NV, Kulkarni PR. Prevalence of obesity in Bombay. *International journal of obesity and related metabolic disorders*, 1992, **16**:367-375.

9. Manson JE et al. Body weight and longevity. A reassessment. *Journal of the American Medical Association*, 1987, **257**:353-358.

10. Bouchard C. Genetics of obesity and its prevention. *World review of nutrition and dietetics*, 1993, **72**:68-77.

11. Neel JV. Diabetes mellitus: a "thrifty" genotype rendered detrimental by "progress"? *American journal of human genetics*, 1962, **14**:353-362.

12. **Kuczmarski RJ.** Prevalence of overweight and weight gain in the United States. *American journal of clinical nutrition*, 1992, **55**(2 Suppl.):495S-502S.

13. **Blokstra A, Kromhout D.** Trends in obesity in young adults in The Netherlands from 1974 to 1986. *International journal of obesity*, 1991, **15**:513-521.

14. **Kuskowska-Wolk A, Bergström R.** Trends in body mass index and prevalence of obesity in Swedish men 1980-1989. *Journal of epidemiology and community health*, 1993, **47**:103-108.

15. **Jalkanen L et al.** Changes in body mass index in a Finnish population between 1972 and 1982. *Journal of internal medicine*, 1989, **226**:163-170.

16. **O'Dea K.** Westernization and non-insulin-dependent-diabetes in Australian Aborigines. *Ethnicity and disease*, 1991, **1**:171-187.

17. **Rissanen AM et al.** Overweight and anthropometric changes in adulthood: a prospective study of 17,000 Finns. *International journal of obesity*, 1988, **12**:391-401.

18. **Williamson DF et al.** The 10-year incidence of overweight and major weight gain in US adults. *Archives of internal medicine*, 1990, **150**:665-672.

19. **Rookus MA et al.** The effect of pregnancy on the body mass index 9 months postpartum in 49 women. *International journal of obesity*, 1987, **11**:609-618.

20. **Rissanen AM et al.** Determinants of weight gain and overweight in adult Finns. *European journal of clinical nutrition*, 1991, **45**:419-430.

21. **Ohlin A, Rossner S.** Maternal body weight development after pregnancy. *International journal of obesity*, 1990, **14**:159-173.

22. **Sobal J, Stunkard AJ.** Socioeconomic status and obesity: a review of the literature. *Psychological bulletin*, 1989, **105**:260-275.

23. *Diet, nutrition, and the prevention of chronic diseases. Report of a WHO Study Group.* Geneva, World Health Organization, 1990 (WHO Technical Report Series, No. 797).

24. **Kahn HS, Williamson DF, Stevens JA.** Race and weight change in US women: the roles of socioeconomic and marital status. *American journal of public health*, 1991, **81**:319-323.

25. **Brown PJ.** *Cultural perspectives on the etiology and treatment of obesity.* In: Stunkard AJ, Wadden TA, eds. *Obesity: theory and therapy*, 2nd ed. New York, Raven Press, 1992:179-193.

26. **Grunberg NE.** Cigarette smoking and body weight: current perspectives and future directions. *Annals of behavioural medicine*, 1989, **11**:154-157.

27. **Hofstetter A et al.** Increased 24-hour energy expenditure in cigarette smokers. *New England journal of medicine*, 1986, **314**:79-82.

28. **Marti B et al.** Smoking and leanness: evidence for change in Finland. *British medical journal*, 1989, **298**:1287-1290.

29. **Baecke JAH et al.** Obesity in young Dutch adults: II, Daily life-style and body mass index. *International journal of obesity*, 1983, **7**:13-24.

30. **Schoenborn CA et al.** *Advance data from vital and health statistics*, No. 154. Hyattsville, MD, United States Department of Health and Human Services, 1985.

31. **Williamson DF et al.** Smoking cessation and severity of weight gain in a national cohort. *New England journal of medicine*, 1991, **324**:739–745.

32. **Seidell JC.** Environmental influences on regional fat distribution. *International journal of obesity*, 1991, **15**(Suppl. 2):31–35.

33. **Williamson DF et al.** Recreational physical activity and ten-year weight change in a US national cohort. *International journal of obesity and related metabolic disorders*, 1993, **17**:279–286.

34. **Hellerstedt WL, Jeffery RW, Murray DM.** The association between alcohol intake and adiposity in the general population. *American journal of epidemiology*, 1990, **132**:594–611.

35. **Suter PM, Schutz Y, Jequier E.** The effect of ethanol on fat storage in healthy subjects. *New England journal of medicine*, 1992, **326**:983–987.

36. **Sjöström L.** *Impacts of body weight, body composition, and adipose tissue distribution on morbidity and mortality*. In: Stunkard AJ, Wadden TA, eds. *Obesity: theory and therapy*, 2nd ed. New York, Raven Press, 1992.

37. **Lindsted K, Tonstad S, Kuzma JW.** Body mass index and patterns of mortality among Seventh-day Adventist men. *International journal of obesity*, 1991, **15**: 397–406.

38. **Troiano RP et al.** The relationship between body weight and mortality: a quantitative analysis of combined information from existing studies. *International journal of obesity and related metabolic disorders* (in press).

39. **Tokunaga K et al.** Ideal body weight estimated from the body mass index with the lowest morbidity. *International journal of obesity*, 1991, **15**:1–5.

40. **Ashley FW Jr, Kannel WB.** Relation of weight change to changes in atherogenic traits: the Framingham Study. *Journal of chronic diseases*, 1974, **27**:103–114.

41. **Williamson DF, Pamuk ER.** The association between weight loss and increased longevity. A review of the evidence. *Annals of internal medicine*, 1993, **119**: 731–736.

42. **Blair SN et al.** Body weight change, all-cause mortality, and cause-specific mortality in the Multiple Risk Factor Intervention Trial. *Annals of internal medicine*, 1993, **119**:749–757.

43. **Manson JE et al.** A prospective study of obesity and risk of coronary heart disease in women. *New England journal of medicine*, 1990, **322**:882–889.

44. **Larsson B.** Regional obesity as a health hazard in men – prospective studies. *Acta medica Scandinavica supplementum*, 1988, **723**:45–51.

45. **Despres JP et al.** Regional distribution of body fat, plasma lipoproteins, and cardiovascular disease. *Arteriosclerosis*, 1990, **10**:497–511.

46. **Dyken ML et al.** Risk factors in stroke: a statement for physicians by the Subcommittee on Risk Factors and Stroke of the Stroke Council. *Stroke,* 1984, **15**:1105–1111.

47. **Barrett-Connor EL.** Obesity, hypertension and stroke. *Clinical and experimental hypertension [A]*, 1990, **12**:769–782.

48. **Staessen J et al.** Body weight, sodium intake and blood pressure. *Journal of hypertension supplement*, 1989, **7**:S19–S23.

49. Schotte DE, Stunkard AJ. The effects of weight reduction on blood pressure in 301 obese patients. *Archives of internal medicine*, 1990, **150**:1701–1704.

50. Karvonen M et al. Cigarette smoking, serum cholesterol, blood pressure and body fatness. Observations in Finland. *Lancet*, 1959, 1:492–494.

51. Stamler R, Ford CE, Stamler J. Why do lean hypertensives have higher mortality rates than other hypertensives? Findings of the Hypertension Detection and Follow-up Program. *Hypertension*, 1991, **17**:553–564.

52. Björntorp P. "Portal" adipose tissue as a generator of risk factors for cardiovascular disease and diabetes. *Arteriosclerosis*, 1990, **10**:493–496.

53. Colditz GA et al. Weight as a risk factor for clinical diabetes in women. *American journal of epidemiology*, 1990, **132**:501–513.

54. Sims EAH et al. Endocrine and metabolic effects of experimental obesity in man. *Recent progress in hormone research*, 1973, **29**:457–496.

55. Liddle RA, Goldstein RB, Saxton J. Gallstone formation during weight-reduction dieting. *Archives of internal medicine*, 1989, **149**:1750–1753.

56. Maclure KM et al. Weight, diet, and the risk of symptomatic gallstones in middle-aged women. *New England journal of medicine*, 1989, **321**:563–569.

57. Hartz AJ, Rupley DC, Rimm AA. The association of girth measurements with disease in 32,856 women. *American journal of epidemiology*, 1984, **119**:71–80.

58. Van Noord PAH et al. The relationship between fat distribution and some chronic diseases in 11,825 women participating in the DOM-project. *International journal of epidemiology*, 1990, **19**:564–570.

59. Davis MA. Epidemiology of osteoarthritis. *Clinical geriatric medicine*, 1988, 4: 241–255.

60. Rissanen A et al. Risk of disability and mortality due to overweight in a Finnish population. *British medical journal*, 1990, **301**:835–837.

61. Osler M. Obesity and cancer. A review of epidemiological studies on the relationship of obesity to cancer of the colon, rectum, prostate, breast, ovaries, and endometrium. *Danish medical bulletin*, 1987, **34**:267–274.

62. Filipovsky J et al. Abdominal body mass distribution and elevated blood pressure are associated with increased risk of death from cardiovascular disease and cancer in middle-aged men. The results of a 15- to 20-year follow-up in the Paris prospective study I. *International journal of obesity and related metabolic disorders*, 1993, **17**:197–203.

63. Zaadstra BM et al. Fat and female fecundity: prospective study of effect of body fat distribution on conception rates. *British medical journal*, 1993, **306**:484–487.

64. Gortmaker SL et al. Social and economic consequences of overweight in adolescence and young adulthood. *New England journal of medicine*, 1993, **329**:1008–1012.

65. Lapidus L et al. Obesity, adipose tissue distribution and health in women – results from a population study in Gothenburg, Sweden. *Appetite*, 1989, **13**: 25–35.

66. Stene-Larsen G et al. Relationship of overweight to hiatus hernia and reflux oesophagitis. *Scandinavian journal of gastroenterology*, 1988, **23**:427–432.

67. **Partinen M, Telakivi T.** Epidemiology of obstructive sleep apnea syndrome. *Sleep*, 1992, **15**(6 Suppl.):S1–S4.

68. **Deurenberg P, Weststrate JA, Seidell JC.** Body mass index as a measure of body fatness: age- and sex-specific prediction formulas. *British journal of nutrition*, 1991, **65**:105–114.

69. **Dowling HJ, Pi-Sunyer FX.** Race-dependent health risks of upper body obesity. *Diabetes*, 1993, **42**:537–543.

70. **Seidell JC et al.** The sagittal diameter and mortality in men: the Baltimore Longitudinal Study on Aging. *International journal of obesity and related metabolic disorders*, 1994, **18**:61–67.

71. **McKeigue PM, Shah B, Marmot MG.** Relation of central obesity and insulin resistance with high diabetes prevalence and cardiovascular risk in South Asians. *Lancet*, 1991, **337**:382–386.

72. **Haffner SM et al.** Incidence of type II diabetes in Mexican Americans predicted by fasting insulin and glucose levels, obesity, and body-fat distribution. *Diabetes*, 1990, **39**:283–288.

73. NIH conference. Gastrointestinal surgery for severe obesity. Consensus Development Conference Panel. *Annals of internal medicine*, 1991, **115**: 956–961.

74. **Goldstein DJ.** Beneficial health effects of modest weight loss. *International journal of obesity and related metabolic disorders*, 1992, **16**:397–415.

75. Methods for voluntary weight loss and control. NIH Technology Assessment Conference Panel. Consensus Development Conference, 30 March to 1 April 1992. *Annals of internal medicine*, 1993, **119**:764–770.

76. WHO MONICA Project. Geographic variation in the major risk factors of coronary heart disease in men and women aged 35–64 years. *World health statistics quarterly*, 1988, **41**:115–138.

8. Thin adults

8.1 Introduction

8.1.1 *Background*

The nutrition and health of adults are of particular importance because it is this age group that is primarily responsible for the economic support of the rest of society. In industrialized countries, although an appreciable proportion of adults are still engaged in activities that require physical stamina and strength, economic productivity depends to a substantial degree on the intellectual and technical skills of the population. In non-industrialized societies, however, where agricultural work is the dominant economic activity, physical capacity and endurance are critical to the ability of adults to sustain the socioeconomic and cultural integrity of their community.

8.1.2 *Terminology*

The terms "stunting" and "wasting" are rarely applied to adults, except in a clinical context where particular individuals may be deemed to be so different in their stature or physical appearance from the rest of society that clinicians employ these descriptive terms without reference to defined cut-off points. Thus "wasting" is usually confined to adults who are ill (in a hospital setting) or enduring extreme conditions, e.g. famine.

Variability in adult weight is recognized as being linked with variation in adult height, which in turn reflects a number of environmental factors active throughout much of childhood. The term "underweight" in adult assessment has therefore been applied to individuals of low body weight relative to height; it is generally expressed in terms of body mass index.

Degrees of underweight have recently been defined as "chronic energy deficiency" (CED), categorized on the basis of BMI (*1, 2*). The term CED was originally applied to adults who were not only underweight for their height but also constrained in their physical activity by inadequate food intakes (*1*); more recently the term has been defined simply in terms of specific levels of BMI (*2*). In this report, however, the condition of low BMI is termed "thinness" graded as mild (grade 1), moderate (grade 2), or severe (grade 3).

Other measures of size
In clinical practice and in population studies, simple additional or alternative measurements to weight and height have been sought. Arm circumference is one such measurement and has also been used together with more sophisticated estimates of muscle circumference obtained by adding a skinfold measurement; however, total circumference at the mid-point of the upper arm (MUAC) is preferred. Measuring MUAC has the advantage that it reflects the mass of just three tissues – bone, muscle, and fat – the last two of which are particularly sensitive to body weight gain

or loss. Changes in arm circumference thus reflect more accurately the increase or decrease of tissue "reserves" of energy and protein (3) than body weight *per se*. By calculating mid-arm muscle circumference (AMC), a more specific measure of the more labile fraction of lean tissue can be obtained. The significance and usefulness of these measurements, used either alone or in association with BMI, are considered later in this section.

8.2 Biological and social significance of anthropometry

8.2.1 *Biological and social determinants of anthropometry*

The average stature of adults varies markedly from country to country. Environmental conditions and childhood nutrition interact with the genetic potential of the individual to determine increase in height and eventual attained stature. Differences in adult height therefore reflect long-term differences in the socioeconomic conditions of different groups in most developed and developing countries. However, as socioeconomic differences within a society attenuate, so the differences in adult height are reduced. The relationships between height and socioeconomic circumstances are more readily seen by monitoring the height of children.

Adult height usually declines with age. This reflects not only the steady, age-related decrease in the width of both the intervertebral discs and the lumbar vertebral bodies (see section 9) but also the impact of the greater height of better-grown younger cohorts. Thus, where socioeconomic impact on adult height has been small over the past 70 years, the differences between the heights of adults aged 20 and 60 years are also small. This contrasts with data on adults in Japan, for example, where there has been a marked secular increase in the height of children and where the discrepancy between the height of 20- and 60-year-old adults is substantial.

Table 37
Daily physical activity level of Rwandan women according to body mass index[a]

	Daily physical activity level[b]			
Body mass index	Monday–Friday	Saturday	Sunday	Average
≤ 17.0	1.51	1.51	1.44	1.50
17.1–17.5	1.57	1.55	1.48	1.55
17.6–18.6	1.63	1.59	1.52	1.61
18.7–23.8	1.67	1.66	1.57	1.65
23.9–26.1	1.69	1.67	1.58	1.67

[a] Data from François P, unpublished report to Food and Agriculture Organization of the United Nations, Rome, 1990.
[b] Expressed as multiples of basal metabolic rate. Average values obtained over a 1-year period.

Once adult stature has been achieved, biological impacts on height are limited to disease states, e.g. Cushing disease or ankylosing spondylitis, or to environmental processes that accentuate bone loss and osteoporosis.

In contrast to the effects on height, changes in nutritional intake and in health can have a major impact on body weight. Seasonal changes in food availability and in physical activity produce fluctuations in both average weight and the population distribution of weights, and any illness that induces anorexia, elevated metabolic rates, or preferential catabolic loss of lean tissue will also produce a fall in body weight. This makes the monitoring of adult weight or some alternative index of body mass a useful tool for assessing the impact of illness, food shortage, or unusual physical demands. Other factors, such as cigarette smoking and drug and alcohol dependence are also usually associated with lower body weight.

8.2.2 *Biological and social consequences of anthropometry*

Adult height has long been recognized as a predictor of work capacity, and formal studies now confirm this relationship. However, height and weight are closely correlated, and in practice work capacity is predicted better by total body weight than by height. The relationship between work capacity and height is therefore indirect. Women's height and weight also predict a variety of outcomes of pregnancy, such as dystocia and low birth weight (see section 3).

Individual adaptation

Individuals of low body weight change the allocation of time and energy to different productive and leisure-time activities. Data collected for the National Food Consumption and Household Budget Survey in Rwandan women[1] reveal that physical activity levels in women with BMI < 17.6 are significantly lower, and the length of time taken for rest each day greater, than those in heavier women (see Table 37). The women of lower weight allocate fewer days to heavy labour; an inverse relationship is thus apparent between BMI and the time allocated to heavy work. Obligatory work needs, however, are still met.

Studies in Ethiopia and in India also show very low levels of physical activity in adult men with BMI 18-19 and women with BMI 17-18 (2); work output is sustained at only 2-4.5 hours per day.[2] Men with a very low BMI (<16) show even lower levels of activity.

---

[1] François P. Unpublished report to the Food and Agriculture Organization of the United Nations, Rome, 1990.

[2] See also:

Norgan NG et al. *The determinants of the biological impact of seasonality on energy nutritional status in a rural Karnataka (South India) agricultural cycle.* Unpublished report to International Food Policy Research Institute, Washington, DC, 1993.

Branca F et al. *Seasonality in agriculture: evidence of its nutritional impact. A case study in southern Ethiopia.* Unpublished report to International Food Policy Research Institute, Washington, DC, 1993.

During seasonal food shortages, adults reduce their energy intakes and increase their expenditure of energy on productive work; for example, to complete jobs such as planting and hoeing, individuals will adjust the time allocated to work and home activities, giving more time to work and expending less energy on home activities and leisure (4). This is an important form of behavioural adaptation, with a pattern that may be different in undernourished and well nourished individuals. When semi-starvation occurs without the need to maintain work output for survival, there is a considerable fall in spontaneous activity (5). However, if it is essential that some work be continued, there is a change in the activity pattern, with a substitution of low-cost for high-cost discretionary activities (6).

The nature of behavioural adaptation can vary. Guatemalan men with low muscle mass who were assigned substantial agricultural workloads took a significantly longer time to walk home after work, and spent about 3 hours/day in sleeping (during the daytime), sitting, playing cards, or other sedentary activities (7) (see Table 38). In contrast, better nourished, age-matched men did not sleep during the daytime, were active at home, and played soccer, thereby remaining physically active for a significantly greater proportion of the day.

The dramatic reduction in physical activity in conditions of acute energy deprivation is an important survival mechanism and seems to be induced by the process of weight loss. Thus, male volunteers in the USA who semistarved for 6 months to achieve a BMI of 16.5 (5) were far less active than African individuals with a similar BMI who had never achieved a BMI as high as the original US levels (20–25) or who had reduced their weight more slowly. Once weight is stabilized, however, and dietary energy is available for physical work, very thin individuals can maintain a certain amount of activity even if their work capacity and productivity are impaired. The distinctions, if any, between the extent of lethargy induced by weight loss *per se* and that associated with a low BMI have not been explored.

Table 38
Allocation of time to activities among well nourished and undernourished rural Guatemalan men[a]

	Time (min) spent daily				Distribution of time (%)		
	walking to work	walking from work	daytime rest	nighttime sleep	Work	Other[b]	Daytime rest
Undernourished	25	40	173	530	27	24	12
Well nourished	20	22	0	498	16	50	0

[a] Modified from reference 7.
[b] Apart from time devoted to sleeping or personal care activities.

Fluctuations in body weight during seasonal changes in food availability have a different impact on the body composition of adults of low body weight than on those of greater weight; the former group lose proportionally more lean tissue (see section 8.4.2) and are therefore compromised to a greater extent in their general health and work capacity. No formal assessment has yet been made of the degree to which the seasonal susceptibility to infection, lethargy, or work impairment is exacerbated in those of low body weight.

Societal changes in behaviour at low body weights
Energy deprivation with consequent weight loss has profound effects on societal behaviour (8). Much depends on the traditions of the society and whether the limitation on food supply is viewed as normal and expected, e.g. as a result of seasonal changes, or as abnormal and life-threatening. As food becomes increasingly scarce, communal activity tends to decline, men migrate in search of alternative employment, and food is hoarded by individual households rather than being shared. Innovative effort is selectively concentrated on preserving and diversifying food stocks, to the detriment of community facilities.

8.3 Anthropometry as an indicator of nutritional and health status

8.3.1 *Work capacity*

Physiological studies have shown that muscle mass is an important determinant of physical work capacity, measured and expressed as maximal oxygen consumption (VO_2 max.) during graded tests of increasingly severe physical intensity. In physically strenuous work, positive correlations have been found between work capacity and work performance: taller individuals with larger body and muscle mass have consistently been shown to have a higher work capacity and work performance than short individuals. However, when work capacity is expressed per kg body weight or per kg active tissue mass, the evidence is less clear. Thus, the overall size of an individual can be important: in heavy activities such as cane-cutting, logging, mining, and certain agricultural activities, the total weight of the body can also be used to power particular tasks, so that the heavier individual is again at an advantage (9). This is illustrated in Table 39, taken from studies conducted in India (10).

In studies of migrant agricultural labourers, Desai (11) was able to show deficits in work capacity that were associated with thinness and short stature.

8.3.2 *Work productivity*

Individuals of low body weight are more likely to fail to appear for work because of illness or exhaustion. Physical training can substantially improve work capacity, but inactivity leads to rapid and substantial reductions in the ability to sustain heavy work.

Table 39
Effect of body weight, height, and body mass index on productivity of male industrial workers[a]

Height (metres)	Productivity, expressed in productivity units		
	Body weight 40-50 kg[b]	Body weight 50-60 kg[b]	Body weight > 60 kg[b]
< 1.60	2875 (18.0)	3250 (22.0)	–
1.60-1.70	2850 (16.5)	3250 (20.0)	3750 (23.0)
> 1.70	–	3325 (19.0)	–

[a] Source reference *10*; used with the permission of the American Society for Clinical Nutrition.
[b] Figures in parentheses denote mean BMI of the group.

The link between low body weight and poor work productivity is complicated by the individual's motivation and health status. Determination to maintain work output can lead to thinner people sustaining hard work but at a higher proportion of their maximal oxygen capacity. The additional stress is then apparent as elevated heart rates at the same level of oxygen consumption and higher blood lactate levels resulting from the smaller muscle mass working harder. In a comparison of Brazilian adolescent boys (*12*), those with a mean BMI below 17 exhibited oxygen consumption levels and gross efficiency of work under the test conditions similar to those of their more affluent counterparts who were of mean BMI 20, but showed greater stress. Men from rural areas of Hyderabad, India, with BMI below 18.5 showed work capacities (expressed in body weight terms) and increments of mechanical efficiency similar to those of better nourished urban men (BMI >20). However, correcting the results for body weight differences revealed that the total work capacity of the lighter individuals was substantially lower than that of their urban counterparts; a similar workload had thus imposed a greater stress on those with low BMI (*13*).

Behavioural differences are also apparent at work. In a study of Guatemalan men, two groups undertook heavy standardized agricultural tasks such as woodcutting, land clearing, and hoeing for 3-6 days. The group with a smaller lean body mass and muscle mass were able to do the same amount of work as the better nourished group, but took considerably more time to complete it (397 ± 123 min/day compared with 235 ± 40 min/day) and performed the tasks at a less intense level (4.6 ± 0.8 kcal$_{th}$/min compared with 5.1 ± 0.2 kcal$_{th}$/min)[1] (*7*). A similar

---

[1] 1 cal$_{th}$ = 4.184 J.

slowing of work in men with low BMI was observed in Kenyan road-workers (*14*). Thus there seems to be a continuous gradient in work capacity and productivity that is linked to body weight, and particularly to lean tissue and muscle mass. This is reflected in the differences in work output at different values of BMI (Table 40) reported in a study of Colombian men (*15*).

8.3.3 *Mortality at low body weight*

Developed countries
In attempting to define a level of weight or BMI below which impairments become apparent, an analysis of mortality data might be appropriate, since the link between body weight and mortality has been used extensively in defining the importance of overweight. In a series of studies in industrialized societies, the relationship between weight and mortality has been shown to be J-shaped, with an increase in mortality among adults with relatively low BMI (19-20). Systematic analysis of 25 major studies (*16*) showed two principal sources of bias in this relationship between thinness and excess mortality. The first was failure to control for cigarette smoking, which is strongly associated with low body weight because it reduces appetite and increases the body's metabolic rate. Moreover, smoking is a major risk factor: mortality rates are high among smokers. The second source of bias was the failure to eliminate early mortality from the analysis of thin adults, many of whom may have already been ill when measured and therefore more likely to have lost weight and died.

Information derived from the Build and Blood Pressure Study (*17*) provides strong supporting evidence for weight loss in the early years following inception of life insurance policies being due to pre-existing disease (*18*). Even the extensive Framingham Study was unable to show any increased risk among underweight individuals, after adjustment for early deaths of non-smokers (*19*). In a study by the American Cancer Society (*20*), a similar trend towards better survival over time was also observed among thin individuals.

Table 40
Reduction in aerobic work capacity associated with low BMI in Colombian men

Category	BMI	VO$_2$ max.	
		litres/min	ml/kg per min
Controls	24.0	2.8	47
Mild malnutrition	21.3	2.1	41
Moderate malnutrition	20.0	1.9	35
Severe malnutrition	17.7	1.0	28

In the Honolulu Heart Programme Study (*21*), mortality rates among men aged 45–68 years were highest in the lightest and heaviest quintiles. Deaths in the heaviest quintile were caused primarily by coronary heart disease, whereas those in the lightest two quintiles related to cancer and "other causes". When BMI at age 25 (median value 19.8) was used to predict future mortality, men in the lightest quintile had the lowest mortality in middle age, provided that they did not lose weight (*19*). This has been confirmed in other studies on thin, non-smoking men who were not suffering from any clinical disorder (*22, 23*). Among non-smoking women in the USA, with no pre-existing diseases (such as coronary artery disease, stroke, cancer), the relationship between BMI and fatal and non-fatal coronary artery disease in all five quintiles is direct and proportional to BMI, with the lightest quintile having a BMI <21. It may be concluded that, after selection of non-smokers and exclusion of early deaths, the relationship between BMI and mortality in industrialized societies is no longer J-shaped.

Since all the mortality studies were conducted in economically developed countries and involved predominantly white "middle-class" adults, it is unknown whether the results are applicable to other racial or ethnic groups. Moreover, most studies have been conducted only on men.

In developed countries, unintentional weight loss has a profound impact on subsequent morbidity and mortality. In a prospective study of 91 patients with involuntary weight loss, for example, 25% died during the first year following the initial visit by the researchers (*24*). In patients with cancer, weight loss is directly related to early mortality as well as responsiveness to treatment (*25*), and weight loss has long been used to estimate surgical risk (*26-28*).

In previously healthy individuals who voluntarily semistarve themselves, low BMI is compatible with life. In one study, volunteers semistarved for 24 weeks and attained a BMI of 16.5; none died (*5*). However, the sample size was small. Moreover, volunteers lost only 15% of their lean tissue, and the critical figure seems to be close to 50%. In an analysis of men and women with anorexia nervosa, the BMI of dying women was about 11 and of men about 13 (*29*). Thus, in highly favourable environments, where the chances of opportunistic infections are low, survival is compatible with very low BMI.

Developing countries
Evidence on the relationship between low BMI and mortality in developing countries is extremely scarce, although recent data for Indian men (*30*) show a progressive increase in mortality rates below a BMI of 18.5, with an almost threefold higher rate after 10 years for those with BMI below 16 (Table 41).

Clearly these men could have been ill before being measured, so it is difficult to assign any causal significance to the relationships. Nevertheless, if it can be assumed that immune competence is compromised in those

Table 41
Annual death rates in Indian men monitored over a 10-year period[a]

Initial BMI	≥ 18.5	17–18.49	16–16.99	< 16.0
Annual death rate (deaths/1000)	12.1	13.2	18.9	32.5

[a] Based on data from reference *30*.

with a low BMI, susceptible low-weight individuals may succumb to the prevalent life-threatening diseases. More prospective epidemiological studies in this field are needed in the developing world.

8.3.4 *Morbidity and low body weight*

Developed countries
Malnutrition among adults in hospitals and nursing homes is common in many developed countries (*31–35*), and the prevalence of significant malnutrition may exceed 25%. Two forms of malnutrition may be seen: adult marasmus, and the malnutrition associated with low serum albumin, which is analogous to kwashiorkor in children. Both of these adult conditions are almost invariably secondary to disease. Hypoalbuminaemic malnutrition usually results from the metabolic effects of injury, inflammation, or infection, rather than from dietary protein deficiency, and the cause is usually clinically obvious. Marasmic individuals or those with significant weight loss also react badly to injury and infection, and have a poorer outcome than normal individuals. They develop longer and more severe episodes of hypoalbuminaemia and associated immune incompetence (*36*). The marasmic patient in a healthy environment, however, is not particularly susceptible to infection unless he or she is malnourished. By contrast, hypoalbuminaemia is a sign, as in developing countries, that the body is responding to infection and therefore losing more lean tissue, particularly muscle, than fat. Measurement of serum albumin levels is thus a valuable simple tool for assessing the overall health status of the individual patient.

Developing countries
There has been little research on the links between low body weight or BMI and episodes of illness in adults in developing countries. Table 42 summarizes the prevalence of "sickness events" according to five classes of BMI among women in Rwanda.[1]

The number of days per year spent in illness increases dramatically in individuals whose BMI is below 18.6. Table 42 also presents data on the number of days per year spent in bed (where 16 hours extra in bed is considered as equivalent to one whole day in bed); this number was disproportionally higher in those with low BMI. A study in Bangladesh (*37*)

---
[1] François P. Unpublished report to the Food and Agriculture Organization of the United Nations, Rome, 1990.

Table 42
Body mass index and sickness events in women in Rwanda[a]

BMI range	No. of days ill per year	Percentage of days per year with sickness events	Equivalent days in bed[b]
≤ 17.0	77	20	40
17.1–17.5	58	16	40
17.6–18.6	29	8	12
18.7–23.8	14	4	7
23.9–26.1	14	4	7

[a] Data from François P, unpublished report to the Food and Agriculture Organization of the United Nations, Rome, 1990.
[b] Equivalent day = 16 hours of daytime spent in bed.

Table 43
Proportion of adults of different body mass index spending time ill in bed in Brazil in 1989[a]

	Proportion (%) of adults spending time ill in bed			
	Men		Women	
BMI range	5–7 days	8–14 days	5–7 days	8–14 days
< 16.0	1.0	< 0.1	5.1	4.5
16.0–16.9	1.0	2.8	2.2	2.9
17.0–18.4	1.4	1.6	0.4	0.8
18.5–19.9	0.6	0.5	0.6	0.9
20.0–24.9	0.4	0.6	0.8	0.6
25.0–29.9	0.5	0.6	1.1	0.6
≥ 30	0.1	< 0.1	1.1	0.9

[a] Reproduced from reference 38 with the permission of the publisher.

showed that the percentage of men who failed to work because of illness also increased with declining BMI, and a Brazilian study (38) showed a U-shaped relationship between reported illness and BMI (Table 43).

This trend is particularly evident for individuals with BMI below 17. In the very large Brazilian sample a gradient effect for those who have spent 8–14 days in bed in the previous two weeks is still evident at a BMI below 18.5. Whether this signifies the effect of disease on low body weight or vice versa can be clarified only by careful and extensive prospective studies, but it seems obvious that in the less developed countries individuals with BMI below 18.5 are at some extra risk, which increases if BMI falls below 17.0.

Figure 58
Ethnic differences in the relationship between average sitting height and average stature in samples of adult men[a]

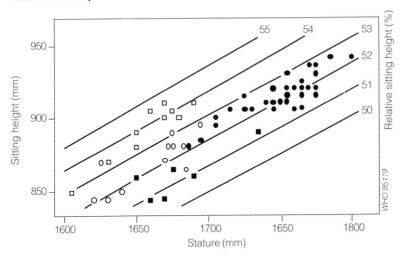

Key to samples:
● = European (including samples of predominantly European descent)
○ = Indo-Mediterranean
□ = Western Pacific
■ = African

[a] Reproduced from reference *40* by kind permission of the publisher, Taylor & Francis.

8.4 Interpretation of anthropometry

8.4.1 *Considerations of body shape*

Individuals with low body weight are usually of short stature, and allowance should be made for this in assessing overweight (see section 7) and underweight. Since BMI is independent of height, it is a more appropriate measurement for most populations than weight alone (*39*). Problems arise, however, in adults whose shape differs from the norm, particularly those whose legs are shorter or longer than might be expected for their height.

The most common index of shape is the Cormic index, which is defined as the ratio of sitting height (crown–rump length) to height (*SH/H*) (*40*). It provides a measure of the relative length of the trunk and the legs and varies between individuals and groups; ethnic differences exist in both size and Cormic index. A typical ratio in those of predominantly European and Indo-Mediterranean[1] descent is 0.52–0.53, but populations in Western Pacific regions have values of 0.54, and African populations somewhat lower values of 0.51 to 0.52 (Fig. 58).

---

[1] Includes countries of the eastern Mediterranean region and the Indian subcontinent.

The Cormic index in women seems to be approximately 0.005 higher than that in men, although this is not well attested in the literature. In different populations, a BMI difference of 1 corresponds to a 0.01 difference in the *SH/H* ratio (*41*). Australian Aborigines have long legs and a BMI 2.0 units lower than Europeans, but the same sitting height and overall body weight. Similarly, South American people tend to have short legs relative to the length of the trunk, with a high ratio of sitting height to height and a higher BMI for their weight than European and Indo-Mediterranean people. Care should therefore be taken in groups and individuals with unusual leg length to avoid classifying them inappropriately as thin or overweight.

There is a linear, but only very moderate, correlation between BMI and height; correlation coefficients range between −0.01 and 0.23 in different ethnic and sex groups (*42*). BMI may therefore be considered as essentially independent of height. It should be noted, however, that, for values of height below 1.50 m or above 1.90 m, a strong non-linearity between BMI and height has been reported (*42*). Interpretation of BMI values for the very tall and the very short should thus be cautious, as the values would be height-biased.

8.4.2 *Low body weight and body composition*

The body can be considered as composed of two compartments – the energy-dense fat tissue, and the lean body mass, which consists largely of muscles and visceral organs plus supporting tissues. For their height, women's bodies have a higher percentage fat content and a lower muscle mass than men's, and women's urinary creatinine–height index (*43*) is lower than that of men.[1] When weight is lost, both adipose tissue and lean tissue (muscle) are used for fuel, but the proportion of lean tissue lost depends on the amount of fat stored (*44*): the greater the mass of adipose tissue, the smaller the loss of lean tissue on starvation. Ferro-Luzzi, Branca & Pastore (*45*) have described this relationship. Because women have a greater fat mass but smaller muscle mass than men of equivalent weights, they lose less lean tissue; Fig. 59 shows this preferential loss of fat in women and the increasing amounts of lean tissue lost as body weight and BMI fall.

The proportion of lean tissue, and specifically muscle tissue, in the body is determined by both genetic and environmental factors. Ethnic differences are apparent, with Papua New Guinean men and women having higher values of lean body mass (LBM) and a smaller percentage of fat than Ethiopians or Indians (*1, 46*). Whether the LBM of adult Ethiopians or Indians is affected by early nutritional conditions is unclear; there has been insufficiently detailed analysis of LBM of, for example, well nourished Indian children growing on the NCHS 50th

---

[1] Defined as the individual's 24-hour urinary creatinine excretion as a fraction of the value for a normal individual of the same height.

Figure 59
Proportion of body weight lost (or gained) represented by lean tissue according to body mass index at the beginning of the weight loss (or gain) period[a]

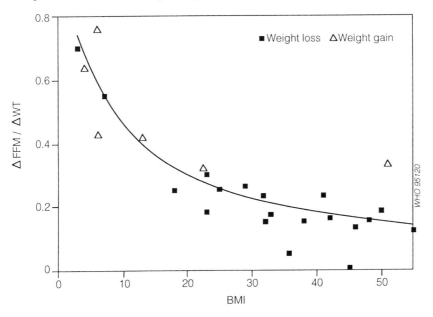

△ FFM / △ WT = (change in fat-free mass)/(weight change)

[a] Adapted from reference *45* with the permission of the publisher.

percentile and well nourished Indian adults with a BMI of 22–23. Under nutritional stress, populations with a smaller body fat mass lose more LBM and can thus be expected to lose weight more rapidly than others.

Training with isometric techniques leads to hypertrophy of muscle, a feature of body-builders and of athletes involved in sports that require the application of intense power over short periods of time (e.g. weight-lifters, sprinters). Isotonic training, on the other hand, leads to very modest changes in muscle mass, although some increase in mid-arm muscle circumference (AMC) can be observed in most athletes compared with non-athletes. Deconditioning is readily induced by cessation of training and in the event of prolonged bed-rest.

In clinical and public health settings, the preferential loss of lean tissue that results from tissue catabolism and gluconeogenesis in both acute and chronic infections is of particular significance. Individuals with a high fat content may lose substantial amounts of lean tissue – particularly muscle – during illness, and it is this loss of the protein-rich tissues, which are responsible for control and maintenance of organ metabolism, that is the determining factor in the individual's survival at low body weight.

When an individual is ill, e.g. with an infection, not only does the muscle mass begin to fall but there is also a dramatic change in the fatiguability of muscle and in the maximum power that can be achieved (*47*). It is relatively simple to test muscle power and endurance by measuring the strength and sustainability of the handgrip (*47, 48*).

Starvation and semistarvation studies on humans and experimental animals have convincingly shown that most organs contribute, in variable proportion, to the loss of body weight; the brain and the spinal cord are notable exceptions (*3, 5*). Animal experiments indicate that atrophy of the organs occurs as early as that of the muscle and in parallel with loss of body weight (see Fig. 60). The organs of concentration camp prisoners and famine victims, estimated to have lost between 25% and 45% of their original weight, weighed between 52% (spleen) and 80% (heart) of normal (*5*).

The weight loss of most organs is accompanied by cytological changes, ranging from cloudy swelling and degenerative changes to mitochondrial brown atrophy. The heart is compromised and becomes susceptible to arrhythmia, anaemia develops because of reduced erythropoiesis, and the capacity of the liver to handle drugs, metabolites, hormones, or toxic substances in the diet becomes impaired. In addition, while the mucosa and other physical barriers to microbial or parasitic entry are remarkably well preserved, the immune system itself is depressed. With a defective immunological response, the stress of even a mild infection is magnified,

Figure 60
Effects of semistarvation on organ weight in the rat[a]

Note: Semistarvation was produced by lowering daily food intake by two-thirds for 6 weeks. The animals were then allowed to recover by gradually restoring food intake. Selected organ weights are plotted as a percentage of baseline weight vs. percentage of initial body weight.

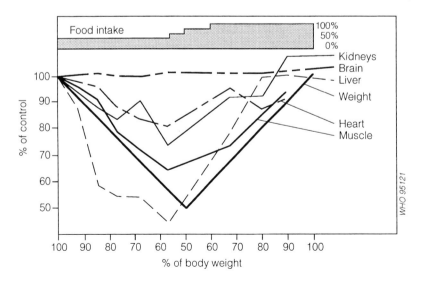

[a] Reproduced from reference *3* by permission of Blackwell Scientific Publications, Inc.

and there is progressive development of widespread life-threatening conditions, such as septicaemia, parasitaemia, or miliary tuberculosis. The interaction between nutritional status and immune competence is also clearly seen in individuals infected with human immunodeficiency virus (HIV), who display marked nutritional deterioration as their disease progresses; malnutrition exacerbates the disease and is often the determinant of death when 50% of the normal lean tissue has been lost (3, 49).

8.5 Using anthropometry in individuals

In men and non-pregnant women, a single measurement of body weight or BMI is of limited use for assessing the individual's risk of ill-health or likely benefit from medical intervention or supplementary feeding. A better predictor of individual risk is the degree of unintentional weight loss of an adult. This risk relates to perioperative morbidity and mortality, as well as to mortality rates in population studies. More refined indices of nutritional status in weight-losing adults include the serum albumin concentration as a general index of stress or infection, and MUAC, AMC, or the creatinine–height index as a measure of muscle mass (50, 51). Functional tests of muscular strength (e.g. grip strength) can also be used for assessing an acute deterioration in health (47). Appropriate oral, enteral, or intravenous refeeding elicits an improvement in grip strength within days; circumferential measurements of the arm and the creatinine–height index, however, respond more slowly over a period of weeks (52).

8.6 Using anthropometry in populations

8.6.1 Targeting interventions

Low body weight or low BMI has been used for targeting supplementary feeding programmes in pregnancy. Selective benefits derive from supplementing thin women (see section 3), but as yet there are no published studies that have selected adults of low body weight or BMI within a population for interventions.

8.6.2 Assessing response to an intervention

Mean adult BMI and BMI distributions can be used to assess the impact of social, health, or agricultural interventions. For example, adults in a deprived area of Zimbabwe who were provided with special food allowances to counteract their perceived food insecurity had a surprisingly high mean BMI; only a negligible proportion had BMI values below 18.5 (2). Secular changes in the BMI distribution of Tunisian adults of low income also suggested an impact of an intervention that provided subsidized edible oils (53). Social and medical programmes in Nepal have also resulted in improvements in adult BMI. Studies such as these, together with demonstrable cyclic, seasonal changes in BMI (45), emphasize the responsiveness of this measure to general changes in the food security of a population. Whether or not arm circumference measurements prove equally useful will depend both on their reproducibility and on the general validity of their relationship to BMI (see section 8.7.2).

8.6.3 *Ascertaining determinants of malnutrition*

Deficiencies of energy, protein, and several micronutrients (e.g. zinc) can lead to a fall in body weight, which may reflect changes in lean body mass and/or fat mass. To discriminate between changes in these two components requires selective measurements of body fat (e.g. triceps skinfold thickness) or of lean body mass (e.g. AMC or creatinine–height index). In adults, the dominant cause of a reduction in body weight is a fall in food intake, caused either by the unavailability of sufficient food to meet energy needs or by anorexia.

8.6.4 *Nutritional surveillance*

Measuring the body weight of adults in developing countries has only recently been recognized as an important means of objectively assessing the degree of nutritional or other socioeconomic deprivation in a population. An unusually low range of BMI can be a useful pointer to the special needs of the population of a particular area, and a changing BMI profile may demonstrate that the population is being adversely affected by social or economic changes (e.g. during structural adjustment).

The distribution of BMI in a population can provide valuable guidance for the planning of long-term development programmes, especially in agriculture and health. Programmes that aim to improve total food supply can be directed specifically towards populations with low BMI, whereas a population with "normal" BMI may require only the limited nutritional improvements necessary to counteract anaemia and other selective nutritional deficiencies.

If a population distribution of BMI is established, further monitoring during times of threat to food availability will reveal the extent to which the population is being affected. Where body weights are near or above normal, food insecurity may result in a shift to the left in the BMI distribution and an increasing proportion of adult BMI falling to between 18.5 and 20. If the average BMI is already as low as 18.5, responsible agencies will be aware of the need for rapid intervention in the event of the food supply being threatened by war or natural disaster.

Management of existing food aid programmes in settings such as refugee camps can be facilitated by anthropometric monitoring of adults, rather than of children alone. This will provide an indication of the potential capacity of adults to contribute physically to the work of rehabilitation and development schemes. Moreover, monitoring of adults may provide a more accurate picture of the adequacy of emergency feeding programmes; the susceptibility of malnourished children in refugee camps and other deprived environments to epidemic infection may confound attempts to discriminate between adequacy of food supply and adequacy of other public health measures.

8.6.5 *Thinness as a public health problem*

It is normal for there to be a relatively small proportion of thin individuals within any population, but an excessive proportion may indicate the presence of food insecurity or the catabolic consequences of widespread infectious diseases, such as AIDS and tuberculosis. Even when the food supply is adequate or environmental stress limited, excessive thinness points to the vulnerability of certain members of the population, with marginal energy reserves, in the event of drought, seasonal food shortages, or epidemics.

The proportion of the population with low BMI that would define a public health problem is closely linked to available resources for correcting the problem, the stability of the environment, and government priorities. About 3–5% of a healthy adult population have a BMI below 18.5; the Expert Committee suggested the following classification of the public health problem of low BMI, based on BMI distribution in adult populations worldwide (see Fig. 61):

Low prevalence (warning sign,
monitoring required):   5–9% of population with BMI <18.5

Medium prevalence
(poor situation):   10–19% of population with BMI <18.5

Figure 61
BMI distribution of various adult populations worldwide (both sexes)

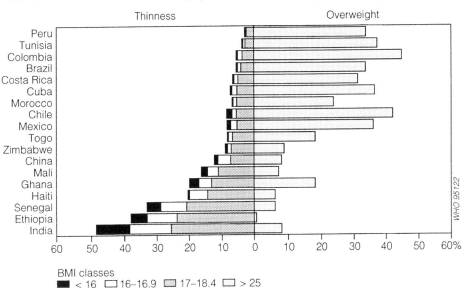

BMI classes
■ < 16 ☐ 16–16.9 ▨ 17–18.4 ☐ > 25

High prevalence
(serious situation):   20–39% of population with BMI <18.5

Very high prevalence
(critical situation):   ≥40% of population with BMI <18.5

This classification is somewhat arbitrary, but reflects the distribution of BMI in many populations of developing countries and endeavours to take into consideration the societal consequences of the functional impairments commonly associated with low BMI.

8.7 Guidelines for use of anthropometric indicators

8.7.1 *Use of BMI with simple cut-off points*

For affluent societies, there are no recognized reference standards that satisfactorily define the lower limit of desirable body weight except in terms of mortality. From Fig. 61 it is evident that BMI values vary widely, depending on the populations assessed. It is also worth noting that, as the proportion of the population with low BMI decreases, there is an almost symmetrical increase in the proportion with BMI above 25. This indicates a tendency for a population-wide shift as socioeconomic conditions improve, with overweight replacing thinness. The dynamics of this shift have been only imperfectly described, but there is consistent evidence that, in the first stages of transition, the wealthier sectors of the society show an increase in the proportion of people with high BMI, which is concurrent with the continued presence of thinness among the less wealthy. The distribution changes again in the later phases of the transition, with an increase in the prevalence of high BMI among poorer people. Appropriate data for generating a reference set of weights can be obtained only if a population has a plentiful supply of food, if children's growth is unimpaired by recurrent infections, and if young adults are free of disease. By the same token, a population that tends to be overweight is unsuitable for use as a reference standard.

There is increasing evidence (*54, 55*) that dietary fat content may contribute to the propensity to gain weight in adult life, which is particularly evident in middle-age. Low levels of physical activity also appear to be a contributing factor. Thus, when a reference population is to be chosen, a group of relatively young, physically active adults should be selected for identifying the lower limits of "normality". Adults enlisted in the armed forces are medically screened and generally physically fit, and may therefore form an appropriate group. In a selected group of soldiers in the British army (*56*), mean BMI of men aged 25–40 years was 24.6; for women aged 25–35 it was 22.7. Respective values of – 2 SD were 19.0 and 17.5.

Finding an appropriate society where adults in general are not inactive, not on a high-fat diet, and not subject to severe intercurrent infections or food shortages is difficult. For example, of the population of the USA, about 10% of men and 15% of women aged 25–40 had a BMI over 30 according to the NHANES surveys during the 1970s (*57*). At this age, those with a high BMI are known to be at substantial risk of premature death from chronic diseases; this population is therefore clearly unsuitable for use as a WHO reference population.

Systematic survey of the Chinese population revealed the smallest range of BMI yet identified (*53, 58*). The Chinese are active, have a dietary fat content that averages about 14% of energy intake, and do not have major epidemic infections, chronic diseases, or food shortages. In 1982, representative samples from 25 different provinces of China showed surprisingly little variation in BMI distribution. Among those aged 20–39 years, the mean and – 2 SD values were 20.9 and 17.1 for men and 21.5 and 16.9 for women (see Table 44) (*58*).

Since no prospective analysis of any differential increase in risk has yet been undertaken in Chinese with a low BMI, it would seem best to rely on pragmatically derived cut-offs of BMI rather than to specify limits based on the Chinese as the reference population. A BMI below 16 is known to be associated with a markedly increased risk of ill-health, poor physical performance, lethargy, and even death, so this cut-off point has validity as an extreme limit. Moreover, BMI below 17 has been linked with a clear-cut increase in illness in adults studied in three continents, and is therefore a further reasonable value to choose as a cut-off point for moderate risk. The proposal of a single cut-off point of 18.5 for specified mild deficiency in both sexes has less experimental support, but seems a reasonable value to use pending further comprehensive studies. The choice of these three cut-off points was adopted by a working group of the International Dietary Energy Consultative Group, who were asked to propose new definitions for chronic energy deficiency in adults (*1*), and was endorsed by a more recent IDECG meeting (*59*). The Food and

Table 44
Age trend of mean body mass index in a sample of the Chinese population[a]

	Men		Women	
Age groups (years)	Mean BMI	SD	Mean BMI	SD
20–29	20.6	1.7	21.2	1.9
30–39	21.2	2.1	21.7	2.7
40–49	21.4	2.7	21.7	2.9
50–59	21.2	2.4	22.0	3.6
60–69	20.9	2.9	21.7	3.7
≥ 70	20.9	3.1	20.6	3.5

[a] Reproduced from reference *58* with the permission of the publisher.

Table 45
Sequential assessment for the epidemiological diagnosis of different grades of chronic energy deficiency (CED)[a]

1. Measure BMI	2. Measure intake or expenditure for PAL estimation *with* the predicted BMR[b]	Group	Presumptive diagnosis[c]
≥ 18.5			Normal
17.0–18.49	≥ 1.4	A	Normal
	< 1.4	B	CED grade I
16.0–16.99	≥ 1.4	C	CED grade I
	< 1.4	D	CED grade II
< 16.0			CED grade III

[a] Reproduced from reference *1* with the permission of the publisher.
[b] PAL = physical activity level, BMR = basal metabolic rate.
[c] For confirmation of the diagnosis and for use in clinical research it is necessary to measure individual BMRs in groups A–D to allow for the appreciable inter-individual variability. At a BMI above 18.5 or below 16.0, the diagnoses can be based on BMI values alone.

Agriculture Organization of the United Nations has also adopted these cut-off points and is using them in an extensive series of worldwide analyses designed to provide an estimate of the prevalence of malnutrition (*53*).

Although the original specification of chronic energy deficiency incorporated a measure of energy turnover as well as BMI, as shown in Table 45, subsequent detailed activity studies suggest that BMI values alone could be used to assess deficiency (*2*).

As mentioned in section 8.1.2 and in Annex 1, the Expert Committee described the condition of low BMI as thinness, with the following three grades:

grade 1: BMI 17.0–18.49 (mild thinness)

grade 2: BMI 16.0–16.99 (moderate thinness)

grade 3: BMI <16.0 (severe thinness)

Annexes 2 and 3 of this report provide complete and more simplified versions, respectively, of BMI tables that will facilitate the utilization of this index in the field. A nomogram is also provided in Annex 2 (Fig. A2.1).

8.7.2 *Arm and arm muscle circumference*

Body fat content can be predicted from measurement of the triceps skinfold thickness but is not particularly useful for diagnosing protein-energy malnutrition because fat is more readily expendable than fat-free mass and correlates poorly with physiological function (*60*), hospital morbidity, or mortality (*61, 62*). The principal value of the skinfold measurement is for calculating the AMC or arm muscle area (AMA), with or without a correction for the bone area.

Frisancho (*57*) developed a series of standards for mid-upper arm circumference and arm muscle area from a multi-stage, stratified survey (1971–1980) of nearly 44 000 children and adults in the USA. He also devloped the Frame Index 2, calculated as [elbow breadth (mm)/stature (cm)] × 100, which allows the individual to be assigned to one of three frame size categories – small, medium, or large. In adult men, a sharp rise in both MUAC and AMA from 18 to 30 years of age was noted; these measurements declined progressively after the age of 40. Women, however, showed a slow, steady rise in MUAC and AMA throughout adult life. The changes in arm circumference and calculated muscle area paralleled weight gains, and were seen in adults of all three frame sizes. The pattern of changes in arm measurements is consistent with those of muscle and other lean tissues, contributing the expected 38% to weight change in adult life (*63*). Given the recognized high BMI values even of young adults in the USA, it seems unwise to use these data as a reference.

Even for other populations for which relevant medical or other health information exists, few data are as yet available that relate to measurements of MUAC and AMA. In the absence of defined cut-offs for these measurements based on health criteria, an alternative method for developing cut-off points is to relate arm measurements to the BMI of individuals in different populations and then choose circumferential values that are equivalent to the existing BMI cut-off. These circumferential measurements may then be considered as practical alternatives to BMI measurements in field studies where there are instrumental or organizational limitations. In due course, it may also become possible to assess the benefits of combining arm measurements with BMI to provide a more specific index of nutritional status (*64*).

The relationship between MUAC and BMI for groups of adults from eight developing countries, for athletes, and for hospital patients in the USA is illustrated in Figs 62 and 63. The athletes comprised 137 track and field athletes and 63 wrestlers and weightlifters who participated in the 1964 Olympic Games and the 1958 Commonwealth Games (*65*). The hospital patients were receiving aggressive nutritional support for severe protein–energy malnutrition complicating critical illness (Bistrian BR, personal communication). The figures show very close agreement between anthropometric measurements in all communities, with a robust and linear correlation (except for male patients) between MUAC and BMI. Clinical patients present a different pattern, with a lower increase in MUAC for each BMI increment. The eight developing communities show slopes and intercepts reasonably similar to each other but different from those of the athletes and clinical patients. Data for these eight communities were combined to produce an overall regression line, and

Table 46

Classification of BMI classes by mid-upper arm circumference for men in seven developing countries[a]

MUAC (cm)	BMI classes				Row total
	< 16	16-16.99	17-18.49	≥ 18.5	
	n (%)	n (%)	n (%)	n (%)	
< 22.4	141 (88)	64 (43)	70 (21)	41 (2)	316
22.4-23.1	8 (5)	28 (19)	44 (13)	52 (3)	132
23.2-24.3	8 (5)	28 (19)	76 (23)	161 (9)	273
> 24.3	3 (2)	29 (19)	139 (42)	1513 (86)	1684
Column total (%)	160 (100)	149 (100)	329 (100)	1767 (100)	2405

[a] China, India, Mali, Papua New Guinea, Senegal, Somalia, Zimbabwe.

Table 47

Classification of BMI classes by mid-upper arm circumference for women in eight developing countries[a]

MUAC (cm)	BMI classes				Row total
	< 16	16-16.99	17-18.49	≥ 18.5	
	n (%)	n (%)	n (%)	n (%)	
< 21.4	110 (75)	61 (38)	54 (13)	37 (2)	262
21.4-22.1	23 (15)	31 (19)	74 (18)	71 (3)	199
22.2-23.2	10 (7)	43 (27)	118 (29)	188 (8)	359
> 23.2	3 (2)	26 (16)	156 (39)	2060 (87)	2245
Column total (%)	146 (100)	161 (100)	402 (100)	2356 (100)	3065

[a] China, Ethiopia, India, Mali, Papua New Guinea, Senegal, Somalia, Zimbabwe.

the MUAC equivalents of the three BMI cut-offs were derived from this line. The MUAC cut-off values that correspond to the BMI cut-off points are given in Tables 46 and 47. It is apparent that MUAC is a reasonable predictor of BMI for the lowest and highest BMI categories, with over 70% correctly classified; prediction of BMI categories of 16.0-16.99 and 17.0-18.49 from arm measurement, however, is relatively poor.

At cut-offs of 24 cm in men and 23 cm in women, the sensitivity of MUAC for BMI <18.5 was 73% and 74% respectively; corresponding figures for specificity were 86% and 87%, and for positive predictive value 65% and 64%.

From a regression of BMI versus MUAC, it was estimated that the average MUAC is about 24 cm in people with BMI <18.5. It is likely that, at a BMI of less than 18.5, individuals with MUAC greater than 24 cm – a group that probably includes a larger proportion of "thin but healthy people" – will fare better than those with a smaller MUAC.

Unlike the US data, no relationship between MUAC and adult age was found in the communities studied, nor was any relationship seen between MUAC and height.

Limited analysis of the relationship between AMA and BMI in these population groups showed no better correlation than that between BMI and MUAC. Although discrimination between changes in lean and fat tissue may be helpful in assessing an individual's nutritional state, the data suggest that MUAC alone may be as helpful a measure as AMA for general population studies. However, AMC is of greater significance in dealing with individuals in clinical studies, because its reduction is directly related to the severity of disease. Muscle is known to be lost preferentially in infection as amino acids are transferred to visceral

Figure 62

Relationship between mid-upper arm circumference and body mass index in seven groups of adult men from developing countries, one group of athletes, and one group of clinical patients

Note: The overall regression line includes only those from developing countries.

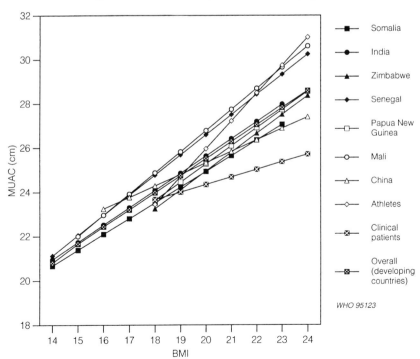

Figure 63

Relationship between mid-upper arm circumference and body mass index in eight groups of adult women from developing countries, and one group of clinical patients

Note: The overall regression line includes only those from developing countries.

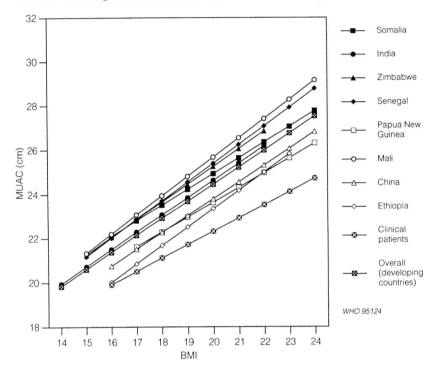

organs to produce acute-phase proteins and to support other functions, such as immune activity. The decline in measured muscle mass can therefore be rapid and profound, and Heymsfield et al. have shown that, if AMA is reduced to 10 cm^2, death invariably occurs in both men and women (66).

In a clinical setting, AMC below the 5th US percentile established by Frisancho (57) (which is approximately 80% of the standard) indicates adult malnutrition (67). The AMC correlates with both serum albumin and percentage weight loss (68, 69); AMA is considered by some to better reflect the volume associated with the mass of skeletal muscle (3), but it relies essentially on the same measurement as AMC. A triceps skinfold thickness of 1–2 mm, a total body fat of 1–3 kg, or a bone-corrected AMA of 9–10 cm^2 are all pointers to imminent death from inanition (3).

8.7.3 *Populations for which the guidelines may not be appropriate*

Male soldiers in the British army show a clear tendency for some weight gain between the ages of 18 and 25 years (56), and this may reflect the final stages of maturation. In enlisted women, however, this weight gain does not occur until about 30 years of age; they are probably unusually active and may also consciously control any weight gain. The NHANES data from the USA (*57*) and other population-representative data on BMI from China (*58*), Cuba (*70*), India (*71*), and Viet Nam (*72*) show that men between the ages of 18 and 25 years have a mean BMI 0.2–1.6 lower than that of men aged 26 to 40 years; at –2 SD, however, the difference is only 0.2–0.7 units. In women aged 18–25 years, the difference in mean BMI from those aged 26–40 years is more variable (0–1.8). Given the difficulty of establishing appropriate limits of BMI in young adults aged 18 to 25 years, particular care is needed to avoid the misclassification of a large proportion of people in this age group as mildly or moderately thin.

Rather than a reduction in the cut-off for grade 1 thinness from 18.5 to 18.0, it is recommended that this age group be examined separately from older cohorts in population studies and results subjected to prudent interpretation. This approach may need revision in the light of further evidence, with the cut-off point being set at a different level.

8.8 Recommendations

8.8.1 *For practical implementation*

For Member States
The new information relating low adult weights to impaired physical capacity, productivity, and health demonstrates the importance of any government's being aware of the range of BMI values within its country. It is therefore recommended that, as part of general surveillance, adult weight and height are routinely measured in health, nutrition, and general community development programmes.

For WHO
WHO should ensure that, in accordance with the recommendation of the FAO/WHO International Conference on Nutrition (Rome, December 1992) to incorporate nutritional objectives in all development programmes, adult anthropometry be included with other measures in such programmes.

8.8.2 *For future research*

Further research is needed in the following areas:

1. To establish more conclusively the validity of BMI cut-off points, by examining the various functional outcomes of low BMI. More precisely, there is a need to document the nature of the relationship between low BMI and immunocompetence as a modulator of susceptibility to infectious diseases and of their severity. Such studies will need to control for confounding factors, notably concomitant micronutrient deficiencies.

2. To assess the value of arm circumference measurement, used alone or in conjunction with BMI, as an indicator of nutritional status and food sufficiency in a community. Such assessment should also address the issue of precision.

3. To evaluate BMI cut-off points for ages 18 to 25 years, for which lower cut-offs may be deemed appropriate.

4. To improve understanding of the effects of low BMI on the composition of lean body mass, e.g. whether the integrity of the mass and composition of lean tissues inevitably compromised by low BMI.

5. To test the usefulness of adult BMI in different settings, especially in populations in which morphotype differs significantly from the norm.

6. To test the usefulness of adult BMI in conjunction with child anthropometry to discriminate between general issues of public health and household food security.

References

1. James WPT, Ferro-Luzzi A, Waterlow JC. Definition of chronic energy deficiency in adults. Report of a working party of the International Dietary Energy Consultative Group. *European journal of clinical nutrition*, 1988, **42**:969-981.

2. Ferro-Luzzi A et al. A simplified approach of assessing adult chronic energy deficiency. *European journal of clinical nutrition*, 1992, **46**:173-186.

3. Heymsfield SB et al. Anthropometric assessment of adult protein-energy malnutrition. In: Wright RA, Heymsfield SB, eds. *Nutritional assessment*. Oxford, Blackwell, 1984:27-82.

4. Immink MDC. Economic effects of chronic energy deficiency: In: Schurch B, Scrimshaw NS, eds. *Chronic energy deficiency: consequences and related issues*. Lausanne, International Dietary Energy Consultative Group, 1987: 153-174.

5. Keys A et al. *The biology of human starvation, Vol. 1*. Minneapolis, University of Minnesota Press, 1950.

6. Gorsky RD, Calloway DH. Activity pattern changes with decrease in food energy intake. *Human biology*, 1983, **55**:577-586.

7. Torún B et al. Energy supplementation and work performance: summary of INCAP studies. In: Kim WA et al., eds. *Proceedings of the XIVth International Congress of Nutrition, Seoul, Korea, August 20-25, 1989*. Seoul, International Union of Nutritional Sciences, 1989:306-309.

8. Bayliss-Smith TP. The integrated analysis of seasonal energy deficits: problems and prospects. *European journal of clinical nutrition*, 1990, **44**(Suppl. 1): 113-121.

9. Shetty PS, Soares MJ, James WPT. Body mass index – its relationship to basal metabolic rates and energy requirements. *European journal of clinical nutrition*, 1994, **48**(Suppl. 3):S28-S38.

10. Satyanarayana K et al. Body size and work output. *American journal of clinical nutrition*, 1977, **30**:322-325.

11. **Desai ID.** Nutritional status and physical work performance of agricultural migrants in southern Brazil. In: Kim WA et al., eds. *Proceedings of the XIVth International Congress on Nutrition, Seoul, Korea, August 20-25, 1989.* Seoul, International Union of Nutritional Sciences, 1989:297-301.

12. **Desai ID et al.** Marginal malnutrition and reduced physical work capacity of migrant adolescent boys in Southern Brazil. *American journal of clinical nutrition*, 1984, **40**:135-145.

13. **Satyanarayana K, Venkataramana Y, Rao SM.** Nutrition and work performance: studies carried out in India. In: Kim WA et al., eds. *Proceedings of the XIVth International Congress on Nutrition, Seoul, Korea, August 20-25, 1989.* Seoul, International Union of Nutritional Sciences, 1989:302-305.

14. **Latham MC.** Nutrition and work performance, energy intakes and human wellbeing in Africa. In: Kim WA et al., eds. *Proceedings of the XIVth International Congress on Nutrition, Seoul, Korea, August 20-25, 1989.* Seoul, International Union of Nutritional Sciences, 1989:314-317.

15. **Spurr GB.** Physical activity, nutritional status and physical work capacity in relation to agricultural production. In: Pollitt E, Amante P, eds. *Energy intake and activity.* New York, Liss, 1984:207-261.

16. **Manson JE et al.** Body weight and longevity. A reassessment. *Journal of the American Medical Association,* 1987, **257**:353-358.

17. *Build and blood pressure study.* Chicago, Society of Actuaries, 1959.

18. **Garrison RT, Castelli WP.** Weight and thirty-year mortality of men in the Framingham Study. *Annals of internal medicine,* 1985, **6**(Pt 2):1006-1009.

19. **Harris T et al.** Body mass index and mortality among nonsmoking older persons. The Framingham Heart Study. *Journal of the American Medical Association*, 1988, **259**:1520-1524.

20. **Lew EA, Garfinkel L.** Variation in mortality by weight among 750 000 men and women. *Journal of chronic disease*, 1979, **32**:563-576.

21. **Rhoads GC, Kagan A.** The relation of coronary disease, stroke, and mortality to weight in youth and in middle age. *Lancet*, 1983, i:492-495.

22. **Sidney S, Friedman GD, Siegelaub AB.** Thinness and mortality. *American journal of public health*, 1987, **77**:317-322.

23. **Linsted K, Tonstad J, Kuzma JW.** Body mass index and patterns of mortality among Seventh-Day Adventist men. *International journal of obesity*, 1991, **15**:397-406.

24. **Marton KI, Sox HC, Krupp JR.** Involuntary weight loss: diagnostic and prognostic significance. *Annals of internal medicine*, 1981, **324**:1839-1844.

25. **Dewys WD et al.** Prognostic effect of weight loss prior to chemotherapy in cancer patients. Eastern Cooperative Oncology Group. *American journal of medicine*, 1980, **69**:491-497.

26. **Studley HO.** Percentage of weight loss. A basic indicator of surgical risk in patients with chronic peptic ulcer. *Journal of the American Medical Association*, 1936, **106**:458-460.

27. **Seltzer MH et al.** Instant nutritional assessment: absolute weight loss and surgical mortality. *Journal of parenteral and enteral nutrition,* 1982, **6**:218-221.

28. Windsor JA, Hill GL. Weight loss with physiologic impairment. A basic indicator of surgical risk. *Annals of surgery*, 1988, **207**:290-296.

29. Henry CJK. Body mass index and the limits of human survival. *European journal of clinical nutrition*, 1990, **44**:329-335.

30. Naidu AN, Rao NP. Body mass index: a measure of the nutritional situation in Indian populations. *European journal of clinical nutrition*, 1994, **48**(Suppl. 3): S131-S140.

31. Weinsier RL et al. Hospital malnutrition. A prospective evaluation of general medical patients during the course of hospitalization. *American journal of clinical nutrition*, 1979, **32**:418-426.

32. Bistrian BR et al. Protein status of general surgical patients. *Journal of the American Medical Association*, 1974, **230**:858-860.

33. Shaver HJ, Loper JA, Lutes RA. Nutritional status of nursing home patients. *Journal of parenteral and enteral nutrition*, 1980, **4**:367-370.

34. Reinhardt GF et al. Incidence and mortality of hypoalbuminemic patients in hospitalized veterans. *Journal of parenteral and enteral nutrition*, 1980, **4**:357-359.

35. Willard MD, Gilsdorf RB, Price RA. Protein-calorie malnutrition in a community hospital. *Journal of the American Medical Association*, 1980, **243**:1720-1722.

36. Fischer JE, Ghory MJ. Protein depletion and immunity in the hospitalized patient. In: Wright RA, Heymsfield S, eds. *Nutritional assessment.* Oxford, Blackwell, 1984:111-129.

37. Pryer J. Body mass index and work disabling morbidity: results from a Bangladeshi case study. *European journal of clinical nutrition*, 1993, **47**:653-657.

38. de Vasconcellos MTL. Body mass index: its relationship with food consumption and socioeconomic variables in Brazil. *European journal of clinical nutrition*, 1994, **48**(Suppl. 3):S115-S123.

39. Keys A et al. Indices of relative weight and obesity. *Journal of chronic diseases,* 1972, **25**:329-343.

40. Pheasant S. *Body space: anthropometry, ergonomics and design.* London, Taylor & Frances, 1986.

41. Norgan NG. Population differences in body composition in relation to BMI. *European journal of clinical nutrition*, 1994, **48**(Suppl. 3):S10-S27.

42. Lee J, Kolonel LN, Hinds MW. Relative merits of the weight-corrected-for-height indices. *American journal of clinical nutrition*, 1981, **34**:2521-2529.

43. Mendez J, Buskirk ER. Creatinine-height index. *American journal of clinical nutrition*, 1971, **24**:385-386.

44. Forbes GB. Lean body mass-body fat interrelationship in humans. *Nutrition reviews*, 1987, **45**:225-231.

45. Ferro-Luzzi A, Branca F, Pastore G. Body mass index defines the risk of seasonal energy stress in the Third World. *European journal of clinical nutrition*, 1994, **48**(Suppl. 3):S165-S178.

46. Norgan NG. Body mass index and body energy stores in developing countries. *European journal of clinical nutrition*, 1990, **44**(Suppl. 1):79-84.

47. Lopes J et al. Skeletal muscle function in malnutrition. *American journal of clinical nutrition*, 1982, **36**:602–610.

48. Hill GL et al. Malnutrition in surgical patients. An unrecognised problem. *Lancet*, 1977, **i**:689–692.

49. Kotler DP, Wang J, Pierson RN. Body composition studies in patients with the acquired immunodeficiency syndrome. *American journal of clinical nutrition*, 1985, **42**:1255–1265.

50. Buzby GP, Mullen JL. Analysis of nutritional assessment indices. Prognostic equations and cluster analysis. In: Wright RA, Heymsfield S, eds. *Nutritional assessment.* Oxford, Blackwell, 1984:141–155.

51. Bistrian BR. Nutritional assessment of the hospitalized patient: a practical approach. In: Wright RA, Heymsfield S, eds. *Nutritional assessment.* Oxford, Blackwell, 1984:183–205.

52. Russell D et al. A comparison between muscle function and body composition in anorexia nervosa: the effect of refeeding. *American journal of clinical nutrition*, 1983, **38**:229–237.

53. Shetty PS, James WPT. *Body mass index: a measure of chronic energy deficiency in adults.* Rome, Food and Agriculture Organization of the United Nations, 1994 (Food and Nutrition Paper No. 56).

54. Tremblay A. Human obesity: a defect in lipid oxidation or in thermogenesis? *International journal of obesity, 1992,* **16**:953–957.

55. Dreon DM et al. Dietary fat: carbohydrate ratio and obesity in middle-aged men. *American journal of clinical nutrition.* 1988, **47**:995–1000.

56. Durning JVGA, McKay FC, Webster CI. *A new method of assessing fatness and desirable weight for use in the Armed Services.* Unrestricted report to Army Department, Ministry of Defence, United Kingdom, 1984.

57. Frisancho AR. *Anthropometric standards for the assessment of growth and nutritional status.* Ann Arbor, University of Michigan Press, 1990.

58. Ge K et al. The body mass index of Chinese adults in the 1980s. *European journal of clinical nutrition*, 1994, **48**(Suppl. 3):S148–S154.

59. James WPT, Ralph A, eds. The functional significance of low body mass index. *European journal of clinical nutrition*, 1994, 48(Suppl. 3): 1–190.

60. Bistrian BR. Interaction of nutrition and infection in the hospital setting. *American journal of clinical nutrition*, 1977, **30**:1228–1235.

61. Harvey KB et al. Biological measures for the formulation of a hospital prognostic index. *American journal of clinical nutrition*, 1981, **34**:2013–2022.

62. Mullen JL et al. Implications of malnutrition in the surgical patient. *Archives of surgery*, 1979, **114**:121–125.

63. Forbes GB et al. Deliberate overfeeding in women and men: energy cost and composition of the weight gain. *British journal of nutrition*, 1986, **56**:1–9.

64. James WPT et al. The value of arm circumference measurements in assessing chronic energy deficiency in Third World adults. *European journal of clinical nutrition* 1994, **48**:883–894.

65. Tanner JM. *The physique of the Olympic athlete.* London, Allen & Unwin, 1964.

66. Heymsfield SB et al. Anthropometric measurement of muscle mass: revised equations for calculating bone-free arm muscle area. *American journal of clinical nutrition*, 1982, **36**:680–690.

67. Bistrian BR. Anthropometric norms used in assessment of hospitalized patients. *American journal of clinical nutrition*, 1980, **33**:2211-2214.

68. Bistrian BR et al. Prevalence of malnutrition in general medical patients. *Journal of the American Medical Association*, 1976, **235**:1567-1570.

69. Young GA, Hill GL. Assessment of protein-calorie malnutrition in surgical patients from plasma proteins and anthropometric measurements. *American journal of clinical nutrition*, 1987, **31**:429-435.

70. Berdasco A. Body mass index values in the Cuban adult population. *European journal of clinical nutrition*, 1994, **48**(Suppl. 3):S155-S164.

71. *India data derived from output tables of a contract between FAO and the National Institute of Nutrition.* Hyderabad, National Institute of Nutrition, 1991.

72. Giay T, Khoi HH. The use of body mass index in the assessment of adult nutritional status in Vietnam. *European journal of clinical nutrition*, 1994, **48**(Suppl. 3):S124-S130.

9. **Adults 60 years of age and older**

9.1 Introduction

9.1.1 *Background*

The demographic situation

For the purposes of this report, the term "elderly" is applied to those aged 60 years and over, who represent the fastest-growing segment of populations throughout the world. In developing countries, the percentage of elderly tends to be small although the absolute numbers are often large: in 1990 there were more than 280 million people aged 60 or over – 58% of the world's elderly – living in less developed regions. The proportion of elderly is rising more rapidly in developing countries than in developed ones; by the year 2020 it is expected that almost 70% of the world's elderly people will be in developing countries, with the absolute number exceeding 700 million compared with 318 million in the more developed regions (*1*). Factors responsible for this changing pattern of population aging include a rapid decline in both fertility and premature mortality (*2*). Declining fertility is particularly apparent in some developing countries such as China, Cuba, and Uruguay, although fertility levels in others such as Bangladesh, Kenya, and Zaire remain high (*3*).

A clear example of population aging is provided by China. Since the founding of the People's Republic of China in 1949, the average life span of the Chinese has increased from 35 to 70 years. A rapid decline in fertility in the past 10 to 15 years has resulted in a large reduction in the proportion of the population under 15 years in addition to the large increase in the numbers of elderly (*4*). Within the older population, the numbers over 80 years of age are increasing the most rapidly and will grow significantly faster than numbers of those between 60 and 70 years during the next few decades.

Other demographic changes that accompany population aging are sex differences in longevity, urbanization, and the composition of the labour force. In most countries, older women outnumber older men and the percentage of women in each age group is steadily increasing. The urbanization that has been an important trend in the past half-century has seen the migration of younger people from rural areas to cities, resulting not only in larger urban populations but also a disproportionately older population in rural areas, especially in developing countries. In developing countries without a compulsory retirement age, people continue to work past the age of 60 or 65 years. With increasing industrialization, however, this is likely to change as workers shift from agricultural activities to industrial production and service occupations (*3*).

The demographic characteristics of the elderly themselves are also likely to be different in the future from what they are at present. The changes that take place will have an enormous impact on health services demanded and provided in all countries, but especially in developing countries, where economic development is uneven and resources are more limited than in industrialized nations.

Anthropometry and aging
Height. Decline in height with age has been noted in studies throughout the world (5). The rate of decline is 1–2 cm/decade and more rapid at older ages (6). It is particularly apparent in sitting height and is the result of vertebral compression, change in height and shape of the vertebral discs, loss of muscle tone, and postural changes. Results of cross-sectional studies may be confounded by the secular increases in height among younger cohorts in industrialized countries and in some developing countries (7): older cohorts have a lower mean stature by comparison with younger cohorts, in addition to the real physical loss in stature evident in longitudinal studies. In Japan, where there has been a large increase in average stature since 1947, this effect is seen particularly clearly. Height-related differences in survival rates may also affect results of cross-sectional studies but this remains to be investigated further. A longitudinal study of 70-year-olds in Gothenburg, Sweden (6), studied serial changes in height, weight, and BMI for the age interval 70 to 82

Table 48
Longitudinal changes in height, body weight, and body mass index of men and women aged 70–82 years[a]

Age (years)	Women ($n = 172$)			Men ($n = 110$)		
	Height (cm)	Weight (kg)	Body mass index	Height (cm)	Weight (kg)	Body mass index
70	160.2 ± 5.7	66.9 ± 10.5	26.1 ± 3.9	174.8 ± 6.5	79.4 ± 9.6	26.0 ± 2.9
	$p < 0.001$	$p < 0.001$	$p < 0.05$	$p < 0.001$	$p < 0.001$	not significant
75	159.3 ± 5.6	65.4 ± 10.3	25.8 ± 4.0	173.4 ± 6.5	77.5 ± 10.0	25.8 ± 3.1
	$p < 0.001$	$p < 0.001$	not significant	$p < 0.001$	$p < 0.001$	$p < 0.05$
79	158.3 ± 5.7	64.0 ± 10.6	25.5 ± 4.0	172.8 ± 6.5	76.0 ± 10.3	25.5 ± 3.3
	$p < 0.01$	not significant	not significant	not significant	$p < 0.001$	$p < 0.001$
81	158.0 ± 5.9	63.7 ± 11.0	25.5 ± 4.4	172.8 ± 6.4	74.6 ± 10.3	25.0 ± 3.3
	$p < 0.001$	$p < 0.001$	$p < 0.01$	$p < 0.001$	not significant	not significant
82	157.7 ± 5.8	62.7 ± 10.7	25.2 ± 4.2	172.4 ± 6.5	74.4 ± 10.0	25.0 ± 3.2

[a] Reproduced from reference 6 with the permission of Food & Nutrition Press Inc., Trumbull, CT, USA.

years; results are given in Table 48. This type of change, however, may vary from population to population depending upon various environmental and genetic factors.

Weight. Weight also declines with age, but the pattern of change is quite different from that of height and varies by sex (5). In affluent countries, the average weight of both men and women increases through middle age. Weight gains in men tend to plateau at around 65 years and weight generally declines thereafter; in women, however, the weight increases are frequently greater and the plateau occurs about 10 years later than in men. In non-European indigenous populations, such as Australian Aborigines, the increase in average weight in the middle years is not evident, but the decline at older ages is. Data on underprivileged populations are limited.

Body weight varies not only among individuals but also within a given individual during aging. Reduction in body water content has been reported as an important cause of decline in weight after 65 years, and was decribed in a Swedish longitudinal study of a small number of 70-year-olds (8). Changes accompanying the weight loss include a decline in muscle cell mass, and in cell mass in general, which is more pronounced in men.

Body mass index. Like weight, average body mass index in industrialized populations tends to increase in middle age and stabilizes somewhat earlier in men than in women. In men, the plateau may begin at 50-60 years or even at 70 years of age; in women it starts at 70 years or later. Both sexes generally show a decrease in average BMI after 70-75 years of age (5, 9, 10).

These trends have been observed in Europeans and populations of European ancestry, but may vary with environmental and genetic factors among different ethnic groups. The relationship between BMI and fat and muscle mass changes with age. Data from NHANES I and II have shown that BMI is more highly correlated with subcutaneous fat (estimated by subscapular skinfold) in younger than in older men and women, and with muscle mass in older than in younger adults (11). Thus, a young person with a high BMI is likely to have more subcutaneous fat than a person with a relatively low BMI value. However, BMI may have different significance in elderly individuals and young adults, because of the reduction in height with age, and it is uncertain whether current height or young adult height is the better for deriving this index.

It should be emphasized that BMI may not decline with age; indeed, it may be higher at age 70 and above than at younger ages because of the age-related changes in both height and weight and morphological changes in the vertebral column that result from osteopenia and increased curvature. Morphological changes in the spine influence mobility, balance, and sometimes also respiration. With extensive vertebral changes, height measurement cannot be accurate and has little value.

Body composition. Significant changes in fat-free mass and patterns of fat distribution occur with aging. Cross-sectional studies show a slow, progressive redistribution of fat in the elderly, with subcutaneous fat on the limbs tending to decrease and intra-abdominal fat to increase. The former is reflected in a decline in calf, thigh, triceps, and biceps skinfolds (*5, 12*) and the latter by an increase in abdomen:hip circumference ratio (AHR). Women accumulate more subcutaneous fat than men and lose it at a later age (*5*). Computed tomography scans have shown that fat weight is similar in middle-aged and older men but that there is less subcutaneous fat and significantly more intra-abdominal fat in older men (*13*). The same investigators also reported more fat between and within muscles in older men.

The Baltimore Longitudinal Study of Aging in the USA measures a large sample of volunteer adults every 2 years. A number of indices have been computed, including the ratio of subscapular skinfold to triceps skinfold; this index compares subcutaneous fat at a trunk site with that at an extremity site. There are large sex differences in the ratio, which is greater for men at all ages than for women, and increases with age in men but not in women (*14*).

Using underwater weighing of 200 healthy Swedish men and women aged 45–78 years, Bjorntorp & Evans (*15*) reported changes in the percentage of weight that is represented by body fat. At 45–49 years, men averaged 25% fat; this seemed to stabilize at 38% at age 60–65 years. Women had more body fat than men at 45–49 years (30%) and stabilized at an average of 43% at 55–59 years. Between 60 and 78, neither men nor women showed much change in percentage body fat.

9.1.2 *Population variation in anthropometry*

Child growth and maturation vary significantly among populations, and these early differences are not diminished in adult populations, which may be even more heterogeneous (*7*). In any given population, individual variation is also increased because of variable rates of aging from person to person and from physiological system to physiological system within the same individual. The broad heterogeneity of the elderly must therefore be taken into consideration in any study of this segment of the population.

Data from various elderly populations throughout the world have been compared (see Table 49) to examine the distribution of anthropometric parameters (*16*).[1] The variation in sex-specific distribution by geographical region/ethnic group, age, and health status was investigated. Analysis of height-for-age in 19 studies with adequate population data revealed wide geographical and ethnic differences. Of those aged 70–79

---

[1] Much of the material published in reference *16* represents background work originally undertaken for the purposes of the Expert Committee meeting.

years, Guatemalans had the lowest mean height and Americans (USA), Dutch, and Swedes the highest. Height decreased with age in all populations; differences ranged from 1.9 to 6.7 cm in men and from 2.0 to 6.0 cm in women. See Table 50.

The listed populations showed a decrease in BMI with increasing age (see Table 51). In most populations, BMI is greater in women than in men, and the distribution by age groups shifts to the left, especially in

Table 49
Sample characteristics of study sites included in analysis of elderly populations[a]

Original study	Location and/or population		Age range (years)	Sample size
Brazilian National Survey of Health and Nutrition, 1989	Brazil	national sample	60–108	4419
Nutritional Assessment of Guatemalan Ambulatory Elderly	Guatemala	one rural location	60–103	202
Longitudinal Study of Health and Social Support in the Hong Kong Chinese Elderly Cohort	Hong Kong		70–100	977
Nutrition in Old Age in Italy	Italy	17 locations	60–97	921
Italian Nutrition Examination Survey of the Elderly (INESE)	Italy	five locations	65–95	1248
Survey of Health and Living Status of the Elderly in Taiwan, 1989	China (Province of Taiwan) national sample		60–97	3818[b]
Established Populations for Epidemiologic Studies of the Elderly (EPESE)	USA	East Boston Iowa	65–90+	3164[b] 3647
NHANES I Epidemiologic Follow-up Study (NCHS-US)	USA	national sample	60–86	3695
IUNS Study of Food Habits in Later Life	Australia	Anglo-Australians Greek descent	60–79 70–104	111 186
	China	Beijing Tianjin	60–95 70–96	264 441
	Greece	Sparta	70–94	70
	Sweden	Johanneberg	69–91	204
Chinese Nationwide Nutrition Survey	China	national sample	60–94	1764
Melbourne Chinese Health Study	Australia	Chinese descent	60–80	68
Rotterdam Elderly Study	Netherlands	Rotterdam	60–103	3752
Mini-Finland Health Survey	Finland	national sample	60–90 +	2126

[a] Reproduced from reference 16 with permission.
[b] Self-reported weight and height.

Table 50

Mean and standard deviation of height (in cm) by age group and geographical location[a]

Location	Age group (years) 60–69	70–79	≥ 80
Men			
Australia (Anglo-Australians)	168.2 ± 10.0[b]	164.0 ± 10.0	–
Australia (Chinese descent)	162.8 ± 5.3[b]	165.0 ± 7.5[b]	–
Australia (Greek descent)	–	165.2 ± 6.4[c]	163.3 ± 6.7
Brazil	165.0 ± 11.0	163.0 ± 10.0	162.0 ± 8.2
China (Beijing)	161.8 ± 4.4	161.6 ± 3.9	–
China (nationwide)	162.1 ± 6.7	160.8 ± 7.7	155.4 ± 6.8[b]
China (Province of Taiwan)	165.6 ± 7.1	164.9 ± 8.6	165.2 ± 8.9
China (Tianjin)	–	166.0 ± 6.0	164.2 ± 6.2
Finland	169.7 ± 11.9	168.7 ± 6.2	167.4 ± 6.4
Greece (Sparta)	–	165.9 ± 6.2	165.9 ± 6.4[b]
Guatemala (rural area)	155.1 ± 5.2	156.0 ± 5.7	153.2 ± 6.8[b]
Hong Kong	–	161.9 ± 6.0	161.7 ± 8.0
Italy (5 locations)	165.5 ± 6.1[d]	164.3 ± 6.7	161.8 ± 6.3
Italy (17 locations)	164.0 ± 7.4	162.2 ± 6.7	160.1 ± 6.8
Netherlands (Rotterdam)	175.1 ± 6.4	172.6 ± 6.4	170.8 ± 7.3
Sweden	–	174.1 ± 5.7	172.9 ± 5.0[b]
USA (East Boston)	170.4 ± 7.9[d]	167.6 ± 7.3	166.9 ± 7.3
USA (Iowa)	176.0 ± 6.6	175.3 ± 6.8	175.0 ± 7.6
USA (national sample)	174.0 ± 6.7	172.0 ± 6.6	170.6 ± 6.6
Women			
Australia (Anglo-Australians)	165.3 ± 8.6	166.4 ± 8.0	–
Australia (Greek descent)	–	149.9 ± 5.3	148.6 ± 6.0
Brazil	152.0 ± 7.4	150.0 ± 7.9	149.0 ± 8.9
China (Beijing)	156.0 ± 4.4	154.6 ± 3.8	–
China (nationwide)	150.6 ± 6.1	148.3 ± 6.3	146.3 ± 7.3
China (Province of Taiwan)	154.8 ± 5.9	153.9 ± 6.1	153.1 ± 5.8
China (Tianjin)	–	152.8 ± 5.9	150.4 ± 6.3
Finland	157.0 ± 5.7	154.7 ± 5.7	153.0 ± 6.3

Table 50 (*continued*)

Location	Age group (years)		
	60-69	70-79	≥ 80
Women (*continued*)			
Guatemala (rural area)	142.9 ± 6.2	139.7 ± 6.6	139.6 ± 5.5[b]
Hong Kong	–	148.4 ± 6.4	145.6 ± 7.2
Italy (5 locations)	153.2 ± 6.3[d]	151.4 ± 6.1	150.6 ± 7.0
Italy (17 locations)	152.5 ± 6.7	150.5 ± 6.5	147.5 ± 6.9
Netherlands (Rotterdam)	163.0 ± 6.2	159.4 ± 6.6	157.2 ± 6.2
Sweden	–	161.1 ± 1.8	157.9 ± 5.6
USA (East Boston)	157.7 ± 6.6[d]	157.2 ± 6.6	156.2 ± 7.8
USA (Iowa)	161.8 ± 6.1[d]	161.3 ± 6.6	161.3 ± 6.5
USA (national sample)	160.6 ± 5.9	159.1 ± 6.0	158.4 ± 5.9

[a] Reproduced from reference *16* with permission.
[b] Sample size < 25.
[c] Age group 74-79 years.
[d] Age group 65-69 years.

Table 51
Mean and standard deviation of body mass index by age group and geographical location[a]

Location	Age group (years)		
	60-69	70-79	≥ 80
Men			
Australia (Anglo-Australians)	27.7 ± 4.3[b]	26.6 ± 3.4	–
Australia (Chinese descent)	22.5 ± 2.8	22.9 ± 2.7	–
Australia (Greek descent)	–	28.0 ± 3.6[c]	27.0 ± 3.7
Brazil	23.7 ± 5.4	22.9 ± 5.0	22.4 ± 4.1
China (Beijing)	25.5 ± 3.9	24.2 ± 3.5	–
China (nationwide)	20.8 ± 3.0	21.7 ± 3.9	20.9 ± 2.6[b]
China (Province of Taiwan)	23.0 ± 3.7	22.5 ± 3.9	22.6 ± 4.6
China (Tianjin)	–	22.2 ± 3.3	21.0 ± 3.8
Finland	26.0 ± 3.7	25.6 ± 3.7	24.3 ± 3.9
Greece (Sparta)	–	27.4 ± 4.4	25.2 ± 2.9[b]
Guatemala (rural area)	21.3 ± 2.6	20.2 ± 2.2	19.6 ± 2.3

Table 51 (continued)

Location	Age group (years)		
	60-69	70-79	≥ 80
Men (continued)			
Hong Kong	–	21.2 ± 3.4	20.6 ± 4.2
Italy (5 locations)	26.9 ± 3.7[d]	26.5 ± 3.8	25.1 ± 3.6
Italy (17 locations)	26.6 ± 4.6	25.5 ± 4.3	25.1 ± 3.7
Netherlands (Rotterdam)	25.9 ± 2.9	25.8 ± 3.3	24.9 ± 3.4
Sweden	–	25.3 ± 3.2	24.8 ± 3.3
USA (East Boston)	26.8 ± 4.2[d]	26.4 ± 4.2	25.0 ± 4.1
USA (Iowa)	26.2 ± 3.6[d]	25.6 ± 3.7	23.9 ± 3.3
USA (national sample)	26.4 ± 4.0	25.6 ± 3.7	24.6 ± 3.8
Women			
Australia (Anglo-Australians)	26.1 ± 5.0	25.6 ± 3.0	–
Australia (Greek descent)	–	30.7 ± 5.1	27.8 ± 6.1
Brazil	25.8 ± 6.7	25.0 ± 7.4	23.9 ± 4.9
China (Beijing)	25.5 ± 5.3	23.0 ± 3.5	–
China (nationwide)	21.7 ± 3.9	20.7 ± 3.6	19.6 ± 3.1
China (Province of Taiwan)	23.4 ± 3.8	22.9 ± 3.9	21.8 ± 4.7
China (Tianjin)	–	22.1 ± 4.1	21.5 ± 4.3
Finland	27.8 ± 4.5	26.8 ± 4.5	25.6 ± 4.0
Guatemala (rural area)	22.4 ± 3.3	21.4 ± 4.4	20.7 ± 4.1[b]
Hong Kong	–	22.4 ± 4.0	20.9 ± 3.6
Italy (5 locations)	29.0 ± 5.0[d]	28.4 ± 5.3	26.6 ± 4.7
Italy (17 locations)	28.6 ± 4.5	28.5 ± 5.4	26.9 ± 5.0
Netherlands (Rotterdam)	26.8 ± 4.1	27.1 ± 4.3	27.0 ± 4.2
Sweden	–	24.1 ± 4.4	23.9 ± 4.0
USA (East Boston)	27.7 ± 5.7[d]	27.4 ± 5.5	25.5 ± 5.4
USA (Iowa)	26.1 ± 4.5[d]	25.2 ± 4.4	22.8 ± 4.0
USA (national sample)	26.5 ± 5.3	25.7 ± 4.9	24.5 ± 5.0

[a] Reproduced from reference 16 with permission.
[b] Sample size < 25.
[c] Age group 74-79 years.
[d] Age group 65-69 years.

women (see Fig. 64). If height is unchanged, a decrease in BMI reflects mostly a decrease in body weight; however, when height also decreases, as it does in the elderly, changes in BMI are smaller than they would be in younger age groups with stable height.

Body mass index varies widely among elderly populations (Table 51). Among men there appear to be two clusters, with samples from Central and South America and of individuals of Chinese descent having considerably lower BMI than others. Women appear to fall into three clusters: the lowest BMI values were among those of Chinese origin (in most studies) and in rural Guatemala, the next highest values were in Brazil, northern Europe, and the USA, and among Anglo-Australians, and highest values occurred among Australians of Greek origin.

Among the 19 studies considered, plus some additional data from Japan and the Philippines, differences were found in the prevalence of thinness (BMI <18.5) and overweight (BMI ≥30) (see Fig. 64). Prevalence of thinness in 70–79-year-old men ranged from 0% (in Anglo-Australians, Australians of Greek descent, Greeks in Sparta, and Swedes) to 18% (Japanese). Among women of the same age group the range was 0% (Anglo-Australians, Australians of Greek descent, Greeks in Sparta) to 28% (Filipinos in Manila). A similar pattern of increase with age in the prevalence of thinness in both men and women was evident in the majority of studies.

Most studies show that the distribution of BMI among those reporting poor health extends further to the left than it does among those reporting very good/excellent health. However, some studies show considerable overlap in the left-hand side of the distributions of those reporting poor health and those reporting excellent health. In national surveys in Italy and the USA, the BMI distribution of those reporting poor health also extends further to the right than those in the other groups. In contrast, in the Hong Kong study, the distribution of those reporting excellent health extends further to the right than those in the other groups (Fig. 65).

9.1.3 *Anthropometry as an indicator of nutritional and health status*

Anthropometric characteristics of individuals and populations are simple and strong predictors of future ill health, functional impairment, and mortality; in turn, they may be modified by disease. For these reasons, anthropometric data are used in many contexts to screen for or monitor disease. In the elderly, however, anthropometry is a relatively new tool and thus difficult to evaluate. The comparative analysis of world populations discussed above suggests that the predictive power of anthropometric indicators relative to a specific outcome is likely to vary with a number of factors such as age-related biological changes, illness, secular changes, childhood diseases, lifelong practices (smoking, diet, exercise), and socioeconomic factors.

Figure 64
Distribution of body mass index

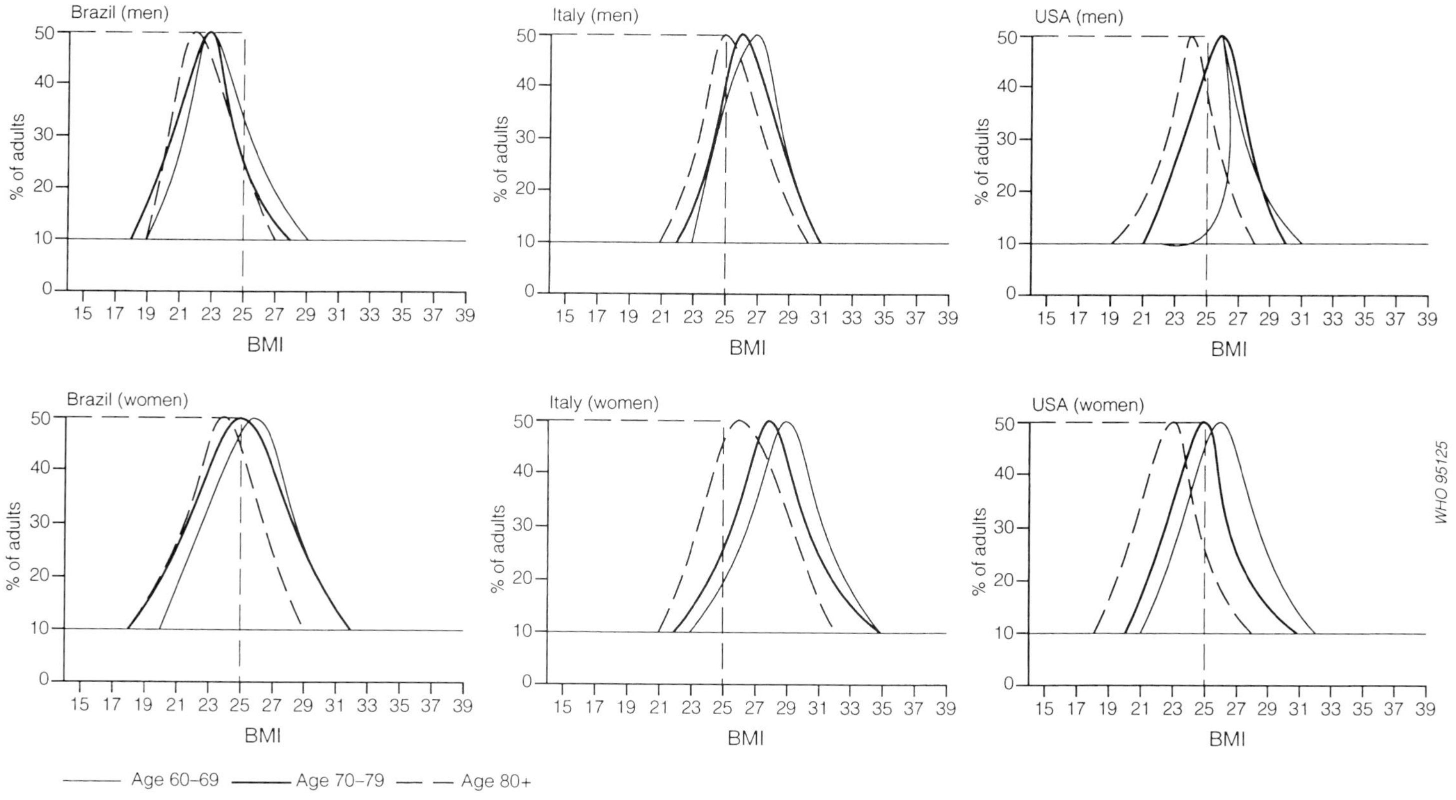

WHO 95125

Age 60–69 ——— Age 70–79 ——— Age 80+

Figure 65

Distribution of body mass index by self-reported health status

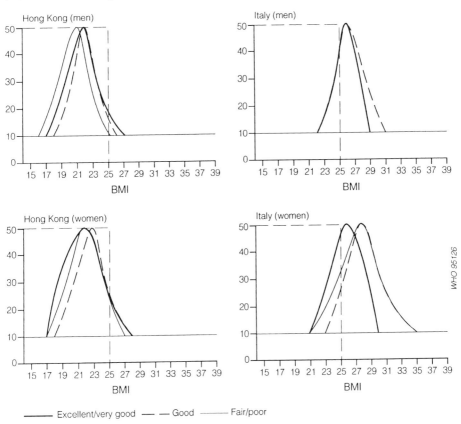

——— Excellent/very good — — Good ———— Fair/poor

Among middle-aged adults (50-65 years) overweight is an important public health problem in many countries and in some the combined prevalence of grade 2 and 3 overweight (BMI ≥30) (see section 7) is as high as 40%. For individuals over 65 years of age the health risk of overweight is unclear; in fact, population data indicate that moderate overweight at older ages is associated with lower mortality (*17*). Among those older than 80 years, thinness and loss of lean body mass may be a more significant problem than overweight. Whether a high abdomen:hip ratio is a risk factor among the elderly is unclear.

Evidence from both acute and chronic illness, as well as from starvation studies, indicates that both lean and fat body mass play a role in determining health status and outcome. Lean body mass is the single most important predictor of survival in critical illness (*18*), and is a significant predictor of outcome in malignancy, AIDS, and some acute illnesses. Data collected by physicians in the Warsaw ghetto during the Second World War have shown that, in starvation, loss of more than 40% of baseline lean body mass is fatal. This same critical figure seems to apply also to AIDS and to normal aging (*19*). The physiological basis for this limit is not clear, but presumably a substantial loss of lean mass reduces body cell mass below the minimum level necessary to maintain physiological function. Current data also indicate that nutritional therapy in illness affords important physiological benefits long before there is measurable improvement in lean body mass, but that return to normal physiological function is not achieved until body composition begins to normalize. These research findings reinforce the argument for applying anthropometry to clinical situations. It should also be noted that serum albumin level is an important predictor of survival in healthy ambulatory adults, even within the normal range of 3.5 to 5.0 g/dl (20).

In contrast, there appears to be no benefit in maintaining fat mass except as an energy reserve during times of nutritional privation. The importance of fat mass lies in the risks it confers for the development of chronic diseases. This, too, underlines the value of estimating fat mass separately from lean mass, in order to classify individuals with respect to health risks and the need for intervention.

Height, weight, and BMI are good indicators for risk of morbidity and mortality, at least in young and middle-aged adults. In Norway, Waaler (9, 10) looked at the relationship between mortality and these variables in a sample of nearly 1.7 million individuals. A strong negative association was noted between height and all-cause mortality, with higher mortality in shorter individuals; this may be a reflection of socioeconomic influences earlier in life. The relationship between BMI and all-cause mortality was U-shaped (see Fig. 66). It should be noted that BMI declined after 70 years and that this cohort and older ones represent survivors. Causes of death associated with low BMI are tuberculosis, obstructive lung disease, and cancer of the lung and stomach; those associated with high BMI are cerebrovascular disease, cardiovascular disease, diabetes, and, in men, colon cancer. In the majority of the elderly, the nadir of the curve was at 21–27 and 23–27 for men and women, respectively.

A U-shaped relationship between BMI and mortality has also been reported for Finnish men (21). Lowest mortality occurred at a somewhat higher BMI among men over 75 years of age than among younger men, but the curve showed excess mortality at the tails of the distribution. Among thin men mortality from cardiovascular causes increased with BMI in the younger cohorts but not in those aged 55–90. A U-shaped relationship between BMI and mortality was also apparent in young women, but was more uncertain for older women, who showed little variation in mortality with BMI. Overweight did not reduce life expectancy in Finnish women aged 65–79 years (22); indeed, a modest degree of overweight seemed to be protective against death. The most favourable BMI was 27–31, a considerably higher figure than was found in Norway.

A follow-up study in Finland of 95 men and 431 women over 85 years of age showed that low BMI was a more important predictor of risk of death than high BMI (*23*). Highest 5-year mortality was reported in the group with BMI <20.0 and the lowest in the group with BMI >30.0. It was concluded that overweight ceases to be a risk factor for death in this age group.

Figure 66
Relationship between 10-year mortality and body mass index in different age groups[a]

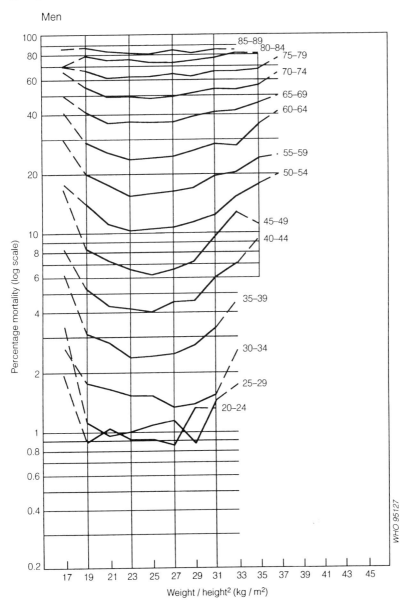

Men

^a Reproduced from reference 9 with the permission of the publisher.

387

Figure 66 (*continued*)

Women

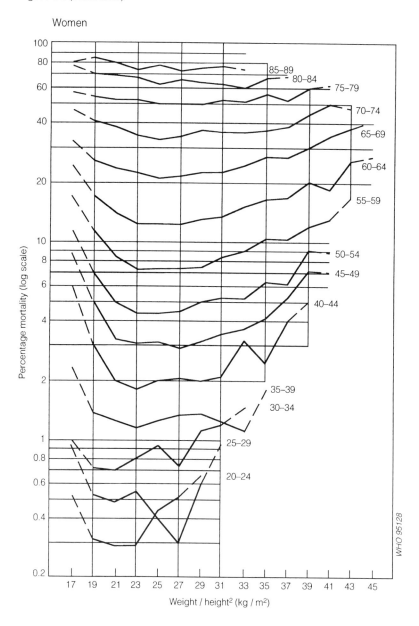

Similar results from a follow-up to the NHANES I in the USA revealed that the moderate additional risk of death associated with weight apparent in older men was not apparent in older women (*24*). When analysis was controlled for poverty, smoking, and elevated blood pressure, high BMI was associated with somewhat increased mortality risk in white men and no increased risk in white women. Other analyses of these data suggested that, compared with older people of moderate BMI, heavier and very thin white women and non-smoking white men were at increased risk of death (*25*). In the Framingham Heart Study in the USA, there was a positive relationship between BMI and mortality in non-smoking men and women over 65 years of age in follow-up studies of from 1 to 23 years (*26*). Survival was lower among individuals in the 70th percentile for BMI (28.5 for men, 28.7 for women) than among thinner individuals with moderate BMI. Those who were overweight at 65 but not at 55 years of age were at lower risk of death than those who gained 0–9% BMI, and those who lost 10% of BMI were at almost twice the risk.

Both overweight and thinness appear to carry risk for mortality, but in the elderly thinness carries a greater risk than overweight. Weight change, especially involuntary weight loss, also poses considerable risk, which may interfere with the interpretation of the data from large studies.

9.1.4 *Interpretation issues in the elderly*

Menopause is an aging phenomenon that influences women's health and is often accompanied by an increase in weight and adiposity. However, the median age of menopause varies among populations. In a randomly sampled group of women in Massachusetts, USA, it was 51 years (*27*), which is also the approximate mean age among European women. There are sparse data from other regions, which show a mean age of 42 years among Mayans and of 46–47 years among uneducated, rural Javanese (*28*).

Differences between young people and the elderly in the relationships between weight and other variables are due, in part, to the influence on body size and fatness of the normal physiological effects of aging, such as loss of height, osteoporosis, changes in the amount and distribution of subcutaneous adipose tissue, and alterations in tissue elasticity and compressibility. There is a considerable lack of understanding of the functional and health-related implications of anthropometric indicators in older people. Moreover, the redistribution of body fat from the extremities to visceral areas in the elderly hampers the adequate estimation of body composition when anthropometric models based on younger adults are applied. Data derived from magnetic resonance imaging or computerized tomographic scanning of the elderly reveal not only a progressive redistribution of fat from the extremities to the visceral area but also the replacement of muscle tissue by intramuscular fat (*29*); this is not reflected in anthropometric measurements of subcutaneous fat. It should therefore be kept in mind that use of anthropometry in the elderly may well result in underestimation of body fat, and that this phenomenon is absent from the young healthy reference population so often used to validate scientific methodology. The use of anthropometric techniques in older adults must be validated on individuals of the appropriate ages. It is unlikely that present methods can avoid this bias.

Traditional measurements of body size may also fail to provide adequate estimates of nutritional status or the effects of nutritional intervention in the elderly. For example, an increase in abdominal circumference with age may reflect shortening of the trunk due to osteoporosis or other spinal deformities: as the length of the trunk decreases, the abdomen increases in girth. In elderly women, there is a significant negative correlation between abdominal circumference and sitting height (30).

On retirement, men in developed countries tend to spend an increasing amount of time in sedentary activities (31), which may explain some of the age-related loss of fat-free mass. A significant negative correlation between age and calf circumference is noted in elderly men, but not in women, and may be due to general loss of muscle in response to the reported greater reduction in physical activity among men than women. Calf circumference is considered the most sensitive measure of muscle mass in the elderly.

A number of intrinsic limitations are common to the use of anthropometry in all age groups; these include the effect of body fluid changes on weight, skinfolds, and circumferences, and the inability of sick people to stand for height measurements. In the elderly, there are certain additional constraints, such as the difficulty of obtaining measurements of weight, height, and other anthropometric variables when a large proportion of the population of interest is unable to walk or stand. From a clinical standpoint, however, the elderly are often the most important target population for intervention. Surrogate measures, such as knee height or arm span, have therefore been developed for use with bed-fast or chair-fast individuals (see section 9.4). In addition, problems in the interpretation of anthropometric data in the elderly may arise from selective survivorship in cross-sectional studies.

9.2 Using anthropometry in individuals

There is a lack of agreement on the clinical usefulness of anthropometry in the elderly for prognosis and for evaluating response to treatment. In individuals who are not in ideal health, and especially elderly individuals, anthropometry suffers from several limitations, in both application of the methods and interpretation of the results. Age-related changes in height should be taken into consideration when metabolic, circulatory, endocrine, and nutritional parameters are related to BMI. More training, standardization of techniques, and good quality equipment will improve the quality of measurements, but the clinician still needs to recognize the limitations of anthropometry in the elderly.

9.2.1 Screening for interventions

Health assessment of an elderly person to evaluate specific risks should include medical and dietary histories, laboratory measurements (e.g. haemoglobin, serum albumin, serum lipids), cellular immune response tests, and anthropometric measurements. Overweight, emaciation, or rapid changes in adipose and muscle tissues are of particular concern. The prevalence of overweight increases with age and results in the loss of mobility (*31*) and an increased burden on cardiovascular and pulmonary function. Increases in weight in elderly men are associated with significant changes in fasting glucose, uric acid levels, and forced vital capacity. Increased adipose tissue on the trunk is independently associated with risk factors for chronic diseases, including glucose intolerance, hyperlipidaemia, and hypertension. Loss of muscle tissue resulting from chronic protein–energy undernutrition increases the risk of morbidity and mortality, partly because it is frequently associated with depressed immune function. General muscle strength, gait, and balance may also be impaired in the elderly, thus increasing the risk of falls and consequent injury (*32*).

Body weight is the sum of all aspects of body composition and is a rough measure of total body energy stores; changes in weight therefore usually parallel energy and protein balance. Weight losses or gains, or a relative change in weight of greater than 10% over a period of less than 6 months, are considered clinically significant. Despite its clinical and nutritional importance, however, body weight is frequently not recorded for elderly people receiving nutritional support because of mobility problems, illness, or unavailability or unreliability of equipment.

The recommended cut-off point for low BMI of 18.5 for adults (see section 8) may be relevant for the elderly, at least from 60–69 years, but whether different cut-offs are more appropriate in individuals of 70 or more years of age is uncertain. Individuals with BMI below this threshold level may be eligible for nutritional supplements. For individuals classified as overweight, the BMI cut-off of 30 recommended for adults (see section 7) may also be considered as a health risk marker, at least in those under the age of 70, who may be considered for counselling in diet and nutrition. When there is no pre-existing chronic disease, older individuals who have remained overweight are probably best advised to maintain their weight; for individuals with pre-existing disease, however, weight control associated with overall clinical treatment is recommended. All groups should be encouraged to increase both physical activity and nutrient density in order to maintain or augment lean body mass.

9.2.2 *Assessing response to an intervention*

The anthropometric measurements that are useful in classifying individuals according to their initial nutritional status and risk often differ from those that are useful for following people over time or for assessing their response to an intervention. The differences arise from the greater importance of accuracy and appropriate reference data for initial classification, in contrast to the precision that is essential in follow-up studies.

Evaluation of the success of an intervention programme often necessitates repeated anthropometric measurements. For clinical purposes it may be assumed that height does not change during follow-up, unless the period is very prolonged. Weight, from which BMI is derived, is the most important single anthropometric measurement. A gain in weight may be caused by an increase in total body water (in oedema, ascites, etc.) or by an increase in fat; conversely, an involuntary loss of weight suggests a loss of lean body mass, with attendant concerns about diagnosis and prognosis. Although there is evidence that weight declines after the age of about 70 years, it is reasonable to set maintenance of weight (within 10% of usual body weight) as a clinical goal.

Body circumferences and skinfold thicknesses are useful for initial classification of patients, but are generally not sufficiently precise for short-term follow-up and monitoring. The interpretation of a small change in triceps skinfold or mid-arm muscle area is difficult, while a change from, for example, the 25th to the 50th percentile, is too insensitive for general use. Yearly changes in BMI, triceps skinfold, mid-arm circumference, and arm muscle area were documented in a longitudinal study of elderly white men and women (*13*). Annual rates of change were small and may have reflected changes in skin compressibility or measurement error or both, in addition to actual changes in body composition. It is unlikely that these measurements will really change if weight does not, and the simplicity of measuring and interpreting a change in weight makes body weight the measurement of choice for short-term follow-up. However, if there is an increase in weight due to ascites or oedema, the clinician may wish to assess somatic protein stores, in which case calf circumference is probably the most useful measurement, being independent of changes occurring in the abdomen.

9.2.3 *Assessment of functional ability*

Assessment of functional ability is important in the evaluation of older people; it is generally rated in terms of daily routine activities as walking, dressing, and eating. At the time of clinical assessment, a variety of simple functional tests may also be performed, including grip strength, 10-metre walking time, time to rise from a chair, and ability to stand on one leg. These tests are good predictors of independence of function, and generally correlate with lean body mass and muscle mass (*32*).

Some evidence suggests that loss of lean body mass predicts functional status, especially in the elderly. Muscle strength, for example, is one of the best predictors of independence and mobility (*29*), and strength is directly determined by the amount of muscle mass (*33*). Thus, functional status and, especially, change in body composition as determined anthropometrically may be extremely helpful in predicting the ability of the elderly to live independently, or to indicate their need for interventions such as nutritional programmes, assistance with daily activities, or even institutionalization.

Poor nutritional status and changes in body composition are believed to be associated with increasing problems of balance and gait in the elderly and thus with risk of falls (*34*). It was shown in one study of aging that fallers had poorer nutritional status than non-fallers, and that nearly all anthropometric measurements, except triceps skinfold, were significantly decreased in men with balance problems (*32*).

9.3 Using anthropometry in populations

9.3.1 *Targeting interventions*

In the public health setting, anthropometry is used to identify groups in need of intervention and to assess response to an intervention; to ascertain determinants or consequences of thinness and overweight; and as a surveillance tool. Population monitoring is more common when there is risk of acute undernutrition, as in the event of war or natural disaster, and the elderly may serve as a sentinel for the entire population. In elderly populations where resources are limited, there is a potential use for triage of need for health care.

Decisions on the implementation of population-wide interventions are made on the basis of anthropometric cut-offs. However, cut-offs developed from samples of younger adults (see sections 7 and 8) are considered provisional for the elderly, since a given BMI does not necessarily imply the same amount of body fat and muscle (*11*), and therefore does not carry an equal health risk, in younger and elderly individuals. The cut-off for undernutrition or thinness is 18.5, and that for overweight, proposed only for ages 60–69 years, is 30. Beyond individual problems of mobility, the health risks of overweight at greater ages are uncertain.

Prevalence of short stature is of considerable interest in population surveys. Short stature is common in Central and South America and much of the developing world, and this may have implications for the interpretation of anthropometry, and possibly for health status, in the elderly. Such populations are likely to have suffered nutritional privations and high rates of infectious diseases in early childhood.

There is little experience of anthropometry of the elderly in field settings in developing countries, largely because of lack of priority for surveys of the elderly in nations dominated by concern for the pressing problems of maternal and child health. Since an increasing proportion of the world's elderly live in developing countries, it is recommended that any survey of adult populations include anthropometric screening of the elderly.

9.3.2 *Assessing response to an intervention*

Interventions in an elderly population may not be expected to produce such obvious responses as, say, increased growth in height among children. The likely response would be a reduction in morbidity and mortality at a specific age. A typical example of intervention would be an exercise programme in a nursing home, designed to improve balance and reduce the incidence of falls. Studies of interventions of this nature are currently being carried out in a number of affluent populations.

9.3.3 *Ascertaining the determinants of thinness and overweight*

In addition to the determinants of adult overweight and thinness already discussed in sections 7 and 8, determinants specific to the elderly are prevalence of depression, institutionalization, injury resulting from falls, poverty, solitary living, illness, and social support networks. However, there is a lack of comprehensive biological and social data in these areas, especially from developing countries.

The importance of monitoring weight in institutionalized settings in developed countries has been stressed in studies by Dwyer et al. (*35*) and Potter et al. (*36*). In the first of these, patients were weighed on admission to nursing homes and again 2 years later; 73% of them either lost or gained at least 4.5 kg. Four-year survival rate was lower among patients who lost weight than among those who gained or remained stable. Lowest mortality occurred at moderate overweight.

9.3.4 *Ascertaining the consequences of thinness and overweight*

Monitoring shifts in the distribution of BMI may reveal changes in the health status of the population. A shift to the left (lower BMI values), for example, may be a warning of impending risk for the entire population. Conversely, in populations with a high prevalence of thinness, a shift of the BMI distribution to the right may be indicative of an improvement in health status. It should be noted, however, that *any* alteration in the distribution of BMI in the elderly may also be due to a cohort effect; a shift to the right may also point to an increasing risk of cardiovascular disease, site-specific cancer, diabetes, and loss of mobility, while a lowering of BMI values is associated with infectious diseases and famine.

9.3.5 *Nutritional surveillance*

Population surveys have often failed to include the elderly, and this situation may be worsened by the reluctance of older people to be measured or interviewed. It is recommended not only that the elderly be included in surveillance, but also that they be specifically targeted for nutritional surveillance since they may be prone to hidden deficiencies that can be corrected by nutritional and health programmes. The elderly should be recognized as a group at risk and as one that may signal nutritional problems in the population as a whole. In long-term planning, efforts should be made to maintain or improve quality of life for the elderly. For this purpose, the ability of the individual to live independently and the proportion of the population capable of a degree of independence in the activities of daily living should be recorded as additional information.

The functional ability of aging individuals varies considerably, and a healthy 80-year-old is not comparable to a healthy 60-year-old. A concept of functional age, similar to that of maturational age of adolescents, should be considered for use in the elderly, but needs further development. For nutritional surveillance of those aged 60 years and more, anthropometric data should ideally be presented by 5-year age groups, but 10-year grouping is more realistic. Biological age groups would be even more appropriate but present difficulties since different organ systems age at different rates and there are no reliable biomarkers of aging. Because anthropometry varies markedly according to sex in the elderly, all data must be analysed by sex.

9.4 Methods of taking measurements

The cooperation of the individual is essential to any anthropometric assessment, but where there is a lack of formal education or where adult children are over-protective of their elderly parents this may be difficult to obtain. Fear of pain and inconvenience are also potential barriers to compliance with the necessary procedures. In randomized studies, the community may fail to understand why some people are to be measured and others not; in such cases, it may cause fewer problems to measure all individuals but use data only for those who were preselected. Communication is essential, and community leaders should be fully consulted. Employing local residents as part of the study team often inspires confidence within the community.

The methods described below include those for individuals confined to bed (bed-fast) or to a chair or wheelchair (chair-fast), which are particularly relevant for elderly populations. However, certain methods may be unsuitable for use in the field or in some developing countries. For other recommended measurements and derivation of indices, such as BMI, that are not specific to the elderly, see Annex 2. Complete and more simplified versions of BMI tables, which will facilitate the utilization of this index, can be found in Annexes 2 and 3, respectively. A nomogram is also provided in Annex 2 (Fig. A2.1).

Note: For consistency with the recommended reference data, arm circumferences and skinfolds should be measured on the right side of the body.

9.4.1 *Weight*

Weighing chair-fast and bed-fast individuals
If an elderly person can sit but is unable to stand, a movable wheelchair scale can be used; the individual should sit upright in the centre of the chair. It is also possible to adapt a pair of bathroom scales to accommodate a wheelchair.

Bed scales incorporating a weighing sling are available for determining the weight of bed-fast patients. The individual is positioned comfortably in the weighing sling, and the sling is raised slowly until the individual is fully suspended. One important drawback is that chair and bed scales are expensive instruments.

Estimating weight from anthropometry

Weight can be estimated by anthropometric means when it cannot be measured directly because of an individual's infirmity or injuries, such as fractures requiring traction or casting. Weight estimates can also be used for calculating indices such as BMI or for estimating energy expenditure.

Weight can also be estimated from calf circumference, knee height, mid-upper arm circumference, and subscapular skinfold. The following equations have been developed for the elderly in the USA (*37*):

Weight (men) = (0.98×calf circ.) + (1.16×knee height)
+ (1.73×MUAC) + (0.37×subscap. skinfold) – 81.69

Weight (women) = (1.27×calf circ.) + (0.87×knee height)
+ (0.98×MUAC) + (0.4× subscap. skinfold) – 62.35

These equations estimate weight within 95% confidence limits of 8.96 kg and 7.60 kg for men and women respectively. Using these equations is not an ideal solution, but may be a reasonable approach in patients who cannot be moved (e.g. after hip fracture). However, since they were developed for the USA, the equations may not be appropriate for use elsewhere, and it may be necessary to develop population-specific equations.

9.4.2 *Height*

At present, there are no guidelines regarding the degree of spinal curvature that would invalidate the measurement of height, but there are obviously individuals whose height should not be measured because of kyphosis or other postural problems. In such cases, height should be estimated or – preferably – knee height should be used as a surrogate. Arm span has also been used as a surrogate for height, but may be less satisfactory than knee height because of joint stiffness in the elderly and because the number of joints involved can reduce the accuracy of measurement. Arm span is also believed to yield young adult height rather than the current (reduced) height of the older individual, since there is little reduction in the length of long bones with aging.

Knee height

The following equations have been developed for estimating height from knee height for white and black Americans aged 60–80 years (*38*):

Height (white men) = (2.08 × knee height) + 59.01

Height (white women) = (1.91 × knee height) – (0.17 × age) + 75.00

Height (black men) = (1.37 × knee height) + 95.79

Height (black women) = (1.96 × knee height) + 58.72

The standard errors are rather large: 7.84 cm for white men, 8.82 cm for white women, 8.44 cm for black men, and 8.26 cm for black women. The equations were developed from a selected population living in the USA and may be inappropriate for other populations; it may therefore be necessary to develop population-specific equations.

Knee height may also be used as an independent measurement, since it is not affected by height loss due to vertebral compression.

It can be measured with a sliding broad-blade calliper: the shaft of the calliper is held parallel to the shaft of the tibia and pressure is applied to compress the tissues. Measurements are recorded to the nearest 0.1 cm, and two measurements taken in immediate succession should be within 0.5 cm of each other.

Height estimated from knee height can be used to derive BMI as an index of the degree of overweight in almost all elderly persons.

For measuring the knee height of an elderly person seated in a wheelchair it is important that the leg is supported so that the knee and ankle are each bent to a 90° angle. Kneeling at the side of the lower leg, the observer places the fixed blade of the calliper under the heel of the foot. The shaft of the calliper is positioned so that it passes over the lateral malleolus and just posterior to the head of the fibula. The movable blade is placed over the anterior surface of the thigh, above the condyles of the femur, about 4.0 cm proximal to the patella. The shaft of the calliper is held parallel to the shaft of the tibia and pressure is applied to compress the tissues.

Bed-fast individuals should lie supine, with the knee and ankle each bent to 90°. Standing to the side of the lower leg, the observer places the fixed blade of the calliper under the heel of the foot, and positions the shaft of the calliper so that it passes over the lateral malleolus and just posterior to the head of the fibula. The movable blade is placed over the anterior surface of the thigh, above the condyles of the femur, about 4.0 cm proximal to the patella. The shaft of the calliper is held parallel to the shaft of the tibia and pressure is applied to compress the tissues.

Arm span
Arm span is a further alternative measurement for use when it is impossible to measure actual height, although – as mentioned – it yields an estimate more closely correlated with young adult height. The individual should stand against a wall, with the arms extended laterally. The arms should be kept at shoulder height during the measurement, although this may be difficult in older people. The measurement is made with a measuring tape at least 2 metres long, with an observer at each end of the tape, and recorded to the nearest 0.1 cm.

Arm span can also be measured with the subject supine, but this presents some difficulty and is a less accurate method.

9.4.3 *Calf circumference*

Calf circumference is considered to provide the most sensitive measure of muscle mass in the elderly, and is superior to arm circumference. It indicates the changes in fat-free mass that occur with aging and with decreased activity (*31, 39*).

To measure the calf circumference of an elderly person seated in a wheelchair it is important that the leg is supported so that the knee and ankle are each bent to a 90° angle. Kneeling at the side of the calf, the observer passes a loop of the measuring tape around the calf, moving it up and down to locate the largest circumference.

A similar procedure is followed for the bed-fast individual. Lying supine, the patient bends the knee to a 90° angle with the sole of the foot resting on the bed or examination table. It may be helpful to place a sandbag under the foot for support. Standing at the side of the calf, the observer places a loop of the measuring tape around the calf, moving it up and down to locate the largest circumference.

9.4.4 *Subscapular skinfold thickness*

Subscapular skinfold thickness is measured with the bed-fast individual lying on the left side with the left arm extending from the front of the body. The trunk should be in a straight line, the legs should be bent and slightly tucked up, and the right arm should rest along the trunk, palm down. An imaginary line through the acromion processes should be perpendicular to the bed. The skinfold thickness is measured just posterior to the inferior angle of the right scapula. The observer gently grasps a double fold of skin and subcutaneous adipose tissue between the fingers and thumb, on a line from the inferior angle of the right scapula to the right elbow. Grasping the skinfold separates subcutaneous adipose tissue from the underlying muscle. The calliper is positioned perpendicular to the length of the skinfold and the jaws of the calliper are applied medial to the fingers, at a point lateral and just inferior to the inferior angle of the scapula.

9.4.5 *Mid-upper arm circumference*

The circumference of the upper arm is measured at its mid-point, located after bending the right elbow to a 90° angle and placing the forearm palm down across the trunk. The upper arm should be approximately parallel to the trunk. Using a measuring tape, the observer identifies and marks the mid-point of the arm, halfway between the tip of the acromion process and the tip of the olecranon process. The skin should be marked at this point before the arm is repositioned for the circumference measurement. The right arm is then extended alongside the body, with the palm facing upwards. It should be raised slightly off the surface of the bed or examination table by placing a sandbag or towel under the elbow, and the hand is placed through the loop of an inelastic, flexible tape measure. At the marked mid-point the tape is pulled just snug around the arm without compressing the tissues. The circumference is recorded to the nearest 0.1 cm, and successive measurements should be within 0.5 cm of each other.

9.4.6 *Triceps skinfold thickness*

Triceps skinfold thickness is measured with the bed-fast individual lying on the left side, with the left arm extending from the front of the body. The trunk should be in a straight line, the legs should be bent and tucked up slightly, and the right arm should rest along the trunk, palm down. An imaginary line through the acromion processes should be perpendicular to the bed. The skinfold thickness measurement is taken on the back of the right arm over the triceps muscle, at the level marked as the mid-point for measurement of MUAC; repeated measurements can vary markedly if they are made at different sites. The observer gently grasps a double fold of skin and subcutaneous adipose tissue between the fingers and thumb, about 1.0 cm from the marked level. The fold of skin must be on the back of the arm, in the midline and parallel to the long axis of the upper arm. Grasping the skinfold separates subcutaneous adipose tissue from the underlying muscle. The jaws of the calliper are placed perpendicular to the length of the skinfold at the level of the marked mid-point, and the observer should bend down to read the calliper to avoid errors due to parallax.

9.5 Sources and characteristics of reference data

Appropriate use of anthropometry requires the comparison of data from individuals with data from healthy people of the same age, sex, and – as far as possible – genetic and environmental background. Currently available normative data, however, rarely include the very old. Even the US Second National Health and Nutrition Examination Survey (NHANES II), which is the most comprehensive data set for anthropometry, does not include people over 74 years of age (*40*). Another data set, the Metropolitan Life tables, much used in the USA, does not include life insurance policy holders over the age of 59 years and is thus of no value for the elderly. Canadian normative data cover people up to the age of 70 years, data from Japan people of more than 80 years (*41*), and United Kingdom data people up to 64 years (*42*). Few normative data exist for the elderly in developing countries, and there is no evidence that what is normal for, say, a 75-year-old man in the USA is also normal for a 75-year-old man in a developing country.

The Expert Committee considered the validity of various data sets for use as references, applying the criteria that data should be presented by 10-year age groups and by sex; that means, standard deviations, and percentiles should be available for each anthropometric parameter and age group; and that data for people over 80 years of age should be included (since it was felt that data from people in their 60s should not be extrapolated to those in their 80s). Moreover, the population-based sample should be free from major disabilities and living in a healthy environment, although it would be likely to contain some unhealthy individuals, since most elderly people probably have one or more disease conditions. The definition of health used to select the sample has a major influence on the reference data. The high prevalence of disease and multiple disease conditions in the elderly means that very few, if any, individuals are completely free of disease. An additional confounder is the influence of differential survivorship as age increases. There may also be significant cohort differences in the elderly: the elderly of today grew up under quite different conditions from those who will be elderly 20 or 40 years hence.

Table 52 summarizes some of the few population-based data sets and their characteristics. The data of Master et al. (*43*), though old, appear to be still much in use in clinics in the USA, and have the advantage of avoiding use of indices such as BMI – the tables give weight range for each inch of height. However, their present-day application may not be entirely appropriate: many of those included in the original sample were born in the last century and grew up under very different socioeconomic conditions from today's elderly.

Recognizing the limitations of available reference data, the Expert Committee did not recommend universal reference data at this time but, rather, the collection of data to describe local levels and patterns. For those countries that have no local data or that lack the resources to develop them, the Committee recommended use of the NHANES III data for comparison between different population groups. The NHANES III survey collected data over the period 1988–1991 on a sample of 600 elderly individuals (equal numbers of whites, blacks, and Hispanics) with no upper age limit and with oversampling of the oldest age-group.

Two levels of implementation are relevant here: use of the recommended measurements and use of available reference data. It should be recognized that many of the available reference data have limitations, but could be used by countries that lack such data for initial evaluation of the status of their elderly populations; this could provide some early indications of future problems. These data are pertinent if used exclusively as reference data for comparison purposes, that is, to compare means and standard deviations across populations. They are not for use as standards. This distinction is especially important, and the Expert Committee expressed particular concern regarding the applicability of any available data to other populations. Different populations show large geographical and ethnic variation in height, weight, and BMI, much of which reflects differences in lifestyle and environment throughout life, genetic differences, and – to an uncertain extent – differences in health status.

Table 52

Reference data for adults aged 60 years and over

Location (and name) of study	Population characteristics	Sample size	Ages (years)	Parameters	Comments	Reference
USA	Whites; nationwide sample	2925 men 2694 women	65–94	Height, weight, body surface area, weight range for each inch of height	Sample drawn from all socioeconomic strata. Height and weight measured in inches and pounds	43
USA	Whites and blacks; randomly sampled	1261 men 1392 women	60–74	Height, weight, sitting height, triceps and subscapular skinfolds, MUAC, elbow breadth, BMI, AMA	Random sampling; data presented as means and percentiles	40
Japan	Asians; nationwide sample	110 men 526 women	60–80 +	Height, weight, triceps and subscapular skinfolds	Means and SDs	41
China (Chinese Nationwide Nutrition Survey)	Asians; nationwide sample	796 men 968 women	60–94	Height, weight, BMI	Means, SDs, percentiles	16
USA	Whites; Ohio sample	119 men 150 women	65–90	Height, weight, knee height, triceps and subscapular skinfolds, arm and calf circumferences, BMI, AMA	Percentiles, charts	44
Sweden	Whites; Uppsala sample	> 250 for each 10-year age group	60–80	Height, weight, weight-for-height	Data for 1964–1971; SDs; not random sample	45

Table 52 (continued)

Location (and name) of study	Population characteristics	Sample size	Ages (years)	Parameters	Comments	Reference
Italy	Whites; 5 small towns in 5 regions	522 men 725 women	65–95	Height, weight, BMI, arm circumference, triceps, biceps, iliac, and subscapular skinfolds, AMA	Percentiles	46
Brazil (Brazilian National Survey of Health and Nutrition)	Mixed; nationwide sample	4419	60–70	Height, weight, BMI		16
Europe (EURONUT-SENECA Study on Nutrition and the Elderly)	Whites born 1913/1914 and 1917/1918; 19 towns	2586	70–75	Height, weight, BMI, triceps skinfold, arm circumference, AMA, waist: hip ratio		47
Guatemala (Nutritional Assessment of Guatemalan Ambulatory Elderly)	Ladinos; urban and rural	202	60–103	Height, weight, BMI		16
Hong Kong (Longitudinal Study of Health and Social Support in the Hong Kong Chinese Elderly Cohort)	Asians	977	70–100	Height, weight, BMI		16
Italy (Nutrition in Old Age in Italy)	Whites; 17 sites	921	60–97	Height, weight, BMI		16
Italy (Italian Nutrition Examination Survey of the Elderly)	Whites; 5 sites	1248	65–95	Height, weight, BMI		16

Table 52 (continued)

Location (and name) of study	Population characteristics	Sample size	Ages (years)	Parameters	Comments	Reference
China (Province of Taiwan)	Asians	3818	60-97	Height, weight, BMI		16
USA (Established Populations for Epidemiologic Studies of the Elderly)	Whites; Boston and Iowa	3164 (Boston) 3647 (Iowa)	65-90 +	Height, weight, BMI		16
IUNS Study of Food Habits in Later Life[a]						
Australia[a]	Whites	111	60-79	Height, weight, BMI, arm, waist, and hip circumferences, skinfolds		48
Sweden[a]	Whites	204	60-91	Height, weight, BMI, arm, waist, and hip circumferences, skinfolds		48
China[a]	Asians	441	70-96	Height, weight, BMI, arm, waist, and hip circumferences, skinfolds		48
Australia[a]	Greek descent	186	70-104	Height, weight, BMI, arm, waist, and hip circumferences, skinfolds		48

Table 52 (*continued*)

Location (and name) of study	Population characteristics	Sample size	Ages (years)	Parameters	Comments	Reference
IUNS Study of Food Habits in Later Life[a] (*continued*)						
Greece[a]	Whites; Sparta	70	70-94	Height, weight, BMI, arm, waist, and hip circumferences, skinfolds		48

[a] The IUNS Study of Food Habits in Later Life includes populations in four countries.

9.6 Recommendations

9.6.1 *For practical implementation*

For Member countries

Member countries are encouraged to collect anthropometric data on adults aged 60 years and above, and to monitor the health of this sector of the population through anthropometric surveys at regular intervals. It is important that countries extend their knowledge of the anthropometric characteristics and health status of the elderly. Special attention should be paid to selection criteria in choosing population-based samples, taking into consideration the heterogeneity of the elderly and the high prevalence of chronic conditions that may affect nutritional status.

For WHO

The Expert Committee recommends that a further consultation be organized by WHO, several years hence, to review the current recommendations in the light of available new data.

9.6.2 *For future research*

Numerous gaps exist in knowledge of the use of anthropometry to assess physical status in the elderly. It has been a common practice to extrapolate data collected on young adults to the elderly, yet it is not known to what extent comparison in the elderly has the same meaning as similar comparison in younger individuals or how this affects interpretation in the case of the elderly. The Expert Committee identified the following areas of research as essential for improving the use of anthropometry in the elderly.

Body composition
1. Establishing determinants of changes in body composition in the elderly.
2. Determining the best methods of measuring body composition in the elderly.
3. Determining the relationship between body composition and morbidity and mortality in the elderly.
4. Investigating and validating different methods of determining body composition, such as bioelectrical impedance.
5. In populations of short stature and stocky build, BMI values may indicate relative affluence and adequate nutrition. Conversely, in populations with relatively long legs compared with the trunk, BMI may indicate undernutrition in individuals who are in fact healthy. It is therefore important to determine whether different cut-off points for BMI should be used in such populations, or whether a different measurement or index should be used.
6. Determining what, other than nutritional interventions, can be done to alter body composition and reduce loss of fat-free mass.

7. Evaluating the use of ultrasound to measure fat in areas that cannot be measured by anthropometric means.
8. Determining why muscle mass is lost with age and the types of muscle changes that occur.
9. Carrying out prospective studies of the abdomen:hip circumference ratio, which is an important predictor of morbidity in the elderly.
10. Determining whether undernutrition is a greater health problem than overweight in the elderly, and whether the health risk changes with age.
11. Determining the prevalence of low (18.5) and high (30) BMI among the elderly.

Body size
1. Determining whether height is the best measurement in the elderly, in view of its age-related decrease, and whether another measurement would give better information on body length. Also determining whether a better index (than BMI) would be one in which body weight is related to some parameter other than height.
2. Determining whether the side of the body (left or right) on which measurements are taken makes a difference in the elderly.
3. Determining whether arm span is as valid a measurement as knee height as a surrogate for height and whether it can be reliably measured in bed-fast individuals.
4. Assessing whether current height or young adult height should be used in deriving indices such as BMI.
5. Determining the age-related changes in BMI and BMI distribution in different populations and assessing whether BMI has the same meaning in every population.
6. Determining whether tall individuals lose height more rapidly than short individuals.

Value of anthropometry
1. Assessing how accurately body composition in the elderly can be estimated by anthropometric methods.
2. Determining what further information anthropometry can yield on health risk and disability.
3. Determining the role of anthropometry in measuring increased function after exercise training.
4. Establishing the different contributions of environmental factors and lifestyle throughout life and of genetic factors to the geographical and ethnic variations in height, weight, and BMI across populations. Determining the extent to which much of the variation across populations is the result of differences in disease and health status. Determining whether population-specific or universal reference data should be used to assess nutritional and health status in the elderly.
5. Identifying the situations in which health status can be evaluated by anthropometry and assessing what anthropometry can reveal about specific health outcomes in the elderly.

6. Determining what factors can be identified in early adulthood that might be markers for risk of mortality later in life.
7. Longitudinal studies of BMI and its components – fat-free mass and fat mass. Determining whether fat distribution provides a better indicator of cardiovascular morbidity and mortality in the elderly, and whether the increase of intra-abdominal fat indicates an increased risk of morbidity or whether it is protective. Data are also needed on lean body mass other than shortly before death as a predictor of long-range morbidity or mortality.
8. If high BMI is a protective factor with regard to total mortality in the elderly, determining the relative contributions to this of fat and lean body mass.

References

1. *World population prospects 1992.* New York, United Nations, 1993.

2. McNicoll G. Consequences of rapid population growth: overview and assessment. *Population and development review*, 1984, **10**:177–240.

3. Kinsella K, Suzman R. Demographic dimensions of population aging in developing countries. *American journal of human biology*, 1992, 4:3–8.

4. Keyfitz N, Flieger W. *World population growth and aging.* Chicago, University of Chicago Press, 1990.

5. Rossman I. Anatomic and body composition changes with aging. In: Finch CE, Hayflick L, eds. *Handbook of the biology of aging.* New York, Van Nostrand Reinhold, 1977:189–221.

6. Svanborg A, Eden S, Mellstrom D. Metabolic changes in aging: predictors of disease. The Swedish experience. In: Ingram DK, Baker GT, Shock NW, eds. *The potential for nutritional modulation of aging.* Trumbull, CT, Food and Nutrition Press, 1991:81–90.

7. Eveleth PB, Tanner JM. *Worldwide variation in human growth*, 2nd ed. Cambridge, Cambridge University Press, 1990.

8. Steen B, Lundgren BK, Isaksson B. Body composition at age 70, 75, 79 and 81 years: a longitudinal population study. In: Chandra RK, ed. *Nutrition, immunity and illness in the elderly.* New York, Pergamon, 1985.

9. Waaler HT. Height, weight and mortality. The Norwegian experience. *Acta medica Scandinavica supplementum*, 1984, **679**:1–56.

10. Waaler HT. Hazard of obesity – the Norwegian experience. *Acta medica Scandinavica supplementum*, 1988, **723**:17–21.

11. Micozzi MS, Harris TM. Age variations in the relation of body mass indices to estimates of body fat and muscle mass. *American journal of physical anthropology*, 1990, **81**:375–379.

12. Chumlea WC et al. Changes in anthropometric indices of body composition with age in a healthy elderly population. *American journal of human biology*, 1989, **1**: 457–462.

13. Borkan GA et al. Age changes in body composition revealed by computed tomography. *Journal of gerontology*, 1983, **38**:673–677.

14. **Shimokata H et al.** Studies in the distribution of body fat: I. Effects of age, sex and obesity. *Journal of gerontology*, 1989, 44:M66-M73.

15. **Bjorntorp P, Evans W.** The effect of exercise on body composition. In: Watkins J, Roubenoff R, Rosenberg IH, eds. *Body composition: the measure and meaning of changes with aging.* Boston, Foundation for Nutritional Advancement, 1992.

16. **Ad Hoc Committee on the Statistics of Anthropometry and Aging.** Variation in weight, height and BMI in geographically diverse samples of older persons. *International journal of obesity and related metabolic disorders* (in press).

17. **Andres R.** Mortality and obesity: the rationale for age-specific height–weight tables. In: Andres R, Bierman EL, Hazzard WR, eds. *Principles of geriatric medicine.* New York, McGraw-Hill, 1985.

18. **Hill GL.** Body composition research: implications for the practice of clinical nutrition. *Journal of parenteral and enteral nutrition,* 1992, **16**:197-218.

19. **Roubenoff R, Kehayias JJ.** The meaning and measurement of lean body mass. *Nutrition reviews,* 1991, 49:163-175.

20. **Phillips A, Shaper AG, Whincup PH.** Association between serum albumin and mortality from cardiovascular disease, cancer, and other causes. *Lancet,* 1989, ii:1434-1436.

21. **Rissanen A et al.** Weight and mortality in Finnish men. *Journal of clinical epidemiology*, 1989, 42:781-789.

22. **Rissanen A et al.** Weight and mortality in Finnish women. *Journal of clinical epidemiology*, 1991, 44:787-795.

23. **Mattila K, Haavisto M, Rajala S.** Body mass index and mortality in the elderly. *British medical journal*, 1986, **292**:867-868.

24. **Tayback M, Kumanyika S, Chee E.** Body weight as a risk factor in the elderly. *Archives of internal medicine*, 1990, **150**:1065-1072.

25. **Cornoni-Huntley JC et al.** An overview of body weight of older persons, including the impact on mortality. The National Health and Nutrition Examination Survey. I – Epidemiologic follow-up study. *Journal of clinical epidemiology*, 1991, 44:743-753.

26. **Harris T et al.** Body mass index and mortality among nonsmoking older persons. *Journal of the American Medical Association*, 1988, **259**:1520-1524.

27. **Brambilla DJ, McKinlay SM.** A prospective study of factors affecting age at menopause. *Journal of clinical epidemiology*, 1989, 42:1031-1039.

28. **Flint M, Samil RS.** Cultural and subcultural meanings of the menopause. *Annals of the New York Academy of Sciences*, 1990, **592**:134-148.

29. **Fiatarone MA et al.** High-intensity strength training in nonagenarians. Effects on skeletal muscle. *Journal of the American Medical Association*, 1990, **263**: 3029-3034.

30. **Chumlea WC, Roche AF, Webb P.** Body size, subcutaneous fatness and total body fat in older adults. *International journal of obesity*, 1984, **8**:311-317.

31. **Patrick JM, Bassey EJ, Fentem PH.** Changes in body fat and muscle in manual workers at and after retirement. *European journal of applied physiology and occupational physiology*, 1982, 49:187-196.

32. **Vellas B et al.** A comparative study of falls, gait and balance in elderly persons living in North America (Albuquerque, NM, USA) and Europe (Toulouse, France): methodology and preliminary results. In: Vellas B et al., eds. *Falls, balance and gait disorders in the elderly.* Paris, Elsevier, 1992.

33. **Frontera WR et al.** A cross-sectional study of muscle strength and mass in 45- to 78-year-old men and women. *Journal of applied physiology*, 1991, **71**:644-650.

34. **Vellas B et al.** Malnutrition and falls. *Lancet*, 1990, **336**:1447.

35. **Dwyer JT et al.** Changes in relative weight among institutionalized elderly adults. *Journal of gerontology*, 1987, **42**:246-251.

36. **Potter JF, Schafer DF, Bohi RL.** In-hospital mortality as a function of body mass index: an age-dependent variable. *Journal of gerontology,* 1988, **43**:M59-M63.

37. **Chumlea WC, Roche AF, Steinbaugh ML.** Anthropometric approaches to the nutritional assessment of the elderly. In: Munro HN, Danford DE, eds. *Nutrition, aging and the elderly.* New York, Plenum Press, 1989.

38. **Chumlea WC, Guo S.** Equations for predicting stature in white and black elderly individuals. *Journal of gerontology,* 1992, **47**:M197-M203.

39. **Conceicao J et al.** Etude des marqueurs anthropométriques au sein d'une population de 224 sujets âgés vivant en maison de retraite. [Study of anthropometric indicators among a population of 224 elderly subjects living in a retirement home.] *L'Année gérontologique*, 1993, **23**:26-34.

40. **Frisancho AR.** *Anthropometric standards for the assessment of growth and nutritional status.* Ann Arbor, MI, University of Michigan Press, 1990.

41. **Ministry of Health and Welfare.** Physical proportion of the Japanese, 1987. *Diabetes research and clinical practice,* 1990, **10**(Suppl. 1):S103-S112.

42. **Burr ML, Phillips KM.** Anthropometric norms in the elderly. *British journal of nutrition.* 1984, **51**:165-169.

43. **Master AM, Lasser RP, Beckman G.** Tables of average weight and height of Americans aged 65 to 94 years. *Journal of the American Medical Association*, 1960, **172**:658-662.

44. **Chumlea WC, Roche AF, Mukherjee D.** Some anthropometric indices of body composition for elderly adults. *Journal of gerontology*, 1986, **41**:36-39.

45. **Karlberg J, Mossberg HO.** Weight-for-height standards in adulthood. *Journal of internal medicine*, 1991, **229**:303-308.

46. **Melchionda N et al.** Epidemiology of obesity in the elderly: CNR multicentric study in Italy. *Diabetes research and clinical practice,* 1990, **10**(Suppl. 1): S11-S16.

47. **de Groot LCPGM, van Staveren WA, Hautvast JGAJ,** eds. EURONUT-seneca. Nutrition and the elderly in Europe. First European Congress on Nutrition and Health in the Elderly. *European journal of clinical nutrition*, 1991, **45**(Suppl. 3): 1-196.

48. **Wahlqvist M et al.** Development of a survey instrument for the assessment of food habits and health in later life. In: Moyal MF, ed. *Dietetics in the 90s. Role of the dietician/nutritionist.* London, John Libbey Eurotext, 1988:235-239.

10. Overall recommendations

10.1 For Member States

1. Current practices and programmes should be evaluated to determine how anthropometry may be used most effectively to improve the health and nutrition of individuals and populations.

2. The Expert Committee's recommendations should be implemented by adapting general guidelines for anthropometric applications, including the setting of cut-off values, and by training appropriate personnel to use the recommended techniques within existing programmes of health and nutrition screening, public health interventions, and preventive services.

3. Anthropometry should be employed in national and local surveillance systems, and coupled with appropriate assessment of remediable causes and intervention targets in order to guide policies and programmes in health and other sectors.

4. The implementation of research recommendations should be supported in order to achieve better understanding and use of anthropometric indicators, and to develop international anthropometric reference data to improve health and nutrition.

10.2 For WHO

1. WHO should encourage the use of anthropometry as a social and technical instrument for assessing health and nutritional status, and more broadly for evaluating social and economic conditions and the impact of development.

2. WHO should facilitate and support the accomplishment of the recommendations for Member States by providing expert consultation, appropriate training and related materials, and technical assistance.

3. WHO should develop guidelines for the implementation of the Expert Committee's recommendations in the context of existing WHO programmes in areas such as nutrition, adolescent health, human reproduction, health of the elderly, and cardiovascular diseases, and encourage the participation of WHO collaborating centres.

4. WHO should support the recommended research agenda on the use of anthropometry to improve health and nutrition of individuals and populations worldwide.

5. WHO should foster the development of international anthropometric reference data and values, and appropriate anthropometric indicators of health, nutrition, and social and economic welfare throughout life.

10.3 For research

1. Practicable methodologies for setting locally appropriate cut-off levels for anthropometric indicators should be developed, taking account of the prevalence of the conditions to be addressed and the resources available locally for interventions.

2. Anthropometric indicators should be developed for specific uses: to assess past or present threats to health, to predict risk, to predict benefit from interventions, and to reflect responses to interventions or other influences.

3. Methods should be developed that allow assessment and monitoring of national problems of stunting, thinness, and overweight; this should be done within the context of health and nutritional surveillance and other relevant programmes, so that the information may be linked to policy formulation, and programme planning and implementation.

4. The theory and practice of anthropometric monitoring in individuals should be developed with a view to improving preventive and curative health services.

5. Appropriate international reference data for anthropometry from birth to adolescence should be developed.

Acknowledgements

Special acknowledgement was made by the Committee to Dr M. de Onis, Nutrition, WHO, Geneva, Switzerland; Dr J.-P. Habicht, Cornell University, Ithaca, NY, USA; Dr J.H. Himes, University of Minnesota, Minneapolis, MN, USA; Dr J.C. Seidell, National Institute of Public Health and Environmental Protection, Bilthoven, Netherlands; and Dr C.G. Victora, University of Pelotas, Pelotas, Brazil, who were instrumental in the preparation and proceedings of the meeting.

Particular thanks were expressed for the extensive contributions made by the following people:

Dr K.V. Bailey, Nutrition, World Health Organization, Geneva, Switzerland; Dr B.R. Bistrian, Division of Clinical Nutrition, New England Deaconess Hospital, Boston, MA, USA; Dr N. Butte, Department of Pediatrics, Children's Nutrition Research Center, Houston, TX, USA; Dr K. Dewey, Program in International Nutrition, University of California, Davis, CA, USA; Dr E. Frongillo, Division of Nutritional Sciences, Cornell University, Ithaca, NY, USA; Dr W.P.T. James, Rowett Research Institute, Aberdeen, Scotland; Dr A. Kelly, Department of Community Health, Trinity College, Dublin, Ireland; Dr L. Launer, Department of Epidemiology and Biostatistics, Erasmus University Medical School, Rotterdam, Netherlands; Dr G.C.N. Mascie-Taylor, Department of Biological Anthropology, University of Cambridge, Cambridge, England; Dr N. Norgan, Department of Human Sciences, University of Technology, Loughborough, England; Dr D. Pelletier, Division of Nutritional Sciences, Cornell University, Ithaca, NY, USA: Dr K. Rasmussen, Division of Nutritional Sciences, Cornell, NY, USA; Dr P. Shetty, London School of Hygiene and Tropical Medicine, London, England.

The Committee also acknowledged with thanks the valuable contributions made to its work by the following institutions and persons:

The Concerted Action on Nutrition and Health of the European Community (EURONUT); University of Vienna, Vienna, Austria; Department of Cooperation, Ministry of Foreign Affairs, Rome, Italy; National Institute of Nutrition, Rome, Italy; Wageningen Agricultural University, Wageningen, Netherlands; Ramón Areces Foundation, Madrid, Spain; Ministry of Health, Madrid Spain; Medical School, University of Geneva, Geneva, Switzerland; Centers for Disease Control and Prevention, Atlanta, GA, USA; Cornell University, Ithaca, NY, USA; Fogarty International Center, Bethesda, MD, USA; International Center for Research on Women, Washington, DC, USA; National Institute on Aging, National Institutes of Health, Bethesda, MD, USA; School of Public Health, University of Minnesota, Minneapolis, MN, USA; United Nations Children's Fund, New York, USA; United States Agency for International Development, Washington, DC, USA; Wellstart International, San Diego, CA, USA.

Dr T. Achard, Paediatrician, Neuchâtel, Switzerland; Dr R.K. Anand, Professor of Pediatrics, TN Medical College, Bombay, India; Dr M.A. Anderson, Office of Health, United States Agency for International Development, Washington, DC, USA; Dr R. Andres, Gerontology Research Center, National Institute on Aging, National Institutes of Health, Baltimore, MD, USA; Dr T. Arbuckle, Laboratory Centre for Disease Control, Health and Welfare Canada, Ottawa, Canada; Professor S. Baba, Hyogo Institute for Research in Adult Diseases, Akashi, Japan; Dr C. Barba, Institute of Human Nutrition and Food, College of Human Ecology, Laguna, Philippines; Dr R. Baumgartner, Clinical Nutrition Research Laboratory, University of New Mexico School of Medicine, Albuquerque, NM, USA; Dr C. Beall, Department of Anthropology, Case Western Reserve University, Cleveland, OH, USA; Dr. G. Beaton, Department of Nutritional

Sciences, University of Toronto, Toronto, Canada; Dr J.G. Bezerra Alves, Maternal and Child Institute of Pernambuco, Recife, Brazil; Dr R. Bhatia, Programme and Technical Support Section, United Nations High Commission for Refugees, Geneva, Switzerland; Dr G. Blackburn, Nutrition/Metabolism Laboratory, New England Deaconness Hospital, Boston, MA, USA; Dr M. Bloem, Helen Keller, International, Dhaka, Bangladesh; Dr G. Bray, Department of Medicine, Louisiana State University, Baton Rouge, LA, USA; Dr K. Brown, Program in International Nutrition, University of California, Davis, CA, USA; Dr C. Brownie, Department of Statistics, North Carolina State University, Raleigh, NC, USA; Dr S. Burger, Helen Keller International, New York, NY, USA; Dr R. Buzina, Nutrition, World Health Organization, Geneva, Switzerland; Dr N. Cameron, Department of Anatomy, University of Witwatersrand, Johannesburg, South Africa; Dr C. Chumlea, Division of Human Biology, Wright State University, Yellow Springs, OH, USA; Dr T. Cole, Dunn Nutrition Centre, Cambridge, England; Dr M. Dawes, Department of Public Health and Primary Care, University of Oxford, Oxford, England; Professor J.-P. Despres, Physical Activity Sciences Laboratory, Laval University, Quebec, Canada; Dr P. Deuronberg, Department of Human Nutrition, Agricultural University, Wageningen, Netherlands; Dr S. Diaz, Department of Physiology and Embryology, Catholic University of Chile, Santiago, Chile; Dr A. Dugdale, Human Nutrition Research Group, University of Queensland, Herston, Australia; Dr J.V.G.A. Durnin, Institute of Physiology, University of Glasgow, Glasgow, Scotland; Dr N. Dusitsin, Department of Obstetrics and Gynaecology, Chulalongkorn University, Bangkok, Thailand; Dr J. Dwyer, Human Nutrition Research Center on Aging, Tufts University, Boston, MA, USA; Dr O. Eiben, Department of Anthropology, Eotvos Lorand University, Budapest, Hungary; Dr F. Falkner, Maternal and Child Health, University of California, Berkeley, CA, USA; Ms B. J. Ferguson, Adolescent Health, World Health Organization, Geneva, Switzerland; Dr H. Friedman, Adolescent Health, World Health Organization, Geneva, Switzerland; Dr E. Gladen, National Institute of Environmental Health Sciences, National Institutes of Health, Research Triangle Park, NC, USA; Dr R. Goldenberg, Department of Obstetrics and Gynecology, University of Alabama, Birmingham, AL, USA; Dr T. Greiner, International Child Health Unit, University Hospital, Uppsala, Sweden; Dr R. Gross, Community Nutrition Training Programme, University of Indonesia, Jakarta, Indonesia; Dr R. Guidotti, Maternal and Child Health and Family Planning, World Health Organization, Geneva, Switzerland; Dr T. Harris, National Institute on Aging, National Institutes of Health, Bethesda, MD, USA; Dr F. Haschke, Salzburg Federal Hospital Children's Clinic, Salzburg, Austria; Dr J. Hautvast, Department of Human Nutrition, Agricultural University, Wageningen, Netherlands; Dr M. Hediger, Department of Obstetrics and Gynecology, University of Medicine and Dentistry of New Jersey, Camden, NJ, USA; Dr S. Heymsfield, Department of Medicine, Columbia University School of Medicine, New York, NY, USA; Dr E. Jéquier, Faculty of Medicine, Institute of Physiology, University of Lausanne, Lausanne, Switzerland; Dr U. Jonsson, Nutrition Section, United Nations Children's Fund, New York, NY, USA; Dr J. Karlberg, Department of Paediatrics, University of Hong Kong, Hong Kong; Dr W. Keller, formerly of Nutrition, World Health Organization, Geneva, Switzerland; Dr Keyou Ge, Institute of Nutrition and Food Hygiene, Chinese Academy of Preventive Medicine, Beijing, China; Dr N. Krebs, University of Colorado Health Sciences Center, Denver, CO, USA; Professor R.A. Kronmal, Department of Biostatistics, University of Washington, Washington, DC, USA; Dr S. Kumanyika, Center for Biostatistics and Epidemiology, Hershey, PA, USA; Dr R. Kumar, Department of Paediatrics, M.L.B. Medical College, Jhansi, India; Dr K. Kurz, International Center for Research on Women, Washington, DC, USA; Dr J. Kusin, Department of Health and Disease Control, Royal Tropical Institute, Amsterdam, Netherlands; Dr T. Kwok, Department of Medicine for the Elderly, Crawley Hospital, Crawley, England; Dr R. Largo, Growth and Development Centre, University Children's Clinic, Zurich, Switzerland; Dr S. Lederman, Center for Population and Family Health,

Columbia University, New York, NY, USA; Dr F. Mardones, World Bank, Washington, DC, USA; Dr J. Martinez, Programme for Control of Diarrhoeal Diseases, World Health Organization, Geneva, Switzerland; Dr R. Martorell, Center for International Health, Emory University, Atlanta, GA, USA; Dr J. Mason, Administrative Committee on Coordination, Subcommittee on Nutrition, World Health Organization, Geneva, Switzerland; Dr M. Mazariegos, CESSIAM, Ear and Eye Hospital, Guatemala City, Guatemala; Dr K. Michaelsen, Research Department of Human Nutrition, The Royal Veterinary and Agricultural University, Copenhagen, Denmark; Dr M. Micozzi, Department of Defense, Armed Forces Institute of Pathology, Washington, DC, USA; Dr C. Monteiro, Department of Nutrition, University of São Paulo, São Paulo, Brazil; Dr C. O'Gara, Expanded Promotion of Breastfeeding Program, Wellstart, Washington, DC, USA; Dr A. Paul, Dunn Nutrition Centre, Cambridge, England; Dr J. Pearson, Gerontology Research Center, National Institute on Aging, National Institutes of Health, Baltimore, MD, USA; Ms J. Peerson, Program in International Nutrition, University of California, Davis, CA, USA; Dr L.A. Persson, Department of Epidemiology and Public Health, Umea University, Umea, Sweden; Dr S. Petersen, Department of Neonatology, State University Hospital, Copenhagen, Denmark; Dr F.X. Pi-Sunyer, Division of Endocrinology, Diabetes and Nutrition, St Luke's Roosevelt Hospital Center, New York, NY, USA; Dr C. Plato, Gerontology Research Center, National Institute on Aging, National Institutes of Health, Baltimore, MD, USA; Dr C. Powell, Tropical Metabolic Research Unit, University of the West Indies, Mona, Jamaica; Dr R.J. Prineas, Department of Epidemiology and Public Health, University of Miami, Miami, FL, USA; Dr L. Proos, Department of Paediatrics, Uppsala University, Uppsala, Sweden; Dr J. Rivera, National Institute of Public Health, Morelos, Mexico; Dr A. Roche, Division of Human Biology, Wright State University, Yellow Springs, OH, USA; Dr W. Rogan, National Institute of Environmental Health Sciences, National Institutes of Health, Research Triangle Park, NC, USA; Dr M.-F. Rolland-Cachera, Institut Scientifique et Technique de la Nutrition et de l'Alimentation (INSERM), Paris, France; Dr I. Rosenberg, Human Nutrition Research Center on Aging, Tufts University, Boston, MA, USA; Dr R. Roubenoff, Human Nutrition Research Center on Aging, Tufts University, Boston, MA, USA; Dr L. Salmenpera, Jorvi Hospital, Espoo, Finland; Dr D. Sanders, Public Health Programme, University of the Western Cape, Belleville, South Africa; Dr F. Savage-King, Programme for Control of Diarrhoeal Diseases, World Health Organization, Geneva, Switzerland; Dr K. Scanlon, Division of Nutrition, Centers for Disease Control and Prevention, Atlanta, GA, USA; Dr T. Scholl, Department of Obstetrics and Gynecology, University of Medicine and Dentistry of New Jersey, Camden, NJ, USA; Dr P.M. Shah, Maternal and Child Health and Family Planning, World Health Organization, Geneva, Switzerland; Dr R. Shephard, School of Physical and Health Education, University of Toronto, Toronto, Ontario, Canada; Dr N. Solomons, CESSIAM, Eye and Ear Hospital, Guatemala City, Guatemala; Dr E. Sommerfelt, Demographic and Health Surveys, Macro International, Columbia, MD, USA; Dr A. Sorenson, National Institute on Aging, National Institutes of Health, Bethesda, MD, USA; Dr A. Stunkard, Obesity Research Group, University of Pennsylvania, Philadelphia, PA, USA; Dr K. Sullivan, Center for International Health, Emory University School of Public Health, Atlanta, GA, USA; Dr A. Svanborg, Clinical Science, University of Illinois at Chicago, Chicago, IL, USA; Dr M. Tayback, Center on Aging, Johns Hopkins University, Baltimore, MD, USA; Dr S. Thorslund, Department of Medicine, Finspang Hospital, Finspang, Sweden; Dr J. Tobin, Gerontology Research Center, National Institute on Aging, National Institutes of Health, Baltimore, MD, USA; Dr A. Tomkins, Institute of Child Health, University of London, London, England; Dr R. Trowbridge, Division of Nutrition, Centers for Disease Control and Prevention, Atlanta, GA, USA. Dr E. Urbankova, Department of Obstetrics and Gynaecology, Faculty Hospital, Martin, Slovakia; Dr J. Van den Broeck, Centre for Human Genetics, Louvain, Belgium; Dr W. van Staveren, Department of Human Nutrition, Agricultural University,

Wageningen, Netherlands; Dr M.A. van't Hof, Department of Medical Statistics, Catholic University, Nijmegen, Netherlands; Dr B. Vellas, Centre for Geriatric Medicine, Toulouse, France; Dr R. Wallace, Department of Preventive Medicine and Environmental Health, University of Iowa, Iowa City, IA, USA; Dr J. Waterlow, Emeritus Professor of Human Nutrition, London School of Hygiene and Tropical Medicine, London, England; Dr R. Whitehead, Dunn Nutrition Centre, Cambridge, England; Dr W. Willett, Department of Nutrition, Harvard School of Public Health, Boston, MA, USA; Professor D.F. Williamson, Division of Nutrition, Centers for Disease Control, Atlanta, GA, USA; Dr P. Winichagoon, Mahidol University, Nakhon Pathom, Thailand; Dr D.L. Yeung, Corporate Nutrition, Heinz Company of Canada Ltd, North York, Ontario, Canada; Dr Zamzam Al-Mousa, Nutrition Unit, Department of Public Health, Al-Shaab, Kuwait; Professor P. Zimmet, International Diabetes Institute, Caulfield, Victoria, Australia.

The Committee expressed special appreciation to Mrs Julie Johnston and Ms Monika Blössner for their valuable contributions to the preparation and running of the meeting.

Annex 1
Glossary of terms and abbreviations

This glossary provides brief definitions of terms and abbreviations used in the report. More detailed definitions may be found in specialized dictionaries, and many of the terms are more fully discussed in the relevant sections of this report.

abdominal circumference
Circumference of the trunk, which reflects intra-abdominal and subcutaneous fat. Preference has been given in this report to circumference of the abdomen rather than the waist (the narrowest part of the trunk). The recommended measurement protocol is described in Annex 2.

abdominal fatness
Fat deposition, primarily visceral, reflected in a large abdominal circumference, especially relative to hip or lower body circumferences.

abdomen:hip ratio
The ratio of abdominal circumference to hip circumference. See measurement protocols in Annex 2.

adolescence
The period extending from the earliest signs of pubescence to the achievement of adult status.

adolescent spurt
A transient period of rapid somatic growth during pubescence, occurring about 2 years earlier in girls than in boys. See section 6.

adiposity
A descriptive term (from adipose tissue or fat) referring to the relative contribution of fat to body composition.

adult voice
The attainment of adult voice, a maturational indicator for boys. See section 6 and Annex 2.

AGA
See *appropriate for gestational age.*

AMA
See *arm muscle area.*

AMC
See *arm muscle circumference.*

appropriate for gestational age (AGA)
Birth weight in the normal range, based on percentile definitions related to gestational age. See section 4.

arm muscle area (AMA)
The estimated cross-sectional area of the muscle in the upper arm, calculated from the triceps skinfold thickness and arm circumference. See Annex 2 for derivation.

arm muscle circumference (AMC)
The estimated circumference of the muscle in the upper arm, calculated from triceps skinfold thickness and arm circumference. See Annex 2 for derivation.

attributable risk
The proportion of a population outcome due to an exposure. For example, the proportion of deaths from diarrhoea that can be attributed to malnutrition. This measure is derived by subtracting the rate of the outcome (usually incidence or mortality) among the unexposed from the rate among the exposed individuals.

AV
See *adult voice.*

B2
Breast stage 2. A stage in the maturation of the breast in females. See Annex 2 for description, and section 6.

BMI
See *body mass index.*

body mass index (BMI)
A measure of body mass relative to height, calculated as weight $(kg)/height^2$ (m^2).

breast-milk substitute
Any food marketed or otherwise represented as a partial or total replacement for breast milk, whether or not suitable for that purpose.

catch-up growth
Rapid, compensatory growth during rehabilitation from prior nutritional deficits or illness.

complementary feeding
Provision of both breast milk and solid (or semi-solid) food to a child.

complementary food
Any food, whether manufactured or locally prepared, suitable as a complement to breast milk or to infant formula, when either becomes insufficient to satisfy the nutritional requirements of the infant. Such food is also commonly called "weaning food" or "breast milk supplement".

exclusive breast-feeding
The feeding of an infant only with breast milk from his/her mother or a wet nurse, or expressed breast milk, and *no other* liquids or solids except vitamins, mineral supplements, or medicines in drop or syrup form.

fatness
The relative amount of body fat.

GA
See *gestational age.*

G3
Genital stage 3. For boys, a stage in the maturation of the genitalia. See Annex 2 for description, and section 6.

gestational age (GA)
Duration of pregnancy, usually expressed in weeks. See section 3.

growth faltering
The negative departure of a child's growth path. Failure to gain, or actual loss of, weight; a weight gain less than a specified value over a given period.

growth velocity
The rate of growth over a specified period, e.g. 5 cm/year.

indicators
Relate to the use or application of indices and are often constructed from them. For example, the proportion of children below a certain level of weight-for-age is widely used as an indicator of nutritional status. See section 2.

indices
Indices are combinations of measurements necessary for their interpretation. For example, a value for weight alone has no meaning unless it is related to age or height. Thus, weight and height may be combined to produce the body mass index. See section 2.

intrauterine growth retardation (IUGR)
Birthweight below a given low percentile cut-off for gestational age. See section 4.

IUGR
See *intrauterine growth retardation.*

large for gestational age (LGA)
Birthweight above a given high percentile cut-off for gestational age. See section 4.

last menstrual period (LMP)
The recalled first day of the last normal menstrual period before the amenorrhea associated with pregnancy; used in dating the beginning of pregnancy. See section 3.

LBW
See *low birth weight.*

LGA
See *large for gestational age.*

LMP
See *last menstrual period.*

low birth weight (LBW)
Birth weight < 2500 g

low height-for-age
Height < –2 SD of the sex-specific reference data relative to age. See section 5.

low weight-for-age
Weight < –2 SD of the sex-specific reference data relative to age. See section 5.

low weight-for-height
Weight < –2 SD of the sex-specific reference data relative to height. See section 5.

maturation
The process of achievement of adult status in structure or function.

menarche
The onset of menses (menstruation) in adolescent girls. The age at which menarche occurs is an indicator of maturational timing. See section 6.

menopause
Natural menopause is considered to have occurred in a woman after 12 consecutive months with no menses.

mid-upper arm circumference (MUAC)
The circumference of the upper arm measured at the mid-point between the tip of the acromial process and the tip of the olecranon process.

MUAC
See *mid-upper arm circumference.*

NCHS
National Center for Health Statistics. A governmental agency in the USA charged with collection and distribution of national data related to health.

NCHS/WHO growth reference data
Reference data for height and weight of children in the USA, originally collected by the National Center for Health Statistics and recommended for international use by WHO.

net gestational weight gain
During pregnancy, the total maternal weight gain minus the infant's birth weight.

net gestational rate of gain
During pregnancy, the net gestational weight gain/gestational age.

nomogram
A graphical device to allow rapid determination of an index (such as BMI), avoiding the need for detailed calculations.

obesity
A state of excess body fat storage (There is no agreement about cut-off points for the percentage of body fat that constitutes obesity.) See sections 6 and 7.

overall rate of gestational weight gain
During pregnancy, the total maternal weight gain/gestational age.

overweight
Excess weight relative to height. For adults, this report recognizes the following three grades of overweight, as judged by BMI:

grade 1: BMI 25.00–29.99

grade 2: BMI 30.00–39.99

grade 3: BMI $\geq$ 40.00

peak height velocity
The maximum rate of growth in stature occurring during the adolescent spurt. See section 6.

point of flexion
The most acute bend in a curve, especially with regard to curves of rates of risk. (The term "inflection" has a very specific meaning in mathematics and was therefore considered inappropriate for most uses considered in this report.)

predominant breast-feeding
Breast milk as an infant's predominant source of nourishment, but with the possible addition of water and water-based drinks (sweetened and flavoured water, teas, infusions, etc.), fruit juice, oral rehydration salts (ORS) solution, drop and syrup forms of vitamins, minerals, and medicines, and ritual fluids (in limited quantities). With the exception of fruit juice and sugar-water, no food-based fluid is admitted by this definition.

prepregnancy weight
Maternal weight measured before conception.

preterm delivery
Birth at < 37 weeks of gestation.

prevalence
The proportion of a population with a disease or condition. See section 2.

pubescence
The period of development of secondary sex characteristics from childhood patterns to adult patterns.

rate of short-term gestational weight gain
During pregnancy, the maternal weight gain between two prenatal visits divided by the gestational age interval between visits.

relative risk
The ratio of the risk of disease or death in one group (exposed) to the risk in another group (unexposed). Groups are often defined by exposure to detrimental factors.

Rohrer's ponderal index
In newborns, an index characterizing body proportions. See Annex 2 for derivation, and section 4.

sexual maturation
The attainment of adult patterns of secondary sex characteristics and reproductive functions. See section 6.

sexual maturation ratings (SMR)
Ratings or stages of the development of secondary sex characteristics, based on quantitative and qualitative changes in pubic hair, breast development in females, and pubic hair, genitalia and voice in males.

SGA
See *small for gestational age.*

shortness
A descriptive term for low height-for-age, without implication of causes.

skeletal maturation
The maturation of the bones of the skeleton, primarily described by changes in shape of primary and secondary centres of ossification from radiographs, and terminating in the fusion of epiphyses of long bones and the cessation of longitudinal growth.

small for gestational age (SGA)
Birthweight below a given low percentile cut-off for gestational age. SGA and intrauterine growth retardation (IUGR) are not strictly synonymous: some SGA infants (e.g. those born to short mothers) may represent merely the lower extreme of the "normal" fetal growth distribution, while other infants who meet the criteria for AGA may have actually been exposed to one or more growth-inhibiting factors. In individual cases, however, it is usually very difficult to ascertain whether or not the observed birth weight is the result of restricted *in utero* growth; classification of an infant as IUGR is thus based, de facto, on the established cut-off for SGA. See section 4.

spermarche
The onset of production of sperm cells by adolescent males.

standard deviation score
See *Z-score.*

stunted
Term applied to individuals whose height-for-age is low as the result of the past process of stunting.

stunting
The process of failure to reach linear growth potential as a result of inadequate nutrition and/or poor health. See section 5.

supplementary feeding programme
A programme providing food or meals additional to the regular family diet, often for younger children who are at risk of inadequate nutrition.

therapeutic feeding programme
Intensive feeding in a supervised or clinical setting for children found to be significantly wasted because of starvation or diseases.

thinness
Insufficient body mass relative to height as indicated by low BMI. For adults, this report recognizes the following three grades of thinness:

grade 1: BMI 17.0–18.49 (mild)

grade 2: BMI 16.0–16.99 (moderate)

grade 3: BMI <16.0 (severe)

Thinness in adolescents is defined as BMI <5th percentile for age.

total gestational weight gain
The difference between final maternal weight, measured or recalled immediately before delivery, and measured or recalled prepregnancy weight.

underweight
See *low weight-for-age*, and section 5.

wasting
See *low weight-for-height.* Describes a recent or current severe process leading to significant weight loss, usually as a consequence of acute starvation and/or severe disease. See section 5.

weaning process
The progressive transfer from breast milk as the sole source of an infant's nourishment to the usual family diet.

weight cycling
Repeated weight gain and loss in an individual, which may be intentional or unintentional and may lead to net gain, net loss, or no overall change.

Z-score (standard deviation score).
The deviation of an individual's value from the median value of a reference population, divided by the standard deviation of the reference population. See sections 2 and 5.

Annex 2
Recommended measurement protocols and derivation of indices

1. Introduction

The manner in which anthropometric and related data are collected requires careful attention. Correct procedures for obtaining the basic measurements are central to the appropriate use and interpretation of anthropometry. The use of specified protocols accomplishes several objectives: it ensures that measurements are comparable with reference data, facilitates interpretation of results, provides a basis for training and standardization of data collectors, and maximizes the reliability of measurements.

This annex provides the basic information necessary for collecting measurements recommended for use in the various age and physical status groups. Specific techniques and details of applications and interpretation of the measurements are provided within the main sections of the report. More complete discussions of anthropometric protocols for many of the recommended measurements and for measurements that may be used for other purposes may be found elsewhere (*1, 2*). To be consistent with the recommended reference data, arm circumference and skinfolds should be measured on the right side of the body.

Training data collectors is important for the proper use of anthropometry, and various publications provide procedures for standardization – ensuring that all observers take measurements in the same way (*3, 4*). It is also important that training curricula cover issues of sensitivity to local customs, dress, and practices of modesty, especially where proper measurement will require the exposure of certain parts of the body. Many problems in this area may be avoided by using observers of the same sex as the subjects.

For almost all age groups, it is recommended that age, sex, height, and weight are recorded; other measurements may be restricted to a single group (e.g. fundal height in pregnancy, attainment of adult voice in adolescence). Table A2.1 may be used to identify all measurements recommended for a particular age or status group or to identify the group or groups in which a specific measurement is advocated.

2. Determination of age and sex

2.1 *Chronological age*

Since many of the recommended measurements and reference data are considered in terms of chronological age, accurate age determination is important, especially for very young children and during adolescence because of the rapid rates of growth. In many areas, birth date is formally registered, and chronological age can be obtained through interviews and

Table A 2.1
Measurements recommended for use in particular age and status groups

Measurement	Age or status group							
	Pregnancy	Newborn	Infancy	Childhood	Adolescence	Adult, overweight	Adult, thinness	Elderly
Age	X	X	X	X	X	X	X	X
Sex	X	X	X	X	X	X	X	X
Gestational age	X	X						
Symphysis-fundus height	X							
Height	X			X	X	X	X	X
Sitting height							X	X
Length		X	X	X				
Weight	X	X	X	X	X	X	X	X
Circumferences								
Head		X	X	X				
Arm	X			X			X	X
Chest		X						
Abdomen						X		X
Hip						X		X
Calf	X							X

Table A 2.1 (*continued*)

Measurement	Age or status group							
	Pregnancy	Newborn	Infancy	Childhood	Adolescence	Adult, overweight	Adult, thinness	Elderly
Skinfold thicknesses								
Triceps					X		X	X
Subscapular	X				X			X
Thigh	X				X			X
Maturational indicators								
Menarcheal status					X			
Breast stage 2 (B2)					X			
Genital stage 3 (G3)					X			
Adult voice (AV)					X			
Derived indices								
Weight loss					X		X	X
Body mass index	X				X	X	X	X
Ponderal index		X						
Abdomen:hip ratio						X		X
Arm muscle circumference							X	
Arm muscle area							X	

verified from records, if necessary. Where birth dates are not commonly known or recorded, efforts should be made to approximate age as accurately as possible; some approaches based on local cultural designations or calendar-related events have been successful in this regard (5). Except in emergency situations, however, children's age should not be approximated according to height or weight: small children are likely to be considered younger than they are, and prevalence of undernutrition will therefore be underestimated.

Counting the number of deciduous teeth in young children may be appropriate for assigning them to age groups, but is an unsatisfactory method for individuals because of the wide variation in the timing of deciduous eruption (6). Eruption of permanent teeth in adolescents is more sensitive to environmental influences than that of deciduous teeth in younger children; counting the number of permanent teeth in adolescents will result in underestimation of chronological age in populations whose overall somatic maturation has been delayed by environmental factors (7). Moreover, variation in the timing of permanent tooth eruption makes this an inappropriate method of estimating chronological age of the individual. Assessment of the recommended maturational indicators will allow grouping of adolescents into general categories that may be useful for interpreting anthropometric data, but is not appropriate for estimating chronological age in individuals.

2.2 *Gestational age*

For newborns, gestational age should be assessed, and may be considered as the number of completed weeks since the first day of the last normal menstrual period (LMP). The LMP date is obtained by interviewing the mother carefully. Alternatively, when ultrasound equipment is available, early (<20 weeks) ultrasonic measurements of fetal dimensions can improve the estimate of gestational age (8).

2.3 *Sex*

Because of the systematic differences in anthropometric dimensions at most ages, recommended reference data are reported separately for males and females. The collected data should therefore include the sex of individuals concerned. Distinctions between sexes will usually be obvious, although parents or other family members may need to be consulted in the case of small children.

3. Measurement protocols

3.1 *Height, sitting height, length, and weight*

Height (adapted from reference 2)
The measurement of height requires a vertical board with an attached metric rule and a horizontal headboard that can be brought into contact with the uppermost point on the head. The individual to be measured

should be barefoot or in thin socks and wearing little clothing so that the positioning of the body can be seen. He or she should stand on a flat surface, with weight distributed evenly on both feet, heels together, and the head positioned so that the line of vision is perpendicular to the body. The arms hang freely by the sides, and the head, back, buttocks, and heels are in contact with the vertical board. Anyone who cannot stand straight in this position should be positioned vertically so that only the buttocks and the heels or the head are in contact with the vertical board. The individual is asked to inhale deeply and maintain a fully erect position. The movable headboard is brought onto the topmost point on the head with sufficient pressure to compress the hair. For consistency with methods used to collect the recommended reference data, no additional upward pressure is exerted on the mastoid processes. The height is recorded to the nearest 0.1 cm.

Two measurers are needed to determine the height of children aged 2–3 years. One measurer places a hand on the child's feet to prevent lifting of the heels and to keep the heels against the vertical board, and makes sure the knees are extended with the other hand. The second lowers the headboard and observes the height reading.

Note: See section 9.4.2 for height measurements in the elderly.

Sitting height (adapted from reference 2)
The measurement of sitting height requires a table and an anthropometer or measuring stick with a horizontal headboard. The individual sits on the table with the legs hanging unsupported over the edge and with the hands resting on the thighs. The posture is as erect as possible, and the line of vision parallel to the ground. It is useful for the measurer to apply gentle pressure with the right hand over the lumbar area and the left hand, simultaneously, on the superior part of the sternum; this reinforces the erect position. Gentle upward pressure on the mastoid processes ensures the fully erect seated posture.

The anthropometer is positioned vertically in the midline behind the subject so that it nearly touches the back. The measurer's left hand is placed under the subject's chin to assist in holding the proper position, and the right hand moves the blade of the anthropometer onto the vertex (the topmost point of the head). The subject is instructed to take a deep breath, and the measurement is made just before he or she exhales and recorded to the nearest 0.1 cm.

Length (adapted from reference 2)
Two observers are required to measure recumbent length. The subject lies in a supine position on a recumbent length table or measuring board. The crown of the head touches the stationary, vertical headboard. The subject's head is held with the line of vision aligned perpendicular to the plane of the measuring surface. The shoulders and buttocks are flat against the table top, with the shoulders and hips aligned at right angles

to the long axis of the body. The legs are extended at the hips and knees and lie flat against the table top, and the arms rest against the sides of the trunk. The measurer ensures that the legs remain flat on the table and shifts the movable board against the heels. In infants, care is taken to extend the legs gently. The length is recorded to the nearest 0.1 cm.

Weight (adapted from reference 2)
During infancy, a levelled pan scale with a beam and movable weights is preferred. Other types of scales may be used where pan scales are unavailable; all types should be regularly calibrated. Birth weight should be determined within 12 hours of birth. The infant, with or without a diaper, is placed on the scales so that the weight is distributed equally about the centre of the pan. When the infant is lying or suspended quietly (which may require patience), weight is recorded to the nearest 10 g. When an infant is restless, it is possible to weigh the mother while she is holding the infant and again without the infant, but this procedure is unreliable, partly because the mother's weight will usually be recorded to the nearest 100 g. If a diaper is worn, its weight is subtracted from the observed weight: reference data for infants are based on nude weights.

An individual who is able to stand without support is weighed using a levelled platform scale with a beam and movable weights. He or she stands still in centre of the platform, with the body weight evenly distributed between both feet. Light indoor clothing can be worn, but shoes, long trousers, and sweaters should be removed. The weight of the remaining clothing is not subtracted from the observed weight when the recommended reference data are used; however, if heavy clothing must be worn during weighing because of cultural constraints, adjustments should be made before weight measurements are interpreted. Weight is recorded to the nearest 100 g.

Individuals, other than infants, who cannot stand unsupported by reason of disability can be weighed using a beam chair scale or bed scale. If an adult weighs more than the upper limit on the beam, a compensating weight can be suspended from the left-hand end of the beam and the measurer must then determine how much weight must be placed on the platform for the scale to record zero. When the subject is reweighed, this compensatory weight is added to his or her measured weight.

Note: See section 9.4.1 for weight measurements in the elderly.

3.2 *Circumferences*

Measurements of body circumferences require a flexible but inelastic (non-stretchable) graduated tape measure.

Head circumference (adapted from reference 2)
Head circumference is measured with the infant held or seated on the lap of the mother or care-taker. Objects such as hairpins are removed from

the hair. The tape is positioned just above the eyebrows and placed posteriorly to give the maximum circumference. It is pulled sufficiently tight to compress hair and yield a measure that "approximates" cranial circumference. The measurement is recorded to the nearest 0.1 cm.

Mid-upper arm circumference (adapted from reference 2)
For measurement of MUAC the subject stands erect, with the arms hanging freely at the sides of the trunk, the palms towards the thighs. Loose clothing without sleeves is worn to allow total exposure of the arm and shoulder area. The circumference is measured at the midpoint of the arm. To locate the midpoint, the subject's elbow is flexed to 90° with the palm facing upward. The measurer locates the lateral tip of the acromion at the shoulder, and a small mark is made at the identified point. The most distal point on the olecranon process of the ulna (at the point of the elbow) is located and marked. A measuring tape placed over these two marks is used to find the midpoint between them, which is marked.

With the subject's arm relaxed, the elbow extended and hanging just away from the side of the trunk, and the palm towards the thigh, the tape is placed around the arm and positioned perpendicular to the long axis of the arm at the marked midpoint. With the tape snug to the skin but not compressing soft tissues, the circumference is recorded to the nearest 0.1 cm.

Note: See section 9.4.5 for measurements in the elderly.

Chest circumference (adapted from reference 2)
An infant is measured when held or seated on the lap of the mother or care-taker; the chest should be bare. The arms are abducted slightly to permit passage of the tape around the chest. When the tape is snugly in place, the arms are lowered to their natural position at the sides of the trunk. Chest circumference is measured at the level of the fourth costosternal (rib) joints, counting the number of ribs from above. The measurement is made in a horizontal plane to the nearest 0.1 cm at the end of a normal expiration.

Abdominal circumference (adapted from references 2 and 9)
The subject stands comfortably with his or her weight evenly distributed on both feet, and the feet about 25–30 cm apart. The measurement is taken midway between the inferior margin of the last rib and the crest of the ilium, in a horizontal plane. Each landmark should be palpated and marked, and the midpoint determined with a tape measure and marked. The observer sits by the side of the subject and fits the tape snugly but not so tightly as to compress underlying soft tissues. The circumference is measured to the nearest 0.1 cm at the end of normal expiration.

Hip (buttocks) circumference (adapted from reference 2)
Wearing only nonrestrictive briefs or underwear, or a light smock over underwear, the subject stands erect with arms at the sides and feet

together. The measurer sits at the side of the subject so that the level of maximum extension of the buttocks can be seen, and places the tape measure around the buttocks in a horizontal plane. An assistant may be needed to help position the tape on the opposite side of the subject's body. The tape is snug against the skin but does not compress the soft tissues. The measurement is recorded to the nearest 0.1 cm.

Calf circumference (adapted from reference 2)
The subject sits on a table so that the leg to be measured hangs freely; alternatively, he or she stands with the feet about 20 cm apart and weight distributed equally on both feet. The tape measure is positioned horizontally around the calf and moved up and down to locate the maximum circumference in a plane perpendicular to the long axis of the calf. The tape is in contact with the skin over the whole circumference but does not indent the skin. The measurement is recorded to the nearest 0.1 cm. During infancy and in the elderly, calf circumference can be measured with the subject supine and the knee flexed to 90°.

Note: See section 9.4.3 for further details of measurements in the elderly.

3.3 *Skinfold thicknesses*

Skinfolds should be measured using skinfold callipers, such as Lange or Holtain callipers, that provide standardized pressure at all jaw openings. Some plastic models are available and may be preferred for non-research purposes. General guidelines for measuring skinfolds should be consulted for those inexperienced in these methods (*1, 2*).

Triceps skinfold (adapted from reference 2)
The triceps skinfold is measured in the midline of the posterior aspect of the arm, over the triceps muscle, at a level midway between the lateral projection of the acromion process at the shoulder and the olecranon process of the ulna (at the point of the elbow). With the elbow flexed to 90°, the midpoint is determined by measuring the distance between the two landmarks using a tape measure; it is marked on the lateral side of the arm. Except for infants and the handicapped, the subject should be measured standing, with the arm hanging loosely and comfortably at the side. The calliper is held in the measurer's right hand. A vertical fold of skin and subcutaneous tissue is picked up gently with the left thumb and index finger, approximately 1 cm proximal to the marked level, and the tips of the callipers are applied perpendicular to the skinfold at the marked level. Measurements are recorded to the nearest 0.5 mm (Lange callipers), 0.2 mm (Holtain callipers), or smallest unit of graduation.

Note: See section 9.4.6 for measurements in the elderly.

Subscapular skinfold (adapted from reference 2)
The subscapular skinfold is picked up gently on a diagonal, inclined infero-laterally at approximately 45° to the horizontal plane in the natural

cleavage lines of the skin. The site is just inferior to the inferior angle of the scapula. The subject stands comfortably erect, with the arms relaxed at the sides of the body. To locate the site, the measurer palpates the scapula, running the fingers inferiorly and laterally along its vertebral border until the inferior angle is identified. For some subjects, especially the obese, gently placing the arm behind the back will help identify the site. The calliper jaws are applied 1 cm infero-lateral to the thumb and finger raising the fold, and the thickness is recorded to the nearest 0.5 mm (Lange callipers), 0.2 mm (Holtain callipers), or smallest unit of graduation.

Note: See section 9.4.4 for measurements in the elderly.

Thigh skinfold (anterior) (adapted from reference 2)
The thigh skinfold site is located in the midline of the anterior aspect of the thigh, midway between the inguinal crease and the proximal border of the knee cap (patella). The subject flexes the hip to assist location of the inguinal crease. The thickness of the vertical fold is measured while the subject stands. The body weight is shifted to the other foot while the leg on the measurement side is relaxed with the knee slightly flexed and the foot flat on the floor. The calliper jaws are applied about 1 cm distal to the fingers holding the fold, and the thickness of the fold is recorded to the nearest 0.5 mm (Lange callipers), 0.2 mm (Holtain callipers), or the smallest unit of graduation.

3.4   *Maturational indicators in adolescence*

More complete descriptions and discussions of stages of secondary sexual characteristics used as maturational indicators may be found elsewhere (*10, 11*).

Menarcheal status (girls) (adapted from reference 12)
Menarcheal status is determined by interview. At the time of questioning each subject is asked her age (or her date of birth) and whether she has begun to menstruate. A knowledge of local language and terminology for referring to menstruation is necessary so that the information obtained is correct.

B2 – Breast development (girls) (adapted from references 10 and 11)
Breast stage 2 (B2) is an arbitrary stage in the process of areolar and breast development in adolescence. It is the breast bud stage, characterized by elevation of the breast and papilla as a small mound, in contrast to the lack of palpable breast tissue in childhood; areolar diameter is enlarged and areolar tissue is elevated.

G3 – Genital development (boys) (adapted from references 10 and 11)
Genital stage 3 (G3) is an arbitrary stage in the process of development in size and shape of penis and scrotum in adolescence. It is characterized

by enlargement of the penis, especially in length, compared with the childhood form; enlargement of testes and descent of the scrotum are also evident.

Voice change (boys) (adapted from reference 13)
The recommended maturational indicator is the attainment of the adult voice (sometimes designated AV). It is important to specify that for the recommended uses, the voice change noted is not the so-called "breaking" or husky adolescent voice, but the attainment of the adult voice. The pitch and resonance of the voice has adult characteristics. It may be helpful for assessment to have boys read or recite a chosen text.

3.5 *Other measurements*

Fundal height (symphysis–fundus height) (adapted from reference 14)
A measuring tape of nonelastic material is required. The distance between the upper border of the symphysis pubis to the superior fundus uteri is recorded to the nearest 0.1 cm.

4. Derived indices

The following seven recommended indices are derived from the basic measurements:

- *Percentage weight loss*, or weight change, is calculated as:

$$\frac{\text{previous weight - current weight}}{\text{previous weight}} \times 100$$

Weight must be measured in the same units on all occasions.

- *Sitting height: height ratio* is expressed as a decimal fraction:

$$\frac{\text{sitting height (cm)}}{\text{height (cm)}}$$

- *Body mass index (BMI)* is calculated as:

$$\frac{\text{weight (kg)}}{\text{height}^2 \text{ (m}^2)}$$

Body mass index may be calculated directly from observed measurements of weight and height, determined from a nomogram (Fig. A2.1), or derived from Table A2.2.

- *Ponderal index (Rohrer's) (PI)* for newborn is calculated as:

$$\frac{\text{birth weight (g)}}{\text{birth length}^3 \text{ (cm}^3)} \times 100$$

Figure A 2.1

Nomogram for obtaining body mass index from height, *H* (cm), and weight, *W* (kg)[a]

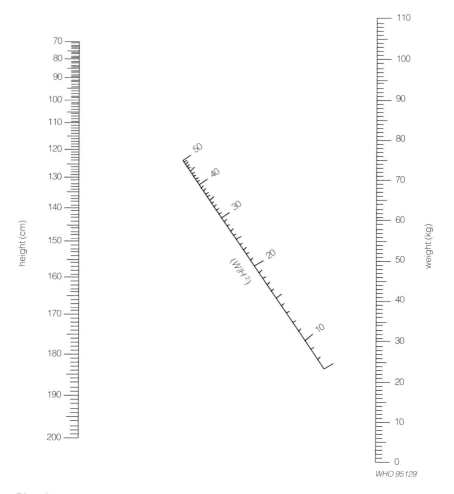

WHO 95129

Directions

1. Locate the person's height on the left column. Numbers in this column *increase* going down the scale.
2. Locate the person's weight on the right column. Numbers in this column *decrease* going down the scale.
3. Lay a ruler or straightedge so that it touches these two points – height and weight.
4. Note where the straightedge crosses the slanted line between these two columns. This is the body mass index value.
5. Enter the body mass index value in the person's record.

[a] Adapted from reference *16* with the permission of the American Society for Clinical Nutrition.

Table A 2.2

Body mass index for selected heights and weights

Weight	Height (cm)																																																		
(kg)	140	141	142	143	144	145	146	147	148	149	150	151	152	153	154	155	156	157	158	159	160	161	162	163	164	165	166	167	168	169	170	171	172	173	174	175	176	177	178	179	180	181	182	183	184	185	186	187	188	189	190
31	15.8	15.6	15.4	15.2	14.9	14.7	14.5	14.3	14.2	14.0	13.8	13.6	13.4	13.2	13.1	12.9	12.7	12.6	12.4	12.3	12.1	12.0	11.8	11.7	11.5	11.4	11.2	11.1	11.0	10.9	10.7	10.6	10.5	10.4	10.2	10.1	10.0														
32	16.3	16.1	15.9	15.6	15.4	15.2	15.0	14.8	14.6	14.4	14.2	14.0	13.9	13.7	13.5	13.3	13.1	13.0	12.8	12.7	12.5	12.3	12.2	12.0	11.9	11.8	11.6	11.5	11.3	11.2	11.1	10.9	10.8	10.7	10.6	10.4	10.3	10.2	10.1												
33	16.8	16.6	16.4	16.1	15.9	15.7	15.5	15.3	15.1	14.9	14.7	14.5	14.3	14.1	13.9	13.7	13.6	13.4	13.2	13.1	12.9	12.7	12.6	12.4	12.3	12.1	12.0	11.8	11.7	11.6	11.4	11.3	11.2	11.0	10.9	10.8	10.7	10.5	10.4	10.3	10.2	10.1									
34	17.3	17.1	16.9	16.6	16.4	16.2	16.0	15.7	15.5	15.3	15.1	14.9	14.7	14.5	14.3	14.2	14.0	13.8	13.6	13.4	13.3	13.1	13.0	12.8	12.6	12.5	12.3	12.2	12.0	11.9	11.8	11.6	11.5	11.4	11.2	11.1	11.0	10.9	10.7	10.6	10.5	10.4	10.3	10.2	10.0						
35	17.9	17.6	17.4	17.1	16.9	16.6	16.4	16.2	16.0	15.8	15.6	15.4	15.1	15.0	14.8	14.6	14.4	14.2	14.0	13.8	13.7	13.5	13.3	13.2	13.0	12.9	12.7	12.5	12.4	12.3	12.1	12.0	11.8	11.7	11.6	11.4	11.3	11.2	11.0	10.9	10.8	10.7	10.6	10.5	10.3	10.2	10.1	10.0			
36	18.4	18.1	17.9	17.6	17.4	17.1	16.9	16.7	16.4	16.2	16.0	15.8	15.6	15.4	15.2	15.0	14.8	14.6	14.4	14.2	14.1	13.9	13.7	13.5	13.4	13.2	13.1	12.9	12.8	12.6	12.5	12.3	12.2	12.0	11.9	11.8	11.6	11.5	11.4	11.2	11.1	11.0	10.9	10.7	10.6	10.5	10.4	10.3	10.2	10.1	
37	18.9	18.6	18.3	18.1	17.8	17.6	17.4	17.1	16.9	16.7	16.4	16.2	16.0	15.8	15.6	15.4	15.2	15.0	14.8	14.6	14.5	14.3	14.1	13.9	13.8	13.6	13.4	13.3	13.1	13.0	12.8	12.7	12.5	12.4	12.2	12.1	11.9	11.8	11.7	11.5	11.4	11.3	11.2	11.0	10.9	10.8	10.7	10.6	10.5	10.4	10.2
38	19.4	19.1	18.8	18.6	18.3	18.1	17.8	17.6	17.3	17.1	16.9	16.7	16.4	16.2	16.0	15.8	15.6	15.4	15.2	15.0	14.8	14.7	14.5	14.3	14.1	14.0	13.8	13.6	13.5	13.3	13.1	13.0	12.8	12.7	12.6	12.4	12.3	12.1	12.0	11.9	11.7	11.6	11.5	11.3	11.2	11.1	11.0	10.9	10.8	10.6	10.5
39	19.9	19.6	19.3	19.1	18.8	18.5	18.3	18.0	17.8	17.6	17.3	17.1	16.9	16.7	16.4	16.2	16.0	15.8	15.6	15.4	15.2	15.0	14.9	14.7	14.5	14.3	14.2	14.0	13.8	13.7	13.5	13.3	13.2	13.0	12.9	12.7	12.6	12.4	12.3	12.2	12.0	11.9	11.8	11.6	11.5	11.4	11.3	11.2	11.0	10.9	10.8
40	20.4	20.1	19.8	19.6	19.3	19.0	18.8	18.5	18.3	18.0	17.8	17.5	17.3	17.1	16.9	16.6	16.4	16.2	16.0	15.8	15.6	15.4	15.2	15.1	14.9	14.7	14.5	14.3	14.2	14.0	13.8	13.7	13.5	13.4	13.2	13.1	12.9	12.8	12.6	12.5	12.3	12.2	12.1	11.9	11.8	11.7	11.6	11.4	11.3	11.2	11.1
41	20.9	20.6	20.3	20.0	19.8	19.5	19.2	19.0	18.7	18.5	18.2	18.0	17.7	17.5	17.3	17.1	16.8	16.6	16.4	16.2	16.0	15.8	15.6	15.4	15.2	15.1	14.9	14.7	14.5	14.4	14.2	14.0	13.9	13.7	13.5	13.4	13.2	13.1	12.9	12.8	12.7	12.5	12.4	12.2	12.1	12.0	11.9	11.7	11.6	11.5	11.4
42	21.4	21.1	20.8	20.5	20.3	20.0	19.7	19.4	19.2	18.9	18.7	18.4	18.2	17.9	17.7	17.5	17.3	17.0	16.8	16.6	16.4	16.2	16.0	15.8	15.6	15.4	15.2	15.1	14.9	14.7	14.5	14.4	14.2	14.0	13.9	13.7	13.6	13.4	13.3	13.1	13.0	12.8	12.7	12.5	12.4	12.3	12.1	12.0	11.9	11.8	11.6
43	21.9	21.6	21.3	21.0	20.7	20.5	20.2	19.9	19.6	19.4	19.1	18.9	18.6	18.4	18.1	17.9	17.7	17.4	17.2	17.0	16.8	16.6	16.4	16.2	16.0	15.8	15.6	15.4	15.2	15.1	14.9	14.7	14.5	14.4	14.2	14.0	13.9	13.7	13.6	13.4	13.3	13.1	13.0	12.8	12.7	12.6	12.4	12.3	12.2	12.0	11.9
44	22.4	22.1	21.8	21.5	21.2	20.9	20.6	20.4	20.1	19.8	19.6	19.3	19.0	18.8	18.6	18.3	18.1	17.9	17.6	17.4	17.2	17.0	16.8	16.6	16.4	16.2	16.0	15.8	15.6	15.4	15.2	15.0	14.9	14.7	14.5	14.4	14.2	14.0	13.9	13.7	13.6	13.4	13.3	13.1	13.0	12.9	12.7	12.6	12.4	12.3	12.2
45	23.0	22.6	22.3	22.0	21.7	21.4	21.1	20.8	20.5	20.3	20.0	19.7	19.5	19.2	19.0	18.7	18.5	18.3	18.0	17.8	17.6	17.4	17.1	16.9	16.7	16.5	16.3	16.1	15.9	15.8	15.6	15.4	15.2	15.0	14.9	14.7	14.5	14.4	14.2	14.0	13.9	13.7	13.6	13.4	13.3	13.1	13.0	12.9	12.7	12.6	12.5
46	23.5	23.1	22.8	22.5	22.2	21.9	21.6	21.3	21.0	20.7	20.4	20.2	19.9	19.7	19.4	19.1	18.9	18.7	18.4	18.2	18.0	17.7	17.5	17.3	17.1	16.9	16.7	16.5	16.3	16.1	15.9	15.7	15.5	15.4	15.2	15.0	14.9	14.7	14.5	14.4	14.2	14.0	13.9	13.7	13.6	13.4	13.3	13.2	13.0	12.9	12.7
47	24.0	23.6	23.3	23.0	22.7	22.4	22.0	21.8	21.5	21.2	20.9	20.6	20.3	20.1	19.8	19.6	19.3	19.1	18.8	18.6	18.4	18.1	17.9	17.7	17.5	17.3	17.1	16.9	16.7	16.5	16.3	16.1	15.9	15.7	15.5	15.3	15.2	15.0	14.8	14.7	14.5	14.3	14.2	14.0	13.9	13.7	13.6	13.4	13.3	13.2	13.0
48	24.5	24.1	23.8	23.5	23.1	22.8	22.5	22.2	21.9	21.6	21.3	21.1	20.8	20.5	20.2	20.0	19.7	19.5	19.2	19.0	18.8	18.5	18.3	18.1	17.8	17.6	17.4	17.2	17.0	16.8	16.6	16.4	16.2	16.0	15.9	15.7	15.5	15.3	15.1	15.0	14.8	14.7	14.5	14.3	14.2	14.0	13.9	13.7	13.6	13.4	13.3
49	25.0	24.6	24.3	24.0	23.6	23.3	23.0	22.7	22.4	22.1	21.8	21.5	21.2	20.9	20.7	20.4	20.1	19.9	19.6	19.4	19.1	18.9	18.7	18.4	18.2	18.0	17.8	17.6	17.4	17.2	17.0	16.8	16.6	16.4	16.2	16.0	15.8	15.6	15.5	15.3	15.1	15.0	14.8	14.6	14.5	14.3	14.2	14.0	13.9	13.7	13.6
50	25.5	25.1	24.8	24.5	24.1	23.8	23.5	23.1	22.8	22.5	22.2	21.9	21.6	21.4	21.1	20.8	20.5	20.3	20.0	19.8	19.5	19.3	19.1	18.8	18.6	18.4	18.1	17.9	17.7	17.5	17.3	17.1	16.9	16.7	16.5	16.3	16.1	16.0	15.8	15.6	15.4	15.3	15.1	14.9	14.8	14.6	14.5	14.3	14.1	14.0	13.9
51	26.0	25.7	25.3	24.9	24.6	24.3	23.9	23.6	23.3	23.0	22.7	22.4	22.1	21.8	21.5	21.2	21.0	20.7	20.4	20.2	19.9	19.7	19.4	19.2	19.0	18.7	18.5	18.3	18.1	17.9	17.6	17.4	17.2	17.0	16.8	16.7	16.5	16.3	16.1	15.9	15.7	15.6	15.4	15.2	15.1	14.9	14.7	14.6	14.4	14.3	14.1
52	26.5	26.2	25.8	25.4	25.1	24.7	24.4	24.1	23.7	23.4	23.1	22.8	22.5	22.2	21.9	21.6	21.4	21.1	20.8	20.6	20.3	20.1	19.8	19.6	19.3	19.1	18.9	18.6	18.4	18.2	18.0	17.8	17.6	17.4	17.2	17.0	16.8	16.6	16.4	16.2	16.0	15.9	15.7	15.5	15.4	15.2	15.0	14.9	14.7	14.6	14.4
53	27.0	26.7	26.3	25.9	25.6	25.2	24.9	24.5	24.2	23.9	23.6	23.2	22.9	22.6	22.3	22.1	21.8	21.5	21.2	21.0	20.7	20.4	20.2	19.9	19.7	19.5	19.2	19.0	18.8	18.6	18.3	18.1	17.9	17.7	17.5	17.3	17.1	16.9	16.7	16.5	16.4	16.2	16.0	15.8	15.7	15.5	15.3	15.2	15.0	14.8	14.7
54	27.6	27.2	26.8	26.4	26.0	25.7	25.3	25.0	24.7	24.3	24.0	23.7	23.4	23.1	22.8	22.5	22.2	21.9	21.6	21.4	21.1	20.8	20.6	20.3	20.1	19.8	19.6	19.4	19.1	18.9	18.7	18.5	18.3	18.0	17.8	17.6	17.4	17.2	17.0	16.9	16.7	16.5	16.3	16.1	15.9	15.8	15.6	15.4	15.3	15.1	15.0
55	28.1	27.7	27.3	26.9	26.5	26.2	25.8	25.5	25.1	24.8	24.4	24.1	23.8	23.5	23.2	22.9	22.6	22.3	22.0	21.8	21.5	21.2	21.0	20.7	20.4	20.2	20.0	19.7	19.5	19.3	19.0	18.8	18.6	18.4	18.2	18.0	17.8	17.6	17.4	17.2	17.0	16.8	16.6	16.4	16.2	16.1	15.9	15.7	15.6	15.4	15.2
56	28.6	28.2	27.8	27.4	27.0	26.6	26.3	25.9	25.6	25.2	24.9	24.6	24.2	23.9	23.6	23.3	23.0	22.7	22.4	22.2	21.9	21.6	21.3	21.1	20.8	20.6	20.3	20.1	19.8	19.6	19.4	19.2	18.9	18.7	18.5	18.3	18.1	17.9	17.7	17.5	17.3	17.1	16.9	16.7	16.5	16.4	16.2	16.0	15.8	15.7	15.5
57	29.1	28.7	28.3	27.9	27.5	27.1	26.7	26.4	26.0	25.7	25.3	25.0	24.7	24.3	24.0	23.7	23.4	23.1	22.8	22.5	22.3	22.0	21.7	21.5	21.2	20.9	20.7	20.4	20.2	20.0	19.7	19.5	19.3	19.0	18.8	18.6	18.4	18.2	18.0	17.8	17.6	17.4	17.2	17.0	16.8	16.7	16.5	16.3	16.1	16.0	15.8
58	29.6	29.2	28.8	28.4	28.0	27.6	27.2	26.8	26.5	26.1	25.8	25.4	25.1	24.8	24.5	24.1	23.8	23.5	23.2	22.9	22.7	22.4	22.1	21.8	21.6	21.3	21.0	20.8	20.5	20.3	20.1	19.8	19.6	19.4	19.2	18.9	18.7	18.5	18.3	18.1	17.9	17.7	17.5	17.3	17.1	16.9	16.8	16.6	16.4	16.2	16.1
59	30.1	29.7	29.3	28.9	28.5	28.1	27.7	27.3	26.9	26.6	26.2	25.9	25.5	25.2	24.9	24.6	24.2	23.9	23.6	23.3	23.0	22.8	22.5	22.2	21.9	21.7	21.4	21.2	20.9	20.7	20.4	20.2	19.9	19.7	19.5	19.3	19.0	18.8	18.6	18.4	18.2	18.0	17.8	17.6	17.4	17.2	17.1	16.9	16.7	16.5	16.3
60	30.6	30.2	29.8	29.3	28.9	28.5	28.1	27.8	27.4	27.0	26.7	26.3	26.0	25.6	25.3	25.0	24.7	24.3	24.0	23.7	23.4	23.1	22.9	22.6	22.3	22.0	21.8	21.5	21.3	21.0	20.8	20.5	20.3	20.0	19.8	19.6	19.4	19.2	18.9	18.7	18.5	18.3	18.1	17.9	17.7	17.5	17.3	17.2	17.0	16.8	16.6
61	31.1	30.7	30.3	29.8	29.4	29.0	28.6	28.2	27.8	27.5	27.1	26.8	26.4	26.1	25.7	25.4	25.1	24.7	24.4	24.1	23.8	23.5	23.2	23.0	22.7	22.4	22.1	21.9	21.6	21.4	21.1	20.9	20.6	20.4	20.1	19.9	19.7	19.5	19.3	19.0	18.8	18.6	18.4	18.2	18.0	17.8	17.6	17.4	17.3	17.1	16.9
62	31.6	31.2	30.7	30.3	29.9	29.5	29.1	28.7	28.3	27.9	27.6	27.2	26.8	26.5	26.1	25.8	25.5	25.2	24.8	24.5	24.2	23.9	23.6	23.3	23.1	22.8	22.5	22.2	22.0	21.7	21.5	21.2	21.0	20.7	20.5	20.2	20.0	19.8	19.6	19.4	19.1	18.9	18.7	18.5	18.3	18.1	17.9	17.7	17.5	17.4	17.2
63	32.1	31.7	31.2	30.8	30.4	30.0	29.6	29.2	28.8	28.4	28.0	27.6	27.3	26.9	26.6	26.2	25.9	25.6	25.2	24.9	24.6	24.3	24.0	23.7	23.4	23.1	22.9	22.6	22.3	22.1	21.8	21.5	21.3	21.0	20.8	20.6	20.3	20.1	19.9	19.7	19.4	19.2	19.0	18.8	18.6	18.4	18.2	18.0	17.8	17.6	17.5
64	32.7	32.2	31.7	31.3	30.9	30.4	30.0	29.6	29.2	28.8	28.4	28.1	27.7	27.3	27.0	26.6	26.3	26.0	25.6	25.3	25.0	24.7	24.4	24.1	23.8	23.5	23.2	22.9	22.7	22.4	22.1	21.9	21.6	21.4	21.1	20.9	20.7	20.4	20.2	20.0	19.8	19.5	19.3	19.1	18.9	18.7	18.5	18.3	18.1	17.9	17.7
65	33.2	32.7	32.2	31.8	31.3	30.9	30.5	30.1	29.7	29.3	28.9	28.5	28.1	27.8	27.4	27.1	26.7	26.4	26.0	25.7	25.4	25.1	24.8	24.5	24.2	23.9	23.6	23.3	23.0	22.8	22.5	22.2	22.0	21.7	21.5	21.2	21.0	20.7	20.5	20.3	20.1	19.8	19.6	19.4	19.2	19.0	18.8	18.6	18.4	18.2	18.0
66	33.7	33.2	32.7	32.3	31.8	31.4	31.0	30.5	30.1	29.7	29.3	28.9	28.6	28.2	27.8	27.5	27.1	26.8	26.4	26.1	25.8	25.5	25.1	24.8	24.5	24.2	24.0	23.7	23.4	23.1	22.8	22.6	22.3	22.1	21.8	21.6	21.3	21.1	20.8	20.6	20.4	20.1	19.9	19.7	19.5	19.3	19.1	18.9	18.7	18.5	18.3
67	34.2	33.7	33.2	32.8	32.3	31.9	31.4	31.0	30.6	30.2	29.8	29.4	29.0	28.6	28.3	27.9	27.5	27.2	26.8	26.5	26.2	25.8	25.5	25.2	24.9	24.6	24.3	24.0	23.7	23.5	23.2	22.9	22.6	22.4	22.1	21.9	21.6	21.4	21.1	20.9	20.7	20.5	20.2	20.0	19.8	19.6	19.4	19.2	19.0	18.8	18.6
68	34.7	34.2	33.7	33.3	32.8	32.3	31.9	31.5	31.0	30.6	30.2	29.8	29.4	29.0	28.7	28.3	27.9	27.6	27.2	26.9	26.6	26.2	25.9	25.6	25.3	25.0	24.7	24.4	24.1	23.8	23.5	23.3	23.0	22.7	22.5	22.2	22.0	21.7	21.5	21.2	21.0	20.8	20.5	20.3	20.1	19.9	19.7	19.4	19.2	19.0	18.8
69	35.2	34.7	34.2	33.7	33.3	32.8	32.4	31.9	31.5	31.1	30.7	30.3	29.9	29.5	29.1	28.7	28.4	28.0	27.6	27.3	27.0	26.6	26.3	26.0	25.7	25.3	25.0	24.7	24.4	24.2	23.9	23.6	23.3	23.1	22.8	22.5	22.3	22.0	21.8	21.5	21.3	21.1	20.8	20.6	20.4	20.2	19.9	19.7	19.5	19.3	19.1
70	35.7	35.2	34.7	34.2	33.8	33.3	32.8	32.4	32.0	31.5	31.1	30.7	30.3	29.9	29.5	29.1	28.8	28.4	28.0	27.7	27.3	27.0	26.7	26.3	26.0	25.7	25.4	25.1	24.8	24.5	24.2	23.9	23.7	23.4	23.1	22.9	22.6	22.3	22.1	21.8	21.6	21.4	21.1	20.9	20.7	20.5	20.2	20.0	19.8	19.6	19.4
71	36.2	35.7	35.2	34.7	34.2	33.8	33.3	32.9	32.4	32.0	31.6	31.1	30.7	30.3	29.9	29.6	29.2	28.8	28.4	28.1	27.7	27.4	27.1	26.7	26.4	26.1	25.8	25.5	25.2	24.9	24.6	24.3	24.0	23.7	23.5	23.2	22.9	22.7	22.4	22.2	21.9	21.7	21.4	21.2	21.0	20.7	20.5	20.3	20.1	19.9	19.7
72	36.7	36.2	35.7	35.2	34.7	34.2	33.8	33.3	32.9	32.4	32.0	31.6	31.2	30.8	30.4	30.0	29.6	29.2	28.8	28.5	28.1	27.8	27.4	27.1	26.8	26.4	26.1	25.8	25.5	25.2	24.9	24.6	24.3	24.1	23.8	23.5	23.2	23.0	22.7	22.5	22.2	22.0	21.7	21.5	21.3	21.0	20.8	20.6	20.4	20.2	19.9
73	37.2	36.7	36.2	35.7	35.2	34.7	34.2	33.8	33.3	32.9	32.4	32.0	31.6	31.2	30.8	30.4	30.0	29.6	29.2	28.9	28.5	28.2	27.8	27.5	27.1	26.8	26.5	26.2	25.9	25.6	25.3	25.0	24.7	24.4	24.1	23.8	23.6	23.3	23.0	22.8	22.5	22.3	22.0	21.8	21.6	21.3	21.1	20.9	20.7	20.4	20.2
74	37.8	37.2	36.7	36.2	35.7	35.2	34.7	34.2	33.8	33.3	32.9	32.5	32.0	31.6	31.2	30.8	30.4	30.0	29.6	29.3	28.9	28.5	28.2	27.9	27.5	27.2	26.9	26.5	26.2	25.9	25.6	25.3	25.0	24.7	24.4	24.2	23.9	23.6	23.4	23.1	22.8	22.6	22.3	22.1	21.9	21.6	21.4	21.2	20.9	20.7	20.5
75	38.3	37.7	37.2	36.7	36.2	35.7	35.2	34.7	34.2	33.8	33.3	32.9	32.5	32.0	31.6	31.2	30.8	30.4	30.0	29.7	29.3	28.9	28.6	28.2	27.9	27.5	27.2	26.9	26.6	26.3	26.0	25.6	25.4	25.1	24.8	24.5	24.2	23.9	23.7	23.4	23.1	22.9	22.6	22.4	22.2	21.9	21.7	21.4	21.2	21.0	20.8
76	38.8	38.2	37.7	37.2	36.7	36.1	35.7	35.2	34.7	34.2	33.8	33.3	32.9	32.5	32.0	31.6	31.2	30.8	30.4	30.1	29.7	29.3	29.0	28.6	28.3	27.9	27.6	27.3	26.9	26.6	26.3	26.0	25.7	25.4	25.1	24.8	24.5	24.3	24.0	23.7	23.5	23.2	22.9	22.7	22.4	22.2	22.0	21.7	21.5	21.3	21.1
77	39.3	38.7	38.2	37.7	37.1	36.6	36.1	35.6	35.2	34.7	34.2	33.8	33.3	32.9	32.5	32.0	31.6	31.2	30.8	30.5	30.1	29.7	29.3	29.0	28.6	28.3	27.9	27.6	27.3	27.0	26.6	26.3	26.0	25.7	25.4	25.1	24.9	24.6	24.3	24.0	23.8	23.5	23.2	23.0	22.7	22.5	22.3	22.0	21.8	21.6	21.3
78	39.8	39.2	38.7	38.1	37.6	37.1	36.6	36.1	35.6	35.1	34.7	34.2	33.8	33.3	32.9	32.5	32.1	31.6	31.2	30.9	30.5	30.1	29.7	29.4	29.0	28.7	28.3	28.0	27.6	27.3	27.0	26.7	26.4	26.1	25.8	25.5	25.2	24.9	24.6	24.3	24.1	23.8	23.5	23.3	23.0	22.8	22.5	22.3	22.1	21.8	21.6
79	40.3	39.7	39.2	38.6	38.1	37.6	37.1	36.6	36.1	35.6	35.1	34.6	34.2	33.7	33.3	32.9	32.5	32.0	31.6	31.2	30.9	30.5	30.1	29.7	29.4	29.0	28.7	28.3	28.0	27.7	27.3	27.0	26.7	26.4	26.1	25.8	25.5	25.2	24.9	24.7	24.4	24.1	23.8	23.6	23.3	23.1	22.8	22.6	22.4	22.1	21.9
80	40.8	40.2	39.7	39.1	38.6	38.0	37.5	37.0	36.5	36.0	35.6	35.1	34.6	34.2	33.7	33.3	32.9	32.5	32.0	31.6	31.3	30.9	30.5	30.1	29.7	29.4	29.0	28.7	28.3	28.0	27.7	27.4	27.0	26.7	26.4	26.1	25.8	25.5	25.2	25.0	24.7	24.4	24.2	23.9	23.6	23.4	23.1	22.9	22.6	22.4	22.2
81	41.3	40.7	40.2	39.6	39.1	38.5	38.0	37.5	37.0	36.5	36.0	35.5	35.1	34.6	34.2	33.7	33.3	32.9	32.4	32.0	31.6	31.2	30.9	30.5	30.1	29.8	29.4	29.0	28.7	28.4	28.0	27.7	27.4	27.1	26.8	26.4	26.1	25.9	25.6	25.3	25.0	24.7	24.5	24.2	23.9	23.7	23.4	23.2	22.9	22.7	22.4
82	41.8	41.2	40.7	40.1	39.5	39.0	38.5	37.9	37.4	36.9	36.4	36.0	35.5	35.0	34.6	34.1	33.7	33.3	32.8	32.4	32.0	31.6	31.2	30.9	30.5	30.1	29.8	29.4	29.1	28.7	28.4	28.0	27.7	27.4	27.1	26.8	26.5	26.2	25.9	25.6	25.3	25.0	24.8	24.5	24.2	24.0	23.7	23.4	23.2	23.0	22.7
83	42.3	41.7	41.2	40.6	40.0	39.5	38.9	38.4	37.9	37.4	36.9	36.4	35.9	35.5	35.0	34.5	34.1	33.7	33.2	32.8	32.4	32.0	31.6	31.2	30.9	30.5	30.1	29.8	29.4	29.1	28.7	28.4	28.1	27.7	27.4	27.1	26.8	26.5	26.2	25.9	25.6	25.3	25.1	24.8	24.5	24.3	24.0	23.7	23.5	23.2	23.0
84	42.9	42.3	41.7	41.1	40.5	40.0	39.4	38.9	38.3	37.8	37.3	36.8	36.4	35.9	35.4	35.0	34.5	34.1	33.6	33.2	32.8	32.4	32.0	31.6	31.2	30.9	30.5	30.1	29.8	29.4	29.1	28.7	28.4	28.1	27.7	27.4	27.1	26.8	26.5	26.2	25.9	25.6	25.4	25.1	24.8	24.5	24.3	24.0	23.8	23.5	23.3
85	43.4	42.8	42.2	41.6	41.0	40.4	39.9	39.3	38.8	38.3	37.8	37.3	36.8	36.3	35.8	35.4	34.9	34.5	34.0	33.6	33.2	32.8	32.4	32.0	31.6	31.2	30.8	30.5	30.1	29.8	29.4	29.1	28.7	28.4	28.1	27.8	27.4	27.1	26.8	26.5	26.2	25.9	25.7	25.4	25.1	24.8	24.6	24.3	24.0	23.8	23.5
86	43.9	43.3	42.7	42.1	41.5	40.9	40.3	39.8	39.3	38.7	38.2	37.7	37.2	36.7	36.3	35.8	35.3	34.9	34.4	34.0	33.6	33.2	32.8	32.4	32.0	31.6	31.2	30.8	30.5	30.1	29.8	29.4	29.1	28.7	28.4	28.1	27.8	27.5	27.1	26.8	26.5	26.3	26.0	25.7	25.4	25.1	24.9	24.6	24.3	24.1	23.8
87	44.4	43.8	43.1	42.5	42.0	41.4	40.8	40.3	39.7	39.2	38.7	38.2	37.7	37.2	36.7	36.2	35.7	35.3	34.9	34.4	34.0	33.6	33.2	32.7	32.3	32.0	31.6	31.2	30.8	30.5	30.1	29.8	29.4	29.1	28.7	28.4	28.1	27.8	27.5	27.2	26.9	26.6	26.3	26.0	25.7	25.4	25.1	24.9	24.6	24.4	24.1
88	44.9	44.3	43.6	43.0	42.4	41.9	41.3	40.7	40.2	39.6	39.1	38.6	38.1	37.6	37.1	36.6	36.2	35.7	35.3	34.8	34.4	33.9	33.5	33.1	32.7	32.3	31.9	31.6	31.2	30.8	30.4	30.1	29.7	29.4	29.1	28.7	28.4	28.1	27.8	27.5	27.2	26.9	26.6	26.3	26.0	25.7	25.4	25.2	24.9	24.6	24.4

Table A 2.2 *(continued)*

Weight	Height (cm)																																																		
(kg)	140	141	142	143	144	145	146	147	148	149	150	151	152	153	154	155	156	157	158	159	160	161	162	163	164	165	166	167	168	169	170	171	172	173	174	175	176	177	178	179	180	181	182	183	184	185	186	187	188	189	190
89	45.4	44.8	44.1	43.5	42.9	42.3	41.8	41.2	40.6	40.1	39.6	39.0	38.5	38.0	37.5	37.0	36.6	36.1	35.7	35.2	34.8	34.3	33.9	33.5	33.1	32.7	32.3	31.9	31.5	31.2	30.8	30.4	30.1	29.7	29.4	29.1	28.7	28.4	28.1	27.8	27.5	27.2	26.9	26.6	26.3	26.0	25.7	25.5	25.2	24.9	24.7
90	45.9	45.3	44.6	44.0	43.4	42.8	42.2	41.6	41.1	40.5	40.0	39.5	39.0	38.4	37.9	37.5	37.0	36.5	36.1	35.6	35.2	34.7	34.3	33.9	33.5	33.1	32.7	32.3	31.9	31.5	31.1	30.8	30.4	30.1	29.7	29.4	29.1	28.7	28.4	28.1	27.8	27.5	27.2	26.9	26.6	26.3	26.0	25.7	25.5	25.2	24.9
91	46.4	45.8	45.1	44.5	43.9	43.3	42.7	42.1	41.5	41.0	40.4	39.9	39.4	38.9	38.4	37.9	37.4	36.9	36.5	36.0	35.5	35.1	34.7	34.3	33.8	33.4	33.0	32.6	32.2	31.9	31.5	31.1	30.8	30.4	30.1	29.7	29.4	29.0	28.7	28.4	28.1	27.8	27.5	27.2	26.9	26.6	26.3	26.0	25.7	25.5	25.2
92	46.9	46.3	45.6	45.0	44.4	43.8	43.2	42.6	42.0	41.4	40.9	40.3	39.8	39.3	38.8	38.3	37.8	37.3	36.9	36.4	35.9	35.5	35.1	34.6	34.2	33.8	33.4	33.0	32.6	32.2	31.8	31.5	31.1	30.7	30.4	30.0	29.7	29.4	29.0	28.7	28.4	28.1	27.8	27.5	27.2	26.9	26.6	26.3	26.0	25.8	25.5
93	47.4	46.8	46.1	45.5	44.8	44.2	43.6	43.0	42.5	41.9	41.3	40.8	40.3	39.7	39.2	38.7	38.2	37.7	37.3	36.8	36.3	35.9	35.4	35.0	34.6	34.2	33.7	33.3	33.0	32.6	32.2	31.8	31.4	31.1	30.7	30.4	30.0	29.7	29.4	29.0	28.7	28.4	28.1	27.8	27.5	27.2	26.9	26.6	26.3	26.0	25.8
94	48.0	47.3	46.6	46.0	45.3	44.7	44.1	43.5	42.9	42.3	41.8	41.2	40.7	40.2	39.6	39.1	38.6	38.1	37.7	37.2	36.7	36.3	35.8	35.4	34.9	34.5	34.1	33.7	33.3	32.9	32.5	32.1	31.8	31.4	31.0	30.7	30.3	30.0	29.7	29.3	29.0	28.7	28.4	28.1	27.8	27.5	27.2	26.9	26.6	26.3	26.0
95	48.5	47.8	47.1	46.5	45.8	45.2	44.6	44.0	43.4	42.8	42.2	41.7	41.1	40.6	40.1	39.5	39.0	38.5	38.1	37.6	37.1	36.6	36.2	35.8	35.3	34.9	34.5	34.1	33.7	33.3	32.9	32.5	32.1	31.7	31.4	31.0	30.7	30.3	30.0	29.6	29.3	29.0	28.7	28.4	28.1	27.8	27.5	27.2	26.9	26.6	26.3
96	49.0	48.3	47.6	46.9	46.3	45.7	45.0	44.4	43.8	43.2	42.7	42.1	41.6	41.0	40.5	40.0	39.4	38.9	38.5	38.0	37.5	37.0	36.6	36.1	35.7	35.3	34.8	34.4	34.0	33.6	33.2	32.8	32.4	32.1	31.7	31.3	31.0	30.6	30.3	30.0	29.6	29.3	29.0	28.7	28.4	28.0	27.7	27.5	27.2	26.9	26.6
97	49.5	48.8	48.1	47.4	46.8	46.1	45.5	44.9	44.3	43.7	43.1	42.5	42.0	41.4	40.9	40.4	39.9	39.4	38.9	38.4	37.9	37.4	37.0	36.5	36.1	35.6	35.2	34.8	34.4	34.0	33.6	33.2	32.8	32.4	32.0	31.7	31.3	31.0	30.6	30.3	29.9	29.6	29.3	29.0	28.7	28.3	28.0	27.7	27.4	27.2	26.9
98	50.0	49.3	48.6	47.9	47.3	46.6	46.0	45.4	44.7	44.1	43.6	43.0	42.4	41.9	41.3	40.8	40.3	39.8	39.3	38.8	38.3	37.8	37.3	36.9	36.4	36.0	35.6	35.1	34.7	34.3	33.9	33.5	33.1	32.7	32.4	32.0	31.6	31.3	30.9	30.6	30.2	29.9	29.6	29.3	28.9	28.6	28.3	28.0	27.7	27.4	27.1
99		49.8	49.1	48.4	47.7	47.1	46.4	45.8	45.2	44.6	44.0	43.4	42.8	42.3	41.7	41.2	40.7	40.2	39.7	39.2	38.7	38.2	37.7	37.3	36.8	36.4	35.9	35.5	35.1	34.7	34.3	33.9	33.5	33.1	32.7	32.3	32.0	31.6	31.2	30.9	30.6	30.2	29.9	29.6	29.2	28.9	28.6	28.3	28.0	27.7	27.4
100			49.6	48.9	48.2	47.6	46.9	46.3	45.7	45.0	44.4	43.9	43.3	42.7	42.2	41.6	41.1	40.6	40.1	39.6	39.1	38.6	38.1	37.6	37.2	36.7	36.3	35.9	35.4	35.0	34.6	34.2	33.8	33.4	33.0	32.7	32.3	31.9	31.6	31.2	30.9	30.5	30.2	29.9	29.5	29.2	28.9	28.6	28.3	28.0	27.7
101				49.4	48.7	48.0	47.4	46.7	46.1	45.5	44.9	44.3	43.7	43.1	42.6	42.0	41.5	41.0	40.5	40.0	39.5	39.0	38.5	38.0	37.6	37.1	36.7	36.2	35.8	35.4	34.9	34.5	34.1	33.7	33.4	33.0	32.6	32.2	31.9	31.5	31.2	30.8	30.5	30.2	29.8	29.5	29.2	28.9	28.6	28.3	28.0
102				49.9	49.2	48.5	47.9	47.2	46.6	45.9	45.3	44.7	44.1	43.6	43.0	42.5	41.9	41.4	40.9	40.3	39.8	39.4	38.9	38.4	37.9	37.5	37.0	36.6	36.1	35.7	35.3	34.9	34.5	34.1	33.7	33.3	32.9	32.6	32.2	31.8	31.5	31.1	30.8	30.5	30.1	29.8	29.5	29.2	28.9	28.6	28.3
103					49.7	49.0	48.3	47.7	47.0	46.4	45.8	45.2	44.6	44.0	43.4	42.9	42.3	41.8	41.3	40.7	40.2	39.7	39.2	38.8	38.3	37.8	37.4	36.9	36.5	36.1	35.6	35.2	34.8	34.4	34.0	33.6	33.3	32.9	32.5	32.1	31.8	31.4	31.1	30.8	30.4	30.1	29.8	29.5	29.1	28.8	28.5
104						49.5	48.8	48.1	47.5	46.8	46.2	45.6	45.0	44.4	43.9	43.3	42.7	42.2	41.7	41.1	40.6	40.1	39.6	39.1	38.7	38.2	37.7	37.3	36.8	36.4	36.0	35.6	35.2	34.7	34.4	34.0	33.6	33.2	32.8	32.5	32.1	31.7	31.4	31.1	30.7	30.4	30.1	29.7	29.4	29.1	28.8
105						49.9	49.3	48.6	47.9	47.3	46.7	46.1	45.4	44.9	44.3	43.7	43.1	42.6	42.1	41.5	41.0	40.5	40.0	39.5	39.0	38.6	38.1	37.6	37.2	36.8	36.3	35.9	35.5	35.1	34.7	34.3	33.9	33.5	33.1	32.8	32.4	32.1	31.7	31.4	31.0	30.7	30.4	30.0	29.7	29.4	29.1
106							49.7	49.1	48.4	47.7	47.1	46.5	45.9	45.3	44.7	44.1	43.6	43.0	42.5	41.9	41.4	40.9	40.4	39.9	39.4	38.9	38.5	38.0	37.6	37.1	36.7	36.3	35.8	35.4	35.0	34.6	34.2	33.8	33.5	33.1	32.7	32.4	32.0	31.7	31.3	31.0	30.6	30.3	30.0	29.7	29.4
107								49.5	48.8	48.2	47.6	46.9	46.3	45.7	45.1	44.5	44.0	43.4	42.9	42.3	41.8	41.3	40.8	40.3	39.8	39.3	38.8	38.4	37.9	37.5	37.0	36.6	36.2	35.8	35.3	34.9	34.5	34.2	33.8	33.4	33.0	32.7	32.3	32.0	31.6	31.3	30.9	30.6	30.3	30.0	29.6
108								50.0	49.3	48.6	48.0	47.4	46.7	46.1	45.5	45.0	44.4	43.8	43.3	42.7	42.2	41.7	41.2	40.6	40.2	39.7	39.2	38.7	38.3	37.8	37.4	36.9	36.5	36.1	35.7	35.3	34.9	34.5	34.1	33.7	33.3	33.0	32.6	32.2	31.9	31.6	31.2	30.9	30.6	30.2	29.9
109									49.8	49.1	48.4	47.8	47.2	46.6	46.0	45.4	44.8	44.2	43.7	43.1	42.6	42.1	41.5	41.0	40.5	40.0	39.6	39.1	38.6	38.2	37.7	37.3	36.8	36.4	36.0	35.6	35.2	34.8	34.4	34.0	33.6	33.3	32.9	32.5	32.2	31.8	31.5	31.2	30.8	30.5	30.2
110										49.5	48.9	48.2	47.6	47.0	46.4	45.8	45.2	44.6	44.1	43.5	43.0	42.4	41.9	41.4	40.9	40.4	39.9	39.4	39.0	38.5	38.1	37.6	37.2	36.8	36.3	35.9	35.5	35.1	34.7	34.3	34.0	33.6	33.2	32.8	32.5	32.1	31.8	31.5	31.1	30.8	30.5
111										50.0	49.3	48.7	48.0	47.4	46.8	46.2	45.6	45.0	44.5	43.9	43.4	42.8	42.3	41.8	41.3	40.8	40.3	39.8	39.3	38.9	38.4	38.0	37.5	37.1	36.7	36.2	35.8	35.4	35.0	34.6	34.3	33.9	33.5	33.1	32.8	32.4	32.1	31.7	31.4	31.1	30.7
112											49.8	49.1	48.5	47.8	47.2	46.6	46.0	45.4	44.9	44.3	43.8	43.2	42.7	42.2	41.6	41.1	40.6	40.2	39.7	39.2	38.8	38.3	37.9	37.4	37.0	36.6	36.2	35.7	35.3	35.0	34.6	34.2	33.8	33.4	33.1	32.7	32.4	32.0	31.7	31.4	31.0
113												49.6	48.9	48.3	47.6	47.0	46.4	45.8	45.3	44.7	44.1	43.6	43.1	42.5	42.0	41.5	41.0	40.5	40.0	39.6	39.1	38.6	38.2	37.8	37.3	36.9	36.5	36.1	35.7	35.3	34.9	34.5	34.1	33.7	33.4	33.0	32.7	32.3	32.0	31.6	31.3
114												50.0	49.3	48.7	48.1	47.5	46.8	46.2	45.7	45.1	44.5	44.0	43.4	42.9	42.4	41.9	41.4	40.9	40.4	39.9	39.4	39.0	38.5	38.1	37.7	37.2	36.8	36.4	36.0	35.6	35.2	34.8	34.4	34.0	33.7	33.3	33.0	32.6	32.3	31.9	31.6
115													49.8	49.1	48.5	47.9	47.3	46.7	46.1	45.5	44.9	44.4	43.8	43.3	42.8	42.2	41.7	41.2	40.7	40.3	39.8	39.3	38.9	38.4	38.0	37.6	37.1	36.7	36.3	35.9	35.5	35.1	34.7	34.3	34.0	33.6	33.2	32.9	32.5	32.2	31.9
116														49.6	48.9	48.3	47.7	47.1	46.5	45.9	45.3	44.8	44.2	43.7	43.1	42.6	42.1	41.6	41.1	40.6	40.1	39.7	39.2	38.8	38.3	37.9	37.4	37.0	36.6	36.2	35.8	35.4	35.0	34.6	34.3	33.9	33.5	33.2	32.8	32.5	32.1
117														50.0	49.3	48.7	48.1	47.5	46.9	46.3	45.7	45.1	44.6	44.0	43.5	43.0	42.5	42.0	41.5	41.0	40.5	40.0	39.5	39.1	38.6	38.2	37.8	37.3	36.9	36.5	36.1	35.7	35.3	34.9	34.6	34.2	33.8	33.5	33.1	32.8	32.4
118															49.8	49.1	48.5	47.9	47.3	46.7	46.1	45.5	45.0	44.4	43.9	43.3	42.8	42.3	41.8	41.3	40.8	40.4	39.9	39.4	39.0	38.5	38.1	37.7	37.2	36.8	36.4	36.0	35.6	35.2	34.9	34.5	34.1	33.7	33.4	33.0	32.7
119																49.5	48.9	48.3	47.7	47.1	46.5	45.9	45.3	44.8	44.2	43.7	43.2	42.7	42.2	41.7	41.2	40.7	40.2	39.8	39.3	38.9	38.4	38.0	37.6	37.1	36.7	36.3	35.9	35.5	35.1	34.8	34.4	34.0	33.7	33.3	33.0
120																49.9	49.3	48.7	48.1	47.5	46.9	46.3	45.7	45.2	44.6	44.1	43.5	43.0	42.5	42.0	41.5	41.0	40.6	40.1	39.6	39.2	38.7	38.3	37.9	37.5	37.0	36.6	36.2	35.8	35.4	35.1	34.7	34.3	34.0	33.6	33.2
121																	49.7	49.1	48.5	47.9	47.3	46.7	46.1	45.5	45.0	44.4	43.9	43.4	42.9	42.4	41.9	41.4	40.9	40.4	40.0	39.5	39.1	38.6	38.2	37.8	37.3	36.9	36.5	36.1	35.7	35.4	35.0	34.6	34.2	33.9	33.5
122																		49.5	48.9	48.3	47.7	47.1	46.5	45.9	45.4	44.8	44.3	43.7	43.2	42.7	42.2	41.7	41.2	40.8	40.3	39.8	39.4	38.9	38.5	38.1	37.7	37.2	36.8	36.4	36.0	35.6	35.3	34.9	34.5	34.2	33.8
123																		49.9	49.3	48.7	48.0	47.5	46.9	46.3	45.7	45.2	44.6	44.1	43.6	43.1	42.6	42.1	41.6	41.1	40.6	40.2	39.7	39.3	38.8	38.4	38.0	37.5	37.1	36.7	36.3	35.9	35.6	35.2	34.8	34.4	34.1
124																			49.7	49.0	48.4	47.8	47.2	46.7	46.1	45.5	45.0	44.5	43.9	43.4	42.9	42.4	41.9	41.4	41.0	40.5	40.0	39.6	39.1	38.7	38.3	37.8	37.4	37.0	36.6	36.2	35.8	35.5	35.1	34.7	34.3
125																				49.4	48.8	48.2	47.6	47.0	46.5	45.9	45.4	44.8	44.3	43.8	43.3	42.7	42.3	41.8	41.3	40.8	40.4	39.9	39.5	39.0	38.6	38.2	37.7	37.3	36.9	36.5	36.1	35.7	35.4	35.0	34.6
126																				49.8	49.2	48.6	48.0	47.4	46.8	46.3	45.7	45.2	44.6	44.1	43.6	43.1	42.6	42.1	41.6	41.1	40.7	40.2	39.8	39.3	38.9	38.5	38.0	37.6	37.2	36.8	36.4	36.0	35.6	35.3	34.9
127																					49.6	49.0	48.4	47.8	47.2	46.6	46.1	45.5	45.0	44.5	43.9	43.4	42.9	42.4	41.9	41.5	41.0	40.5	40.1	39.6	39.2	38.8	38.3	37.9	37.5	37.1	36.7	36.3	35.9	35.6	35.2
128																					50.0	49.4	48.8	48.2	47.6	47.0	46.5	45.9	45.4	44.8	44.3	43.8	43.3	42.8	42.3	41.8	41.3	40.9	40.4	39.9	39.5	39.1	38.6	38.2	37.8	37.4	37.0	36.6	36.2	35.8	35.5
129																						49.8	49.2	48.6	48.0	47.4	46.8	46.3	45.7	45.2	44.6	44.1	43.6	43.1	42.6	42.1	41.6	41.2	40.7	40.3	39.8	39.4	38.9	38.5	38.1	37.7	37.3	36.9	36.5	36.1	35.7
130																							49.5	48.9	48.3	47.8	47.2	46.6	46.1	45.5	45.0	44.5	43.9	43.4	42.9	42.4	42.0	41.5	41.0	40.6	40.1	39.7	39.2	38.8	38.4	38.0	37.6	37.2	36.8	36.4	36.0
131																							49.9	49.3	48.7	48.1	47.5	47.0	46.4	45.9	45.3	44.8	44.3	43.8	43.3	42.8	42.3	41.8	41.3	40.9	40.4	40.0	39.5	39.1	38.7	38.3	37.9	37.5	37.1	36.7	36.3
132																								49.7	49.1	48.5	47.9	47.3	46.8	46.2	45.7	45.1	44.6	44.1	43.6	43.1	42.6	42.1	41.7	41.2	40.7	40.3	39.9	39.4	39.0	38.6	38.2	37.7	37.3	37.0	36.6
133																									49.4	48.9	48.3	47.7	47.1	46.6	46.0	45.5	45.0	44.4	43.9	43.4	42.9	42.5	42.0	41.5	41.0	40.6	40.2	39.7	39.3	38.9	38.4	38.0	37.6	37.2	36.8
134																									49.8	49.2	48.6	48.0	47.5	46.9	46.4	45.8	45.3	44.8	44.3	43.8	43.3	42.8	42.3	41.8	41.4	40.9	40.5	40.0	39.6	39.2	38.7	38.3	37.9	37.5	37.1
135																										49.6	49.0	48.4	47.8	47.3	46.7	46.2	45.6	45.1	44.6	44.1	43.6	43.1	42.6	42.1	41.7	41.2	40.8	40.3	39.9	39.4	39.0	38.6	38.2	37.8	37.4
136																										50.0	49.4	48.8	48.2	47.6	47.1	46.5	46.0	45.4	44.9	44.4	43.9	43.4	42.9	42.4	42.0	41.5	41.1	40.6	40.2	39.7	39.3	38.9	38.5	38.1	37.7
137																											49.7	49.1	48.5	48.0	47.4	46.9	46.3	45.8	45.3	44.7	44.2	43.7	43.2	42.8	42.3	41.8	41.4	40.9	40.5	40.0	39.6	39.2	38.8	38.4	38.0
138																												49.5	48.9	48.3	47.8	47.2	46.6	46.1	45.6	45.1	44.6	44.0	43.6	43.1	42.6	42.1	41.7	41.2	40.8	40.3	39.9	39.5	39.0	38.6	38.2
139																												49.8	49.2	48.7	48.1	47.5	47.0	46.4	45.9	45.4	44.9	44.4	43.9	43.4	42.9	42.4	42.0	41.5	41.1	40.6	40.2	39.7	39.3	38.9	38.5
140																													49.6	49.0	48.4	47.9	47.3	46.8	46.2	45.7	45.2	44.7	44.2	43.7	43.2	42.7	42.3	41.8	41.4	40.9	40.5	40.0	39.6	39.2	38.8
141																													50.0	49.4	48.8	48.2	47.7	47.1	46.6	46.0	45.5	45.0	44.5	44.0	43.5	43.0	42.6	42.1	41.6	41.2	40.8	40.3	39.9	39.5	39.1
142																														49.7	49.1	48.6	48.0	47.4	46.9	46.4	45.8	45.3	44.8	44.3	43.8	43.3	42.9	42.4	41.9	41.5	41.0	40.6	40.2	39.8	39.3
143																															49.5	48.9	48.3	47.8	47.2	46.7	46.2	45.6	45.1	44.6	44.1	43.6	43.2	42.7	42.2	41.8	41.3	40.9	40.5	40.0	39.6

- *Abdomen:hip ratio (AHR)* is expressed as a decimal fraction:

$$\frac{\text{abdominal circumference (cm)}}{\text{hip circumference (cm)}}$$

- *Arm muscle circumference (AMC)* is estimated from arm circumference (AC) and triceps skinfold thickness (TSF), assuming a circular and concentric model (*15*):

AMC (cm) = AC (cm) - [$\pi \times$ TSF (cm)]

- *Arm muscle area (AMA).* Cross-sectional arm muscle area is estimated from arm circumference (AC) and triceps skinfold thickness (TSF), assuming a circular and concentric model (*15*)

$$\text{AMA (cm}^2) = \frac{[AC - (\pi \times TSF)]^2}{4\pi}$$

Corrections of AMA for estimated bone areas in each sex are recommended for some purposes:

$$\text{Bone-free AMA (cm}^2)\ \text{for men}\ = \frac{[AC - (\pi \times TSF)]^2}{4\pi} - 10$$

$$\text{Bone-free AMA (cm}^2)\ \text{for women}\ = \frac{[AC - (\pi \times TSF)]^2}{4\pi} - 6.5$$

References

1. Cameron N. *The measurement of human growth.* London, Croom Helm, 1984.

2. Lohmann TG, Roche AF, Martorell R, eds. *Anthropometric standardization reference manual.* Champaign, IL, Human Kinetics Books, 1988.

3. *Measuring change in nutritional status.* Geneva, World Health Organization, 1983.

4. *Assessing the nutritional status of young children.* New York, United Nations, 1990.

5. Jelliffe DB, Jelliffe EFP. *Community nutritional assessment.* Oxford, Oxford University Press, 1989.

6. Delgado H et al. Nutritional status and the timing of deciduous tooth eruption. *American journal of clinical nutrition,* 1975, **28**:216-224.

7. Hagg U, Taranger J. Dental development, dental age and tooth counts. *Angle orthodontist,* 1985, **55**:93-107.

8. Kramer MS et al. The validity of gestational age estimation by menstrual dating in term, preterm, postterm gestations. *Journal of the American Medical Association,* 1988, **260**:3306-3308.

9. *Measuring obesity: classification and description of anthropometric data. Report on a WHO Consultation on the Epidemiology of Obesity, Warsaw, 21–23 October 1987.* Copenhagen, WHO Regional Office for Europe, 1989 (unpublished document EUR/ICP/NUT 125, obtainable on request from WHO Regional Office for Europe, 8 Scherfigsvej, 2100 Copenhagen 0, Denmark).

10. Tanner JM. *Growth at adolescence,* 2nd ed. Oxford, Blackwell, 1962.

11. Van Wieringen JC et al. *Growth diagrams 1965 Netherlands.* Groningen, Wolters-Noordhoff, 1971.

12. Eveleth PB, Tanner JM. *Worldwide variation in human growth, 2nd ed. Cambridge, Cambridge University Press, 1990.*

13. Hagg U, Karlberg J, Taranger J. The timing of secondary sex characteristics and their relationship to the pubertal maximum of growth in boys. In: Carlson DS, ed. *Orthodontics in an aging society.* Ann Arbor, MI, Center for Human Growth and Development, 1989:167-179.

14. Belizan JM et al. Diagnosis of intrauterine growth retardation by a simple clinical method: measurement of uterine height. *American journal of obstetrics and gynecology,* 1978, **131**:643-646.

15. Heymsfield S et al. Anthropometric assessment of adult protein-energy malnutrition. In: Wright RA, Heymsfield S, eds. *Nutritional assessment.* Boston, Blackwell, 1984:27-82.

16. Roche AF et al. Grading body fatness from limited anthropometric data. *American journal of clinical nutrition,* 1981, **34**: 2831-2838.

Annex 3
Recommended reference data

This annex contains tables of reference data, recommended by the Expert Committee, that have not been widely distributed by WHO previously. The NCHS/WHO reference data for the weight and height of children have been previously published by WHO (1), and have also been distributed separately as the annex to that publication. Individual sections of the report concerning age and physical status groups should be consulted for rationales, recommended cut-offs, and interpretation of the reference data.

Table A3.1
Mid-upper arm circumference (cm): combined sexes, 6–60 months[a]

Age (months)	–3 SD	–2 SD	–1 SD	Median	+1 SD	+2 SD	+3 SD
6	10.9	12.0	13.2	14.3	15.5	16.7	17.8
7	11.0	12.2	13.4	14.6	15.7	16.9	18.1
8	11.2	12.4	13.6	14.8	16.0	17.2	18.3
9	11.3	12.5	13.7	14.9	16.2	17.4	18.6
10	11.5	12.7	13.9	15.1	16.3	17.5	18.8
11	11.6	12.8	14.0	15.2	16.5	17.7	18.9
12	11.7	12.9	14.1	15.4	16.6	17.9	19.1
13	11.7	13.0	14.2	15.5	16.7	18.0	19.2
14	11.8	13.1	14.3	15.6	16.8	18.1	19.4
15	11.9	13.1	14.4	15.7	16.9	18.2	19.5
16	11.9	13.2	14.5	15.8	17.0	18.3	19.6
17	12.0	13.2	14.5	15.8	17.1	18.4	19.7
18	12.0	13.3	14.6	15.9	17.2	18.5	19.8
19	12.0	13.3	14.6	15.9	17.2	18.5	19.8
20	12.1	13.4	14.7	16.0	17.3	18.6	19.9
21	12.1	13.4	14.7	16.0	17.3	18.7	20.0
22	12.1	13.4	14.7	16.1	17.4	18.7	20.0
23	12.1	13.4	14.8	16.1	17.4	18.8	20.1
24	12.1	13.5	14.8	16.1	17.5	18.8	20.1
25	12.2	13.5	14.8	16.2	17.5	18.8	20.2
26	12.2	13.5	14.9	16.2	17.5	18.9	20.2
27	12.2	13.5	14.9	16.2	17.6	18.9	20.3
28	12.2	13.5	14.9	16.3	17.6	19.0	20.3
29	12.2	13.6	14.9	16.3	17.6	19.0	20.4

Table A3.1 *(continued)*

Age (months)	-3 SD	-2 SD	-1 SD	Median	+1 SD	+2 SD	+3 SD
30	12.2	13.6	14.9	16.3	17.7	19.0	20.4
31	12.2	13.6	15.0	16.3	17.7	19.1	20.4
32	12.2	13.6	15.0	16.4	17.7	19.1	20.5
33	12.3	13.6	15.0	16.4	17.8	19.1	20.5
34	12.3	13.7	15.0	16.4	17.8	19.2	20.6
35	12.3	13.7	15.1	16.4	17.8	19.2	20.6
36	12.3	13.7	15.1	16.5	17.9	19.3	20.6
37	12.3	13.7	15.1	16.5	17.9	19.3	20.7
38	12.3	13.7	15.1	16.5	17.9	19.3	20.7
39	12.4	13.8	15.2	16.6	18.0	19.4	20.8
40	12.4	13.8	15.2	16.6	18.0	19.4	20.8
41	12.4	13.8	15.2	16.6	18.1	19.5	20.9
42	12.4	13.8	15.3	16.7	18.1	19.5	20.9
43	12.4	13.9	15.3	16.7	18.1	19.6	21.0
44	12.5	13.9	15.3	16.8	18.2	19.6	21.1
45	12.5	13.9	15.4	16.8	18.2	19.7	21.1
46	12.5	13.9	15.4	16.8	18.3	19.7	21.2
47	12.5	14.0	15.4	16.9	18.3	19.8	21.2
48	12.5	14.0	15.5	16.9	18.4	19.8	21.3
49	12.5	14.0	15.5	17.0	18.4	19.9	21.4
50	12.6	14.0	15.5	17.0	18.5	20.0	21.4
51	12.6	14.1	15.5	17.0	18.5	20.0	21.5
52	12.6	14.1	15.6	17.1	18.6	20.1	21.6
53	12.6	14.1	15.6	17.1	18.6	20.1	21.6
54	12.6	14.1	15.6	17.2	18.7	20.2	21.7
55	12.6	14.1	15.7	17.2	18.7	20.3	21.8
56	12.6	14.1	15.7	17.2	18.8	20.3	21.9
57	12.6	14.1	15.7	17.3	18.8	20.4	21.9
58	12.6	14.2	15.7	17.3	18.9	20.5	22.0
59	12.6	14.2	15.8	17.3	18.9	20.5	22.1
60	12.6	14.2	15.8	17.4	19.0	20.6	22.2

[a] Median and standard deviations (cm). Reference data are based on the first and second National Health and Nutrition Examination Surveys (NHANES I and II) in the United States of America.

Table A3.2
Mid-upper arm circumference (cm): boys, 6–60 months[a]

Age (months)	-3 SD	-2 SD	-1 SD	Median	+1 SD	+2 SD	+3 SD
6	11.5	12.6	13.8	14.9	16.1	17.3	18.4
7	11.6	12.7	13.9	15.1	16.3	17.5	18.6
8	11.7	12.8	14.0	15.2	16.4	17.6	18.8
9	11.7	12.9	14.2	15.4	16.6	17.8	19.0
10	11.8	13.0	14.2	15.5	16.7	17.9	19.1
11	11.9	13.1	14.3	15.6	16.8	18.0	19.3
12	11.9	13.2	14.4	15.7	16.9	18.1	19.4
13	12.0	12.2	14.5	15.7	17.0	18.2	19.5
14	12.0	13.3	14.5	15.8	17.1	18.3	19.6
15	12.1	13.3	14.6	15.9	17.1	18.4	19.7
16	12.1	13.4	14.6	15.9	17.2	18.5	19.8
17	12.1	13.4	14.7	16.0	17.3	18.6	19.8
18	12.1	13.4	14.7	16.0	17.3	18.6	19.9
19	12.2	13.5	14.8	16.1	17.4	18.7	20.0
20	12.2	13.5	14.8	16.1	17.4	18.7	20.0
21	12.2	13.5	14.8	16.1	17.5	18.8	20.1
22	12.2	13.5	14.9	16.2	17.5	18.8	20.1
23	12.2	13.5	14.9	16.2	17.5	18.9	20.2
24	12.2	13.6	14.9	16.2	17.6	18.9	20.2
25	12.2	13.6	14.9	16.3	17.6	18.9	20.3
26	12.3	13.6	14.9	16.3	17.6	19.0	20.3
27	12.3	13.6	15.0	16.3	17.7	19.0	20.4
28	12.3	13.6	15.0	16.3	17.7	19.1	20.4
29	12.3	13.7	15.0	16.4	17.7	19.1	20.4
30	12.3	13.7	15.0	16.4	17.8	19.1	20.5
31	12.3	13.7	15.1	16.4	17.8	19.2	20.5
32	12.3	13.7	15.1	16.5	17.8	19.2	20.6
33	12.4	13.7	15.1	16.5	17.9	19.2	20.6
34	12.4	13.8	15.1	16.5	17.9	19.3	20.6
35	12.4	13.8	15.2	16.5	17.9	19.3	20.7
36	12.4	13.8	15.2	16.6	18.0	19.3	20.7

Table A3.2 *(continued)*

Age (months)	-3 SD	-2 SD	-1 SD	Median	+1 SD	+2 SD	+3 SD
37	12.4	13.8	15.2	16.6	18.0	19.4	20.8
38	12.4	13.8	15.2	16.6	18.0	19.4	20.8
39	12.5	13.9	15.3	16.7	18.1	19.5	20.9
40	12.5	13.9	15.3	16.7	18.1	19.5	20.9
41	12.5	13.9	15.3	16.7	18.1	19.6	21.0
42	12.5	13.9	15.4	16.8	18.2	19.6	21.0
43	12.5	14.0	15.4	16.8	18.2	19.7	21.1
44	12.5	14.0	15.4	16.8	18.3	19.7	21.1
45	12.6	14.0	15.4	16.9	18.3	19.8	21.2
46	12.6	14.0	15.5	16.9	18.4	19.8	21.3
47	12.6	14.0	15.5	17.0	18.4	19.9	21.3
48	12.6	14.1	15.5	17.0	18.4	19.9	21.4
49	12.6	14.1	15.6	17.0	18.5	20.0	21.4
50	12.6	14.1	15.6	17.1	18.5	20.0	21.5
51	12.6	14.1	15.6	17.1	18.6	20.1	21.6
52	12.6	14.1	15.6	17.1	18.6	20.1	21.6
53	12.6	14.1	15.7	17.2	18.7	20.2	21.7
54	12.6	14.2	15.7	17.2	18.7	20.2	21.8
55	12.6	14.2	15.7	17.2	18.8	20.3	21.8
56	12.6	14.2	15.7	17.3	18.8	20.4	21.9
57	12.6	14.2	15.8	17.3	18.9	20.4	22.0
58	12.6	14.2	15.8	17.3	18.9	20.5	22.1
59	12.6	14.2	15.8	17.4	19.0	20.6	22.2
60	12.6	14.2	15.8	17.4	19.0	20.6	22.2

[a] Median and standard deviations (cm). Reference data are based on the first and second National Health and Nutrition Examination Surveys (NHANES I and II) in the United States of America.

Table A3.3
Mid-upper arm circumference (cm): girls, 6–60 months[a]

Age (months)	-3 SD	-2 SD	-1 SD	Median	+1 SD	+2 SD	+3 SD
6	10.4	11.5	12.7	13.9	15.0	16.2	17.4
7	10.6	11.8	13.0	14.1	15.3	16.5	17.7
8	10.8	12.0	13.2	14.4	15.6	16.8	18.0
9	11.0	12.2	13.4	14.6	15.8	17.0	18.2
10	11.1	12.3	13.6	14.8	16.0	17.2	18.4
11	11.3	12.5	13.7	15.0	16.2	17.4	18.6
12	11.4	12.6	13.9	15.1	16.4	17.6	18.8
13	11.5	12.7	14.0	15.2	16.5	17.7	19.0
14	11.6	12.8	14.1	15.4	16.6	17.9	19.2
15	11.7	12.9	14.2	15.5	16.7	18.0	19.3
16	11.7	13.0	14.3	15.6	16.8	18.1	19.4
17	11.8	13.1	14.4	15.7	16.9	18.2	19.5
18	11.8	13.1	14.4	15.7	17.0	18.3	19.6
19	11.9	13.2	14.5	15.8	17.1	18.4	19.7
20	11.9	13.2	14.5	15.8	17.2	18.5	19.8
21	11.9	13.3	14.6	15.9	17.2	18.5	19.8
22	12.0	13.3	14.6	15.9	17.3	18.6	19.9
23	12.0	13.3	14.7	16.0	17.3	18.6	20.0
24	12.0	13.4	14.7	16.0	17.4	18.7	20.0
25	12.0	13.4	14.7	16.1	17.4	18.7	20.1
26	12.1	13.4	14.7	16.1	17.4	18.8	20.1
27	12.1	13.4	14.8	16.1	17.5	18.8	20.2
28	12.1	13.4	14.8	16.1	17.5	18.9	20.2
29	12.1	13.5	14.8	16.2	17.5	18.9	20.3
30	12.1	13.5	14.8	16.2	17.6	18.9	20.3
31	12.1	13.5	14.9	16.2	17.6	19.0	20.3
32	12.1	13.5	14.9	16.3	17.6	19.0	20.4
33	12.2	13.5	14.9	16.3	17.7	19.0	20.4
34	12.2	13.6	14.9	16.3	17.7	19.1	20.5
35	12.2	13.6	15.0	16.3	17.7	19.1	20.5
36	12.2	13.6	15.0	16.4	17.8	19.2	20.5

Table A3.3 *(continued)*

Age (months)	-3 SD	-2 SD	-1 SD	Median	+1 SD	+2 SD	+3 SD
37	12.2	13.6	15.0	16.4	17.8	19.2	20.6
38	12.2	13.6	15.0	16.4	17.8	19.2	20.6
39	12.3	13.7	15.1	16.5	17.9	19.3	20.7
40	12.3	13.7	15.1	16.5	17.9	19.3	20.7
41	12.3	13.7	15.1	16.6	18.0	19.4	20.8
42	12.3	13.8	15.2	16.6	18.0	19.4	20.8
43	12.4	13.8	15.2	16.6	18.1	19.5	20.9
44	12.4	13.8	15.2	16.7	18.1	19.5	21.0
45	12.4	13.8	15.3	16.7	18.1	19.6	21.0
46	12.4	13.9	15.3	16.7	18.2	19.6	21.1
47	12.4	13.9	15.3	16.8	18.2	19.7	21.2
48	12.4	13.9	15.4	16.8	18.3	19.8	21.2
49	12.5	13.9	15.4	16.9	18.3	19.8	21.3
50	12.5	14.0	15.4	16.9	18.4	19.9	21.4
51	12.5	14.0	15.5	17.0	18.4	19.9	21.4
52	12.5	14.0	15.5	17.0	18.5	20.0	21.5
53	12.5	14.0	15.5	17.0	18.6	20.1	21.6
54	12.5	14.0	15.6	17.1	18.6	20.1	21.7
55	12.5	14.1	15.6	17.1	18.7	20.2	21.7
56	12.5	14.1	15.6	17.2	18.7	20.3	21.8
57	12.5	14.1	15.7	17.2	18.8	20.3	21.9
58	12.5	14.1	15.7	17.3	18.8	20.4	22.0
59	12.5	14.1	15.7	17.3	18.9	20.5	22.1
60	12.5	14.1	15.7	17.3	18.9	20.5	22.2

[a] Median and standard deviations (cm). Reference data are based on the first and second National Health and Nutrition Examination Surveys (NHANES I and II) in the United States of America.

Table A3.4
Percentiles of BMI-for-age: male adolescents, 9–24 years[a]

Age (years)	Percentiles				
	5th	15th	50th	85th	95th
9	14.03	14.71	16.17	18.85	21.47
10	14.42	15.15	16.72	19.60	22.60
11	14.83	15.59	17.28	20.35	23.73
12	15.24	16.06	17.87	21.12	24.89
13	15.73	16.62	18.53	21.93	25.93
14	16.18	17.20	19.22	22.77	26.93
15	16.59	17.76	19.92	23.63	27.76
16	17.01	18.32	20.63	24.45	28.53
17	17.31	18.68	21.12	25.28	29.32
18	17.54	18.89	21.45	25.92	30.02
19	17.80	19.20	21.86	26.36	30.66
20-24	18.66	20.21	23.07	26.87	31.26

[a] Reference data are based on the first National Health and Nutrition Examination Survey (NHANES I) in the United States of America (2, 3).

Table A3.5
Percentiles of BMI-for-age: female adolescents, 9–24 years[a]

Age (years)	Percentiles				
	5th	15th	50th	85th	95th
9	13.87	14.66	16.33	19.19	21.78
10	14.23	15.09	17.00	20.19	23.20
11	14.60	15.53	17.67	21.18	24.59
12	14.98	15.98	18.35	22.17	25.95
13	15.36	16.43	18.95	23.08	27.07
14	15.67	16.79	19.32	23.88	27.97
15	16.01	17.16	19.69	24.29	28.51
16	16.37	17.54	20.09	24.74	29.10
17	16.59	17.81	20.36	25.23	29.72
18	16.71	17.99	20.57	25.56	30.22
19	16.87	18.20	20.80	25.85	30.72
20-24	17.38	18.64	21.46	26.14	31.20

[a] Reference data are based on the first National Health and Nutrition Examination Survey (NHANES I) in the United States of America (2, 3).

Table A3.6
Percentiles of triceps skinfold thickness: male adolescents, 9–18 years[a]

Age years	Percentiles						
	5th	10th	25th	50th	75th	90th	95th
9.0	4.8	5.5	6.7	8.4	11.1	14.6	17.8
9.5	4.8	5.5	6.7	8.6	11.5	15.5	18.7
10.0	4.9	5.6	6.8	8.8	11.9	16.4	19.8
10.5	4.9	5.6	6.9	9.0	12.4	17.4	20.8
11.0	4.9	5.6	7.0	9.3	12.8	18.3	21.8
11.5	5.0	5.7	7.0	9.4	13.2	19.1	22.7
12.0	4.9	5.7	7.1	9.6	13.4	19.8	23.4
12.5	4.9	5.6	7.1	9.6	13.6	20.2	23.9
13.0	4.8	5.6	7.0	9.6	13.5	20.3	24.1
13.5	4.6	5.4	6.8	9.4	13.3	20.1	24.0
14.0	4.5	5.3	6.6	9.1	13.0	19.6	23.7
14.5	4.3	5.1	6.4	8.7	12.5	19.0	23.2
15.0	4.1	4.9	6.2	8.4	12.0	18.2	22.7
15.5	3.9	4.7	5.9	8.0	11.5	17.4	22.1
16.0	3.8	4.6	5.8	7.7	11.2	16.8	21.6
16.5	3.8	4.5	5.6	7.4	10.9	16.2	21.3
17.0	3.8	4.5	5.6	7.3	10.9	16.0	21.3
17.5	3.9	4.5	5.7	7.3	11.1	16.1	21.6
18.0	4.2	4.6	5.9	7.5	11.7	16.6	22.3

[a] Reference data are based on the Health Examination Survey, and the first National Health and Nutrition Examination Survey (NHANES I) in the United States of America (4).

Table A3.7
Percentiles of triceps skinfold thickness: female adolescents, 9–18 years[a]

Age years	Percentiles						
	5th	10th	25th	50th	75th	90th	95th
9.0	6.0	6.8	8.4	11.0	14.1	18.5	21.2
9.5	6.0	6.8	8.5	11.2	14.5	19.1	22.0
10.0	6.1	6.9	8.6	11.4	15.0	19.8	22.8
10.5	6.2	7.0	8.8	11.6	15.4	20.4	23.5
11.0	6.3	7.2	9.0	11.9	15.9	21.1	24.2
11.5	6.4	7.3	9.2	12.2	16.4	21.6	24.9
12.0	6.6	7.6	9.5	12.6	16.9	22.2	25.6
12.5	6.7	7.8	9.8	12.9	17.5	22.8	26.2
13.0	6.9	8.0	10.1	13.3	18.0	23.3	26.8
13.5	7.1	8.3	10.4	13.7	18.5	23.8	27.4
14.0	7.3	8.5	10.7	14.1	19.0	24.2	28.0
14.5	7.5	8.8	11.1	14.5	19.5	24.7	28.5
15.0	7.7	9.1	11.4	14.8	20.0	25.1	29.0
15.5	7.9	9.3	11.8	15.2	20.5	25.5	29.4
16.0	8.0	9.6	12.2	15.6	20.9	25.9	29.8
16.5	8.2	9.8	12.5	16.0	21.3	26.3	30.1
17.0	8.4	10.0	12.8	16.3	21.7	26.7	30.4
17.5	8.5	10.2	13.2	16.6	22.0	27.0	30.7
18.0	8.6	10.4	13.5	17.0	22.2	27.3	30.9

[a] Reference data are based on the Health Examination Survey, and the first National Health and Nutrition Examination Survey (NHANES I) in the United States of America (4).

Table A3.8
Percentiles of subscapular skinfold thickness: male adolescents, 9–18 years[a]

Age years	Percentiles						
	5th	10th	25th	50th	75th	90th	95th
9.0	3.2	3.7	4.0	4.9	6.4	10.4	13.6
9.5	3.2	3.7	4.0	5.0	6.6	10.9	14.4
10.0	3.3	3.8	4.1	5.0	6.8	11.4	15.2
10.5	3.4	3.8	4.2	5.2	7.0	11.8	15.9
11.0	3.4	3.9	4.3	5.3	7.2	12.2	16.6
11.5	3.5	3.9	4.4	5.4	7.4	12.6	17.2
12.0	3.6	4.0	4.5	5.6	7.6	13.0	17.9
12.5	3.6	4.1	4.6	5.7	7.9	13.4	18.5
13.0	3.7	4.2	4.8	5.9	8.1	13.8	19.1
13.5	3.8	4.3	5.0	6.1	8.4	14.2	19.7
14.0	3.9	4.4	5.1	6.3	8.6	14.6	20.3
14.5	4.0	4.6	5.3	6.5	8.9	15.1	20.9
15.0	4.2	4.7	5.5	6.7	9.2	15.5	21.5
15.5	4.3	4.8	5.7	7.0	9.5	16.1	22.1
16.0	4.4	5.0	5.9	7.2	9.9	16.6	22.7
16.5	4.6	5.2	6.1	7.5	10.2	17.3	23.3
17.0	4.8	5.4	6.4	7.8	10.6	18.0	24.0
17.5	4.9	5.5	6.6	8.2	11.0	18.7	24.6
18.0	5.1	5.7	6.8	8.5	11.4	19.5	25.3

[a] Reference data are based on the Health Examination Survey, and the first National Health and Nutrition Examination Survey (NHANES I) in the United States of America (4).

Table A3.9
Percentiles of subscapular skinfold thickness: female adolescents, 9–18 years[a]

Age years	Percentiles						
	5th	10th	25th	50th	75th	90th	95th
9.0	3.6	4.0	4.6	5.8	8.4	13.6	17.2
9.5	3.7	4.0	4.8	6.1	8.9	14.5	18.2
10.0	3.8	4.1	5.0	6.4	9.4	15.3	19.2
10.5	4.0	4.3	5.2	6.7	9.9	16.2	20.2
11.0	4.1	4.5	5.4	7.0	10.4	17.0	21.2
11.5	4.3	4.6	5.7	7.3	11.0	17.8	22.2
12.0	4.5	4.8	5.9	7.7	11.5	18.6	23.2
12.5	4.6	5.1	6.2	8.1	12.1	19.3	24.1
13.0	4.8	5.3	6.4	8.4	12.6	20.1	25.0
13.5	5.0	5.5	6.7	8.8	13.2	20.8	25.8
14.0	5.2	5.7	7.0	9.2	13.8	21.5	26.6
14.5	5.4	5.9	7.2	9.5	14.3	22.1	27.4
15.0	5.5	6.2	7.4	9.9	14.8	22.7	28.1
15.5	5.7	6.3	7.7	10.2	15.4	23.2	28.7
16.0	5.8	6.5	7.9	10.6	15.8	23.7	29.2
16.5	6.0	6.7	8.1	10.9	16.3	24.2	29.7
17.0	6.1	6.8	8.2	11.2	16.7	24.6	30.1
17.5	6.2	7.0	8.4	11.5	17.1	24.9	30.4
18.0	6.3	7.0	8.5	11.7	17.5	25.1	30.6

[a] Reference data are based on the Health Examination Survey, and the first National Health and Nutrition Examination Survey (NHANES I) in the United States of America (*4*).

Table A3.10
Adult weights and heights corresponding to recommended cut-off values for body mass index

Height (cm)	BMI								Height (cm)
	16.0	17.0	18.5	20.0	22.0	25.0	30.0	40.0	
	Thinness					Overweight			
	Body weight (kg)								
140	31.4	33.3	36.2	39.2	43.1	49.0	58.8	78.4	140
141	31.8	33.8	36.8	39.8	43.7	49.7	59.6	79.5	141
142	32.3	34.3	37.3	40.3	44.4	50.4	60.5	80.7	142
143	32.7	34.8	37.8	40.9	45.0	51.1	61.3	81.8	143
144	33.2	35.3	38.4	41.5	45.6	51.8	62.2	82.9	144
145	33.6	35.7	38.9	42.1	46.3	52.6	63.1	84.1	145
146	34.1	36.2	39.4	42.6	46.9	53.3	63.9	85.3	146
147	34.6	36.7	40.0	43.2	47.5	54.0	64.8	86.4	147
148	35.0	37.2	40.5	43.8	48.2	54.8	65.7	87.6	148
149	35.5	37.7	41.1	44.4	48.8	55.5	66.6	88.8	149
150	36.0	38.2	41.6	45.0	49.5	56.3	67.5	90.0	150
151	36.5	38.8	42.2	45.6	50.2	57.0	68.4	91.2	151
152	37.0	39.3	42.7	46.2	50.8	57.8	69.3	92.4	152
153	37.5	39.8	43.3	46.8	51.5	58.5	70.2	93.6	153
154	37.9	40.3	43.9	47.4	52.2	59.3	71.1	94.9	154
155	38.4	40.8	44.4	48.1	52.9	60.1	72.1	96.1	155
156	38.9	41.4	45.0	48.7	53.5	60.8	73.0	97.3	156
157	39.4	41.9	45.6	49.3	54.2	61.6	73.9	98.6	157
158	39.9	42.4	46.2	49.9	54.9	62.4	74.9	99.9	158
159	40.4	43.0	46.8	50.6	55.6	63.2	75.8	101.1	159
160	41.0	43.5	47.4	51.2	56.3	64.0	76.8	102.4	160
161	41.5	44.1	48.0	51.8	57.0	64.8	77.8	103.7	161
162	42.0	44.6	48.3	52.5	57.7	65.6	78.7	105.0	162

Table A3.10 *(continued)*

Height (cm)	BMI								Height (cm)
	16.0	17.0	18.5	20.0	22.0	25.0	30.0	40.0	
	Thinness					Overweight			
	Body weight (kg)								
163	42.5	45.2	49.2	53.1	58.5	66.4	79.7	106.3	163
164	43.0	45.7	49.8	53.8	59.2	67.2	80.7	107.6	164
165	43.6	46.3	50.4	54.5	59.9	68.1	81.7	108.9	165
166	44.1	46.8	51.0	55.1	60.6	68.9	82.7	110.2	166
167	44.6	47.4	51.6	55.8	61.4	69.7	83.7	111.6	167
168	45.2	48.0	52.2	56.4	62.1	70.6	84.7	112.9	168
169	45.7	48.6	52.8	57.1	62.8	71.4	85.7	114.2	169
170	46.2	49.1	53.5	57.8	63.6	72.3	86.7	115.6	170
171	46.8	49.7	54.1	58.5	64.3	73.1	87.8	117.0	171
172	47.3	50.3	54.7	59.2	65.1	74.0	88.8	118.3	172
173	47.9	50.9	55.4	59.9	65.8	74.8	89.8	119.7	173
174	48.4	51.5	56.0	60.6	66.6	75.7	90.8	121.1	174
175	49.0	52.1	56.7	61.3	67.4	76.6	91.9	122.5	175
176	49.6	52.7	57.3	62.0	68.1	77.4	92.9	123.9	176
177	50.1	53.3	58.0	62.7	68.9	78.3	94.0	125.3	177
178	50.7	53.9	58.6	63.4	69.7	79.2	95.0	126.7	178
179	51.3	54.5	59.3	64.1	70.5	80.1	96.1	128.2	179
180	51.9	55.1	59.9	64.8	71.3	81.0	97.2	129.6	180
181	52.4	55.7	60.6	65.5	72.1	81.9	98.3	131.0	181
182	53.0	56.3	61.3	66.2	72.9	82.8	99.4	132.5	182
183	53.6	57.0	62.0	67.0	73.7	83.7	100.5	134.0	183
184	54.2	57.6	62.6	67.7	74.5	84.6	101.6	135.4	184

Table A3.10 *(continued)*

Height (cm)	16.0	17.0	18.5	20.0	22.0	25.0	30.0	40.0	Height (cm)
	Thinness					Overweight			
	Body weight (kg)								
185	54.8	58.2	63.3	68.5	75.3	85.6	102.7	136.9	185
186	55.5	58.8	64.0	69.2	76.1	86.5	103.8	138.4	186
187	56.0	59.5	64.7	69.9	76.9	87.4	104.9	139.9	187
188	56.6	60.1	65.4	70.7	77.8	88.4	106.0	141.4	188
189	57.1	60.7	66.1	71.4	78.6	89.3	107.1	142.9	189
190	57.8	61.4	66.8	72.2	79.4	90.3	108.3	144.4	190

For easy reference and calculation of BMI values corresponding to recommended cut-offs, first find the height of the individual in the left- or right-hand column. The weights given in the row for that height correspond to various recommended cut-off values for adult BMI. Weights for two normal BMI values are also included.

Interpretation
BMI <16.00 indicates grade 3 thinness
BMI 16.0–16.99 indicates grade 2 thinness
BMI 17.0–18.49 indicates grade 1 thinness

BMI 18.5–24.99 is the normal range for an individual

BMI 25.0–29.99 indicates grade 1 overweight
BMI 30.0–39.99 indicates grade 2 overweight
BMI ≥ 40.00 indicates grade 3 overweight

References

1. *Measuring change in nutritional status.* Geneva, World Health Organization, 1983.

2. Must A, Dallal GE, Dietz WH. Reference data for obesity: 85th and 95th percentiles of body mass index (wt/ht^2). *American journal of clinical nutrition,* 1991, **53**:839–846.

3. Must A, Dallal GE, Dietz WH. Reference data for obesity: 85th and 95th percentiles of body mass index (wt/ht^2) – a correction. *American journal of clinical nutrition,* 1991, **43**:773.

4. Johnson CL et al. *Basic data on anthropometric measurements and angular measurements of the hip and knee joints for selected age groups 1-74 years of age.* Washington, DC, Department of Health and Human Services, National Center for Health Statistics, 1981 (Vital and Health Statistics, Series 11, Publication No. (PHS) 81-1669).